Praise for *Buddhists: Understanding Buddhism Through the Lives of Practitioners*

"This volume invites readers to understand what it can mean to be a Buddhist. Rather than approaching Buddhism as an abstract entity by means of texts and doctrines that form a coherent and fixed system, these humanistic accounts enable one to situate and comprehend various ways in which people have actually *lived* and thereby impacted Buddhist tradition. One comes away from reading this book with a knowledge of how Buddhism is a force that is fluid, diverse, and distinctive in its countless iterations."

John Holt, Bowdoin College

"In the past there has been a tendency in Western books to approach Buddhism through its doctrines, in particular some of its more intellectually elite and perhaps more controversial philosophical doctrines. On the other hand, in the Western 'popular' press and culture Buddhism is sometimes seen as a fairly loose collection of 'new-agey' ideas and attitudes about compassion and reincarnation often presented with little potential for radical transformative impact on lives. Todd Lewis has for many years been in the forefront of a contemporary approach to Buddhism among scholars that seeks to reorient our understanding of Buddhism around what Buddhists *do*: the way in which Buddhist doctrines and experiences themselves interact with Buddhist lives and actual living Buddhism. The present comprehensive collection looks at the interface between what Buddhists do and Buddhist biographies, the specific way of living Buddhism expressed in the lives of a wide range of 'eminent' and also (until now) perhaps less well-known Buddhists, past and present. I know of no other book in Buddhists Studies quite like this, and it should make fascinating reading for those who really want to understand what makes Buddhists and Buddhism 'tick,' not as a collection of abstract ideas but as an actual lived way of being in the world and looking forward to the world(s) to come. Great stuff – this book is highly recommended!"

Paul Williams, University of Bristol, author of
Mahāyāna Buddhism: The Doctrinal Foundations

Buddhists

Understanding Buddhism Through the Lives of Practitioners

Edited by

Todd Lewis

WILEY Blackwell

This edition first published 2014
©2014 John Wiley & Sons Ltd

Registered Office
John Wiley & Sons Ltd, The Atrium, Southern Gate, Chichester, West Sussex, PO19 8SQ, UK

Editorial Offices
350 Main Street, Malden, MA 02148-5020, USA
9600 Garsington Road, Oxford, OX4 2DQ, UK
The Atrium, Southern Gate, Chichester, West Sussex, PO19 8SQ, UK

For details of our global editorial offices, for customer services, and for information about how to apply for permission to reuse the copyright material in this book please see our website at www.wiley.com/wiley-blackwell.

The right of Todd Lewis to be identified as the author of the editorial material in this work has been asserted in accordance with the UK Copyright, Designs and Patents Act 1988.

All rights reserved. No part of this publication may be reproduced, stored in a retrieval system, or transmitted, in any form or by any means, electronic, mechanical, photocopying, recording or otherwise, except as permitted by the UK Copyright, Designs and Patents Act 1988, without the prior permission of the publisher.

Wiley also publishes its books in a variety of electronic formats. Some content that appears in print may not be available in electronic books.

Designations used by companies to distinguish their products are often claimed as trademarks. All brand names and product names used in this book are trade names, service marks, trademarks or registered trademarks of their respective owners. The publisher is not associated with any product or vendor mentioned in this book.

Limit of Liability/Disclaimer of Warranty: While the publisher and editor have used their best efforts in preparing this book, they make no representations or warranties with respect to the accuracy or completeness of the contents of this book and specifically disclaim any implied warranties of merchantability or fitness for a particular purpose. It is sold on the understanding that the publisher is not engaged in rendering professional services and neither the publisher nor the author shall be liable for damages arising herefrom. If professional advice or other expert assistance is required, the services of a competent professional should be sought.

Library of Congress Cataloging-in-Publication Data applied for
Hardback ISBN: 978-0-470-65817-8
Paperback ISBN: 978-0-470-65818-5

A catalogue record for this book is available from the British Library.

Cover image: Ts'ampa Nawang. Photograph by Nicolas Sihlé. Reprinted with permission. Asian woman praying with incense sticks © szefei/iStock, Little Tibetan monks © beemore/iStock

Set in 9.5/11.5pt Minion by Laserwords Private Limited, Chennai, India
Printed and bound in Malaysia by Vivar Printing Sdn Bhd

1 2014

Contents

Notes on Contributors ix
Preface xiii
Acknowledgments xv

    Introduction 1
    Todd Lewis

Part I   Buddhists in the Earliest and Medieval Eras   11

1 The Female Householder Mallika 13
    Kristin Scheible

2 Bhadda Kundalakesa: The Ex-Jain 21
    Alice Collett

3 Two Noted Householders of the Buddha's Time: *Upasika* Vishakha and *Upasaka* Anathapindika 29
    Todd Lewis

4 Nagarjuna: The Great Philosopher 39
    Joseph Walser

5 Who Is Uncle Donpa? 52
    David J. Cooper

6 Ma-chig Lab-dron: Mother of Tibetan Buddhist Chod 62
    Michelle J. Sorensen

Part II   Buddhist Lives in the West   71

7 I.B. Horner and the Twentieth-Century Development of Buddhism in the West 73
    Grace G. Burford

8 Takyu: A Young Buddhist Nun at a Ch'an Temple in the English Midlands 80
    George D. Chryssides

9 Refuge and Reconnection: One Lao Woman's Story 87
    Stewart Jobrack

10	Conversion, Devotion, and (Trans-)Mission: Understanding Ole Nydahl *Burkhard Scherer*	96
11	Noah Levine: Punk Rocker and Buddhist Meditation Teacher *Brooke Schedneck*	107
12	Legendary Beat Poet: Allen Ginsberg *Tony Trigilio*	115
13	Dr. Stephen John Fulder: Founder of Vipassana in Israel *Joseph Loss*	124
14	Amala Sensei: Zen Priest *Sally McAra*	133

Part III Buddhist Lives in South and Southeast Asia — 145

15	Pawinee Bunkhun: The Life of a Thai Buddhist *Upasika* *Rachelle M. Scott*	147
16	Mahasi Sayadaw of Burma *Bradley S. Clough*	157
17	Corporal Monk: Venerable Sudinna's Journey from the Sri Lankan Army to the Buddhist Sangha *Daniel W. Kent*	165
18	The Lure of Renunciation and the Ways of the World: Maechii Wabi of Thailand *Sid Brown*	172
19	Becoming a Theravada Modernist Buddhist in Contemporary Nepal *Lauren Leve*	179

Part IV Buddhist Lives in the Himalayan Region — 191

20	Tenpe Gyaltsen: The Fifth Jamyang Zhepa *Paul K. Nietupski*	193
21	A Female Tibetan Buddhist Diviner in Darjeeling *Tanya M. Zivkovic*	201
22	Tsultrim Zangmo: A Twenty-First-Century Tibetan Buddhist Woman in South Asia *Tsultrim Zangmo and Michelle J. Sorensen*	209
23	Bakula Arhat's Journeys to the North: The Life and Work of the 19th Kushok Bakula in Russia and Mongolia *Vesna A. Wallace*	218
24	Hunger, Hard Work, and Uncertainty: Tashi Dondrup Reminisces on Life and Death in a Tibetan Village *Geoff Childs*	228
25	Benefiting the Doctrine and Sentient Beings: The Life of a Tibetan Lineage Master and the Ethos of Altruistic Action *Nicolas Sihlé*	236
26	Living Practical Dharma: Chomo Khandru and the Himalayan Bon Tradition *Sara Shneiderman*	246

27 Excavating the Stories of Border-Crossing Women Masters in Modern Buddhism: The
    Oral Biography of Pelling Ani Wangdzin and Her Family   257
    Amy Holmes-Tagchungdarpa

Part V   Buddhist Lives in East Asia   **265**

28 The Life of a Contemporary Japanese Buddhist Priest: Protecting the Dharma and
    Ensuring Its Flow with All of One's Strength   267
    Naoyuki Ogi

29 Toshihide Numata: Igniting the Flame of the Dharma   274
    Naoyuki Ogi

30 Seno'o Giro: The Life and Thought of a Radical Buddhist   280
    James Mark Shields

31 Building a Culture of Social Engagement: Nichiren Buddhism and Soka Gakkai Buddhists
    in Japan   289
    Anne Mette Fisker-Nielsen

32 Blood and Teardrops: The Life and Travels of Venerable Fazun   296
    Brenton Sullivan

33 A Modern Chinese Laywoman: Dumplings, Dharani, and Dedication – Honest Auntie Li
    Tries to Be a Good Buddhist   305
    Alison Denton Jones

Index   317

For an alternative table of contents that, for the purposes of teaching, arranges the biographies into the various schools of Buddhism, please go to www.wiley.com/go/lewisbuddhism.

Notes on Contributors

George D. Chryssides is Honorary Research Fellow in Contemporary Religion at the University of Birmingham, UK, and was formerly Head of Religious Studies at the University of Wolverhampton, UK. He has published extensively on new religious movements and has a particular interest in new expressions of Christianity and Buddhism.

Sid Brown, Professor at Sewanee, the University of the South in Tennessee, focuses on the lived experience of Buddhism. Her first book, *The Journey of One Buddhist Nun* (2001), is a biography of a modern Thai female renunciant, and her second, *A Buddhist in the Classroom* (2009), views classroom teaching through a Buddhist lens, exploring the ethical quandaries, lived experiences, and intimacy of teaching. Brown has been studying Buddhism since being introduced to it by the Antioch Buddhist Studies Program in 1982. During her years earning her B.A. from Emory, her M.A. from Florida State University, and her Ph.D. from the University of Virginia, she researched and lived in India, Sri Lanka, Japan, and Thailand. More recently her work has turned to Buddhist views and rituals associated with environmental concerns and animals.

Grace G. Burford, Ph.D., is Professor of Religious Studies at Prescott College, USA, and the author of *Desire, Death, and Goodness: The Conflict of Ultimate Values in Theravada Buddhism* (1991) and numerous articles on Buddhist-Christian studies. She is currently writing a biography of twentieth-century British scholar of Buddhism I. B. Horner.

Geoff Childs holds a Ph.D. in Anthropology and Tibetan Studies from Indiana University and is an Associate Professor of Anthropology at Washington University in St. Louis who specializes in studying the interconnections between demographic processes, economic changes, and family transformations in the highlands of Nepal and the Tibet Autonomous Region, China. His recent collaborations with physical anthropologists aim to document out-migration and population decline in Himalayan communities of Nepal, investigate the links between genetic adaptation to high altitude and reproductive outcomes, and examine the association between adaptation to high altitude, mother's milk, and infant growth.

Bradley S. Clough teaches about Asian religions (with a focus on Buddhism) at the University of Montana, USA. He has written many articles on different facets of Buddhism and has a forthcoming book from Cambria Press titled *Noble Persons' Paths: Diversity and Controversy in Theravāda Buddhism*.

Alice Collett is a Senior Lecturer at York St. John University. She received her M.A. from the University of Bristol in 1999 and her Ph.D. from Cardiff University in 2004. Since then she has worked in various universities in North America and the United Kingdom. She has published several articles on women in early Indian Buddhism and a recent edited volume titled *Women in Early Indian Buddhism: Comparative Textual Studies* (2013). She has just completed work on a monograph entitled *Pāli Biographies of Buddhist Nuns*, which was supported by an Arts and Humanities Research Council fellowship award.

David J. Cooper is a doctoral student focusing on Tibetan Buddhism in the Department of Religious Studies at the University of California, Santa Barbara, USA. His research interests include humor, religious literature and folklore, and monastic life.

Anne M. Fisker-Nielsen is a social anthropologist with reference to Japan. She is particularly interested in Buddhist theory, civil society, political participation, and the issue of religion and the secular in the modern nation state. She teaches at the School of Oriental and African Studies, University of London. Fisker-Nielsen has undertaken long-term and firsthand research in Japan, in particular with the Buddhist organization Soka Gakkai and the Clean Government Party (Komeito). Her recent book, *Religion and Politics in Contemporary Japan: Soka Gakkai Youth and Komeito* (2012), is a study of grassroots-level political engagement in a group whose value orientation is derived from Nichiren Buddhism.

Amy Holmes-Tagchungdarpa is an Assistant Professor in the Department of History at the University of Alabama, USA. She is the author of *The Social Life of Tibetan Biography: Textuality, Community and Authority in the Lineage of Tokden Shakya Shri* (forthcoming) and essays on Tibetan, Chinese, and Himalayan social and cultural history.

Stewart Jobrack teaches anthropology at the Ohio State University-Marion, USA. He is writing a Ph.D. dissertation on the practice of Theravada Buddhism among Lao refugees and immigrants in the United States.

Alison Denton Jones is a lecturer on Social Studies at Harvard University, USA, specializing in cultural and institutional developments in contemporary Buddhism in Chinese societies. Her dissertation, "A modern religion? The state, the people, and the remaking of Buddhism in urban China today," examines lay Buddhism in a single Chinese city.

Daniel W. Kent is a visiting Assistant Professor of Asian religions at Whitman College in Walla Walla, USA. Dr. Kent has lived and researched in Sri Lanka for over four years. His primary research interests include Buddhism and war, Buddhist ethics, and Buddhist nationalism.

Lauren Leve is Associate Professor in the Department of Religious Studies at the University of North Carolina at Chapel Hill, USA. An anthropologist by training, she has been conducting ethnographic research on Theravada Buddhism in Nepal since 1990. Her research is driven by concerns with the cultural dynamics of globalization, particularly the relations between political and economic liberalization, ethical personhood, and religious change. She is also interested in the globalization of *vipassana* meditation, human rights and democracy, gender, Buddhist modernity, and nongovernmental organizations and the developmental state.

Todd Lewis is Professor of World Religions at the College of the Holy Cross. His primary research since 1979 has been on Newar Buddhism in the Kathmandu Valley, Nepal. He is the author of many articles on this tradition, and is the coauthor of *World Religions Today* (fourth edition 2011). His most recent translation, *Sugata Saurabha: A Poem on the Life of the Buddha by Chittadhar Hridaya of Nepal* (2010), received awards from the Khyentse Foundation and the Numata Foundation as the best book on Buddhism published in 2010.

Joseph Loss teaches in the Sociology and Anthropology Department at Bar-Ilan University, Israel. He has published on the history of Israeli anthropology (*Anthropological Quarterly*) and on Israeli Buddha-dhamma (*Nova Religio*). His most recent article addresses the issue of a converted Buddhist identity. It appeared in the collection *Kabbalah and Contemporary Spiritual Revival* (2011).

Sally McAra is an adjunct research associate in the School of Art History, Classics and Religious studies at Victoria University, New Zealand. She has researched and written several works about Buddhism in the West. She is Secretary of the New Zealand Buddhist Council and is a member of the Auckland Zen Centre.

Paul K. Nietupski is a professor of Asian religions at John Carroll University, USA. His recent publications include *Labrang Monastery: A Tibetan Buddhist Community on the Inner Asian Borderlands 1709–1958* (2011) and contributions to a coedited volume titled *Reading Asian Art and Artifacts: Windows to Asia on American College Campuses* (2011).

Naoyuki Ogi has written many articles for various periodical publications on Buddhism. He is a 14th-generation Buddhist priest of the Choshoji Temple (Pure Land School) in Japan and is connected with the International Affairs Section of Bukkyo Dendo Kyokai (Society for the Promotion of Buddhism) in Tokyo. He graduated from Ryukoku University and the Theological Union/Institute of Buddhist Studies located in Berkeley, California, USA. He also completed a 2010–11 residential fellow program at Harvard Divinity School, USA.

Brooke Schedneck is Lecturer in Buddhist Studies at the Institute of Southeast Asian Affairs at Chiangmai University, Thailand. She holds a Ph.D. in Asian Religions from Arizona State University. Her main scholarly interests include the intersection of Buddhism and modernity as well as the emerging global Buddhist landscape. Her most recent project explores the history of modern *vipassana* meditation, specifically investigating Thailand's international meditation centers. The title of her monograph through Routledge's series Contemporary Asian Religions is *Thailand's International Meditation Centers: Tourism and the Global Commodification of Religious Practices* (2014). She has been published in *The Buddhist Studies Review*, *The Pacific World Journal*, *The Journal of Contemporary Religion*, and *Contemporary Buddhism* and maintains a research website called Wandering Dhamma (www.wanderingdhamma.org).

Kristin Scheible earned a Ph.D. from Harvard University, USA, in 2006 and is Assistant Professor of Religion at Bard College, USA. Her area of expertise is Theravada Buddhist literature; her research revolves around the work of narratives in the genre of historical literature (*vamsa*) in the Pali language, and her current book project is on the Pali *Mahavamsa*. Her most recent publications include "Priming the lamp of *dhamma*: the Buddha's miracles in the Pāli *Mahāvamsa*" in the *Journal of the International Association of Buddhist Studies* (2011) and "'Give me my inheritance': Western Buddhists raising Buddhist children" in *Little Buddhas: Children and Childhoods in Buddhist Texts and Traditions* (2012).

Burkhard Scherer is Chair in Comparative Religion, Gender and Sexuality at Canterbury Christ Church University, UK, and specializes in Buddhist philosophy, queer theory, and the globalization of Buddhism(s). Among Professor Scherer's books are *Buddhismus* (2005) and *Queering Paradigms* (2010).

Rachelle Scott is an Associate Professor of Religious Studies at the University of Tennessee. She received her Ph.D. in Religion from Northwestern University in 2002. Her first book, *Nirvana for Sale? Buddhism, Wealth, and the Dhammakāya Temple in Contemporary Thailand* (2009), examines the relationships between wealth and Buddhist piety in Theravada Buddhism and in contemporary Thailand. Dr. Scott is currently working on her second book project, *Gifts of Beauty and Blessings of Wealth: The New Prosperity Goddesses of Thailand*, which focuses on the emergence of new narratives about female spirits within contemporary Thai religious practice. Her research examines how these cults are linked in complex ways to representations of Thailand's past, present, and future, as well as to issues of religious authority, economic development, cultural globalization, and sexuality.

James Mark Shields is Associate Professor of Comparative Humanities and Asian Thought at Bucknell University, USA, and Japan Foundation Visiting Research Fellow at the International Research Center for Japanese Studies, Japan (2013–14). He was educated at McGill University, Canada; the University of Cambridge, UK; and Kyoto University, Japan. He conducts research on modern Buddhist thought, Japanese philosophy, comparative ethics, and the philosophy of religion. He is author of *Critical Buddhism: Engaging with Modern Japanese Buddhist Thought* (Ashgate, 2011) and coeditor of *Teaching Buddhism in the West: From the Wheel to the Web* (2003), and is currently completing a book on progressive and radical Buddhism in Japan.

Sara Shneiderman is Assistant Professor of Anthropology and South Asian Studies at Yale University, USA. Her research explores the relationships between political discourse, ritual action, and crossborder mobility in producing identities and shaping social transformation in the Himalayan regions of Nepal, India, and China's Tibetan Autonomous Region. Her forthcoming book is titled *Rituals of Ethnicity: Thangmi Identities across Himalayan Borders*, and she has published several articles on the themes of Nepal's Maoist movement and ongoing political transformation; ethnic classification, affirmative action, and the politics of recognition in South Asia; and borders and citizenship in the Himalaya.

Nicolas Sihlé is an anthropologist specializing in the Tibetan cultural area and in the comparative anthropology of Buddhist societies. He has taught anthropology at the University of Virginia, USA, and is now a full-time researcher at the Centre for Himalayan Studies at the CNRS (Centre National de la Recherche Scientifique) in France. He has carried out fieldwork over a total of more than three years in Tibetan communities, and is the author of a forthcoming book on Tibetan tantrists: *Rituels bouddhiques de pouvoir et de violence: La figure du tantriste tibétain* (Buddhist rituals of power and violence: the figure of the Tibetan tantrist). His current work focuses on communities of tantrists in post-Mao, northeast Tibet (among which he has been carrying out fieldwork since 2003) and on the larger, collective project of an anthropology of Buddhism. He is also the editor of a collective research blog, *The Himalayas and Beyond* (http://himalayas.hypotheses.org).

Michelle J. Sorensen recently completed her Ph.D. at Columbia University, USA. Her dissertation is titled "Making the old new again and again: legitimation and innovation in the Tibetan Buddhist Chöd tradition." Her publications include "The body extraordinary: embodied praxis, Vajrayogini, and Buddhist Gcod" in *Tibetan Studies: An Anthology* (2006); "Cutting to the chase: the problem of 'mind' in the context of gCod" in *Mahayana Buddhism: History and Culture* (2008); "Mahāmudrā Chöd? Rangjung Dorjé's commentary on *The Great Speech Chapter* of Machik Labdron" in *Wading into the Stream of Wisdom* (2012); and "Translation and vestige" in *Sagar* (2013). She is currently a Visiting Assistant Professor at the University of Mississippi, USA.

Brenton Sullivan is a Ph.D. candidate in the Department of Religious Studies at the University of Virginia, USA. His dissertation research is focused on the growth of the Geluk school of Tibetan Buddhism in Amdo (Northeastern Tibet) and, in particular, on the history of the influential Monguor monastery known as Gonlung Jampa Ling (Ch. Youning si).

Tony Trigilio is a Professor of English at Columbia College Chicago. His books include the critical monograph *Allen Ginsberg's Buddhist Poetics* (2012) and the anthology *Visions and Divisions: American Immigration Literature, 1870–1930* (coedited with Tim Prchal, 2008). He is the author of five volumes of poetry, the most recent of which is *White Noise* (2013). He coedits the poetry journal *Court Green* and is a former editor for the academic book-review journal *The Beat Review*.

Vesna A. Wallace is a Professor of Buddhist Studies in the Department of Religious Studies at the University of California, Santa Barbara, USA. The areas of her specialization are Indian and Mongolian Buddhist traditions. She received her M.A. in Asian Languages and Literature from the University of Washington, USA, and her Ph.D. in South Asian Studies from the University of California, Berkeley, USA. In addition to the languages of India, she studied classical and modern Mongolian and classical Tibetan. She has authored and translated four books on Indian Buddhism and published many articles on Indian and Mongolian Buddhism. She is a recipient of many grants and awards, including the Silver Medal bestowed by Mr. Elbegdorj, the President of Mongolia, for her contribution to the friendship of peoples.

Joseph Walser is Associate Professor of Religion at Tufts University, USA. His first book, *Nagarjuna in Context* (2005), examines what Nagarjuna's writings would have meant in their immediate social contexts. He is currently investigating the intersections of Buddhism and Brahmanism in ancient India, and the origins of Mahayana Buddhism among Brahmin Buddhists.

Tanya M. Zivkovic is a social anthropologist whose research explores notions of body and life course through death, relics, reincarnation, and biographical representations. She is a Research Fellow in the Department of Anthropology, University of Adelaide, Australia.

Preface

The genesis of this book goes back to my interdisciplinary graduate training, and especially the last class offered in fieldwork methods at Columbia University by Margaret Mead. In her inimitable way, she forced her students to consider a variety of research methods, including taking life histories. When I did so as part of my own first fieldwork in Nepal from 1979 to 1982, I collected information on a large sample of Buddhist merchants, and found these biographies to be rich and illuminating on a variety of topics.

A further push toward proposing this volume came through inspiration from subsequent publications on the anthropology of life histories, such as *Lives: An Anthropological Approach to Biography* (1991) by L.L. Langness and Gelya F. Franks. After reading Reinhold Loeffler's *Islam in Practice: Religious Beliefs in a Persian Village* (1986) and seeing how the religious beliefs and practices of Muslims vary widely in rural Iran, I wondered about a similar project for Buddhists. Just as these life histories make it impossible to imagine any monolithic construction of Islam and Muslims, this volume was conceived as providing similar insights about Buddhism and Buddhists.

To balance the textual resources available in courses that traditionally focus primarily on the doctrines and practices of Buddhist philosophers and saints, I wondered whether students could benefit from biographies sampling a broader community of adherents. Could a book of biographies of Buddhists provide instructors with a resource that would allow greater attention to typical Buddhists? To this end, I put out a call on various academic list-servs for scholars (scholars of Buddhism, anthropologists, historians) to compose short life histories of Buddhists, from antiquity until the present day. I also solicited leading scholars for contributions to achieve both historical and geographical balance. The present volume puts specific human faces to who is, and what it means to be, a Buddhist.

In addition, on the book's web site (www.wiley.com/go/lewisbuddhism) there is a listing of sources containing longer, book-length Buddhist biographies: the narrative of the Buddha's life found in traditional and modern writings; accounts of the hundreds of former lives he lived before his last life, when he reached enlightenment; and the longer accounts of the lives of various saints and scholars that have been translated from the vast archive of traditional Buddhist texts into English.

This volume was also inspired by StoryCorps, an oral-history initiative begun a decade ago in the United States. Across the country, this project has at various sites offered a studio and a technician for individuals who want to interview another person for an hour; the result is that the individuals get a CD copy of the conversation, with the recording archived in perpetuity in the Library of Congress. Culling cases from among the tens of thousands of interviews, a series of books has been published from this program, revealing the brilliance of its design as well as a magnificent diversity of lives of ordinary people being lived today. In one such volume, *Listening*

Is an Act of Love: A Celebration of American Life from the StoryCorps Project, the editor, Dave Isay, summarizes the foundational ideas on which this biography project was built:

> That our stories – the stories of everyday people – are as interesting and important as the celebrity stories we're bombarded with by the media every minute of the day ... That if we take the time to listen, we'll find wisdom, wonder and poetry in the lives and stories of the people all around us.[1]

This volume falls into this tradition. Its ambition is to give insight into what it means to be a Buddhist, imagining how this tradition has attracted human devotion for over 2500 years.

Todd Lewis
Holden, Massachusetts
February 2014

Note

1 Isay, D. (2007) *Listening Is an Act of Love: A Celebration of American Life from the StoryCorps Project*, Penguin, London: 1.

Acknowledgments

I would like to express my thanks to all the contributors who responded to the call for biographies, and who carried on in an extended process of writing and revising their narratives.

I must express my gratitude to the teachers who shaped my own development as a scholar interlinking religious studies and anthropology, including Robert Murphy, Marvin Harris, Gerald Berreman, Stanley Tambiah, Ainslie Embree, Gregory Schopen, and Theodore Riccardi Jr.

I am especially grateful to the Simon Guggenheim Foundation for a fellowship that enabled me to complete the research on this project, and to the College of the Holy Cross for granting a sabbatical leave to complete the editing.

I am indebted to Rebecca Harkin, commissioning editor at Wiley Blackwell, who saw the originality and promise in this volume and who supported it through the chaotic process of assembling so many parts by so many contributors. The exacting copyediting of Hazel Harris made this book clearer and better in every way.

Introduction

Todd Lewis

"Buddhism" is a single word, a noun that refers to one of the world's great religious traditions. It is an English term that implies a singularity. But no religions are monolithic. This pluralism is especially true in the case of Buddhism, as there never was any institution, single figure, or group of spiritual leaders that could prescribe conformity, or enforce it, across Asia or beyond. Monks, kings, and patrons adapted Buddhist tradition to their localities, transplanting it into many social and cultural environments, from the tropical regions of South and Southeast Asia to the high-altitude Tibetan Plateau; from the trade routes of India to the Confucian societies of East Asia; and then, in recent centuries, from Asia into Europe and the Americas.

This diversity presents a challenge for the student of this important tradition, the world's first missionary religion. Its spread on both the silk and sea routes of antiquity was at the center of one of the most important crosscultural connections in world history, linking South Asia to East Asia. Imagining how Buddhism was, and is, *lived* by actual Buddhists across this vast religious geography is indeed quite daunting.

All that we have now to inform us about Buddhist tradition are four sources: texts in translation, the cumulative record of art and architecture, thousands of inscriptions from Buddhist monuments, and ethnographic records of Buddhist societies.[1] Central to most courses are texts rendered into English, and these should be read critically, informed with historical and sociological imagination. Why? Because Buddhist texts were written down by the literate elite in societies in which literacy was rare. Their authors were not typical Buddhists, but members of the sangha, the monastic order. And these monk-authors tended to be most interested in the rules of the order, doctrinal exposition, and often the fine points of meditative technique or philosophical argument.

Remarkably few Buddhist texts, in fact, address the religious interests or practices of the householders, the men and women who constituted 95 percent or more of almost every known Buddhist community.[2] Their lifeworlds were only rarely a celibate monk-writer's focus.[3] So, when we read the texts in translation, we are almost always sampling topics that were of prime interest to only a minority of Buddhists.

This divide was common to all world religions, especially before the modern era. There was the elite: the saints, the great thinkers, a small group of what the sociologist Max Weber called the "religious virtuosi." They naturally draw our attention. And, as intellectual readers, we are drawn to the beliefs and spiritual practices of these Buddhists, some of whom are among the greatest figures in the history of religion. The records of the Buddhist elite's teachings, the philosophers' systems of doctrinal thought, the saints' mind-boggling asceticism, and the wealth of spiritual practices designed to guide persons to reach complete enlightenment (*samyak sambodhi*) – all are worthy of study. These remarkable realms of Buddhist tradition – with their insights into mind and consciousness, their formulations of the existential challenges human beings face, their vision of society centered on compassion, and so on – stand among the most sublime accomplishments in the record of humanity's religious history.

⌘

Most students who take Buddhism courses wish to acquire deeper understanding of Buddhist philosophies, philosophers, and forms of meditation, and it is important to broaden and deepen their spiritual imaginations. This book is based on the assumption that there are also *other goals* to realize in the study of Buddhism. The first is to understand typical Buddhists, past and present. It is easy for elite text-based representations to reduce Buddhism to philosophy and reduce the humanity of Buddhist devotees to intellect. This is a naïve, ivory-tower misconception. To use an ivory-tower analogy: just as the courses, scholarly interests, and activities of the philosophy faculty in a college or university might be of special interest to some, no one would conclude that the history of an academic institution should be determined by what this department wrote in journals or taught in its classrooms.

Our goal in this textbook is to foster curiosity about how the history of Buddhist societies unfolded, recognizing that there were always individuals involved in the economic, political, and institutional realms of tradition. To approach these central historical phenomena means looking to the lives of typical Buddhists, those 95 percent of every society who were *not* monks, *not* philosophers or saints, but who followed the "Triple Jewels," taking refuge in the Buddha, dharma, and sangha. How did kings and queens, farmers, workers, merchants, housewives, husbands, and patrons live Buddhist lives? Only by having some idea about these "typical Buddhists" can we adequately comprehend what Buddhism contributed to Asian societies and what it now contributes across the globalized world and in the West.

So, to go beyond the virtuoso traditions, students need to study Buddhism not as a vague, disembodied abstraction but as a vibrant, multifaceted phenomenon embraced by a broad sample of adherents. Humans are so different, born with diverse talents and shaped by varying experiences; they are diverse by gender and in their economic class, factors affecting how they have engaged with their social surroundings and religions. The template of the bell curve (Figure I.1) is useful to display the universal pattern of the range of beliefs that humans adopt in adhering to any world religion. Although it is impossible to graph this spectrum with precision, paying attention to how religion exists for the elite, the average believer, and the hardly observant is a valuable exercise. In our diagram, the vertical axis plots the percentage of believers and the horizontal axis is a measure of belief vitality and ritual attendance. On the left side are the elite, whose lifestyle embodies complete commitment to the highest religious ideals. They are "all in." Examples include the Tibetan Buddhist nun doing a three-year cave meditation retreat; the Zen monk who undergoes *sesshin*, a period of ultra-intense *zazen* (sitting meditation), treating ten days as a single day, not sleeping, to achieve *satori* (enlightenment); or the *Abhidharma*-philosopher-monk who devotes his life to categorizing all the ways that the Buddha's analysis can be applied to the processes

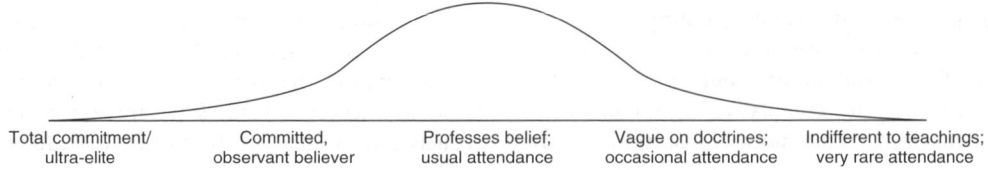

Figure I.1 A bell curve showing the universal pattern of the range of beliefs that humans adopt in adhering to any world religion.

of consciousness. On the far right are those Buddhists who are indifferent to doctrine or who disbelieve all or large parts of the dharma. (Yes, their presence is also universal; a record of skeptics and disbelievers is found in the early Buddhist canonical texts.) In between is a broad spectrum of individuals whose lives are led to greater or lesser degrees by Buddhist thought, ethical norms, and ritual practices.

This bell curve of diverse human beings who vary in their spiritual maturity is also a central Buddhist view of the world. The Buddha did not imagine or treat his disciples as the same, but assumed they possessed a wide range of aptitudes. Being attentive to the natural existence of human variance caused by karma can provide insight into how Buddhism became a great world religion, one that captured the imagination and elicited the loyalty of the full spectrum of believers in every society. Attending to the complexity of any Buddhist community can also provide clues about how and why the tradition declined or changed over its history in given times and places.

For the college student and the growing audience of westerners interested in Buddhism, it is easy to construct a historical vision of this tradition from the perspective of the spiritual and philosophical elite alone. Even though a historian can rightly point out that monks, nuns, philosophers, and virtuoso spiritual seekers have constituted only a small minority of Buddhists past and present, it has been on them that most textbooks place major focus. Taking only a small portion of the "bell curve" of all Buddhists as representing the whole tradition is neither historically apt nor adequate to convey the fullness of what Buddhist tradition has been or is today. Thus, one purpose of this book is to provide a series of representative life histories that broaden the student's awareness of the diversity among Buddhists and forms of Buddhism.

⌘

This book of Buddhist biographies provides a series of new sources for students of Buddhism; it assumes they will also be reading a textbook and texts in translation that introduce the doctrinal foundations, from the time of Buddhism's origins through the luxuriant varieties of interpretations and related spiritual practices that evolved over the subsequent 2500 years.[4] With this in mind, only two doctrinal topics shall be discussed here as they provide a foundation for the content of this volume: the canonical teachings that define the natural diversity of individuals and their practices in Buddhist communities; and the dual fields of legitimate religious practice in them, the transcendental and the pragmatic.

The Eightfold Path and the Gradual Path

The tradition itself clearly acknowledges the need to address the inherent diversity within a Buddhist society. Buddhaghosa (370–450), the great Buddhist monk and scholar, who resided in Sri Lanka, set forth an influential overview of Buddhist tradition called the Eightfold Path. This core synopsis of the faith is based on how he organized a Buddhist's necessary progression through stages:

- Morality: right speech, right action, right livelihood.
- Meditation: right mindfulness, right concentration, right effort.
- *Prajna*: right views, right inventions.
- Nirvana.

Every student of Buddhism must grasp this organization of the tradition. Buddhaghosa's schema teaches us that a Buddhist life is founded on (1) the development of moral character. One speaks truthfully, acts morally, and makes a living without harming other beings. Right action also includes ritual actions and meritorious donations. Thus, moral living defines being a Buddhist for most adherents. Further, we can see that a disciplined moral life is the necessary foundation for successfully undertaking meditation. Knowing that traditionally this defined being "a good Buddhist" for 95 percent of a population makes understanding Buddhism in practice, and "a typical Buddhist," quite straightforward.

Until the modern era, it was only select monks and nuns who moved on to the next stage (2), the practice of meditation. Here Buddhism offers two modes of mind cultivation. The first is trance or practices that lead to calming states of consciousness. The second is mindfulness, the intense focus on discerning what is truly real in individual experience: seeing reality as impermanent, seeing embodied life as inevitably immersed in suffering, and viewing there to be no soul within to anchor human experience.

To the extent that meditation is successful, the individual develops (3) *prajna*, a capacity to discern the real from the many delusions that we succumb to due to desire and anger. Here we see that one has to make a huge effort, and keep to one's intention to reach enlightenment. When *prajna* is perfected, the one who has fully "calmed the mind and discerned the real" experiences (4) nirvana.

⌘

The early texts also recommend how teachers should progress in introducing doctrinal teachings and spiritual practices to their disciples. The ancient tradition specified what was called the "Gradual Path" (*anupurvikatha*), which lays out the specific progress a typical Buddhist should make as a "good Buddhist":

1 making donations (*dana*) for earning merit (*punya*);
2 moral instruction (*shila*);
3 the value of reaching heaven (*svarga*);
4 the evil that comes from demerit (*pap*) and life devoted only to pleasure;
5 the value of renunciation;
6 study of the Four Noble Truths.[5]

This paradigm directs all varieties of persons to work through stages and pursue a gradual, systematic advancement toward enlightenment, a path that assumes a series of lifetimes. In the Pali Canon, manuals for instructors take care to define some texts as pertaining to "mundane" issues and others to the "supramundane"; some teachings apply to "ordinary persons" and others to "adepts"; but, significantly, the teaching guides do not regard these as separate religious paths but as one path with many levels and applications.

This Gradual Path framework envisions society as a multipoint hierarchy of individuals, who vary according to their karma and spiritual capacities, and teachers, who try to match each individual with the best practice for them. Working within the logic of the Gradual Path, too, we find the central ideal that Buddhists are interdependent and linked through ritual and patronage, which connects advanced practitioners with others moving along the Gradual Path. In his teachings, the Buddha was a "communalist" in cultivating both monastics and householders; Buddhist communities succeeded when the latter supported the former, who in return guided them by preaching the dharma. This fundamental exchange is central to the sociological imagination of Buddhism. The biographies depict both householders and monastics conscientiously attending to their respective roles.

This book has been assembled to provide case studies that cover the entire spectrum of the Buddhist bell curve. It will also reveal the great diversity of monastic careers and the common pattern of individuals moving along the Gradual Path – sometimes from householder to the sangha and back. We can follow notable and obscure nonmonastics who try to find meaning and wellbeing in their lives by "taking refuge." Through the genre of the biography, we can follow individuals through the logic of their lives as they negotiate the choices, tensions, and rewards of living as Buddhists. It is here where this textbook's thick description of Buddhist lives can also go beyond the particularities of learning about this tradition, and open up deeper levels of crosscultural understanding. As anthropologists L.L. Langness and Gelya Frank have written,

> The acts of empathy that arise in attempting to understand the reality of people sometimes very different from ourselves can be a real transformative process. Such acts of empathy, whether fully successful or not in actually simulating the other person's experience, help us break down the barriers of ego and identity that give us each the illusion of somehow standing separate and apart from the flow of human consciousness through the millennia.[6]

Pragmatic and Transcendental Buddhism

The dharma includes the teachings that lead elites to realize nirvana; it also includes the means of merit-making to advance in *samsara*. The tradition's canonical narratives – found in *jatakas*, *avadanas*, and stories in ritual texts – also convey the pragmatic role of the dharma in Buddhist communities. The Buddha's words convey the ultimate truth in expositions, but some words specifically revealed by the Buddha can also change the world: repel evil and create good, protecting those who take refuge in it. Curing illness, repelling demons, attracting luck and auspiciousness, and protecting kings and kingdoms are the pragmatic effects of taking refuge in the Buddha, his dharma, and the sangha. As an early Mahayana text, the *Mahavastu*, states, "For verily Dharma protects the one who lives by dharma, as a large umbrella protects us in time of rain."[7]

⌘

The stories in this volume illustrate how the dominant religious orientation in Buddhist communities has been the accumulation of merit. The logic of Buddhist institutional history in every locality has been shaped by those householders and monastics seeking to make merit the hope for current happiness and better rebirth either as a human being or a god. Students should read these texts dealing with merit and the practical ethos of proper human striving, as there are important passages that cover the details and ethos of pragmatically living a Buddhist life as a householder. One example is found in the fourth book of the Pali Canon's *Anguttara-nikaya*. It explicitly treats the issue of merit and the householder's life, as the Buddha instructs the good Buddhist to seek the "Four Conditions":

There are these four conditions which are desirable, dear, delightful, hard to win in the world. Which four? ...

[1] *Wealth* being gotten by lawful means ...
[2] *Good reputation* among kinsmen and teachers
[3] *Long life* and attain a great age ...
[4] When the body breaks up, on the other side of death may I attain a happy *birth in a heaven*![8]

The text then proceeds to specify how the moral and wealthy Buddhist householder should do the "Four Good Deeds":

Now, ... with the wealth acquired by energetic striving, amassed by strength of arm, won by hard work, honestly and lawfully earned, is the doer of four deeds. What are the four?

[1] [He] makes himself happy and cheerful, he is a contriver of perfect material *happiness* [of others]: his mother and father, his children and wife, his servants and workmen, his friends and comrades. This ... is the first opportunity seized by him, turned to merit and fittingly made use of.
[2] Then again, the ... disciple ... with that wealth finds *security* for himself from all misfortunes whatsoever, such as may happen by way of fire, water, the king, a robber, an ill-disposed person ...
[3] Then again ... the disciple ... is a maker of *five ritual offerings* (*bali*): to relatives, guests, hungry ghosts, to the king, and to the gods (*devata*) ...
[4] Then again, the ... disciple ... offers *gifts to all such recluses and brahmins* who abstain from sloth and negligence, who are bent on kindness and forbearance, who tame the one self, calm the one self ... which has the highest results, a gift heavenly, resulting in happiness and leading to heaven.[9]

The actions and ideals in life articulated here can be seen in the biographies of this volume and are evident in Buddhist householders concerned with family, wealth, rituals, and protection. Many seek to turn wealth into merit. Buddhist merit-making can "cheat death" by in future lifetime(s) reuniting couples after death and reuniting individuals with their former wealth. Merit-making is also not strictly individualistic, as actions by kin, patrons, shipmates, monks, and kings can affect the destinies of others. It is noteworthy how important the act of transferring merit is – to the recently dead, distant kin, or to benefit all beings – in the lives of devout Buddhist householders.

Finally and emphatically, the Buddha here and in many sermons recognized rebirth in a heaven as a legitimate and exalted religious goal to strive for as well. This aspiration was historically neither rare nor even confined to householders. The best example of this aspiration to be reborn in heaven is found in the life of the previously mentioned monk-scholar Buddhaghosa, one of the greatest and most exceptional intellectuals in the tradition's history. He commentated on most of the Pali Canon, and his long composition, the *Visuddhimagga* ("The Path to Purification"), provides a detailed, step-by-step guide to the stages to enlightenment and is one of the greatest

Buddhist treatises. In the postscript to this work, Buddhaghosa states that he hopes that the merit he has earned by writing the *Visuddhimagga* will allow him to be reborn in heaven and to abide there until the next Buddha Metteyya (Maitreya) appears, so he can hear his teaching and then attain enlightenment. Even such a virtuoso felt he could not attain nirvana in his lifetime, but only afterward. For him, heaven was a sufficient goal, and all he could imagine attaining.

For many monastics and most householders across the Buddhist world, "doing Buddhism" is centered on merit-making (often collective in practice and effect) and on showing respect for local deities, and is focused on earning rebirth in heaven.

A historically and sociologically informed overview of how Buddhism is lived in individual lives falls into four interlocking tracks of legitimate Buddhist striving:

1 pragmatic wellbeing, via rituals and merit-making;
2 moral cultivation, via donations, pure conduct, and compassionate acts;
3 better rebirth (human or in a heaven), via merit-making and merit transfer;
4 seeking nirvana, via meditation.

In the biographies in this volume, the reader should be alert to how, through merit rituals, Buddhism fosters family ties, encourages an "energetic striving" after economic success, promotes the worship of hungry ghosts and local gods, justifies the rightful seeking after worldly happiness and security, applauds the religious virtues of faith and heaven-seeking, and underlines the virtue of being a donor and patron. All are sound Buddhist ideals. This pragmatic conception of the dharma, however defined by local tradition, shaped the successful domestication of Buddhism from Sri Lanka to the Himalayas, from central Asia to Japan, and from Beijing to Ohio. Analyzing the Four Good Deeds alongside the Four Noble Truths as textual distillations of normative Buddhism is essential for understanding Buddhism with historical imagination.

To see the relevance of both of these central doctrines, students should read the popular canonical (or postcanonical) narratives called *jatakas*. There are over six hundred, which attests to their popularity and use. In each, the actions of the future Buddha Shakyamuni – who is reborn as an animal, spirit, or human – convey the realities of karmic cause and effect, the role of rituals, how beings reappear in each others' lives, and how to pursue the ideal of experiencing nirvana in the future. These stories were used in sermons, depicted on monastery walls, and acted out in festivals that conveyed the dharma as truth and power to householders and monks from antiquity onward.[10]

⌘

Students should be aware of a common, and false, Western stereotype that Buddhism is only a philosophy and not a religion. Its corollary is to dismiss rituals as contradicting the pure teaching of the Buddha, seeing them as concessions to the ignorant masses. In the texts quoted above, of course, the Buddha belies this modern misconception, specifically recommending ritual offerings to gods and hungry ghosts as good, compassionate deeds for householders. In these biographies as well, what is obvious is that rituals are integral to the central practice of making merit and taking part in the living tradition. Moreover, precisely defined rituals characterize the ordination of monastics and the regular activities in their communal lives. The donations that provide the material necessities that allow monks and nuns to live in the sangha are made in ritual ceremonies. The Buddha himself identifies specific recitations of his words that monastics must recite in rituals (called *paritta* in the Theravada world, *raksha* in the Mahayana) to create worldly, pragmatic protection from a host of dangers to people and communities. Death rites are especially elaborate, as are the procedures for introducing many forms of meditation. Anyone who lives in an Asian community where the tradition is found quickly and decisively comes to know that it is through ritual that adherents live their Buddhist lives.

That the monastic elite do not segregate themselves from pragmatic concerns of their communities is illustrated by a tradition in Thailand. There, the *Abhidharma*, the third division of the Pali Canon, is a focus of both transcendental analysis and pragmatic concerns. While these texts provide detailed distillations of the Buddha's teachings, and so serve as guidelines for erudite scholarly analysis or meditative practice, in Thailand there is also another use for these "working texts." These same texts are central to common rituals: monks recite the *Abhidharma* at funerals and these texts are donated to temples as an act of merit-making; further, the sacred syllables from parts of these texts are used in chants to generate protective powers. Here we see the literal confluence of the transcendental and the pragmatic in living Buddhism.

⌘

In summary, taking refuge in Buddha, the dharma, and the sangha meant following a tradition that offered various means by which the Buddha's words and Buddhism's saints' ritual actions could exert control over the powers of the universe. In this way the dharma was a force for good that could both resist troubles (disease, misfortunes) and promote worldly prosperity. As the Chinese scholar Yun-hua Jan noted about Buddhism in practice, "From an insider's viewpoint, ... recitation [of mantras] is extremely powerful, and in certain cases, it is claimed to be even more powerful and preferable than either a philosophical understanding or the excellence in moral disciplines."[11] On the ground and in individual lives, Buddhist traditions offered both inspiration and worldly benefits.

Thus, Buddhists are rightly concerned with experiencing the transcendental goal of nirvana, most thinking it far off in distant life; most also attend to the natural spiritual law of karma, and also central to Buddhist identity is faith in the pragmatic powers of the Buddhas and bodhisattvas enlisted through ritual. Lofty moral values and blissful fruits of meditation certainly must have impressed and converted some; but the dharma's control over the powers that ensure health, wealth, progeny, and peace had a powerful appeal in securing the faith's success in contexts as different as nomadic pasturelands, urban enclaves, and subsistence-farming villages. This conjunction of the transcendental and pragmatic has always been a feature of Buddhism wherever it has thrived in history.

⌘

The content of this book was contributed by the scholars who responded to various internet calls soliciting short biographies of Buddhists from any era. Some are based on textual studies, others on historical or anthropological research.[12] In this book's sample can be seen a cross-section of where research on Buddhism has been concentrated in recent decades. Despite efforts to seek out scholars who could write about those skeptical or half-hearted adherents on the right-hand side of the bell curve, few biographies were forthcoming in this area, while there was a plethora of submissions tipping toward the left-hand side. This is understandable: traditional Buddhist writers of every age had virtually no interest in writing up accounts for posterity of the hardly devout, and modern academic scholars working with texts thereby have no sources to draw upon. A few historians familiar with documented communities have provided such examples, and the reader will meet the legendary Tibetan rogue Uncle Donpa in Chapter 5.

Preceding each biography is a brief introduction by the editor that alerts the reader to the person's historical context or how the biography connects with the important themes discussed above, and also introduces any special issues that are found in the chapter. For each life history, the authors were asked to include three sections: background on the individual and any interpretive themes to be developed; a biography conveyed in a vivid, creative manner; and a short conclusion highlighting how this individual's life relates to understanding the Buddhist tradition generally.

⌘

In surveying the belief patterns of the world's Buddhist communities, and in reading about the lives of Buddhists in this volume, the student is challenged both by the sheer diversity of doctrinal expression and by the complexity of Buddhism's systematic thought. Such an outpouring of writing from a tradition that held the ultimate reality to be beyond words! Buddhism's great migration across Asia, and beyond, has entailed the translation of texts, ideas, ethical norms, and rituals into non-Indic societies, communities with divergent languages and cultures. In becoming a world religion that adapted to all these contexts, Buddhism in practice promoted compassionate, medically advanced, disciplined, mercantile, and literate societies. Like other great world religions, Buddhism has shown that its understanding of human suffering and its causes, its transformative meditation traditions, and its vision of a compassion-centered civilization have enduring relevance, especially in the midst of changes that have shaken the modern and postcolonial world. This book's biographies serve to make this tradition understandable in human terms through an exceptionally diverse collection of Buddhists' lives. Composed by noted scholars, these biographies have been compiled to provide the student with what traditional stories told in Buddhist communities for millennia have also sought: to ground the teachings in the struggles of life in order to promote understanding.

References

Covil, L., Roesler, U., and Shaw, S. (eds) (2010) *Lives Lived, Lives Imagined: Biography in Buddhist Traditions*, Wisdom, Boston, MA.

Jan, Y.-H. (1977) The power of recitation: an unstudied aspect of Chinese Buddhism. *Studi Storico Religiosi*, 1, 299.

Jones, J.J. (1952) *The Mahavastu*, vol. 2, Luzac and Co., London.

Langness, L.L. and Frank, G. (1981) *Lives: An Anthropological Approach to Biography*, Chandler and Sharp, Novato, CA.

Lewis, T.T. (1997) The anthropological study of Buddhist communities: historical precedents and ethnographic paradigms, in *Anthropology of Religion: A Handbook* (ed. S. Glazier), Greenwood Press, Westport, CT, pp. 319–67.

Sassoon, V. (ed.) (2012) *Little Buddhas: Children in Buddhist Societies*, Oxford University Press, New York.

Schober, J. (ed.) (1997) *Sacred Biography in the Buddhist Traditions of South and Southeast Asia*, University of Hawaii Press, Honolulu.

Schopen, G. (1991) Archaeology and Protestant presuppositions in the study of Indian Buddhism. *History of Religions* 31 (1), 1–23.

Woodward, F.L. (trans.) (1992) *The Book of Gradual Sayings*, vol. 2, Pali Text Society, Oxford.

Further Reading

Isay, D. (ed.) (2007) *Listening is an Act of Love: A Celebration of American Life from the StoryCorps Project*, Penguin, New York.

Isay, D. (ed.) (2012) *All There Is: Love Stories from StoryCorps*, Penguin, New York.

Isay, D. (ed.) (2012) *Mom: A Celebration of Mothers from StoryCorps*, Penguin, New York.

Isay, D. (ed.) (2013) *Ties that Bind: Stories of Love and Gratitude from the First Ten Years of StoryCorps*, Penguin, New York.

Loeffler, R. (1988) *Islam in Practice: Religious Beliefs in a Persian Village*, SUNY Press, Albany.

Loy, D.R. (2010) *The World is Made of Stories*, Wisdom, Boston, MA.

Notes

1 The "first draft" of the history of Buddhism has been almost exclusively informed by the content of texts, as archaeology and art history remain marginal in academic Buddhist studies. The problems with this textual bias have been discussed by Gregory Schopen (1991). A few preliminary efforts have been made to marshal the transcultural record of ethnographic studies (e.g., Lewis 1997).

2 Tibet is the exception; there, in recent centuries before 1949, up to 25 percent of the population were members of the sangha.

3 One would expect that the literature of any world religion would address the central need of attending to the enculturation of children. Not so in the case of Buddhism. In fact there is almost no mention of children. Recent attention to the place of children in the tradition is found in a collection of essays (Sassoon 2012).

4 A collection of essays in Schober (1997) is devoted to the role of biography in the lives of Buddhists in South and Southeast Asian history. A treatment of the role of narratives in Buddhist tradition appeared in *Lives Lived, Lives Imagined: Biography in Buddhist Traditions*, a volume edited by Covil, Roesler, and Shaw (2010).

5 Note here how the ancient teachers do *not* recommend what a modern student in a Buddhism

course often begins with, the doctrines contained in the Four Noble Truths.
6 Langness and Frank 1981: 154.
7 Jones 1952: 77.
8 Woodward 1992: 74, numbering and emphasis added.
9 Woodward 1992: 75–6, numbering and emphasis added.
10 In the website associated with this book, a bibliography of *jatakas* in English translation is compiled. In a sense, each *jataka* is a biography of the future Buddha in a separate lifetime, as he worked his way up in *samsara*, making mistakes but ultimately finding rebirth as a prince in his last life, when he finally realized the ultimate truth.
11 Jan 1977: 299.
12 The student is also urged to sample book-length Buddhist biographies, almost all on saints, that provide a richer and more nuanced level of detail, beginning with the central narrative of Shakyamuni, the Buddha. In the website for this textbook, there is a listing of recommended biographies for this purpose.

Part I
Buddhists in the Earliest and Medieval Eras

1
The Female Householder Mallika

Kristin Scheible

Editor's Introduction

There are quite a few notable women whose lives are recounted in the earliest texts. Some were most intimately connected to the Buddha's life story, such as Queen Maya, who gave birth to him; her sister, the Queen Mahapajapati, who nursed and cared for him and later pestered him for acceptance into his order; his wife Yasodhara, who loved him; and Sujata, who provided the nourishment that enabled him to press forward to his final realization of nirvana. There was also the merchant wife Vishakha (see Chapter 3), who was first and foremost among women patrons and builder of the Purva Vihara in Shravasti. And then there were the eminent *theris*, women arhats whose influential poetic, personal accounts of their lives have been preserved in the canonical *Therigatha* ("Verses of Female Saints").

This chapter's subject is a devout follower of the Buddha, and her unusual life moves from low-caste street vendor to becoming favorite queen of Pasenadi, the king of Kosala. As skillfully constructed here from scattered canonical references and commentaries, Mallika's actions and her destiny in past and future rebirths become subjects that elicit many important discourses by the Buddha. These incidents center on karma, the effects of merit and demerit, the reality of spouses being united repeatedly over lifetimes, and the ways that character traits, too, carry over to future lifetimes. One surprising peculiarity in the Buddhist reckoning of merit-making is that the holier the recipient (needy or not), the greater the quantity of merit earned. Knowing this helps to explain how Mallika's gift to the Buddha, the highest of all spiritual beings, could have led to such an extraordinary and rapid rags-to-riches transformation in her life.

Buddhists: Understanding Buddhism Through the Lives of Practitioners, First Edition. Edited by Todd Lewis.
© 2014 John Wiley & Sons, Ltd. Published 2014 by John Wiley & Sons, Ltd.

What this biography also highlights is how much the tradition preserves, and highlights, the Buddha's preaching to kings and courtiers. He was a skillful and determined leader of a missionary movement built on moral foundations, and so it should not be surprising that his encounters with political leaders, and their wives, find a common place in the Buddhist canon. It might also surprise the student that such an exemplary person as Queen Mallika, immediately after her charmed and virtuous life, was reborn in a horrible Buddhist hell (if only for a short time), due to an incident with a dog. But such is the logic of karma and its ripening (*vikalpa*) in the world of *samsara*.

Introduction: Mallika's Historical, Geographical, and Cultural Context

India, the birthplace of Buddhism, looked far different at the time of the Buddha from how it does today. It would have been much less populated, and 16 *mahajanapada* (independent republics and kingdoms) dotted the landscape.[1] It was a time of social change, upheaval even. At this time, as historian Romila Thapar has suggested, republics were "parting company with Vedic orthodoxy,"[2] which set the stage for new voices, such as those of women and non-Brahmins, to make an impact.[3] The Buddha was one of a number of itinerant teachers who sought refuge in the jungle forests but whose teaching was centered in cities. The early community surrounding the Buddha drew from various sectors of society, disrupting the traditional caste-based transmission of religiosity in favor of a different authority, that of the Tri Ratna: the Buddha as its teacher, the Dharma that was his teaching, and the sangha, his community of monks. This social shift may not seem radical to a reader today, but it was radical for the period under consideration, when women's roles and caste roles had been clearly defined and were rigid.

Supporting the Buddha and his sangha financially were his benefactors: merchants with their fortunes from trade and the kings who exchanged their patronage for dharma teaching. The Buddha frequently stayed in Sravasti, the capital of the *mahajanapada* Kosala. King Pasenadi (Skt. Prasenajit) was the king of Kosala, and the focus of our chapter here, Mallika, was one of Pasenadi's queens and herself a devout patron of the Buddha. The Tri Ratna were already established by the time Mallika convinced her husband to convert to Buddhism. Through various episodes in Mallika's life, we can see how taking refuge in the Buddha, dharma, and sangha would have been understood in quite a literal way; more than once during a time of crisis, Mallika would seek out the Buddha for support. While she may have been typical in her faith, Mallika was not at all typical for a laywoman of her time, as she had access to the Buddha himself. The name Mallika is embedded in a canonical list of the most notable female householders (*upasika*).[4] Mallika also appears in a list of seven people, "famous even to the gods," who performed extraordinary acts of devotion that bore fruit in their lifetimes.[5]

Mallika was just a wife and layperson, albeit a queen and devoted supporter of the Buddha. According to canonical and commentarial accounts, her life story was interwoven with the Buddha's, and such proximity to the central biography of Buddhism warrants our attention. She was a queen, but not a singular one – she was one of a few queens of Pasenadi, although she was low born. She had sex with a dog (and enjoyed it). She argued with her husband, taunted him, and upstaged him. She was not, ostensibly, a Buddhist moral exemplar, and yet the most often pronounced expression of the Buddhist version of the Golden Rule comes embedded in her story. Unfortunately, Mallika's biography is not present in a coherent, chronologically sound, narratively coherent way. Instead, Mallika's story is revealed in bits and pieces, each a fragment with edges to explore, each a new surface to reflect some light on the morally didactic material conveyed within.

Mallika's Biography

Over a half-century ago, with an eye toward discerning social history, the scholar I.B. Horner (whose biography is included in this textbook; see Chapter 7) called for a careful examination of laywomen's lives as represented in the earliest Buddhist texts. She cast about and discovered a trove of information, albeit in scraps scattered throughout the canonical materials:

> Then, too, there was Queen Mallikā, chief consort of King Pasenadi of Kosala, with whom the Buddha converses now and again; and Nakulamātā, the pious and devoted wife of Nakulapita. And this is typical: such records exist but they are scattered through the Vinaya and the Nikāyas. These, then, have to be searched and carefully sifted in order to build up any reliable picture of the position held by lay-women at the time and the place to which this literature purports to refer.[6]

To find Mallika, let alone cobble together her biography, requires the "sifting" I.B. Horner called for, and some text-to-text jumping – premodern Buddhist "biographies" jump genres and become attached to, and assumed into, new works. Mallika is a character caught in the Buddha's own community, a karmic net that is cast and recast with characters shuffling between roles and recurringly related in birth after birth. Sometimes Mallika's present-day experiences are explained through a story of a past life of the Buddha, and sometimes they are explained by the Buddha, peering into her past lives. References to Mallika weave in and out of early stories, and that is how Mallika's story begins: she makes an appearance in the frame story of the *Kummasapinda Jataka* (415), where the Buddha himself provides details of her previous life.

Mallika was the beautiful and good daughter of the chief garland maker in Savatthi. As a 16-year-old, she once made her way to a garden with some of her friends. She carried three portions of gruel in her basket, a biographical element that connects this story with others.[7] Leaving town, she passed the Buddha on his way into town; he caught her eye, and she was motivated to offer him her gruel, which he accepted. This pleased Mallika, who then dropped at his feet to pay respect, "rapt in joy" (*pitim gahetva*). This act prompted a smile from the Buddha; asked about this marked reaction, he explained, "Ananda, the fruit from this offering of gruel will be that this girl will on this very day become the chief queen of the King of Kosala." Later that day, when the King Pasenadi of Kosala was riding by, exhausted after a battle with rival king Ajatasattu of Magadha, he was diverted by the singing of a charming young woman.

Remarkably, her rapidly ripened merit was such that, rather than run away, Mallika approached the king and held his attention by physically holding his horse's nose steady. They had a brief courtship; the king ascertained that she was unmarried and paused to rest while she held his head on her lap. He unhesitatingly brought her in a procession with his army back to her home in Savatthi, but it didn't end there. That evening, a chariot was sent for her, and Mallika was brought to the palace, presented with jewels, anointed, and made the chief queen. "From that day forward she was the dear, pleasing, and dutiful wife of the King ... and beloved of the Buddhas." Her good fortune became the talk of the town, and even sparked conversation within the early sangha about the "virtue of the Buddhas" that made her meteoric social rise possible.

What catches our own notice about Mallika, the person imagined in the literature, is that she caught the Buddha's attention, then the king's attention, and then the people's (and sangha's) attention. At first glance, the fetching story of a low-born woman rising when she attracts the king appears to be typical, a commonly employed narrative hook. But her allure is not ultimately attributable to her singing, good looks, or charming personality; what is decisive is the force of merit that is earned by a donation to the Buddha. Fittingly, the *jataka* tale that is introduced by this frame story reveals that gifts of basic (even unsalted) gruel to earlier Buddhas also resulted in better births for the givers. The other effect of this story is to introduce the queen as having a special place in the Buddha's own circle of devotees. Her privileged position, even as a laywoman, is an effect of the Buddha's own position, and this bond sets up more didactic encounters where her righteousness and loyalty to the Buddha are highlighted. To *upasikas* like Mallika, the profound, important truths are revealed about how future destiny in *samsara* is connected to an individual's action in the here and now.

Mallika was inspired to take refuge after she directly asked the Buddha about the cause of differences she perceived in those around her:

how can one woman have it all, being beautiful, wealthy, and skillful, while another can be beautiful but poor and not skillful, and another unattractive, wealthy, and skillful, and another unattractive, poor, and not skillful? The Buddha explained that traits perceived in this life are the result of actions in past lives; physical attributes are reflections of one's moral cultivation through time. Beauty, wealth, and skillfulness are caused by lack of anger, generosity, and lack of envy in past lives, whereas unattractiveness, poverty, and unskillfulness are the result of past experiences of anger, stinginess, and envy. Mallika then determined she would strive to be good to her subjects; generous to the sangha, Brahmins, and poor; and not envious of others.[8] She showed her great generosity not only by giving regular alms but also by building a large, ebony-lined hall for the sangha, which was used for religious discussions.

Although she may have strived for excellent behavior, there were a few instances when her behavior was less than exemplary. A story of an unintentional indiscretion, followed by a lie to cover it up from the scrutiny of the king, adds texture to her biography while it stands out as one of the strangest incidents in early Buddhist literature. The setting is the Queen in her bath, then:

> [a dog] ... saw the queen bend down and [it] started to perform an indecent act with her. Though she took no active part, it was not a fitting thing. However, since there are none who reject such gratification, the queen endured the pleasure.[9]

When the king confronted her about this "indecent act," she actively denied it. Even when the king pushed her to confess, after her misbehavior with her body and then in her speaking, she refused and instead concocted a story about how images double themselves in the bath house and deceive the viewer. She reported that the king himself had appeared in a compromising position when she looked upon him from the same vantage point, and convinced him he had simply seen something that didn't occur. Privately, of course, she knew she had lied, and through offerings to the Buddha she hoped to mitigate the consequences of her vile actions. The story concludes with her thoughts on her indecent act and her lies, which will cause her rebirth in the Avici hell, among the worst in the Buddhist cosmos.

Her attempt to assuage her husband aside, Mallika was not always a complacent wife. At least three heated arguments with her husband provided opportunities for the Buddha to teach. In each, the Buddha intervenes as an effective peacemaker. The frame story for the *Sujata Jataka* explains that, once, King Pasenadi was extraordinarily angry with Mallika, and completely ignored her. The Buddha came to know of it, and went to the palace on his alms rounds. Instead of accepting the alms from the king, he covered his bowl and asked after Mallika. The king complained that she was spoiled by the new privileges she enjoyed. The Buddha simply reminded him that it had been the king himself who had raised her to such a position, and that he should put up with the offense. He advised that they live in peace together. When the sangha asked about it, the Buddha explained that this was not the first time he had interceded in their marital disputes – in a past life, when the future Mallika had been a fruit-seller's daughter and had caught that king's eye, the king had similarly raised her up as chief queen. One day back then she upset this king because she didn't recognize the fruit in his bowl as being the type she had hawked before becoming queen. That king – who would become Pasenadi in a future birth – also took offense at how prideful she had become and ordered her away from him. The then future Buddha had intervened at that point, too, explaining the king's complicity in her change of status, thus enabling the king to forgive her haughtiness as he had a hand in its creation.[10]

Another time, the king was angry with Mallika; again he blamed her overweening pride, but this time the root of the argument was said to be in an offense of "conjugal rights," where she felt ignored. The frame story is much like that in the *Sujata Jataka*: Mallika does not appear for the almsgiving, the king complains about her, and the Buddha tells him to get over it, explaining through a previous life story. In this case, in their past lives, the Buddha had been king Bhallatiya, who had come upon two heavenly spirits called *kinnaras* (the future Pasenadi and Mallika) embracing emotionally. The *kinnaras* explained that, 697 years before, a storm-flooded river had separated them for just one miserable night, and that remembering that night brought forth such emotion. By reminding the king and Mallika of their love in the current life, and as it carried over from a shared past life, the Buddha acted again as an effective peacemaker.[11]

In the frame story of the *Sambula Jataka*, the sangha discusses the hot topic of the day, how Mallika had risen in life as a result of her gift of gruel to the king and how she was an exemplary devoted and faithful wife. The Buddha explained that even in a past life she had been so devoted: she was once the chief consort of the crown prince Sotthisena, who was so affected by leprosy that he left the palace to hide in the wild. The dutiful Sambula followed him and ministered to his every need. When she was almost abducted by a demon, the deity Sakka intervened. When she returned to Sotthisena's side, Sotthisena tested her faithfulness and she swore she was true to him alone. She affirmed this in the ancient Indic ritual called "An Act of Truth," in which she proclaimed that, if she were telling the truth, Sotthisena's leprosy would be healed. Then it was. They returned so that Sotthisena could reign, but soon his head was turned by other women and Sambula was jilted. Sotthisena's father, the former king (who would be the Buddha in the future), thereupon reminded his son of Sambula's unswerving dedication in his time of need and thus brought the two back together.[12] Here again, loyalty and devotion are important traits for Buddhist householders.

The stories reveal a keen mind at work; Mallika is smart. Once when the Buddha's attendant Ananda is sent to the palace to explain the dharma to the queens, Mallika proves a quick study while Queen Vasabha is not at all.[13] Sometimes, however, Mallika is too smart for her own good, but it is for a greater good that her intelligence causes trouble. In one story from a *Dhammapada* commentary, Mallika outshines, even humiliates, her husband: "Mallika called the king a simpleton for putting his faith in brahmins and took him to the Buddha, and while the king sat trembling, asked the questions for him and had them explained."[14] Here, Mallika is an agent for understanding and for the greater good of others. In the frame story of the *Mahasupina Jataka*, King Pasenadi seeks out Brahmins to interpret his 16 ominous dreams.[15] The Brahmins propose exorbitant sacrifices "everywhere four roads meet," and as they make their preparations they find reasons to petition the king for even more. "'Large sums of money, and large supplies of food of every kind will be ours,' thought the exultant brahmins."[16] In the story, Mallika at first just seems curious as to why the Brahmins keep petitioning the king (and why the king allows them to). Her suspicions ultimately prompt the king to seek out the advice of "the chief Brahmin of the world," the Buddha himself, who puts the king's mind at ease as he explains that his dreams point to the far future, that they have been dreamed by kings of the past, and that the unnecessary fears of the kings of the past gave the greedy Brahmins an excuse to prescribe costly sacrifices then as well.

The *Piyajatika Sutta*[17] opens with a householder overcome with grief over the death of his son; he finds the Buddha, who notes the householder's compromised faculties (*te indriyanam annathattan ti*). The householder exclaims that of course he is beside himself; he has just lost his son, which makes him unable to eat and draws him to the cemetery, where he cries out, "Where have you gone?" The Buddha counsels, "That's the way it is, householder. That's the way it is – for sorrow, lamentation, pain, distress, & despair are born from one who is dear, come springing from one who is dear."[18] But this householder rejects the Buddha's position, and accepts an alternative consolation from some gamblers who assure him that it is happiness and joy that arise from the loss of a dear one. Word spreads of the conversation, and, when it reaches the king of Kosala himself, Pasenadi wonders what the Buddha's teaching really is. Naturally, he consults Queen Mallika about the statement that sorrow and so on arise from a dear one, and specifically attributes the statement to "your contemplative, Gotama." Mallika responds, "If that was said by the Blessed One, great king, then that's the way it is."[19] Her apparently flippant deference to the Buddha piques the king's ire, and he snipes:

> No matter what Gotama the contemplative says, Mallikā endorses it: "If that was said by the Blessed One, great king, then that's the way it is." Just as, no matter what his teacher says, a pupil endorses it: "That's the way it is, teacher. That's the way it is." In the same way, no matter what Gotama the contemplative says, Mallikā endorses it: "If that was said by the Blessed One, great king,

then that's the way it is." Go away, Mallikā! Out of my sight![20]

Though her faith in the Buddha's truthfulness is unswerving, Mallika nonetheless sends a trusted Brahmin to ask the Buddha directly if he had, in fact, said that. Having provoked the king's anger, yet not wanting to lose an argument, shrewd Mallika wants to be sure. The Brahmin's petition for confirmation provides the Buddha with an opportunity to elaborate. Citing examples drawn from many personal experiences, the Buddha reveals the underlying universal truth that attachment to the dead leads only to grief. Now armed for a further confrontation with her king, Mallika adapts the Buddha's universal lesson to her particular situation, exemplifying Buddhist practice. She convinces the king of the statement's veracity by applying it to his own life, and what might his feeling be should he lose his own beloved dependents, princess Vajiri, his other queen (Vasabha), and his son Vidudhaba, as well as herself ("Am I dear to you?" *Piya te ahan ti*?) and the king's subjects. The king is thus drawn more deeply toward the Buddha's teaching, as he sees its applicability within his own life experience.

In this long textual account, we see the power of story, both inside and outside the text, to disseminate the dharma. The story of Mallika's gruel-giving and the story of the Buddha's seemingly dispassionate words of advice are said to have spread rapidly among the people – it is a public airing of private relations. Many people have loved and lost, and this universal experience gives rise to the truism that loving excessively is a source of long-term sorrow. The repetition of the stories of the people catalyzes understanding. But what Mallika does is analogous to and illustrative of the power of biography: she adapts the common, universal narrative of love and loss to the very particular life experiences of the king himself. Of course he would feel an especial regard for his own progeny; of course his faculties would be diminished should harm come their way. Putting a human face on the abstract teaching makes the lesson stick in King Pasenadi's mind and sways him to the Buddha's doctrines. And the special salience of this biography applies to the reader of this story, who is brought inside the text.

A vignette located in several places in the Pali Canon, known as the *Mallika Sutta*, opens with King Pasenadi and Queen Mallika together in an upper level of the palace:

"Tell me, Mallika, is there anyone dearer to you than the self?"[21]

"To me, Maharajah, there is no other dearer to myself than the self. But to you, Maharajah, is there anyone dearer than the self?"

"To me also, Mallika, there is no other dearer than the self."[22]

Clearly anticipating an exchange of affection, Pasenadi appears mystified that his beloved queen would not find him – the king, her love – more cherished than herself! He visits the Buddha, who listens to him recount the exchange with Mallika and uses it as an opportunity to share his wisdom in the form of an *udana*, or "inspired utterance":

Having traversed all directions within the mind,
No one is found more dear than oneself.
As everyone holds one's self the most dear,
One who loves himself should not harm another.[23]

This verse suggests a primary existential orientation based on the self as a moral agent. Ethical reckoning begins with self-conception and understanding. It appeals to common sense: don't be violent, because you understand what violence feels like in your own life; as you are your own most dear person, each other person understandably holds himself most dear. The Buddha himself looked to his extensive life, the stories of his past lives, and the moments that made sense of his present to reveal something pertinent to present situations.

Reciprocity often predominates in Buddhist stories: when Mallika met the king, "she did him a (good) turn" by letting him rest in her lap; the king's reciprocity is to install her as chief queen. So when, on the upper story of the palace, she replies to the king's query that there is no one more dear to her than herself, this direct and forthright answer surprises the king. Then she goes further by turning the question back to him, and his reflection is what drives further insight, beyond the romantic surface to existential depth. King Pasenadi is said to ponder:

I, who am king, ruler of the earth, indwell, after conquering it, this great circle of the earth as its owner. As far as I am concerned, it is fitting that I do not behold another dearer than the self. But this outcaste, being inferior from birth, (yet) who was installed by me in an exalted position, does not hold me, who am her lord, likewise dear. She says, face to face with me, that "The self alone is dearer." "How hard, truly, is this one," and, having lost his self-possession, reproved her, saying: "Surely for you the Three Jewels are dearer."

The queen's response reveals that even good intentions in fact have roots in reflecting on the only spiritual story that really matters in the long journey *samsara*, that of the self's destiny. Mallika explains that, while she holds the Three Jewels dear, she does so in order to secure for herself the benefits of better rebirth as she proceeds with the cumulative self-cultivation that she hopes will result in "the bliss of freedom."[24] The story of one's life is central to the ultimate reckoning of what is most valued.

Within the narrative strands of her life, Mallika exemplifies ideal householder characteristics such as loyalty, devotion, and generosity. She is also held up as the ideal wife in five traits: always rising before her husband; always going to bed after him; always obeying his commands; always being polite; and using only kind words. Through her we see that, if a person can align his or her life toward the Three Refuges, the process can be transformative. While early in her stories she lies to and argues with her husband, the later Mallika is praised as a model of feminine virtue, someone who plumbs the profundity of the dharma, especially the nature of suffering, in her honest declaration that she holds herself most dear. Clinging excessively to that which is dear is the cause of suffering, as is explored in the *Piyajatika Sutta*, and it is this theme that returns in the *Raja* or *Kosala Sutta*,[25] where the king himself is immersed in grief over Mallika's death.

Stories from her life, especially that of her death, become templates to explore the details of how karma works, with intentions and in actions, and the characteristics that develop through time to build a good person.

Pasenadi was visiting the Buddha when a messenger brought the distressing news of Queen Mallika's sudden death. His response was visceral: "He sat there miserable, sick at heart, his shoulders drooping, his face down, brooding, at a loss for words."[26] The story of her death, whispered to the king, provides the grounds within the narrative for the Buddha to explain that all the sorrow the king feels ultimately is for no good. The Buddha also anticipates Pasenadi's likely question about her rebirth location; unwilling to cause the king more pain by revealing her inevitable if short-term rebirth in the Avici hell, the Buddha repeatedly causes him to forget to ask. Only after Mallika had then been reborn in the Tusita heaven on the eighth day did the Buddha reveal her location, and he used her story to reflect on death and decay.

Reflections on How This Individual's Life Relates to the Buddhist Community

Reconstructing a life from Mallika's narrative scraps underscores the utility of biography in helping to construct Buddhists outside the text, even in the current day. Just as the Buddha's past-lives narratives literally construct his Buddha body (by narrating his cultivation of perfections), so the narratives of the past, narrative present, and future lives of Mallika construct her body as a subject for teaching the dharma. Her character, as is the case for everyone in the Buddhist understanding of karma, develops through time and through life experiences. And her character still continues to teach core values and about the workings of karma.

References

Bhikkhu, T. (trans.) (2011) Piyajatika Sutta: from one who is dear. *Access to Insight*, October 15, www.accesstoinsight.org/tipitaka/mn/mn.087 .than.html (accessed January 20, 2014).

Bhikkhu, T. (trans.) (2012) Kosala Sutta: the Kosalan. *Access to Insight*, February 12, www.accessto insight.org/tipitaka/an/an05/an05.049.than.html (accessed January 20, 2014)

Cowell, E.B. (ed.) (1963 [1895–1913]) *The Jātaka or Stories of the Buddha's Former Births*, 7 vols, Pali Text Society, London.

Chalmers, R. (trans.) (1895) *The Jataka*, vol. I (ed. E.B. Cowell), Cambridge University Press, Cambridge.

Fausbøll, V. (1877–97) *The Jātaka, together with Its Commentary*, 7 vols, Kegan Paul, Trench, Trubner, London.

Francis, H.T. (trans.) (1905) *The Jataka*, vol. V (ed. E.B. Cowell), Cambridge University Press, Cambridge.

Francis, H.T. and Neil, R.A. (trans.) (1897) *The Jataka*, vol. 3, tr. by H.T. Francis and R.A. Neil, Allen and Unwin, London.

Hardy, E. (ed.) (1899) *Anguttara-nikaya*, Part IV, Pali Text Society, London.

Horner, I.B. (1982) Women in early Buddhist literature: a talk to the All-Ceylon Buddhist Women's Association Colombo, Colombo, Sri Lanka, January 18, 1961. *The Wheel*, 30, www.accesstoinsight.org/lib/authors/horner/wheel030.pdf (accessed January 6, 2014).

Malalasekera, G.P. (1974 [1937]) *Dictionary of Pali Proper Names*, Routledge & Kegan Paul, Boston, MA.

Masefield, P. (trans.) (1994–5) *The Udana Commentary (Paramatthadipani nama Udanatthakatha)*, Sacred Books of the Buddhists, vols. 43 and 45, Pali Text Society, Oxford.

Obeyesekere, R. (2001) *Portraits of Buddhist Women: Stories from the Saddharmaratnāvaliya*, SUNY Press, Albany.

Rouse, W.H.D. (trans.) (1901) Bhallātiya Jātaka, in *The Jataka*, vol. IV (ed. E.B. Cowell), Cambridge University Press, Cambridge.

Steinthal, P. (ed.) (1982) *Udāna*, Pali Text Society, London.

Thapar, R. (1966) *A History of India*, vol. 1, Penguin, Baltimore, MD.

Woodward, F.L. (trans.) (1987) *The Minor Anthologies of the Pāli Canon, Part II: Udāna: Verses of Uplift and Ittivuttaka: As It Was Said*, Pali Text Society, London.

Notes

1. See Thapar 1966: 50.
2. Thapar 1966: 51.
3. Thapar continues, "this trend is also apparent from at least one brahman source, which describes certain republican tribes as degenerate *kshatriyas* and even *shudras*, because they have ceased to honour the brahmans and to observe Vedic ritual" (1966: 51).
4. Hardy 1899: 197.
5. *Milindapanha* 115: 291, www.tipitaka.org/romn (accessed January 16, 2013).
6. Horner 1982.
7. See the third story in *Jatakamala*, or *Kathasaritsagara* xxvii.
8. Hardy 1999: 197.
9. Obeyesekere 2001: 162.
10. Francis and Neil 1897: 13–15.
11. Rouse 1901: 271–5.
12. Francis 1905: 48–53.
13. Malalasekera 1974: 455.
14. Malalasekera 1974: 455.
15. Chalmers 1895: 187–94.
16. Chalmers 1895: 187.
17. Bhikkhu 2011.
18. Bhikkhu 2011.
19. Bhikkhu 2011.
20. Bhikkhu 2011.
21. "Atthi nu kho te Mallike koc' añño attanā piyataro?" (Steinthal 1982: 47). *Attana* means "yourself."
22. Woodward 1987: 56.
23. Masefield 1994–5: 729–30.
24. Masefield 1994–5: 730.
25. Bhikkhu 2012.
26. Bhikkhu 2012.

2
Bhadda Kundalakesa
The Ex-Jain

Alice Collett

Editor's Introduction

There are many texts from early Indian Buddhism that include evidence of female practice, and other figures from this early period are included in this volume. While there is much evidence that, like all ancient religions, the tradition founded by the Buddha assumed that men were innately superior in most matters, including spiritual aptitude, it eventually evolved to allow women to enter the sangha. From then on, the sangha was a refuge for women. This chapter focuses on a biographical account of one of these early and influential Buddhist woman monastics, Bhadda Kundalakesa.

This precise, scholarly chapter raises issues that students should be aware of as they read these story narratives. Being the product of several or more centuries of oral transmission and countless retellings, what ended up as a written text in a modern collection must be read critically, not as naked history but as redacted by unknown editors, some of whom were as interested in telling a good tale as in preserving a pure historical tradition. The fact that this enlightened woman is found in accounts across the earliest strata of Buddhist literatures does suggest that she may well have been a contemporary of the Buddha.

This biography gives insight into the context of ancient northeast India at a time when the Buddha and many other wandering teachers were criss-crossing the early cities and trade routes of that area, attracting communities of followers and debating with each other, with their disciples sometimes switching teachers. There are also insights about the role of women at the time, the age of marriage, and how the Buddhist movement succeeded in attracting, inspiring, and even celebrating women's spiritual attainments.

Buddhists: Understanding Buddhism Through the Lives of Practitioners, First Edition. Edited by Todd Lewis.
© 2014 John Wiley & Sons, Ltd. Published 2014 by John Wiley & Sons, Ltd.

Introduction

It would appear from the Sanskrit, Chinese, and Tibetan texts that the women whose lives are recounted or whose stories are told in the Pali literature were known across all the schools of early Buddhism, as the same or very similar stories appear elsewhere. The evidence about women in the early tradition includes, for example, a well-known text of verses attributed to "elder nuns" (*theris*) who were apparently direct disciples of the historical Buddha; a list of preeminent nuns and a similar list of distinguished laywomen; stories of the conversion to Buddhism and women's attainment of complete awakening; and narrative accounts of women's lives.

This chapter focuses on a biographical account of one of these Buddhist nuns, Bhadda Kundalakesa. According to the textual accounts, Bhadda was a historical figure who lived during the time of Gotama Buddha and was one of his disciples. Several Indian Buddhist texts contain accounts of Bhadda, but in this chapter I focus on just the Pali literature. The main part of the chapter recounts the longest and most detailed account of her life, from a fifth-century commentarial text, the *Manorathapurani*.[1] This text is a commentary on an earlier canonical text – the *Anguttara-nikaya*. Following this biography of Bhadda's life, I compare this later work to other accounts of her. Firstly, I discuss verses attributed to her in the *Therigatha*, or "Verses of Elder Nuns," a composite text that may contain parts that date to the time of the Buddha himself. I also look at the biography of Bhadda's life in the *Theri-Apadana*, a text composed around the second century BCE that has some interesting differences from the later commentarial work. To conclude, I compare the *Manorathapurani* biography with analogous ones in other Pali commentaries dating to a similar period.

The *Manorathapurani* account begins, as is typical for the text, by noting Bhadda Kundalakesa's distinguished ability – that she is foremost in quick realization, or higher knowledge (*khippabhinna*). Then there is some cataloging of her past lives, under previous Buddhas. The woman (who becomes Bhadda) was born into a noble family in the town of Hamsavati during the eon of Buddha Padumuttara. When she heard Buddha Padumuttara declare a nun to be foremost in quick intuition, she made a resolve to attain that same distinction. After transmigrating for a hundred thousand eons in the worlds of gods and men, she was reborn, during the time of Buddha Kassapa, in the house of Kiki, a king of Benares, as one of his seven daughters. In devotion to Buddha Kassapa, she lived an ethical and celibate life for twenty thousand years. Following that, having transmigrated among worlds of gods and men in the interval between one Buddha and another, she was reborn in the era of Gotama Buddha in the city of Rajagaha, to the family of a wealthy merchant, and given the name Bhadda.

On that same day, in that same city, a son was born to the king's priest. At the moment of his birth, the weapons in the entire city, beginning with those at the king's palace, began to glow brightly. Early next morning, going to the king's family, the priest asked whether the king had slept well. The king replied, "Teacher, how could we sleep well this day, fear arises in us seeing the weapons in the palace glowing brightly all night long." The priest replied, "Great king, don't let this be cause for concern. It was not only the weapons at your palace that glowed brightly but those all over the city." The king asked why this had happened and the priest told him, "A child was born in our house under the robber's star. He has arisen as an enemy of the entire city, that is his sign. This is not misfortune for you especially, but if you wish we will take him away." The king replied that, as long as the boy presented no harm to him or his family, there was no need to take him away. The child was named Sattuka ("enemy").

Bhadda grew up in the wealthy merchant's house, while Sattuka grew up in the house of the king's priest. From the time Sattuka was able to walk and run around, he would steal whatever he found and bring it home until his parents' house was full. His father was not able to stop him, even after threatening him. Years later, when Sattuka was older, his father, seeing he could not prevent Sattuka from doing this, provided him with the necessary clothes and tools for housebreaking and sent him off to earn his living this way. This he did, and soon across the entire city there was not a house he had not robbed.

One day, the king was out in the city in his chariot and he asked his charioteer, "Why is it that breaches can be seen in every single house in the city?" The charioteer replied, "King, in this city is a thief named Sattuka who breaks through walls and takes the family's property." The king sent for the city watchman and asked him why this thief had not been apprehended. The city watchman replied that they were not able to find him. The king said, "If this thief is not seized today, I will have you punished."

The watchman sent men all over the city. The thief was caught red-handed, carrying stolen goods from a house, and was taken to the king. The king ordered that the robber be taken from the city and killed. The city watchman took him forth, according to the king's command, beating him with a thousand blows at points along the way, and took him to the south gate of the city.

At that moment, Bhadda[2] had opened her window and was looking out because of the noise made by the crowd. She saw the thief Sattuka being led away. Clasping both hands to her heart, she threw herself on her bed. As she was the only daughter of the family, her relatives could not bear even the slightest troubled look on her face, so seeing her lying there they asked her what was the matter. "Did you see that thief being led away to execution?" she asked, "If I have him I will live, not having him will be the death of me." They were not able to console her in any way so her father went to the city watchman and bribed him with a thousand pieces of gold, asking him to set the thief free as his daughter had her heart set on him. The watchman agreed, and delayed the execution until sunset. Then he had another man brought out from the prison, had Sattuka's bonds untied, sent him to the house of Bhadda's father with some servants, and had the other man led away to be killed.

Deciding to fulfill his daughter's wishes, her father had Sattuka bathed in perfumed water, adorned with jewels, and sent to the upper part of the house. Bhadda, happy that her wishes were fulfilled, adorned herself with jewels and went about her duty of serving her husband. After a few days had passed, Sattuka thought, "These jewels and ornaments she wears will be mine! I will find a way seize these gems!" At a time they were sitting happily near one another, he said to Bhadda, "There is something I should say." The merchant's daughter, with a happy mind, like someone who had received a thousand gifts, said, "Speak freely, my lord." He said, "You thought you saved my life, but when I was seized I prayed to the goddess inhabiting the mountain on which thieves are killed that if my life was saved I would give offerings. It was because of her my life was saved, so we should prepare offerings." Bhadda, thinking she would fulfill his wishes, had offerings prepared, adorned herself with all her jewels, got into the cart with her husband and off they went. Once there, she began to climb intending to make offerings to the goddess of the mountain. Satukko thought, "With everyone going up the mountain, I will not have the opportunity to seize the jewels," so he gave Bhadda the offering bowl to take and he went on up the mountain. He said no loving words to Bhadda while talking with her, and from his manner she understood his intentions. He said to her, "Bhadda, take off your garment and make a bundle of those jewels you are wearing." "Husband, what did I do wrong?" "Do you think I came to make an offering? I could tear out that goddess' liver and eat it! I came under pretense because I covet your jewels." Bhadda replied that, as they were now husband and wife, the jewels belonged to both of them equally, not just to her. After agreeing to hand them over she asked that just one final desire of hers be granted, that, still dressed in all her jewels, he allow her to embrace him, once face to face and once from behind. He agreed to this, and after their first embrace, going to embrace him from behind, she instead pushed him off the precipice, and he fell to his death. Seeing this happen, the goddess of the mountain uttered this verse:

Not in all situations is a man wise,
A woman can be wise too, watchful here and there.
Not in all situations is a man wise,
A woman can be wise too, should she think for only a moment.

Realizing that she could not now go home, Bhadda decided that she would instead become a renouncer and join an ascetic order. She went to the Jain order, and asked to be admitted. They asked her, "What type of ordination will you take?" and she asked for the highest form of ordination. They ordained her by pulling out her hair with a Palmyra thorn. And, when the hair grew back, it grew out very curly, and so she came to be called Kundalakesa ("curly hair").

Undertaking practice, she easily grasped all the teachings in the place she had been ordained. Seeing there was nothing further to be learned there, she wandered from royal city to village and town, going where there were learned ones and learning all they had to offer. It came to be that soon no one could give answers to her questions because of her advanced learning. Not finding anyone able to debate with her, entering a village or town she would make a pile of sand at the gate, stand a branch of a *jambu* tree in it, and say to nearby children, "If anyone is able to debate with me, let them trample down this branch." If after seven days no one had trampled it down, she would take it and depart.

During this time, the Buddha was staying at the Jeta Grove, near Savatthi. One day, Kundalakesa also arrived in Savatthi. Entering into the city, she stood the branch in a pile of sand as before, and instructed the children as before. Just then, the Buddha's disciple, Sariputta,[3] was entering the city alone, the community of monks having gone in ahead of him. Seeing the *jambu* branch in the mound of sand he asked: "Why is this here?" The children told him, and so he instructed the children to trample it down, which some of them did. Kundalakesa, having finished her alms round in the city, was leaving and saw that the branch had been trampled. When she heard it was Sariputta's doing, she thought: "Indeed, he must be a great man daring to trample the branch. I will obviously be inferior to him and not be able to outshine him in debate. I must go to town and inform the community." And so everyone in the city, in all districts, came to know of this.

Now Sariputta, having finished his alms round in the city, sat down at the foot of a tree. Then Kundalakesa, followed by a great crowd, approached Sariputta, greeted him in the customary respectful way and stood to one side. She asked, "Blessed Teacher, was it you who had my branch trampled?"

"Yes, it was I," he replied. Kundalakesa responded: "So it be, Blessed Teacher, let us debate, you and I." Sariputta consented, asking her who should put the first questions. Bhadda asked first, questioning him on all matters on which she was learned. Supplying good answers, Sariputta dispensed with all her questions easily. Not able to defeat him, she fell silent. Sariputta then said: "You have asked many questions, now let me ask you just one."

"Ask it, Blessed Teacher."

"What is one?"

"Blessed Teacher, I do not know."

"If you do not know even as little as this, how can you know anything else?" Defeated in debate, Bhadda fell at Sariputta's feet, asking to become his disciple. Sariputta informed her that she would do better to become a disciple of his own teacher, the Buddha. So, in the evening, she went into the presence of the Buddha as he was teaching; she prostrated herself fully before him, and stood respectfully to one side. The Buddha, to enable her to destroy that which holds her back from cultivating spiritual insight, spoke this verse from the *Dhammapada*:

> Better than a thousand verses of meaningless words,
> is one word of a verse which, having heard it, brings peace.

At the end of the recitation of this verse, as Bhadda stood there she attained the state of an *arahant*. The Buddha consented to her ordination, so she joined the nuns in their nunnery and renounced the world. Afterward, the Buddha's disciples discussed the greatness of Bhadda Kundalakesa, to have attained the state of an *arahant* after hearing only one verse. The Buddha placed Bhadda as foremost in quick realization.

The Biographical Details of Bhadda Kundalakesa in Other Texts

As mentioned above, Bhadda Kundalakesa is known from a variety of texts and although her biography is identifiably hers in other texts – that is, many elements of it remain the same – there are significant differences in the various accounts. In the remainder of this chapter, I look briefly at other accounts of her.

Therigatha

There are verses attributed to Bhadda Kundalakesa in the *Therigatha*, a canonical collection of verses of elder nuns who are considered to have been direct disciples of the historical Buddha.

The text contains accounts apparently authored by the nuns themselves, telling of their struggles for (religious) liberation. The verses of Bhadda in the *Therigatha* are as follows:

> Hair cut, wearing dirt, with one robe, I wandered previously, thinking there was fault where there was no fault, and that there was no fault where there was fault.
> Leaving from my daytime dwelling on Mount Gijjhakuta, I saw the stainless Buddha, attended by his community of monks.
> Having bent the knee, having paid homage, I stood face to face with him, hands in the gesture of respect. "Come, Bhadda," he said, that was my ordination.
> I traveled over Anga and Magadha, Vajji, Kasi, and Kosala. Free from debt, for 50 years I enjoyed the alms of the kingdoms.
> Indeed, this lay disciple is wise and has produced much merit, this one who gave a robe to Bhadda, who is now free from all bonds.[4]

The allusion to one robe in the first verse refers to Jainism. This is a difference between the two traditions according to the early literature – Buddhist renouncers owned and wore either two or three robes, and the Jainas that had robes had only one (others of them would wander naked). The next refrain in that verse, "thinking there was fault where there was no fault, and that there was no fault where there was fault," also refers to Bhadda's previous religious persuasion. Now, as a Buddhist, she sees that the beliefs she held as a Jain practitioner were at fault and that they were not in accord with the way things are as she now understands them and, to her mind, now understands them properly.

Theri-Apadana

In the version of Bhadda Kundalakesa's story in the *Theri-Apadana*, many of the elements are the same as the *Manorathapurani* version above; however, they are told in a much less embellished and shorter form. In the *Theri-Apadana*, Bhadda Kundalakesa's account begins with her birth during the time of Buddha Padumuttara and her aspiration to become a disciple foremost in quick realization. Following that her birth as one of the seven daughters is recounted and then her present existence. In this version, the fatalistic underpinning of the relationship between Bhadda and Sattuka as expressed in the *Manorathapurani* version is missing. The long prolegomenon to their meeting in the narrative above, which begins with them both being born on the same day in the same city, is replaced in the *Theri-Apadana* version with just two short verses that sum up their meeting and marriage:

> Seeing a thief being led away for execution, I became infatuated with him. My father had him released for a thousand coins.
> Seeing my state of mind, my father gave him to me. I had trust in him, and was devoted and affectionate towards him.[5]

This difference between the two accounts is an important one, as the earlier account in the *Theri-Apadana* presents the course of events as circumscribed around a woman's free choice to choose her own marriage partner. The fatalistic turn in the later commentarial narrative circumvents this. However, that the narrative revolves around this key point in the *Theri-Apadana* version highlights circumstances not often considered to have been a reality for women in ancient India. Contemporaneous Brahmanical literature from the period prescribes rules for behavior and domestic duties for women, and according to these texts women were often betrothed as early as three months old and married before puberty to a man chosen for them by their parents. This type of marital arrangement appeared to have largely been the norm and is attested to in some texts, through the apparent voices of young girls distraught at not having been married off by the time they reached puberty. Stephanie Jamison translates some such passages:

> She saw her period (had come) unexpectedly. The child became ashamed of menstruating while in a maidenly state.[6]

> "My period has arrived and no husband has been chosen for me.
> What happened; What is to be done?"[7]

However, as well as this story of Bhadda Kundalakesa, there is some evidence from Buddhist literature that suggests that the social stricture that all female children should be married before puberty to a man chosen for them by their parents was not as pervasive as has been considered to be the case. As Bhadda chose her own marriage partner, and this is attested to in all versions of her narrative, and glossed as fate only in the *Manorathapurani* version, she either was not betrothed at an early age or was allowed to renege on the family's promise. The thief was very much her own choice, a decision born from sudden infatuation, not a considered decision made in consultation with her parents and, given the consequences, not a good choice either. However – and surprisingly, given assumptions about parental control of marital arrangements at the time – her parents appeared to have supported her decision to wed a social delinquent, even at acute financial cost. Unfortunately, Bhadda's age at the moment of her infatuation and subsequent marriage is not stated in any of the life accounts. Women were often married as children in ancient India and, in both Buddhist and Brahmanical literature, there was a notion of a time of "coming of age" that was the time for children to take up adult duties. It appears that, although the notion of "coming of age" was popular, what was considered to be the appropriate age at which this occurred varied, in some cases being as young as seven or eight and in other cases being 12 or 13, the onset of puberty. There is some evidence that, at this time in some early communities, children or young women were given choices other than marriage. For example, there is a Buddhist story of a woman who became a learned Brahmin because, leading up to and at the moment of coming of age, she was identified as extremely intelligent.[8] Other Buddhist literature refers to girls or young women who at this time made a decision to "go forth" as a Buddhist or Jain practitioner and in other accounts are said to choose to become a lay follower of the Buddha, seemingly instead of marriage and as a precursor to taking ordination later in life.

The *Theri-Apadana* account of the life of Bhadda Kundalakesa has one striking difference from other accounts. In the *Theri-Apadana* account Bhadda's conversion to become a follower of the Buddha is entirely different. Sariputta, so key to Bhadda's conversion in other accounts, is missing from this account. In the *Theri-Apadana*, Bhadda is converted when she has a particular experience. The somewhat ambiguous text reads as follows:

> Dogs seized a human hand that had been cut off, dropped it close to me and went away. Seeing the sign, I received the hand that was full of maggots.[9]

Dogs, it would appear from early Indian literature, could be aggressive, and, as cremation as a death rite was the norm, partially decomposing bodily parts were not an uncommon sight. But the crux of the verse is Bhadda's response to this incident; it caused her to reassess. In the satirical refrain, the hand full of maggots seems to represent Jain doctrine. As soon as Bhadda realizes that, in fact, those doctrines she holds true are a festering mass of inconsistencies and falsities, she immediately seeks a new teacher and is directed to the Buddha.

The change to the narrative in later versions of the story may have come about because the pun and the inherent satire of the verse were lost on later redactors. The new version, of conversion through debate, both maintains some of the original thrust of the *Theri-Apadana* version and upholds the spirit of it. In the version in which Bhadda Kundalakesa is converted through dialogue with Sariputta, the prologue to the debate paints Bhadda as an intelligent woman, highly skilled in learning and articulate discourse. She is so learned and skilled in the art of debate that none can match her, and, it would appear, few dare to. Her conversion comes about as Sariputta triumphs in their exchange. He does this by putting a question to her that she cannot answer – "what is just one?" This is a question recorded in other parts of the Pali Canon as one of the ten questions for novices. The answer to the question is not a profound one; the answer is that all beings subsist on food. However, the point is rather that Sariputta demonstrated an ability to outwit Bhadda in debate, and by doing so was the catalyst for her conversion.

Biographies of Bhadda Kundalakesa in other commentaries

The two other Pali commentaries that tell Bhadda Kundalakesa's biography are the commentary on the *Therigatha* and the commentary on the

Dhammapada. There is also a similar story in the *Sulasa Jataka*, although in this case the protagonist is not Bhadda but a courtesan. The biographies in the *Therigatha* and *Dhammapada* commentaries are essentially the same story as in the *Manorathapurani*, but with both slight and more major differences. The *Dhammapada* commentary tells us only of Bhadda's present life, while the *Therigatha* commentary recounts her previous births, mirroring the narrative of the *Manorathapurani*. But neither of the other two commentarial accounts proffer the fatalistic underscore to her relationship with Sattuka found in the *Manorathapurani*. In these instances, again her choice is her own. Another interesting difference between the commentarial accounts is the attribution of exemplary quick wit to Bhadda. In the *Therigatha* commentary, as in the *Manorathapurani*, she realizes Sattuka's intention to kill her as they ascend the mountain. In the *Dhammapada* commentary, however, she remains blind to his true intentions until he reveals them to her himself, which rather seems to undermine both her otherwise apparent strong perceptive ability and the ensuing verses on women's wisdom. One final slight difference – an amusing one – in the commentarial narratives comes again from the *Dhammapada* commentarial account. In this version, Bhadda is understood to have been such a formidable debater that whenever men know she was in town, fearful of being drawn into debate with her, they would run away!

Conclusion

The Pali biographies of Bhadda Kundalakesa outlined above overlap both with regards to the story arc and in detailing specific episodes in the narrative. However, although this might seem to suggest some historical accuracy to the biographical account as a whole and some episodes in particular, this cannot be substantiated. Evidence from early manuscript fragments and from studies of Buddhist manuscript cultures, and detailed study of these preserved textual accounts of early Buddhist women clearly demonstrate that it is important to question the level of historical accuracy in these early records. The extant texts have undergone long processes of oral and written transmission, and both conscious and unconscious changes to the biographical accounts will have happened along the way, sometimes it seems even to the extent that a biography usually associated with one particular nun in one tradition comes to be associated with a different nun in another. Nevertheless, the person of Bhadda Kundalakesa lives on in the extant literature, and her life story remains a source of inspiration to Buddhist monks and nuns today.

References

Collett, A. (2009) Somā, the learned Brahmin. *Religions of South Asia* 3 (1), 93–109.

Jamieson, S.W. (1996) *Sacrificed Wife/Sacrificer's Wife: Women, Ritual and Hospitality in Ancient India*, Oxford University Press, Oxford.

Further Reading

Barnes, N.J. (2002) Women and Buddhism in India, in *Women in Indian Religions* (ed. A. Sharma), Oxford University Press, Oxford, pp. 38–69.

Blackstone, K.R. (2000) *Women in the Footsteps of the Buddha: Struggles for Liberation in the Therīgāthā*, Motilal Banasidass, Delhi.

Collett, A. (ed.) (2013) *Women in Early Indian Buddhism: Comparative Textual Studies*, Oxford University Press, New York.

Collett, A. (forthcoming) *Pāli Biographies of Buddhist Nuns*.

Lilley, M.E. (ed.) (2006 [1925–7]) *Therī-Apadāna*, in *The Apadāna, Parts I & II*, Pali Text Society, London.

Neumaier, E.K. (2004) Women in the Buddhist traditions, in *Women and Religious Traditions* (ed. L.M. Anderson and P.D. Young), Oxford University Press, Oxford, pp. 80–107.

Sponberg, A. (1992) Attitudes toward women and the feminine in early Buddhism, in *Buddhism, Sexuality and Gender* (ed. J. Ignacio Cabezon), SUNY Press, Albany, pp. 3–36.

Oldenburg, H. and Pischel, R. (eds) (1999 [1883]) *Theragāthā-Therīgāthā*, in *The Thera- and Therīgāthā: Stanzas Ascribed to Elders of the Buddhist Order of Recluses*, Pali Text Society, Oxford.

Walleser, M. (ed.) (1973 [1924]) *Manorathapūraṇī*, in *Manorathapūraṇī: Buddhaghosa's Commentary on the Aṅguttara-Nikāya*, vol. 1: *Eka-nipatā-vaṇṇanā*, Pali Text Society, London.

Notes

1 The *Manorathapurani* account in this chapter is a partial translation and a partial paraphrase, with some slight abridgment.
2 Here, as in some other places in the *Manorathapurani*, Bhadda is called Subhadda.
3 The name Sariputta is not used in this text, although in other texts it is. Here he is called Dhammasenapati ("captain of the teachings").
4 *Therigatha* 107–11.
5 *Theri-Apadana* 23–4.
6 *Mahabharata* III.290.3 as cited in Jamieson 1996: 238.
7 *Mahabharata* I.77.6 as cited in Jamieson 1996: 238.
8 Collett 2009.
9 *Theri-Apadana* 38–9.

3
Two Noted Householders of the Buddha's Time
Upasika *Vishakha and* Upasaka *Anathapindika*

Todd Lewis

Editor's Introduction

The legendary patrons of the Buddha and his movement featured in this chapter are associated with the building of the first permanent monastic residences for the sangha. These patrons are Anathapindika, whose gold coins purchased the lovely forested land on which he built the Jetavana monastery in Shravasti, and Vishakha, who sold her dowry jewelry to build the spacious grounds of the Purva Arama ("Eastern Monastery") in that same city. These were among the first instances of householders providing places of accommodation and spiritual practice in peaceful natural settings near one of the most important cities of ancient India. In acquiring these donations, the sangha came to possess the resources necessary to be a true refuge to men and women wishing to renounce householder life and become monks or nuns. The Buddha subsequently spent the majority of his yearly monsoon retreats in Shravasti, dwelling in one of these beloved monasteries.

Vishakha and Anathapindika were from the merchant caste, and are rightly portrayed as being among the wealthiest individuals of the region at the time the Buddha lived. Their prominence among the earliest disciples reveals two insights about Buddhist history. First, the rise of the tradition, and its later success, was due to the patronage of merchants. If you look at a map showing the early trade routes in South Asia, they will coincide almost exactly with the network of early Buddhist monasteries. The second insight to be drawn from the prominence of merchants such as the two featured here is that such merchants became model householders for Buddhists over the subsequent two millennia of Buddhist history. Along with

Tapussa and Bhallika, the caravan traders who offered the Buddha his first alms after reaching enlightenment, Vishakha and Anathapindika were widely featured in Buddhist monastic art and popular storytelling across Asia.

The appellation *upasaka* (fem. *upasika*) applied to both subjects is an important one in every Buddhist society. It can be translated as "devout householder." In some places in the earliest texts, the Buddha refers to his sangha as a "fourfold sangha" consisting of the celibate renunciant monks and nuns, and then the male and female *upasakas*. Across the Buddhist world up to the present, these special householders can be seen working to support the monastics and their monasteries, making donations, organizing rituals and festivals, and often managing the institution's finances. Some *upasakas* are also known for their 24-hour residence at monasteries on the *uposatha* days, which fall on each full moon and new moon; wearing white robes, they take on additional vows (not to eat after noon; no sexual relations; no entertainments, jewels, or other finery) and listen to sermons, and many sleep in the monastery. It is these "devout householders" who in many eras and places have held Buddhist communities together.

This chapter contains an excerpt from *Sugata Saurabha*, a modern life of the Buddha written by the poet Chittadhar Hridaya of Nepal (1982).[1] Taken from its chapters 14 and 17, these biographies within this long account provide a close personalized treatment of these two important merchant patrons. Although a modern composition, this work of epic poetry was composed in traditional couplets, "perfumed" with the devotion of its author, who uses a variety of other Indic poetic conventions. Where the classical sources are silent, he also inserts details of daily life drawn from his own Newar community, in Kathmandu, Nepal. The tradition of poetic storytelling found in *Sugata Saurabha* is found in Buddhist story narratives; it is composed for an unhurried reader who follows the author's skillful composition of scenes, looks for the wit in the dialog, and savors the rich details of daily life and the subtleties of his characters. In this manner, the reader here should feel the determined devotion the Buddha aroused in Anathapindika at their first meeting and then in the merchant's negotiations with Prince Jeta for his forest grove; she should also identify with the devout and spunky Vishakha, who knows her own worth, stands her ground as a Buddhist with her father-in-law, and is undeterred in erecting a fitting monastery for the sangha.

Anathapindika the *Upasaka*

When the Buddha was residing in the Sitavana Monastery
Together with his *sangha* of noble disciples in Rajagriha
The generous one whose name became famous as "Anathapindika the Devout Householder"
Came to visit a merchant at home there and consult with him.

He found his merchant friend busy as if preparing for a wedding or a rice-feeding ceremony,
Hurrying here and there as if the king of Magadha were arriving at his invitation.
So he asked – "As you have no time even to talk today, what is the celebration?"
His friend replied, "Yes, the Lord with the *sangha* is coming tomorrow,
So I am sorry to keep you waiting here, elder brother! Please do not mind."

Then Anathapindika also wished to see
  first-hand this Lord called "Buddha."
Although he had heard people speaking
  very highly of this teacher
He did not yet believe him so worthy
  because he never witnessed his greatness.
He thought to himself, "I will subject him
  to a real test now:
If he calls me by true name, I can certify
  that he is an omniscient Lord."
After a while, once he finished his evening
  meal, he said – "Gentleman! Take a torch
And let us go now to have our *darshan*[2] of
  the Tathagata."
But the merchant smiled and said – "It is
  not yet time to go meet the Buddha."
So Anathapindika went to bed with
  "Buddha, Buddha" on his mind.

Meeting the Buddha

He rose from his bed many times that night,
  thinking the morning had dawned.
Finally, he set off to the place where the
  Buddha was staying.
That night, for some unknown reason,
  Rajagriha's city gates were wide open,
But with darkness everywhere, not a single
  house could be discerned beyond the city.
Although his hair stood on end and his ears
  echoed with shrill sounds,
He nevertheless set off from there full of
  devotion.
When he reached Sitavana, he sighted the
  Lord from afar who
Having arisen from bed early, was taking a
  morning walk in the nearby open
  grounds.
After he went there, hurrying to see the
  divine teacher,
The Lord of Sages said, "Come here,
  Sudatta!"[3] and invited him to sit nearby.
Since no one there knew his true name, he
  said, "How could the Buddha know it!"
Feeling amazed by this, he promptly bowed
  to the Buddha's feet.
With all doubts and suspicions regarding
  the Buddha banished from his mind
He felt great faith and humbly asked the
  Tathagata if he was feeling well.
The Lord replied, "One who is clean and
  pure remains undisturbed;
One whose mind is pacified is peaceful;
One who is desire-less sleeps soundly, and
  always dwells at ease."
The son of Shuddhodana[4] also spoke on
  other topics, one after the other.
Although he was a householder, due to his
  natural wisdom he understood
Many things that people with wandering
  thoughts due to ignorance fail to
  comprehend …
With great devotion he then said with both
  hands folded –
"I have come to take refuge in the Buddha,
  his teaching, and the *sangha*.
Please come together with all the monks in
  the *sangha*, Lord!
Favor me with the blessing of serving you
  and the *sangha* food and drink the day
  after tomorrow!"
The Lord Buddha smiled cheerfully and
  rays of light gleamed here and there
And after having his invitation accepted
  with silence, the householder left him.
After he learned of this, the Rajagriha
  merchant turned to Sudatta and said,
"Elder Brother! Whatever foods and
  money that may be needed, please take
  mine."
"Trouble yourself not as I have enough
  provisions for the Buddha's meal
And the *sangha*'s; but if you desire, do assist
  by supplying the necessary workers." …
Meanwhile, the merchant had various
  sumptuous dishes prepared in the
  kitchen,
While Sudatta on his part readily dispersed
  money like water pouring from his hands.
That day when the Lord was guest of honor
  in the Rajagriha merchant's house,
Next day it was the turn of the Shravasti[5]
  merchant to provide a meal for the Lord.
After he with his own hands served the
  foods to them,
Once the monks finished eating their lunch,
  he made a proposal –

"I know it makes no difference to you,
  Lord!
Whether you reside in a magnificent
  building or under a tree
Nevertheless, I intend to build a
  monastery

For you to stay in when you sojourn in Shravasti."

In this way, after seeing this outpouring of heartfelt generosity and devotion
Shakyamuni smiled and recognizing his strong desire, replied –
"Riches remain unsteady like a flash of lightning, although
You now are surrounded by wealth and are bent on charitable giving,
You feel happy in righteousness and it is no wonder that you have found the right view!"
The Lord highlighted for him the importance of generosity with further illustrations –
"One offering a gift of robes offers beauty, a giver of food offers strength,
But the one offering dwellings to religious persons gives them everything."
After having accompanied the Lord back to the monastery
The merchant took leave, bowed to him, and departed cheerfully.

Building the Jetavana monastery

How blessed is Anathapindika who, though at the outset ignorant,
Perfected himself in acquiring wisdom and returned to Shravasti pure-minded.
There he looked for a suitable site where he could build a monastery and
Found Jeta's forest a very pleasant site and formed the wish to purchase it straight away.
So he visited the palace of Prince Jeta, the owner, in order to buy it.
But found Prince Jeta was steadfastly unwilling to give it up.
Still the householder made a second respectful request, "[Sell] your forest to me,
Noble Son! I ask humbly that you give it as I intend to build a monastery."
Jeta replied to him, "If you are intent on taking my woodland for a dwelling
You must do just this, merchant! Spread gold coins over all the land you want to buy."

"All right!" he said and sent his men to fetch an enormous quantity of gold coins there.
But after finding them inadequate to cover the entire tract, "Bring more, quickly,"
He commanded so that Prince Jeta, when he heard this, thought to himself –
"This work must certainly be superb, or why else pour out gold coins like grains of sand!"
So he spoke forthrightly – "Enough, Noble Merchant! You have laid out so many coins that
I will donate the rest of the land on my own. Please take as much as you need."
After hearing him say this, the householder expressed great delight and said –
"If it is so, 'Jeta's Forest Monastery'[6] will be the name given it."
In that woodland park, he had a large and splendid temple[7] built
With numerous monk-quarters, meditation halls, pretty buildings,
Strolling grounds, gathering halls, fire pits, storerooms, *bahi*,
Water taps, open roof pavilions, bathrooms, toilets, courtyards, pools and tanks.
The monastery symbolized Anathapindika's affluence,
Or a palace belonging to the earthly king of the wealth, Kuvera,
Yet also it was symbolic of the glory of that beautiful country, Koshala,
Even as holy and sanctified as the place where the Tathagata attained Buddhahood.
Adjoining this monastery, there were many rest houses constructed by others.
One poor man undertook a project there thinking, "I must do something great."
Though he erected walls with the bricks fashioned and baked with his own hands
Since he lacked the mason's art, the wall nearing completion collapsed.
Many times did he attempt to erect it again, but it collapsed again before completion!
Feeling frustration, the poor man thumped his head with his own fists and requested –

"Fine robes, sumptuous foods, wholesome
  medicines, and houses for shelter,
To those who can give these to them, let
  the monks give needed advice."
The Blessed One, having come to know
  this, sent for all of his monks there
And gave these instructions: "Be it a
  shelter, rest house, dormitory, or
  courtyard –
To whomever wishes to build it and has
  obtained the consent of the community
  for it
One monk must attend to giving him
  advice where necessary."
Meanwhile, the merchant had a pavilion
  properly erected for the Teacher's
  coming,
A house for offerings[8] was also
  constructed, with fences put up where
  necessary.
Completed, the whole area was decorated
  with garlands and flags fluttering
  "*jigijigi*,"
As the grounds echoed with the playing of
  many different musical instruments.
The merchant together with his relations
  went to conduct Shakyamuni there
And halted overnight in the rest house
  which he himself had built for public use.
When he reached Rajagriha, he learned
  that the Great Recluse was in Vaishali
So he went there and brought the Buddha
  back with him.
When he returned to his own hometown,
  the streets were chock-a-block with
  musicians
Who had come to receive and accord them
  a festive welcome.
All the invited guests and relatives
  assembled there as well
Chanting hymns in praise of Sugata that
  resounded well in their ears.
A woman was seen there sweeping clean
  the street redolent with smoking
  incense,
Where home-spun cloth spread on the
  road honored him with a white-carpet
  welcome.
Those who wore rich clothes and precious
  ornaments
And who cascaded down handfuls of
  puffed rice
And waters perfumed with five scents
  along the street,
They also incited the gaze of those fond of
  commenting on the ornaments worn by
  others.
But at the sight of the Blessed One, they
  bowed their heads low in respect for
  him,
And promptly cast rice toward him, both
  out of reverence and to still their
  restlessness.
For these reasons, the central city of
  Shravasti wore a festive look
And the Dharmaraja[9] was taken on a
  bejeweled lion throne with great pomp.

*Ritual offerings to the sangha
and the dedication of the monastery*

After washing their feet and performing a
  puja of five offerings,[10]
The merchant, merchant's wife, and their
  relatives gave each monk a rice-filled
  bowl.
The merchant also offered each an alms
  bowl filled with sweets,
As his wife donated cooked rice from a
  rice basket using a ladle.
It was husked rice, unhusked rice and
  monetary gifts that the sons offered,
As daughters-in-law gave out trays in
  which the eight auspicious sweets[11]
  were placed.
The grandsons also offered alms bowls
  filled with fried wheat flour and
  pastries,
Followed by daughters who gave out
  wheat, peas, black beans, lentils, and
  other grains.
Grandchildren gave bags with rice and
  lentils along with bagged rice and
  pulses and so on,
Still other offerings were made by near
  and dear ones who came –
Some placed white rice pudding on lotus
  leaf plates, some offered milk,
Some offered molasses placed in earthen
  bowls, some salt and cups of oil.
Some donated fruits like jackfruit,
  pomegranate, pears, etc.,
Others gave tooth sticks, chalkstone
  pieces, still others various fruits.

Some prepared sets of robe cloth saying,
"This one is suitable for making a robe,"
Some carried ropes, cords, brooms, and sticks; some gave needles and thread.
Some filled freshly baked earthen jugs with pure water,
Some were busy helping others in their work such as carrying things, and so on.
At the very end, the very generous merchant Anathapindika, the householder,
With great devotion made an offering holding a brick and clod of earth while saying –
"Whatever it may be rightly called, this is a donation to the *sangha* of shelter;
Today, therefore, please accept this well-made 'Jetavana monastery.'"
Outstretching his hands and accepting his offering of brick and earth
The Blessed One then spoke highly of *dana* (religious gifts).

Buddha's praise for the virtue of householder generosity

"Some give liberally desiring earthly pleasures; some to gain wealth,
Some for the reason of glory, some in order not to appear miserly,
Some for being transported into heaven, but these are not your reasons for giving."
Exclaiming "Blessed One!" the householder fell at the Lord's feet, overcome with faith.
Sugata gave to him who knew the dharma the name "Great Lay Disciple"[12] [and said:]
"Thank you, householder, thank you," then explained the importance of generosity –
"*Dana* is an ornament in this world, it is *dana* that ends unrighteousness,
Dana is the ladder to heaven, it is *dana* that brings peace of mind."

Vishakha the *Upasika*

When she was a young girl just at the threshold of her youth,
A bathing festival was being celebrated in the city of Saketa one day so
She went with companions of her own age.
While going to a large bathing pool in a group but
Before they had reached the bathing spot, it rained very heavily
So her friends rushed inside a rest house in fear of being drenched.
Soaked to the skin, Vishakha still proceeded cautiously along the lane
Stepping deliberately, as if she had something that could have been easily spilled.
A group just then arriving from Shravasti in quest of a suitable bride
Who were also just then stranded in the rain there saw her –
They observed all her charming qualities, her age, beauty, character, disposition.
To note how civil she was in speaking, they initiated a conversation –
"Good Lady, why do you seem to be elderly?" To this Vishakha replied –
"Why Uncles! What has made you say such a thing to me?"
They smiled and answered – "See Young Lady! All your friends
Arrived here without getting wet, but we see that only you have soaked clothes,
Were you chased by cows in the road that made you take so long?"
Looking down, she made a quick-witted and cheerful reply –

"As I do have dresses and plenty of them,
Since daughters are like earthen pots, always displayed for sale,
If by any chance my arms or feet are maimed
I will be a spinster, no matter how good my virtues and conduct."[13]

After hearing her say this, they thought – "This is one of immeasurable worth."
Staying there until it stopped raining, the women went to bathe in the pool.
After bathing, all of them returned to their respective homes.
Following close behind her, the marriage brokers reached her house.

Marriage negotiations

Her father Dhananjaya, having treated them with utmost respect, said,
"Please come in. Do sit down. Where have you come from and what can I do for you!"
They said, "For no other reason than for the great merchant Mrigara:
We have come to inquire about your daughter Vishakha's horoscope."[14]
The merchant replied, "Fine. Please do since we need to marry off our daughter.
What really matters is not wealth but an upright family, since we are such a family."
No sooner had he uttered this than his wife came in and
Set out before them dishes of fried eggs and sweets, saying, "Eat, please eat."
Having received a well-made horoscope and a good reception
The marriage brokers went back to Shravasti very much delighted.
Her horoscope was so replete with auspicious signs, it matched even before detailed study,
So whole betel nuts and confections[15] were dispatched to Saketa city per local custom.

Wedding rituals

Once her mother had completed all the formalities and just prior to bidding her daughter farewell
She shared the secrets the bride needed to know to get on well in her husband's home.
Her father also spoke to [the groom's] eight persons present there – "Please listen.
In the home to which she is going, whatever mistakes my daughter makes in her work,
Please be kindly disposed to show her sympathy, Gentlemen!"
They assented to his request and said – "Certainly we promise this, so do not worry."
Then they adorned Vishakha with ornaments worth nine *crores*[16] of rupees
That were given along with a cartload of dowry that was pulled by yoked oxen …
When they reached Shravasti, all the city's citizens there who could
Went out to see Vishakha, her ornaments, her beauty and her grace.
Their common conversation became, "See how lucky [the groom] Purnavardhana is!
Is this not a law of nature: water flows and adds to the already vast ocean?"[17]

The incident of the naked ascetics

Many days after the formal conclusion of the wedding feast
Mrigara [the father-in-law] one day had his house crowded by a gathering of naked ascetics.[18]
Vishakha was called to pay her respects to their respected holiness,[19]
So having heard the word "saint"[20] mentioned, she promptly went there.
At the sight of the naked ones sitting there, she exclaimed, "So these are Arhats?"
Then turned her back on them and went away, shaking her head's plaited hair.
The naked ones were enraged by her remark – "Could you not find any other!
Why bring a Buddhist bride into your home? Drive her out of your house at once."
"I beg your pardon, reverends! Please forgive the child's mistake," he said.
Afterwards, they were all cheered up and departed one by one.

A Buddhist monk's visit and a family feud

Another incident transpired while the merchant was eating rice pudding on a gold plate
And a Buddhist monk came to beg and stood at his doorstep.
Vishakha noted his arrival, but was too bashful to address her father-in-law directly,
So without speaking, she went outside to draw her father-in-law's attention to see him.

But since he still did not notice him and only just went on eating,
After a long while, Vishakha stepped forward and said politely to the monk –
"Please step in, Reverend Sir! My father-in-law here was eating some old ... "
Having already been infuriated by her earlier remark,
This comment only further fanned the flames of his anger.
He wrathfully placed the plate on the floor and gave orders to his servant –
"Take it away, and at the same time also expel her immediately to her own house."
But who could drive her away? Everyone there was charmed by her.
She replied – "Father-in-law! Since our wedding was not a mock wedding
How can we be parted at your whim since I still do have a mother and father;
Please send for the eight city leaders and after consulting with them,
If I am found guilty, you may do whatever you please."
"All right," he said and then sent for the eight and they all came there.
Upon their questioning, Vishakha gave them her answer as follows –
"Well uncles! Even when a monk with an alms bowl in hand came to the door
My father-in-law kept eating without any regard for him, so I said to him –
'Please step in, monk! My father-in-law is eating his previously accumulated merit.'"[21]
They then asked, "Respected Merchant! What fault do you see in this?"
The merchant then accused her of having various other defects
But she explained each, calling upon the ten [marriage] secrets her mother had imparted.
"Thank you, Lakshmi,[22] thank you," they said and after they all left,
The daughter-in-law said, "Now I must return to my parental home."
The chastised merchant then looked at his daughter-in-law's face and said –
"Don't be troubled at heart, daughter-in-law! You can forget the whole matter."

Vishakha's hosts the Buddha and monks

Chaste Vishakha smiled and said, "I am not troubled at heart for any other reason
But that I want very much to have a *darshan* of the Buddha or his monks."
After her father-in-law gave her permission to support any religion she wished to,
The next day she invited the pre-eminent Sage to come with the *sangha* to her house.
Once she had rinsed their hands and feet[23] and given them places to sit
She sent for him and said, "It would be fitting if father-in-law served the meal."
But ... he stayed away and sent a message, "The daughter-in-law may serve the meal herself."
Later, after he was sent for again and told, "The Jina[24] is about to preach the *dharma*,"
Mrigara appeared there grudgingly, remaining at a considerable distance.
He soon found how great was the Lord's preaching! With every point made clear to him,
He become a "stream-enterer"[25] while only listening from a considerable distance.
"I take refuge in the Lord," he declared and hurried up to him, bowing at his feet.
In Shakyamuni's presence, he looked at his daughter-in-law and said with hands together –
"You from this day have become my mother, daughter-in-law!"
So her name has been "Mrigara Mata"[26] since that day.

A visit to Jetavana, ornaments, and a vow

Well, as this is the same chaste Vishakha who was in the monastery,
It was she who one day came to make *dana* offerings and take the eight vows.[27]
Before going inside the monastery, she removed all her ornaments
And as she gave them to her maid, she said – "I will put them on again when I return."

When she came out after attending the
exposition on the teaching
The maidservant forgot to collect the
ornaments placed just outside the
monastery.
After they left, she told her maid, "Give
me the ornaments," but the maid froze
still
Then said – "Well, I forgot to collect them,
but I'll soon be back with them all." …
After returning home, she sent for some
goldsmiths and showed them the
ornaments,
Who valued them at nine *crores* of
rupees, excluding one *lakh*[28] for
workmanship.
She tried to sell them, but no one there
could buy them, so she bought them
herself
And brought them to the monastery in
carts filled with coins equal in value to
the ornaments.

Donation of the "Eastern Monastery"

The Buddha said, "Thank you for making
such a *dana* offering, one so fine,
Vishakha! You may build another
monastic residence near the eastern
gate."
After saying, "Fine, Tathagata, fine." She
first bought a plot of land with that
money,
Then embarked upon the work of
constructing the monastery.
One day, having learned that the Lord was
to depart, she went there and asked,
"The supervision of this monastery work,
Reverend! Who can do it now?"
The Lord of the World left five hundred
monks behind including Maudgalayana
As those who would be supervisors of the
construction work.
In due course when it was fully
constructed with two stories and one
hundred cells
When completed, the large "Eastern
Monastery"[29] was exceedingly lovely to
behold.
That monastery was very finely decorated
and fully furnished,
From the well-made carpets to the
festooning flags fluttering
phura-phura …
After traveling in the area, Sugata
returned to Shravasti,
As everyone came to see Vishakha's
monastery there …
Vishakha arranged a festival to declare the
monastery open, having spent all nine
crores,
Then she also offered each of the monks a
new set of fine robes to wear.
After she gave them all their meals for
three consecutive months during the
monsoon retreat,
On the full moon day of *Kathina*,[30] with
surpassing devotion she gave the
buildings as *dana*.
As this monastery is symbolic of the faith
and devotion of that lady merchant,
To those asserting "Women are only
hindrances to the *dharma*," this
provides an answer.

References

Lewis, T. and Tuladhar, S.M. (trans.) (2010) *Sugata Saurabha: A Poem on the Life of the Buddha by Chittadhar Hridaya of Nepal*, Oxford University Press, New York.

Further Reading

Dutt, S. (2008) *Buddhist Monks and Monasteries of India: Their History and Their Contribution to Indian Culture*, Motilal, New Delhi.

Heng-ching, S. (1994) *Sutra on Upasaka Precepts*, Numata Center for Buddhist Translation & Research, Berkeley, CA.

Ishigami, Z. (1990) *Disciples of the Buddha*, Kosei, Tokyo.

Lewis, T. (1993) Newar–Tibetan trade and the domestication of the *Simhalasārthabāhu Avadāna*. *History of Religions* 33 (2), 135–60.

Thera, N. (2003) *Great Disciples of the Buddha: Their Lives, Their Works, Their Legacy*, Wisdom, Boston, MA.

Notes

1. The biographies that constitute this chapter are drawn from Lewis and Tuladhar (2010). The translation has been abridged and simplified for clarity in a few places for use in this volume.
2. "Sighting," a term applied to images of the divine as well as living teachers.
3. The given personal name for Anathapindika.
4. I.e., the Buddha.
5. I.e., Anathapindika.
6. Jetavana Arama.
7. *Mandira*.
8. *Dana-shila*.
9. Dharma King" – i.e., the Buddha.
10. *Pancopacara puja*. An Indic offering designed to please the five senses, consisting of five things: rice, flowers, red powder, a lit wick, and incense.
11. These are eight sweets that symbolize the eight auspicious symbols.
12. *Maha-upasaka*.
13. In other words, she needs to be careful not to injure herself; the state of her clothes is secondary.
14. A negotiation of a marriage match begins in Nepal (and across South Asia) with a check of the prospective couple's astrological compatibility. This is usually done by an astrologer, who examines the individual horoscopes that are made soon after birth.
15. The poet uses Newar terms. Here again it is *lakha*, a set of 24 pieces of sweet pastry and betel nuts given by the family of the groom to the bride once a marriage is settled.
16. One *crore* means ten million.
17. In other words, the rich get richer, in property and good fortune.
18. Though "naked ascetics" is vague and could suggest Jains, Ajivakas, or other ascetics, we soon learn that it is the first group.
19. Lit. "have *darshan* of them."
20. *Arhat*.
21. Note that when comparing the two utterances the poet has written for Vishakha, in her second or testimonial recounting, the word *punya* ("merit") is inserted after "old," changing the implied meaning from food to a colloquial statement about karma.
22. A good wife is regarded as the goddess of wealth incarnate in Newar culture by both Hindu and Buddhist families.
23. The text says that she "washed their hands and feet" but this must be taken to mean that she poured water for them to rinse them, as touching a woman would be a violation of the *Vinaya* law.
24. The poet here repeatedly uses "Jina," an honorific that both Jains and Buddhists have used to refer to their great leaders. The choice of epithets here shows Vishakha's (and the poet's) clever choice of words designed to lead the father-in-law there.
25. *Shrotapatti*, "stream-enterer," a person regarded as having no more than seven lives left until he or she reaches nirvana.
26. "Mother of Mrigara." This curious and idiosyncratic usage is canonical, with the merchant attesting to the fact that, as a mother brings a boy to maturity, here Vishakha has brought his spiritual development decisively to maturity.
27. On *Uposatha* days (full and no moon days) as well as on eighth lunar days, devout Buddhist householders reside in the monastery for the day, wear white clothes, and vow to take eight of the ten main monastic rules. One of these, to eschew adornments, explains Vishakha leaving behind her ornaments in the monastery.
28. One *lakh* means 100,000.
29. Purva Arama.
30. The Buddhist end-of-monsoon retreat day, when householders donate robes and other requisites to the sangha.

4

Nagarjuna
The Great Philosopher

Joseph Walser

Editor's Introduction

Nagarjuna's life probably spanned the second half of the second century and the beginning of the third. Accounts of his life, all written centuries after his death, are strikingly diverse, mixed with legends, and utterly contradictory. The wide range of accounts of his life, along with the relative paucity of hard evidence relating to it, has led some scholars to conclude that we must be content either to believe next to nothing about Nagarjuna's life or to doubt whether a person with this name existed at all. The scholar authoring the biography in this chapter rejects these alternatives; he draws from texts, inscriptions, art, and archaeological data to construct a cogent narrative of Nagarjuna and his sociocultural contexts. A model of creative interdisciplinary historiography, this chapter sheds light on one of the key figures in the history of Buddhism while also helping us to imagine the complexity of Buddhism in ancient India.

To say Nagarjuna was a pivotal figure in the history of Buddhist thought is an understatement: he actively promoted a budding Mahayana movement and was the first celebrity Buddhist philosopher to bring Buddhist ideas into a philosophical arena that was dominated by Hindu philosophers. He is credited with founding a philosophical school, the "Madhyamaka" (Middle Way), whose adherents applied rigorous logical reasoning to try to establish that all things are "empty" of their own nature and hence not different from nirvana. Accordingly, nirvana is not otherworldly but can exist only in the here and now; language is inevitably "samsaric" – tinged with ignorance and the imprint of desire. So it is not through the inevitably distorted web of constructed language that one can realize enlightenment, but only in the silent, wordless direct apperception of the truth through meditation. Virtually all Mahayana traditions look back to Nagarjuna as one of the foundations of the Mahayana tradition, and his works are still read, and revered, across Asia.

This chapter also causes us to consider Nagarjuna as a man with a social and hence caste identity. Although he was one of the world's greatest philosophers and a thinker whose arguments guided the subsequent history of Mahayana Buddhism across Asia, this chapter also indicates how his voice was influential in speaking in support of Buddhist ritualism, patronage, and ethical principles. Addressing the king, Nagarjuna clearly states what is the classic Buddhist approach to adopting the Buddhist path: until he is able to understand the full doctrine and practice meditation, the king should practice charity, ethics, and patience. Although this biography is inevitably speculative given the lack of explicit concrete sources, it grants us a detailed understanding of what it meant to be a Buddhist in the early historical period.

Introduction

Despite his fame, it is very difficult to give a straightforward narrative account of Nagarjuna's life,[1] but this is not due to lack of such narratives. The problem is that there are simply too many of them, and they tend to reflect more of the concerns of the communities that preserved them centuries after his life than particularly accurate accounts about Nagarjuna himself. Further, the hagiographical accounts themselves disagree on the most basic details, such as where he lived. Some accounts place him in Kashmir, but some assert that he lived elsewhere in central or southern India.

Of course, as with anything in the early historical period in India, the degree to which one is willing to accept a given "fact" of Nagarjuna's life will largely be a function of one's tolerance for uncertainty.[2] Nevertheless, there is considerable heuristic value in thinking about the biographical clues that we *do* have, since the implications of even the most basic details of Nagarjuna's life shed light not only on his own writing but also on the lives of a whole host of other groups of people in second-century India. Thinking about Nagarjuna as a man (and not simply as a philosopher) offers insight about what it meant to be a Buddhist in the early historical period.

The points about Nagarjuna about which we may be reasonably certain are: that he lived sometime in the second century CE; that he began his career in Mathura, north India; that he was a Buddhist monk; that he was born a Brahmin belonging to one of the Yajurveda branches; and that he moved to Andhra Pradesh later in life and took up some kind of advisory role to King Yajna Shri Satkarni sometime after 170 CE.

Second-Century Mathura

We can make a lot of sense out of Nagarjuna's writings if we place him in the context of second-century Mathura, the ancient (and still-extant) city located some 90 miles south-southeast of Delhi. This major city is the only place in India where there is second-century archaeological evidence indicating the presence of all the philosophical schools, Buddhist and non-Buddhist, that Nagarjuna engages in his magnum opus, *Root Verses on the Middle* (*Mula Madhyamaka Karika*). So it was in Mathura where the need to address each of these schools would have been most pressing. At this time, Mathura was an important center of commerce that was located on a regional trade route that connected the Gangetic Plain in the north to leading areas in south India.[3] Though Buddhism, Jainism, and early Brahmanical religions had been there for some time, the area was dominated until the first century by devotional cults focusing on *yaksas* and especially serpent deities called *nagas*.⁴

Beginning in the first century, the archaeological record indicates that more and more Buddhist, Jain, and Brahmanical temples were being built; *naga* and *yaksa* cults were slowly being incorporated into the three expanding religions as well as moving from public spaces into domestic spaces.⁵ Mathura was thus both cosmopolitan and multireligious, with adherents of one religion living among adherents of other religions. Individuals might worship at the Buddhist monastery, but then most of your life would likely be spent frequenting shops owned by patrons of the local Shiva temple or hanging out with your neighbor who belonged to a Jain householder association (*gana*), perhaps complaining about taxes or the local school where your children were classmates. Further, there is some evidence that a single site could be considered sacred by *naga* worshippers, Brahman priests, and Buddhist monks simultaneously, much like sacred places across South Asia are still regarded today.

Buddhism itself in Mathura then was also increasingly multisectarian. It should be noted, though, that, while the traditional Buddhist histories depict the development of Buddhism as the outgrowth and branching out of a number of what we might call "sects" or "schools" (for lack of better terms), clear identifiers of these divisions are rarely found in the archaeological record. Most monasteries were simply known by their primary patron or the local ruler. Beginning in the first century CE, however, dedicatory inscriptions at a number of monasteries in Mathura do begin to record a special sectarian affiliation. The majority appear to have been Mahasamghika monasteries or their affiliates.⁶

It is likely that monasteries began to highlight their particular sectarian affiliations more aggressively when an outside group new to the region was brought into Mathura from the northwest by King Rajuvula (or by his family members, Kharahostes and Shodasa) sometime immediately after 29 CE. These Buddhist newcomers were the Sarvastivadins, a widespread and popular monastic school, but in Mathura they found themselves in a rather awkward position. On the one hand, they were the favorites of the new king and were given a monastery and land immediately adjacent to the royal palace to settle on. They may even have served as palace scribes who spread the local use of the *kharosthi* alphabet, which was used in the subcontinent's northwest. Further, the land that they occupied was taken away from the Mahasamghikas and the king made sure that it would never be returned to them by writing his wishes in stone on a Mathura lion capital inscription.⁷ This sudden loss of prestige, land, and concomitant revenue appears to have naturally incited resentment among the long-established Mahasamghikas.

Mahayana Traditions in Mathura

There is no mention of the word "Mahayana" in any inscription from Mathura at this time (or ever). This is not particularly surprising, since Mahayana in the early centuries was not a sectarian affiliation but appears to have been understood to be a kind of textual commitment that could be taken on within any monastery.⁸ That said, Falk has shown that there was a distinct interest, especially in Mathura, in the creation of images and the worship of "bodhisattvas" (Buddhas in the making) from the beginning of the Kushana dynasty (127 CE).⁹ While evidence for a cult of bodhisattvas may or may not be evidence for Mahayana traditions, it cannot be denied that all early Mahayana texts assume their audience already knows what a bodhisattva is and appear to have been seeking recruits among communities that already believed in bodhisattvas other than Shakyamuni, the historical Buddha.

While there does seem to be some connection between interest in bodhisattvas and early Mahayana, exponents also seem to have another trait: connections to Brahmin communities. Although this Mahayana movement was self-consciously Buddhist, the archaeological evidence indicates cultural elements that seem strongly influenced by Brahmanical traditions. For example, Falk has shown that the early depictions of bodhisattvas at Mathura – especially their head coverings (*ushnisha*) – bear features grounded in Vedic traditions specifically related to sovereignty.¹⁰

If Nagarjuna had been a Buddhist monk in this environment, we should expect his writings to reflect and speak to this situation. His *Root Stanzas on the Middle* rather famously argue that all phenomena are empty (*shunya*) of their own-nature (*svabhava*), a thesis that was derived from the budding *Perfection of Wisdom* (*Prajnaparamita*) literature, written perhaps a generation earlier. While the doctrine of emptiness itself had come to be understood as central to *Perfection of Wisdom* literature, Nagarjuna uses it to formulate an attack on idiosyncratic Sarvastivadin doctrines, since neither the Mahasamghika sects nor the Sammitiyas were particularly committed to the proposition that phenomena had such an "empty nature" except in the most nominal sense.[11] Given this, some scholars have argued that Nagarjuna's arguments would not have been very convincing to the Sarvastivadins.[12] Whether this is true or not is not particularly relevant since, in the Mathura context, Nagarjuna was not writing for them. Instead, he was probably writing in a Mahasamghika monastery. In these contexts, his arguments about emptiness can be interpreted as: "if we accept the Mahayana arguments about emptiness, then we will have a strong philosophical position to argue against them (these newly arrived Sarvastivadins)." It should be noted that, although Nagarjuna directly attacks Sarvastivadin theses, nothing else he says ever directly contradicts what the Mahasamghikas or the Sammitiyas were teaching at the time.

While it is likely that the earliest statements of Mahayana philosophy, the *Perfection of Wisdom* treatises, were written in Mathura a generation or two before Nagarjuna (quite possibly in his own community), this new philosophical-literary movement met resistance at the outset. Possibly this was due to the outsider Sarvastivadins challenging what they perceived to be a Brahmanical metaphysics as part of their efforts to draw clearer borders between Buddhism and Brahmanism. Afraid of being left on the wrong side of the border, Buddhists of the Brahmin caste such as Nagarjuna promoted the Great Vehicle, not as a hybrid of Buddhism and Brahmanism but as the very core of Buddhist orthodoxy, the Middle Way. It is now time to paint a portrait of what a Mathura monk's life of that time might have been.

Monastic Life in Mathura

A monk, by any definition at the time, would have been an individual who took the full set of monastic vows governing body, speech, and mind. These vows were codified in the *pratimoksha*, the list of vows that were to be recited communally every fortnight on full moon and no moon days. While there are some differences in the *pratimokshas* between the Sarvastivadins and the other sects found at Mathura, these differences would not have amounted to much in terms of the expected behavior for a monk or nun. That said, we should not assume that all monks were alike any more than we should assume that all lay Buddhists were alike.[13]

It appears that the main distinction apparent in early Mathura in the first three centuries CE would have been the distinction between the Sarvastivadin monasteries and the rest of the sects. As mentioned above, the Sarvastivadins came with an invading king and were patronized by his dynasty. This pattern of patronage continued well into the Kushana dynasty of the second and third centuries and the vast majority of patrons of the Huviksha monastery at Jamalpur were recent foreign migrants.[14] Given the connection between the Sarvastivadins and the local dynasty, it is not surprising to find donations made by the recent immigrants to support the sovereign; even the non-Kushana donors at the site record family names that reflect nomadic family structures and not the more local Brahmanism-inflected caste and clan (*gotra*) affiliations. These inscriptions made by the new residents contrast distinctly with the patrons of the other Buddhist monasteries as well as those of Brahmanical and Jain temples, whose frequent mention of caste and clan display individuals with distinctively local roots.

Of course, not all donors were laypeople. Monks and nuns in ancient India, while restricted in their *use* and *possession* of wealth, were not forbidden from having it. Presumably, a wealthy monk or nun's fungible wealth would be held by their families.[15] This wealth could then be used for specified purposes such as buying a robe, a bowl, or a monastic residence. In fact, it was quite common for monks and nuns to be patron donors to a monastery and not just its fundraisers. It is only through their recorded donations that we know much of anything about these activities of such monks and nuns from this time period. One such donation at the Sarvastivadin Huviksha monastery reveals the number of monastic specializations available to a monk or nun. As Basu has noted:

> A majority of the inscriptions indicates that the project of the year 77 was primarily undertaken by monks whose particular titles indicate their specialized role as ascetics and preachers. Joint donors of a pillar base, the monks Suriya and Buddharaksita, for example, were practitioners of meditation while another donor monk, Budhishreshtha, whose name if parsed, would mean "the foremost in reasoning," identified himself as a preacher... who knew the fourfold scriptures... Dharmmadatta, another donor, also called himself a preacher, instructor of dharma or a *dharmakathaka*. These monastic titles indicate that these monks played a more specialized role than the ordinary [monk]. The... title *caturvvidya* ["with fourfold-knowledge"], for example, refers to a monk with knowledge of the fourfold scriptures, a direct reference to the title adopted by Vedic specialists in reciting the four Vedas... Further, among itinerant monks, donors were identified as *prahanikas* (masters in meditation) and even had names such as Suriya that were unusual for Buddhist monks.[16]

This donation record points to a number of monastic specializations: the preacher, the textual specialist, and the meditator. Each of these specializations can be found in Buddhist literature (although *prahanika* is an unusual term for a meditator) and they appear to have been well established at this time if not before. What the Buddhist monastic rules stress about similar monastic vocations (they also specifically mention the forest dwellers, the elders, and those who live only on food collected during begging rounds) is that engaging in one of these more narrow vocations in no way absolved one from ordinary monastic chores and responsibilities.[17] Indeed, a monk could not get out of basic maintenance of the monastic facilities by claiming that he had some special status by virtue of his vocation. These inscriptions suggest that the Buddhist monastic living appears to have developed with an eye to parallel developments in local Brahmanical and Jain traditions. Indeed, we do not have a strong reason to assume that monks such as Suriya (mentioned above) would have made a strong distinction between Buddhism and Brahmanism.

Basu also argues that we need not assume that adopting an identity as "Buddhist" back then even included something like "conversion":

> In addition to varying regional origins, social backgrounds, ethnic identities, and occupational affiliations, patrons, especially laymen, were also differentiated according to religious identity, even as donors to the Buddhist monastery... Although as patrons, local naga worshipers and Kushana officials were all members of a larger Buddhist entity, they were not, strictly speaking, Buddhists. This points to a more loosely defined identity that held together multiple patronage groups at the site of the Huvishka vihara. *Sanghhaprakrtas* [laypeople formally affiliated with the monastery] were the only lay donors identified by distinctly Buddhist names, which indicates their status as converts and points to their integration within the monastic community. By contrast, the remaining lay patrons – both local and foreign – do not appear to have formally joined the monastery as converts. A majority of non-Buddhist names attested for lay patrons suggests that in spite of their patronage to the Buddhist monastery and their close relationship with donor monks, there was little change in self-perception among lay patrons.[18]

So what would all this have meant for a monastic author such as Nagarjuna? To begin with, our understanding of the patrons gives us some indication of what ideas would be circulated in the monastery where they resided. If a monastery's patrons were largely local, with generations of shared ties based on caste and their Brahmanical rituals making offerings to ancestors, a sermon mocking these practices or its traditions could easily be taken to be mocking the *people* who engaged in them. But this same anti-Brahmanical, antiritual sermon would have gotten a more sympathetic hearing among Sarvastivadin immigrants who wished to display themselves as distinct from and superior to the local population. If we then consider that most patrons of Buddhism would not necessarily have considered "Buddhism" to be their primary identifier (i.e., they were patrons, not converts), they could quite simply take their devotional actions and patronage elsewhere.

The fact that Mathura seems to have had two quite distinct patronage pools (one Brahmanical and local, the other non-Brahmanical and translocal) means that any monastic ambitious author such as Nagarjuna had to interpret or select Buddhist scripture in a manner consonant with his patrons, yet respond to those on the other side of the divide. The Sarvastivadins may have been the minority, but they also had strong affiliations in the local Kushana administration. Anything Nagarjuna wrote had to negotiate its own path among these competing interests.

This foray into the social context of Mathura should highlight the fact that a monk could not just write any ideas that came into his head. For a philosopher-monk living under the Vinaya rules, the constraints on writing were very real. If other monks preached, memorized, studied, or otherwise transmitted material that was deemed to be not "word of the Buddha" (*Buddha-vacana*), this would have rendered the offending monk liable to monastic censure. When it came to texts, each Buddhist monastery was the primary apparatus for the production, reproduction, and dissemination of ideas deemed to be "word of the Buddha." The biggest danger to early Mahayana was actually resistance *from the monks themselves*. If they did not approve of a text, it would not be reproduced by the scribes among them. Considering that an average palm-leaf manuscript might last around two hundred years,[19] any new doctrine would require an ongoing commitment of the local monks to reproduce the manuscript as part of its routine maintenance of its Buddhist documents if the doctrine was to survive beyond the life of the medium on which it was written. Initially, the authors of the *Perfection of Wisdom* texts sought to accomplish this by bypassing the monastic mechanism for the reproduction of texts and getting laypeople to memorize or copy texts down into a book. Nagarjuna's arguments for a Mahayana version of emptiness against specifically Sarvastivadin doctrines, then, can be seen as a specific technique to bring Mahayana texts into the normal monastic routine of textual reproduction – at least among those sects opposed to the Sarvastivadins. Only then did the Mahayana tradition grow slowly as a presence in monastic Buddhism.

Nagarjuna, a Brahmin Monk

When a man becomes a Buddhist monk, he does not cease to be a son, a member of a caste, or a subject of his kingdom. Becoming a monk merely adds one more role to his repertoire; ordination does not erase all other roles, nor does it absolve him from all obligations in these circles of relationship. He is still responsible for his family members, responsible for performing rituals for the care of his dead ancestors, and responsible for paying tolls and any taxes if required by the state.[20] Nowhere does the Buddha absolve a monk of any of these obligations should the state wish to impose them. Given these realities, it is relevant to inquire into Nagarjuna's caste.

The monk Kumarajiva's *Life of Nagarjuna*, the earliest biographical account,[21] states that Nagarjuna was born a Brahmin (the highest of the four *varnas*, or castes) in south India. While it is common for biographers of this generation to ascribe the highest caste (the best education and so on) to their subjects, in this case it probably also happens to be true. Nagarjuna was the first Buddhist we know of to write in proper Sanskrit, and he did so at a time when every writer other than Brahmins was writing in forms of Prakrit, greatly simplified languages derived from Sanskrit that were closer to spoken vernaculars.[22] Indeed, a knowledge of classical Sanskrit grammar and of the theories of Sanskrit grammarians is necessary to understand key points in Nagarjuna's philosophy.[23] Beyond mastery of the language, Nagarjuna appears to have some command of Vedic ritual literature and its commentaries.[24]

Now, it might be objected that, if Nagarjuna had been a Buddhist, how could he also have been a Brahmin? Aren't Hinduism and Buddhism distinct categories? But, if we look at the question from a different angle, things are not so clear. The Pali Canon has approximately 4941 sutras in the four main collections (the *Digha, Majjhima, Samyutta*, and *Anguttara Nikayas*). Of these, only a handful can be read as anti-Brahmanical. On the other hand, there are quite a few sutras that even on the harshest reading propose only modifications to Brahmanical religion and even then seem to propose modifications that many post-Vedic-era Brahmanical groups were already adopting. More to the point, many of the Buddha's top disciples are not only presented as being Brahmins but also are addressed by the Buddha himself as "Brahmin!" in every dialogue in which they appear (e.g., Maudgalyayana/Moggallana). In other words, Brahmins who became monks continued to be recognized by the Buddha as Brahmins after ordination. Further, nowhere does the Buddha forbid any of them from performing the rituals that mark them as Brahmins, either in the sutras or in the monastic codes. Hence, while contemporary scholarship uses the word "conversion" rather freely, the term is misleading when applied to second-century India if we understand the term to mean abandoning one's old religion in order to embrace a new one. In fact, it is not at all clear in the second century what percentage of the population understood "Buddhism" and "Brahmanism" to be two different religions.

Of course, the distinguishing of a "Hinduism" from a "Buddhism" has never been a simple matter, in the past or today.[25] It is not clear at what point Buddhists started to preach that Buddhist doctrine was something other than Brahmanical doctrine, but we can only assume that, once the idea was formulated, it would have been adopted by groups who had something to gain in their opposition to the Brahmanical system and would have been *resisted* by those who had something to lose in making this distinction. By all accounts, Brahmins were important constituents early on in Buddhism and, as they became recipients of royal land grants (*brahmadeyyas*) later on, they became even more important as major Buddhist donors. But here the historical context is important: if land-grant-holding Brahmins were crucial to monastic finances, their money came precisely from the fact that they were Brahmins and occupied a key position in Brahmanical ritual and political economy.[26] To abandon this status would be to abandon the very wealth that some Buddhist monasteries had come to rely on.

So how does Nagarjuna's caste status as a Brahmin shed light on his life and writings? First of all, the "absorption into the empty" (*shunyato samadhi*) that Mahayana texts describe as one of the "gates to nirvana" was also shared by Brahmins who memorized and practiced the teachings of the Maitrayani branch of the *Black Yajurveda*.[27] This treatise on yoga in the *Maitrayani Upanishad* (II.4; VI.23, 31; VII.4) states that *brahman* is *shunya* (empty) and *niratman* (either "without a soul" or "without a body"[28]); it also asserts that the one who engages in this yogic meditation "having through the *atman* (the soul) beheld the *atman*, he becomes without *atman*. From this fact, that he is without *atman*, we must conclude that he is without thought, without source; it is the definition of release" (VI.20).[29]

In light of first- and second-century attempts by the Sarvastivadins to draw a boundary between Hinduism and Buddhism by claiming that Hindus believed in a soul (*atman*) and Buddhists believed in soullessness (*anatman*), we can now read Nagarjuna's argument for emptiness in context: it shows not only that the meditative practices that his Brahmin Buddhist community had been practicing for generations were consonant with a central Buddhist teaching, especially the doctrine of no soul, but also that the Brahmin Buddhists passed the ultimate litmus test for Buddhist orthodoxy. Since the Maitrayanis had argued in their *Upanishad* that not only does one become empty upon attaining Brahman but also that the ideal state was to become "soul-less," we can read Nagarjuna's arguments advocating Mahayana to simultaneously be arguments for a continued place for certain Brahmanical communities, and practices, within Buddhism.

Nagarjuna in Andhra Pradesh

The key to dating Nagarjuna to the second century is the testimony of a number of major early sources that connect him to a Satavahana king located in the Deccan in southern India. The problem, of course, is that the Satavahana domain never extended as far north as Mathura. By the second century, the Satavahanas seem to have been largely confined to the east coast around the Krishna River in Andhra Pradesh. So, while Mathura is an ideal site for the sectarian positions Nagarjuna engages in his *Root Verses*, it provides no real clues as to the time of its composition other than the time of the Sarvastivadins (from 40 CE). The famous Buddhist center called Amaravati on the lower Krishna River provides an ideal spot for Nagarjuna's writing of a letter (the *Ratnavali* or *Jeweled Garland*[30]) to a Satavahana king, but it simply does not have any traces of the opponents that so occupied Nagarjuna in the *Root Verses*. What is clear is that the *Jeweled Garland* contains a number of features that suggest a more mature author as well as some intellectual development in comparison to the *Root Verses*. The conclusion is the possibility that Nagarjuna began his career in Mathura (where he wrote the *Root Verses* and the *Dispeller of Disputes*) and then moved to coastal Andhra, where he penned the *Jeweled Garland* and several of the devotional hymns ascribed to him.

But why would Nagarjuna have moved to coastal Andhra Pradesh? Was he running away from Mathura due to friction resulting from his *Root Verses*? Did he go to Andhra in order to spread Mahayana in a new area? Was he invited by a local king with the promise of a Brahmin land grant or of an advisory position in the court? Any are possible. Coastal Andhra in the second century supported many Buddhist monasteries and had deeply ingrained networks of local patronage.[31] At the same time, the Satavahana dynasty was legitimated by the performance of two Brahmanical horses, and a second-century inscription records a certain Jayavarman donating a village to a group of six Brahmins representing prominent Vedic lineages.[32] Clearly patronizing Brahmins and not just Buddhist monasteries was becoming part of the local repertoire of political legitimation. One can certainly imagine an enterprising king seeking political advantage by patronizing a Buddhist monk of a prestigious northern Brahmanical lineage such as Nagarjuna.

It is in the context of the political needs of these sovereigns – kings whose sovereignty was positioned at the intersection of Buddhism and Brahmanism – that we should read Nagarjuna's later writings. There is much of interest in these writings. Amid standard Buddhist teachings on doctrine and ethics, the *Jeweled Garland* contains specific recommendations for royal policy (thus shedding light on at least the expectations on the king in second-century India). Nagarjuna begins his letter to the king by discussing basic Buddhist doctrines, including the doctrine of no self. In his presentation, however, Nagarjuna says that this doctrine is very difficult to understand without overnegating (i.e., it is not so simple as understanding that the soul does not exist, so there is no reason to assume this to be an intrinsically anti-Brahmanical argument). He then goes on to say that, until the king is able to understand the doctrine, he should practice charity and ethical living:

> Therefore as long as the doctrine removing
> the conception of I is not known
> Take heed of the practices
> Of giving, ethics, and patience.[33]

Charity, ethics, and patience are certainly virtues to be cultivated by any Buddhist, but what makes Nagarjuna's discussion especially interesting is the fact that the king is in a very different political and financial position from other Buddhists. Though Nagarjuna's advice could be applied to all, much of the *Jeweled Garland* concerns specifically how the king is to accomplish these virtues *as a wealthy householder and as king*.

Nagarjuna's recommendations are too numerous to be reproduced here, but his recommendations concerning royal charity provide a good illustration of what a Buddhist monk in an advisory role would look like. First of all, Nagarjuna expects royal charity to consist of funding architectural and renovation projects in Buddhist monasteries, constructing religious images, stupas, and monastic cells with lavish adornments. He is also to provide all the necessities for preachers of the doctrine.[34]

In addition to attending to the infrastructure, the king was also expected to support the message of the monasteries, both by directly supporting teachers and by providing media for writing.

> Listen to teachers with homage
> And respect, serve, and pray to them
> Always respectfully revere
> The [other] bodhisattvas.
> You should not respect, revere,
> Or do homage to others, the Forders,
> Because through that the ignorant
> Would become enamored of the faulty.
> You should make donations of pages and books
> Of the word of the King of Subduers [the Buddha]
> And the treatises they give rise to
> Along with their prerequisites, pens and ink
> As ways to increase wisdom.
> Wherever there is a school in the land
> Provide for the livelihood of teachers
> And give lands to them [for their provisions].[35]

Here, Nagarjuna asks the king to support the dissemination of Buddhism through supporting its apparatus of transmission and attempts to dissuade him from supporting its rivals, here identified as "the forders" (*tirthika*).³⁶ Nevertheless, Nagarjuna is certainly not pitching Buddhism against all others, since elsewhere he specifically recommends that the king support multiple "centers of doctrine" and "temples":

> Also you should maintain other centers of doctrine³⁷
> Established by the previous kings –
> All the temples and so forth –
> As they were before.³⁸

It is interesting here that Nagarjuna asks the king not only to provide pens and ink but also to support "schools."³⁹ Buddhism clearly benefited by an expansion of literacy and it would appear that Nagarjuna expected the king to provide for it. That the education might have been public is suggested by the fact that, immediately after the verse, Nagarjuna continues to recommend other public works that only a king can provide: hostels, hospitals, and irrigation tanks.⁴⁰

The king's ethical responsibilities extended to the economy as well. He was not only to provide for the indigent but was also to regulate prices and reduce taxes:

> Provide extensive care
> For the persecuted, the victims of crop failure,
> The stricken, those suffering contagion
> And for beings in conquered areas …
> Protect [the poor] from the pain of wanting [your wealth].
> Set up no [new] tolls and reduce those [that are heavy].
> Also free [traders from other areas] from the afflictions
> That come from waiting at your door.
> Eliminate robbers and thieves
> In your own and others' countries.
> Please set process fairly
> And keep profits level [even during scarcity].⁴¹

Finally, the king was not just to have concern for the welfare of humans in his domain but was even to provide for its animals, insects, and resident hungry ghosts as well.

We also get, in the *Jeweled Garland* and in the devotional hymn, a glimpse of what Buddhist devotional practices would have looked like. This is significant, since most of the Buddhist literature available to us is not directly liturgical, and yet we know that Buddhists chanted and performed other devotions to the Buddha. Indeed, for Nagarjuna's Buddhist contemporaries, he may have been just as famous for his contributions to Buddhist liturgy as he was for his philosophy. In the *Jeweled Garland*, Nagarjuna instructs the king to go three times a day in front of an image of the Buddha and recite a prayer consisting both of praise for the Buddha and a series of promises:

> Therefore in the presence of an image [of the Buddha]
> Or monument [stupa] or something else
> Say these twenty stanzas three times every day
> [what follows is a lengthy prayer].⁴²

Apart from the *Jeweled Garland*, there are also a number of free-standing devotional hymns attributed to Nagarjuna.⁴³ These devotional hymns reveal that for Nagarjuna emptiness was not just a theory argued with detachment but was also part of a larger worldview in which the Buddha might be understood to *be* emptiness, though no less the object of devotion because of it. Three of these hymns, the *Paramarthastava*, the *Niraupamastava*, and the *Dharmadhatustava*, speak of emptiness and of the Buddha in positive terms, displaying a distinct tendency in the direction of the "womb of the Buddha" or "seed of the Buddha" (*tathagatagarbha*) doctrine.⁴⁴ (This is a doctrine that would manifest in much later Zen Buddhism as "the Buddha nature," as well as in the Tibetan Buddhist teachings of "the Great Perfection" (*rDzogschen*).) In context and significantly, the *tathagatagarbha* texts seem to have come from Andhra Pradesh⁴⁵ around the second or third centuries. The doctrine of the "womb of the Buddha," as taught in the *Lion Roar of Srimaladevi* or the *Tathagatagarbha Sutra*, teaches that there is a seed or a kernel of the Buddha within most of us that, under the right circumstances, will blossom into full Buddhahood. Since this essence is, in fact, emptiness itself, the *tathagatagarbha* texts also argue that the historical Buddha only appeared to be born, suffer, and die. In fact, the Buddha only appears to have done all these things. The real Buddha transcends all transformation and apparent multiplicity. He is not dead, but in fact the essence of the cosmos, the absolute Brahmin, just like Krishna in the *Bhagavad Gita* and in the *Pancaratra* portions of the *Mahabharata*. Thus, although Nagarjuna never uses the actual terms in his devotional hymns, his works can be seen as possible precursors to the full-blown Mahayana texts advocating the *tathagatagarbha* doctrine.

Nagarjuna's devotional hymns appear to be addressed to a community whose liturgical practices included singing or chanting praises to the Buddha, understood as an eternal essence that was both immanent to the individual Buddhist as well as being all-pervasive, eternal, and transcendent. This would have been a community in which Brahmins brought up with expectations formed by teachings about Vishnu or Shiva would find the Buddha to be in every way their equal. Again, the proximity of these liturgical hymns and metaphysical doctrines to traditions that were being circulated among the Brahmanical communities would not only have been convenient for local Brahmins; the hymns and the contents of the *Jeweled Garland* would have provided avenues for local kings and administrators to express their piety to a far wider community than if they accepted the proposed boundary between Buddhism and Brahmanism.

Conclusion

In all, what we can discern about Nagarjuna's life is as important for what it tells us about ordinary Buddhists, Hindus, and Mahayanists in second-century India as for what it tells us about Nagarjuna's exceptionality as philosopher and ethical advocate. There is no question that Nagarjuna was brilliant on numerous levels, and his place in philosophical history is well deserved. But his brilliance shines brightest when we understand his philosophy as addressing the real people and institutional concerns of his day – concerns that in many ways are quite similar to our own.

References

Basu, C. (2001) Redefining the nature of cultural religions in early India: early India: Mathura and the meaning of "Kusana" art (1st–3rd centuries AD). Ph.D. diss. University of Pennsylvania.

Basu, C. (2006) Patronage and representation at the Huviska Vihara, a Kusana-period monastery in Mathura. *Studies in History*, 22 (2), 157–79.

Bhattacharya, K. (1980) Nagarjuna's arguments against motion: their grammatical basis, in *A Corpus of Indian Studies: Essays in Honour of Professor Gaurinath Sastri* (ed. A.L. Basham), Sanskrit Pustak Bhandar, Calcutta, pp. 85–95.

Bühler, G. (1962) The Nanaghat inscription. *Archaeological Survey of West India*, 5, 59–74.

Burton, D.F. (1999) *Emptiness Appraised: A Critical Study of Nāgārjuna's Philosophy*, Curzon, Richmond.

Corless, R. (1995) The Chinese life of Nagarjuna, in *Buddhism in Practice* (ed. D. Lopez), Princeton University Press, Princeton, NJ, pp. 525–31.

Falk, H. (2004) The Kaniska era in Gupta records. *Silk Road Art and Archaeology*, 10, 167–76.

Falk, H. (2011) Ten thoughts on the Mathura lion capital reliquary, in *Felicitas: Essays in Numismatics, Epigraphy and History in Honour of Joe Cribb* (ed. B. Shailendra and G.S.J. Cribb), Reesha Books International, Mumbai, pp. 121–44.

Falk, H. (2012) Small-scale Buddhism, in *Devadattiyam: Johannes Bronkhorst Felicitation Volume* (ed. V.F.J. Bronkhorst), Peter Lang, Brussels, pp. 491–517.

Filliozat, J. (1945) La doctrine des brahmanes d'après Saint Hippolyte. *Revue de l'histoire des religions*, 130, 59–91.

Fogelin, L. (2006) *Archaeology of Early Buddhism*, AltaMira Press, Lanham, MD.

Hayes, R. (1994) Nagarjuna's appeal. *Journal of Indian Philosophy*, 22 (4), 299–378.

Hopkins, J. (1998) *Buddhist Advice for Living & Liberation: Nagarjuna's Precious Garland*, Snow Lion, Ithaca, NY.

Ichimura, S. (1992) Re-examining the period of Nagarjuna: Western India, A.D. 50–150. *Journal of Indian and Buddhist Studies*, 40, 1073–9.

Karashima, S. and von Hinuber, O. (2012) *Die Abhisamacarika Dharmah: Verhaltensregeln Für Buddhistische Mönche Der Mahasamghika-Lokittaravadins, Band I*, International Research Institute for Advanced Buddhology, Soka University, Tokyo.

Lüders, H. (1912) *A List of Brahmi Inscriptions*, Superintendent Government Printing, Calcutta.

Mitrikeski, D. (2008) Nagarjuna's religious practices seen through the analysis of his hymns. Ph.D. diss. University of Sydney.

Mitrikeski, D. (2009) Nagarjuna and the *Tathagatagarbha*: a look at some peculiar features in the *Niraupamyastava*. *Journal of Religious History*, 33 (2), 149–64.

Neelis, J. (2011) *Early Buddhist Transmission and Trade Networks: Mobility and Exchange within and beyond the Northwestern Borderlands of South Asia*, Brill, Leiden.

Ruegg, D.S. (1981) *The Literature of the Madhyamaka School of Philosophy in India*, Harrassowitz, Wiesbaden.

Sahni, D.R. and Bahadur, R. (1927–8) Seven inscriptions from Mathura. *Epigraphia Indica*, 19, 65–9.

Sayers, M.R. (2013) *Feeding the Dead: Ancestor Worship in Ancient India*, Oxford University Press, New York.

Schopen, G. (1992) Ritual obligations and donor roles of monks in the Pali *Vinaya*. *Journal of the Pali Text Society*, 16, 87–107.

Singh, U. (2004) Cults and shrines in early historical Mathura (c. 200 BC–AD 200). *World Archaeology*, 36 (3), 378–98.

Tsuchida, R. (1991) Two categories of Brahmins in the early Buddhist period. *Memoirs of the Research Department of the Toyo Bunko*, 49, 51–95.

Van Buitenen, J.A.B. (1962) *The Maitrayaniya Upanisad: A Critical Essay, with Text, Translation, and Commentary* [in English and romanized Sanskrit], Mouton, The Hague.

Walser, J. (2005) *Nagarjuna in Context: Mahayana Buddhism and Early Indian Culture*, Columbia University Press, New York.

Westerhoff, J. (2010) *The Dispeller of Disputes: Nagarjuna's Vigrahavyavartani*, Oxford University Press, Oxford.

Further Reading

Hopkins, J. (1998) *Buddhist Advice for Living & Liberation: Nagarjuna's Precious Garland* [in English], Snow Lion, Ithaca, NY.

Lüders, H. and Janert, K.L. (1961) *Mathura Inscriptions: Unpublished Papers*, Vandenhoeck & Ruprecht, Göttingen.

Nath, V. (2001) *Puranas and Acculturation: A Historico-Anthropological Perspective* [includes passages in Sanskrit], Manoharlal, New Delhi.

Siderits, M. and Katsura, S. (2013) *Nagarjuna's Middle Way: The Mulamadhyamakakarika*, Wisdom, Boston, MA.

Walleser, M. (1979) *The Life of Nagarjuna from Tibetan and Chinese Sources*, Nag, Delhi.

Walser, J. (2005) *Nagarjuna in Context: Mahayana Buddhism and Early Indian Culture* [in English], Columbia University Press, New York.

Walser, J. (2007) The origin of the term "Mahayana" (the great vehicle) and its relationship to the *Agamas*. *Journal of the International Association of Buddhist Studies*, 30 (1–2), 219–52.

Westerhoff, J. (2009) *Nagarjuna's Madhyamaka: A Philosophical Introduction* [in English], Oxford University Press, Oxford.

Young, S. (forthcoming) *Conceiving the Indian Buddhist Patriarchs in China*, University of Hawai'i Press.

Notes

1 The account of Nagarjuna's life that I can offer here will be less of a sustained narrative than a set of points of reasonable certainty and the social and political implications radiating out from those points. In the following, I will discuss these points and talk about the light they shed on both the ideas of Nagarjuna and the larger cultural milieu of his time.

2 Most scholars who write about Nagarjuna are trained in philosophy and tend to be uncomfortable with the murkiness inherent in the historical project of trying to trace the footprints of a man who lived 1800 years ago. The fact remains that, historically speaking, we have to go with the data that we have, not with the data we wish we had – and this means that any historical account of Nagarjuna will have to be presented in terms of statements that are more or less probable.

3 Neelis 2011: 197–200.

4 *Nagas* and *yaksas* were powerful deities with a local and sometimes translocal cult following. Though *yaksas* almost always take human form, *nagas* are most often depicted as cobra-like creatures, often with multiple heads and occasionally with a simultaneous human form represented. In contradistinction to *yaksas*, who could be the tutelary deities of a grove or a city, *nagas* tended to protect bodies of water, such as rivers or water tanks (often constructed and maintained by Buddhist monasteries), and were invoked to bring rain.

5 Basu 2001; Singh 2004.

6 There is one inscription recording the presence of a Sammitiya monastery at "Shri Vihara" (Sahni and Bahadur 1927–8: 67).
7 See Falk 2011: esp. 131ff.
8 This point is explored extensively in Walser (2005: 110–15).
9 Falk 2004, 2012. In fact, the inscription referring to the Sammitiyas was found on a slab (a seat?) that was dedicated along with a bodhisattva "for the worship of all Buddhas" and entrusted to the care of the Sammitiyas (Sahni and Bahadur 1927–8: 67).
10 Falk 2012. While it would not be quite correct to say that the bodhisattva's *ushnisha* was "Brahmanical," I think we should interpret the Mathura bodhisattva figures to embody local visions of sovereignty – with the caveat that sovereignty would probably have been understood through the lens of deities and liturgies that derived from Vedic lineages (*shakha*), not Buddhist ones. See Basu 2006: chapter 2, 58ff.
11 Walser 2005: chapters 6–7.
12 Hayes 1994; Burton 1999.
13 Chandrayi Basu (2001, 2006) has provided us with a detailed discussion of some of the diversity within Buddhist monastic life in Mathura as well as the diversity of the patronage base that supported them.
14 Their Kushana patrons appear in sculptures at the time adorned with their Central Asian clothes, thereby visually maintaining their ethnic distinction from the local population.
15 Schopen 1992; Basu 2006: 165–6.
16 Basu 2001: 129–30.
17 See Karashima and von Hinuber 2012: 130.
18 Basu 2006: 133.
19 It is true that a palm-leaf or birch-bark manuscript might last a very long time (some of the birch-bark manuscripts of the British Library collection have lasted over 2000 years and the palm-leaf manuscript in the Gilgit collection is around 1600 years old). However, in both of these cases, the manuscripts in question were preserved in jars, which was not a universal practice for most of India. Though I have no hard numbers for this, the longevity of a manuscript under normal conditions would probably be much, much shorter, with factors such as humidity, bugs/rodents, and simple turning of the pages leading to the pages wearing out in a much shorter time span.
20 On rituals for the care of dead ancestors, see Sayers (2013). It should be noted, however, that many kings exempted monks, or at least certain monasteries, from taxes and the like. We should not assume that this was always the case.
21 Corless 1995.
22 Ichimura 1992.
23 Bhattacharya 1980.
24 For example, one of the cases that Nagarjuna refers to in his treatise entitled *Dispeller of Disputes* (*Vigrahavyavartani*) states, "If the son is to be produced by the father and if the father is to be produced by this very son, you have to say which produces which in this context." Nagarjuna's auto-commentary rewords the verse to say: "If someone said 'the son is to be produced by the father, and this father is to be produced by this very son ... '" (Westerhoff 2010: 34). Nagarjuna is pointing out what *some people* already say – namely, that the father produces the son and the son produces the father. Who are "those people"? This can only refer to the discussion in a key Brahmanical text of how the creator, Prajapati, gives birth to Fire (Agni), who then returns the favor in a fire sacrifice by (re)producing his father. To cite this tradition, even against non-Buddhist opponents, would require cultural competencies with deep roots in the Vedic tradition. In other words, to be able to bring up this example suggests that Nagarjuna had memorized the text or knew of it from his Brahmanical upbringing.
25 Rather, distinguishing is an *act* that people either do or not do, and (to paraphrase Bourdieu) the distinguishing distinguishes the distinguisher as the kind of person who not only has the competencies and interest to know where to draw the line but also knows which side of it to occupy.
26 see Tsuchida 1991.
27 If Filloziat (1945) is correct that this *upanishad* (or some version of it) was known by Hyppolytus (d. 235) in Rome, then we are probably safe in assuming that it had to have been fairly well established in India during Nagarjuna's lifetime.
28 see Van Buitenen 1962: 99–100.
29 Van Buitenen 1962: 142.
30 See Hopkins 1998.
31 Fogelin 2006.
32 Lüders 1912: inscription 1328.
33 Hopkins 1998: 112.
34 Hopkins 1998: 124–5.
35 Hopkins 1998: 135–6.
36 It is not clear at this point to whom he is referring, although earlier he singled out the Samkhyas, the Vaisheshikas, and the Jains (Hopkins 1998: 102, verse 61) as being inferior.
37 "Centers of doctrine" likely indicates that the king should support the rules and endowments made by the previous kings. The word that Hopkins translates as "temples" (*deva-drona*),

however, does seem to indicate the worship and bathing/anointing of deity images in temples since the feminine, *devadroni*, is an "idol procession" or "ablution."
38 Hopkins 1998: 136.
39 The Sanskrit passage is missing at this point, but the Chinese suggests some kind of hall of learning while the Tibetan more specifically indicates a place or institution where *writing* is taught. It is not clear either from the terminology or from context whether the place of learning and the teachers were assumed to be part of the monastery or were some kind of publically available education in literacy.
40 Hopkins 1998: 124–6.
41 Hopkins 1998: 127.
42 Hopkins 1998: 159.
43 There is mounting evidence that Nagarjuna actually wrote them (Mitrikeski 2008).
44 David Ruegg (1981: 31–2) was perhaps the first to note this.
45 Mitrikeski 2009: 155ff.

5

Who Is Uncle Donpa?

David J. Cooper

Editor's Introduction

In the spectrum of Tibetan Buddhists going from saints to skeptics and nonbelievers, Uncle Donpa seems to occupy a position close to the latter end. Stories about Uncle Donpa are part of the tradition of oral lore that emerged from illiterate and "unofficial" local Tibetan cultures. They spread, through oral tradition and more casual joke-telling, to every segment of Tibetan society and to nearly every region of the Tibetan cultural sphere, where they have long been an important form of entertainment. In this chapter exploring the most widely known and beloved individual in Tibetan folklore, David Cooper skillfully weaves a series of stories about him around a discussion of the multiple ways he has been understood by interpreters right up to the present day.

Traditionally, the tales involving sexual or scatological themes were told with coarse language. The outrageous accounts also never offer an explicit "lesson," and Uncle Donpa's actions are not overtly explained or rationalized. This trickster character belies the impression that Tibetan Buddhists have a blind and unshakable faith in their leaders and traditions; in these tales, we cannot miss a healthy skepticism of religious figures and institutions. Uncle Donpa stories portray those who approach religious elites with blind faith as naïve fools: lamas do not necessarily use their spiritually derived powers for noble purposes, nor do nuns necessarily keep their vows. Beyond these insights, in this chapter we can see how other interpreters in Tibet's multivocalic tradition have tried to understand Uncle Donpa's moral deformities and idiosyncratic actions as nonetheless the work of a bodhisattva or that of a "mad yogin." We finally learn how this cultural hero-rogue has also been inserted into the politics of modern Chinese–Tibetan relations.

Buddhists: Understanding Buddhism Through the Lives of Practitioners, First Edition. Edited by Todd Lewis.
© 2014 John Wiley & Sons, Ltd. Published 2014 by John Wiley & Sons, Ltd.

Introduction

A man walks into a Tibetan Buddhist nunnery ... dressed as a nun. He is interested in obtaining the pleasures of "fresh young virgin nuns" and they, it turns out, are interested in him.[1] Undetected for months, he enjoys his adventures until so many nuns have become pregnant that the abbess suspects an infiltrator. So she orders two walls to be built a few feet from each other and instructs each nun to jump across while she sits below and looks up their robes. The man, ever crafty, pulls his extraordinarily long penis between his legs and ties it up to his belt with a string. He jumps across with the nuns and is not detected. A second time he jumps across and again is not detected. However, on the third attempt, the string breaks and the jig is up. Although he is tied up and punishment seems inevitable, we know that he will inevitably find some clever means of escape.

Who is this man and what on earth is he doing in a book of Buddhist biographies? He seems to be neither a real person nor much of a Buddhist. Many Tibetans would agree, except for those who believe that he was a historical figure. Or a "mad" yogin. Or a bodhisattva. And then there are those who view him as a kind of common man's hero, a critic of the abuses of the powerful ...

This confounding figure is Tibet's most famous trickster, the beloved Akhu ("Uncle") Donpa, gleeful violator of taboos. The stories of his frequent transgressions draw attention to the rules and structures that underlie Tibetan society. But do these stories serve to challenge the rules or do they reinforce them by reminding the hearer why they are necessary? Or perhaps they serve some other purpose. Like fun-house mirrors, Uncle Donpa stories reflect back a grotesque though recognizable image of Tibetan society. What Tibetans have seen in this mirror has varied depending on their perspective. Further, their ideas about who Uncle Donpa is and what his stories mean provide glimpses of various and sometimes competing values in the Tibetan Buddhist world, past and present.

Uncle Donpa and Trickster Tales in Tibet

One Tibetan translator of the famous trickster's tales has written, "you will not find a Tibetan who does not grin luminously when you simply mention the name [Uncle Donpa]."[2] Stories about Uncle Donpa are part of the tradition of oral lore that emerged from illiterate and "unofficial" local Tibetan cultures. They spread, through oral tradition and more casual joke-telling, to every segment of Tibetan society and to nearly every region of the Tibetan cultural sphere, where they have long been an important form of entertainment.

Cultural norms generally dictate that risqué humor must be shared at appropriate times and places, and, as is true in most cultures, Tibetans do not always agree about what is "appropriate." For example, among some contemporary families, tales of Uncle Donpa are forbidden in the home and are considered more appropriate for the tavern. In some communities, the traditional tellers of these tales have been elderly men, whose audiences consist mostly of (highly amused) children.

Because Uncle Donpa's stories emerged in the evolving oral traditions of various local societies and because they were never traditionally recorded, those still in existence today are varied and conflicting. In some cases, his stories are conflated with those of other Tibetan trickster figures, or even with tricksters from Islamic folklore. However, certain characteristics and themes remain consistent in most of the tales. From them, the composite figure that emerges is poor, marginal, and itinerant; he is usually subservient to an invariably corrupt member of the official class – often an aristocrat, ruler, or religious figure. Through deceit and cleverness, he satisfies his base urges while exposing his opponents' vices, and always manages to avoid the harsh punishment that would surely await any actual common person caught in such acts. Traditionally, the tales involving sexual or scatological themes were told with fittingly coarse language. The accounts also never offer an explicit "lesson," and Uncle Donpa's actions are not overtly explained or rationalized, perhaps because explaining a joke is the surest way to spoil it. And yet, these stories carry more weight than the average joke, as evidenced by Tibetans' continuing reflection on and interpretation of their possible meanings.

Uncle Donpa has traditionally been understood in two major ways: as a common man's hero and as a saint in disguise. These two interpretations of his role offer important insights into the traditional relationship between Tibet's ordinary Buddhists and its religious and political elite.

In more recent history, additional interpretations of Uncle Donpa's significance have been suggested: as a historical figure; as an inspiration for advocates of open debate in the public sphere; as a mouthpiece for misogyny; and as a proto-Communist revolutionary. These newer views reflect Tibetan Buddhists' encounters with new worlds and ideas.

Traditional Interpretations

Uncle Donpa as a common man's hero

Uncle Donpa tales frequently draw critical attention to the issue of class, reflecting the stories' social origins in nonelite oral tradition. As a result, Uncle Donpa is often interpreted as a common man's hero whose tales articulate the values of ordinary Tibetan householders while providing a satirical exposé of the traditional religious and political elite from the commoner's perspective. One such story combines both political and religious satire:

> While serving as a king's secretary, Uncle Donpa annoys the king one day, and the king forces him to spend a very cold night naked on the palace roof. Plotting revenge, Uncle Donpa defecates, then covers the feces with white lime dust and stabs it with a stick. After the stick freezes into place, he picks it up and writes something on the bottom of the frozen feces. From his rooftop perch, Uncle Donpa notices the king meditating below before an altar of the Buddha. He drops the feces into the king's lap. Surprised, the illiterate king picks it up. He doesn't know what it is, and wants to know what the writing says. Aware that Uncle Donpa can read, the king calls him down from the roof and orders him a hot breakfast. In a most humble and reverent tone, Uncle Donpa reveals that the substance on the stick is "shit from heaven," and that catching it makes the king the luckiest of all kings. Uncle Donpa then encourages the king to eat a little bit to "get its blessings." Eager to believe Uncle Donpa, the king "touched his forehead, ate a piece of it, and put the rest on his altar," after which Uncle Donpa "saluted and was dismissed."[3]

In the king's act of eating this "holy shit," both secular and religious powers are brought "down to earth." At the same time, Uncle Donpa gets a hot meal and is restored to the king's good graces.

In another Uncle Donpa tale of religious satire, humble commoners encounter a Buddhist high lama:

> A poor farming couple and several field hands are sitting by the roadside taking a break from their work and passing the time by telling dirty jokes and stories. When a "very holy lama" passes by and asks what they are doing, one of them, caught up in the joke-telling mood, inadvertently says, "we're sowing penises in our field."[4] Everyone laughs at this except the lama, whose embarrassment quickly turns to rage. He tells them that their crops *will* turn into penises, and the lama's curse actually causes this to happen.
>
> Destitute without a harvestable crop to feed them, the poor farming couple receives an offer of help from Uncle Donpa, who promises to sell the penis crop and return with enough money to allow the couple to buy more grain than the field normally would have yielded. Armed with only his ingenuity and knowledge of the weaknesses of the powerful, Uncle Donpa plucks up a number of the penises and carts them off to be sold at a nunnery. There, he lays them out on a carpet according to size, promising that these magical penises will satisfy the sexual desires of anyone who buys them. Because it is daytime, the nuns haughtily ignore him.
>
> However, once night falls, nearly all of the nuns return, one by one, to buy the penises. As promised, Uncle Donpa passes the proceeds to the couple, whose penis business ends up being so lucrative that they then go off in search of the holy lama to ask him to place the magic curse on their field every year.[5]

The conflict in both of these stories is rooted in class. The protagonist and his allies are poor peasants and the antagonists are the elite. Our protagonist, Uncle Donpa, is clearly a commoner himself and, in the second story, is motivated to act out of sympathy for those who have been wronged. The powerful are depicted as corrupt and abusive; both king and lama, with little provocation, are quick to use their power to harm, rather than help, the powerless. Likewise, their kindness extends to the poor only when a man like Uncle Donpa can be of use to them. (The king shows generosity toward Uncle Donpa only when he needs to know what has been written in the feces.) Further, the elite are shown to be hypocrites; their corrupt, immoral actions do not match their elevated station in Tibetan society. This is particularly true of the lusty nuns, whose transgressions are intentionally hidden. For these reasons, Uncle Donpa tales work as class-based revenge fantasies where normally unchecked injustices are avenged and the hypocrisy of the powerful perpetrators is exposed. There are two interrelated elements to this interpretation of Uncle Donpa as a common man's hero: the affirmation of the commonsense intelligence of ordinary Tibetans and the articulation of a critique of the elite.

Non-Tibetans often characterize ordinary Tibetan Buddhists as having unshakable faith in their leaders and traditions, but the Uncle Donpa tales suggest that such a characterization is not really accurate. In fact, the tales appear to reflect a healthy skepticism of religious figures and institutions, portraying as foolish those who approach religious elites with blind faith. The first story mocks the gullibility of Tibetans in the face of magical claims, revealing the ease with which religious charlatans can and do operate. In this case, the gullibility and vanity of the king make him easy prey for Uncle Donpa's trickery. In the second story, the message seems to be that "the red robe does not make the monastic." Nuns do not necessarily keep their vows, nor do lamas inevitably use their spiritually derived powers for noble purposes. In order to avoid being victimized by untrustworthy and hypocritical elites, commoners are encouraged to use their commonsense intelligence and cleverness to get along in the world. That these tales reveal a real countercurrent to the dominant Tibetan view of the religious elite is reflected in the popular saying, "When the southern clouds go northwards, [Uncle Donpa] prays for rain."[6] In other words, there is no sense in praying for rain when the sky is clear, no matter what the lamas say.

In traditional Tibet, where religious elites and institutions held the most power culturally and politically and the majority of the people were agricultural laborers tied to the farm estates these elites held, public criticism of the privileged by the common people was taboo and could bring down serious punishment. Only the elite were permitted to publicly criticize their fellow elites. But, in these tales, Uncle Donpa is about as far away from being a member of Tibet's elite as possible and his tales push against that taboo. Likewise, the telling of these stories by ordinary Tibetans can be seen as a challenge to the powerful. For ordinary Tibetans, then, these tales traditionally provided a rare venue for publicly voicing messages challenging the elite. For outsiders, they provide a rare glimpse of what some of those messages were.

That the tales of Uncle Donpa have not only survived but also thrived within Tibet's rigid social system indicates that, like all enduring humor, they push right up to the line without crossing it. Within the tales, there are several mitigating elements that have likely helped to keep them on the safe side of the line. First, satiric humor is a double-edged sword: the fact that it permits open criticism while allowing the critic to retreat behind an "it was just a joke" excuse is both its power and its limitation. Something that is "just a joke" may expose social ills but may be of limited use in real political or social terms. Second, the Uncle Donpa stories are clearly set in a fantasy world. The fact that he acts out and gets away with such outlandish things softens any real-world application of his social criticisms. Finally, although the stories are rife with attacks against the powerful, neither the elite scoundrels nor the institutions they represent are specifically identified. Further, Uncle Donpa's victories are never more than temporary reversals. He does not attempt to reform the behavior of his opponents or to make structural changes of any sort; he simply moves on to the next punch line. For these reasons, it is relatively easy to interpret the satiric depiction of corrupt elites as merely highlighting incidental deviations from a normally fair and just status quo rather than attempting to make a deeper criticism of class-based problems inherent within the social system.[7]

Even so, it is not difficult to see why Uncle Donpa is frequently regarded as a common man's hero. There are no figures in Tibetan folklore who challenge the status quo as much as he does. Although they are socially sanctioned, Uncle Donpa's tales both challenge the taboo against criticizing the elite and clearly reflect the concerns and anxieties of the common people. However limited, this potential challenge to Tibet's elite may have contributed to the development of other interpretations of Uncle Donpa that are more elite-friendly.

Uncle Donpa as a saint in disguise

One such interpretation is that of Uncle Donpa as a religious figure; it is one that ultimately promotes the religious elites' perspective. This "buddhifying" of Uncle Donpa takes this figure – often seen as a dirty scoundrel, critic of elites, and breaker of taboos – and identifies him as a saint in disguise. This process is not completely straightforward, since Uncle Donpa tales themselves contain no explicit "morals" or Buddhist teachings. They also never give the slightest indication that he is a saint – he seems to be quite the opposite. He never performs miracles, even in secret, or does anything else that is typically associated with sainthood. In contrast to the "common man's hero" interpretation, likening Uncle Donpa to a saint requires the imposition of a meaning that is not at all obvious in the stories themselves. One tale in this realm is in the domain of chanting the holy texts, and Uncle has a reputation for being good at this; Tibetan families often invite readers to their homes for several days to read scriptures aloud, believing that this brings good fortune.

> One day, Uncle Donpa is invited to read scriptures for a family in which the father is completely bald. This man is so embarrassed by his baldness that he avoids going out in public.
>
> A couple of days into the reading, Uncle Donpa is growing frustrated because the family has failed to fulfill their obligation to serve him their best food. Indeed, the beans they offer are disgusting, almost inedible; couldn't they offer meat or something Uncle Donpa actually wants? He notices that this family has several sheep, one black one and the rest white. And with that, Uncle Donpa hatches a scheme.
>
> The bald man sits next to Uncle Donpa as he reads. A devoted Buddhist, the man is also illiterate; all he knows about scripture is what has been read to him. So, Uncle Donpa begins to take some liberties with the scripture, loudly adding these words: "If a man is utterly bald / he will grow hair again / if he wears the warm skin of a black sheep." At once, the man is captivated. "Really? Is this true?" Uncle Donpa assures him, "Scripture says so!" Believing this to be true, the man orders someone to kill his black sheep. While the skin is still warm, he quickly puts it on his head. As this "cure" takes effect, Uncle Donpa enjoys mutton for lunch and dinner.[8]

If there is nothing self-evidently saintly about this reader of phony scripture, how can Uncle Donpa be considered a saint? To understand Uncle Donpa in religious terms, his identity and behavior must be analyzed according to existing models of Buddhist holy people. Two of these, the bodhisattva and the "mad" yogin (*naljor nyonpa*, or *rnal 'byor smyon pa*), are the most common. But how can such a leap be made from the apparently profane to the sacred? Even though Uncle Donpa is supposedly a saint "in disguise," he still must have enough in common with traditional saints for this interpretation to be plausible.

When seen as an emanation of a bodhisattva, Uncle Donpa is typically associated with either Avalokitesvara (Chenrezig, *spyan ras gzigs*) or Manjushri (Jampelyang, *'jam dpal dbyangs*). According to this view, he embodies their qualities of compassion and wisdom, respectively, which can manifest in virtually any form, however unusual, to benefit others. In the case, for example, of Manjushri (the bodhisattva of wisdom), Uncle Donpa can be seen as exposing hypocrisy in order to cultivate in others the wisdom to differentiate between appearance and reality.

As a "mad" yogin, Uncle Donpa is associated with the "crazy saint" archetype that has a long history in Tibetan Buddhism. "Crazy saint" behavior in this tradition began with the outlandish antics of some of the great Indian *mahasiddhas*, continued through the activities of the famously anti-institutional Milarepa (*mi la ras pa*, 1052–1135), and reached its wildest and most famous peak with the "mad" yogins of the fifteenth century. In particular, one of these fifteenth-century figures, Drukpa Kunle (*'brug pa kun legs*), sheds light on the interpretation of Uncle Donpa as a "mad" yogin. Not only is Drukpa Kunle by far the most famous model for this "type" but also he and his tales have interfaced with the figure and tales of Uncle

Donpa in a way that reveals a fascinating dialogue between the folk traditions and perspectives of ordinary Tibetans and the literary traditions and perspectives of religious elites.

Parallels between the two characters are so striking that the "mad" yogin Drukpa Kunle often appears to be an overtly religious version of Uncle Donpa. According to one scholar, the recording and propagation of Drukpa Kunle tales may, in part, be the religious elites' response to being challenged by this "aberrant yet beloved trickster of popular culture."[9] Indeed, Drukpa Kunle's tales mimic many elements of the trickster tale but provide a message that is ultimately religious and endorses an elite perspective on society, while subtly negating the secular critique implicit in the original trickster tales. As a result, when Uncle Donpa is interpreted as a "mad" yogin, the focus likewise necessarily shifts away from secular critique and toward religious instruction.

Unlike Uncle Donpa, Drukpa Kunle (1455–c. 1529) was certainly a historical person. He is regarded in hagiographies as a saint of pristine lineage in the Drukpa Kagyu school and the reincarnation of previous masters. But he was also "wild" in many ways, living an unorthodox lifestyle, criticizing the religious elites of his day for hypocrisy, and composing lively, irreverent songs in a colloquial style.

Drukpa Kunle's story has long since entered the oral lore of Tibetan societies, where his tales have been embellished and have grown bawdier over the years to more closely resemble those of Uncle Donpa. In fact, the tales of both figures have become so intertwined that they are often mentioned in the same breath and, sometimes, stories told about one have later come to be told about the other. As figures of Tibetan oral lore, both are famous for graphic sexual and scatological satiric humor. Like Uncle Donpa, Drukpa Kunle wanders from place to place exposing the faults of respectable religious figures. He mocks social conventions, mixing with the people and using vulgar language. He irreverently breaks taboos, indulging in drunkenness and violence at most every turn. Like Uncle Donpa, he is sexually insatiable, and sports a comically large penis, which he modestly refers to as the "Flaming Thunderbolt of Wisdom."[10]

Apart from these similarities between the two characters, the clear religious logic that underlies the tales of Drukpa Kunle is quite different from the implicit principles found in the Uncle Donpa stories. The following story illustrates this.

Drukpa Kunle has agreed to supply the ambrosia (consecrated liquids) for a famous abbot's empowerment ceremony. The abbot is in the middle of purifying the flask that is normally used to hold the liquid when he arrives, but Drukpa Kunle abruptly declares, "The flask will not be needed today." He states that he will provide the ambrosia himself. So he instructs the gathered devotees to close their eyes tightly and hold out their hands. Then he proceeds to urinate a single drop into each outstretched hand from his penis. Those who consume the liquid with an attitude of reverence and devotion find it to be sweet. Others say it is disgusting and tastes like urine, so they spit it out and wipe off their hands. Afterward, those who drank the urine with an attitude of devotion found they "gained power and realization," while those who spat it out only gained "a run of bad luck."[11]

The logic behind all of the Drukpa Kunle tales is that, no matter how disgusting or unethical his actions may appear to ordinary beings, they are in reality the enlightened activity of a Buddhist master who, unconstrained by ordinary notions of "good" and "bad," employs "skillful means" (*upaya*) in order to bring awakening to others. Until seekers rid themselves of the dualistic mind that is attached to reckoning everything as "good or "bad," they cannot reach advanced spiritual awareness.

In order to interpret Uncle Donpa as a "mad" yogin, this same logic must be applied to his tales. In light of this, consider the following Uncle Donpa tale:

Uncle Donpa lusts after his own grown daughter, who still lives with him following his wife's death. When his daughter falls ill for several days, he plots to sleep with her by suggesting that she seek the healing blessing of a very holy lama who lives in a nearby cave. He warns her, though, that this lama has taken a vow to keep his face covered and must not be asked to remove the covering. He then gives her directions to the cave, and quickly heads to the uninhabited cave himself, then sits down and covers his face. When his daughter arrives and tells him about her problems, the "lama" mysteriously instructs her to "join two navels" in order to be cured. When she returns home, Uncle Donpa is waiting for her. When she tells him what the lama has suggested, he tells her it would be embarrassing to make such a request of a stranger, and offers to join his own navel to hers that night. She agrees. That night, they take off their clothes and touch their navels together. Both become filled with the desire to have sex and they do.[12]

In order to apply the logic of the "mad" yogin to this story, the scoundrel disguised as a saint must become a saint disguised as a scoundrel disguised as a saint! Presumably, Uncle Donpa has imparted some high religious teaching or blessing to his daughter. That a religious explanation could be applied to a story depicting behavior so ethically forbidden is not so far fetched, however, when placed alongside similar tales of the taboo-breaking Drukpa Kunle. In fact, one story of Drukpa Kunle has him seducing his own mother, and in several others he kills young children. In all of these cases, however, a teaching is imparted. Those who greet these teachings with absolute faith are rewarded, but those who condemn his behavior using their own common sense or even basic Buddhist principles suffer karmic consequences for their lack of faith. In the seduction of his mother, it is his mother's lust, rather than his own, that is at fault. And, when Drukpa Kunle proclaims that a child he has killed was, in fact, a demon, the boy's parents recognize the wisdom of the slaying and come to have great faith in the lama. (In return, the lama predicts they will have more children.) Applying this inverted religious logic to the Uncle Donpa stories, it is possible to consider that the "shit from heaven" Uncle Donpa dropped in the king's lap *was* intended as a blessing after all. If Drukpa Kunle's urine can be interpreted as a miraculous substance, why not Uncle Donpa's feces? Perhaps the king was not a gullible fool but a paragon of faithful devotion.[13]

Does Uncle Donpa as a "mad" yogin also share the values articulated by Uncle Donpa as a common man's hero? In the "mad" yogin role, he is not a common person who uses his cleverness to get away with breaking society's rules. Rather, though he plays the part of the "everyman," he is an enlightened being, the elite of the elite, whose behavior only affirms that those rules don't apply to him. In every respect, then, interpreting Uncle Donpa as a "mad" yogin negates the values championed by the common man's hero. A satirical, secular, class-oriented critique of elites becomes a metaphysical critique of *samsara* and an exhortation, ultimately, for all to play their part, which, for the common people, means embracing faith over skepticism and the sincerity of one's own religious practice over criticism of the apparent failings of others. In other words, the tales essentially become elite clerical discourse. While the "common man" interpretation continues to exist, the critique of elites is thoroughly contained by this competing model.

One scholar suggests that this process of subordination by incorporation, repeated many times over in Tibetan history, has acted as such an effective "steam valve" that no truly revolutionary movements or figures can be found in traditional Tibet.[14] If there was any potential for an alternative to the elite system, it never gained traction. This is in line with a historical pattern of Buddhist institutions in many cultures, and not just in Tibet. Buddhist traditions have long dominated other regional cultures and subcultures by accommodating and incorporating them into their own overarching system. In Tibet, behind a narrative of "taming the wild," many pre-Buddhist local gods were preserved in this way, although they were said to have been conquered by powerful Buddhist yogins (including Drukpa Kunle) and bound to the service of Buddhism. In this way, worship of more ancient local gods was transmuted into a "higher" Buddhist worship. The wild Uncle Donpa is similarly tamed when he is turned into a "mad" yogin and might be seen, on some deeper level, as not only "civilized" but also a civilizing agent to common people who might be tempted to challenge the elite. This process of "buddhification" of all aspects of Tibetan life was so successful that it is exceedingly rare to find voices from traditional Tibet that express alternatives to the clerical elite. Still, the "wild" man who resists taming and incorporation persists in Uncle Donpa's "common man" guise.

Contemporary Interpretations

Since 1959, the Chinese government that has ruled the Tibetan region has broken the power of the traditional aristocratic class and greatly reduced the influence of the monasteries. The Tibetan government-in-exile and Tibetan refugees have tried to preserve traditional culture while adapting to life in India and elsewhere and coping with the challenges of the "modern globalizing world." Yet Tibetan oral tradition continues to survive, and Uncle Donpa remains very popular with contemporary Tibetans, who now have greater access to tales about him through publications, radio, and television. These new circumstances, a mix of possibilities, tensions, and anxieties, are reflected in four recent interpretations of the trickster. These new interpretations of Uncle Donpa – as historical saint, as protomodernist, as mouthpiece for misogyny, and as proto-Communist – demonstrate that the need to interpret this important figure continues.

Uncle Donpa as a historical saint

Rase Konchok Gyatso (b. 1968), a contemporary Drikung Kagyu lama, claims to have uncovered the "historical" Uncle Donpa, and has attempted to separate the man from what he considers to be the fantastical and ethically dubious accretions to the folk tales. Using textual references to an "Uncle Donpa," the author asserts that Uncle Donpa was in fact an accomplished twelfth-century practitioner of the Drikung Kagyu school. To support his contention, he relies on local tradition from a district south of Lhasa, where there is a rock that is reputed to bear a miraculous imprint left by Uncle Donpa as a mark of his realization. This interpretation can be seen as a formalization of the traditional religious interpretation. Rather than making a vague claim, however, Rase Konchok Gyatso attempts to fit Uncle Donpa specifically within the institutional context of the Drikung Kagyu school. Further, this attempt to differentiate between the historical figure and the rogueish folk hero may indicate that Tibetan scholars and householders in exile now insist on a more historical consciousness and therefore on Uncle Donpa, if he is to be taken seriously, being a historical person.

Uncle Donpa as a protomodernist

Some politically outspoken members of the Tibetan exile community have invoked Uncle Donpa as a model for Western-style open debate in the public sphere. Jamyang Norbu (b. 1949), an important early figure in the development of the Tibetan Youth Congress and an outspoken critic of what he views as the Tibetan government-in-exile's conciliatory approach to China, has explicitly referenced Uncle Donpa as his inspiration in several articles published on the website Phayul.com. For Jamyang Norbu, Uncle Donpa symbolizes honest and open criticism, including criticism of religious and political figures, as a means to progress. This stance, in turn, has met with much resistance. In posted comments in response to criticism of his articles, Jamyang Norbu's defenders also sometimes invoke Uncle Donpa to support his stance. This interpretation of Uncle Donpa as a champion of honest and open criticism might be seen as a reworked "common Tibetan" interpretation.

Uncle Donpa as a mouthpiece for misogyny

Other Tibetans now criticize the social function of the Uncle Donpa tales. Nuns in Dharamshala have complained that the stories, enjoyed by many in the exile community, are defamatory and open nuns to unjustified scrutiny and gossip at a level that monks do not face. Further, the nuns have complained that, since they are already "second-class" monastics in traditional Tibetan life, these stories serve the dominant patriarchal norms that still work against the nuns' desire for respect and support in exile.

Uncle Donpa as a proto-Communist

Some Chinese authors have appropriated Uncle Donpa as a proto-Communist revolutionary. To this end, a set of Uncle Donpa stories collected by Chinese authors from Tibetan informants was published back in 1980. These stories were initially written down in Chinese, after which they were "improved" and then retranslated back into Tibetan.[15] The published version, in Tibetan, is full of Chinese idioms as well as Communist jargon and rhetoric. Predictably, Uncle Donpa becomes a heroic, materialist figure who demonstrates that religion is superstition grounded in the false hopes of exploited "serfs" for a better afterlife. In one story from this collection, an evil lama preys on the superstitions of the common people by promising them heavenly rebirth through the performance of *phowa* (*'pho ba*), the transference of a dying person's consciousness to a celestial Pure Land. Instead, he murders them for pleasure. Uncle Donpa heroically exposes the lama and leads the people to realize the lama's true nature and the folly of their own superstitions. Finally, he leads them in burning this "jackal in monk's robes" alive in a bonfire.[16] The stories in this Chinese collection are neither bawdy nor very funny; the polemic is both too obvious and heavy handed. Explicitly addressing the lack of bawdy material, the editors admit that this element was present in many of the tales. However, they contend it was not a part of the authentic Uncle Donpa stories. They argue that this bawdy material was actually introduced by "reactionary" elements (i.e., the Tibetan government) to deceive the common people and discredit this noble, proto-Communist figure![17]

Conclusions

Both the range of interpretations of Uncle Donpa's significance and the important issues his tales address give him a prominent place in Tibetan culture, past and present. His tales continue to serve as a great source of entertainment and a significant means through which Tibetans (and now others as well) reflect on and argue about class, religion, history, gender, politics, and their own beliefs. Uncle Donpa, ever the trickster, will no doubt continue to inspire new interpretations while always somehow staying just out of reach.

References

A khu bstan pa'i gtam rgyud (1980) Si khron mi rigs dpe skrun khang, Chengdu.

Aris, M. (1987) "The boneless tongue": alternative voices from Bhutan in the context of Lamaist societies. *Past and Present*, 115, 131–64.

Bell, C. (1987) *Portrait of a Dalai Lama: The Life and Times of the Great Thirteenth*, Wisdom, London.

Dorje, R. (1975) *Tales of Uncle Tompa: The Legendary Rascal of Tibet*, Dorje Ling, San Rafael, CA.

Dorje, R. (1997) *Tales of Uncle Tompa: The Legendary Rascal of Tibet*, 2nd edn, Station Hill Arts, Barrytown, NY.

Dowman, K. (1998) *The Divine Madman: The Sublime Life and Songs of Drukpa Kunley*, 2nd edn, Dawn Horse Press, Clearlake, CA.

Further Readings

Dowman, K. (1998) *The Divine Madman: The Sublime Life and Songs of Drukpa Kunley*, 2nd edn, Dawn Horse Press, Clearlake, CA.

Hartley, L.R. and Schiaffini-Vedani, P. (eds) (2008) *Modern Tibetan Literature and Social Change*, Duke University Press, Durham, NC.

Hyde-Chambers, F. and Hyde-Chambers, A. (2001) *Tibetan Folk Tales*, Shambhala, Boston, MA.

Von Schiefner, F.A. (trans.) (2013) *Tibetan Tales Derived from Indian Sources*, Routledge, New York.

Notes

1. Dorje 1997: 30.
2. Dorje 1997: ix. Indeed, his name itself conveys Tibetans' warm regard for this figure: "Uncle" (*Akhu*, or *a khu*) conveys affectionate familiarity as well as a certain respectability, and "donpa" (*ston pa*) means "teacher" or "one who reveals."
3. Dorje 1997: 50.
4. Dorje 1997: 23.
5. Dorje 1997: 36.
6. Bell 1987: 350.
7. While humor certainly plays a role in making these tales more palatable to elites, it should be noted that among Tibetans the joke has also been considered a potent thing. This is reflected in the Tibetan language itself, where one of the words for "joke" (*tenshik*, or *bstan bshig*), sometimes used in reference to satiric critiques of the Uncle Donpa sort, literally means "destruction of the dharma."
8. Dorje 1997: 41.
9. Aris 1987: 131–64, 144–5.

10 Dowman 1998: 96.
11 Dowman 1998: 129.
12 Dorje 1975: 61.
13 Interestingly, there is a history in Tibet of devotees consuming small amounts of urine, or even excrement, of holy lamas.
14 Aris 1987: 145–6.
15 *A khu bstan pa'i gtam rgyud* 1980: ii.
16 *A khu bstan pa'i gtam rgyud* 1980: 193. "Jackal in monk's robes" is also how the fourteenth Dalai Lama has been characterized by some of his Communist Party detractors.
17 *A khu bstan pa'i gtam rgyud* 1980: 2–5.

6

Ma-chig Lab-dron
Mother of Tibetan Buddhist Chod

Michelle J. Sorensen

Editor's Introduction

The subject of this biography is one of the most frequently mentioned women in Tibetan history and culture, considered exemplary for her strength and generosity, a role model for both women and men. A householder who was a wife and mother and a student of noted monks, Ma-chig Lab-dron later became a renunciant, a yogini, and a renowned teacher.

Ma-chig Lab-dron is best known for her articulation and codification of Chod, a tradition grounded in the Mahayana *Perfection of Wisdom* (*Prajnaparamita*) literature, with its praxis designed to cut through ego-clinging and eliminate erroneous patterns of dualistic thinking. The aim of the practitioner is to become unattached to form and to liberate all modes of sensory consciousness – seeing, hearing, smelling, tasting, touching, mental consciousness – by not evaluating their experiences as either positive or negative. When these discriminating mental activities are abandoned, the practitioner is released from attachment, so he or she can rest in the clear state of the pure, self-arisen mind. The Chod texts traced to Ma-chig Lab-dron emphasize that this practice ought to be in accordance with the ideals of the Mahayana bodhisattva, with the ultimate aim being the liberation of all sentient beings from the realm of suffering. This meditation tradition was eventually adopted by all monastic and lay lineages of Tibetan Buddhism, and is the only Buddhist tradition to be transmitted from Tibet back to India.

The biography of Ma-chig Lab-dron gives insight into several common aspects of Tibetan Buddhist tradition. First, we can witness in her aptitude for reading and proficiently reciting the texts the popularity of this practice, as elsewhere in Asia; and, since few householders were literate in premodern Tibet, they would offer payment to those who could read the texts, seeking the great merit and protection that was produced by the recitation of the dharma, a promise and practice that is found in the earliest Buddhist texts. Second, we can understand the ways that a spiritual virtuoso's life is explained and then remembered for posterity: Ma-chig's extraordinary ability at reading is explained as a residual blessing from her previous life; and then in the legends that formed around her birth and her family, we can clearly see the pattern of saints' lives conforming to details of the Buddha's life (supernormal events occurring to mark her birth; speaking right after her birth; a body with a host of extraordinary auspicious marks; etc.). Finally, in Ma-chig's biography we can witness the difficulties Tibetan women have faced in undertaking advanced practices. According to conservative Tibetan beliefs, women could not attain enlightenment unless they were born as a male. There being no ordination lineage for female monastics, Tibetan women lacked means of institutional or material support to dedicate their lives to practice alone. The twists and turns in Ma-chig Lab-dron's biography reflect this context, making her life all the more extraordinary for the great impact her own teaching made across Tibetan Buddhism up to the present day.

Introduction: Life in Tibet during the "Later Spread" of Buddhism (Ninth–Twenfth Centuries)

In the middle of the eleventh century in a remote valley of Tibet, a girl was born to the family of the local chief; she would eventually become known as Ma-chig Lab-dron, the "Singular Mother, the Light of Lab." Ma-chig Lab-dron is remembered to the present day as a woman who became both learned and enlightened in the Tibetan Buddhist tradition.

When we try to imagine what Ma-chig Lab-dron's life was like, it is helpful to think about daily life in Europe during the Middle Ages. In both Europe and Tibet, the majority of people in that period lived simple lives, primarily eating sustenance foods and rarely traveling far from their homes. Communities were organized around family groups and interconnected under the purview of a local chief landowner. The worldviews of most people were influenced more by spiritual beliefs, traditional learning, and direct interactions with nature than by formal education or scientific understanding.[1]

In Ma-chig's time, Tibet was a sparsely populated area of central Asia. The Tibetan Plateau's inhospitable terrain was mostly inhabited by nomads, with scattered settlements that integrated monastic and clan groups. Outside the hierarchies of the monastic institutions and the few ruling clans, it is difficult to trace clearly the contours of social distinctions – such as status and communal roles – for this period. Obviously, since there is a tradition of oral and written biographical sketches of her life, Ma-chig was not an average member of her society but an exemplary individual. From the accounts of her life, Ma-chig appears to have been from an upper-class family and to have lived in a village, as opposed to the rural or nomadic life lived by many of her contemporaries. She occupied a privileged position within her social environment: in addition to records suggesting that she was born to the chief of the local village and his wife, she was literate and had a close relationship with a religious specialist in her village. Especially for a woman of her time, Ma-chig's literacy was unusual: not only was access to education limited but also, unless people were willing to travel, communication and the exchange of ideas were limited. Literacy was scarce; it was usually developed among nobles from important clans, merchants, and those educated within a monastic setting. However, following the decline of Buddhism in Tibet during the first half of the ninth century, the presence and importance of monastic institutions had decreased. Not only would Ma-chig have inhabited a society in which the majority of people were illiterate but also her daily existence was one of basic sustenance in terms of food and clothing, given the harshness of the climate and terrain, even in the relatively fertile area of the Yarlung Valley in southeastern Tibet.

The period of the "later spread" of Buddhism during which Ma-chig lived was a time of "Tibetan renaissance." The Yarlung dynasty – which had ruled during the eighth and ninth centuries on the Tibetan Plateau over much of what constitutes the contemporary region of Tibet – disintegrated, and decentralized political powers and communities developed in its place. During this period, Buddhism was being revitalized by new translations and transmissions of teachings, explicitly distinguished as "new" (*gsar ma*) transmission lineage, in contrast with the "ancient" or "old" ones (*nnying ma*). These political and philosophical shifts supported a variety of religious environments, including both monastic and householder communities of practitioners as well as groups following charismatic teachers; all of these fostered an increased interest in Buddhist teachings. Individuals would travel significant distances under great physical hardship in order to receive spiritual teachings; they would also participate in pilgrimage to visit venerated sites or objects. The rulers of Gu-ge (in eastern Tibet) invited the famous teacher Atisha (980–1054) of Vikramasila monastery (on the Gangetic Plain) to visit their land. After his arrival in 1042, he inspired a revival of the scholastic study of Buddhism and a host of new monastic institutions flourished. A great scholar, Atisha supervised the translation of many Buddhist texts into the Tibetan language. Another notable South Asian Buddhist teacher traveling to the region was Pa-dam-pa Sang-gye (Pha dam pa Sangs rgyas, d. 1117), a renowned practitioner of Buddhist yogas and master of experiential learning through meditation. He is thought to have disseminated dharma teachings to Ma-chig.

The Life Story of Ma-chig Lab-dron

Ma-chig's biography has been the subject of numerous retellings in Tibetan up to the present. The two most popular Tibetan spiritual biographies of Ma-chig[2] have been translated into English several times, in tones ranging from colloquial to scholarly. Working from these and other Tibetan primary sources, we can retrace the broad outlines of her life.

Birth and youth

Most sources record the birthplace of Ma-chig in a village called Tsho-mer in the region of Lab-chi situated in lower Tam-shod in E'i Gang-wa. Although these names do not exist in contemporary Tibet, we can surmise that Ma-chig's childhood residence was in the eastern part of the Yar-lung valley, southeast of Lhasa. Current scholarship has settled on 1055 for her birth and either 1149 or 1154 for her death.

Ma-chig's father, Cho-key Da-wa, was the village chief, suggesting a relatively high social status. Her family appears to have been relatively wealthy and prominent in their community, which consisted of several hundred households. Members of the family were considered strong followers of the Buddhist traditions, and they are remembered as being supportive and charitable to others, treating their subjects and servants with compassion. Her mother, Lung-mo Bum-chen, gave birth to three other children: two sons and a daughter. Lung-mo Bum-chen was 48 when she became pregnant with Ma-chig. Lung-mo Bum-chen's pregnancy was a surprise to her friends and neighbors, and is credited as a blessing resulting from her exemplary life as a Buddhist.

Ma-chig is remembered as being special from birth: she was able to talk with her mother as soon as she was born. She also had marks on her body that are signs in the Buddhist tradition of being an exemplary being, including the auspicious syllable *hrih* on her tongue, a circle of five colors of light that appeared like a third eye on her forehead, and the syllable *a* bathed in white light at the crown of her head. Because of these unusual features, her family was concerned about how people would react to her strangeness, and they kept her away from people.

Beginning when she was a toddler, Ma-chig would make prostrations to the images of the celestial bodhisattva Avalokitesvara, the female embodiment of compassion Tara, and the tantric goddess Vajrayogini, and she did so while reciting the mantras associated with them. She would also recite a single-line summation of the *Perfection* of Wisdom (Prajnaparamita) teachings, another talent considered to be evidence of knowledge carried over from her previous lives. By the age of five, Ma-chig had learned to read and write. Soon after, she could recite the entire text of *The Perfection of Wisdom in Eight Thousand Lines* (*Ashtasahasrika Prajnaparamitasutra*) twice in a single day. By the time she was ten, she could recite the text four times a day, and she could recite it eight times a day when she was 13. When Ma-chig was 13, her mother passed away. She lost her father when she was 16 and her sister when she was 20. Her elder brother, Ke-u-gang Kor-lo-drag, became a respected monk, scholar-translator, and head of a local monastery. Her younger brother inherited her father's role as a local leader.

Complementing her childhood aptitude for ritual performance, Ma-chig took an early interest in Buddhist teachings and became a student of Dra-pa Ngon-she (Grwa pa mngon shes, 1012–90). Her renowned ability to recite the *Perfection of Wisdom* texts as a professional reader allowed her to pursue her studies at this noted teacher's monastery. Skill as a reader of texts has always been a valuable ability in Tibetan Buddhist communities: householders sponsor recitations of Buddhist texts to accumulate merit. Readers were contracted to recite a particular text a specific number of times and donations were made accordingly; such donations supported both the reader and the monastic community. Readers were esteemed for their precision and speed. While performing these rituals as Dra-pa Ngon-she's assistant for several years, Ma-chig also received an education on the teachings associated with the *Perfection of Wisdom* and learned their various commentaries, as well as other traditional Buddhist sutras.

Advanced studies

When Ma-chig was about 20, Dra-pa Ngon-she advised her to continue her studies with Kyo-ton So-nam La-ma, a teacher learned in classical Buddhist philosophy as well as Vajrayana teachings. So-nam La-ma was at one time a monastery teacher, but by the time Ma-chig met him he had turned solely to meditation practice and stayed in mountain retreats. So-nam La-ma encouraged Ma-chig to build on the familiarity she had gained through reciting and studying the *Perfection of Wisdom* teachings, bolstering her efforts to contemplate more deeply the meanings contained in the texts. He eventually gave Ma-chig various sutra and tantra teachings that greatly improved her understanding of the dharma. During this time, Ma-chig also went on pilgrimages to sacred places.

Marriage and motherhood

While she was studying with So-nam La-ma, Ma-chig met an itinerant Indian yogin the texts identify as Thod-pa Ba-re. She became his partner and gave birth to several children.[3] According to later sources, her marriage to Thod-pa Ba-re was a point of controversy, given that she had previously behaved as a spiritual renunciant and had lived as a student at a monastic institution; she was then accordingly referred to as "Lady who had abandoned her vows."

It is unlikely that Ma-chig was ever a fully ordained nun (*dge slong ma*), because the full Buddhist ordination lineage for women never reached Tibet, so women in this region could not be officially ordained nor could they be of the same institutional status as ordained males. This lack of an ordination lineage speaks to how difficult it would be for a woman, especially during this time, to gain a recognized and respected status as a religious expert or spiritual mentor.[4] So, during Ma-chig's time, it was difficult for women to practice the Buddhist dharma since there were few monastic institutions that would offer women a place for their spiritual or scholarly advancement. Even for wealthy female practitioners, remaining at home with their parents was only acceptable for a period of time.[5] The only alternative for a woman was to meet a dedicated male practitioner who was not celibate and become his consort, but the development of her own practice was entirely dependent on the character of her male partner.

Early spiritual career and personal development

According to several traditional sources, at some point fairly early in her adult life, Ma-chig also met and received teachings from the Indian yogi Pa-dam-pa Sang-gye, the well-known teacher of Zhi-je (*zhi byed*), a method for the pacification of suffering. Later in her adult life, Ma-chig left her family and again devoted herself to her own spiritual practice, shaving her head and dressing in the simple clothes symbolizing her choice to live as a renunciant. She spent years traveling to give and to receive teachings. Ma-chig eventually settled in a cave at Zang-ri Kar-mar (*Zangs ri khang dmar*), where a community of men and women gathered who accepted her as their teacher and adopted her methods for seeking enlightenment.

Ma-chig Lab-dron's Teachings

The *Great Speech Chapter* (*Bka' tshoms chen mo*), one of the few extant philosophical works attributed to Ma-chig Lab-dron, contains her personal instructions on the *Perfection of Wisdom* teachings, which she spent her life studying. In this text, Ma-chig cites a well-known section of the *Heart Sutra* (*Prajnaparamitahrdayasutra*), one of the most important *Perfection of Wisdom* texts in Mahayana Buddhism She also provides her own commentary on how to understand this canonical work. As Ma-chig explains:

> As for form, the essence of form is empty. Unattached to form, meditate on emptiness. One who is definitively unattached to form is liberated from the Negative Forces of grasping [things] as permanent. One who does not meditatively cultivate emptiness in mental consciousness is definitively liberated from the Negative Forces of nihilism. The appearances of forms cannot be obstructed, nor grasped as something definitive: they are naturally luminous and clear. [By understanding this,] one's hearing, smelling, tasting, touching, mental consciousness, and so forth, are likewise liberated. As for mental consciousness, it is a Negative Force Without Obstruction. When there are occurrences through the doors of the sense faculties, they are the Negative Forces with Obstruction. Appearances presented to the sense faculties are directly severed through one's intent for self-liberation; without separation, there will be great delusion.[6]

The *Heart Sutra* explains that nothing truly exists, since nothing in the world is permanent or independent of anything else: everything that is perceivable or comprehensible comes into being in relation to other things, and, because of these relationships, nothing is ever unchanging and stable. Since all things we perceive are ultimately empty, it is erroneous to think that there is "something" that can be grasped. Even the concept of "emptiness" is itself empty. A person who understands the impermanence of all things and their lack of essence understands that all things are "naturally luminous and clear." To an enlightened being, the forms of things are mere appearances; an awakened consciousness recognizes the true nature of reality as empty of anything other than impermanent and interconnected phenomena, which we mentally conceptualize as distinct before enlightenment.

According to Ma-chig's commentary on the *Heart Sutra*, one experiences obstructions to one's own awakened consciousness because of the conceptual processes of one's mind: these are the Negative Forces Without Obstruction. But there are also Negative Forces with Obstruction, which refer to the experiences of a person who mistakenly believes that objects exist in some discrete and factual way independent of the mental faculties.

Ma-chig's unique teachings on the Negative Forces – distractions and obstructions that people face in daily life and on the path to spiritual development – were inspired by passages in the *Teaching of the Perfection of Wisdom in Eight Thousand Lines* and its commentary. In the *Perfection of Wisdom* tradition, Negative Forces are represented in the form of Mara, a demonic character who confronts the Buddha and other practitioners with distractions, self-doubt, and other misgivings when they are on the brink of enlightenment. Mara and his minions seek to divert practitioners from becoming enlightened beings. In Ma-chig's commentary on these teachings, she emphasizes that the demonic character of Mara is in fact created by the operations of our own minds:

> As for the manner in which Negative Forces Without Obstruction occur: the manner in which objects occur in the mental consciousness is as good or as bad; the differentiations [made] by one's own discriminative thinking are taught as Negative Forces Without Obstruction. Because one's natural mind does not include grasping a deity as a deity, a spirit as a bad spirit, the hopeful and fearful thoughts of the mental consciousness are one's own Negative Forces that have happened in oneself.[7]

This section from *The Great Speech Chapter* captures one of the teachings that Ma-chig returns to again and again: Negative Forces are nothing other than the workings of the discrimination-making mind. We tend to think dualistically and to evaluate things as positive or negative, especially in relation to how we consider things that affect us; in Ma-chig's analysis, we thus conceptualize beneficial things as "good" (and possibly caused by the influences of "good deities") and harmful things as "bad" (and possibly caused by "bad spirits"). Interrelated with this discriminative thinking is the mistaken belief that all phenomena have an intrinsic identity – that things "are" what they appear to be, outside our perceptions and conceptions. According to Ma-chig, such patterns of thinking are the foundations for our belief in "deities" and "demons." Thus, if we neglect to analyze the mental processes that construct such entities so that they really seem to "be" something independent, the experiences of "hope" and "fear" will also seem to be reactions to external things.

In *The Great Speech Chapter*, these four Negative Forces are discussed at length and expanded on in a variety of contexts. The Negative Forces with Obstruction are said to be caused by a person's affirmative and negative discriminations of sense phenomena. Believing these discriminations to be correct and real is what fetters a person in *samsara* and perpetuates her existence in a world of suffering. In explaining these Negative Forces, Ma-chik cites the *Perfection of Wisdom* teaching: "as for form, the essence of form is empty."[8] She advocates meditation on emptiness as a remedy for these Negative Forces, although she also cautions against making emptiness into something itself, which would result in nihilism. The aim of the practitioner is to become unattached to form and to liberate all modes of her sensory consciousness – seeing, hearing, smelling, tasting, touching, and mental consciousness – by not evaluating their experiences as either positive or negative. Thus, one will be liberated from the Negative Force of grasping things as permanent, which is presented as equivalent to a Negative Force with Obstruction.

Mental consciousness itself is said to be a Negative Force Without Obstruction. While the sensory experiences can become Negative Forces with Obstruction, the mental processes that evaluate and grasp them as something permanent and real are Negative Forces Without Obstruction. Negative Forces Without Obstruction are the differentiations that are made by one's own discriminative thinking. Because one's natural mind does not grasp a deity as a deity or a spirit as a bad spirit, the hopeful and fearful thoughts associated with these entities are Negative Forces that simply originate in one's own mind: they are fabrications that are said to appear "like waves arising from a still ocean." The core of grasping and the source of the Negative Forces is negation and affirmation. When these discriminating mental activities are abandoned, the practitioner is released from the behavior of grasping and can rest in the clear state of the self-arisen mind (*rang byung sems*).

Spiritual Innovator: Chod Tradition

Ma-chig Lab-dron became a Buddhist adept best known for her articulation and codification of the philosophy and praxis of the Chod tradition. Chod teachings are grounded in the Mahayana *Perfection of Wisdom* (*Prajnaparamita*) literature, and they are designed to support practitioners who desire to cut through ego-clinging and eliminate erroneous patterns of dualistic thinking. The teachings of Chod were eventually adopted by many monastic and lay lineages of Tibetan Buddhism; Chod also has a corollary in the Bon religion of Tibet. Chod is said to be the only Buddhist tradition to be transmitted from Tibet to India.

Chod practitioners use various techniques to achieve the aim of cutting through dualistic thinking and ego-clinging, including visualizations, meditations, recitations, physical movements, and music. Chod methodology, in alignment with conventional Buddhist teachings, can be understood as two-fold. One aspect is akin to the Buddhist practice of calmly abiding through experiences of mental turmoil (*samatha*); the other aspect can be seen as parallel to the Buddhist practice of meditative analysis of the constructed nature of one's experiences as being dependent on one's mental conditioning and functioning (*vipassana*). Using these two practices, the practitioner deepens her understanding of the fundamentally empty nature of all phenomena.

The Legacy of Ma-chig Lab-dron

The life stories of this extraordinary saint help us better to understand the difficulties women have faced in pursuing enlightenment within the Tibetan Buddhist tradition. According to conventional Buddhist belief, women could not attain enlightenment without embodiment as a male. In a collection of Ma-chig's teachings popularly referred to as the "Chod Hair-tip Wisdom Teachings" (*Gcod kyi gzhung shes rab skra rtse*), she self-consciously refers to her status as a woman in a Buddhist culture and reacts against this conventional belief: she states that "those, like me, who have taken on an inferior body [i.e., that of a female]" are still able to achieve liberation by "understanding the meaning of the Victorious Mother [*Prajnaparamita*]."⁹ Ma-chig insists that women can attain enlightenment, but she also recognizes their subordinate status within her community.

As with elements of many life stories that are passed from generation to generation, there are aspects of Ma-chig's life story that appear ahistorical or fictional, yet they foster remembrance of her as an exemplary person. For example, Ma-chig's spiritual authority is undergirded by referring to her previous birth as a noble Indian man. The traditional stories of Ma-chig's life mention her previous life as Prince Mon-lam Drup, the son of King Shrisura Arya, a ruler in northern India; this prince would eventually become an ordained Buddhist monk known as Don-drup Zang-po. While the authenticity of this earlier incarnation is a matter of religious faith, Ma-chig's previous existence as a prominent man helps to strengthen her claims to religious authority.

Similarly, the narratives that attempt to establish a direct connection between the well-known Indian Buddhist master Pa-dam-pa and Ma-chig legitimate her status by associating her teachings with a prominent male. Because of her subordinate position as a woman, the transmission lineage that links Ma-chig and Pa-dam-pa functions to legitimate her teachings of Chod as valid and authentically Buddhist. Although it is likely that Ma-chig met Pa-dam-pa and received teachings from him – he was active in the area of Ding-ri and was known to be inclusive of all genders and classes of people – it is not true that he gave her the teachings she would later transmit to others as Chod.

Ma-chig's principal male disciples included Gyal-wa Don-drub, who became a lineage-holder of her teachings. His grandson was To-nyon Sam-drub, known as the "Snowman of Sham-po-gang," and it was he who originated the later tradition of black-hat-wearing Chod practitioners known as "Gang-pa." Quite a few texts in the Tibetan literary archive are traditionally attributed to Ma-chig.¹⁰

Ma-chig's remarkable achievements are attested to by the fact that she is one of the most frequently mentioned women in Tibetan history and culture, considered exemplary for her strength and generosity. As a teacher, Ma-chig was venerated for her wisdom and skill in practicing internal yogas. At some point after her death, Ma-chig came to be remembered as various supramundane entities: as a tantric goddess (yogini), an avatar of Tara, and the embodiment of the *Perfection of Wisdom*. Other texts identify Ma-chig as an embodiment of Ye-she Tso-gyal (757–817), the wife of the early Tibetan king Tri-song De-tsen and the consort of Padmasambhava, the renowned Buddhist master who transmitted Buddhist teachings to Tibet from the Indian subcontinent. Within the Tibetan Buddhist tradition, various people have been recognized as Ma-chig's later emanations, including the Tibetan master Jetsun Rigdzin Chonyi Zang mo (1852–1953) and Tsultrim Allione (b. 1947), an American Buddhist teacher and author.

References

Ma gcig lab sgron (1981a) *Shes rab kyi pha rol tu phyin pa zab mo gcod kyi man ngag gi gzhung bka' tshoms chen mo* [The Great Speech Chapter, the textual tradition of the oral instructions of the profound *Prajnaparamita Chod*], in *Gdams ngag mdzod* (ed. 'Jam mgon kong sprul blo gros mtha' yas), vol. 14, Lama Ngodrup and Sherab Drimey, Delhi, pp. 7–17.

Ma gcig lab sgron (1981b) *Shes rab kyi pha rol tu phyin pa'i man ngag gcod kyi gcod kyi gzhung shes rab skra rtse'i sa gzhung spel ba rin po che'i gter mdzod* (*Gcod kyi gzhung shes rab skra rtse*), in *Gdams ngag mdzod* [A hair's tip of wisdom, a precious treasury augmenting the root teachings in the textual tradition of the oral instructions of Prajnaparamita Chod] (ed. 'Jam mgon kong sprul blo gros mtha' yas), vol. 14, Lama Ngodrup and Sherab Drimey, Delhi, pp. 81–99.

Further Reading

Edou, J. (1996) *Machig Labdron and the Foundations of Chöd*, Snow Lion, Ithaca, NY. (Includes an English translation of the two biographical chapters on Ma-chig Lab-dron from the *Phung po gzan skyur gyi rnam bshad gcod kyi don gsal byed*, with additional materials on the Chod tradition.)

Gyatso, J. (1985) The development of the gcod tradition, in *Soundings in Tibetan Civilization* (ed. B.N. Aziz and M. Kapstein), Manohar, New Delhi, pp. 320–41. (An early academic article noting foundational materials for the study of Chod.)

Kollmar-Paulenz, K. (1998) Ma gcig lab sgron ma: the life of a Tibetan woman mystic between adaption and rebellion. *Tibet Journal*, 23 (2), 11–32. (An article discussing some of the biographical materials on Ma-chig Lab-dron; the author has also contributed a study and German translation of a 19th-century history of Zhi-je and Chod by Chos kyi seng ge.)

Labdron, M. (2003) *Machik's Complete Explanation: Clarifying the Meaning of Chöd: A Complete Explanation of Casting Out the Body as Food (Phung po gzan skyur gyi rnam bshad gcod kyi don gsal byed)* (trans. S. Harding), Snow Lion, Ithaca, NY. (A recent English translation of the *Phung po gzan skyur gyi rnam bshad gcod kyi don gsal byed*, a collection of Chod teachings that includes two biographical chapters on Ma-chig Lab-dron.)

Orofino, G. (2000) The great wisdom mother and the gcod tradition, in *Tantra in Practice* (ed. D.G. White), Princeton University Press, Princeton, NJ, pp. 320–41. (A short introductory essay on Ma-chig Lab-dron and Chod; includes an English translation of a section of the *Great Speech Chapter* (*Bka' tshoms chen mo*).)

Notes

1 A close European counterpart to Ma-chig of Lab is the famous nun Hildegard of Bingen (1098–1179), who was born slightly later in the eleventh century than Ma-chig. Both Hildegard and Ma-chig were composers, philosophers, and spiritual adepts who were influential within and beyond their communities and eras. Unlike Hildegard, who was a cloistered nun whose travels were restricted, Ma-chig was not physically confined to any one place or space – she was able to wander from site to site, following teachers and gathering students. Both Hildegard and Ma-chig flourished within traditional social and religious frameworks, though both also were innovators within their traditions. They both found ways to incorporate their personal experiences of reality into their religious teachings in an effort to help the spiritual development of others.

2 The historical editor was Nam-kha Gyal-tsen (1398–1472) and his account is found in the first two sections of a collection of Chod texts.

3 Sources differ on the number of children that Ma-chig had – from one to three sons and either one or two daughters.

4 In fact, the issue of full ordination continues to be a contentious issue for both Tibetan and non-Tibetan women who follow a celibate path according to one of the institutional Tibetan Buddhist lineages.

5 Nang-sa O-bum is another woman of this period whose life history is known. Her parents eventually arranged for her marriage to a prince who beat her to death. Her life story became the subject of Tibetan musical theater, which recounted how she came back to life with the ability to transmit information about the dead to their living friends and relatives.

6 Ma gcig lab sgron 1981a: 8, my translation.

7 Ma gcig lab sgron 1981a: 8, my translation.

8 "Gzugs ni gzugs kyi ngo bos stong" (*Bka' tshoms chen mo* 7/456; see Ma gcig lab sgron 1981a: 8).

9 Ma gcig lab sgron 1981b: 84, my translation.

10 *The Great Speech Chapter*, *The Supplementary Chapter of Oral Instructions*, *The Quintessential Chapter of the Chöd System of Negative Forces*, *The Common Eightfold Supplementary Section*, *The Uncommon Eightfold Supplementary Section*, and *The Distinctive Eightfold Supplementary Section*. Of these, *The Great Speech Chapter* is the only one that can presently be dated as composed prior to the fourteenth century, through the existence of an annotated outline and a commentary ascribed to the Third Karmapa, Rang-jung Dorje (1284–1339). In his commentary on *The Great Speech Chapter*, the Third Karmapa mentions other texts by Ma-chig that may no longer be extant.

Part II
Buddhist Lives in the West

7
I.B. Horner and the Twentieth-Century Development of Buddhism in the West

Grace G. Burford

Editor's Introduction

Most practitioners of Buddhism in the West, just like most contributors to this textbook, have learned what they know about Buddhism by reading English-language publications and studying Buddhist scriptures translated into English (and other European languages). Through the definitions chosen to gloss key terms from the canonical languages, and the explanations offered of Buddhist teachings and practices, these scholars have exerted a huge influence on how most non-Asians – and even many Asians – have come to think about Buddhism. What did the Buddha teach? Which practices are crucial? How did Buddhism begin and develop? To a large extent, our answers to these questions today reflect the influences of these first generations of Western scholars of Buddhism. This relatively small circle of dedicated intellectuals were drawn to study Buddhism because of their interests in religion, history, philosophy, sociology, and linguistics; they contributed just as much to the establishment of Buddhism in Europe and the Americas as did the Asian teachers who left their home countries to serve Asian immigrant communities and non-Asian converts in the West. Devoted to studying Buddhism through its original sources, they transmitted what they learned to others in a very sympathetic way.

This biography of Isaline B. Horner (1896–1981), a pioneering scholar in this tradition, provides a window into these important figures. Grace Buford's life history also enables us to examine how the understanding of Buddhism fits into the history of British colonialism and how the study of Buddhism became defined almost solely by texts. This thoughtful biography also raises the issue of what "Buddhism" is and what makes a person a "Buddhist."

Buddhists: Understanding Buddhism Through the Lives of Practitioners, First Edition. Edited by Todd Lewis.
© 2014 John Wiley & Sons, Ltd. Published 2014 by John Wiley & Sons, Ltd.

Introduction: Colonial Context, the Centrality of Texts, and the Authority of European Scholarship

How these influential Western scholars approached and understood Buddhism was shaped by the dominant political and social patterns of their times. Colonialism provided the context within which the establishment of Buddhism in the Western imagination occurred, especially in Britain. The British Empire included not only India (the birthplace of Buddhism) but also the adjacent strongholds of Theravada Buddhism, Ceylon (renamed Sri Lanka in 1972) and Burma (also known as Myanmar since 1989). Indeed, several pioneers in the European study of Theravada Buddhism first encountered it during their time in South Asia as British civil servants.

The Europeans and Americans who initially studied Buddhism were fascinated by the Buddhist texts they found in Asian monastic archives, written in ancient languages previously unknown in the West, preserved in a variety of unfamiliar scripts on palm leaves and other exotic media, some recited by monks who knew astoundingly long books of scripture by heart. In a clear sign of the self-superior attitude of colonial rulers, these westerners often perceived the texts as containing the "real" Buddhism, and many of them felt that the Buddhists from whom they got the texts lacked true understanding of the teachings they preserved. Indeed, most colonial-era scholars saw the Buddhists they met as the latest in a long line of religious practitioners responsible for the degradation of "the pure religion" the Buddha originally taught. In an approach modeled on scientific objectivity, these westerners thought they could discover the original, pure religion of the Buddha by examining the texts themselves, deliberately excluding what they saw as the corrupting influence of the Asian Buddhists' interpretations. Largely disinterested in the traditional views of Asian monk-scholars, most preferred to rely on their own linguistic skills and their modern "objective" understanding of history.

Theravada Buddhism and the Pali Canon

For some of these early scholars of Buddhism in the West, the Theravada branch of Buddhism – with its claims to being the original form of Buddhism and to preserving the teachings of the Buddha unchanged since he spoke them – held special appeal. Although these scholars' modern understanding of history led them to doubt that the Theravada Buddhists actually taught and practiced exactly what the Buddha had established nearly 2500 years earlier, the Theravada did seem to have the oldest canon of scriptures, and the consistency of its practices across various areas of Asia did indicate a preference for preservation over innovation. For this subgroup of the westerners studying Buddhism, the scriptures of Theravada Buddhism seemed to offer the most promising avenue to discovering what the Buddha actually said and did – that is, the "original," authentic Buddhism they sought.

The texts that the Theravada Buddhists regard as preserving the words of the Buddha are written in an ancient Indian language called Pali, and we refer to this collection of Buddhist scriptures as the Pali Canon. This collection is the only complete one we have from among the 18 early schools that first arose in South Asia. It includes three main groups of texts: the *suttas*, which document the teachings the Buddha gave; the special instructions the Buddha gave for how the monks and nuns who left home to follow the Buddha's path should live, called the *Vinaya*, or "discipline"; and a collection of more philosophical texts called the *Abhidharma*, or "higher teachings." Over the centuries after these texts were compiled, the Theravada tradition also generated many commentaries and treatises written by monks, also in Pali, on the canonical texts.

The Rhys Davids and the Pali Text Society

It is difficult for us to imagine now how little Europeans and Americans knew about Buddhism 150 years ago. In 1866, when a young British man named Thomas William Rhys Davids (1843–1922) went to Ceylon to work for the British Colonial Service, European scholars knew very little about the Pali Canon or its potential for expanding their understanding of Buddhism. During Rhys Davids' seven years in Ceylon, he learned to read Pali texts under the guidance of several erudite and devout Theravada Buddhist monks,[1] thereby beginning his lifelong study of Buddhism, based on what he found in the Pali texts.

When Rhys Davids returned to England, he continued his study of Buddhism and promoted European scholars' early efforts to edit, translate, and interpret Pali texts. He soon published his first book, a brief guide to Buddhism, which quickly proved very popular.[2] In 1881, Rhys Davids founded the Pali Text Society (PTS). The initial aim of the PTS was to enlist the help of European and Asian scholars who could or were willing to learn to read Pali (always a small group of specialists, even today) to produce printed editions in Pali and translations into English of as many Pali texts as possible. In choosing to devote himself to these efforts, Rhys Davids correctly anticipated that the then-new curiosity in the West about Buddhism would continue to grow. Indeed, Buddhism proved to be appealing, especially in Britain, to many members of the growing middle classes, whose recent access to higher education, increased income, and leisure time were beginning to enable them to explore foreign religions as alternatives to what some saw as the empty materialism of modern science and the mindless dogmatism of Christianity.

When Thomas Rhys Davids died in 1922, his wife, Caroline Augusta Foley Rhys Davids (1857–1942), assumed the primary leadership positions in the PTS, which she occupied until her death. Both of the Rhys Davids recruited as many scholars as they could to volunteer their time and energy to learn Pali so they could edit and translate Theravada Buddhist texts. Women's access to education and scholarship at this time was severely limited, so most of these scholars were men. But, remarkably, there have always been women involved in the work of the PTS. Thomas Rhys Davids taught Pali to Mabel Bode, who contributed significantly to the early work of the PTS. Caroline Rhys Davids, herself a feminist and strong supporter of women's suffrage, made a point of recruiting, training, and cultivating women scholars in the hope that one of them would become her successor at the helm of the PTS. By the time of her death, she had succeeded in this effort. Her protégée was I.B. Horner.

I.B. Horner (1896–1981): Early Life and Education

Isaline B. Horner was born in a suburb of London in 1896 to a financially-well-off, middle-class family. By British societal norms for girls' education at that time, it was unusual that Horner started school around the age of nine and at 16 went to boarding school at Prior's Field School for girls (established 1902).[3] After completing her studies at Prior's Field in 1914, Horner attended one of the two recently established colleges for women at the University of Cambridge, Newnham College. In addition to being on the cutting edge of women's education in Britain, Newnham College and Prior's Field School shared a characteristic that distinguished them from most other schools of their kind for either men or women: they did not require of their students religious affiliation or practice. As Horner would later recall approvingly about her years at Prior's Field, "There was also, subject to one's parents' approbation, freedom not to go to Church."[4] That this met with her parents' approbation seems clear from a 1912 letter from Horner's school mistress to a mistress at Prior's Field. She describes Horner as possessing many worthy characteristics, but regrets that her parents "appear to ignore religious observance." As a result, Horner had "been under no religious influence except at school."[5]

At Newnham College, Horner focused her studies on "moral sciences," i.e., philosophy. In the 1920s, Horner and her grandmother shared an interest in the lectures and publications of Stanton Coit (1857–1944), an American social activist who had become a British citizen in 1903 and who advocated replacing Christian churches with humanist ethical societies. In a letter to her grandmother in 1922, Horner describes herself as "a true daughter of rationalist, scientific Cambridge, and a firm disciple of Kant." She goes on to say that Christians she meets who try to get her to go to church will not succeed, since "only Dr. Coit's Church exists for me."[6]

Encountering Buddhism in Asia

Horner completed her studies at Newnham College in 1917 and stayed on to work in the Newnham library, until 1921. That year the college principal invited Horner to accompany the principal's sister, D.J. Stephen, to India. Stephen was a Christian missionary with an interest in Indian philosophy,[7] whose missionary work focused on establishing schools for Indian women.

Horner's first encounter with Buddhism took place in Ceylon, where she and Stephen stopped over on their way to India. After she had been in India for four months, she wrote, "I long sometimes to get back to the Buddhists … [who] think in a positive way of Peace and Brotherhood and a common humanity."[8] Decades later, Horner would recall that, during the very first days of her first visit to Ceylon, "Buddhism made a very great impact on her."[9] After living and traveling for two years in South Asia (Ceylon, India, and Burma), Horner returned to England in 1923.

Joining the Pali Text Society

Horner's unusually high-quality education, liberal religious views, and early opportunity to spend two years in Asia set her up for the direction her life would follow. Next, a family connection would propel her directly onto that path. A cousin of Horner's grandmother was a close friend of Caroline Augusta Foley, before (and after) she married Thomas Rhys Davids. Once, when Horner was about 12 years old, she had actually met the Rhys Davids at her cousin's house. Thomas Rhys Davids died when Horner was in India, and, by the time Horner returned to England and began to explore her new interest in Buddhism, Caroline Rhys Davids was in charge of the PTS. Horner's cousin put her in touch with Caroline Rhys Davids, who urged her to research and write about women in Buddhism at the time of the Buddha. Horner responded to this suggestion enthusiastically, diving into her initial study of Pali texts and Buddhism that led to her groundbreaking first book, *Women under Primitive Buddhism* (1930), which would remain the only book-length study of women in Buddhism for nearly 50 years.[10] Encouraged by Caroline Rhys Davids, Horner next began to edit for the PTS a multi-volume Pali commentary.[11] During this same period, Horner wrote her second book on Buddhism[12] and began publishing articles about Buddhism in scholarly journals in the United Kingdom and Asia. She also began to give talks about Buddhism to various groups in Cambridge and to contribute articles to Buddhist publications in Ceylon. Over the following decades, Horner would return to South Asia several more times and develop many warm relationships with Theravada Buddhist monks and laypeople there.

Even before her edition of the third volume of the commentary came out in 1938, Horner had already begun her second major PTS project, her translation of the *Vinaya* portion of the Pali Canon. Horner would work on this six-volume translation of the guidelines and instructions for Theravada Buddhist monastic life over the next 28 years.[13]

Assuming Leadership of the Pali Text Society

Caroline Rhys Davids died in 1942. Although she had groomed Horner to take over as both President and Honorary Secretary of the PTS, and the PTS Council members urged Horner to assume both of those positions immediately, Horner insisted that she would accept only the Honorary Secretary role for the time being. But, as Honorary Secretary, Horner did effectively run the organization.[14] In addition to editing and translating Pali texts herself, she actively recruited scholars from Europe, the United States, and Asia to contribute (without compensation) to the PTS's work with texts. Then she would politely but persistently push these scholars, and help them, to complete their PTS projects. She monitored the stocks of PTS books and oversaw the reprinting of out-of-print and revised volumes. Horner single handedly managed the entire process of book production, which required constant correspondence with editors, translators, printers, distributors, and even individual customers who bought their books directly from the PTS. She often packed up the books to be sent out herself, and it was not unusual for PTS customers to turn up at the official PTS address only to discover that it was Horner's home. In addition to selling these visitors the books they came to buy, Horner would often invite them to have tea and discuss their interests in Pali and Buddhism. Eventually, in 1959, Horner did become President, and Honorary Treasurer, of the PTS, positions she held until her death in 1981. In the nearly 40 years that Horner managed the operations of the PTS, she shepherded 56 new PTS volumes and 223 reprints of PTS books through the publication process, in addition to editing four and translating 15 volumes of Pali texts herself.

Participation in Buddhist Groups

All those years that Horner was working tirelessly with European, American, and Asian scholars to ensure the success of the PTS, she was also participating in the life of British Buddhist groups with ties to Theravada Buddhists in Ceylon. One of these groups, the Buddhist Society, began in 1924 when Christmas Humphreys (1901–1983) founded the Buddhist Lodge of the Theosophical Society. Two years later, the Buddhist Lodge separated from the Theosophical Society and began regular publication of a journal, *Buddhism in England*. In 1943, the group changed its name to the Buddhist Society and began calling its publication *The Middle Way*. Issues of *The Middle Way* document Horner's active participation in this group, noting when she was elected to serve in leadership roles in the Society's governance and announcing the countless Buddhist Society-sponsored lectures she gave. *The Middle Way* published transcripts of her talks, as well as articles she wrote about Buddhism, her reviews of books on Buddhism, and excerpts from the Pali texts she was translating.

Humphreys had also had a hand in the founding of London's first Theravada Buddhist monastery and religious center, the London Buddhist Vihara (LBV), in 1926. When the onset of World War II forced the monks of the LBV to return to Ceylon, Horner helped lead the effort that began in 1948 to revive the LBV; it was reestablished in 1955 and continues to operate today. Horner was a frequent speaker at the LBV and, especially in her later years, was treated as a respected elder in the LBV community.

Horner's relations with Humphreys, however, were not always smooth. Horner's purpose in much of her work with these groups was to help these Buddhists understand the teachings of the Buddha that the Pali texts conveyed. In Horner's view, Humphreys did not properly ground his frequent talks and articles on Buddhism in actual Buddhist teachings. As another leading British scholar of Buddhism, Edward Conze (1904–1979), recalled,

> Miss Horner... herself was a fine and meticulous scholar... She and I were taken on as Vice-Presidents because of our scholarly prestige... At Council meetings we watched our President's [Christmas Humphreys'] performance with the amused tolerance one feels for a barker at a country fair... Miss Horner was particularly cross with him because he persisted in treating *The Voice of the Silence*[15]... as an authentic Buddhist scripture of outstanding value.[16]

In addition to the talks Horner delivered to these and other Buddhist groups in London, Cambridge, and Manchester, she was a popular speaker on her trips to South Asia, where she was treated as a sort of Buddhist celebrity for her expertise in the Pali texts and her leadership of the PTS. She was constantly asked to serve on advisory boards and leadership councils of new Buddhist groups in Asia as well as in the United Kingdom and Europe.

Was Horner a Buddhist or just an Advocate of Buddhist Views?

The first generation of European and American scholars of Theravada Buddhism and Pali texts tended not to think of themselves as "Buddhists." Especially for the British scholars who began their studies under the British Empire, Buddhists were the "others" they encountered in far-off lands and in ancient texts. Scholars associated with the PTS in its early decades openly admired, appreciated, and even agreed with what they understood to be the teachings of this religion they studied, but that did not necessarily lead them to self-identify as Buddhists.

Professionally, Horner maintained her position as an intellectual outsider in relation to Buddhism. She wrote her many publications and almost all of her lectures, including the talks she gave to Buddhist groups, from the perspective of a careful scholar, always grounding her accounts of Buddhist teachings in the Pali texts. Yet Horner adopted the mission of the PTS – to make the Pali texts available in the West – and took on the task of explaining the teachings contained in those Theravada Buddhist scriptures with an enthusiasm and commitment that clearly went beyond an academic treatment of these teachings. Horner did occasionally express her advocacy of Buddhism explicitly, especially when her audience comprised Buddhists in Ceylon. For instance, in an article published in the *Buddhist Herald*, a publication of the International Buddhist Study Group in Ceylon, she used Buddhist terminology to construct her argument in a column entitled "Against Materialism." In such instances, Horner presents herself as a member of the Buddhist community addressing her fellow Buddhists. In a message she recorded that was broadcast in Ceylon for Vesak (the annual celebration marking the Buddha's birth, awakening, and death) in 1965, she observes that, because "our *kamma* [Sanskrit: karma] is good," we live in an epoch when we can know the teachings of a Buddha and can celebrate "many a Buddha-day." She goes on to say that we must face the responsibilities that come with living in such an age, namely, "to practice the Teaching and to spread it, but not merely to talk about it or admire it without, each one of us according to his capacity, making of it something real and vital, something prominent in our everyday lives."[17]

Conclusion

A question of identity

If we look at Horner's life, we see her enthusiastic dedication to the global spread of what she understood to be the genuine teachings of the Buddha, her active leadership of Buddhist organizations, and statements like the ones she made in her 1965 Vesak talk. It seems safe to assume that those who attended her Buddhist Society lectures and turned to her articles in *The Middle Way* for expert guidance on following the Buddha's teachings saw Horner as a fellow Buddhist. Likewise, those who participated with her in Buddhist ceremonies that included taking the Three Refuges and Five Precepts, whether at the LBV or at Buddhist temples in Asia, would likely have assumed she was a Buddhist.

On one occasion Horner explicitly denied that she was a Buddhist, because she did not meditate.[18] But many of the people she worked closely with in Asia and the United Kingdom did not meditate either, and she certainly regarded them as Buddhists. Meditation practice is not a universal characteristic of Buddhists that sets them apart from non-Buddhists. In fact, there is no such distinguishing Buddhist practice or belief. The meaning of the term "Buddhist" shifts, depending on who is using it, for what purpose, in what context. Horner's views and actions over her lifetime offer considerable evidence that she adopted a Buddhist worldview, supported Buddhists she came in contact with, and worked tirelessly to promote deeper understanding and wider acceptance of the teachings and practices of Buddhism. In the end, the most compelling evidence that Horner did identify as a Buddhist is that six months before her death she changed her will to specify that she have a Buddhist funeral service. When she died in 1981, Sinhalese monks from the LBV conducted a traditional Ceylonese Buddhist funeral for her that was attended by many Buddhist monks, laypeople, and scholars.

Horner's legacies

Countless scholars, Buddhist monks, and Buddhist householders have relied on I.B. Horner's editions and translations of Pali texts. Her six-volume translation of the Pali Canon's monastic discipline texts (the *Vinaya*) has proven indispensable to English-speaking Buddhist monastics all over the world. Yet Horner's editions and translations of Pali texts are not likely to be her most lasting legacy in the Buddhist world. Such works are inevitably limited by the scope of understanding of the time in which they are produced, and the resulting errors they contain are quickly pointed out by subsequent scholars who work to improve and eventually replace the works of their predecessors. Horner's more lasting impact will probably stem from the facts that her strong leadership and financial support kept the PTS going during her lifetime and that the money she left to the PTS when she died provided a stable financial foundation for this organization that continues to make its work possible to this day.

Horner's other lasting legacy is more subtle, namely her contributions to the continuation of the Buddha-dharma in our world. Through her work for, leadership of, and financial legacy to the PTS; her countless talks and articles on Buddhism addressed to Buddhists and non-Buddhists alike, in the West and in Asia; and her friendships with and generous support of individual Buddhists and Buddhist organizations, Horner spread the teachings of the Buddha. She may not have readily identified herself as a Buddhist, but she certainly enacted the Buddha's directive to his followers to go forth and teach and explain the dharma for the benefit of the many.[19]

References

Conze, E. (1979) *The Memoirs of a Modern Gnostic, Part I*, Samizdat Publishing, Princeton, NJ.

Elliott, M. (2002) *Prior's Field School: A Century Remembered, 1902–2002*, Prior's Field School, Godalming.

Horner, I.B. (n.d.) Correspondence and papers, 1903–80, Faculty of Asian and Middle Eastern Studies, Cambridge University.

Horner, I.B. (1930) *Women under Primitive Buddhism: Laywomen and Almswomen*, Routledge & Kegan Paul, London.

Horner, I.B. (1936) *The Early Buddhist Theory of Man Perfected: A Study of the Arahan*, Williams & Norgate, London.

Horner, I.B. (trans.) (1938–1966) *The Book of the Discipline (Vinaya Pitaka)*, 6 vols, Pali Text Society, London.

Horner, I.B. (ed.) (1933–1938) *Papañcasūdanī (Majjhima-nikāya Commentary)*, 3 vols, Oxford University Press for the Pali Text Society, London.

Iggleden, R.E. and Iggleden, C.W. (1974) Isaline Blew Horner, President of the Pali Text Society: a biographical sketch, in *Buddhist Studies in Honour of I.B. Horner* (ed. L. Cousins, A. Kunst, and K.R. Norman), D. Reidel Publishing, Dordrecht, pp. 1–8.

Rhys Davids, T.W. (1877) *Buddhism: Being a Sketch of the Life and Teachings of Gautama the Buddha*, Society for Promoting Christian Knowledge, London.

Stephen, D.J. (1918) *Studies in Early Indian Thought*, Cambridge University Press, Cambridge.

Wickremeratne, L.A. (1985) *The Genesis of an Orientalist: Thomas William Rhys Davids in Sri Lanka*, Motilal Banarsidass, Delhi.

Notes

1 Wickremeratne 1985: xxiv.
2 Rhys Davids 1877.
3 Prior's Field School continues to educate girls today.
4 Elliott 2002: 13.
5 Horner Correspondence and Papers: F/1.
6 Horner Correspondence and Papers: F/8.
7 See, e.g., Stephen 1918.
8 Horner Correspondence and Papers: F/8.
9 Iggleden and Iggleden 1974: 2.
10 Horner 1930.
11 Horner 1933–8.
12 Horner 1936.
13 Horner 1938–66.
14 The title "Honorary" in the PTS role titles, at least during Horner's lifetime, is misleading. It might have been an honor to be the PTS secretary, but there was never an additional, "actual" secretary doing the day-to-day work behind the scenes for the Honorary Secretary; she did it all.
15 A book written in 1889 by the Russian theosophist Madame Blavatsky.
16 Conze 1979: 73.
17 Horner Correspondence and Papers: L/14.
18 Interview with Sara Boin Webb and personal correspondence with Russell Webb.
19 The well-known passage in which the Buddha instructs his followers to spread the truth (dhamma) he had realized and had taught them can be found in the *Vinaya* (monastic discipline) portion of the Pali Canon (*Mahavagga* I.11.1). Horner translates it as follows in the fourth volume (1951) of *The Book of the Discipline* (*Vinaya Pitaka*) (1938–1966: vol. 4, 28): "Walk, monks, on tour for the blessing of the manyfolk, for the happiness of the manyfolk out of compassion for the world, for the welfare, the blessing, the happiness of devas and men. Let not two (of you) go by one (way). Monks, teach *dhamma* which is lovely at the beginning, lovely in the middle, lovely at the ending. Explain with the spirit and the letter of the Brahma-faring completely fulfilled, wholly pure. There are beings with little dust in their eyes, who, not hearing *dhamma*, are decaying, (but) if they are learners of *dhamma*, they will grow."

8

Takyu

A Young Buddhist Nun at a Ch'an Temple in the English Midlands

George D. Chryssides

Editor's Introduction

This chapter highlights the typical temple practices of Chinese Buddhism, although it is within a diaspora community in England. It is interwoven around the life of a young woman who decided to take ordination at this site, the Fa Yue Monastery. Here at a new temple, we see the prominent focal points of devotee engagement: the centrality of Kwan Yin, the bodhisattva of compassion; worship of Bhaisajyaguru, the medicine Buddha; and the way in which the temple incorporates the Chinese commitment to ancestor veneration associated with the bodhisattva Ksitigarbha. This case study shows the typically flexible relationship between monastic tradition and the domestic interests of its householder devotees, in a mutually supportive context that serves transcendental visions and practical, this-worldly concerns.

This study from England also illustrates how Buddhist tradition in its global spread conforms to the ancient pattern of a home monastery (in Hong Kong) spreading the faith through establishing new branches on its periphery (in this case, rural England). What is also noteworthy is the expression of filial service to elderly parents that moved the nun Takyu to leave the monastery to live closer to them. This action is in fact not unusual: it is normative, and required, in the earliest monastic rule book, the *Vinaya*, showing how Buddhists lauded filial service as a norm shared across Asia, from India to China.

The overview of activities at Fa Yue Monastery illustrates how Buddhism has multiple levels of engagement, incorporating those seeking its ultimate goal of nirvana, those wishing to gain merit for a good present life and better rebirth, and those who seek to avert misfortune or attract pragmatic benefits. Here, as across the globe, Buddhists engage with their tradition for a variety of purposes, ranging from gaining pragmatic benefits to attaining final liberation from the human predicament.

Buddhists: Understanding Buddhism Through the Lives of Practitioners, First Edition. Edited by Todd Lewis.
© 2014 John Wiley & Sons, Ltd. Published 2014 by John Wiley & Sons, Ltd.

Introduction

In 1994 I became acquainted with the Fa Yue Temple[1] in Brierley Hill, near Dudley in the English West Midlands. My wife had noticed a letter in the local newspaper, in which the correspondent referred to the recent conversion of a disused sports pavilion into a Buddhist temple and urged readers to make use of their local sports facilities, lest a similar unhappy fate befell them! We decided to find this pavilion-turned-temple, arriving unannounced, having no contact details of any office-bearer. Despite being unexpected, we received a very warm welcome from the temple secretary – a petite young woman called Wai, later to become the Venerable Takyu Sik.[2] Wai showed us around the temple and spent some time with us. On learning that I frequently took students on field visits, she indicated her willingness to receive students and talk to them. Over the years I have visited the temple, usually – not always – with student groups, and the account of Takyu's life and of the monastery is based on notes taken over a 14-year period between 1994 and 2008, together with a semistructured interview in 2011.

Life History

Takyu's life history cannot be separated from the history of the monastery. Her parents came to England in the 1960s. Since her grandmother had been a devotee of Kwan Yin,[3] she and her parents housed images of this celestial bodhisattva in their respective homes, but they knew almost nothing about Buddhist teachings. Wai's uncle owned a book entitled *The Teaching of the Buddha*, which her grandmother noticed some time in the 1980s; she borrowed it, and was attracted by its ideas. When Wai's mother next visited Hong Kong, she tried to find a copy for herself, aided by Wai's grandfather. The Hong Kong Fa Yue Temple had a book store, which they visited. They did not find the book, but there they met the Dharma Master, who welcomed them cordially. On the family's periodic returns to Hong Kong, they learned more about Buddhism from him.

The Dharma Master enquired whether there were monasteries in England, and was eager to establish one there. Wai's parents undertook the task of finding premises for this purpose. At first they were minded to donate their house at Amblecote to the Master but, because of planning regulations, a change of use from a residential home to a publicly accessible Buddhist monastery was not permitted. Instead, they decided to sell their property and donate the money for this purpose. They looked around the Brierley Hill area to find a suitable property, employing a solicitor to assist them. His search led to the discovery that the Brierley Hill Pavilion was for sale: it had been disused for some 14 years but was capable of being restored and was the right size. The Master came to England in 1989, acquired the building, and succeeded in making a temple there the spiritual focus for the Chinese and Hong Kong diaspora communities. When the temple was officially opened in 1994, the town's mayor was one of the principal guests.

Takyu's official role in the temple is visitors' officer. This involves welcoming students from schools, colleges, and universities to the temple, showing them around, and explaining what Buddhism means. She usually begins by explaining that "Fa Yue" literally means "dharma rain," signifying that the temple's function is to disseminate the teaching of the Buddha, which rains down benevolently on human beings. This is usually followed by an explanation of what being in the sangha entails. The Chinese Mahayana tradition admits women as well as men to the monastic life; both can take vows to live celibately and unmarried.

The monastics of this school observe the traditional Ten Precepts, five of which are binding on the laity: no killing, no stealing, no sexual misconduct, no false speech, and no alcohol. The prohibition on killing extends to all life forms, including insects; however, it does not entail a vegetarian lifestyle: eating meat is not the same as killing the animal. Although the food that the laity prepares at the temple is vegetarian, Takyu believes that Buddhist practice involves accepting whatever food the laity offer, although having a craving for meat would be inappropriate.[4] As a sign of her conversion to Buddhism, Takyu's mother stopped offering meat to Kwan Yin, now that she was worshipping the goddess[5] within a Buddhist context. Takyu says that some worshippers continue to offer meat at Fa Yue Temple, particularly chicken, which is considered a delicacy.

Chinese communities are not renowned for vegetarianism, and such an act is construed as offering one's best to the bodhisattva. Takyu's mother tried to be vegetarian but found that this was not conducive to her health. Takyu points out that the Buddha does not appear to have been vegetarian.

In addition to the publicly disclosed monastic precepts, there are 48 minor precepts. For a householder, the penalty for infringement is not very heavy: one should confess one's misdeeds in front of a Buddha image, or else to a monk or nun. Misconduct by the sangha is more serious: a violation of a major precept must be confessed in front of ten monks; for a minor precept a single monk or nun may hear a confession.

The Monastery

The monastery provides the sangha's accommodation. Its exterior is unpretentious, on account of its previous use. The only hints that it is a Buddhist temple are the Chinese characters above the door, and a large metal urn for lighting incense and making offerings to the hungry ghosts. The former pavilion occupies two stories, the upper one providing the living accommodation for the monks and nuns. It is unusual for male and female members of the sangha to occupy the same monastery, but – as one would expect – the men and women live separated by a corridor. Being residential, the building is named Fa Yue Monastery, but it also has a sanctuary where followers can express their devotion and receive spiritual help. At its busiest, there have been eight monks and nuns in residence, but at the time of writing there are only two nuns living there. Takyu is not one of them, for reasons that will be explained.

The temple's iconography reveals its community's principal interests. In 1994 the central figure was an image of the bodhisattva Kwan Yin inside a glass case, in front of which was a table for offerings of flowers and fruit. Normally an Asian Buddhist temple has protector deities on either side of the entrance, but the design of the converted sports pavilion prevents this, since the external door leads directly into the shrine area. These deities were therefore placed inside the temple, on either side, occupying positions nearest to the entrance.

In 1996 one of the monks, who has now returned to Hong Kong, was visiting the Victoria and Albert Museum in London, where he came across a large statue of Kwan Yin, some 20 feet tall, which was in storage. It was crafted in 1686 and brought to England in 1876. He reckoned that it could be better cared for at the Fa Yue Temple, and approached the authorities, who agreed that the statue could be transported to Brierley Hill, together with a large old bell, on an indefinite loan, renewable at regular intervals. This large statue now dominates the temple area, and the smaller Kwan Yin image has been moved to one side. The sheer size of the acquired Kwan Yin statue meant that it could not go through the temple door until the surrounding woodwork and glass were removed.

Apart from Kwan Yin, a cased image of Bhaisajyu (or Bhaisajyara) is prominent and situated on Kwan Yin's right. This is the medicine Buddha, who is worshipped for healing, and his own distinctive sutras, when recited, are believed to be efficacious.[6] For a modest annual fee, members can purchase a small plaque that is displayed at the back of the case and that is believed to promote health and healing. Healing is different from curing, and Takyu explains that the plaques do not offer miraculous cures for persistent ailments: health should rather be construed as total wellbeing – physical, mental, and spiritual. However, Takyu claims to know of a cancer victim in Hong Kong who was cured of his illness and attributes his cure to Bhaisajyu.

Also in the main temple area are two red and gold pagodas, with compartmentalized shelves containing Buddha images. Their role is in part to do with the temple's ongoing fundraising, and donors believe that sponsoring images such as these earns merit and fosters good luck.

Behind the main temple area, a short passage leads into a smaller shrine, known as the ancestral room. This is a long, narrow area, at the end of which is an image of the Buddha Amitabha. On one's right is an image of the bodhisattva Ksitigarbha, behind which a number of white plaques with small photographs are encased in glass. Ksitigarbha presides over the hells and has taken a vow not to enter full enlightenment until the hells are empty. The photographs here are of members' deceased relatives, whose families can burn incense in front of Ksitigarbha and make offerings of fruit and flowers. This celestial bodhisattva therefore has a special association with the dead and can be invoked to ensure that they have a smooth passage in the afterlife and a good rebirth. The ancestral shrine is the place where members pay due respect to their ancestors. Filial piety is an important Chinese ideal, one of the five cardinal relationships enjoined by Confucius and a principle that permeates all Asian cultures; Buddhists in China, Korea, and Japan have interpreted moral observance as including expressions of filial devotion.

The Ordination

During the monastery's first two years, Wai was its secretary. By then, however, she had decided to become a nun. She explains that a conventional householder's lifestyle seemed increasingly unappealing. People would come to her house and unburden themselves regarding their marital problems: some were unhappily married, others had husbands having extramarital affairs, and several had problems with their children. This caused her to question the conventional institution of marriage and family life, and also introduced some self-doubt: could she be happy with a husband or bring him happiness? Meanwhile, the Dharma Master's dharma talks, accompanied by books and tapes, raised questions for Wai about life's ultimate purpose, and, as she became increasingly familiar with Buddhist doctrines, she saw the monastic life as a preferable alternative.

Wai's ordination took place at the Fa Yue Monastery in the autumn of 1996. The ceremony began at six o'clock in the morning, and my wife and I were invited as guests. Since the ceremony was conducted mainly in Chinese, Wai's brother Geoff and other friends translated for us and made us welcome. Several monks were present, dressed in red and yellow ceremonial robes rather than the brown or black ones normally worn by the sangha. Householders associated with the temple wore black gowns, which is a common practice during Ch'an temple rituals. Wai's parents had a prominent position at a table: parental agreement is a requirement for undergoing ordination. After some chanting, a bowl of water and a razor were brought out, and one of the monks shaved off Wai's hair, a ritual that originated with the Buddha as a sign of his renunciation of the world. It is customary for the laity to present gifts to an ordinand and we had been advised that a modest monetary gift was appropriate, and small red envelopes were provided for this purpose. At the appropriate point in the ceremony the congregation was invited to the platform to present Wai – now Takyu – with their donations.

Toward the end of the ceremony, attendees were invited to kneel in a row in front of a table and place their bared left arm on it. A monk came round with three small pieces of incense for each participant and glued them to their arms; he was followed by a second monk who came around with a taper to light them. Geoff explained that it brought good luck and that one should make a wish for each lump of incense. After some hesitation I decided to take part. Perhaps surprisingly, it was not painful: I merely experienced a sensation of heat on the arm, which swelled afterward, turning red; however, once the swelling subsided, it left permanent scars on the skin! At a later ceremony in Hong Kong, Takyu subjected herself to having nine incense sticks burned into her scalp. She reported that, unlike the good luck ceremony, this was extremely painful, and it left white scar tissue where no hair can grow back, giving a kind of domino pattern on her upper forehead. If one looks closely at a Chinese Buddhist monk's or nun's head, it is not uncommon to see the effects of such incense burning, typically leaving either three or nine dots.

Monastic Temple Religious Practices

Living as a nun in a monastery involves following the monastery's spiritual life. A typical day begins with a morning ritual at around five o'clock (six o'clock in winter). This follows a manual entitled *The Buddhist Liturgy*,[7] and consists of mantra-chanting of homage to Kwan Yin, Amitabha, and Weito; taking the Three Refuges; and a recitation of the *Heart Sutra*. Additionally there is a ceremony at three o'clock called the "evening ritual," although it is in the afternoon. Offerings of fruit, flowers, and water are made. Fruit reminds one to be unselfish (its growth is like a gift); flowers signify impermanence; and water symbolizes purity. This ritual service has components similar to the morning devotion but also incorporates the feeding of hungry ghosts: a small portion of water and rice is taken outside to the incense urn for them. The liturgical manual explains that, because of the efficacy of the mantras, the hungry ghosts are now able to open their mouths and to consume food and drink as ambrosia.

These daily rituals are open to all, but in practice it tends to be only monastics who attend the morning one, owing to its early hour. On full moon days, some householders make a special effort to attend. It is full moon and new moon days that are the most significant: precepts are recited, and participants restrict themselves to vegetarian food. Twice a day the bell is rung 108 times, at morning and evening rituals. The drum and bell are sounded also for the benefit of calling the spirits, since their echoes are believed to reach down to the hells.

Three festivals a year are held in honor of Kwan Yin, and there are celebrations to honor the Buddhas (Bhaisajyu, Amitabha, Maitreya) and bodhisattvas (Samantabhadra, Manjushri, Mahasthama, and Ksitigarbha), all of whom have images in the temple. Additionally, Wesak Day is marked by a grand ceremony that celebrates Shakyamuni Buddha's birth, enlightenment, and death; it falls in spring on the eighth day of the fourth lunar month of the Chinese year. Special ceremonies mark each new moon and full moon. In addition, there are two intensive meditation retreats each year at Fa Yue Monastery. In theory, they should last for seven days, but this has recently been cut down to three. Ch'an (J. Zen) meditation is centered on observation of the breath, thus building up the mind's ability to reach a state of undistracted concentration. Other forms of meditation involve the recitation of the mantras associated with Buddhas and bodhisattvas.

Forms of Pragmatic Buddhism

At the Fa Yue Temple, the quest for pragmatic benefits raised a contentious issue: the use of fortune-telling devices. It is quite common for Buddhist temples across Asia to have metal tubes containing numbered sticks near the main altar. The procedure is for a devotee to shake the tube until one stick emerges and note what its number is; this is thought to correspond to a supernatural answer to a specific question or the features of fate at the moment it emerges. The devotee then goes to a cabinet nearby, where there are dozens of numbered cubbyholes. The devotee retrieves the slip according to the number that emerged on the stick, and tries to understand the cryptic content and apply it in the future. Fa Yue Temple has fortune sticks but uses them in conjunction with four-line poems associated with Kwan Yin, from a text.

This practice turned out to be controversial. Before becoming ordained, Takyu used to speak favorably about these popular pragmatic interests of the congregation, mentioning good luck, good fortune, and longevity. When the temple formally opened in 1994, however, these devices were removed at the Dharma Master's request. The lay members were extremely disappointed, since such oracular consultations are popular. The matter was discussed with the Master, who agreed to reinstate them. Takyu's attitude to this variety of fortune telling is somewhat ambiguous: she describes the activity as "superstitious," and "not part of Buddhism." However, she acknowledges that it is highly popular, and that many members of the congregation have been amazed by the remarkably apt answers and the helpful guidance they have received. For example, quatrain 30 offers the following warning to those who inquire about their ambitions – advice that is spiritual and not merely pragmatic:

My advice to you is please don't be
over-ambitious,
The white crane must beware of the secret
arrow in the mist
Pulling at firewood, you can uncover a hissing
snake –
And one bite from it could bring complete
disaster.[8]

Fa Yue Temple, therefore, offers a means of applying Buddhism to earthly affairs. Takyu believes that the monastic life enables her to do precisely that. Being a nun, she explains, is not like being a hermit, whose lifestyle she would not wish to emulate. She feels she is fortunate as a nun, seeing herself as having the best of both worlds. She does not have to worry about a partner or about children, but she has nieces, whom she sees regularly. She watches television with them and sees programs about the kinds of activities that children enjoy. From time to time, family members have their problems, which they share with her, and she says that she tries to help them through Buddhist teachings. She believes her tradition does not so much provide a ready solution for specific problems but rather offers a way of life to follow that may help to limit such problems from arising and afford a lifestyle that places earthly problems in perspective. Takyu regards her religious occupation as promoting the welfare of others as well as her own spiritual progress.

In 2006 Takyu moved out of the monastery. She now lives in a house on her own on the same street as her parents. Her elderly mother recently contracted diabetes and her father has a heart condition. Although her siblings live in the area, they have to earn their living by running a local Chinese takeaway restaurant, so Takyu feels obliged to play her part in ensuring her parents' wellbeing, believing that parental obligations take precedence over the temple's religious life. In order to look after her parents, she needs to handle money and do the shopping for them; however, this is nothing new, since she previously carried out domestic tasks for the temple.

Takyu's lifestyle and life in the monastery raise issues regarding the forms Buddhism takes. The temple's institutional organization does not readily fall into the idealized textbook descriptions of Ch'an (Zen), which are typically associated with monastic training, or long periods of meditation retreat. The Buddhism of Fa Yue Temple, by contrast, seeks to serve a Chinese diaspora community consisting mostly of householders. All rituals are in Chinese, and the books and DVDs in the temple's small library are almost all in Chinese. Only one westerner attends regularly: he feels welcome but does not understand much of the devotional activities. The only concession to westerners is that the service book has an interlinear English translation.

From the description of the temple given above, the emphasis placed on Kuan Yin and Ksitigarbha will be evident. Kwan Yin is a well-documented focus of Mahayana devotionalism for householders and monastics; although Ksitigarbha is less well known, his image is also found in almost every Buddhist temple in East Asia. Depicted in front of ancestral plaques as a shaven-headed monk with a crown on his head and a large staff in his hand, he is believed capable of forcing open the gates of the Buddhist hells. "Ksitigarbha" literally means "earth store" or "earth womb," alluding to the tradition that Shakyamuni Buddha entrusted Ksitigarbha to be guardian of the earth until the coming of the Buddha Maitreya in the next eon. *The Sutra on the Past Vows of the Earth Store Bodhisattva* recounts Ksitigarbha's past life as a young woman called Kong Mok ("Sacred Girl") who had the task of rescuing her deceased mother from hell. The sutra extols the virtue of filial piety, which Kong Mok illustrates. Takyu's decision to move out of the monastery to look after her mother is therefore a striking example of how such an act is in accordance with Chinese Buddhism.

Conclusion

Fa Yue Monastery exhibits the Buddhist religion in a way that both differs from the forms of Buddhism that westerners have adopted and is largely based on Western literature, with Western assumptions. Takyu's Buddhism is found in England, but it serves a Chinese diaspora community, one that does not set out to attract a Western following. In doing so, it retains numerous distinctively Chinese traits that are not typically found in Western Buddhism: the cults of Ksitigarbha and Bhaisajyu, respect for ancestors, and the value of filial piety. Being a real person living in twenty-first-century Britain, Takyu illustrates how Chinese Ch'an Buddhism can be practiced in real life. While textual figures such as Kong Mok provide a saintly role model for today's believer, the saint represents the ideal to which to aspire rather than the reality of the real-life practitioner. Fa Yue Monastery acknowledges the importance of devotion, morality, and the role of the sangha, yet the way in which all three of these are manifested is flexible and practical. Each householder can decide their level of participation in the devotional practice, what offerings are appropriate, and the extent to which they seek healing or venerate their ancestors.

The folk practice of oracular consultation raises the question of where Buddhism's boundaries lie. In the Fa Yue Temple's congregation, the matter is left unresolved: Takyu insists that these practices are not part of Buddhism, but yet, if they are widely sought after in the context of a Buddhist temple, what else are they? They serve a pragmatic function and are plainly important to followers.

Despite undergoing ordination, which appears to mark a clear boundary between lay and monastic life, Takyu nonetheless not only finds it possible to pursue a lifestyle that fulfills both monastic and familial obligations but also perceives this lifestyle to be a necessary way of pursuing her religion. Takyu insists the monastic life need not involve seclusion but includes interaction with the world outside the monastery. Boundaries between the sangha and the laity are less important than human compassion and filial piety, as symbolized by the central images of Kwan Yin and Ksitigarbha, respectively. Finally, the Fa Yue Monastery and Takyu's biography provide a case study for gaining insight into Buddhism as it is actually practiced by a Chinese community living as a minority in a Western society.

References

Chryssides, G.D. (1999) Buddhism and conscience, in *Conscience in World Religions* (ed. J. Hoose), Gracewing, and University of Notre Dame Press, Leominster, UK, and Notre Dame, IN, pp. 176–99.

Palmer, M., Ramsey, J., and Kwok, M.-K. (1995) *Kuan Yin: Myths and Prophecies of the Chinese Goddess of Compassion*, Thorsons, London.

Sutra Translation Committee of the United States and Canada (1983) *The Buddhist Liturgy*, Buddhist Association of Canada and Young Men's Buddhist Association of America, Thornhill, Ontario, Canada, and New York.

Yü, C.-F. (2000) *Kuan-yin: The Chinese Transformation of Avalokitesivara*, Columbia University Press, New York.

Williams, P. (1989) *Mahayana Buddhism: The Doctrinal Foundations*, Routledge, London.

Further Reading

Chryssides, G.D. (2010) Transcultural migration and new religious movements: a case study of Vipassana, in *Religions et Mondialisation: Exils, Expansions, Résistances* [Globalization: exiles, expansions, resistors] (ed. B. Rigal-Cellard), Presses Universitaires de Bordeaux, Bordeaux, pp. 281–90.

Faure, B. (2009) *Unmasking Buddhism*, Wiley-Blackwell, Oxford.

Fowler, J. and Fowler, M. (2008) *Chinese Religions: Belief and Practices*, Sussex Academic Press, Brighton and Portland.

Pannapadipo, P.P. (2005) *Little Angels: Life as a Novice Monk in Thailand*, Arrow Books, London.

Prebish, C.S. and Keown, D. (2006) *Introducing Buddhism*, Routledge, London.

Notes

1 The name was originally spelled "Fat Yue," but this was later changed. The organization uses both the names "Fa Yue Temple" and "Fa Yue Monastery." In the ensuing discussion, I shall use the former to designate the parts and functions of the temple to which the public normally have access and the latter to refer to the entire premises, which include the monastic quarters. Normally "temple" signifies a public place of devotion and "monastery" a residence for monks and nuns, which typically includes a temple area.

2 I shall use the name Wai to refer to my informant before her ordination, and Takyu to refer to her after she became ordained in 1996. The names are genuine and are used with her permission.

3 The most popular celestial bodhisattva in all places where Mahayana Buddhist culture spread across Asia and now globally. Known in Sanskrit as Avalokitesvara, in Tibetan as Chenrizi, and in Japanese as Kannon. See Yü 2000.

4 Chryssides 1999.

5 The word "goddess" is used in a somewhat loose sense. Kwan Yin, of course, is a bodhisattva in the Buddhist tradition, but clearly she cannot be so described outside that context.

6 Williams 1989: 247–51.

7 Sutra Translation Committee of the United States and Canada 1983.

8 These poems are reproduced in Palmer, Ramsay, and Kwok 1995: 150.

9
Refuge and Reconnection
One Lao Woman's Story

Stewart Jobrack

Editor's Introduction

This biography tracks one main avenue by which Buddhism is spreading into Euro-American communities: immigration by Asians. Like Takyu, the Chinese woman who became a nun in a monastery in rural England (see Chapter 8), here we have the story of "Malayky," who fled Laos during the repression and persecutions inflicted on prominent families after a Communist government took power in 1975. The story of Malayky's traumatic war experiences and her harrowing escape into Thailand, done by taking refuge in a border Buddhist monastery, give this life history special depth and drama.

Like many from across Asia who have immigrated to the West, under duress or not, most immigrant Buddhists have had to face the challenge of recentering their religious identity and meeting their spiritual needs. Few seek out Buddhist centers started by, and run for, westerners. Instead, in hundreds of cities and towns far from their homelands, immigrants from every Buddhist country have gathered, pooled their resources, and created temple-centers. Most follow a typical pattern of moving from humble urban storefronts to converted houses where they have placed Buddha images and created spaces for rituals and meditation. People from the same country have naturally tended to create their own centers, and quite often a Buddhist temple far from home has served as a gathering place for teaching children the home language and culture. Prosperous communities have paid for monks or nuns to immigrate and then reside and maintain their monastic temple.

For many, Buddhist practice plays an integral part in the story of their adjustment to life in the West. As seen in this biography, many immigrants struggle with the stress of serious economic challenges in coping with life in their new country, with

---

Buddhists: Understanding Buddhism Through the Lives of Practitioners, First Edition. Edited by Todd Lewis.
© 2014 John Wiley & Sons, Ltd. Published 2014 by John Wiley & Sons, Ltd.

further pressure felt to remit money back home for their relatives, making savings hard to accumulate. Also stressful are the long separations from family, friends, and native cultures, especially when parents are elderly or siblings suffer difficulties.

In no way, however, is being Buddhist in the West like what it was back home; there it was focused on the monastery, where daily offerings could be made, children educated, monks consulted, goods redistributed, and social life organized. What is also different in Malayky's experience of Buddhism in the United States is her training in meditation practice and having to negotiate her own psychological issues by choosing between medications and meditation.

What is so vividly conveyed here is what remains constant in most Buddhist lives, even in exile: conceptualizing life in terms of karma, and seeking to improve one's own and one's family's destiny through merit-making. Regarding merit-making, Malayky makes the traditional observation that it "is just like you put something in your pack. The more you put, the more you get: it's good marriage, good people, good deeds ... It's karma. It's with you forever." Despite the physical distance from her home and the deaths of her parents, Malayky feels satisfaction in making regular connections to them through acts of merit (donations to monks, charity, etc.) and then transferring the merit to them, even in the afterlife.

Another noteworthy feature of this life history is the manner in which Malayky speaks of the "soul" as the entity that lives on after death. As she reports, "There are souls around in the world. Only we cannot see them. But they see us. They are souls ... sometimes, you close your eyes, it looks like people walk past. When you open your eyes, they are gone. It's kind of like souls [all] around." For the student who has read about the Buddhist doctrine of *anatman*, "no soul," Malayky's words might seem mistaken. But this usage is common in Southeast Asia, where there is a vernacular word for "soul" in Burmese, Thai, and Lao, indicating that "soul" is commonly used by householders to explain the continuity of karma for the living and those who go to their next rebirth. What does this indicate? Abstract definitions matter for philosophers but mean little to the laity; what is primary and central to the Buddhist householder's life is living with karma.

Introduction

In daily practice, Theravada Buddhists in Asia repeat the "taking refuge" Pali verses three times, reaffirming their devotion to the Buddha, the dharma, and the sangha. This happens every Sunday for a group of ethnic Lao in Columbus, Ohio, who chant these words in their local *wat*, a monastic temple they built from a remodeled ranch home purchased in 1987. They are in Columbus because they sought physical, rather than spiritual, refuge; like over three million other people from Vietnam, Cambodia, and Laos, they left their homes after what Americans usually call the "Vietnam War." Beginning in 1975 and continuing through the 1980s, about 12 percent of Laos' population fled. By the time these major population movements ended in the late 1990s, some 1.4 million people from Indochina had been resettled in the United States.[1] Among them are the roughly three thousand Lao currently living in Columbus. They are a small part of that refugee movement. Each refugee and each immigrant has a story. In this chapter, I recount one of them.

Malayky[2] was one of the first people to welcome me to the *wat* in Columbus when I visited there to start my anthropological fieldwork in 2003. She is a particularly patient teacher of Buddhism, and an especially open individual.

Malayky speaks quickly and confidently in a heavily accented English. She sometimes apologizes for her difficulty in finding an English equivalent for a complicated Lao or Pali word. But she speaks with authority about a wide range of issues. Over the years, she and her husband have explained many aspects of Buddhist practice and Lao culture to me. I've talked to them often, and in September 2012 I recorded an open-ended interview with Malayky in which she described her background in Laos and how important Buddhist practice has been to her. Malayky is not representative of all refugees nor is she an expert on Buddhist thought and practice. But her story reveals how Buddhism offers meaning and strength to an ordinary person confronting extraordinarily painful circumstances.

Malayky was born in 1961 in Savannakhet, southern Laos, the fifth of seven children. Her father was a sergeant in the Royal Lao Government's army, and most of her family were connected either to the government or the military. She escaped Laos to Thailand 1981 after the Communist government's policies became increasingly severe. Malayky paints an idyllic scene of childhood life in Laos before this time:

> [I remember] all my sisters and my brothers sitting around together. My dad [would] make breakfast ... He'd get up like five or six in the morning, go to get the fish. He'd cook for the whole family before we'd go to school. We [would] eat together, my dad and the family. And we had a lot of fun. [My dad would] make corn in the morning. Sharing with each other. Growing up, we had a lot of fun. That's what I remember.

This picture fits an image of rural life sold to the West by the tourism industry.[3] But Laos was not pristine. Beginning on a small scale in 1954, US aid first supported a military and police force and soon expanded to the civilian sector. The Royal Lao Armed Forces and the Royal Lao Government were very much dependent on this foreign aid[4] and the influx of money and foreign influence had many consequences. Malayky grew up in this context: "All my family ... growing up ... worked on the ... farm ... After that, all the children, growing up, they lived in town, and they worked for the government. Everybody worked for the army, worked for the Marines."

Despite US military and development aid, and the changes it encouraged in Laos, Buddhist institutions and Theravada practice persisted. Malayky remembers her extended family living in a small village where her grandfather played an important traditional political role. Village life, as it had for generations, was focused on the central institution of the *wat*, where children were educated, goods redistributed, and social life organized.

> My grandfather, grandmother taught me to grow up with the Buddha, to go to the temple. Every day [we were] in the temple. [My grandfather] he is a kind of like ... I don't know how to even call ... [*phu nyi*]. He is like a big person. He is like a captain who lives in the town. Anybody who has problems has to come to see my grandfather. He is like a captain in that county. People who are fighting, people who have problems, have to come to see him. And then let him do something for the family. Yeah. People would often give something to them and then they'd [my grandparents would] have to do something good for the temple.

But Malayky's stories of peaceful village life, and of learning Buddhism from her grandparents and from the Buddhist *bhikkus* (monks) at the *wat*, are punctuated by memories of war.

> They come. I don't know what kind of bombs. Like a fire would come up. Boom. You know and my head, my brain, [explosion sounds]. Every time they bombed, we had, like a big [hole in the] ground. We put some kind of wood on the top and we put land over it to close it ...., like bones [buried] underground. So, we have to go underground, go into the hole. Just like a snake go "poof"! And they [the bombs are] close. Like so close, we could not stay in the house right then.

Even though these events occurred in the late 1960s and early 1970s, they remain raw to her.

> I still have dreams sometimes. Every time I dream like that, I got sweat coming out of my body. And my hearing. [I hear the bombs] sometimes in my ears. I didn't talk about it. I didn't talk in public. When I talked about this story, I'd cry. Sometimes, before, when I talked about this story, I'd cry. Even before, when I talked in school, my teachers cried with me too. You know, every time I talked about it, I'd cry, so I couldn't talk.

In 1975, when Malayky was 14 years old, US support for the Royal Lao Government ended and Vientiane (the capital city of Laos) was declared "liberated" by the Communist Pathet Lao. The Communists began a slow process of transforming Laos into a socialist society. This involved dealing with the many Lao who were associated with the previous regime. Many officers of the Royal Lao army and leaders of the Royal Lao Government willingly went to what were euphemistically called "reeducation camps" or "seminars" for what they believed would be three months. Some remained as long as ten years; some were executed; some died there from the harsh conditions. Finally, the king was pressured to abdicate in November of 1975 and the Lao People's Democratic Republic – a one-party state – was established.[5]

As Malayky finished school and began to explore her career options, the new Communist government was just beginning its efforts to consolidate power throughout Lao society. Part of the process involved compulsory mass meetings in villages, factories, and hospitals.[6] Malayky describes the experience of Communist cadres enforcing the policy of "reeducation" at the hospital where she had just started working:

> I thought I wanted to be a doctor. That's what I thought. That's what I thought I wanted to be my career, my future. [I started with] two years of nursing. [I worked for a] hospital in Pakse in 1978. But something [was] going wrong. Everyone who worked inside [the hospital] over there had to change, had to go to seminar. I didn't trust them [the Communists]. They called family by family. They wanted to know all about your family.

Eventually, they called Malayky's family. Her father, because of his association with the Royal Lao Armed Forces, was imprisoned. Her brother, also with a history in the Royal Lao military, was killed.

> They came to my house and they looked around, moved everything around. Everything. All the clothes. Everything. My dad had World War II clothes in the style of the French. They took all his clothes. They said, "You work for the CIA or something?" They took him to jail. They took my dad to jail. And then my brother ... They killed him. I didn't even see him. I'm sad. Sometimes I [still] have bad dreams. I didn't even know where they took my dad.

Mourning her brother and worried about her imprisoned father, Malayky found the strength to confront a government worker.

> You know, after my dad was gone like that, I didn't know what to do. I started to worry. What should I do? [I thought] my dad is sitting in jail and I can't help him. I went to the government person [and we went to see my dad] ... [When I saw him] I didn't even [recognize] my dad. "Who is that?" Then they said, "This is your dad."
>
> He was so skinny. I didn't know what to do. I was so worried. What could I do? My dad is sitting in a jail. I [decided that I] am going to get him out. I [wasn't] scared even though [the cadre, the government worker] is a strong person. I thought to myself, before I came to the United States, if my dad cannot get out, I will not leave him. Before I leave here, I will not leave until my dad can get out.

Malayky convinced the cadre that her elderly father was no threat to the new regime and, eventually, she arranged his release from prison. Not yet 20 years old and despite her fears, she resolved to leave Laos.

> I didn't know what to do. [I thought] some day I will escape out of this country. But I didn't think I would come to the United States. I didn't see my future here. I wanted to go to France or [maybe] to the United States. But, all my cousins, they escaped already [to the United States]. Because I never moved out from my family, I was kind of scared.

Her escape began by convincing her boss at the hospital that she must take time off work to help her pregnant sister in Vientiane. She hoped to cross the Mekong River into Thailand from there, as had many refugees before her. She arranged two weeks off work but wasn't able to arrange transportation to Vientiane. Finally, just two days before she was due back at work, she was offered a spot on a cargo plane, transporting equipment, people, and a menagerie of animals in one large compartment.

> They put everything in there. They don't have seats. A lot of pigs. A lot of chickens. A lot of animals. But I have to go, no matter what. I have to do something. I went inside. They put cages of

chickens, dogs, everything. You know, monkeys, goats, like big goats. They all smell. They stink. Oh my God. First time in an airplane. First time I left my family. I just prayed. I had never seen Vientiane, either. This was the first time.

Once in Vientiane, Malayky immediately sought out a *wat*. She uses the English word "pray" to describe the Theravada Buddhist ritual she conducted for her parents. "At that time, when I went to Vientiane, I lit two or three candles and prayed at the *wat*. I went and prayed over there. Prayed for my mother and father [so that] they [would] survive and [be] happy."

Escape was, at best, uncertain. She explains the dangerous, delicate process of getting to the riverbank along with a cousin and one of his friends. "We tried to walk slowly. Security, you know, guard, at the river. They walk back and forth, back and forth. If they see us, maybe they can shoot and kill us. They don't want people to escape out from the country."

Unsure of their prospects before they left, the three refugees sought guidance through a kind of divination. Malayky explains the process:

> We made like some kind of … What do you call it? Psychic. We made a good wish before we left. We prayed before we left. We prayed like, "OK I want to go somewhere." If the candle goes down to the ground, I must go. If the candle goes about half down and then blows out, then [we don't go].

Although she sought guidance from divination, Malayky's understanding of Buddhist teaching emphasizes the fundamental role of personal responsibility for one's actions and outcomes. She does not rely fully on supernatural intervention.

> Everything is up to people … It's like people who go to church. They believe God is going to do something. They say God is going to help us out … The people have to do something too. Like you go to work to help yourself, to buy something, to do something for your life. God is not helping you go to work and then get the money for you. Right? You have to help yourself. You have to be yourself. You have to stand up on your own two legs and work for yourself. Work for your family and your children. That's how Buddha taught. Buddha law taught that. You have to stand on your own two legs. You have to work for yourself. You have to do something good for yourself.

Refuge and Reconnection

Through her escape to a refugee camp in Thailand and her eventual resettlement in the United States, Malayky continued to find strength in her understanding and practice of Buddhism. This strength has enabled her to face the challenges of separation from her family with equanimity. She finds strength in the face of suffering and shows little anger toward those who caused it. She claims that her strength comes from inside, but it is enhanced by her understanding of the Buddha's Four Noble Truths and by her actions – including ritual actions. Buddhists talk of "practicing dharma" through the Eightfold Path, which is conceived of as a means to develop skills in order to discipline the mind. Ultimately, skillful practice leads to *nibbana*, enlightenment. In the meantime, the process develops a better, more generous and compassionate person. Malayky's strength, as she sees it, comes from this Buddhist practice and, although there are few systematic studies of the issue, social workers, social scientists, and refugees themselves point to the support that Buddhist beliefs and practices have provided for Southeast Asian refugees.[7] Malayky recounted the way she has felt inner strength in adversity:

> I was strong since I was little, in school and here too. Every time I have a problem, something [some strength] comes up. Even when I went to court, I [stood up] for myself. Even my attorney stood behind me. When I'm standing in the court, something came up. Then I said to the judge, "May I say something?" Bad or not bad. Good or not good. Listen or not listen. And they listened to me. Even if my language is not good, I can explain to people and understand them. Because I am living over here. I am not stealing. I am not lazy. I am working. I pay taxes. I bought a house. I pay taxes for house. I bought a car. I pay taxes for the car. I pay taxes for everything. I don't steal. I don't take favors from the government. I come over and stand on my two legs. And work for myself. For myself and my family. I don't go to the welfare to get something from the people. I stand with own legs. I said that. I just said that to the people in the courtroom.

Buddhism, as Malayky practices it, does more than provide inner strength. The rich Theravada

Buddhist rituals that are a fundamental part of traditional Lao culture provide a mechanism for transcending the gaps of time and space, and for connecting with lost loved ones. Perhaps this is a general quality of all ritual, but it is especially important for the Lao diaspora. It is not only through Skype and cell phones and Facebook that Lao around the world connect with home; Buddhist ritual also helps to construct a transnational space and individuals live in a common "imagined community."

Malayky was in the United States when her father passed away. She learned of the details through phone conversations with her mother, brother, and sister. This provided her with some comfort.

> Before he died, he wore like nice clothes… He liked good, nice clothes. Suit. He liked something clean… You know, how the Marines, they have to wear a nice suit, a flower… to be… like a stronger man. At that time, he wanted to die… he went to buy a suit. He was ready. Live long and never come back. Never like, "Oh, oh oh" [mimicking crying]. Just live long and never come back.

Malayky finds comfort, far from her home, in the reports that her father faced death with equanimity. The expression "live long and never come back" succinctly summarizes the ultimate aspirations for a Buddhist in the Theravada tradition. A person aspires to escape the cycle of birth, death, and rebirth – to "never come back" and rather to achieve *nibbana*. For common, everyday householders, this may take many lifetimes. The fact that her father was "ready" for death suggests to Malayky that he was on a path toward that ultimate goal.

Despite separation and death, Malayky sees her daily actions as directly connected to her father, to her mother, and to her family from past generations. She explains this in terms of the concepts of karma and *boun* (merit). This is symbolically represented in a libation that she and other congregants perform after daily chanting. As water (ideally brought from home) is poured from one vessel to another, people chant these verses, here translated from Pali, transferring the merit they have earned:

> May all beings – without limit, without end – have a share
> in the merit just now made, and in any other merit I have made.
> Those who are dear and kind to
> me – beginning with my mother and father –
> Whom I have seen or never seen; and others, neutral or hostile;
> Beings established in the cosmos – the three realms, the four modes of birth,
> With five, one, or four aggregates – wandering on from realm to realm:
> If they know of my dedication of merit, may they themselves rejoice,
> And if they do not know, may the devas inform them.
> By reason of their rejoicing in my gift of merit, may all beings always live happily, free from animosity.
> May they attain the Serene State, and their radiant hopes be fulfilled.[8]

While the verses she recites refer to "all beings," Malayky thinks of her parents before all others as she pours water and transfers the merit she has earned.

> Every time that I come to the temple, I pray for him [my father]. Let… his soul be happy… Whenever I am doing something, everyday, today, I pray for them [my mother and father]. Whenever I do something, I give something, … I still do that. Everyday. I still do that when I bring the water to the ground, I pray for mother's spirit… There are souls around in the world. Only we cannot see them. But they see us. They are souls. Sometimes you can touch them. You're feeling… you touch, like sometimes, you close your eyes, it looks like people walk past. When you open your eyes, they are gone. It's kind of like souls [all] around.

> I don't care about 100 days, one year, two years. I do it every day. I can… [Merit-making] is just like you put something in your pack. The more you put, the more you got. It's good marriage, good people, good deeds. Something you do, good things… It's karma. It's with you forever.

> Good things, It's not only you, it can go to your children. Or your grandchildren or your great grandchildren forever… It's karma. Something like a kind of fruit. It grows, coming up… It grows – grow, grow, grow forever. That's why people have to study about, learn something about Buddha to understand.

So, on a daily basis, Malayky symbolically reaffirms her connections to the past and to the future. Further, she specifically ties her own actions, the merit she earns, to the wellbeing of her parents, grandparents, and children. This is a reminder that karma transcends the dimensions of time and space and the specific historical events that brought her to Columbus. But those historical events do not disappear. They continue to affect her physical and psychological condition now. Nor do the souls of people from the past disappear, even if the living are not always aware of them. Actions – both in the past and in the present – have consequences that persist.

> For me, before [i.e., earlier in life], I [was] sick. I come over here [to the temple]. I prayed for my health to get better, my mind to get better. Before I [would] get angry, I [would] get upset ... I've got problems with my back. You know. I was scared from there [Laos]. I've got problems from when I left my country. I've got problems with my family, my dad. The Vietnam War, you know ... I'd get pain before, pain so I cannot sleep. Constantly got problems. I had pain and then I had headaches. Problems with the pain and the headaches ...
>
> Every time I have pain here and then it come up through my head and I got headaches. I have dreams. I got bad dreams. Sometimes I dream, I don't know, like people [are] going to kill me. Sometimes I'd go ... to the door and then [there is a] scary something ... Sometimes [in my dreams] I jump into the water and call [for] help. I'd wake up in a sweat.

Malayky sees her Buddhist practice as much more effective than the medication offered by Western doctors. The medication, according to Malayky, is counterproductive. It leads to less awareness, to less mindfulness, to "forgetting karma":

> I talk to [the] doctor. Before, they gave me medicine to control my [pain] ... The more I take medicine, the more my [memories are] forgotten. The more I take, the more it gets worse ... Because the medicine makes people forget everything. If I take more, I do something, I forget. I forget so much. I forget karma. If I meditate, I'm [in] balance.

She uses the metaphor of a computer hard drive that is too full to describe a human mind:

> I look at it this way. For example, the more you put ... in the system on the hard drive. [It's that way with the] mind, too. From the beginning, [as] I am growing up, [put in] until now. My memory is full, right? I want to clean the mind. Now, I come to sit over here. I want to clean the mind. Meditation. I want to clean those bad files out. But I don't want to take medicine. The more I take medicine, the more I get worse. [For] some people, I don't know. But to me, I take medicine everyday before, for my pain, for my head, for everything. Every time I go for a check-up, they give me [medicine]. I leave [it] there. I leave [the] medicine and go to the Buddha.
>
> I breathe in, I go down, down, down, down and it makes me feel more energy. You know. I learned [from] a lot of monks, I learned from the monks' experience. Some monks don't take any medicine because they practice meditation. I use the medicine inside to heal me. When I meditate, I look at what is painful, what caused the pain. Where did it start? Where did it come from? You have to look at what [forgotten] things [that you did] for one day, if you are sick that day. [If you cannot] sleep, eat, or something, then you follow your body. But only the things you can control. You cannot control what happened before you were born.

So the process of "cleaning the hard drive" that Malayky describes is not one of forgetting but a discipline of intense self-examination. The ethics that follow from it also begin with an honest examination of one's own actions rather than evaluating others' behavior:

> You don't compare to anybody. Compare to yourself. It's just for you. If you want to hate this person, no. Hate yourself, too. It comes from you. It is beginning from you ... If you want to say something to a person, say it to yourself first. Is it a good thing to say or not a good thing to say? It starts from yourself. Is it good? Not good? People have different brains ... Observe yourself. Everything will come up. Bad and good inside your heart and mind will come up. You're going learn from it. You're going to learn from [your] body. That's what the monk [taught] today. You have to learn from yourself. Don't complain [about] others. Complain [about] yourself first ... [The monk said] don't look around. Look at yourself.

Malayky finds individual psychotherapy and a comprehensive system of ethics within the institution of the local Buddhist temple. She also finds, through Buddhism, a mechanism to bridge the gaps between her life in Laos and her life in the United States. But Buddhism cannot be isolated from other aspects of her transnational family life. Malayky has never returned to Laos, but she remains involved with life there.

Although Malayky expresses sadness and regret about the separation from her parents, she believes that there is a connection beyond the physical. That connection is maintained through Buddhist practice. She describes the evening of her mother's death in Laos while Malayky was in Columbus:

> You know what, the day [my mother] passed away like the time for us over here was like seven at night. Six in the morning over there in Laos. I just sit like that. I pray. After that, I take the water in the front yard [to transfer merit]. Some kind of a wind came up. I thought [my mother passed away]. Later, my sister told me [she passed away just at that time].

The distances are great. Malayky has never returned to Laos. In 1983 she migrated to Dallas, Texas, where she met her husband. They moved to Columbus in 1985 for better jobs. Her husband's parents and much of his extended family now live in Central Ohio. Malayky's extended family is scattered across the globe. One sister lives in Saskatoon, Saskatchewan. Others of her family remain in Laos.

Malayky could not pursue a career in medicine in the United States, as she had dreamed. But she learned English. She worked hard in factories for years until a back injury made it impossible for her to continue. She and her husband bought a house and they have raised two sons, both of whom are college educated and in professional careers. She is at the *wat* every day, feeding the monks, meditating, studying, participating in ritual life, and helping to create a solid core for the Lao–American community.

Conclusion

In a purely physical sense, Malayky has taken refuge in the United States. In a more fundamental way, she reaffirms on a daily basis that she takes refuge in the Buddha, the dharma, and the sangha. These "Three Refuges" simultaneously aid her in her American life and, paradoxically, connect her to Laos. Through ritual, she connects to family, both living and dead. Through understanding Buddhist teaching and practicing meditation she copes with the trauma of war and dislocation. Through participation in the Buddhist community, she finds a satisfying identity.

References

Canda, E.R. and Phaobtong, T. (1992) Buddhism as a support system for Southeast Asian refugees. *Social Work* 37 (1), 61–7.

Dhammayut Order in the United States (2013) *A Chanting Guide*, 3rd edn, Dhammayut Order in the United States, Valley Center, CA.

Evans, G. (2002) *A Short History of Laos: The Land in Between*, Allen & Unwin, Crows Nest, NSW.

Robinson, W.C. (1998) *Terms of Refuge: The Indochinese Exodus and the International Response*, Zed Books, New York.

Van Esterick, P. (1992) *Taking Refuge: Lao Buddhists in North America. Monographs in Southeast Asian Studies*, York Lanes Press, Toronto.

Further Reading

Access to Insight (2013) What is Theravada Buddhism? www.accesstoinsight.org/theravada.html (accessed January 6, 2014).

Bullit, J. (ed.) (2013) Access to Insight, www.accesstoinsight.org. (A great resource with reliable information about Theravada Buddhism, including translations of selected Pali texts.)

Cadge, W. (2005) Heartwood: The First Generation of Theravada Buddhism in America, University of Chicago Press, Chicago, IL. (A fascinating book about Theravada Buddhism in America. The author looks at its history and studies both an immigrant congregation and a congregation of American converts.)

DeVoe, P.A. (1996) Lao, in *Refugees in America in the 1990s: A Reference Handbook* (ed. D.W. Haines), Greenwood Press, Westport, CT, pp. 259–78. (A concise, clear introduction to Lao culture and the refugee experience.)

Diamond, J. (1989) *Enchantment of the World: Laos*, Children's Press, Chicago, IL.

Evans, G. (2002) *A Short History of Laos: The Land in Between*, Allen & Unwin, Crows Nest, NSW. (A clear, readable introduction to the country's complex history.)

Holt, J.C. (2009) *Spirits of the Place: Buddhism and Lao Religious Culture*, University of Hawaii Press, Honolulu. (The best scholarly book that specifically addresses the unique characteristics of Lao Buddhism.)

Kirsch, A.T. (1985) Text and context: Buddhist sex roles/culture of gender revisited. *American Ethnologist*, 12 (2), 302–20.

Meeker, O. (1959) *The Little World of Laos*, Charles Scribner's Sons, Honolulu, HI.

Numrich, P.D. (1999) *Old Wisdom in the New World: Americanization in Two Immigrant Theravada Buddhist Temples*, University of Tennessee Press, Knoxville, TN. (A comparison of two Theravada Buddhist temples in the United States. Numrich carefully documents how these Sri Lankan and Thai temples adjusted to the American social and cultural setting.)

Van Esterick, P. (1992) *Taking Refuge: Lao Buddhists in North America*, York Lanes Press, Toronto. (A fascinating study of how Lao refugees came to Toronto, Ontario, and then established a Buddhist temple there and adjusted to life in North America.)

Notes

1 Robinson 1998: 2.
2 Not her real name.
3 Two sentences from Laos' official tourism website (www.tourismlaos.org/index.php) in 2012 illustrate this fantasy projection: "Laos is a country as yet untouched by the modern demands, stress and peace [sic] of life. Its beauty lies in the Lao people, century-old traditions and heritage, and its lush pristine landscape."
4 Evans 2002: 101–4.
5 Evans 2002: 169–75.
6 Evans 2002: 176–83.
7 Cf. Canda and Phaobtong 1992; Van Esterick 1992.
8 Dhammayut Order in the United States 2013: 37.

10

Conversion, Devotion, and (Trans-)Mission
Understanding Ole Nydahl

Burkhard Scherer

Editor's Introduction

This biography presents a Danish teacher, Lama Ole Nydahl, who has been one of the most successful institution-builders in the lineage school of Tibetan Buddhism called the Karma Kagyu. It discusses how the organization he founded, the Diamond Way, has become one of the most successful in the world at attracting Western adherents. The chapter charts the path that Nydahl's life took, moving from his discovery of Tibetan Buddhism while traveling in the Himalayas to his authorization from the 16th Karmapa (the reincarnate leader of the Kagyu school) to teach Buddhist doctrine and found the Diamond Way organization; the teachings he acquired; and the support he received from other Tibetan teachers to add the title "lama" to his name. Drawing on Lama Ole's own biographies and Diamond Way publications, the author gives an account of the features of this organization, and especially how it has dealt with the universal problem faced by all founders of religious organizations, especially Euro-Americans claiming to be authentic teachers of the Dharma: the need for legitimation.

In many respects, Nydahl is unique among westerners who now claim the title of lama ("tantric teacher") based on their training in particular Tibetan schools. Having asserted that he is an incarnation of the fierce Buddhist protector Mahakala, he went on pilgrimage across Tibet and wrote a traditional account (*namthar*) about this, conforming to a common practice in Tibetan hagiographic tradition; in it, he identifies places he visited in his previous incarnations and the actions taken, especially in Eastern Tibet. In this way, he has done what hundreds of renowned Tibetan teachers (or their students) have done for centuries: constructing a text authenticating spiritual greatness, revealing miraculous deeds, and bearing witness to the subject's place in an established spiritual lineage. Also highly unusual for a Western lama is Lama Ole's becoming integrally involved in a dispute of succession that still divides the Karma Kagyu school regarding the two contenders for recognition as the 17th Karmapa reincarnation. The Diamond Way and Lama Ole took a side and even helped smuggle their side's claimant from China-held Tibet to India. The chapter also highlights the development of the Diamond Way's hetero-machismo and controversial stands Lama Ole has taken, such as his being an outspoken critic of Islam.

The details of the Tibetan Buddhist world are especially complex and its various schools are confusing to keep straight, even to scholars. What can be learned from this account is how the Diamond Way is traditional in providing many stages for Buddhists to strive for, and how it has built into its programs an orthodox progression for its followers, beginning with the simple and universal Buddhist practice of taking refuge in the Three Jewels to vowing to be a bodhisattva who strives to balance the quest for personal liberation with compassionate action for others. And, for those aspiring to more advanced practices, the Diamond Way offers more complex forms of meditation based upon Mahayana teachings involving identifying oneself with the body-speech-mind of celestial bodhisattvas. Its advanced teaching also includes initiation into the tantric tradition of Cakrasamvara meditation and into the practice of consciousness transfer at death (*phowa*), which can result in rebirth in Amitabha's Pure Land, where enlightenment is then feasible. The Diamond Way's largest centers now include facilities to support those wishing to undertake a three-year meditation retreat in cave-like isolation.

The Diamond Way tradition has also included a variety of ritual practices that are integral to its centers; for them, its leaders have translated Tibetan rituals and chants into modern Western languages, making their meanings accessible. Adhering to a very insistent orthopraxy, Lama Ole Nydahl has been at the center of a Western school that aspires to make Tibetan Buddhism accessible to westerners and yet be a player in the authentic transmission of the Karma Kagyu school of Tibetan Buddhist tradition.

Introduction

Ole Nydahl is one of the most successful lay convert propagators of the Tibetan Buddhist Karma Kagyu (*bKa' brgyud*) school. With over six hundred groups and centers worldwide, Nydahl's Diamond Way is one of the largest Buddhist lay movements, with a particularly strong following in Central and Eastern Europe. Following his personal conversion experience, Nydahl identifies his absolute devotion to his late teacher, the 16th Karmapa hierarch, Rang byung rig pa'i rdo rje (1924–1981), as the root for all his activities. Hence, "conversion," "devotion," and "(trans-)mission" can be viewed as the key elements in Nydahl's life journey.

Unlike other Western Buddhist converts who created new organizations – such as Sangharakshita, the founder of the Friends of the Western Buddhist Order – Nydahl and his wife Hannah (1946–2007) never saw themselves as instigators of a new, specifically Western (or even eclectic) form of Buddhism; instead they have always emphasized the importance of the close, traditional inheritance of their teachings as part of and within the global Karma Kagyu tradition. Their Diamond Way might rightly be described as "missionary" and "neo-orthopraxic."[1] Since its practice is traditional and "technical," the Diamond Way does not qualify to be categorized as predominantly "charismatic;"[2] however, the movement displays to some extent "charismatic" features, including what could be called "Ole-normativity": the tendency to foster uncritical imitation of Nydahl's hetero-machismo, lifestyle, and political views. Unsurprisingly, Nydahl has drawn criticism from Buddhists and non-Buddhists, academics[3] and nonacademics alike, for his seemingly unconventional teaching style, his personal life, and his political involvement in the ongoing schism within the Karma Kagyu school after the death of the 16th Karmapa. In this regard, Ole Nydahl occupies a curious place among the various Western Buddhist teachers of the twentieth and twenty-first centuries.

As a neo-orthopraxic movement, the Diamond Way focuses on "transmission" for its claims of spiritual validation and authenticity. Two autobiographical books form the core of Nydahl's legitimization and transmission accounts: *Entering the Diamond Way* (1999, German original 1979) and *Riding the Tiger* (1992, German original 1990). The books fulfill the function of hagiographies and constitute the narrative dimension of the Diamond Way's cohesion, as this claim of normative transmission is emphasized in almost every public lecture given by Nydahl himself.

In the first of these accounts, *Entering the Diamond Way*,[4] Nydahl describes his encounter with Buddhism. This book entails the foundational narratives of the Nydahls' conversion, spiritual training, and mission (German *Sendung*) narrative for the period 1969–1972. The inspiration for the book is attributed to a suggestion by the 16th Karmapa in 1976. Nydahl later expands upon this version, calling it "a book in the style of Milarepa's life story."[5] The *Mi la'i rnam thar* by gTsang smyon He ru ka, translated famously by Walter Y. Evans-Wentz in 1928, relates the conversion, reformation, and liberation of the notorious black magician and murderer and later famous yogin Milarepa (1040–1123), one of the realized founding figures and a vital link in the transmission lineage of the various Kagyu branches. As a self-proclaimed modern yogi, Nydahl suggests reading his own life story as a modern variation of Milarepa's dramatic transformation.

His second book, *Riding the Tiger*,[6] covers the development of the movement, from Ole and Hannah Nydahl's return to Copenhagen in October 1972 until the early 1990s. Emic source materials for the period after 1990 are less conveniently at hand and consist of numerous articles, interviews, lecture transcripts, newsletters, and so on in dozens of languages.

Early Life: Conversion, Training, and Mission

Born in 1941, Ole Nydahl grew up in the relatively sheltered conditions of a humanistic educated middle-class environment in Lynbgy, north of Copenhagen, Denmark. Nydahl describes himself as "the wildest" child, who enjoyed "climbing the tallest trees and taking on the biggest boys."[7] This characteristic feature continued prominently into adulthood, when Nydahl regularly got into fights and proved to be difficult to handle during his service in the Danish army (1960–1961); while he excelled at the undergraduate level in philosophy, Nydahl ultimately abandoned his academic education in favor of drugs, motorcycles, and boxing.

In 1965, Nydahl got together with his childhood sweetheart, Hannah Christiansen, whom he married in 1968. Experimenting with cannabis, LSD, and other drugs, they smuggled hashish, envisaging themselves then as "liberty fighters for the noble cause of inner freedom." For some of those who knew him, Nydahl was a difficult young man. As one lifelong friend of Nydahl put it, "People always forget: Ole was not really a nice person then."[8] This evaluation balances the later presentation of himself, in which Nydahl interprets his early-life wildness as a natural reflection of his conditioning as a Buddhist protector from previous lives. Nydahl describes himself as a "natural hero"[9] who from early childhood onward had visions of his previous life as a Tibetan officer fighting the Chinese and protecting Tibetan monks and civilians.[10] This hagiographic element intratextually prepares and corroborates Nydahl's claim from 1980 onward to be an emanation of the Buddhist protector deity Mahakala.

Nydahl's charismatic reformation, conversion, and mission narrative is often denoted as his "three years in the Himalayas" becoming the "first western student of the great Tibetan master, His Holiness the 16th Gyalwa Karmapa."[11] His "three years of training" is narratively often constructed such that it invites the comparison (or even implicit identification) with the traditional three-year retreats necessary for adopting the "lama" title. In reality, the time the Nydahls spent in the Himalayas and with the 16th Karmapa was shorter, albeit intense.

Their exposure to Himalayan spirituality and Tibetan Buddhism also developed when they were engaged in their hashish-smuggling activities. On their honeymoon in the summer of 1968, the Nydahls had some paranormal experiences in India and Nepal and saw a picture of the Karmapa for the first time at the Svayambhu Stupa in Kathmandu. Still, this first journey can hardly count as a spiritual quest; despite the cursory interest in Tibetan Buddhism fueled by reading Walter Y. Evans-Wentz's *Tibetan Yoga and Secret Doctrines* (1935), the Nydahls' honeymoon was still just another hippie drug pilgrimage. In the following winter vacation of 1968–69, the Nydahls met their first Tibetan Buddhist teacher, the 'Brug pa Kagyu master Lopon Tsechu Rinpoche (1918–2003). The religious miracle story of this encounter, the lama becoming transparent before Nydahl's eyes, is pivotal to the hagiographical plot element of his personal transformation and is complemented by the first spiritual authorization claim: the Rinpoche blessed them, "transmitting the power of the Kagyupa lineage" to them.[12] This hailed the end of the Nydahls' career as drug dealers; upon returning to Europe, they were arrested and Nydahl had to spend four months in jail. As Hannah Nydahl remembers, prison became a place of purification, reflection, and initial experiments with meditation:

> This was a big turning point in our lives.... During these six weeks, Lopon Tsechu Rinpoche was very clear in our mind, even though we didn't really know anything about Buddhism. We were not allowed to have any personal belongings, save for this one book, *Tibetan Yoga and Secret Doctrines*. That was *the* book for us.... [W]ithout knowing what meditation was, we both started meditating. Probably because of previous habits, we had some experiences, and it felt as if Lopon Tsechu Rinpoche constantly appeared in our mind.[13]

In search of more adventures and the mysterious lama, the couple embarked on their third journey to the Himalayas, which would last two years. In December 1969 they arrived in Kathmandu, meeting Lopon Tsechu Rinpoche and coincidentally the 16th Karmapa. Although Nydahl felt that he had been recognized as a protector by the Karmapa at that time during a Black Crown ceremony in Bauddha, Nepal, it wasn't until September 1970 that the couple stopped using drugs and followed the Karmapa to his seat in exile in Rumtek/Sikkim. It was here where they finally took formal Buddhist refuge. For their first practice, they received protector mantras. According to Nydahl's later recollection, in 1970 the Karmapa also transmitted to them what would become the main practice in the Diamond Way centers around the world: the "three lights meditation" or "Guru-Yoga on the Sixteenth Karmapa," composed in 1959. His earlier hagiographic accounts, however, curiously do not mention this point.

Subsequently, the couple was sent to Sonada/Darjeeling to study and meditate with Kalu Rinpoche (1905–89). While visiting the Karmapa as often as possible, they completed their preparatory meditations (Tib. *sngon 'gro*) within six months. In Tibetan Buddhism, this set of four or five successive meditations prepares practitioners for advanced practices such as tantric "deity yoga."[14] The couple then received the necessary empowerments and explanations for the advanced Guru-Yoga taught by the Eighth Karmapa in the tradition of the Cakrasamvara Yogini-Tantra teachings. From 1986 onward, this practice has been the primary meditation in Nydahl's centers after his students complete the *sngon 'gro*.

Having overstayed their visa once too often, the Nydahls had to leave Sikkim and India; the Karmapa sent them back to Denmark in the fall of 1971; they returned to India for some months in 1972, helping Ayang Tulku in the refugee camps in Southern India and visiting the Karmapa in Rumtek in October 1972, only to be sent home again after only a few days there in order to start a meditation center in Copenhagen. In a letter to Queen Margarethe of Denmark, the Karmapa entrusted the couple to her and describes them as his pupils "who are deeply sincere in their search for the truth." Alluding obliquely to Nydahls' drug past, the Karmapa concludes his recommendation: "We had some remarkable results with young people who are going through the trials of ... a war-torn and drug-deluded generation." Ole Nydahl himself recounted his mission as having a much broader scope: "He [the Karmapa] said that, as first westerners, we now had his blessing for starting centers, and that after the first work in Denmark I would teach in Europe and everywhere."[15]

First Charismatic Phase: Foundations (1972–1982)

In the fall of 1972, Nydahl embarked on his Buddhist teaching career with several lectures in Denmark. Already in November, his missionary activities took him beyond the Danish borders; in teaching and, for the first time, giving Buddhist refuge in Graz (Austria), he set the example for the foundations of many Buddhist centers. Shortly thereafter, one of the most characteristic westernizations within the Diamond Way practice emerged: guided meditations in the local language instead of *puja*s sung in Tibetan. Also during this period, Nydahl developed a prepreliminary practice particular to the Diamond Way: the "short refuge" of 11,111 simplified mantra repetitions preceding the refuge/prostrations (111,111 repetitions) of the introductory entry practice, *sngon 'gro*.

As commissioned by the Karmapa, the Nydahls also started a center in Copenhagen; slowly, groups in Sweden and in Germany were established. When the Dalai Lama visited Denmark in October 1973, Nydahl's center played a key role in the organization of the event and the Nydahls also played an instrumental role in the European visits of Kalu Rinpoche (1974–76) and the Karmapa (1974, 1975, and 1977). In 1976, his missionary efforts brought Nydahl behind the Iron Curtain into Czechoslovakia and Poland, where a group was formed in Krakow.

Concentrating on establishing Diamond Way centers, Nydahl's style indicated clear neo-orthopraxic signs when, in the fall of 1977, he opposed the establishment of a nonsectarian (Tib. *ris med*) center in Hamburg, stating his concern for the purity of the transmission.[16] After the death of the 16th Karmapa in 1981, the Diamond Way continued to expand as Nydahl grew into his teacher role. His own householder lifestyle included joyful, "free-love" promiscuity. This laid the foundations for the continuing and common thread of criticism against Nydahl from traditional Tibetan groups: his own systematically propagated "non-neurotic approach to sexuality." Such critics view this as overemphasizing the place of (hetero)sexuality in religious practice and life; additionally, Nydahl's approach to sexuality is based on pre-/counter-feminist hetero-machismo and gender stereotyping; further, a tension can be observed between his own sexual libertinism and the social and political conservatism he inspires in his followers with his regular support of (center-)right politicians and anti-Islam rhetoric.

During these initial stages, a Western meditation style emerged while Tibetan ritual was maintained and intra-Karma Kagyupa political struggles arose between Kalu Rinpoche, Chime Rinpoche, Ayang Tulku, and the Nydahls. An idea of territorial responsibilities developed in which Nydahl saw himself authorized especially for the Germanic and Slav countries and left France for the monastic Karma Kagyupa. At the same time, a first phase of institutionalization began.

Second Charismatic Phase: Transition (1982–1992)

In its second charismatic phase, from 1982 through the early 1990s, the Diamond Way developed in the face of tribulation, characterized by the tension between charismatic expansion and consolidation. On the one hand, following the death of his own charismatic inspiration, the 16th Karmapa, Nydahl struggled to establish himself as a serious voice among the global, traditional, and celibate monastic institutions that dominated the Karma Kagyupa school. His ultimately successful appropriation of the "lama" title testifies to this process. Organizational tribulations in this period included the 1984 conflict with Chogyam Trungpa's Vajradhatu in the United States and the separation from the original German Karma Kagyupa Association (KKV, founded in 1977) and the subsequent foundation of a separate Kagyupa association in 1989. On the other hand, continuing his missionary drive, Nydahl expanded his characteristically extensive travel schedules; for example, in 1988, he traveled around the globe three times and visited Hungary and the USSR for the first time. In the 1980s, Nydahl, his wife Hannah, and three friends also secretly traveled across Tibet, collecting relics for his centers and consolidating his spiritual legitimization claims by writing a traditional Buddhist narrative of his recognizing places on the Tibetan plateau from his former life in East Tibet.

Important meditation centers in Kuchary (Poland) and Karma Guen (Andalusia/Spain) were founded; the first *phowa* course was held in 1987 in Graz, Austria. *Phowa*, or "conscious dying," is an advanced Tantric meditation, during which practitioners learn to transfer their consciousness at the moment of death to the Pure Land of the Buddha Amitabha. Tibetan Buddhists believe that they can escape the world of *samsara* and achieve a state of mind ("Pure Land") in which they can safely mature to full enlightenment.

The arrival of AIDS and the scandals that rocked Trungpa Rimpoche's Vajradhatu organization (see the Allen Ginsberg biography in Chapter 12) made Nydahl change his promiscuous behavior so that, by the end of the 1980s, he had settled for a single additional intimate partner. From 1990 until 2004, this was Caty Hartung (1965),[17] who also became the organizational manager of the Diamond Way.

The second charismatic phase entailed the emergence and institutionalization of the Diamond Way as a distinctly householder convert movement. Nydahl had become instrumental in the globalization of Tibetan Buddhism. By the beginning of the 1990s, the former drug-smuggling hippie had not only become a reformed character but also a religious missionary, who gradually emerged as a recognized Buddhist teacher: a lama. The Diamond Way also grew in the United States and Central and South America, and Nydahl regularly guided pilgrimages for members/disciples to the holy Buddhist sites in Asia. In 1988, Buddhism was recognized as a religion by the Denmark government, and Nydahl was now authorized to conduct marriages and funerals.

"Twenty Years on the Road": The Making of a Lama

When Nydahl gave Buddhist refuge in 1972 for the first time, it is difficult to say to what extent he was authorized at the time. He claims he received oral instructions from the Karmapa to give refuge and the bodhisattva vow "during his years of practice in the Himalayas."[18] Still, in the first German edition of *Riding the Tiger* (but omitted in the subsequent English and German versions), Nydahl stated that he had told the new Buddhist converts to take refuge with the Karmapa as well; he ended this practice in 1978 when, as he claims, the Karmapa himself deemed this superfluous. It is clear that Nydahl was not sent back in 1972 already as a "lama" in the sense of a traditionally trained and fully qualified Buddhist teacher. Since the 16th Karmapa, in his letter to Queen Margarethe, referred to the Nydahls merely as "trusted pupils," suspicious critics might view Nydahl's hagiographies as hyperbolic self-legitimization. In 1972, by giving refuge, Nydahl created a *fait accompli*.[19]

Nydahl's authorization and spiritual legitimization as an authentic Karma Kagyu teacher is one of the recurrent themes in the Diamond Way's hagiographic narratives. Given the background of the traditional Tibetan hagiographic genre, the "liberation narratives" (Tib. *namthar*), this is rather unsurprising: the construction of authenticity, transmission, and spiritual lineage is one major component of *namthar*. The 1990 original of *Riding the Tiger* contains the vague suggestion that the Karmapa had referred to Nydahl as "lama" from 1978 onward, but this is omitted in later editions; in another passage, Nydahl claims that the Karmapa called him "Lama in accordance with [his] work."[20] This is reflected by the cover texts of his books from 1979 onward, which prominently refer to Nydahl as a "lama."[21] The back cover of the 1985 edition even goes a step further, by vaguely claiming that Nydahl had been "recognized" by the Karmapa.[22] A document written by the Karmapa[23] states, "I have authorised both Ole and Hannah Nydahl to continue to be instructors to the people who are first entering into the understanding and practice of the Buddha Dharma." That the Karmapa's authorization as "instructors" for beginners is not really equal to "qualified lama" is evident from another document labeled "certificate" dated March 26, 1979. In it, the Karmapa states, "I hereby appoint them [Ole and Hannah Nydahl] as teachers of the fundamental teachings [of Buddhism] … I have also empowered them to give refuge and the bodhisattva vow to any person *in the absence of qualified Lamas*."[24] Nydahl comments on this formulation, noting that his wife asked to have it included since "she was afraid that without it we would not get any Rinpoche-visits."[25]

The outside observer with a critical outlook could interpret this as an example of a tendency to prematurely claim spiritual authority, built on hyperbole, self-mystification, and self-aggrandizement. But other interpretations of the opaque legitimization narrative are possible. It seems evident that Nydahl's spiritual development was not finished when he was thrown into the depths of Buddhist missionary work in the West. The first charismatic phase was certainly not only a period of teaching but also – and predominantly – one of further learning, a career not unlike many monks in Tibet who accumulate additional initiations and teachings throughout their lives. In the end, Nydahl became what his activities projected him to be: an externally authenticated teacher.

After the Karmapa's death, Nydahl was finally formally recognized as a "Buddhist Master" by the Shamarpa, the second-highest lama of the Karma Kagyu school. Nydahl's account of the circumstances of having this particular title bestowed on him points to another plausible interpretation of the aforementioned letters the Karmapa wrote in regard to the Nydahls: the tensions between tradition and modernism. In the context of Buddhist Modernism, with its "detraditionalization" that de-emphasizes hierarchies,[26] the emerging Western Karma Kagyu lay movement had become an important factor within Tibetan Buddhist politics. Traditional elements within the school emphasized the conventional training and education of a lama in three-year retreats;[27] this entails a very serious spiritual commitment of isolating oneself for three years, three months, and three days from all outside contact and dedicating oneself to a closed meditation retreat with only occasional contact with the lama supervising the retreat. After receiving the necessary teachings and initiations, practitioners usually dedicate the first year of the retreat to completion of the preparatory practices while the remainder is spent practicing the higher tantric meditations. By contrast, the Nydahls' mission was focused on institution-building, founding "grassroots" centers.

Third Charismatic Phase: The Global Schism and Diamond Way Expansion (1992–2007)

It might not be a complete coincidence that Nydahl's successful recognition by the tradition as a legitimate teacher bearing the title "lama" was finalized in a period of great tribulation for the global Karma Kagyu community. After the death of the 16th Karmapa, tensions between four young regents came to a head in 1992, when three of them recognized the boy Urgyen Trinley, who was born in the Tibetan Autonomous Region of China, as the reincarnation of the late hierarch. They justified their recognition of Urgyen Trinley based on a prediction letter that had allegedly been written by the 16th Karmapa before his demise. The authenticity of this letter was subsequently questioned by the senior regent, who since the fourteenth century has been known as the "Red Hat Karmapa" or the Shamarpa. Against the 14th Shamarpa's wish, Urgyen Trinley was enthroned and support for his recognition came from both the Chinese government and the Dalai Lama – the figurehead of Tibetan Buddhism in exile but who can claim no true authority in matters of recognition within the Karma Kagyu school. The external validations by the two poles of power in the politics of Tibetan Buddhism in exile resulted in the majority of the Tibetan population accepting Urgyen Trinley as the 16th Karmapa's reincarnation. But still, many Karma Kagyu followers found themselves in the middle of a religious and political power struggle. Followers of Urgyen Trinley took control of the monastery of the late 16th Karmapa in Rumtek by force; the Shamarpa enthroned his own candidate, Thaye Dorje, in Delhi a few months later. By 1994, the schism was complete. The Diamond Way had entered the conflict when it organized the escape operation of the second claimant, by then an 11-year-old boy, who was brought out of China and into India. Throughout the whole conflict, Nydahl and the Diamond Way supported the Shamarpa. This alliance proved crucial and has continued alongside the growing global support for Thaye Dorje, despite strong partisan polemics and scholarly contention, especially in the United States.

The global schism certainly stabilized Nydahl's position; politically, he had rendered himself indispensable. The schism also sped up the formal detraditionalization within the Diamond Way. Nydahl called this change necessary and referred to it as the avoidance of "cloistered exoticism"[28]: increasingly, as the practice of the preparatory meditations (sngon 'gro) was emphasized in Diamond Way centers, now only the mantras of traditional chants were recited in Tibetan, and *pujas* sung in Tibetan were generally phased out. Further, the traditional prostrations in front of the altar upon entering the meditation hall were scrapped, Buddhas and bodhisattvas received Western names (e.g., Loving Eyes instead of Chenrezig (Skt. Avalokitesvara)), and the Tibetan refuge formula was done in translation. However, Nydahl's increasing westernization of Tibetan Buddhism constituted a mere repackaging of its orthopraxic content.

In the same period, Nydahl continued the global expansion of the Diamond Way. As of 2003, increasing travel activities in Central and Southern America and the post-Communist countries of Eastern Europe had allowed the movement to grow to more than four hundred centers worldwide. From 1987, the teaching of *phowa* or "conscious dying" became increasingly important and a trademark of Nydahl and the Diamond Way. The annual summer courses held from 1993 to 2007 near Kassel (Germany) drew thousands of followers and also featured teachings and rituals such as tantric initiations/empowerments by lamas loyal to the Shamarpa.

The Nydahls' first Buddhist teacher, Lopon Tsechu Rinpoche, also supported the Diamond Way in these years of expansion. He orchestrated building a considerable number of large, impressive *stupas* at Diamond Way centers throughout Europe, most notably in southern Spain, at the Buddhist retreat center Karma Guen, where the first tantric Kalacakra Stupa outside Asia was inaugurated in 1994.

In the new millennium, the Diamond Way grew further and gained more public recognition: Shamarpa's Karmapa candidate visited Europe for the first time in January 2000 and was received by a large Diamond Way congregation in Düsseldorf, Germany. Also in 2000, the Diamond Way took a prominent role by representing Buddhism in Europe's Expo 2000 and at the 2004 Summer Olympics in Athens. In Hamburg, Warsaw, Budapest, Canberra, and elsewhere, large centers were established; land for new Diamond Way lay retreats was purchased in the Americas and in Greece, Poland, and the Czech Republic. So-called "traveling teachers" were appointed to teach in the Diamond Way centers. Initially only a dozen, their number grew steadily to over 30 in 2003, and as of 2010 there were 232.

Several events hailed the end of expansion and the beginning of a new consolidation: with the death of Lopon Tsechu Rinpoche in June 2003, the Diamond Way lost one of its most charismatic traditional supporters. Then, two months later, Nydahl had a serious parachuting accident. He fractured his right thighbone, damaged his pelvis, and suffered collapsed lungs. Doctors were fighting for his life for several weeks, and then months of rehabilitation followed. Now at the age of 62, Nydahl's hypermasculine, high-adrenaline activities – fast cars, motorcycles, bungee-jumping, sky-diving – seemed to have caught up with him. Still, after a short break, Nydahl again went around the world, this time on crutches, to resume his former teaching schedule, so this accident did not seem to change him much.[29]

One year after the accident, a potential organizational crisis was narrowly avoided, when Nydahl's intimate relationship with Caty Hartung ended. Hartung remained as the Diamond Way manager. Three years later, a major tremor shook Diamond Way when Hannah Nydahl died on April 1, 2007 after a long illness. A very private person, Hannah Nydahl had divided her time between supporting her husband and maintaining contacts with the Asian Karma Kagyu teachers and hierarchy. As a translator and diplomat, she had left the extrovert activities to Ole Nydahl while working in the background. In his letter to students on the same day (*DWN-News* 16/2007), Nydahl described how "losing her is an amputation and the wound is deep": the Diamond Way had clearly entered its ongoing, consolidating late-charismatic period.

Conclusion: Observations on a Late-Charismatic Movement in Transition

Viewed in light of the Tibetan hagiographic tradition of "liberation stories" (*namthar*), Nydahl's life story can be regarded as a modern example of established "crazy-yogin" narratives found within the Karma Kagyu tradition.[30] Some aspects of Nydahl's teachings are directly linked to biographical "scars": his unconventional path toward authenticated spiritual validation as a lama is directly connected to his propagation of a lay

Buddhism based on idealism and friendship. Further, establishing and building up centers is hagiographically argued to be more important than undergoing formal training; this work as a grassroots specialist is also presented as a means to achieve equivalent levels of spiritual realization through Nydahl's compassionately working for the benefit of humanity. Interestingly, rhetorically placing charismatic leadership and Dharma activity above personal meditation retreats does have prominent Tibetan precursors, such as Lama Zhang (1122–93), the founder of the Tsalpa Kagyu lineage.[31]

Nydahl's recipe for the westernization and globalization of Tibetan Buddhism is the "neo-orthopraxic repackaging" of traditional content. Tensions can be observed between Nydahl's missionary charisma and institutionalizing forces.[32] For example, in 2009, Nydahl made an attempt to shake up the hierarchical trend among the rapidly growing number of "traveling teachers." At the same time, due to increasing external criticism, Nydahl has adopted a more rigid approach concerning his followers in matters of political activism ("no politics in the centers") and conduct codes for social media. Further late-charismatic consolidating measures appear to have taken an even more authoritarian and sectarian direction. In the summer of 2010, Nydahl publicly revoked the authority of one particular "traveling teacher" to teach in Nydahl's name, because this teacher had reportedly introduced self-chosen practices of more traditional Tibetan form and style in the centers; subsequently, further prominent, yet out-of-favor, "traveling teachers" within the organization were pushed out. In the summer of 2011, Nydahl even allowed himself a public stand-off with the Shamarpa about a well-intended but ostensibly ill-worded statement, in which this second-highest Karma Kagyu lineage lama had written about Nydahl. Finally, Nydahl-centered sectarianism surfaced openly in August 2012 when, at the Europe Center, one of Nydahl's closest students publicly and directly challenged the spiritual authority of the then-present 17th Karmapa hierarch. Whether recent developments are viewed as cultish, simply clumsy, or even prudent depends on the observer.

One could perceive an authoritarian leadership here and an attempt to consolidate by creating conformism and silencing internal dissidence; from this vantage, the emergence of "Ole-ist" sectarianism appears to be tolerated, at least, just as devotion to unquestioned authority develops in the logic of many modern "cults." By contrast and based on a hermeneutics of trust, one could argue that, in late-charismatic periods, the consolidation of a movement necessarily entails creating and solidifying the highest possible cohesion and communal vision; in this case, this may be necessary in order to carry the movement through the crisis that may arise after Nydahl's death.

Irrespective of the observer's view, it is clear that the unconventional style that determined the first phases of Nydahl's Diamond Way faces challenges as the founder and his circle seek to consolidate and solidify institutional norms. Their view seems to be that conformity and loyalty are necessary for ensuring the long-term stability of this movement. This struggle – coupled with factors such as relations and cooperation with the Tibetan Karma Kagyu hierarchy, the nature and scope of the spiritual authority granted to Nydahl's "traveling teachers" and Diamond Way administrators, and the global cohesion and identity among Nydahl's centers – will be of key interest as the final pages of the Danish lama's legacy are written.

References

Anthony, D. and Ecker, B. (1987) The Anthony typlogy: a framework for assessing spiritual and consciousness groups, in *Spiritual Choices: The Problem of Recognizing Authentic Paths to Inner Transformation* (ed. D. Anthony, B. Ecker, and K. Wilber), Paragon House, New York, pp. 35–105.

Batchelor, S. (1994) *The Awakening of the West: The Encounter of Buddhism and Western Culture*, Parallax Press, Berkeley, CA.

Borup, J. (2005) *Dansk Dharma: Buddhisme og Buddhister i Danmark* [Danish Dharma: Buddhism and Buddhists in Denmark], Forlaget Univers, Højbjerg.

Borup, J. (2007) *Danske Verdensreligioner: Buddhisme* [Danish new religions: Buddhism], Gyldendal, Copenhagen.

Evans-Wentz, W.Y. (1935) *Tibetan Yoga and Secret Doctrines*, Oxford University Press, London, 1935.

Hartung, C. (2003) "Den Wesen nutzen ... ": Ein Interview mit Caty Hartung ["Beings' benefit...": an interview with Caty Hartung]. *Buddhismus Heute*, 35, 40–5.

Klein, E. (1998) *Buddhistische Persönlichkeiten* [Buddhist personalities], Goldmann, Munich.

McMahan, D.L. (2008) *The Making of Buddhist Modernism*, Oxford University Press, New York.

Nydahl, H. (2007) His way was very skilful: Hannah Nydahl on H.H. the 16th Gyalwa Karmapa Rangjung Rigpe Dorje (part 1). *Buddhism Today*, 20, 18–23.

Nydahl, O. (1979) *Die Buddhas vom Dach der Welt: Mein Weg zu den Lamas* [The Buddhas from the roof of the world: my path to the lamas], Diederichs, Munich.

Nydahl, O. (1983) *Når Jernfuglen Flyver* [When the iron bird flies], Borgen, Valby.

Nydahl, O. (1989) *Die Buddhas vom Dach der Welt: Mein Weg zu den Lamas* [The Buddhas from the roof of the world: my path to the lamas], 2nd edn, Octopus, Vienna.

Nydahl, O. (1990) *Über alle Grenzen: Wie die Buddhas in den Westen kamen* [Regardless of borders: how the Buddhas came to the West], Joy Verlag, Saltzburg.

Nydahl, O. (1992) *Riding the Tiger: Twenty Years on the Road – Risks and Joys of Bringing Tibetan Buddhism to the West*, Blue Dolphin, Grass Valley.

Nydahl, O. (1994) *Über alle Grenzen: Wie die Buddhas in den Westen kamen* [Regardless of borders: how the Buddhas came to the West], 2nd edn, Joy Verlag, Saltzburg.

Nydahl, O. (1995) *Die Buddhas vom Dach der Welt: Mein Weg zu den Lamas* [The Buddhas from the roof of the world: my path to the lamas], 3rd edn, Marpa Verlag, Vienna.

Nydahl, O. (1999 [1985]) *Entering the Diamond Way: Tibetan Buddhism Meets the West*, 2nd edn, Blue Dolphin, Grass Valley, CA.

Nydahl, O. (2003) *Die Buddhas vom Dach der Welt: Mein Weg zu den Lamas* [The Buddhas from the roof of the world: my path to the lamas], 4th edn, Aurum, Bielefeld.

Nydahl, O. (2005) *Über alle Grenzen: Wie die Buddhas in den Westen kamen* [Regardless of borders: how the Buddhas came to the West], 3rd edn, Aurum, Bielefeld.

Rawlinson, A. (1997) *The Book of Enlightened Masters: Western Teachers in Eastern Traditions*, Open Court, Chicago, IL.

Saalfrank, E.S. (1997) *Geistige Heimat im Buddhismus aus Tibet: Eine empirische Studie am Beispiel der Kagyüpas in Deutschland* [Spiritual home in Buddhism from Tibet: an empirical study of the Kagyu in Germany], Fabri Verlag, Ulm.

Scherer, B. (2009) Interpreting the Diamond Way: contemporary convert Buddhism in transition. *Journal of Global Buddhism*, 10, 17–48.

Scherer, B. (2011) Macho Buddhism: gender and sexuality in the Diamond Way. *Religion and Gender*, 1, 85–103.

Scherer, B. (2012) Globalizing Tibetan Buddhism: modernism and neo-orthodoxy in contemporary Karma bKa' brgyud organizations. *Contemporary Buddhism*, 13, 125–37.

Yamamoto, C.S. (2009) *Vision and violence: Lama Zhang and the dialectics of political authority and religious charisma in twelfth-century central Tibet*. Ph.D. dissertation. University of Virginia.

Further Reading

Borup, J. (2008) Buddhism in Denmark. *Journal of Global Buddhism*, 9, 27–37.

Caplan, M. (2001) *Halfway up the Mountain: The Error of Premature Claims to Enlightenment*, Hohm Press, Prescott, AZ.

Galanter, M. (1989) *Cults: Faith, Healing, and Coercion*, Oxford University Press, Oxford.

Nydahl, O. (1999) *Entering the Diamond Way: Tibetan Buddhism Meets the West*, Blue Dolphin, Grass Valley, CA.

Nydahl, O. (2008) *The Way Things Are: A Living Approach to Buddhism for Today's World*, O-Books, Winchester, UK, and Washington, DC.

Nydahl, O. (2012) *Buddha & Love: Timeless Wisdom for Modern Relationships*, BRIO Press, Minneapolis, MN.

Nydahl, O. (2012) *Fearless Death: Buddhist Wisdom on the Art of Dying*, BRIO Press, Minneapolis, MN.

Prebish, C.S. and Baumann, M. (eds) (2002) *Westward Dharma: Buddhism beyond Asia*, University of California Press, Berkeley and Los Angeles.

Scherer, B. (2009) Interpreting the Diamond Way: contemporary convert Buddhism in transition. *Journal of Global Buddhism*, 10, 17–48.

Scherer, B. (2011) Macho Buddhism: gender and sexuality in the Diamond Way. *Religion and Gender*, 1, 85–103.

Scherer, B. (2012) Globalizing Tibetan Buddhism: modernism and neo-orthodoxy in contemporary Karma bKa' brgyud organizations. *Contemporary Buddhism*, 13, 125–37.

Notes

1 For a more detailed discussion of aspects of Nydahl's activities, see Scherer (2009, 2011, 2012).
2 In the sense of the Anthony typology (Anthony and Ecker 1987: 39–40).
3 Academic attention to Ole Nydahl and his Diamond Way began in the 1990s (see Scherer 2009: 30). Stephen Batchelor briefly described him as a "sun-tanned Viking" who projects an "ecstatic, sensuous version of Tantric Buddhism" with "fundamentalist and sectarian overtones" (1994: 114). Nydahl received a more balanced, two-page appraisal by Andrew Rawlinson (1997: 462–3). In Germany, Eva Saalfrank's (1997) qualitative ethnographic study on convert identity contains an initial academic evaluation of Nydahl and the Diamond Way. Brief and critical comments by a few continental European religionists follow; Jørn Borup (2005: 156–63; 2007: 46–9) provides a balanced evaluation of Nydahl and the Diamond Way in Denmark.
4 German: 1979 with subsequent editions in 1989, 1995, and 2003; Danish: 1983; English 1985 with a second edition in 1999.
5 "Ein Buch im Stil der Lebensgeschichte Milarepas" (Nydahl 1994: 118 = 2005: 127).
6 German: 1990 with subsequent editions in 1994 and 2005; English: 1992.
7 Klein 1998: 55.
8 Personal communication, 2007.
9 Klein 1998: 60.
10 See, e.g., Nydahl (1999: 2); not in the first edition (1985).
11 Nydahl 1983: back-cover text.
12 Nydahl 1983: 42.
13 Nydahl 2007: 20.
14 The preparatory (or preliminary) practices entail 100,000 or 111,111 recitations each of the refuge formula while doing full-body prostrations (to purify the body); recitation of the hundred-syllable mantra of Vajrasattva (to purify speech and mind); recitation of the *mandala* offering formula (presenting the whole universe to all Buddhas in gratitude and filling the mind with countless positive imprints); and recitation of the formula of devotional praise to the gurus (to prepare the student for the blessings of the higher tantric meditations).
15 Nydahl 1983: 232.
16 Nydahl 1992: 123.
17 See Hartung 2003: 41–2.
18 Ole Nydahl, personal communication, February 2011.
19 Ultimately, the interpretation of Nydahl's action is a question of hermeneutical perspective. With a hermeneutics of suspicion, one could conclude that this act was an ego-inflating assumption of unwarranted spiritual authority; with a hermeneutics of trust, one could view this as an authentic enactment of the Karmapa's wish.
20 Nydahl 1990: 229; 1992: 239.
21 Nydahl 1979 and its 1983 Danish and 1985 English translations; the back-cover text of the second German edition (1989) introduces him only as a "meditation master."
22 What is meant by "recognized" here is unclear. Was it his potential as a teacher, or a more exalted status such as lama ("tantric guru") or even a *tulku* (a consciously reborn realized master)? These titles would later be claimed by Nydahl.
23 Reproduced in Nydahl 1992: 135.
24 Reproduced in Nydahl 1979: 232 but omitted in subsequent editions; emphasis added.
25 Nydahl, personal communication, February 2011.
26 McMahan 2008: 42–4.
27 Prominent Kagyu master active in the West, Kalu Rinpoche, offered these to Western devotees in France from 1976 onward.
28 "Lebensferne Exotik," Nydahl (1990: 365); the passage was left out in the English version (1992).
29 In Nydahl's reflection on the accident in a letter a month after the event, (auto)hagiographical strategies of legitimization were paramount (August 28, 2003, *DWN-News* 34/2003): although he admitted that "the crash is fully my [Nydahl's] own fault" and that "surely to some it is now a relevant question how skilfully my mind is handling the gift of my body," the following account was dramatized by preceding ominous and coinciding sinister events: "it is an open question if it would have been possible to avoid some kind of accident." Nydahl's reflection focused on his fearlessness, his hypermasculinity (he does not call for help), and his compassion: he is mindful and grateful to the paramedics.
30 See Scherer 2009, 2012.
31 Yamamoto 2009.
32 Scherer 2009.

11

Noah Levine
Punk Rocker and Buddhist Meditation Teacher

Brooke Schedneck

Editor's Introduction

With the contemporary world changing so rapidly in so many dimensions of life, from the economic system and employment to the technologies that connect and sustain us, it should not be surprising that many people are experiencing modern life as lacking meaning and marked by suffering. While much has changed since the Buddha's time, it is clear that his teachings that address suffering, define its causes, and prescribe meditation remain edifying to many people in the world today.

The biography in this chapter charts the course of an unconventional teacher whose own suffering early in life was so acute, and his responses to it as a punk rocker so failed, that he attempted suicide. Noah Levine's life was transformed by his exposure to Buddhist meditation and the calm and discernment it produced; after meeting a Western monk, Ajahn Amaro, who told him that he had also once been a punk rock music fan, Levine found his life's mission in integrating the punk worldview and Buddhist meditation. This unlikely combination, which would have made no sense to most traditionalists in the premodern era, nonetheless resonates powerfully with many disaffected people across the world today. Through his books, his retreats, and the two organizations he founded – Against the Stream Buddhist Meditation Society and the Mind Body Awareness Project – Levine now devotes his life to turning around troubled lives. He skillfully leads those drawn to punk's energy of disillusionment and its ethos of mindless escape to entertain new and positive pathways, centered on Buddhist practice.

On the most fundamental level, he points out, the punk movement concurs that there is suffering in life, as in the First Noble Truth; but Levine's originality is in pointing out that the Buddha went further, where punks have not: to understand the causes and conditions of suffering and then to teach a path to freedom through meditation. In Levine's teaching, Buddhist meditation, like the punk culture,

---

Buddhists: Understanding Buddhism Through the Lives of Practitioners, First Edition. Edited by Todd Lewis.
© 2014 John Wiley & Sons, Ltd. Published 2014 by John Wiley & Sons, Ltd.

"rebels"; but, unlike punk's taking solace in drugs and the oblivion of powerful drumbeats, he witnesses to the fact that the Buddha's path can lead to genuine and enduring peace. Levine's movement "Dharma Punx" shows the vitality of Buddhism in Western countries as it is adapting to new environments and creating new communities. Levine writes in a language that speaks to a subculture of individuals as troubled as he once was; he insists that his teachings are traditional, a translation of the Buddha's universal message for those troubled by the state of the world today.

The Religious Biography of Noah Levine

Noah Levine was born in 1971 to "hippie" parents who practiced meditation and were especially inclined to Buddhism. But, as he grew up, Levine reacted against the views of his parents, thinking they were naïve and misguided. Eventually, in the early 1980s, he joined the punk rock scene, a movement that advocated questioning society, rejecting middle-class conventionality, and rebelling against authority. Living in California and socializing with the punk music crowd, he got involved with drugs and even did some jail time for possession of narcotics. While in jail he eventually came to a point where he decided to listen to his father's advice and try meditation. This dramatically changed his life. Levine eventually became a popular meditation teacher for troubled and at-risk youth as well as a punk rock musician for fans throughout America. He has organized meditation groups across the country and regularly meets with youth and adults in juvenile halls and prisons. He established a name for himself among the teachers of Buddhism and meditation in America through his memoir, *Dharma Punx* (2003).

Levine adapted much Buddhist terminology for the particular audience of punk rock youth who follow him. This can be seen in his recent book about Buddhist practice, *Against the Stream* (2007). His goal, he states, is to be of service and to use his life story, his success in turning his own life around, to help others like him. Combining what he feels is a natural link – between the punk rock music ethos and the Buddha's teachings – with his unique way of presenting mindfulness meditation, Noah Levine's Buddhist teachings have resonated with many youth. Therefore, Levine is one of the younger teachers within American Buddhism and his methods and interpretations of the teachings resonate for youth and troubled teenagers. His message speaks to people who probably never thought about Buddhism before, and, because of the way he teaches in person and through books, he has gained many students and followers. He is part of a Buddhist youth movement in the emerging history of the religion in America.

Levine begins his memoir, *Dharma Punx*, by relating his experience to that of his peers. He writes that his life is:

> A story about my generation: the punks, the kids all around the world who searched for meaning and liberation in the age of Reagan, Thatcher, and the Cold War's constant threat of total nuclear annihilation ... Looking at the once idealistic hippie generation who had long since cut their hair, left the commune, and bought into the system, we saw that peace and love had failed to make any real changes in the world. In response, we felt despair and hopelessness, out of which came the punk rock movement.[1]

He describes his life story as "intense," one that takes the reader to punk rock concerts, juvenile detention centers, and the meditation halls. It is part of a larger story of his generation, of people trying to incorporate Buddhist spiritual practices into their lives. Now a meditation teacher and prison volunteer, his transformation has come full circle.

Early Life: Drugs, Alcohol, Jail, and Punk Rock Music

One of Noah Levine's earliest memories was from age five. He used to hide under his house with a knife, promising himself that he could use it to kill himself if things got bad enough. His mother and her boyfriend were creating an abusive and unstable homelife and Levine describes his early despair. Stephen Levine, his father, remembers that as a child Noah had a sadness and world-weariness, and remarked that this kind of suffering can be a preliminary stage for realization and transformation. During his childhood, Levine lived intermittently with his mother in California and his father and stepmother in New Mexico. He writes about his relationship with his father, a well-known author of books on Buddhist meditation:

> I didn't even know what my dad's books were about, I had never even read one – some hippie shit about being nice and passive, I figured. Meditation and all that boring crap. Not for me. Everyone knows that the hippies failed. A bunch of drugged out, dirty rich kids talking about peace and love.[2]

During his adolescent years, Levine felt an overriding dissatisfaction with American society. He recounts his teenage angst and falling into increasing drug and alcohol addiction, how he didn't care about school but only getting high. So he joined his friends to hit the streets, to score drugs and booze as the only escape.

Levine describes his reaction the first time he heard punk rock music this way: "I couldn't believe it; it was like hearing the voice of God. The high energy and fast style of music just made me want to break something, which was how I felt most of the time anyway. I knew from that moment on that I wanted to be a punk rocker too."[3] After this Noah began integrating punk rock ideals into his lifestyle. He attended concerts, hung out with other punk rock kids, and, with a Mohawk haircut, leather jacket, and boots, he outwardly identified himself with this group. But along with this lifestyle also came refuge in more drugs and alcohol.

The increased use of intoxicants set in motion some destructive life patterns. Levine and his friends begin to steal from strangers, family, and friends in order to pay for their drug habits. He writes about how all he cared about was getting his next fix, and this mattered far more than eating or maintaining healthy relationships. Stealing and violence related to drug addiction landed him in jail on numerous occasions. He became familiar with the juvenile correctional system, its routines and people there, spending months at a time in detention.

This is not the typical early life of a Buddhist meditation teacher, but it was precisely this lifestyle that later made Noah Levine effective as such a teacher. He uses his life story and his turning away from troubles as the basis for teaching others, especially those in the same position he once occupied. In his teachings he recounts these low moments, when he lost all connection to family, friends, and even punk music in order to feed his addiction. From this grounding his students can see the power of Buddhist teachings and meditation to transform life.

Turning Point: Becoming a "Spiritual Person"

In his last stay in juvenile hall at age 17, he reached a turning point when he realized that his whole life had become just a quest to escape from reality. He writes that "drowning our teenage angst with drugs, sex, and violence had, in the end, made me lose my punk rock ideals in what became nothing more than the pursuit of oblivion."[4] He later recognized this moment as having hit "rock bottom." Noah's attitude changed this time in detention when he realized that he was the one to blame for his suffering because of his addiction. Before this he had blamed everyone and everything else – his family, society, adults, hippies, police, government – but not himself.

This made him again turn to thoughts of suicide, but this time in his jail cell. He began hitting his head against the cell wall, but, when this failed, he used a prison comb to try to slit his wrists. When the guard found him, he was moved to a padded cell. There he felt even more dejected: "There is nowhere to hide from the life of addiction and crime that I have created. I have failed at being human. I have even failed at taking my own life."[5]

In the midst of this dark period, Noah called his father, who gave him the meditation instructions that would eventually become a crucial part of his life. He had nothing more to lose, so he reluctantly relented and tried calming his mind by counting his breaths, as his father had recommended. This did make him feel a little better, even initially, as the practice gave his mind some relief from constant thinking. During this stint in detention, Levine was also inspired by recovering addicts, who came to tell their stories of healing through the 12-step program invented by Alcoholics Anonymous. Their stories provided hope for recovery; for the first time, Levine was able to admit that he needed help. But at this time he was still not interested in anything spiritual or seemingly associated with hippies, peace, or the Bible – in the punk view he still held, these things are crutches for the weak minded. Levine just felt he needed to stop doing drugs and that, if he could remain sober, he would be okay. After leaving detention, he entered a group home for troubled youth. While living here he felt that he didn't need the recovery program or meditation, but he did decide to stay sober.

In order to stay clear of drugs and alcohol, Levine found a group of friends who were sober too. So he joined the Straight Edge movement, a group that developed out of the Washington, DC, punk scene and whose members wore black Xs painted on the backs of their hands. In the late 1980s, there were many Straight Edge punks within the greater punk and hardcore music counterculture scene. At this time Noah tried to work through the steps of the 12-step program but it was impossible for him to get past one of its basic ideas: surrender to a higher power. He writes: "Getting into Straight Edge probably saved my life. The 12-step program was offering a spiritual solution to my alcoholism that I wasn't ready to accept. Straight Edge was just a bunch of punkers helping each other stay clean through peer support."[6]

After his Straight Edge connection helped him to stay sober, he began to realize that this wasn't enough, that he was still suffering. He was still acting out by spray-painting graffiti throughout his hometown of Santa Cruz, California; when caught, he had to pay fines and do several hundred hours of community service. This was the wakeup call that he needed to work more on recovery. So he decided to take the 12-step recovery program more seriously, getting a sponsor and even starting to pray. He describes this experience:

> I felt like such a jerk. All of my life I had made fun of religious freaks and there I was, on my knees praying … Prayer was like my meditation practice, something I did alone and never talked about. I was actually a little ashamed that I had become so weak that I had stooped to spiritual practice. This was not punk, and certainly didn't fit in with my anti-everything attitude.[7]

But soon he became more used to prayer and meditation as part of his daily life. Through these practices he found more stability in his life. This was the moment when he began to recover in earnest and turn his life toward spiritual practice. He writes of spirituality as his last resort: "Drugs hadn't worked, material accumulation hadn't worked, violence certainly hadn't worked, and the negative attention ego trip of graffiti hadn't worked, gangs and lawlessness had just almost gotten me locked up again."[8] Thus, spiritual practice was his only hope for a better life.

Committing to Buddhism

In 1991 Levine attended his first meditation retreat with well-known teacher and author Jack Kornfield, in order to delve deeper into meditation practice. He admits that at first he felt bored, especially because he was the only 20-year-old there and definitely the only punk rocker. He felt that this was his father's world, but when he started practicing his attitude shifted. One night he heard a dharma talk by Kornfield and everything suddenly became clear "I began to fantasize about becoming a meditation teacher. It was almost as if I just knew that eventually it would happen. One day I would teach. A quiet sense of direction took me to a place I had never been before."[9] At this time also he continued to progress on the 12-step path. As a result of the recovery process, he found he had a new willingness to take suggestions and make changes in his negative behavior; he was now able to forgive and just let go.

Recovery now became a major part of Levine's life as he spent much time making amends to those he had hurt or stolen from. He also began to help others recover from addiction and found work in the medical field, hoping to be of service to others. He regards this time as the opening of a more spiritual worldview: "I had the feeling that my outlook on life was beginning to expand. I was starting to open to the true meaning of life, to have a spiritual perspective on things."[10]

At first he explored spiritualities such as Sufism and Hinduism, but ultimately he found a home in Theravada Buddhism. The Four Noble Truths and the Eightfold Path just felt familiar and right for him. Although he had enjoyed Hindu yoga and Sufi ritual practices, Buddhism made more sense to him. As he wrote of his life at this time when he chose to practice Buddhism:

> My life had truly been transformed in those first couple of years of serious spiritual practice. Many of my negative and destructive behaviors, such as stealing, lying, and all forms of physical violence, began to fall away. The more I practiced kindness and humility, the more the world seemed to appear friendly and manageable.[11]

He next attended another retreat, this one led by a British monk, Ajahn Amaro, whom Levine was very impressed by and who inspired him greatly. This experience made him think about practicing renunciation and becoming a monastic. At first Levine felt intimidated by being around a monk, but he was comforted by the sense of acceptance Ajahn Amaro gave him. He was happy to have completed the retreat and, although it was hard, he immediately wanted to do another because he had seen the possibility of living a happy life as a full-time meditator. Noah writes poignantly about his experiences during these meditation retreats:

> I was really afraid of what I would find in the quiet moments ... I was still afraid of what I might find if I slowed down enough to see what was really behind my negative attitudes and actions. Yet after having practiced meditation for a while I began to truly experience moments of serenity and my fear of peace began to lessen.[12]

He found that the peace he felt could only be found through meditation practice, and that this was a much more lasting experience than the highs he received from drugs. He soon became more involved with the Buddhist communities in his area and read about the Western monastics, especially those in the Ajahn Chah forest lineage of Thailand. He started thinking more seriously about becoming a monk and traveling to Asia.

This time was also the beginning of Noah's particular integration of punk ethics and spiritual practice. His life now consisted of leading and participating in meditation groups and then going out to punk rock shows. Through his reading of Buddhist books he came across a line where the Buddha says that his awakening was "against the stream." This struck him: "That was it, exactly what I was looking for: an inner rebellion that would bring me to liberation ... My early life's external rebellion had only led to more suffering; the Buddhist spiritual path was the perfect way to realize my goal of the real revolution."[13]

Next Levine decided to take his practice further and travel to Thailand, where he could attend longer, rigorous retreats and consider becoming a monk. He thought of this as a pilgrimage and was excited to see places where Buddhism is deeply rooted. He later admitted, however, that he had held unrealistic expectations of "exotic" and "timeless" Asia and that he had expected that staying at the monastery would automatically bring him peace; this did not happen. At first, he visited the famous international forest monastery Wat Pah Nanachat, where Thai and foreign monks resided. His excitement came to an end when he realized he was not really ready for its demanding practices, and he left after only staying one night. He then traveled to the south of Thailand to be with his friends, but felt guilty for not carrying through with his plan. But he eventually learned to enjoy his time in Asia and surrender to the fact that he was not ready to take ordination. Instead he learned that his life should be lived in the world, and focused on service.

Mixing Punk with Buddhism: The Teaching Style of Noah Levine

Upon returning from his travels in Asia, Levine began leading meditation groups at his house, as there was a growing interest in spiritual exploration among many in the punk and hardcore scene. This allowed Levine to complete his intention to share Buddhist teachings with his peers. He also thought seriously about teaching meditation more regularly and so attended a teacher training program for mindfulness-based stress reduction, with an eye to bringing this teaching into juvenile halls and prisons.

Just when he started to think that his life as a teacher was falling into place and he felt a sense of purpose, he read his father's new book about

Buddhist practice, *A Year to Live: How to Live This Year as if It Were Your Last* (1998). Through this book, Levine was inspired to take a year off and practice as if he really had one more year to live. He took seriously this opportunity to prepare for death, and during this year spent time on a number of meditation retreats, touring India, interspersed with being in the company of friends and family. At this time he also got a number of tattoos and found that, rather than conflicting with his teaching persona, they have actually helped. As he wrote:

> I loved that fact that being visibly tattooed set me apart from the mainstream. I had awakened from the delusion of wanting to fit in so that I could be of service ... Being heavily tattooed with images of Buddhas and religious icons has actually helped me to spread the Dharma rather than hindered me.[14]

Through this break and its Buddhist practice, Levine realized that he could be much more peaceful and that his relationship with the world and his own mind had changed for the better. He continually reflected on how far he had come since he had tried to commit suicide in that jail cell. Because of his decision to use his life to help others, he chose to go into the counseling field, finish college, and then complete a master's degree in counseling psychology.

At this stage Levine tried to integrate Buddhist meditation and the punk rock worldview even further, feeling that they could add up to one whole. With his friends who practiced meditation and also frequented punk rock shows, he talked extensively about Buddhism and life. Levine used to feel that spiritual practice would take him away from the punk scene but now he felt even more connected to punk music. In his view, both come from the same dissatisfied energy and the same search for freedom. One can answer this search through loud musical drumbeats and drugs or through spiritual practice. When his teacher, Ajahn Amaro, told Levine that in his youth he was also a punk rock music fan, they agreed that dharma and punk could support each other. The punk movement is clear about the First Noble Truth: there is suffering in life. But few punks take this where the Buddha did, to understand the causes and conditions of the suffering and see that there is a path to freedom. Levine also found that, although both can be seen as manifestations of rebellion, Buddhist meditation "rebels" against one's own ignorance. This is what is most difficult and most fulfilling about mindfulness practice (*vipassana*) – it points one inward and to a place beyond bondage to suffering.

Through his sustained practice and interest in service, Levine next got involved with teaching in the family programs at Spirit Rock Meditation Center in Woodacre, California, where Jack Kornfield also teaches. He also worked on a rite-of-passage program for teenagers at the San Francisco Zen Center and started running a series of day-long meditation retreats for youth. He has enjoyed teaching this age group but knows that his ultimate task is to help incarcerated youth and adults. To pursue this, he took leave from teaching at these Buddhist centers and joined a friend's project working with adults in prison. As he has written of his experience there, "I knew I had planted the seeds of mindfulness, the greatest gift I could ever give. I had no idea what would come from those seeds, whether they would be watered and grow into deeply rooted Bodhi trees or just be a few minutes of relaxation in a difficult time in their lives."[15]

In his teaching Buddhism, Noah identifies himself as a punk rock meditation teacher, infusing the ideas of rebellion and dissatisfaction present in both. In the documentary film about his life, *Meditate and Destroy* (2007), Levine is heard saying, "Buddhism isn't just for hippies anymore." His role in spreading meditation and Buddhism is as a translator of an ancient tradition into a modern language and into a specific subculture. He also states that his goal is to inspire people to investigate and not throw away the teachings of the Buddha because they think of them as "mystical" or "hippie-like." In the film, Noah's mentors Jack Kornfield and Ajahn Amaro state their view that he is teaching in an authentic way and that Buddhists need this kind of diversity among its teachers because the world is diverse.

Noah's students now, instead of taking drugs and committing acts of violence, turn to meditation practice as a nonviolent form of revolution. He leads others in finding positive channels for their urge to rebel against society.

Noah Levine's mission now is to make Buddhist teachings available and accessible to his peers, and especially to those in the punk rock scene. At the same time, he sees himself reconnecting Buddhism to its rebellious and radical roots. He feels that, instead of corrupting Buddhism, he is putting two like things together. In his second book, *Against the Stream*, Levine's evolved teaching style is evident. Calling the book a "field guide for the front lines of the revolution"[16] and nicknaming the Buddha, Siddhartha Gautama, as "Sid," he goes on to present Buddhist teachings in a unique if irreverent way. He calls the Buddha and all Buddhists "spiritual revolutionaries" and breaks up his book into sections such as "Basic Training," "Boot Camp," and "The Revolutionary Manifesto." He also makes clear the traditional Buddhist view that meditating in order to "wake up" is not a selfish activity but benefits all beings. In line with this he calls the Buddha a rebel and the path of Buddhism a refuge available for all rebels, malcontents, and searchers after the truth. He connects the life story of the Buddha to the experiences of present-day spiritual seekers, identifying Buddhism as an experiential, nondogmatic religion.

In 2008, Levine founded the Against the Stream Buddhist Meditation Society, which is based in California but has a number of affiliated groups throughout North America. These groups call themselves "Dharma Punx," after Levine's memoir of the same title. This book inspired the formation of these groups, which are led either by Levine himself or his trainees. The mission of these groups is to fight an inner battle against ignorance and express it outwardly through punk rock music.

Levine also founded a nonprofit organization called the Mind Body Awareness Project, which since 2000 has taught meditation to at-risk youth in detention halls, clinics, high schools, and group homes. All of these activities now realize his vow to be of service to the world, an intention he had when he first started to meditate. His teaching style has introduced a whole new generation and type of people to Buddhist practice.

Noah Levine's Life Story and Its Relation to the Buddhist Tradition

Noah Levine's life is part of the recent history of Buddhism in America. His life story must be contextualized within the countercultural movements of the 1960s and 1970s. Levine and others reacted against their parents' generation and what they thought was the naïve way they looked at the world; in opposition to them, they devoted themselves to punk music and its lifestyle. Buddhism in Western countries is continuously being reinterpreted as it emerges in new forms in new environments. Levine's movement of "Dharma Punx" communities is one of the ways Buddhism is being adapted to American culture. His message coalesces with the punk lifestyle and speaks to his generation and to many younger people who identify with it. Levine writes in a language that speaks to youth troubled like he once was. But Levine still calls his message traditional, as the Buddha's message is universal. His mission is to repackage the dharma and offer its benefits to newcomers.

References

Levine, N. (2003) *Dharma Punx*, HarperOne, New York.

Levine, N. (2007) *Against the Stream: A Buddhist Manual for Spiritual Revolutionaries*, HarperSanFrancisco, San Francisco, CA.

Levine, S. (1998) *A Year to Live: How to Live This Year as if It Were Your Last*, Three Rivers Press, New York. (A guide to appreciating life, used by Noah Levine in developing his practice.)

Further Reading

Against the Stream: Buddhist Meditation Society, http://againstthestream.org. (The informative website of the Against the Stream Buddhist Meditation Society, founded by Noah Levine.)

Dharma Punx: Official Homepage, www.dharmapunx.com. (The official website of the book by Noah Levine.)

Griffin, K. (2004) *One Breath at a Time: Buddhism and the 12 Steps*, Rodale Books, Emmaus, PA.

Kornfield, J. (2009) *The Wise Heart: A Universal Guide to the Universal Teachings of Buddhist Psychology*, Bantam, New York. (An interesting work that describes the teachings of the Buddha that relate to psychology.)

Mind Body Awareness Project, www.mbaproject.org. (The website of this nonprofit organization, which provides mindfulness meditation training for youth.)

Notes

1. Levine 2003: ix.
2. Levine 2003: 42.
3. Levine 2003: 11.
4. Levine 2003: 59.
5. Levine 2003: 2.
6. Levine 2003: 71.
7. Levine 2003: 83.
8. Levine 2003: 84.
9. Levine 2003: 87.
10. Levine 2003: 103.
11. Levine 2003: 105.
12. Levine 2003: 109.
13. Levine 2003: 128.
14. Levine 2003: 175.
15. Levine 2003: 244.
16. Levine 2007: xii.

12

Legendary Beat Poet
Allen Ginsberg

Tony Trigilio

Editor's Introduction

The poems of Allen Ginsberg join those of Gary Snyder and the novels of Jack Kerouac as central to the Beat movement, which developed in the 1950s and 1960s, all three authors bringing Buddhism to many in the antiwar counterculture. Ginsberg's Buddhism was both the product and producer of a larger cultural embrace of Asian religion in the postwar United States. His popularity as a poet, along with his candor about Buddhism in his poems, came at a time when Americans were moving from traditional Western religions to explorations of Asian religions on a scale never seen before in American history. Ginsberg's originality is seen, in part, with his incorporating into his poems the Buddhist theory that certain sounds (mantras) have the capacity to open the mind and alter reality. He wielded his mantra-clad poems against the Vietnam war and other causes, connecting language and action.

This chapter explains how Allen Ginsberg's identity as a Buddhist was a product of his early curiosity about the various Buddhist traditions, and the various countries where they had developed over the centuries. We see how his personal journey moves from unsystematic personal studies to travels across Asia, culminating with his close, religious 15-year relationship with Chogyam Trungpa, founder of the Vajradhatu organization in Boulder, Colorado. Trungpa represents one of the innovative and pioneering figures who brought Tibetan Buddhism to the United States, and Ginsberg became a close collaborator in programs at Naropa University, one of its important institutions.

Ginsberg's life is a case study in the vicissitudes of the Tibetan tradition of spiritual cultivation called "Guru-Yoga." Found as well in other Mahayana traditions such as Zen, this path is entered into by a student for whom a teacher-guru becomes not just a guide but the primary focus of the student's spiritual experience. Ginsberg adopted Trungpa as such a guru, accepting him with complete trust, expecting that

---

Buddhists: Understanding Buddhism Through the Lives of Practitioners, First Edition. Edited by Todd Lewis.
© 2014 John Wiley & Sons, Ltd. Published 2014 by John Wiley & Sons, Ltd.

his teaching methods would be both enlightened and benevolent. The latter's erratic behavior, alcoholism, and then an incident involving abusive treatment of disciples at a retreat caused the poet to re-examine his relationship with Vajradhatu and his teacher.

Early discussions of Allen Ginsberg's life that draw upon his early poetry can easily see in it an often careless accumulation of various Orientalist stereotypes woven into a hedonistic, superficial awareness of Buddhist and Hindu ideas. Consideration of the entire arc of his work through to the final collections of poetry, however, indicates a deeper, nuanced understanding of Buddhist doctrines. In his finest compositions, we can see the culmination of Ginsberg's determined attempts to apply Buddhism to questions of impermanence, desire, and loss – topics with which all serious poets and spiritual practitioners inevitably struggle.

Introduction

Allen Ginsberg (1926–97) was one of the most popular US poets of the twentieth century and one of the century's most well-known North American Buddhist writers. His epic poem "Howl" (published in 1956) is a touchstone long poem in the Anglo-American canon and is widely considered the poem that, along with Jack Kerouac's 1957 novel *On the Road*, established the Beat Generation as a significant movement in postwar US literature. Ginsberg's influence also was important in other major schools of twentieth-century American poetry, including the poetry of the San Francisco Renaissance, the Black Mountain poets, the Confessionals, and the New York School poets. Ginsberg's effect on American culture was felt more widely than that of any other poet of his era. He was a vital figure in the gay civil rights movement in the United States and was one of the leaders of the antiwar, drug decriminalization, and antinuclear movements of the 1960s and 1970s.

Ginsberg saw poetry foremost as an intervention in sacred language. As such, no understanding of his life can be complete without an exploration of his Buddhist study and practice. He was raised in a Socialist-Communist Jewish household in Paterson, New Jersey, and began studying Buddhism in the mid-1950s. His early works, from "Howl" through his poems of the late 1960s, were deeply influenced by his personal study of Buddhism and this led to major Buddhist-influenced transformations in his poetics, including, most importantly, his incorporation of mantra speech in his poems. This use of sacred language synthesized Western and Asian religious traditions. Beginning with *Mind Breaths: Poems, 1972–1977*, Buddhism became one of the primary organizing principles of his work.

Ginsberg formalized his Buddhist training with Tibetan lama Chogyam Trungpa Rinpoche after taking bodhisattva vows from him in 1972, and studied with Trungpa until the lama's death in 1987. His work with Trungpa included readings of the major texts of the Tibetan Mahayana and Vajrayana traditions, especially those that taught the Tibetan graduated path to enlightenment, or *lam rim*. At the request of Trungpa, and in collaboration with fellow poet Anne Waldman, he cofounded the Jack Kerouac School of Disembodied Poetics in 1974 at Naropa Institute (now Naropa University), the first accredited Buddhist college in the United States. Ginsberg was the first major poet in the United States to study and practice in Trungpa's "Crazy Wisdom" school, in which primal human desire, in all its potential excesses, functions as a vehicle of enlightenment rather than as a state of mind that must be overcome and controlled. In 1989, Ginsberg became a student of Tibetan lama Gelek Rinpoche, also a tantric teacher, and this guru–student relationship continued until the poet's death in 1997.

A Poet's Jewish Roots and Buddhist Beginnings

Asked by the *Jerusalem Post Magazine* to describe his feelings about his son's Buddhism, the poet's father, Louis Ginsberg (a poet himself of some renown in the early twentieth century), said: "People ask him why he, as a Jew, follows the Buddhists, and he says he wants to preach idealism of the human race, to take the best of all religions. I say that's a good idea, but before I do that, I want to study more and explore more of my own Jewish heritage."[1] Yet, for his son Allen, Judaism was inextricable from Buddhism. Indeed, Ginsberg's experiments with voice and form that produced "Howl," an epic in the Anglo-American lineage of poetic prophecy, were themselves indebted to the poet's study of Hebrew prophecy. His Buddhist study led to the innovative "one speech-breath-thought" poetics of "Howl," in which each new strophe in the poem was crafted to evoke Buddhism's sacred tripartite structure of body-speech-mind. During this early stage of his career, Ginsberg made the most of what he could from the limited Buddhist sources around him. His knowledge of Buddhism was a product of his curiosity about the various Buddhist traditions, the various cultures from which they emerged; but, like much of his work prior to his studies with Trungpa, he was adopting Buddhist ritual and practice in the absence of formal instruction from a qualified teacher.

For the first half of his career, through the early 1970s, Ginsberg practiced a self-taught religious hybrid of Judaism and Buddhism while seeking a Buddhist teacher who could straddle both religious traditions. Indeed, Ginsberg's description of his father's poems in his introduction to Louis Ginsberg's poetry collection *Morning in Spring and Other Poems* (1970) was as much an account of Louis' poetics as it was an expression of Allen's own hybridized religious and artistic impulses: "Would that all sons' fathers were poets! For the poem and world are the same. Place imagined by consciousness, and the squared exact forms of these poems are tiny models of Hebrew-Buddhist Universes rhyming together in Imagination."[2] As enthused as Ginsberg might have been about Jewish–Buddhist hybridity, he nevertheless would describe his lack of a Buddhist teacher during this early period of North American postwar Buddhism with some regret: "Nobody knew much about zazen ... It was a great tragedy. If somebody had just taught us how to sit, straighten the spine, follow the breath, it would've been a great discovery."[3]

The Buddhist practice of Ginsberg's fellow Beat poet, Gary Snyder, stands in contrast to Ginsberg's early years without a Buddhist teacher. Snyder studied Zen formally in Asian monasteries during Ginsberg's early Buddhist autodidactic period; and, even after Ginsberg formalized his instruction with Trungpa, Snyder often seemed to be the more studious practitioner of Buddhism, as can be seen in the correspondence between the two writers. Snyder's and Ginsberg's letters demonstrate shared, mutual respect for each other's Buddhist practice. Their letters suggest, too, that Snyder was an informal Buddhist mentor for Ginsberg. In a September 1976 letter from Ginsberg to Snyder, for instance, Ginsberg explains his difficulties coming to terms with the most basic of Buddhist principles, the lack of a creator god, and his discussion of this doctrinal issue reflects how much more advanced Ginsberg himself saw Snyder's practice to be: "Trungpa's teaching of non-theism seems to have penetrated my skull finally. It does seem strange that for 20 years I've been yapping about God. Why didn't you tell me to shut up."[4]

The roots of Ginsberg's interest in literary-religious visionary hybridism can be traced back to 1948, his last year as an undergraduate student at Columbia University. His reported vision of the British Romantic poet William Blake that occurred that year is the fulcrum for understanding Ginsberg's religious biography. The poet was alone in his Harlem apartment, where he lived while finishing his degree at Columbia University, and had just finished masturbating.[5] He claimed to hear Blake's voice reciting the poem "Ah, Sun-flower." Later, in a 1966 interview with *The Paris Review*, Ginsberg described the voice as an "auditory hallucination."[6] For Ginsberg, this auditory hallucination – his physical experience of the voice of one of the foremost poets of the sacred in the Anglo-American tradition – was tantamount to a religious experience. The altered state of consciousness the poet claimed to feel as a result of the auditory hallucination returned periodically throughout that week. He later entered the Columbia University bookstore and experienced what mystics of nearly all religious traditions have themselves described: a sublime and visionary awakening in which the taken-for-granted, intractable barrier between self and other became porous. Describing this breakdown of subject–object distinctions in the

Paris Review interview, Ginsberg recalled that everyone in the bookstore "all had the consciousness, it was like a great unconscious that was running between all of us that everybody *was* completely conscious."[7]

The Blake vision both inspired and constrained Ginsberg's religious and artistic development. On one hand, the vision affirmed for Ginsberg that he indeed was a poet writing in the visionary company of Anglo-American poetic prophecy. The Blake vision was a catalyst that produced groundbreaking poems such as "Howl" and "Kaddish" (published in 1961), but it also led to his spending the next 15 years trying to reproduce the Blake vision, often through drug use rather than disciplined spiritual practice.

Asian Pilgrimage, Tibetan Influences, Antiwar Expressions

After meeting Tibetan lama Dudjom Rinpoche during Ginsberg's travels to India in 1962–63, the poet understood his attachment to reproducing the Blake vision was actually preventing him from re-experiencing the state of visionary consciousness that originally occurred in his Harlem apartment. In the dedicatory remarks to his *Indian Journals: March 1962–May 1963* (1970b), Ginsberg invoked Dudjom Rinpoche's advice on the Blake vision: "If you see anything horrible don't cling to it[,] if you see anything beautiful don't cling to it." The remark is a conventional representation of the Buddhist Middle Way, to be sure; but Ginsberg's use of it as an introductory dedication that would frame the entirety of *Indian Journals* suggests just how important it was to his spiritual and artistic development. In fact, Dudjom Rinpoche uttered these words at precisely the time in Ginsberg's career when he most needed to hear them. This admonition on attachment represented a crucial turning point for Ginsberg, artistically and spiritually, and the poet repeated it frequently in interviews and lectures, emphasizing that it helped him move forward as a poet and freed him to study the basic Buddhist principles of nonduality and impermanence.

The effect of the Asia trip on Ginsberg's religious consciousness cannot be underestimated, for it was here that he also confronted the fraught relationship between his sexual identity as a gay man and his emergent Buddhist-Jewish religious consciousness. His most memorable long poems of this period, "Angkor Wat" and "The Change: Kyoto-Tokyo Express" (both written in 1963), chart the development of a discourse that would overcome his body anxieties as he abandoned his early, mistaken belief that he could not be a Buddhist without renouncing sexual desire. In these poems, Ginsberg crafted a "Queer Dharma" middle way between the poles of sex and renunciation, ecstasy and asceticism.[8] As dramatized in Ginsberg's re-envisioning of the Buddha's *Satipatthana Sutta* in "The Change," Buddhism was significant in Ginsberg's development of a visionary rhetoric that was communitarian rather than self-cherishing – one that would replace absorption with one's own body with an identification with the sense-based experiences of others.

In the poem "Wichita Vortex Sutra" (published in 1966), Ginsberg first incorporated Buddhist mantra speech to create a sacred language that would envision the end of the Vietnam War. Inspired by his reading of the *Heart Sutra*, the short Mahayana text on emptiness, Ginsberg attempted in "Wichita Vortex Sutra" to remake a language that, he felt, had been essentialized as propaganda – "language abused by war," as he describes it in the poem – into a revivified language crafted to bring readers closer to the sacred. The poet's Buddhist study inspired an aesthetic that fused sacred speech, political speech, and avant-garde poetic language.[9] Ginsberg later argued that his study of mantra influenced "Wichita Vortex Sutra" to such an extent that the poem itself was an effort to "make a series of syllables that would be identical with a historical event."[10] The poem dramatized Ginsberg's effort to create a Buddhist-inspired language for redemption in an era ravaged by war: "I lift my voice aloud, / make Mantra of American language now, / I here declare the end of the War!"[11] As he would later explain, Ginsberg's pacifist mantra in "Wichita Vortex Sutra" was his response to what he saw as the US military establishment's own governing mantras:

Where they [US President Lyndon Johnson and his military advisers] say "I declare – We declare war," they can say "I declare war" – their mantras are black mantras, so to speak. They pronounce these words, and then they sign a piece of paper, of other words, and a hundred thousand soldiers go across the ocean. So I pronounce my word, and so the point is, how strong is my word?[12]

For Ginsberg, this linguistic strategy was more than just an exercise in agitprop. It was instead an effort to "make Mantra of American language now" – to infuse the English language with the non-dual sensibility of the Buddhist mantra.

The war did not officially end for the United States until 1973, and, like many in the New Left at the time, Ginsberg was politically dispirited by the continuation of violence in Vietnam and on the home front in the last few years of the war. By now, Ginsberg had become a popular poet who had fused lyricism and politics throughout his entire career; but it was perhaps unrealistic for him to expect that he could remove himself from political discourse or diminish his media visibility, as in his 1966 poem "Iron Horse," in which Ginsberg had fantasized about a total retreat from worldly affairs.

Problems at Naropa Institute and with Chogyam Trungpa

During a time when Ginsberg might have retreated utterly into political quietism, events were transpiring – both at a personal level and, institutionally, at Naropa – that would make such retreat impossible. In 1975, a major Buddhist scandal erupted during a Vajrayana retreat supervised by Trungpa in Snowmass, Colorado. The poet W.S. Merwin and his companion Dana Naone were subjected by Trungpa and his followers to treatment so severe that Merwin would later characterize it as a "psychic rape."[13] Although not present at Snowmass, Ginsberg was upset by what happened there, and this event came to threaten the existence of Naropa.

The events were as follows. Entering the last month of the three-month seminary retreat, Trungpa organized a Halloween party as a cathartic night of revelry before the group was to undertake the retreat's grueling final period. At the Halloween party, Trungpa ordered that some of his students be stripped of their clothing in order to experience, physically, the naked vulnerability of mind required to begin the practice of the most advanced Vajrayana path. Trungpa stripped off his own clothes and ordered one of his students to bring Merwin and Naone from their quarters to the meditation hall so they would be naked. When the two refused to be taken to the meditation hall, their telephone lines were disconnected and a group of Trungpa's students crowded into the hallway and the balcony outside their room – in essence, trapping Merwin and Naone in their living quarters. Merwin tried to fight off the students with a broken wine bottle (his assailants would require hundreds of stitches for their wounds), but the two were outnumbered. Eventually, they were taken to the meditation hall and their clothes forcibly removed. In a meeting with Trungpa the next day, Merwin and Naone decided to continue their participation in the retreat, despite their harrowing experience. As they explained it, they had finished two-thirds of the retreat and they felt the benefits of Trungpa's tantric teachings were important enough to finish the final one-third, even under these difficult circumstances.

The Snowmass incident and its aftermath are crucial to forging a more complete understanding of Ginsberg's religious biography. Merwin and Naone initially did not speak publicly about what happened at Snowmass, but rumors about what had happened spread in the North American Buddhist community. Although Ginsberg was touring with Bob Dylan and the Rolling Thunder Revue at the time, he nevertheless was associated with Snowmass by dint of his highly visible associations with Trungpa, Naropa, and the contemporary poetry community that Merwin represented. He had by now become one of the most visible spokespersons for Trungpa and Naropa in the North American Buddhist community.[14]

Ginsberg initially defended Trungpa's actions. However, this incident eventually caused him to question the central Vajrayana Buddhist concept of guru devotion. In its ideal form, guru devotion is a version of the Buddhist teacher–student relationship in which the student is so dependent upon the spiritual teacher (guru) that the student transfers his/her guiding conceptual frame of reference from the self to the guru: as the embodiment of enlightenment, the guru is the standard by which the student negotiates the path to enlightenment. Guru devotion can create a relationship in which the guru is more than just a guide and becomes the focus of the student's spiritual experience. After Snowmass, Ginsberg began to question precisely his degree of trust in Trungpa as his guru. As he wrote in a June 22, 1980 journal entry: "I used to boast no identity! Now why am I stuck with the accusation of a fixed identity as Trungpa's sucker? Am I?... Should I renounce Trungpa and retire to my farm?"[15]

Ginsberg's self-questioning in the journal was also sparked by fallout from a 1979 interview with poet Tom Clark, later reprinted in Clark's *The Great Naropa Poetry Wars* (1980). In remarks he later would disavow (he assumed Clark would give him the chance to edit the interview before publication), Ginsberg alarmed readers with an interpretation of guru devotion that seemed beyond the reach of civil law. Responding to Clark's argument that unchecked guru devotion could lead to dangerous imbalances of power between teacher and student, Ginsberg replied that Clark's "reference to cultural artifacts like the Bill of Rights" oversimplified the spiritual and psychological complexities of guru devotion.[16] The interview with Clark occurred within a year of the Peoples Temple massacre in Jonestown, Guyana; and, in the context created by the spiritual abuse of power that led to Jonestown, Ginsberg's comments about Merwin and Naone could not have seemed more insensitive: "Strip 'em naked, break down the door! Anything – symbolically! I mentioned privacy before – the entrance into Vajrayana is the abandonment of all privacy. And the entry onto the Bodhisattva path is total – you're saying, 'I no longer have any privacy ever again.'"[17]

One of Ginsberg's biographers, Michael Schumacher, would later explain, "Of all the statements made by Ginsberg during the course of the interview, this one would be the most damaging."[18] The concern in the North American Buddhist community was not entirely with the accuracy of Ginsberg's interpretation of Vajrayana practice; indeed, a case could be made that, as one presses deeper into Vajrayana practice, one must indeed relinquish liberal humanist identifications with privacy. Instead, many of Ginsberg's fellow Buddhists, and many of his readers, were troubled that one of the West's most politically active poets could abandon his seemingly sophisticated understanding of power relations in obedience to the hierarchies of a religious community that seemed to be ruled autocratically by one person, Trungpa.

Ginsberg suffered from headaches and nightmares, and writer's block, after Snowmass. Continued abuses of power within Trungpa's Buddhist community after Trungpa's death in 1987 only made matters worse: Trungpa's successor, Osel Tendzin (Thomas Rich), promiscuously slept with students, even when he knew he was infected with HIV. One of these students contracted the virus from him. Ginsberg's notebooks and correspondence from this period document an effort to save Trungpa's Vajradhatu organization from itself, on one hand working to protect the organization from the stigma of Osel Tendzin's actions while on the other imploring the organization's senior students to acknowledge that Osel Tendzin's moral authority as a religious leader had been compromised as a result of what he had done. As in the Snowmass incident, Ginsberg tried to remedy a situation for which he was not directly responsible but with which he was identified because he was the most visible representative of Trungpa's Vajradhatu community. In 1989, Ginsberg left the Vajradhatu organization for Gelek Rinpoche's Jewel Heart organization, and his new teacher became a stabilizing force for Ginsberg's religious practice.

Last Years

In the final years of his life, Ginsberg's study of Buddhist nonduality and impermanence led to greater experiments in poetic language and form. Experiments such as his "American Sentences" (published in his 1994 poetry collection *Cosmopolitan Greetings*) are themselves hybrid haiku-Anglo-American urban nature poems, and poems such as "Is About" (published in his 1999 poetry collection *Death and Fame*) read as postmodern explorations of the virtues and limitations of language's mediation of perception and experience. In *Death and Fame*, his final book, Ginsberg revisits his reputation as the poet who celebrates the body, re-examining this reputation within the framework of Buddhist teachings on the universal suffering of aging. Ginsberg was now writing about bodily illness as he was dying of liver cancer. An aging poet and tantric practitioner, Ginsberg marked the passing of his impermanent body in language that dramatized the body's abjection with unflinching candor, as in poems such as "Here We Go 'Round the Mulberry Bush," "Excrement," "Bowel Song," "Hepatitis, Body Itch … ," "Scatalogical Observations," "I Have a Nosebleed … ," and "This Kind of Hepatitis Can Cause Ya."

Ginsberg died on April 5, 1997, surrounded by Gelek Rinpoche and several monks and senior practitioners from the Jewel Heart organization, who performed traditional Tibetan Buddhist death rituals at his bedside for the following 24 hours. As far back as 1991, Ginsberg had been preparing for the death process with Gelek Rinpoche, who advised Ginsberg that he "should concentrate as befit[s] the level of Buddhist practice he had attained by that time and meditate on the idea of compassion for all sentient beings. Practicing those thoughts so that he could use them during his final moments became one of [Ginsberg's] goals."[19] Funeral services were held the day after his death at the Jewel Heart Center in New York City. The following Monday, a service was held at Trungpa's Shambhala Center, where the Jewish Kaddish prayer for the dead was included in the Buddhist service. After Ginsberg was cremated, some of his ashes were buried next to his father at Gomel Chesed Cemetery in Newark, New Jersey. Gelek Rinpoche scattered some of the ashes at the Jewel Heart Center in Ann Arbor, Michigan. Some of the poet's ashes (mixed with his those of his life partner, Peter Orlovsky, who died in 2010) were buried by Trungpa's students near a stupa at the Shambhala Mountain Center in Colorado.

Ginsberg's Buddhism was both the product and producer of a larger cultural embrace of Asian religion in the postwar United States. Ginsberg's popularity as a poet, along with his candor about Buddhism in his poems, came at a time when Americans were moving from traditional Western religions to Buddhism in numbers never seen before. Richard Hughes Seager observes that, since the late 1950s, "Buddhism in the United States has been transformed from the religion of a relatively small number of Asian Americans and an esoteric preoccupation of a much smaller European avant-garde into what amounts to a mass movement."[20] Ginsberg's visibility as a popular writer and media figure contributed in no small part to what Seager describes as the growth of this "mass movement": perhaps Ginsberg's greatest contribution to American Buddhism is that he served as a bridge between countercultural and mainstream Buddhisms in the United States. As Gelek Rinpoche argued in his eulogy to Ginsberg: "The actual Dharma practice which affects millions of people's lives, he [Ginsberg] made possible to take root, through all these efforts that he made."[21]

Allen Ginsberg's contribution to American Buddhism cannot be assessed outside the context of his relationship with Trungpa, the most well known countercultural Buddhist teacher in the postwar United States and the founder of Naropa. As important as Trungpa was to Ginsberg and postwar countercultural spiritual seekers, he was a polarizing figure all the same. Indeed, as Buddhist scholar Charles S. Prebish explains, in a discussion that otherwise praises Trungpa's deft abilities to engage Buddhist practitioners no matter what their level of practice, "Trungpa's well-publicized reputation and unpredictability seemed to require at least a bit of caution from all who had not known him previously."[22] Prebish's remarks about the ambivalence of the Buddhist community toward Trungpa is standard for how Ginsberg's Buddhism has been received by scholars and historians. Because Ginsberg's religious influences drew from so many disparate sources, it would be easy to take him at his word that he was only a "flaky Buddhist."[23] However, to assume Ginsberg's tongue-in-cheek characterization is self-evident would be as inaccurate as taking the Beat Generation mythos at its word and presuming that he was an American Buddhist lay master. The truth is somewhere between these two poles: like any serious Buddhist practitioner, Ginsberg struggled to apply his Buddhism to everyday lived experience, and this struggle was in itself a manifestation of the seriousness of his Buddhist commitment. As discussed above, his early curiosity about Buddhism led him to incorporate Buddhist texts and contexts, along with those of Judiasm, into his earliest poems, but he did not begin any kind of systematic study and practice of Buddhism until he formalized his training with Trungpa. By then, he had already brought many readers to Buddhism as part of what Robert S. Ellwood has described elsewhere as an emergent "glossolalia" of American religious practice in the 1960s.[24] As both a popular culture media figure and a poet – a rare combination in any era, but especially in the twentieth century – he is one of the most significant figures in what John Whalen-Bridge and Gary Storhoff in 2009 termed "Buddhist American literature": Ginsberg was one of the first, and the most widely read, Buddhist American literary artists of the twentieth century.

References

Clark, T. (1980) *The Great Naropa Poetry Wars*, Cadmus Editions, Santa Barbara, CA.

Ellwood, R.S. (1994) *The Sixties Spiritual Awakening: American Religion Moving from Modern to Postmodern*, Rutgers University Press, New Brunswick, NJ.

Fields, R. (1992) *How the Swans Came to the Lake: A Narrative History of Buddhism in America*, 3rd edn, Shambhala, Boston, MA.

Gefen, P.S. (1971) My son the guru, my father the poet. *Jerusalem Post Magazine*, July 9, 8–11.

Gelek Rinpoche (1999) *Odyssey to Freedom* [transcription of 1997 lectures], Jewel Heart, Ann Arbor, MI.

Ginsberg, A. (1970a) Confrontation with Louis Ginsberg's Poems, in *Morning in Spring and Other Poems*, Morrow, New York, pp. 11–20.

Ginsberg, A. (1970b) *Indian Journals: March 1962–May 1963*, Dave Haselwood and City Lights, San Francisco, CA.

Ginsberg, A. (1980) Improvised poetics: interview with Michael Aldrich, et al., in *Composed on the Tongue: Literary Conversations, 1967–1977*, Grey Fox, San Francisco, pp. 18–62.

Ginsberg, A. (1994) *Cosmopolitan Greetings: Poems 1986–1992*, HarperCollins, New York.

Ginsberg, A. (1999) *Death and Fame: Last Poems, 1993–1997*, HarperCollins, New York.

Ginsberg, A. (2001) *Spontaneous Mind: Selected Interviews, 1958–1996* (ed. D. Carter), HarperCollins, New York, pp. 17–53.

Ginsberg, A. (2006) *Collected Poems, 1947–1997*, HarperCollins, New York.

Ginsberg, A. and Snyder, G. (2009) *The Selected Letters of Allen Ginsberg and Gary Snyder*, Counterpoint Press, Berkeley, CA.

Leyland, W. (ed.) (1998) *Queer Dharma: Voices of Gay Buddhists*, Gay Sunshine, San Francisco, CA.

Morgan, B. (2006) *I Celebrate Myself: The Somewhat Private Life of Allen Ginsberg*, Viking, New York.

Prebish, C.S. (1999) *Luminous Passage: The Practice and Study of Buddhism in America*, University of California Press, Berkeley, CA.

Sanders, E. (ed.) (1977) *The Party: A Chronological Perspective on a Confrontation at a Buddhist Seminary*, Poetry, Crime, and Culture Press, Woodstock, NY.

Schumacher, M. (1992) *Dharma Lion: A Critical Biography of Allen Ginsberg*, St. Martin's Press, New York.

Seager, R.H. (1999) *Buddhism in America*, Columbia University Press, New York.

Trigilio, T. (2012) *Allen Ginsberg's Buddhist Poetics*, Southern Illinois University Press, Carbondale.

Whalen-Bridge, J. and Storhoff, G. (2009) *The Emergence of Buddhist American Literature*, SUNY Press, Albany.

Further Reading

Dougherty, J. (1987) From society to self: Ginsberg's inward turn in "Mind Breaths." *Sagetrieb* 6 (1), 81–92.

Ginsberg, A. (1966) Reflections on the mantra. *Back to Godhead* 1 (3), 5–9. [Reprinted in B. Morgan (ed.) (2000) *Deliberate Prose: Selected Essays, 1952–1995*, HarperCollins, New York, pp. 148–50.]

Ginsberg, A. (1983) Introduction, in *First Thought, Best Thought: 108 Poems* (Chögyam Trungpa), Shambhala, Boulder, CO, pp. xi–xviii.

Ginsberg, A. (2000) Meditation and poetics, in *Deliberate Prose: Selected Essays, 1952–1995* (ed. B. Morgan), HarperCollins, New York, pp. 262–73.

Ginsberg, A. and Ginsberg, L. (2001) *Family Business: Selected Letters between a Father and Son* (ed. M. Schumacher), Bloomsbury, New York.

Goss, R.E. (1999) Buddhist studies at Naropa: sectarian or academic? *American Buddhism: Methods and Findings in Recent Scholarship* (ed. D.R. Williams and C.S. Queen), Curzon, Richmond, pp. 215–37.

Hyde, L. (ed.) (1984) *On the Poetry of Allen Ginsberg*, University of Michigan Press, Ann Arbor.

Kamenetz, R. (1994) *The Jew in the Lotus: A Poet's Rediscovery of Jewish Identity in Buddhist India*, Harper, San Francisco, CA.

Miles, B. (1989) *Ginsberg: A Biography*, HarperCollins, New York.

Perloff, M. (1990) A lion in our living room: reading Allen Ginsberg in the eighties, in *Poetic License: Essays on Modernist and Postmodernist Lyric*, Northwestern University Press, Evanston, IL, pp. 199–230.

Tonkinson, C. (ed.) (1995) *Big Sky Mind: Buddhism and the Beat Generation*, Riverhead, New York.

Trigilio, T. (2000) *"Strange Prophecies Anew": Rereading Apocalypse in Blake, H.D., and Ginsberg*, Fairleigh Dickinson University Press, Madison, NJ.

Trungpa, C. (1991) *Crazy Wisdom*, Shambhala, Boston, MA.

Vendler, H. (1996) American X-rays: forty years of Allen Ginsberg's poetry. *New Yorker*, 4 (November), 98–102.

Whittemore, R. (1984) From "Howl" to OM, in *On the Poetry of Allen Ginsberg* (ed. L. Hyde), University of Michigan Press, Ann Arbor, pp. 200–2.

Notes

1 Gefen 1971: 11.
2 Ginsberg 1970a: 18–19. As further evidence of Ginsberg's attraction to hybridity, this assertion that his father's poems are "tiny models of Hebrew-Buddhist universes" is itself framed with the Anglo-American tradition of poetic prophecy and the debt this tradition owes to Hebraic prophecy. In this passage, Ginsberg claims his father as a fellow hybridized poet in the prophetic line, and authorizes this claim with his own particular revision of the book of Numbers 11:29, from the Hebrew Bible.
3 Fields 1992: 214.
4 Ginsberg and Snyder 2009: 182.
5 It is no insignificant detail that the alleged vision occurred after Ginsberg had masturbated: for Ginsberg, a poet in the tradition of Blake and Walt Whitman, the Platonic separation of body and soul was a false dichotomy that inhibited rather than inspired religious expression. For Ginsberg, the desired and desiring body was crucial to the making of poems.
6 Ginsberg 2001: 36–7.
7 Ginsberg 2001: 42.
8 My use of the phrase "Queer Dharma" is indebted to Winston Leyland's (1998) book of the same name, *Queer Dharma: Voices of Gay Buddhists*.
9 Ginsberg's strategy in the poem was inspired by the *Heart Sutra*'s teachings on emptiness but also took its cue from complex experiments with linguistic performativity that later would become an influence on the avant-garde Language Poets of the late twentieth century.
10 Ginsberg 1980: 46.
11 Ginsberg 2006: 407.
12 Ginsberg 1980: 47.
13 Sanders 1977: 56–7.
14 My account herein of the Snowmass incident is drawn from Clark (1980) and Sanders (1977). I discuss in greater detail the effects of Snowmass on Ginsberg's Buddhist poetry in my *Allen Ginsberg's Buddhist Poetics* (2012).
15 Schumacher 1992: 649.
16 Clark 1980: 53.
17 Clark 1980: 60.
18 Schumacher 1992: 639.
19 Morgan 2006: 615.
20 Seager 1999: 232.
21 Gelek Rinpoche 1999: 301.
22 Prebish 1999: 159–60.
23 Late in his career, Ginsberg frequently characterized himself in interviews as a "flaky Buddhist." This ironic, self-deprecating representation also appears in the opening lines of his 1996 poem "Multiple Identity Questionnaire": "I'm a jew? a nice Jewish boy? / A flaky Buddhist" (Ginsberg 2006: 1103).
24 Ellwood 1994: 6.

13

Dr. Stephen John Fulder
Founder of Vipassana in Israel

Joseph Loss

Editor's Introduction

This chapter focuses on a teacher of *vipassana* Buddhist meditation in Israel, and it illustrates the extent to which the tradition has spread to nearly every nation in the world today. The characteristics of Buddhism in Israel, as sketched here, also demonstrate the universal truism about this religion's global diaspora: it adapted successfully by conforming to the unique patterns of sociocultural development in the host country. Unlike most other countries to which Buddhism has spread, Israel has almost no Asian refugee populations that would have imported the faith through immigration; in addition, the subject of this chapter, Stephen Fulder, is like many residents of Israel a Jewish migrant whose original ethnic identity is British. His own Buddhist experiences in the West and his contacts there and in South Asia provided the content and methods for his developing a new institution and tradition of practice in Israel. Last, we observe how Fulder's portrayal of *vipassana* meditation is not in conflict with the majority population's Jewish identity, and created no conflicts or cognitive dissonance among those who would join the programs. Leaders of the Buddhist community from the ancient period onward likewise modified the tradition's norms to promote the spread of the dharma; the Buddha himself averted conflicts with kings, military officers, and merchants, and later monk leaders in East Asia were astute to conform to the majority's culture's core values, adopting the ancestor-veneration practices central to local cultures.

In following Stephen Fulder's journey, we can witness another common effect of seriously exploring a religion other than one's own: as a nonpracticing Jew, his deepening immersion in Buddhist meditation eventually took him "back" to his Jewish roots in reconsidering the meaning and importance of celebrating the Sabbath. Taking the time to slow down and live more simply for a day each week was revitalized as an important spiritual practice.

Buddhists: Understanding Buddhism Through the Lives of Practitioners, First Edition. Edited by Todd Lewis.
© 2014 John Wiley & Sons, Ltd. Published 2014 by John Wiley & Sons, Ltd.

A final insight to be garnered from this unusual case study is how Buddhist groups do not naturally cooperate in spreading the dharma. In fact, as with competing Christian denominations across the world, and different monastic schools competing for patrons in Asian countries today, we likewise observe in Israel the institutional competition between Tovana, the meditation organization founded by Fulder, and the global Vipassana school founded by the renowned teacher S.N. Goenka (1924–2013). Here as elsewhere, there is no historical precedent or local basis for Buddhists uniting under a single leader or institution.

Background

Until the early 1990s Israeli culture had had only two notable encounters with Buddha-dhamma. The first was embodied by David Ben-Gurion, the first prime minister of Israel (established 1948), who had an intellectual interest in Buddhism.[1] Ben-Gurion's visit to Burma in 1961 brought Yitzhak Navon, the secretary of Ben-Gurion's bureau at the time and future fifth president of Israel, to spend three days in meditation practice under the guidance of Sayagyi U Ba Khin. The second encounter came in the form of a Zen center on the Mountain of Olives in Jerusalem led by a Japanese Zen monk – Do Kyu San – and managed by Hannah and Ernest Zeidner, a German Jewish couple, during the 1970s. This center attracted several dozen Israelis.

While Buddhism first arrived in Western countries in the nineteenth century, mainly through immigration, and global forms of Buddhism have been flourishing in the West since the 1970s as a result of immigration and conversion,[2] it was only in the early 1990s that the first significant wave of Buddha-dhamma practice in Israel began. Several local branches of global organizations by then were established and their scope of activity steadily increased. An unprecedented variety of Buddha-dhamma traditions are currently enriching Israeli culture. Among them the Vipassana traditions appear to be the most popular.

This ascension of mindfulness practitioners began with three experienced practitioners who organized parallel courses in Israel. The first was probably Dalya Tamir, who in 1990 initiated a short course in Kibbutz Tzova with a Vipassana teacher from abroad. Later she organized several additional Vipassana courses with Fred Von Allmen before immigrating to the United States in 1992. Another course was put together in 1991 by Eilona Ariel, a student of Satya Narayan Goenka, in the tradition of the Burmese lay teacher

Figure 13.1 Stephen Fulder. Reprinted with permission.

Sayagyi U Ba Khin. Ariel subsequently organized a growing number of yearly courses and finally established the popular Israel Vipassana Trust. In the same year Stephen Fulder organized another Vipassana course in Israel at his private house in the unique communal Galilee village, Clil. At the time Fulder had already had a long experience in *vipassana* practice under the guidance of U Ba Khin's followers, mainly Sayamagyi Daw Mya Thwin (Mother Sayamagyi).

Fulder was born in 1946 in London to an Orthodox Jewish family of German refugees who found asylum in England just before World War II. Even at an early age, Fulder found the Jewish religion oppressive and rebelled against his parents' tradition. Similar to early Zionists in Europe he was motivated to free himself from the insecurities of former generations of Jews. However, he did not take the Zionist path of so-called Jewish political liberation but rather a spiritual path of inner liberation. In 1966, just after he began to study in Oxford for a degree in biochemistry, he arrived in California for a summer job at Stanford University only to find himself amid an ecstatic creative and psychedelic counterculture in which the norm was critiquing existing social conventions. In retrospect, he sees this visit as his spiritual initiation. For Fulder, the most important lesson of that time was that, in his words, "reality is more than meets the eye."

Like many of his "baby-boomer" generation, Fulder hitchhiked all the way from London to Lahore and back. This visit to India impressed him so much that he had to return. Unlike the popular image of the drifting hippie, Fulder was experimenting with aspects of the counterculture but still developing a professional career. The next time he went to India was in 1975, after he had completed a Ph.D. in molecular biology, researching the aging process. He came to teach Ph.D. students in biochemistry for three months at Banaras Hindu University in Varanasi, Uttar Pradesh. Then, he stayed on for another six months in a small room on the banks of the holy Ganges only to enjoy what he called "the sense of worship, the devotion of the *sadhus* and the spirituality of daily life of the local residents."[3] What most inspired him and appealed to him in the Indian spirituality was the vision and practice aimed at total transformation through rebuilding the personality. Although at the time he was not involved in any formal spiritual practice, it is clear in retrospect that he was probably more than ready to embark on his lifelong Buddhist journey. This journey seemingly took him in two different or even opposing directions – away to non-Jewish spiritual practices and "back" to his Jewish roots. However, for Fulder himself these directions would not be less than compatible and even mutually reinforcing.

Toward the end of his stay, he joined a Vipassana meditation course with Goenka. The course was hard work with moments of special flavor. Once the course was over he had a feeling of wonder, awe, and magic of the ordinary that reminded him of former psychedelic experiences. Still, he felt especially empowered. From this point on, Fulder became a devoted participant in numerous Vipassana courses. Yet, it took several years before it became clear to him that his way in life was indeed Buddhist.

In England he met Rachel, the woman of his life and the future mother of their three daughters, and followed her to Israel. Although he was not motivated by national sentiments, his Jewish identity entitled him to an immediate Israeli citizenship. Moreover, growing up in England on the ideas of European enlightenment, he believed that politics and religion should be separated or would end up in mutual corruption.

Nevertheless, Stephen and Rachel married in 1976 in Jerusalem in an Orthodox Jewish ritual. Fulder was disappointed to learn there is no such thing as a Buddhist wedding. A year later their first daughter was born, and for the next five years the Fulder family lived parts of each year in Jerusalem and London, with Fulder teaching at Hadassah Hospital and in London at London University. While in Jerusalem, the small family was part of a community that was led by John Woods, whose house served as their center, yet each family lived in distinct homes. Woods was a dedicated Gandhian who challenged materialistic norms. The families in the community used to hold joint activities such as the cooperative buying of food, preparing meals, and baking bread for local people in need.

In 1981 the urban collective moved to Galilee in the north of Israel for the purpose of conducting a social experiment by establishing an alternative community, named Clil. They bought plots of land from residents of the neighboring Arab and Druze towns of Abu Snan and Yirka. They were committed to simple living conditions and to ecological principles in the spirit of Mahatma Gandhi. Fulder built the family's house by himself out of simple local materials and learned to farm the land. During their first seven years they lived with no electricity. While the founders subscribed to values that were neither Western Bourgeois nor Zionist, the establishment of Clil fitted into the government plan to Judaize the Galilee. Summing up the first 30 years in Clil, Fulder said that, while it was a constructive experience on a personal level, the project failed in terms of establishing a viable alternative community.

In parallel, Fulder continued to develop a successful career as a researcher, consultant, and writer in the fields of complementary medicine and medicinal plants, on which he has published 14 books and dozens of articles, both academic and popular. He is often invited to speak at international conferences and meetings, and is on the editorial board of the *Journal of Alternative and Complementary Medicine*. He has worked as an adviser for the herbal and pharmaceutical industries as well as for nongovernmental organizations. He is currently involved in the preservation and commercial development of traditional Greek–Arabic medicine.

Western Meditation

During the first ten years in Clil, Fulder was traveling abroad to England and the United States for the sake of Vipassana courses about three times a year. Against the background of an almost complete absence of Buddhist practice and Vipassana courses in Israel, in 1991 he initiated a course at his house. He invited John Coleman, one of U Ba Khin's authorized teachers, to teach that course. In the following years he organized additional courses, first at his home and later in a Christian monastery in Ein Karem, a village near Jerusalem. It was a period of exploration for Fulder. While preparing for the first course, Fulder realized that the world of Vipassana is much more varied than he ever imagined as a student of Goenka. For the next courses, Fulder invited various teachers, such as Christopher Titmuss, Stephen Batchelor, Lama Surya Das, and Fred Von Allmen, but it was in Titmuss' approach that he found a spring of inspiration. Thus, Titmuss became Fulder's main teacher.

The early courses ran solely on donations, which were used to cover expenses and support the teachers. However, Fulder and friends in the Buddha-dhamma in 1994 established a formal association called Tovana, which "disseminates spiritual teachings and practices derived from the Buddhist teachings, the Dharma."[3] *Tovana* literally means "insight"; it is actually a Hebrew translation of the English gloss of the Pali term *vipassana*, rather than a direct translation from Pali.[4]

The first Vipassana course in Israel led by Titmuss was an eye opener for Fulder and for other practitioners. His approach was nondogmatic, open, and investigative yet respectful to tradition, and this set the path of Tovana for years to come. For instance, Titmuss introduced into Tovana's courses the practice of *sanzen*, a Zen question-and-answer session between a teacher and a practitioner with the intention to open up students to deeper realizations during the course of dialogue. Titmuss used to come two or three times a year for years and had a profound influence on the direction Tovana took. In the early 2000s, he initiated a new and experiential Dharma Facilitators Program that ran for two years and allowed experienced practitioners who experienced Buddha-dhamma mainly through Vipassana courses to be exposed to other aspects of its wisdom.

Many other visiting teachers in Buddha-dhamma courses in Israel have been of Western origin and the main language through which Buddha-dhamma has been conveyed to Israeli practitioners is the global lingua franca – English. As a result, many Buddhist concepts infiltrated into the practitioners' daily Hebrew discourse in their English form – defilement, attachment, non-self, mind, emptiness, among many others. In addition, a prominent feature of the practitioners' discourse is the modern Western emphasis on scientific authority and individualistic legitimization. In fact, Stephen Fulder himself embodies this quality of Western meditation. He is an Englishman who practiced Buddha-dhamma prior to his immigration to Israel and became one of the leading figures and pioneers in naturalizing the Buddha-dhamma in Israel.

From One Man's Project to a Community

The first courses Stephen Fulder organized and later the Tovana courses both sought two goals: his becoming an effective Buddha-dhamma teacher and the development of a community of Vipassana practitioners. Continuing the momentum of the courses in Clil and in the Christian monastery in Ein Karem, participants in these courses formed groups that met in private homes for the purpose of group meditation. Around 1995, one of these groups that met in the northern city of Karmiel invited Fulder to give them meditation instructions and Buddha-dhamma teachings. Soon, the number of invitations from groups of practitioners grew. Later, the development of Tovana as a mechanism for setting up courses freed Fulder from organizational tasks to focus mainly on teaching courses, first as an assistant teacher alongside foreign senior teachers and later teaching by himself or accompanied by other local assistant teachers. Thus, in a gradual process encouraged by students on the one hand and Titmuss on the other, Fulder became the first and main local teacher for Tovana.

Over the course of the first ten years, Fulder was responsible for all of the important decisions taken in Tovana and mainly for the decisions regarding the teachers to be invited by the association. However, the beginning of the twenty-first century saw the induction of two new local teachers. Several years later three additional teachers were inducted. These new teachers took some of the burden of decision-making off Fulder's shoulders.

Since its inception Tovana has relied mainly on volunteer work and its scope of activity has grown along the years. It currently holds hundreds of formal and informal events each year. The training of local teachers enabled an expansion and diversification of Buddha-dhamma events throughout the country. Tovana's events vary in length, from weekly meetings of one or two hours with or without a teacher to meditation courses that last one or two weeks. Recently, the association has aspired to have a permanent retreat center but this has not yet become a reality.

Thus, forces "from below" and "from above" merged in the process of Fulder becoming a teacher. Such a process is characteristic of Tovana, a highly democratic association with an informal relationship between teachers and practitioners. This may be the main difference between Tovana and the other large Israeli Vipassana organization – Israel Vipassana Trust – that is directly following Goenka's tradition.

Influenced by yet Ambivalent toward Goenka

Goenka's Vipassana courses were extremely influential both on Fulder and on the general Buddha-dhamma scene in Israel, but they elicited ambivalent attitudes. While appreciating Goenka's personal charisma, spiritual authority, and organizational skills as well as the conditions for practice offered in the courses that are put together by the Israel Vipassana Trust, Fulder's Buddhist trajectory deviated from Goenka's exclusively Buddhist path. In a similar fashion, for many Jewish-Israeli Buddha-dhamma practitioners, Goenka's Vipassana course served as their first impressive and influential acquaintance with Buddha-dhamma practices, teachings, and experiences. However, after participating in one or more of Goenka's courses in Israel or abroad, many of them look for other Buddha-dhamma venues. Some find their Buddhist home in Tovana and others in other Buddha-dhamma groups in Israel. Many do conform to Goenka's instructions and do not seek other Buddhist groups for their practice. One of the main components of Goenka's ethos is his instruction to the participants in his courses to avoid other Buddha-dhamma teachings and practices besides his. The explicit reasoning is the claim that spiritual progress can be achieved only by adhering to one kind of practice and that Goenka's interpretation of the Buddha-dhamma is the one and only true interpretation.[5]

While Tovana is loosely affiliated to the network of Insight Meditation Society[6] centers and teachers and is open to all Theravada-inspired Buddhist traditions as well as Hindu Advaita-Vedanta influences, the Israel Vipassana Trust is strongly devoted to Goenka as its sole focus; he alone is their guiding teacher and the Trust uses Goenka's recordings for meditation instructions and dharma talks. Through its commitment to Goenka's detailed mandatory protocol regarding almost every aspect of the association's activity, the Israel Vipassana Trust has emerged as a highly hierarchical and bureaucratic structure.

The instruction regarding exclusivity, which faithful followers of Goenka once softened by calling it his "recommendation," now carries a sanction against violators. This instruction was perceived by many Israeli practitioners to be an unacceptable demand. More than that, voluntary obedience to formal impersonal rules runs against the core of contemporary Jewish-Israeli habitus.[7] Fulder's countercultural views regarding blind conformity are to some degree similar to the wider Jewish-Israeli attitude to rules.

A few years after establishing Tovana and organizing courses with various teachers, Fulder wished to join another course by Goenka. He applied for a course run by the Israel Vipassana Trust and was accepted. In his application form he had to list his former experience with other meditation practices. As a result, at the end of the course he was called to the assistant teacher,[8] who questioned Fulder regarding his future intentions. He told Fulder that if he continued to practice with other teachers he could not attend Goenka's courses again. For Fulder, this demand was outrageous. He felt that such a demand contradicted the teachings of the Buddha and so he never returned to hear Goenka's teachings.[10]

However, the Vipassana courses by Goenka at times drew larger numbers of participants than other Buddha-dhamma associations in Israel due to their low cost and as a result of his group's skillful outreach.[11] Goenka's ethos assumes that Buddha-dhamma is priceless and therefore that retreats should not have any fees. According to Goenka's mandatory universal protocol, an applicant for a Vipassana course should not be charged a fee to be accepted. Only on the last day of a course are new participants introduced to the concept of *dana* (generosity) and during the dharma talks of that day they are persuasively asked to contribute.

At the beginning of the twenty-first century the number of participants in Tovana's events began to drop, probably due to the competition with the Israel Vipassana Trust and Dharma Friends of Israel, a large association focused on Tibetan Buddhism. Trying to imitate the centuries-old practice of providing alms to Asian monks, both associations did not charge a fee to participate in their events but rather asked for voluntary donations at the end. At the same time, dedicated practitioners of Tovana, some of them ex-Goenka practitioners, appreciated the donation system and wanted to change Tovana's funding system to be the same. This initiative from below was accepted favorably by Christopher Titmuss and Stephen Fulder. As a result, Fulder led a long process of planning, discussion, thinking, and practice on the issue of *dana* and its various possible implementations. The process also involved the rest of Tovana's teachers. Yet, the decision was taken by the general assembly of practitioners. The process culminated in the decision by Tovana at the beginning of 2004 to run its courses purely on donation. This move proved to be an immediate success. The number of participants almost doubled and the expenses were covered as before.

As in many other issues dealt with by his soft and inclusive approach, Fulder did not take a hard line on the issue of donations, which he calls in his teachings, "an economy of the heart." When invited to teach the Buddha-dhamma in non-Tovana forums, Fulder does not set any standard remuneration fee.

Relation to Judaism

Goenka's continual insistence that his *vipassana* path is "not religious" is especially attractive for Jews[12] and probably was so for young Fulder. In his basic course, Goenka tells the story of his acquaintance with Buddha-dhamma and his hesitations with regard to issues of religious identity. He was born a Hindu and was confident that he must never convert. The solution was found in changing his view of Buddha-dhamma. If *vipassana* is not labeled as a religion, then the threat of conversion is diminished. Such an attitude resonates with a similar concern that accompanies many non-Buddhist Jews who found their way to Buddha-dhamma.

It was only after many years of practicing Buddhist meditation, and probably as a result of it, that Fulder realized that his struggle against his Jewish identity was not really necessary. He therefore began to look for ways in which the Buddhist and the Jewish teachings could enrich each other in his daily life. For instance, the Shabbat (Saturday) is a day of great importance for him. Although he does not consider himself a religious person and observing Shabbat in Israel is a mark of being an observant Jew, Fulder finds the practice of observing Shabbat similar to Buddhist meditation practice and courses. In both, the quality of stopping regular activities and diversions is central. Thus, Fulder embodies in his daily practice a nonreligious yet nonsecular identity.

Like many other religious and nonreligious individuals and communities, Fulder is selective in what he takes from the Jewish tradition. Similar to most Jewish-Israeli practitioners, his relation to Buddha-dhamma is nonreligious and does not share the Jewish-Israeli obsession with identity. For him, as a practitioner of Buddha-dhamma, any identities that the individual may ascribe to himself or have ascribed to him by others are mere "windows" through which larger truths may be revealed, rather than exclusive things one has to hold and cherish.

Politics

Viewing the Palestinian–Israeli conflict as the major cause of suffering in Israel and Palestine, Fulder was involved in initiating several projects aimed at healing the suffering and hatred on both sides. The first initiative was the "People to People" monthly two-day workshops with 15 participants from each side. The workshops took place in Nablus in the Occupied Palestinian Territories. Fulder's partner was a Palestinian woman who ran a therapeutic kindergarten for traumatized Palestinian children. Although the workshops achieved dramatic transformations in the perceptions and actions of some Israelis and some Palestinians, after three years the Palestinian Authority insisted that the workshops be part of an official process that must demonstrate clear structural, rather than individual, outcomes. The result was that the workshops were halted.

The second initiative was a response to an unexpected racist and violent outburst expressed in a Tovana course led by Titmuss and Fulder on July 2001, less than a year after the outbreak of the second Intifada (Palestinian uprising) in October 2000. One of the Jewish participants in the course shocked the teachers and the other participants when she expressed a wish for the death of all Arabs. It made them realize that Buddha-dhamma practice is not a perfect vaccine against violence and racism. Therefore, they were moved into action. They looked for possible ways to express their Buddha-dhamma path in favor of reconciliation and peace, and decided to adapt the peaceful actions taken by Buddhist monks at times of war in Asia. They held Jewish–Palestinian silent peace walks, some lasting several hours, some several days, all around Israel and less often in the Occupied Palestinian Territories. A new association was established to support these activities – Shvil Zahav ("Middle Way") – in which Fulder played a leading role.

While the activities and discourse of Shvil Zahav were aimed at allowing middle-class Jewish-Israelis of the moderate left a way out of their feelings of helplessness and resignation resulting from the collapse of the Oslo peace process, the joint actions with Palestinians forced them to cross boundaries in ways that were and still are unimaginable for most middle-class Israeli Jews. For instance, during the height of the second Intifada, Shvil Zahav activists regularly visited villages near the Palestinian city of Jenin to meet Palestinian counterparts. At that time, Jenin was considered by mainstream Hebrew media as the most dangerous hub of terror in the Palestinian West Bank. These meetings were effective in dispelling the belief in so-called "uncontrolled Palestinian hatred," a common perception among Jewish-Israelis. Shvil Zahav lost momentum after several years, but it gave birth to several further Buddhist initiatives in pursuit of peace: a "Cease Fire of the Heart" to consider peaceful solutions to the Israeli–Palestinian conflict; a free clinic in the eastern part of the divided Palestinian town of Barta'a; and other initiatives published and promoted by the *Engaged Dharma* blog, which aims to be "a virtual platform for the vision and variety of engaged Dharma activities in Israel."[13]

Some Concluding Remarks

Unlike most Buddha-dhamma practitioners in Israel, Stephen Fulder is an English baby boomer with a clear English accent. Nevertheless, he embodies several main characteristics of Israeli Buddha-dhamma. First, in contrast to the popular view of Buddha-dhamma that assumes that it simply came to Israel from the Asian global periphery, much evidence shows that its arrival in Israel was mediated by Euro-American groups. Second, before opening up to the rich world of Buddha-dhamma, Fulder was guided by U Ba Khin's followers, especially Goenka, whose courses are one of the main gates through which Buddha-dhamma has been adopted in Israel. Third, rejecting the rigid rules of Goenka, Fulder has attracted those Israelis who dislike formal and impersonal rules. Last, by releasing his resistance to the Jewish tradition and finding some Jewish practices inspiring, Fulder exemplifies the common nonsecular and nonreligious position among Jewish-Israeli Buddha-dhamma practitioners.

References

Baumann, M. (1997) The Dharma has come west: a survey of recent studies and sources. *Journal of Buddhist Ethics*, 4, 194–211.

Baumann, M. (2001) Global Buddhism: developmental periods, regional histories, and a new analytical perspective. *Journal of Global Buddhism*, 2, 1–43.

Clasquin, M. (2002) Buddhism in South Africa, in *Westward Dharma: Buddhism beyond Asia* (ed. C.S. Prebish and M. Baumann), University of California Press, Berkeley, pp. 152–62.

Federman, A. (2009) His Excellency and the monk: a correspondence between Nyanaponika Thera and David Ben-Gurion. *Contemporary Buddhism*, 10 (2), 197–219.

Golden, D. (2006) Structured looseness: everyday social order at an Israeli kindergarten. *ETHOS*, 34 (3), 367–90.

Loss, J. (2010) Explicit non-religious and implicit non-secular localization of religion: Buddha-Dhamma in Israel. *Nova Religio*, 13 (4), 84–105.

Pagis, M. (2008) Cultivating selves: vipassana meditation and the microsociology of experience. Ph.D. thesis. University of Chicago.

Rocha, C. (2006) *Zen in Brazil: The Quest for Cosmopolitan Modernity*, University of Hawaii Press, Honolulu.

Further Reading

Boorstein, S. (1998) *That's Funny, You Don't Look Buddhist: On Being a Faithful Jew and a Passionate Buddhist*, HarperCollins, New York.

Kamenetz, R. (2007) *The Jew in the Lotus: A Poet's Rediscovery of Jewish Identity in Buddhist India*, HarperCollins, New York.

Loss, J. (2011) Between universalism and relativism: the acquiring of a continuously liberating self by Buddha-Dhamma Israeli practitioners, in *Kabbalah and Contemporary Spiritual Revival* (ed. B. Huss), Ben-Gurion University Press, Beer-Sheva, pp. 329–56.

Obadia, L. (2002) Buddha in the promised land: outlines of the Buddhist settlement in Israel, in *Westward Dharma: Buddhism beyond Asia* (ed. C.S. Prebish and M. Baumann), University of California Press, Berkeley, pp. 177–88.

Pagis, M. (2011) Producing intersubjectivity in silence: an ethnography of meditation practices. *Ethnography*, 11, 309–28.

Notes

1 Federman 2009.
2 Baumann 1997, 2001.
3 Interview with Stephen Fulder, July 16, 2011.
4 http://tovana.org.il/en.
5 This is one example among many of the mediation of Euro-American culture in the process of the adoption of Buddha-dhamma in Israel. More than that, it is a characteristic of the adoption of Buddhism in other places on the global margins of the West, such as Brazil (Rocha 2006) and South Africa (Clasquin 2002).
6 However, in a private conversation, Robert Sharf, a scholar of Buddhist studies who used to practice with Goenka in the 1970s, told me that he does not recall such a rule of exclusivity existing until the mid-1970s. Prior to that, many of Goenka's Western students studied with both Goenka and Munindra (in Mahasi Sayadaw's line), as well as with other Vipassana teachers, with Goenka's support.
7 A Theravada-centered meditation group founded in Barre, central Massachusetts, in 1975, that

was pivotal in establishing regular Vipassana programs and retreats and in training certified teachers based upon the group's founders' training in Thailand and Burma. Significantly, the Insight Meditation Society's founding teachers were all Jewish Americans.

8 Golden 2006.
9 Goenka's recordings are considered to be the main teacher in every course run by the Israel Vipassana Trust.
10 While engaging in ethnographic research among Buddha-dhamma practitioners in Israel, I ran into a number of Goenka's "old students," namely those who had participated in at least one basic ten-day Vipassana course. Many told me that, when applying for additional courses, they preferred to lie regarding their diverse former meditation practice rather than be denied future access to additional courses.
11 The Israel Vipassana Trust constantly advertises its courses in Tel Aviv's weekly local newspaper free of charge and has an entry in the Israeli Yellow Pages. A moving documentary – *Doing Time, Doing Vipassana* – made in the mid-1990s by two of the Israeli teachers of the Israel Vipassana Trust on Goenka's courses in Indian prisons was broadcast on Israeli television and is often used in various outreach events run by the association. A book by William Hart, a Jewish-American teacher of Goenka's tradition – *The Art of Living: Vipassana Meditation as Taught by S.N. Goenka* – was translated into Hebrew in 1994 and became a must-read for the association's practitioners.
12 Loss 2010: 89–90. According to Michal Pagis (2008: 10), who studied in Goenka centers, "the demand for [Goenka's] *vipassana* courses in Israel was the highest [compared to other Goenka centers] in the world when compared to the size of the population."
13 http://engagedharma.wordpress.com.

14

Amala Sensei[1]
Zen Priest

Sally McAra

Editor's Introduction

This subject of this essay is a Zen priest and teacher, Amala Sensei (Charlotte Wrightson, b. 1958), who is based in the city of Auckland, New Zealand. This chapter explores how someone raised in a middle-class Anglican family came to spend over a decade undertaking intense and disciplined Zen training at the Rochester Zen Center, then follows her path to becoming a member of the third generation of Western Zen teachers. In the modern globalization of Buddhism, the "pioneers" were either westerners who engaged in training in Asia and returned home to teach, or Asian teachers who visited or resided in the West (i.e., Judeo-Christian countries), and trained successors. In this chapter, we reach the "third generation" of Western teachers, as Amala Sensei trained with Roshi Bodhin Kjolhede, student of pioneering Roshi Philip Kapleau, and then brought his lineage to New Zealand.

In this compelling account of a woman ordained as a Zen teacher, the author focuses on the key elements in Amala's "finding the dharma path" that are widely shared by thousands of other committed Western Buddhist practitioners: realization that her inherited religion was inconsistent and lacked something spiritual; influences from protest movements and the 1960s counterculture that questioned established norms and institutions; an attraction to the contemplative life and spaces; fascination with the mind (perhaps begun with experiences with psychedelic drugs); and the necessity of dealing with a variety of personal issues.

Western transplantation of Buddhist tradition has succeeded to such an extent that there are now meditation centers in most major cities of the West, from all the schools of Asian Buddhism. While this transmission of the dharma has been impressive and the numbers of those Americans who have now experienced Buddhist meditation has grown, a consistent problem has been in sustaining the integrity of these new institutions without abiding by the norms of the canonical *Vinaya*, especially its rule of celibate monasticism. Abuses of power and sexual misconduct, while not universal, have been widespread among both Asian and Western teachers of all the Asian schools. Few scandals, however, have involved women teachers.

In this biography, we glimpse both the beauties and difficulties of making a life as a Western Zen lineage-holder and teacher. Lacking the monastic buildings and endowments that were integral to sustaining the tradition in Asia, and in a country where patrons are still few, it is no easy matter to transmute a person's spiritual vitality and the wish to serve others into a sustainable life. Such is the contemporary reality of women teachers today such as Amala Sensei that her religious vocation is not founded on traditional monastic vows but is being built on the strength of her marriage. While Buddhist traditionalists might find much to criticize in these developments, at times and places even in Asia, the tradition has been sustained by married men and women. In modern Nepal and Japan, and for almost a millennium in the Himalayan Nyingmapa tradition, successful Mahayana communities have been led by married monks and their wives. In considering them, and modern pioneers such as Amala Sensei, we can witness the application of the highly praised Mahayana principle of *upaya* (skillful means), which a bodhisattva should utilize in the work of spreading the dharma.

Background

In the 1960s, the post-World War II "baby-boomer" generation began entering adulthood. In the West during the late 1960s through the 1970s, some baby boomers began questioning "the establishment," referring to those with political and financial power who act in their own misguided, materialistic self-interest, at the expense of the environment and its inhabitants.

Countercultural movements emerged, involving various forms of activism and protest movements relating to pacifism, environmentalism, feminism, and antiracism (shaped in part by the civil rights movement). Many baby boomers also explored alternative lifestyles and spiritual traditions. This counterculture had a major influence on what Charles Prebish terms "the American Buddhist movement,"[2] which can be extended internationally to encompass many contemporary Buddhist movements. Further, over the past three decades, many non-Buddhists have incorporated Buddhist techniques such as meditation and mindfulness into their lives in a secular context, to address issues such as stress, depression, and chronic illness. One study found that many Americans, while not identifying as Buddhist, incorporate elements of Buddhist teachings into their worldview.[3] Indeed, discussing the baby-boomer generation's tendency toward eclectic spiritual seeking in the United States, Roof notes that Buddhism is among the biggest-selling categories of religious books.[4]

Thus, from the 1960s onward, Western interest in Buddhism has flourished, especially among the progressive, educated middle classes, resulting in the establishment of numerous international Buddhist networks; branches of many of these groups now have centers in New Zealand. Some of these networks are allied to a particular school or lineage, such as Tibetan Buddhism.[5] Others create their own independent synthesis from several Buddhist traditions.[6] Each Buddhist group tends to relate more intensively to its affiliate groups overseas than to other Buddhist groups in the same city. The Auckland Zen Centre, along with several "sister" centers in other countries, is affiliated with the Rochester Zen Center (RZC) in upstate New York.

However, unlike in the United States, where many well-established Zen centers have developed residential communities and training

Figure 14.1 Roshi Bodhin Kjolhede and Sensei Amala Wrightson on the occasion of her dharma transmission ceremony in Auckland, February 2012. Photograph by Doug Casement, 2012. Reprinted with permission.

programs, groups in New Zealand are still small. The fact that Zen had such a minimal presence in New Zealand in the 1980s led Amala and her husband Richard von Sturmer to travel to Rochester for training. I resume her story after a short introductory note about notions of "elites" in Buddhism, Buddhist modernism, and the repackaging of modern Zen.

Buddhist modernism, elite Buddhism, and the "repackaging" of Zen

The concept of elite Buddhism, as used in this volume, refers to "virtuoso" Buddhist practitioners: accomplished meditators, teachers, and scholars, past and present, whose lives are exceptional when compared with the vast majority of people who identify as Buddhist. These elite Buddhists are usually monks who have spent years specializing in meditative training in monasteries or isolated hermitages, often relying on lay supporters for their material needs. They are elites in that they are privileged, protected, and highly respected. In traditional Buddhist cultures, most people believe that only monks (and, among monks, only a few virtuosi who specialize in meditation) can become enlightened, by means of extensive meditation practice. The majority of traditional lay Buddhists do not meditate, instead engaging in their religion via ritual, ethical conduct, and service to their community's monastics.[7]

Modernist forms of Buddhism, in contrast, undergo a kind of "democratization"[8] in that they emphasize that laypeople, male or female, can meditate and attain enlightenment. In this sense, modernist Buddhism attempts not to be "elite," making enlightenment available to all. Indeed, Amala told me that she was uncomfortable with the word "elite" in relation to Zen; she associated it with the exclusivism of a privileged few, contrary to the motivation to benefit all beings that Mahayana Buddhism teaches. Further, in New Zealand, where the ideology of equality is widely espoused, the term "elite" often has negative connotations.

However, Amala also emphasized how important it is for New Zealand Zen to develop the facilities to support people who devote themselves to full-time spiritual cultivation.[9] This in effect creates specialists, thus fitting both Lewis' and Jan Nattier's use of the term "elite."[10] Lewis' use of the term focuses on the role of specialized practitioners/teachers within the world of Buddhism, while Nattier's use situates meditation specialists within the broader, non-Buddhist social context, in that she highlights how Buddhist teachings on meditation appeal to people from relatively privileged backgrounds (often, but not exclusively, middle class, educated, white, etc.).[11] A further context that is worth bearing in mind is that what Western Buddhists think of as authentic "Buddhism" is actually drawn from specific approaches that have come to the West via twentieth-century Asian reformists.[12] These reformers, who were often middle-class intellectuals (elite in Nattier's sense of the word), sought to rid Buddhism of its "cultural accretions" and to focus on attaining *bodhi* (awakening), dismissing as less authentic the Buddhism of those who seek worldly benefits, magical aid, or better conditions in a future rebirth. Zen has undergone such reforms.

In Japan, Zen has certain culturally specific elements, including "strict uniformity, inflexible routine, almost military sense of order and discipline,"[13] as well as a rigid hierarchy, institutionalized sexism, and even physical violence.[14] All of these elements, McMahan supposes, should make Zen practice unthinkable to people from cultures "characterized by democratic ideals, reverence for individual freedom, and suspicion of authority and hierarchy."[15] McMahan explains this irony by showing how Zen has been "repackaged" and adapted to Western cultural norms, so that it is represented "as a condition of mind separable from historical tradition and East Asian cultural forms."[16] Yasutani Roshi (1885–1973), a Japanese Zen priest, was one such reformist; he combined elements of Soto and Rinzai practice and made full-time Zen training available to householders in Japan, where *zazen* (sitting meditation) had formerly been reserved for a few temples and monasteries.[17] Philip Kapleau (1912–2004) was among an early cohort of non-Japanese to embark on this reformed style of Zen, training with Yasutani for over a decade in Japan before he returned to the United States to found the RZC in 1966.

Coming to the Path

The RZC is among the oldest Zen centers in the United States, and in its early days earned itself a reputation as "the 'boot camp' of American Zen"[18] due to the intensity of the training there. Kapleau compiled a book consisting of translations of Yasutani's teachings and other material, in *The Three Pillars of Zen*, which was first published in 1965 and has been reprinted and issued in several subsequent editions and translated into ten languages, placing it among the most influential texts on Western Zen.[19] Its popularity contributed to the growth of the RZC. Indeed, Amala and Richard were among the many who trained there as a result of reading this book.

The pair first visited the RZC during the 1980s, entering full-time residential training (see below) between 1989 and 2003 and becoming students of Bodhin Kjolhede, a disciple of Kapleau. Roshi Bodhin Kjolhede (b. 1948 in Detroit) has been abbot since Kapleau's retirement in 1986. Thus it was Roshi Bodhin who ordained Amala as a priest in 1999, authorized her to teach independently in 2004, and gave her dharma transmission in New Zealand in 2012. In the RZC's lineage, Zen priests undergo a novitiate and an ordination ceremony but take fewer precepts than nuns and monks.[20] Further, unlike their monastic counterparts, priests may be in a relationship or marriage, but they should not take on the priest role while a primary caregiver for small children, since at that time the family needs to be their priority. As Amala explains, "[in our lineage] becoming ordained as a priest involves making a vocational commitment; ... you dedicate your life to serving the Dharma fulltime."[21]

During her 13-plus years of training, Amala served on the RZC staff in various roles, including Acting Spiritual Director and Head of Zendo (the Spiritual Director's main assistant). Amala and Richard returned to New Zealand in late 2003 to establish the Auckland Zen Centre; she is its Spiritual Director while Richard assists her as Head of Zendo. Since then, Amala has worked full time as a Zen teacher. She teaches introductory meditation workshops and gives *teishos* (dharma talks) and *dokusan* (private interviews), and several times a year she and Richard conduct *sesshins*.[22] She is a member of the American Zen Teachers' Association and maintains links with Rochester, returning every year or so to attend *sesshin* with her own teacher and to conduct *sesshins* at the RZC and elsewhere.

Amala's religious duties include both traditional roles (e.g., ceremonies from the Buddhist calendar and memorial and funeral services) and Western adaptations (e.g., rites of passage such as weddings, which in Japan would be conducted by Shinto rather than Buddhist priests).[23] In the wider community, she gives talks and meditation workshops at universities, serves as the Buddhist chaplain at a university, and participates in inter-Buddhist activities (chairing the executive committee of the New Zealand Buddhist Council, which she cofounded in 2007) and programs of multifaith dialogue (in the Auckland Interfaith Council). She advocates "engaged Buddhism,"[24] maintaining that "the [Buddhist] precepts must come to permeate all our interactions, all our choices, including how we spend our money, and how we participate in the democratic process."[25]

In 1998, the year before her public ordination, Amala gave two "Coming to the Path" talks at the RZC. Normally the incumbent teacher gives *teisho* each Sunday; sometimes senior students will give a "Coming to the Path" talk: a personal narrative about how they came to be involved in Zen. In her first talk, she spoke about an experience that happened at about four years of age that she considered to have sustained her through the years.

> I was sitting in my parents' garden. ... I was sitting on a rug, on the lawn, and there was also a little bowl of water sitting in front of me. Suddenly everything became very still. And the grass was a green, green, green, green, and the sky was an absolutely blue blue, and everything shone and radiated. And right at the center of all this was a stillness and a kind of crystal clarity.[26]

This experience gave her a glimpse that it is possible to awaken to the mind's "fundamental purity and clarity."[27] After describing this moment of lucidity, Amala added that "this experience ... has over the years given me a lot of faith, and sustained me through a lot of ... difficulties."[28]

The remainder of Amala's two 1998 talks detail her experience of being part of an Anglican church while also attending a Catholic primary school during the 1960s; being an adopted child; experiences during her teens with drugs and then theater; and anxieties about the threat of global annihilation during the Cold War. Each of these things added urgency to her search, leading to her years of intensive training and eventual ordination as a Zen priest.

The spiritual seekers of the baby-boomer and subsequent generations who either became Buddhist or incorporated aspects of Buddhist practice into their lives often expressed dissatisfaction with the religion of their parents (typically Christianity or Judaism) or with the overly materialistic emphasis of secular society. In this vein, exposure at an early age to two distinct forms of Christian culture and doctrine led Amala to a deep questioning. During her childhood she loved the nuns and quietly aspired to become one herself. The atmosphere of the convent also appealed to her:

> If we forgot our lunch we would get sent down to the convent, the house, to get one of the sisters to make us some sandwiches. And ... it reminds me of the [Rochester] Zen Center, there were these beautiful shiny wooden floors and staircases, and figures in different places, and this sense of a life of discipline and quiet.[29]

At the same time, the competing claims of Anglicanism and Catholicism led her to ask questions about "different ways of believing";[30] that is, why different groups claimed knowledge of the absolute truth. She maintains that turning to Zen was not a reaction against her religious upbringing. Regarding Catholicism, she considered the nuns to be "really strong, independent women"[31] who were "great ... female role models, ... who had found a path that they really lived." Regarding her parents' progressive Anglican church, she found the priests' sermons "inspiring and intelligent," and from her parents and the Christian communities she learned about kindness and "having responsibility for others, and making your beliefs real in how you live and act in the world. And that's what I'm most grateful to my parents for, the spirit of service ... which is I think the essence of Christianity. Love."[32] But, like many of her contemporaries, Amala was puzzled by apparent contradictions in Christian teachings, and concluded that humans had "created God because we needed him to provide meaning." Her turning away from Christianity was partly the "teenage thing of reacting against what your parents believe," but she stresses that the bigger factor was simply "leaving it behind as it didn't have meaning."

Alongside her religious questioning, the fact that she was adopted as a baby influenced her life path. In Amala's second talk in 1998, she reflected on the psychological effects of having been adopted: "I grew up with a nagging sense of feeling illegitimate, of somehow being a non-person, lacking a place in the world. And I felt compelled to kind of prove myself, to be someone."[33]

She explained that one of the difficulties facing adopted children is that "knowing where you're going is very much tied up ... to knowing where you come from. So if you're confused about that, you don't feel grounded."[34] Looking back, she considered her childhood to have been permeated with a subconscious fear of abandonment:

> It's very natural for children to want security ... from their parents, because they know they can't survive without them. And what happens with an adopted child is that you know that losing your parents is a reality. It's happened once; it could happen again. So you grow up with this fear, and you somehow want to do something to control it. ... And for me, the strategy when I was small was to be good. Somehow that if I was really good, my parents would want me and I'd be safe.[35]

The urge to be a "good child" entailed being more controlled and responsible than was typical for her peers. She adds, "I ... took refuge in my school work and my intellect. ... You could say in some ways that I missed out on that childhood wildness and spontaneity." She said:

> Adopted children can be super-sensitive to their parents' wishes. They really try somehow to fulfill what their parents want from them. ... I was lucky in that my parents were very loving, and their desires for me were pretty healthy ones, so I don't think any great damage was done by this. But always the flip-side of this kind of compliance is defiance. And you just internalize it – the good is on the outside, and the defiance builds up inside, and I think eventually it has to come out. ... If you are always looking to please other people, then you really don't know what pleases you and what you need to do.[36]

This led her into rebellious behavior during her early and mid-teens, during which time she experimented with drugs and had boyfriends that her parents "loathed." Experimentation with psychedelic drugs was common in the 1960s and 1970s and it was this that stimulated interest in heightened mental states, leading for some to an interest in Buddhist and other Eastern religions. Various influential Western Buddhist teachers of the baby-boomer generation began their spiritual quest in this way,[37] including Amala's own teacher, who says that the accounts of awakening that he had read in *The Three Pillars* resonated with his own experiences with drugs:

> Mescaline had revealed a world of cosmic love, ordinarily obscured by false appearances, in which every individual was a breathtakingly unique expression of ultimate worth. These hallucinogenic experiences had been transitory, but now with the promise of enlightenment, I thought, they could be recovered and secured.[38]

Amala's teenage interest in psychedelics was more than just rebellion; with hindsight, she considers that it also convinced her about the importance of understanding the mind: "Drugs were a factor in [my] realizing that the mind is absolutely the key to our lives. Everything depends on it." However, the fleeting experience that these drugs provide is dangerous because, although it allows access to "new levels of the mind, ... you haven't got any equipment for integrating that experience into your life and certainly not the maturity to do it. ... So it can actually be very damaging in the long run, especially if you keep taking drugs over an extended period."[39]

While in her teens, she also became involved in a school drama club. Through her interest in experimental theater she met her future husband Richard at age 19. He had been in London and, according to one account, returned to New Zealand in 1977 "charged with the new punk movement that flourished there. He assembled a troupe of 'actors' and they rehearsed a series of theater/music pieces revolving around his poetry and showmanship."[40] This troupe called itself "The Plague," and Amala dropped out of university and joined as a vocalist and had a managerial role when the group toured New Zealand. She said, "it was very, very high energy, very loud, ... mostly pretty angry lyrics."[41] The group played at an alternative music festival called Nambassa in January 1979 and made an impact by performing naked except for full-body paint. Amala told me that their work in The Plague and later in a cabaret group called Inside Information was "a reaction about how repressed New Zealand felt then, during the Muldoon era."[42] These fringe art/theatrical groups were an element in the wider countercultural reaction against conservative politics and social norms in New Zealand.

Amala and Richard later attended a drama school in Italy from 1981 to 1982 but were disappointed with it, and their living conditions were difficult. At a time when they had reached a crisis point, they read *The Three Pillars of Zen*. Prior to this, they had been aware of Zen as the source of inspiration for Noh drama and haiku poetry, but "reading [*Three Pillars*], feeling so stuck, we suddenly realized ... that Zen actually was something you did ... It was so exciting to read these stories of ordinary people – not sages living in the mountains – but ordinary westerners taking up Zen practice and being transformed by it. These stories were extremely inspiring."[43]

Consequently, in 1982 they attended an "Introduction to Zen" workshop offered by Philip Kapleau in Stockholm, Sweden, and the following day, a day-long period of *zazen* had a great impact:

> The most important experience I had during that day was sometime in the middle of the afternoon when suddenly I [heard] the sounds outside like I'd never heard them before. A car door slamming, somebody talking to somebody else, trees in the wind, and it was, I don't know what I can say, it suddenly made me realize how cloudy my mind was, if now I was hearing things so clearly. And I had the same experience again [at the RZC]. I can still vividly remember being out in the dorms, about to brush my teeth, turning on the tap, and hearing this water. Really hearing the water. And this was enough, really, to make me have great faith in this practice. Not only was my mind cloudy, but there was something you could do that would wipe away the clouds.[44]

At this juncture, the pair took up Zen practice in earnest. Back in New Zealand, they continued *zazen* and ran a small Zen group from Richard's father's house. They engaged in various creative pursuits, including a theatrical duo called The Humanimals that made two experimental films and performed original work; Amala also resumed university studies, completing an M.A. in Italian literature in 1988. Zen was attractive not only because of the increased clarity it gave her but also for similar reasons that theater had appealed: because it was an "antidote to that lack of spontaneity"[45] of her childhood. Through Zen practice, she has said, "There is a source which is deeper than the controlling elements that create a lack of spontaneity. Ideas about 'self' drop away and there is just pure action."

Paradoxically perhaps, the disciplined and very structured aspects of Zen training provided what Amala sought in her own search for freedom and spontaneity: from an overly self-disciplined child to teenage rebellion, then to drama, and then to Zen. Amala has referred to this as the paradox of finding freedom in Zen's form and discipline, as there is freedom in the structure of dance choreography or a piece of music.

The other important aspect of Buddhism that has deepened its appeal in the counterculture is that it promises a solution to human problems: if people can transform their own minds, they will be able to bring about transformation in society. Like many of her contemporaries, in her early adulthood Amala was haunted by a concern about global problems such as the Cold War and the potential for mass extermination via nuclear war: "My conscious reason for getting involved in Zen ... was the suffering and violence in the world, especially in terms of poverty and the arms race."[46] The feeling of global peril motivated her to "sit down and face a wall." This expression not only refers to engaging in *zazen* but also to being present with whatever "comes up," including painful inner matters that one may have been avoiding. By the late 1990s, nuclear war no longer seemed such a big threat, but other environmental issues, including the consequences of human-induced climate change, continue to remind her about the value of Zen practice beyond her own personal sphere. To "wipe away the clouds" in her own mind was also to work on eliminating the deep causes of suffering in the wider world:

> With the nuclear issue, it was also to do with my feeling of powerlessness to stop that insane situation, but recognizing at the same time, that the source of that insanity was people's greed and fear and hatred, and that I could do something about those things in myself. I might not be able to stop the United States or the USSR from stockpiling weapons of mass destruction, but I could go to the source of that impulse in myself.[47]

In 1986, Amala and Richard attended three weeks of training in Rochester. The possibility of becoming a Zen priest occurred to Amala at this time. During that time, Kapleau ordained two women and one man. "I found myself crying and saying, 'Oh, this is what I want to do with the rest of my life.' And from then on, I knew that was what I wanted to do: become a priest."[48] They returned in 1988 for two seven-day *sesshins*, also attending *sesshins* conducted by teachers visiting New Zealand. Following this, Amala entered full-time residential training at the RZC in 1989. The daily routine began with a 5:15 a.m. wakeup for two rounds of *zazen* and a chanting service. After breakfast the residents engaged in their various jobs.[49] During the day and into the evening there were other meditation sessions. As well as this daily routine, every month or so, the center offered regular *sesshins*. She felt like she had found what she had always wanted to do:

> I just loved the discipline of it, ... and also to be able to do that much sitting [*zazen*], I felt just so fortunate to be able to do that. Also the other part of it, was being in a really strong community with a lot of support for the training, and also a very international community with people from all over the world, from Europe and Mexico, Canada, all other parts of the United States as well. So it was also very stimulating to be in that environment...; I mean any time you live in community you have problems develop between people, but this sense that everybody was working on themselves, and sincerely doing that, really seemed wonderful. And the physical environment, too, the Center *zendo*, other spaces, the garden, all really supported the practice.[50]

Several circumstances made full-time Zen training possible for Amala. As a couple, she and her husband Richard prioritized their lives differently from most of their peers, choosing not to have children and for a long time not living in a private household in order to engage in Zen training at Rochester, far from their New Zealand home. Further, the RZC was well established enough to provide full-time, residential training and provide for trainees' basic material needs. If they had stayed at Rochester, they would have continued to live in a dedicated Zen training environment. Instead, however, they returned to New Zealand in 2003 and, with the many challenges that it entails, began to establish a Zen center.

Conclusion

Amala's account of her childhood illustrates how someone from a non-Buddhist environment could develop the foundations for an exceptional commitment and motivation to become a full-time Buddhist priest and teacher. Zen practice in the West, somewhat repackaged, offered Amala both elements that were familiar from her childhood and aspects that had been lacking. The key elements of Amala's "coming to the path" narrative are similar to those of other committed Western Buddhist practitioners, for example:

- feeling that one's inherited religion lacked something or was inconsistent (seeing that the "different ways of believing" she encountered in Catholicism and Anglicanism were relative, not absolute truths);
- being attracted to contemplative environments (the nuns' convent and the RZC);
- fascination with the human mind (via experimentation with psychedelic drugs and theater, and later through Zen), and, alongside this, seeking a means to overcome mental afflictions (including a sense of ungroundedness that came from being adopted);
- influence from the countercultural/protest movement that questioned secular materialism and sought alternatives to established norms and institutions.

These personal elements help to answer the question of how she became a Zen priest. But we should also relate her story to our understanding of contemporary Buddhism.

The fact that Amala engaged in many years of specialized training; has been formally recognized as a priest, teacher, and lineage-holder; and now has her own Zen center situates her among the upper tiers of Western Buddhist practitioners. Nonetheless, her story demonstrates the need for flexibility in conceptualizing Buddhist elites. Firstly, it does so with regard to the "two-tiered" model that represents Buddhist communities as consisting of a narrow upper tier of celibate religious specialists and a lower, broader tier of laypeople. Amala is a married, ordained priest, a role that is less monastic than a nun but far more specialized than that of a lay Buddhist. However, we should note that, although the divide between monastics and laypeople is indeed sharply defined in many traditional Buddhist communities, cross-cutting it is not unprecedented; indeed, in Tibet, Nepal, Kashmir, and Japan, married monk-priests led or lead Buddhist communities. A further innovation in many westernized orders of Buddhism is their insistence on the equality of men and women, bringing us to a second reason to broaden our understanding of Buddhist elites. For a married female, becoming a priest was unimaginable in Japanese Zen; modernized, reformed Zen made this possible. With regard to both the monastic–lay divide and her gender, Amala's role as a married female priest provides an example of a kind of Buddhist leader/specialist that cross-cuts the lay and monastic categories.

Many Western Zen centers have been developing a specialized, semimonastic setting with opportunities for residential training. The Rochester model of priesthood provides an opportunity for full-time, vocational training (people may also engage in this training without seeking ordination; arrangements vary in other Zen lineages). The partner or spouse of a priest, if they have one, can serve as a valuable source of emotional and sometimes financial support, given the lack of the kind of monastic institution that would support religious specialists in these ways in more traditional settings. Such relationships facilitate the emergence of new kinds of elites in contemporary Buddhism. As Amala told me, Zen practice in the West is still "a work in progress"; its practitioners are "finding out by doing," through trial and error, what it means to be a Zen priest in the United States, New Zealand, and elsewhere.

References

Batchelor, S. (2002) Foreword, in *Zig Zag Zen: Buddhism and Psychedelics* (ed. A.H. Badiner and A. Grey), Chronicle Books, San Francisco, CA, pp. 9–11.

Chunn, M. and Chunn, J. (1995) *The Mechanics of Popular Music: A New Zealand Perspective*, GP Publications, Wellington.

Hart, W. (2011) *The Art of Living: Vipassana Meditation as Taught by S.N. Goenka*, HarperOne, New York.

Kapleau, P. (2000 [1966]) *The Three Pillars of Zen: Teaching, Practice, and Enlightenment* (ed. R.P. Kapleau), Anchor Books, New York.

Keown, D. (2003) *Oxford Dictionary of Buddhism*, Oxford University Press, Oxford.

Kjolhede, B. (2000) Standing by enlightenment without resting in it, in *Zen Teaching, Zen Practice: Philip Kapleau and* The Three Pillars of Zen (ed. K. Kraft), Weatherhill, New York, pp. 121–33.

Kraft, K. (2000) Introduction, in *Zen Teaching, Zen Practice: Philip Kapleau and* The Three Pillars of Zen (ed. K. Kraft), Weatherhill, New York, pp. 7–18.

Lifton, B.J. (1994) *Journey of the Adopted Self: A Quest for Wholeness*, Basic Books, New York.

McAra, S. (2007) *Land of Beautiful Vision: Creating a Buddhist Sacred Place in New Zealand*, University of Hawaii Press, Honolulu.

McAra, S. (2009) A "stupendous attraction": materialising a Tibetan Buddhist contact zone in rural Australia. Ph.D. thesis. University of Auckland.

McMahan, D. (2002) Repackaging Zen for the West, in *Westward Dharma: Buddhism beyond Asia* (ed. C. Prebish and M. Baumann), University of California Press, Berkeley, pp. 218–29.

McMahan, D. (2008) *The Making of Buddhist Modernism*, Oxford University Press, Oxford and New York.

Nattier, J. (1995) Visible and invisible: Jan Nattier on the politics of representation in Buddhist America. *Tricycle*, 5 (1), 42–9.

Nonomura, K. (2008 [1996]) *Eat, Sleep, Sit: My Year at Japan's Most Rigorous Zen Temple* (trans. J.W. Carpenter), Kodansha International, Tokyo.

Prebish, C. (1998) Introduction, in *The Faces of Buddhism in America* (ed. C.S. Prebish and K.K. Tanaka), University of California Press, Berkeley and Los Angeles, pp. 1–10.

Redmond, G. (2004) Are psychedelics the true Dharma? A review essay of *Zig Zag Zen: Buddhism and Psychedelics. Journal of Buddhist Ethics*, 11, 94–113.

Rocha, C. (2006) *Zen in Brazil: The Quest for Cosmopolitan Modernity*, University of Hawaii Press, Honolulu.

Roof, W.C. (1999) *Spiritual Marketplace: Baby Boomers and the Remaking of American Religion*, Princeton University Press, Princeton, NJ.

Sharf, R. (1995a) Buddhist modernism and the rhetoric of meditative experience. *Numen*, 42, 228–83.

Sharf, R. (1995b) Sanbokyodan: Zen and the way of the new religions. *Japanese Journal of Religious Studies*, 22 (3–4), 417–58.

Wrightson, A. (1998a) Coming to the Path talk 1, talk given at Rochester Zen Center, January 25.

Wrightson, A. (1998b) Coming to the Path talk 2, talk given at Rochester Zen Center, May 3.

Wrightson, A. (2008) Interview with Hugh Kemp in Wellington, February 26.

Wrightson, A. (2010) Interview with Sally McAra, September 22.

Wuthnow, R. and Cadge, W. (2004) Buddhists and Buddhism in the United States: the scope of influence. *Journal for the Scientific Study of Religion*, 43 (3), 361–78.

Further Reading

Arai, P. (1999) *Women Living Zen: Japanese Soto Buddhist Nuns*, Oxford University Press, Oxford. (This work provides insight into the lives of female Japanese Zen practitioners.)

Covell, S. (2005) *Japanese Temple Buddhism: Worldliness in a Religion of Renunciation: Topics in Contemporary Buddhism*, University of Hawaii Press, Honolulu.

Hickey, S. (2010) Two Buddhisms, three Buddhisms, and racism. *Journal of Global Buddhism*, 11, 1–25. (An article discussing diversity in Buddhism.)

Kemp, H. (2008) Taking up the practice: conversion and Buddhist identity in New Zealand. Ph.D. thesis. Victoria University of Wellington. (A study of convert Buddhists that includes material from an interview with Amala.)

McAra, S., Metcalf, F., and Halafoff, A. (forthcoming) Buddhism in Australia, Canada, New Zealand and the USA, in *The Wiley-Blackwell Companion to South and Southeast Asian Buddhism* (ed. M Zimmerman), Wiley-Blackwell. (A work that will provide a wider sociological context for understanding the lives of Western Buddhists.)

Spuler, M. (2002) The development of Buddhism in Australia and New Zealand, in *Westward Dharma: Buddhism beyond Asia* (ed. C. Prebish and M. Baumann), University of California Press, Berkeley, pp. 139–51. (Further background on Buddhism in New Zealand.)

Notes

1. For consistency, I refer to her as Amala, the Sanskrit name she received when she was ordained.
2. Prebish 1998: 9.
3. Wuthnow and Cadge 2004.
4. Roof 1999: 99.
5. McAra 2009.
6. McAra 2007.
7. McMahan 2008: 183.
8. McMahan 2008: 242.
9. Amala Sensei, personal communication, March 2011.
10. See the Introduction and Nattier 1995.
11. However, most non-Buddhist westerners have little or no contact with practicing Buddhists. If they were to enter a typical Western Zen center, they would be more likely to consider it an odd fringe group than an elite one.
12. Sharf 1995a; see also McMahan 2008.
13. McMahan 2002: 218.
14. Nonomura 2008.
15. McMahan 2002: 218.
16. McMahan 2002: 228.
17. Sharf 1995b: 426, 434–6.
18. Kjolhede 2000: 125.
19. Kraft 2000: 7.
20. While Buddhist monks and nuns of various lineages take 218 or more vows, in Amala's order, priests take the same 16 precepts as laypeople, plus the vow to dedicate their lives to the Buddha-dharma and to the welfare of all sentient beings.
21. Wrightson 2008.
22. Intensive group meditation retreats, typically lasting between two and seven days and entailing ten or more hours of daily *zazen*.
23. Rocha (2006: 176–83) discusses the creation of Buddhist wedding and baby-naming ceremonies among non-Japanese Brazilians.

24 Engaged Buddhism seeks to apply Buddhist teachings to address problems relating to the welfare of humans, animals, and the environment (Keown 2003: 86). The term is attributed to Vietnamese monk Thich Nhat Hanh, who in the 1960s sought solutions to the war then ravaging his country through exploring how Buddhist teachings could help peace activists (Keown 2003: 86).
25 Personal communication, December 2010. All subsequent quotes from Amala Roshi are from personal communications, unless otherwise noted.
26 Wrightson 1998a.
27 This expression describes the mind's "original" state and is from Yasutani Roshi's advice on a meditation practice involving counting the breath (in Kapleau 2000: 144): "The fundamental purity and clarity of the mind is obscured by the ceaseless waves of thought which pitch and toss about in it; consequently we falsely see ourselves as individual existences confronted by a universe of multiplicities. *Zazen* is a means of stilling these waves so that our inner vision can be brought into accurate focus."
28 Wrightson 1998a.
29 Wrightson 1998a.
30 Wrightson 2008.
31 Wrightson 1998a.
32 Wrightson 2008.
33 Wrightson 1998b.
34 Her discussion about being adopted is informed by her reading of a book called *Journey of the Adopted Self: A Quest for Wholeness* (Lifton 1994), which she cites elsewhere in her talk.
35 Wrightson 1998b.
36 Wrightson 1998b.
37 Batchelor 2002; see also Redmond 2004.
38 Kjolhede 2000: 122.
39 Wrightson 2008.
40 Chunn and Chunn 1995: 6.
41 Wrightson 2010.
42 Wrightson 2010. Rob Muldoon was prime minister from 1975 to 1984. The political conservatism of his National Party meant that New Zealand sent sports teams to Apartheid South Africa and supported the United States' involvement in the Vietnam War.
43 Wrightson 2008.
44 Wrightson 1998b.
45 Wrightson 1998b.
46 Wrightson 2008.
47 Wrightson 2008.
48 Wrightson 2010.
49 The RZC usually has around 20 full-time residents, and there is sufficient work to keep them occupied. In return the Center provides their accommodation and food, and, in some cases, a stipend.
50 Wrightson 2010.

Part III

Buddhist Lives in South and Southeast Asia

15

Pawinee Bunkhun
The Life of a Thai Buddhist Upasika

Rachelle M. Scott

Editor's Introduction

The biography of this modern Thai woman reflects the diversity of religious practices in Thailand and offers a case study of what can define an *upasika*, an exemplary householder. Throughout Pawinee Bunkhun's life, the foundation of her religious activities has been similar to that of most Thai Buddhists, focused on making merit in order to receive health and happiness in this life and to secure a favorable birth in the next one. She has a monastic temple in Bangkok where she regularly contributes donations and effort, and she goes on periodic traditional group pilgrimages across the country to visit noted shrines, images, and relics, to secure the classic benefits householders have always sought: the transcendental (merit) and the pragmatic (healing, protection, long life).

Stories from the Pali texts told by the monks extol laypersons who receive beneficial results from acts of generosity, from giving a simple bowl of rice (the story of Sujata's gift to the Buddha) to donating grand monasteries (see the biographies of Anathapindika and Vishakha in Chapter 3). These gifts enabled the Buddha and other monks to follow lives of renunciation; without them, today monks would have had to work in order to survive, which would take them away from their life of spiritual cultivation. Stories of exemplary donors from the past are retold in Thai temples through Buddhist narratives and Buddhist art. In fact, the most popular *jataka* (past life) in Thailand is the Vessatara *jataka*, the story of the Buddha's penultimate life as Prince Vessatara, who perfects generous giving through the relinquishment of his kingdom, and even his children and wife. Each year this story is retold in most Thai temples, including the Bun Phra Wes festival in northern Thailand.[1]

Buddhists: Understanding Buddhism Through the Lives of Practitioners, First Edition. Edited by Todd Lewis.
© 2014 John Wiley & Sons, Ltd. Published 2014 by John Wiley & Sons, Ltd.

But, as she has gotten older, and as an urban and well-educated woman alert to changing opportunities for householders, Pawinee has engaged in a variety of practices that were not available in the small town of her birth. A clear marker of being an *upasika* is her immersion in formal studies of the *Abhidharma* – the third portion of the Pali Canon, concerned with advanced analysis of the doctrine – as are her avidly reading popular vernacular books on Buddhism and her commitment to regular meditation practice. The seven books in the Theravada *Abhidharma* all focus on the various "physical and mental events" (*dhammas*) that are the building blocks of the individual's experience of reality. As the author points out, modern institutional development in education has enabled and expanded the opportunities for monks and householders to together study the very old tradition of *Abhidharma* inquiry. And, while Pawinee Bunkhun has known about the basics of meditation practice since she was a little girl, it was only after she retired that she incorporated formal meditation practice into her religious life. While advanced studies and meditation deepened her awareness of the analytical and spiritual dimensions of the tradition, they did not displace making offerings to monks or reading popular Thai translations of Buddhist texts.

This perceptive portrait of Pawinee Bunkhun's life bears witness to the operative use of the Buddhist categories *kushala* (skillful) and *akushala* (unskillful) to evaluate the ethical and spiritual effect of past or future personal actions. As all intentional acts of body, speech, and mind lead to karmic seeds being planted and inevitably ripening (*vipakha*), a careful and wise Buddhist will often ask himself or herself whether a course of action will lead to *kushala* or *akushala vipalka*. Most Thais used the concept of karma to explain why so many innocent people died as a result of the tsunami of 2004, which was one of Southeast Asia's worst natural disasters, and to emphasize how the power of karma stretches across many lifetimes. As Pawinee has reminded the author on more than one occasion, "we are all ancients," and we should never view life only in terms of the present one.

Introduction

In the middle of one of Bangkok's notorious rainy-season deluges, I met a Thai Buddhist laywoman whose life embodies both traditional and modern forms of religiosity. On that day, I was visiting the old city section of Bangkok. I had been in the capital for only a few days, and I had wanted to see some of the main tourist sites, especially the Grand Palace, which houses Wat Phra Kaew (the temple of the Emerald Buddha) and Wat Pho, a temple known for both its large reclining Buddha image and its school of traditional Thai massage. In my eagerness to view these sights that day, I forgot to take an umbrella with me. My forgetfulness proved to be a boon.[2] After touring the exhibits at the National Museum, I walked toward the Grand Palace. The sky quickly turned from dark gray to menacing black, and rain began to pour down without mercy. I, like many other stranded Bangkok residents, quickly ran to the nearest shelter, which happened to be a narrow canopy over a bus stop bench. After about an hour, the rain finally ceased, and I continued to walk toward the Grand Palace. Since I was famished by this time, I decided to stop for a quick bowl of noodle soup (*kuaitiaow nam*). As I sat enjoying the warmth of the soup, I noticed a sign for Mahachulalongkorn Buddhist University, one of the two Buddhist universities in Thailand. In fact, the University and the historic temple adjacent to it, Wat Mahathat, were directly across from the noodle shop. I simply could not resist a quick diversion into the temple grounds before proceeding to Wat Phra Kaew and the Emerald Buddha.

As I wandered through the numerous buildings of the temple, a friendly elderly man asked me a few questions about myself and then escorted me to the International Office, where monks are trained to participate in missionary activities around the world. Inside the office, I met the head monk and his attendants. He was curious about my research on contemporary Thai Buddhism and instructed one of his lay devotees, Pawinee Bunkhun,[3] to help me. She graciously accepted this directive with a characteristic Thai smile. On that day, she guided me through Wat Phra Kaew and Wat Pho, and then later saw me safely home. In the ensuing months and years, she introduced me to Thai Buddhism through her eyes – through the eyes of an urban, educated, modern laywoman who embraces both traditional and modern forms of religious practice. She invited me to travel all across Thailand with her and her cadre of close-knit work and temple friends. We visited Buddhist sites, participated in religious ceremonies, and spent many hours chatting with monks. On these occasions, I saw her engage in a variety of lay practices, from offering food to monks and venerating Buddha images to attending weekly classes on *Abhidharma* philosophy.

For many people living in North America and Europe, meditation is synonymous with Buddhism. When one thinks about Buddhist practice, one envisions a Buddhist monk sitting with his legs crossed as he breathes in deeply. The Buddhist monk, with his colored robes and shaven head, has, in fact, become a popular image in new media, from Kleenex commercials in America to Japanese-inspired global anime characters. Discourses on "karma," "mindfulness," and "enlightenment" have become a part of our global lexicon. In the process, however, the importance of other forms of Buddhist practice are often overlooked or undervalued in the Western imagination of Buddhism. By focusing on the religiosity of Pawinee Bunkhun, this chapter will showcase the religious practices of a Thai laywoman, shedding light on issues of gender, modernity, and the diversity in Thai Buddhist practice.

Pawinee Bunkhun was born in Phitsanulok, Thailand, on August 20, 1951. Phitsanulok is located in the northern region (Pak Nua) of Thailand about 214 miles north of Bangkok. The city of Phitsanulok served for a brief period of time as the capital of the Ayutthaya Kingdom during the reign of King Borommatrailokanat (King Trailok; r. 1448–88).[4] Today, Phitsanulok is known for its houseboats along the Nan River, the famed temples of Wat Phra Si Ratana Mahatat and Wat Chulamani, its Buddha-image-casting factory, and its close proximity to the Sukhothai Historical Park. Pawinee speaks fondly of growing up in Phitsanulok and visiting the various Buddhist sites in the region around her hometown.

She left Phitsanulok for the capital of Bangkok (Thai: Krungthep) in 1969 to pursue a bachelor's degree in sociology from the highly esteemed Chulalongkorn University. After receiving her B.A. and M.A. in sociology, she married, had two sons, and entered the Thai civil service. She worked for the government's development office from the time of her graduation until her retirement in 2011. In the over 40 years that Pawinee has lived in the wider Bangkok area, she has seen the city undergo dramatic changes, from its population explosion (from 3.1 million to approximately 12 million residents in the wider Bangkok area) to its rise as one of the commercial centers of Southeast Asia.

Pawinee's religious life reflects both her diverse upbringing and her experiences as a modern, educated, and urban woman. Pawinee's parents were of Chinese ancestry, and many of her earliest memories of Buddhist practice reflect this heritage. She recalls her parents chanting "Namo Amito Fo" (an essential practice in Chinese forms of Pure Land Buddhism), venerating Jow Mae Kwan Im (Guan Yin, the bodhisattva of compassion), and paying respect to her ancestors at the household shrine. At the same time, her family also participated in activities that are commonly associated with Thai Theravada practice. Pawinee remembers attending rituals at Theravada temples with her family; hearing monks chant the sacred language of Pali; learning how to *wai* (show respect) properly to monks, teachers, parents, and others; and learning how to make offerings to monks. In the public schools, Theravada Buddhism is taught as a part of Thai history, and so it became a part of Pawinee's history as well. In fact, when she was 13 years old, she won a student award for her paper on Asanha Bucha day (Asalha Puja day), a day that commemorates the Buddha's first sermon after his awakening. Her paper addressed the significance of the holiday to both the sacred biography of the Buddha and to Thai culture. Pawinee's broad religious background reflects the diversity of religious practice in Thailand and the fact that many Thais of Chinese descent embrace Thailand's Theravada heritage as part of their national and religious identities.

For most of her life, Pawinee's religious practice has focused on traditional forms of Buddhist householder practice, especially on making merit (*tam bun*) and being a good person (*khon di*), but she has supplemented these core practices with serious doctrinal study as well. While at Chulalongkorn University, she became enthralled with the writings of Ajahn Buddhadasa (1906–93), a modernist monk who focused on social ethics and religious reform.[5] Since that time, Pawinee has considered Ajahn Buddhadasa to be one of the most important monks in Thailand's modern history and has regularly attended ritual events at Wat Chonprathan Rangsarit in the northern Bangkok suburb of Nothaburi, a temple that has a long association with Ajahn Buddhadasa's central temple, Suan Mokkh ("Garden of Liberation") in the southern Thai city of Surat Thani. In addition to her temple activities, Pawinee began a formal study of *Abhidharma* philosophy over ten years ago. This deepened her awareness of the philosophical and analytical dimensions of the tradition, but it did not displace the other aspects of her popular practice. Pawinee's religious life today reflects a range of interests and practices, from offering food, books, and photographs to monks to venerating Buddha images, meditating with friends, and reading Thai translations of Buddhist Studies texts, such as Walpola Rahula's famous book, *What the Buddha Taught*.[6]

Lay Buddhism in Thailand

The Buddhist tradition has flourished in Thailand for well over a thousand years, and today over 90 percent of Thais are practicing Buddhists. One reason for the success of the tradition in Thailand is the historically strong relationship between the monastic order (Pali *sangha*) and householders.

Many scholars have defined this relationship as symbiotic: the lay community supports the *sangha* through gifts of food, clothing, and shelter, while in return the monastic community gives instruction on the *dhamma* (Pali; Skt. *dharma*; the teachings of the Buddha) to the laity and serves as a field for the cultivation of merit. Thai Buddhists commonly believe that gifts to monks produce merit or beneficial results (Thai *bun*) for the giver, including a long, healthy, and prosperous life. Acts of generous giving to the *sangha* reflect Thai notions of ethical conduct as well as the Buddhist notion of karma (Thai *gam*). One common Thai saying reflects this central idea: *tam dee, dai dee; tam chua, dai chua* (do good, receive good; do evil, receive evil). This is the Buddhist version of moral and ethical causality.

Buddhist ethics is based on the idea that not only do actions have consequences but also actions are the results of particular states of mind. Buddhist doctrine connects these states of mind to verbal, mental, and bodily processes. As the *Dhammapada*, an anthology of early Buddhist teaching, states: "If a man speaks or acts with an impure mind, suffering follows him as the wheel of the cart follows the beast that draws the cart ... If a man speaks or acts with a pure mind, joy follows him as his own shadow."[7] These causal relations provide the foundation for much of the tradition's teachings on householder and monastic practice. The *Vinaya*, the code of conduct for monks, lists the 227 rules for fully ordained monks to observe, all of which seek to fashion a spiritually disciplined person through the careful and sustained awareness of an individual's own verbal, mental, and bodily processes (from collecting food to dealing with other renouncers).

Lay men and women are often reminded to observe the five precepts (*panca sila*) at Buddhist gatherings: refraining from taking life, stealing, sexual misconduct, lying, and the consumption of intoxicants. While Buddhists have varying degrees of commitment to these precepts and widely different views on the specifics of their interpretation (for instance, does the first precept mandate vegetarianism?), there is consensus, nevertheless, on the importance of these precepts for Buddhist practice.[8] On most ritual occasions, laypersons will recite all five precepts following the recitation of the triple refuge: "I take refuge in the Buddha; I take refuge in the dhamma; I take refuge in the sangha." This constitutes one core part of lay participation in formal acts of the sangha. Many Buddhists, including Pawinee, view the act of simply repeating and trying to follow the precepts as a meritorious or karmically beneficial action.

Pawinee frequently classifies difficulties in her life as "*akusul-vipak*" (*akusala-vipakha*; "ripening of unskillful, [past/bad action]"). According to Pawinee, this idea is so embedded within everyday thinking that she and all of her friends will instantly say "*akusul-vipak*" when an unfavorable event occurs, such as falling down the stairs or stepping in a hole. She thinks that knowledge of the laws of karma helps her to take responsibility for her actions and to not blame others for misfortune.

It is common for Thai Buddhists to link differences in wealth, health, and personal success to the workings of karma. When Pawinee developed bronchitis after a week of meditating outdoors in the north of Thailand, for instance, a monk told her to *tam bun* (make merit) to help her overcome her sickness. The monk's instructions reflected the notion that Pawinee's sickness and health were the results of karmic action and demonstrated the centrality of merit-making in the practice of Buddhism in Thailand. Anthropologists have noted that several practices are considered to be especially efficacious in the accumulation of extraordinary merit (Pali *punna*; Thai *bun*), from ordaining as a monk to building temples or stupas.[9] Women are able to participate in all of these activities except ordination since there are no authorized fully ordained nuns (*bhikkhuni*) in the Theravada tradition. Women do renounce the world but their pious acts are often regarded with ambivalence. As a result, many Thai Buddhists do not classify becoming a woman renunciant (*maechii*) as an act of extraordinary merit-making.

Pawinee, along with many lay Buddhists, associates acts of generous giving (*dana*) to the monastic community with making merit. In fact, Pawinee taught me how to properly offer food to monks during our first few visits to temples. For her, this ritual constituted my first instruction in Buddhist practice. While many practitioners in the West begin their Buddhist practice with meditation, in Buddhist countries, initial lessons often focus on the karmic benefits of *dana*.

Today, laypersons across Thailand do acts of *dana* daily. The most common *dana* is the offering of food to monks. Thai monks depend entirely on the support of householders for their food, shelter, medicine, and other requisites. Many monks continue the traditional practice of collecting food on alms rounds (Thai *bindabat*; Pali *pindapata*) in the morning, while others, especially those in larger monasteries, receive food brought to them by donors. Pawinee frequently gives to monks at her local temple as well as to monks at other temples. During her routine temple visits, Pawinee frequently offers beverages, sweets, fruits, and other snacks at any time of day, sometimes serving food at the formal meal times just after sunrise and right before noon. In so doing, she feels that she serves a role similar to that of a mother or caregiver who attends to the every need of a loved one. On her birthday, she offers a large meal for a group of monks in order to secure special blessings and good karma for the next year. These acts are done in a highly ritualized manner, with her gift-giving accompanied by formal bowing in which she is careful not to touch the monk. On Sundays and Buddhist holy days, laypersons will often eat after the monks have received their food. Pawinee is especially fond of the curried Chinese noodles (*khanom jin*) that are frequently cooked at temples and are readily available at street stalls near the entrance to temples. The offering and consumption of food at Buddhist temples creates a familial atmosphere that reinforces the bonds between monks and their lay supporters.

Bonds among householders are also strengthened during religious journeys, which Buddhists view as yet another means for the accumulation of merit. In ancient India, places that were associated with the life of the Buddha became early pilgrimage sites. These included the location of his birth (Lumbini), awakening (Bodhgaya), first sermon (Isipatana), and death (Kusinara). Following the Buddha's death, these and other locations became important not only for their association with the once-living Buddha but also for their possession of Buddha relics. Bodily relics became important objects for veneration after the Buddha's death, and they continue to be the focus of devotional activity for all Buddhists.[10]

As the Theravada tradition developed in South and Southeast Asia, new places of pilgrimage emerged in the Buddhist landscape. Many of these places were thought to possess bodily relics. Over time, iconic images of the Buddha were also considered a type of relic; as such, many of these representations, especially ones that were unique or grand, became the focus of popular pilgrimage as well. In Thailand, Buddhist practitioners will often visit Buddhist temples that possess remarkable relics, Buddha images, and stupas (memorial monuments that contain relics), as well as those that are associated with popular monks.

Pilgrimage plays a significant role in the life of Pawinee Bunkhun. She has traveled extensively throughout Thailand, visiting small temples as well as grand ones. Each place offers an opportunity for merit-making. I have accompanied her on several of these trips, which are typically a combination of enjoyable travels (*pai tiao*, "to go out") and religious practice. These trips often focus on eating foods of a specific area, such as seafood along the coast or sticky rice in the northeast, or at restaurants renowned for a particular kind of food. They also involve acts of everyday tourism, from seeing cultural performances – such as crocodile shows, traditional Thai dancing, or calypso cabarets – to visiting national and local historical monuments. On one occasion, we went on a bus trip with a group of local monks and laypersons from Wat Mahathat to a provincial temple in Suphanburi. We spent the first half of the day engaged in merit-making activities (such as listening to monks chant and give lessons on the dhamma, making monetary donations, and offering food to fish in a temple pond) and the second half of the day exploring national and religious monuments in the area. The day included formal acts of religious devotion along with conversations about music, food, and even soccer. (Many monks in Thailand are avid fans of international soccer!) That particular day represented the ways in which religious practice is interwoven into the actions and concerns of everyday life. It is often difficult, if not impossible, to distinguish between so-called "religious" and "secular" activities since any activity can be infused with religious context, meaning, or bodily gestures.

Pawinee has also traveled to other Buddhist countries, including Burma, Laos, Cambodia, Sri Lanka, and India. Most of these trips have been arranged through her associations with Wat Mahathat, one of Bangkok's largest and most significant temples. Wat Mahathat is a temple in the Mahanikai lineage of the Thai sangha, and it is well known for its Buddhist university, Mahachulalongkorn University, with which most of Thailand's scholar-monks are associated. Due to Pawinee's association with Wat Mahathat, she has been able to meet a number of scholar-monk dignitaries during her trips. Of all of the religious trips that she has taken, Pawinee singles out her pilgrimage to India in 1997 as the most significant. Like many other trips, lay representatives from Wat Mahathat arranged and managed the trip; the main purpose of the trip was to visit the principal pilgrimage sites associated with the Buddha's life, and this was the reason why Pawinee decided to participate. While there, she met a high-ranking monk from Wat Mahathat who became a friend and spiritual guide to her; it was he who directed her toward *Abhidharma* studies, which became an important part of her religious practice later in life. Although he is no longer residing at Wat Mahathat in Bangkok, Pawinee makes regular trips to visit him at his new temple in the Ayutthaya area, where he is now the abbot.

Pawinee views all of these religious acts – offering food to monks, listening to the dhamma, and visiting Buddhist sites – as acts that demonstrate her respect for the triple gem (the Buddha, the dhamma, and the sangha). She often conveys this respect through the bodily act of *krap wai* (Skt. *Namaskara*; the placing of one's palms together and bowing) to Buddha images and monks. This act is ubiquitous throughout Thailand, from children showing respect to their teachers in the morning to hotel attendants greeting their guests, but this bodily action possesses a special significance when the object of one's respect represents the triple gem.

Many Thais also pay respect to local gods and spirits as well as to their ancestors. Every morning, for instance, Pawinee pays respect to the spirit shrine outside her house, which contains icons of an elderly man and woman. For her, the shrine facilitates her ability to pay respect to her deceased mother-in-law, who purchased the house where she lives, and to pay respect to others who have had a positive impact on her life: all of her teachers from elementary school through college; King Rama V, who founded her university and who is viewed as the great modernizer of Thailand; and all of the spirits who reside near her home, whom she petitions to help keep her sons safe and happy.

Gender and Buddhism

Pawinee's experiences as a Buddhist have been shaped, in part, by her gender. As a woman, the cultural expectation is that she will be a good lay Buddhist: she will make merit, support the monastic institution, and be an ethical person. In addition, many Thai Buddhists might add that she should be a good mother to sons who may one day enter the sangha. While there are many similarities between the practices of all householders, the gender distinction is always present. For instance, laymen have a degree of physical intimacy with monks that shapes their interactions with them. But women are not allowed to touch monks. When offering an item to a monk, a woman should never place the object directly in his hand; when walking around a monk, a woman must be very cautious so as to not inadvertently touch him or his robe. These cultural injunctions against physical contact between women and monks are meant to uphold the *Vinaya* rules and maintain the mental purity of monks, reinforcing the norms of male spiritual superiority.

In the nineteenth century, many early Western Buddhist scholars described Buddhism as an egalitarian religion since during its early history it allowed women to ordain as renouncers and because it generally promoted the idea that women were capable of achieving the highest attainments within the religion.[11] During the time of the historical Buddha, few women renounced the world. It was not a path that was generally prescribed within ancient Indian culture. Only a few religious groups allowed it, and, according to canonical accounts of the first Buddhist nun, Mahapajapati, the Buddha himself was reluctant to admit women into the monastic order. He allowed it only after insisting that Mahapajapati and all subsequent *bhikkhuni* (fully ordained nuns) would accept a series of additional rules that clearly placed them under the authority of the male sangha.[12] Given their secondary status, it is not surprising that the order of officially recognized *bhikkhuni* died out centuries later in the Theravada tradition.

A few women in Theravada societies today do renounce the world. In Thailand, they are called *maechii*, and they typically practice the eight precepts of a layperson.[13] While the male monastic elite does not recognize them as official nuns (*bhikkhuni*), they nevertheless are renouncers: they leave their families, shave their heads, and don white robes. Since many people do not recognize them as "fields of merit" (the idea that giving to monks will reap karmic rewards), they struggle to receive financial support. The figure of the female renouncer, therefore, is not a common ideal, and many women face significant hardship when they decide to renounce. Men, in contrast, may choose to renounce, with their families' consent, at any time, from an early age (typically around the ages of 11 or 12) until death. In the past, many young boys received an education by entering the sangha as novices and being trained within the temple schools.[14] Moreover, it used to be commonly held that a man was suitable for marriage only after he had spent at least one monsoon rain retreat as a monk. The term for such a man is *khon suk* (a ripe man), while those who had not spent time as a monk were deemed *khon dip* (an unripe man).[15]

The vast majority of women in Thailand and elsewhere, therefore, continue to practice Buddhism as laywomen. In the textual tradition of Theravada Buddhism, there are a number of female lay Buddhists who provide models of exemplary practice. In Thailand, Queen Camadevi of Haripunjaya is exalted as a great patron of the Buddhist tradition. She, like many ideal monarchs, supported and promoted the growth of Buddhism; for this she received many boons, including health and happiness.[16] In contemporary Thailand, Queen Surikit and her daughter Princess Maha Chakri Sirindhorn continue to embody the ideal of royal generosity.

The practices of these exemplary women, as well as those of ordinary laywomen, focus on acts of merit-making, which demonstrate the quality of their character. Pawinee describes many of her activities, both those that are explicitly religious and those that reflect Buddhist virtues, as acts of *tam bun*. For example, she views her following of the five precepts, especially her stance against the consumption of alcohol and other drugs, as a meritorious act. At the same time, she views her activities as a mother – rearing children to be ethical and responsible social beings and teaching them the value of respect for elders – as religious actions. In addition, many mothers of monks with whom I have spoken refer to their parenting as an essential part of their sons' religious paths; this connects their religious actions directly to the continuation of the sangha and the Buddha's teachings. Moreover, many monks feel indebted to their parents for their care, support, and guidance; as a result, many demonstrate their gratitude by dedicating the merit gained from ordination to their parents, and many give it exclusively to their mothers.

Abhidharma Studies

When I first met Pawinee in 1998, she had recently begun a course of *Abhidharma* (higher dhamma or advanced philosophy/psychology) study at Wat Mahathat, one of Bangok's oldest and most prestigious temples. She had been advised by the director of the program to undertake the series of courses offered at Wat Mahathat in order to gain a deeper understanding of the doctrinal tradition. She started this program in 1998 and completed it in 2007. She credits the course with teaching her about the Buddha's most profound teachings on the mind and reality.

While most Theravada Buddhists would claim that the *Abhidharma* texts contain the essence of the Buddha teachings, and so serve as guidelines for scholarly analysis, in Thailand there is a long tradition of also using *Abhidharma* texts for ritual purposes. These texts are commonly chanted at funerals and donated to temples as an act of merit-making; in addition, sacred syllables from the texts are used for ritual protection.[17] In fact, the focus on Abhidhamma studies by both monks and laypersons has been one feature of the modernization of Buddhism in Thailand.[18]

Phra Kitthivuttho reestablished the Abhidhamma Foundation at Wat Mahathat in the 1960s. This was the result, in part, of the introduction of the modern Burmese study of Abhidhamma by Phra Phimontham in the 1950s.[19] The curriculum for *Abhidharma* studies, as of 2002, focused on three categories of learning: beginning (*jula-aphithaamikatri*), intermediate (*majjhima-aphithaamikatri*), and advanced (*maha-aphithaamikatri*). Students had the option of either attending class every weekday or taking special intensive classes every Saturday and Sunday. Since Pawinee worked during the week, she chose the intensive classes on the weekends. While the full course takes seven and a half years to complete (the first section takes eighteen months and the remaining two sections take three years each), many students, including Pawinee, take slightly longer as they may have breaks between the sections. Following the completion of each unit, participants are tested on their knowledge and the scores are publicly posted. Pawinee passed all of her exams but always found them difficult and the least desirable part of her studies.

Pawinee's class consisted of monks, nuns, laymen, and laywomen. While the distinctions between monks and laywomen were maintained in the class (monks would sit separately from laywomen), Pawinee commented that it seemed strange to be studying the *Abhidharma* texts alongside monks, the preservers of the tradition. She noted, however, that the monks were typically young (early to mid twenties) while the ages of her fellow lay students ranged significantly, from college-aged students to elderly retirees. She became close friends with many of her classmates and she continues to engage in religious practices with them. On one occasion, for instance, we celebrated the Chinese New Year in Bangkok's Chinatown (Yaowarat) with one of Pawinee's classmates. We went to Wat Traimit, which houses the famed five-ton golden Buddha statue, where we offered money and received blessings from a resident monk.

Most recently, Pawinee and several of her *Abhidharma* classmates have embarked on a course of meditation practice with an international organization (the head monk is from Canada but the organization has links with temples across the globe). While Pawinee has known the basics of meditation practice since she was a little girl, it is only now, after she has retired, that she has incorporated formal meditation practice into her religious life. Unlike many famous forest monks who are known for their prolonged practices in isolation, however, Pawinee's meditation experiences frequently occur with her friends, at a temple in Bangkok or a forest retreat outside

Chiang Mai. She links her meditation practice to both her formal study of *Abhidharma* philosophy and her intent to make as much merit as possible in the remaining years of her present life.

Conclusion

Pawinee Bunkhun's religious life reflects the diversity of Buddhism in contemporary Thailand. On the one hand, many of her religious activities focus on making merit in order to receive health and happiness in this life and to secure a favorable birth in the next one. In this respect, her religious practice fits the pattern of most lay Buddhists in Thailand today. On the other hand, her religious life also reflects the ways in which the lay practice has changed over the past century. As a modern, urban, and well-educated layperson, Pawinee engages in a variety of practices that would not have been a relevant part of religious life in Phitsanulok, the place of her birth, 60 years ago. Her commitment to *Abhidharma* studies, her reading of popular vernacular books on Buddhism, and her international tours of Buddhist sites all reflect new dimensions of Buddhist practice in contemporary Thailand. While many descriptions of Thai Buddhism focus on a distinction between "traditional" Buddhism and "modern" Buddhism, Pawinee's religiosity demonstrates the provisional nature of such distinctions and challenges us to rethink our assumptions about lay practice in contemporary Thailand.

References

Collett, A. (2006) Buddhism and gender: reframing and refocusing the debate. *Journal of Feminist Studies in Religion*, 22 (2), 55–84.

Collins, S. and McDaniel, J. (2010) Buddhist "nuns" (*mae chi*) and the teaching of Pali in contemporary Thailand. *Modern Asian Studies*, 44 (6), 1373–408.

Germano, D. and Trainor, K. (2004) *Embodying the Dharma: Buddhist Relic Veneration in Asia*, SUNY Press, Albany.

Harvey, P. (2000) *An Introduction to Buddhist Ethics: Foundations, Values and Issues*, Cambridge University Press, Cambridge.

Jackson, P.A. (1987) *Buddhadāsa: Theravada Buddhism and Modernist Reform in Thailand*, Silkworm Press, Chiang Mai.

Jackson, P.A. (1989) *Buddhism, Legitimation, and Conflict: The Political Functions of Urban Thai Buddhism*, Institute of Southeast Asian Studies, Singapore.

Kaufman, H.K. (1960) *Bangkhuad: A Community Study in Thailand*, J.J. Augustin, Locust Valley.

Lang, K.C. (1986) Lord Death's snare: gender-related imagery in the *Theragāthā* and the *Therīgāthā*. *Journal of Feminist Studies in Religion*, 2 (2), 63–79.

Mascaro, J. (trans.) (1973) *The Dhammapada*, Penguin, London.

McDaniel, J.T. (2008) *Gathering Leaves and Lifting Words: Histories of Buddhist Monastic Education in Laos and Thailand*, University of Washington Press, Seattle, WA.

Swearer, D.K. (1995) *The Buddhist World of Southeast Asia*, SUNY Press, Albany, NY.

Swearer, D.K. (2010) *The Buddhist World of Southeast Asia*, 2nd edn, SUNY Press, Albany.

Swearer, D.K. and Premchit, S. (1998) *The Legend of Queen Cāma: Bodhiraṃsi's Cāmadevīvaṃsa, a Translation and Commentary*, SUNY Press, Albany.

Tambiah, S.J. (1970) *Buddhism and the Spirit Cults in Northeast Thailand*, Cambridge University Press, Cambridge.

Vathanaprida, S. and MacDonald, M.R. (1994) *Thai Tales: Folktales of Thailand*, Libraries Unlimited, Englewood, CO.

Wyatt, D.K. (2003) *Thailand: A Short History*, Yale University Press, New Haven, CT.

Further Reading

Cook, J. (2010) *Meditation in Modern Buddhism: Renunciation and Change in Thai Monastic Buddhism*, Cambridge University Press, Cambridge.

Gethin, R. (1998) *The Foundations of Buddhism*, Oxford University Press, Oxford.

Keyes, C. and Daniel, E.V. (eds) (1983) *Karma: An Anthropological Inquiry*, University of California Press, Berkeley, CA.

Kitiarsa, P. (2012) *Mediums, Monks, and Amulets: Thai Popular Buddhism Today*, University of Washington Press, Seattle.

McDaniel, J. (2011) *The Lovelorn Ghost and the Magical Monk: Practicing Buddhism in Modern Thailand*, Columbia University Press, New York.

Rahula, W. (1959) *What the Buddha Taught*, Grove Press, New York.

Scott, R. (2009) *Nirvana for Sale? Buddhism, Wealth, and the Dhammakāya Temple in Contemporary Thailand*, SUNY Press, Albany.

Swearer, D. (1995) *The Buddhist World of Southeast Asia*, SUNY Press, Albany.

Notes

1. Tambiah 1970.
2. In Thailand, this would not be viewed as a coincidence but rather the result of my previous good deeds (merit).
3. The author created this pseudonym to protect the identity of Pawinee Bunkhun, who is not a public figure.
4. Wyatt 2003.
5. Jackson 1987.
6. *What the Buddha Taught* is a book that has frequently been used in Buddhism courses in Western universities over the past few decades. The book presents a modernist reading of Buddhism emphasizing the philosophical and ethical dimensions of the tradition. Walpola Rahula (1907–97) was a Buddhist monk and scholar from Sri Lanka.
7. Mascaro 1973.
8. Harvey 2000.
9. Kaufman 1960; Tambiah 1970.
10. Germano and Trainor 2004.
11. Collett 2006.
12. Lang 1986.
13. A few *maechii* in Thailand do follow the ten training precepts of a novice, but this practice is more common in Burma and Sri Lanka.
14. Swearer 1995: 48.
15. Vathanaprida and MacDonald 1994: 118.
16. Swearer and Premchit 1998.
17. McDaniel 2008; Swearer 2010.
18. Collins and McDaniel 2010.
19. Jackson 1989.

16
Mahasi Sayadaw of Burma

Bradley S. Clough

Editor's Introduction

The Burmese master scholar, teacher, and practitioner Mahasi Sayadaw (1904–1982) was one of the most influential Buddhist monks of the modern era. His life provides insight into the different varieties of religious occupation those taking ordination into the sangha can choose. We follow this young Burmese man's life from his taking vows as a novice at age six, through his rise to prominence as a gifted young scholar, his full ordination at age 20, and then his adoption of the *dhutangas*, the intensive ascetic lifestyle recommended but not required by the Buddha for those inclined to the practices he himself took to as he sought enlightenment as a young man. During this time, Sayadaw retreated to engage in intensive meditation that lead to nirvana realization. Recognized for his attainments as a scholar and practitioner, he devoted his life to both of the two classical poles of life in the Buddhist sangha: the life of study (*pariyatti*) and the life of spiritual practice (*patipatti*). The first side of this dichotomy presents the domesticated sangha: village dwellers, literary specialists, and preachers; the other side defines a cluster associated with reform: living apart from society, meditation, and a strict disciplinary rectitude.

In addition to producing over 60 books on Buddhist doctrine and meditation practice, Sayadaw became a major spiritual teacher who spread insight into meditation practice. Backed by a wealthy donor, he did this through founding a large network of meditation centers in Burma and throughout South and Southeast Asia, with disciples spreading the centers to Japan and the West as well. While Mahasi Sayadaw succeeded in reaching the highest traditional accomplishments (nirvana realization, scholarship, meditation teacher), his life must also be understood as attuned to the needs of the modern era, when the advocates of "Protestant Buddhism" called for, and rewarded, teachers who would make the mindfulness meditation practices that even few monks traditionally undertook available to hundreds of thousands of householders. While traditionalists in the sangha criticized Sayadaw for teaching that nirvana could be realized in a short time by following his methods, it is certain that this remarkable monk energized several generations of modern Buddhists across Asia and made Buddhist meditation accessible to interested Western Buddhists.

The Early Life of Mahasi Sayadaw

The child who would become known as Mahasi Sayadaw was born in 1904 in Seikkhun, a prosperous village about seven miles west of the town of Shwebo in Upper Burma.[1] His parents, self-sufficient farmers, sent the young boy to Pyinmara Monastery in Seikkhun in order for him to receive an early monastic education, as was the custom in rural areas of Burma. When he was 12 years old, the boy was admitted into the monastic community (*sangha*) as a novice (*samanera*). His first teacher, U Adicca, gave him the novice's name Shin Sobhana ("Auspicious [One]"), which is given only to those who demonstrate a particular grace and dignity in their demeanor. His senior teachers were responsible for educating novices in both secular and religious subjects, and Shin Sobana showed himself to be adept in both areas of study. Eventually he received the elder novice title of *koyingyi* and became known as Koyin Sobhana. Koyin Sobhana continued his studies under Sayadaw U Parama at Thugyi-kyuang Monastery, one of the renowned cluster of monasteries in the town of Ingyin-taik. After a short period of study under Sayadaw U Arcara at the Shwe-Theindaw Monastery, he became a *rahan* or fully ordained monk on November 26, 1923.

For monks of the Theravada Buddhist tradition of South and Southeast Asia, there is a premium placed on learning the authoritative scriptures of the tradition, which have been composed in the Pali language, and over the next three years U Sobhana, as he was now known, took and easily passed the full gamut of Pali scriptural examinations administered by the Burmese government. During this time, U Sobhana strictly followed the standard monastic rules (*Vinaya*), which Theravada teaches are the foundation of a career, one that ideally goes on to meditation practice and the attainment of realization of spiritually liberating insight (*panna*). In addition, once on this path, he also took on extra ascetic practices optional for monks, the *dhutangas*.[2]

Ashin Sobhana next went to Mandalay, a city noted for its preeminence in *pariyatti* or Buddhist learning, and there he continued scriptural studies under many high *sayadaws*.[3] He had been studying in Mandalay for about a year when he was called by the head of the Taik-kyaung monastery in Taungwainggale, Moulmein, to assist him in the teaching of his pupils.

Striving for a balance between learning (*pariyatti*) and practice (*patipatti*), Ashin Sobhana not only was becoming a great student and teacher based on learning but also had a deep interest in meditation practice. In Theravada Buddhism, the highest, liberating form of meditation is "insight cultivation" (*vipassana-bhavana*); this technique is also known as "mindfulness" (*sati*). Concordant with this, Ashin Sobhana had developed a deep interest in the key Pali text on meditation, known as the *Great Sermon on the Foundations of Mindfulness* (*Mahasatipatthana Sutta*). This led him not only to studying this text rigorously but also to taking up practice of its subject, insight meditation under the noted master Mingun Jetawan Sayadaw in neighboring Thaton.

Ashin Sobhana's intensive practice of this method led him to mastery of it in four months. His biography speaks of his attaining "complete purification of body and mind" through the acquisition of the seven "limbs of enlightenment:"[4] mindfulness (*sati*); investigation of the doctrine (*dhamma-vicaya*); energy (*viriya*); joy (*piti*); tranquility (*passaddhi*); concentration (*samadhi*); and equanimity (*upekkha*). So, as asserted in his authorized biography, Ashin Sobhana attained the highest goal of nirvana (Pali: *nibbana*) realization at the remarkably young age of 34. It is said that he also successfully transmitted the method of practice to three disciples at Seikkhun while on a visit there in 1938. Soon, however, he was called to return to Taungwainggale to take charge of the monastery upon the death of its abbot and there he continued his teaching and textual studies. In 1941 he passed the *Dhammacarya* ("Teacher of the Doctrine") exam with his usual level of quickness and success.

The Japanese invasion of Burma in 1942–1945 forced Ashin Sobhana to return to Seikkhun, where he taught the doctrinal and practical techniques of the "Four Foundations of Mindfulness" to a growing number of followers at the Mahasi Monastery there. His leadership role there led him to take the title of Mahasi Sayadaw. The number of *vipassana* yogis (insight meditators) sitting with him continued to greatly increase. Eventually, his pupils prevailed upon him to write down his teachings and the result was the monumental *Manual of Vipassana Meditation*. This comprehensive work in two volumes totaling 950 printed pages soon became the most authoritative treatise in Burma on mindfulness cultivation. Mahasi became renowned in the Shwebo-Sagaing region for both his erudition and his success as a meditation teacher.

During the time following the publication of this magnum opus, there appeared on the scene a famously devout and rich layperson named Sir U Thwin. He wanted to set up a new major meditation center, one to be led by a teacher of proven virtue and ability. After listening to a discourse on *vipassana* by Mahasi and observing his serene and dignified demeanor, U Thwin believed he had found the ideal master. On November 13, 1947, U Thwin established the Buddha Sasananuggaha Association on a large plot of land in the capital city of Rangoon and proposed that the prime minister invite Mahasi to direct the meditation center to be built there and named Sasana Yeiktha. For the next two years, Mahasi divided his time between the monasteries in his native Seikkhun and Taungwainggale, but in November of 1949 Prime Minister U Nu personally invited him to the Sasana Yeiktha, thus beginning his 29-year career as its director. The Sasana Yeiktha became a novel institution in that it had not only monastic structures for monks but also living quarters for laity. That the laity had a center specifically designed to foster *their* meditation training and where they would train alongside monks was an entirely new innovation in the Theravada Buddhist world. Within a few years of the establishment of the main center at Rangoon, over a hundred similar meditation centers sprang up throughout Burma, led by members of the *sangha* trained by Mahasi.[5] Centers based on his method spread to other Theravada countries: Thailand, Sri Lanka, Cambodia, and India. According to 1972 census numbers reported in Mahasi's biography, Burma had over 700,000 monastic and lay yogis involved in meditation training at Mahasi Sayadaw's centers and Thailand had over a million!

In recognition of his distinguished scholarship, spiritual attainments, and teaching accomplishments, in 1952 the President of the Union of Burma gave Mahasi the prestigious official title of *Agga Maha-Pandita* (meaning "Highest Great Teacher"). In 1953 Mahasi was part of a Burmese delegation to Thailand and Cambodia sent to help organize the historic Sixth Council (*Chattha Sangayana*). With delegates from across the world, it began in 1954 with the extremely ambitious goal of publishing a definitive text of the entire Pali Canon as well as all of the Pali commentaries and subcommentaries. Mahasi had two extremely important positions at this Council, which was held over a period of three years. First, he was the *Pucchaka* or "Chief Questioner," who was responsible for verifying where each canonical *sutta* or sermon was delivered, for whose sake it was given, and for what purposes it was preached. He was also an *osana*, one of the project's final "editors." In this capacity, the task was the final revising and reprinting of the Pali Canon. Mahasi was part of this process from start to finish and he also was the sole final proof corrector. And, because of his practical experience, he was also assigned the position of sole editor of the commentaries on the most important Theravada treatise on training, Buddhaghosa's fifth-century work, the *Visuddhimagga*.[6] Based on his great expertise on this work, Mahasi in 1957 wrote an introduction (*nidana-katha*) to the *Visuddhimagga*, in which he sought to correct what he saw as numerous misinterpretations of the author and the work that were made in the Harvard University Press edition (1950) of the text. Further, in the late 1950s and early 1960s, he completed a four-volume translation of the *Visuddhimagga* into Burmese. This was followed in subsequent years by a four-volume commentary on the same text. The 1950s also saw him ceaselessly giving lectures on this text and its "great commentary" (*maha-tika*) at Sasana Yeiktha in Rangoon.

Besides the many scholarly and practical achievements discussed so far, it is important to discuss Mahasi's missionary work as well. In 1956–7, he was part of a delegation to Japan, where interest in Theravada Buddhism had grown in this Mahayana country, in the wake of the Sixth Theravada Council. In the mid-1950s, he led a mission to Indonesia to promote Theravada Buddhism there as well, and there he also consecrated monastic boundaries (*simas*), initiated novices (*samaneras*), and ordained monks (*bhikkhus*). In 1957, he sent a delegation of his teachers to Sri Lanka (formerly Ceylon) with the express purpose of reviving insight meditation there. Mahasi himself followed up on this in 1959 when he went to Sri Lanka and presided over the opening of 12 permanent and 17 temporary meditation centers that his disciples established there.[7] Later in 1959 he traveled to India, again with the purpose of giving practical teachings on insight meditation. A major part of this trip was the sermons he gave to "untouchable" converts there. In the early 1960s, he visited Thailand, where over three hundred centers had been opened that followed his methods of mindfulness/insight meditation. There were an estimated one million individuals involved in programs there as of 1964.

From the late 1960s to his rather sudden death of a severe heart attack in 1982, Mahasi Sayadaw continued an active schedule of giving teachings on the *Visuddhimagga* and the *Mahasatipatthana Sutta* in order to educate as many people as possible on his way of practicing insight meditation. These teachings were mostly given in Burma, but his missionary activities continued in centers across South and Southeast Asia, and between 1979 and 1981 spread to new places such as Nepal, the United States, Britain, and several continental European countries. To the end, he also continued his scholastic pursuits, having published 67 scholarly volumes by the time of his death.

Monastic Ordination and Ascetic Practices

The first issue that might be raised in the life of Mahasi is the early age – six years – at which he was sent to the monastery. This was not so unusual for rural Burmese boys seeking an education, but in more urban areas public secular schools were a more likely option. When anthropologist Melfred Spiro analyzed Burmese men's reasons for entering the monkhood, he found the three major reasons for doing so were religious motives, the desire to escape the hardships and suffering of life, and the wish for an easier life.[8] Donald Swearer more recently noted others: besides gaining an education, there are the motives of acquiring "a higher social status, a response to social custom and pressure, and repayment of a filial debt, especially to one's mother."[9] Since Mahasi's family was fairly prosperous, though, their decision would likely have been based on their Buddhist values.

In the Theravada countries of Southeast Asia, monastic tenure usually reflects the individual's motivation for ordination. It has been a long-held custom in these countries for young men to take the novice ordination (*pabbajja*) near the age of puberty, remain a monk for a few months or years, and then return to lay life. As Swearer observes, such practice is akin to Christian confirmation and Jewish bar/bat mitzvah, a rite of passage to adulthood and a passage into one's religio-social community.[10]

Mahasi's career represents a different choice with respect to full ordination (*upasampada*) at the age of 20 into the life of a monk (*bhikkhu*), in order to engage in a full-time and lifetime pursuit of the religion's highest goal, *nibbana*. Like all other monks, monks with such a goal in mind take a vow of celibacy and live a life that minimizes attachment to worldly things. In this way, the Theravada monks of Southeast Asia observe the "time-honored tradition of the Middle Way" so that a monastic career does not ordinarily involve excessive ascetic practices.[11] Here again, however, Mahasi chose the elite path within the customs of Theravada monasticism, the *dhutangas*. These are deprivations to doggedly purify oneself from all obstacles to experiencing *nibbana*, undermining attachment to food, clothing, and shelter. Some of the *dhutangas* are taken by all monks, such as wearing only three robes, going for all alms, and taking one meal per day; other practices are exclusive to followers of the *dhutangas*, such as wearing patched-up robes, sleeping in a seated position, and being satisfied with whatever dwelling one comes upon, whether that be a tree in the forest or a cemetery. Mahasi's biography does not specify how long he kept to these ascetic practices, but the fact that he took them at the very beginning of his career as a fully ordained *bhikkhu* indicates the great seriousness he had with respect to removing the obstacles to *nibbana* as quickly as possible.

Another issue that arises in Mahasi's biography is his sense of vocation as a monk. Ideally speaking, the tradition holds that there are three stages in the progress of a monk: learning (*pariyatti*) the wording of the dhamma (Skt. *dharma*); practicing (*patipatti*) the dhamma; and penetrating (*pativedha*) the dhamma and realizing its goal. In our reading we see that Mahasi's career was marked by pursuit of all three of stages. From his precocious success in the national Pali exams in his early twenties, from his travels to Mandalay to study under Burma's leading scholar-monks, from his prolific writing career (which had a special emphasis on commenting on the practical texts, the *Mahasatipatthana Sutta* and the *Visuddhimagga*), and from his role as a redactor of the Pali Canon and its commentaries at the Sixth Theravada Council, it is clear that *pariyatti* was central to Mahasi Sayadaw's career. In his emphasis throughout his career on the practical application of texts such as the *Mahasatipatthana Sutta* and the *Visuddhimagga*, and in his setting up of hundreds of meditation centers throughout the Theravada world, it is evident that *patipatti* was also of equal importance to his life's mission. And, if the claim in his biography and the testimonies of thousands of his students and his disciples' students are true, it seems that he was responsible for the deep penetration of the dhamma, *pativedha*, for a great many people.

Such a career, however, of balancing the pursuits of learning and practice that lead to a final "penetration" or realization of the spiritually liberating truth is a very unusual one in the context of Theravada history, especially in modern times. In examining the history of Theravada Buddhist soteriology, one can identify a number of conflicts that significantly determined what particular teachings and practices would gain primacy. The chief division of the *sangha* that has stood out most prominently in shaping the nature of Theravada Buddhism has been the bifurcation of learning (*pariyatti*) and praxis (*patipatti*). Not only were these two different vocations but also the former has been the preferred focus of *sangha* life. It is true that the tradition of "practice," associated with the residential vocation of forest-dwelling (*arannavasi*), has always been regarded as a legitimate branch of the *sangha*; but, for the rank-and-file monastics, the life of "learning" associated with the residential vocation of village-dwelling (*gamavasi*), and its corresponding occupational vocations of scholarship (*ganthadhura*) and preaching (*dhammakathika*), has been favored by sangha leaders. In the history of Theravada Buddhism, the first is called *ganthadhura*, the "burden/vocation of books," and it denotes the learning and teaching of dhamma; the second is called *vipassanadhura*, the "burden/vocation of (insight) meditation." While monks ideally both studied texts *and* cultivated purity through meditation, most have specialized in one vocation. So, in practice, *vipassanadhuras* have not usually preached and *ganthadhuras* have infrequently meditated.[12]

Because *ganthadhura* and its attendant responsibilities have necessitated residence near laity and considerable contact with them, most monks of this vocation have lived in urban or village areas and are also known by the residential designation *gamavasi* or "village dwellers." The *ganthadhura* monks have studied texts not only to edify themselves and maintain the integrity of established Buddhism but also to act as transmitters of the Buddhist tradition. This brings us to the second type of *ganthadhura*, who orally disseminates the basic principles of dhamma to the laity. In fulfilling this purpose by instructing them in the authentic dhamma and acting as vehicles through which the sacred power of the dhamma becomes available to them, these teachers have been most responsible for spreading the central values of Buddhism, albeit in an attenuated and moderated form, among householders. Another service performed by book-monks for householders is ritual: the chief Theravada ritual is the *paritta*, recitations of specific words given by the Buddha to impart protection to individuals and spread auspiciousness in specific places such as homes and businesses.

In the modern era up to the present day, biographies of prominent monks have testified to how this traditional separation of careers, and separate realms of monastic residence, is no longer so clear. Not all forest monks have been rigorous ascetic meditators and the forest retreats have produced some of Theravada's most outstanding scholars. Although forest monks are estimated to comprise less than 5 percent of the *sangha* in Theravada countries, the great spiritual masters remain extremely important for their embodiment and exemplification of the Buddhist ideal of attaining liberation. Contemporary accounts from these countries frequently refer to monks and householders seeing the determination, piety, and integrity of the forest monks with awe and respect. Most laypersons regard them as the closest approximation to the traditional ideal of the *arahant* (Skt. *arhat*), and as living proof of the validity of the silent and solitary life of monks pursuing detachment, meditation, and final realization. For many Theravadins, Mahasi Sayadaw was one such individual.

The Lay Meditation Movement

Mahasi Sayadaw was a leader in a new movement in Theravada Buddhism, in an era when meditation had waned in the Theravada world, which was beset with all the traumas and disruptions of colonial rule. Sayadaw's movement not only reintroduced meditation in monastic circles but also brought significant numbers of laypeople to the intensive practice of mental cultivation (*bhavana*). While other Burmese teachers – namely Ledi Sayadaw and U Ba Khin – were also instrumental players in this movement, Mahasi and his disciples, in their work at Sasana Yeiktha and at hundreds of other centers throughout the Theravada world, were certainly central figures in initiating hundreds of thousands of householders into the serious cultivation of the mind.

With respect to Mahasi's leadership in the lay meditation movement, three major features of his teaching are noteworthy. As Robert H. Scharf has noted, Mahasi and his followers have asserted the superiority of what has been called the "bare insight" method, sometimes going as far as to say that it is the one and only path to liberation.[13] His technique claims to provide direct entry into the path of insight (*vipassana*), without necessitating prior training in tranquility meditation (*samatha*), which involves absorbing oneself in the rarefied states of meditative trance states (*jhana*) that serve to calm and concentrate the mind and body to high degrees. This claim contradicts the long-accepted teaching – promoted by the authoritative commentator Buddhaghosa (c. 370–450 CE) and with the support of many passages in the Pali Canon – that training in *samatha* is the necessary foundation of Buddhist meditation. To be specific, Buddhaghosa held that achievement of at least the four *jhanas* of the realm of form (*rupadhatu*) is a necessary, essential foundation for successful *vipassana* practice. Some traditionalist monk-scholars additionally insist that, for *vipassana* to lead to realization, there must beforehand be the further accomplishment of entering the four attainment levels (*samapattis*) of the formless realm (*aruppadhatu*), up to the stage of accomplishing the "cessation of thoughts and feelings" (*sanna-vedayita-nirodha-samapatti*).[14] In contrast, Mahasi and his movement have maintained that merely entering into absorption in the first *jhana* provides the practitioner with a sufficient level of one-pointed tranquility. Further, they have said that this lesser requisite degree of proficiency in *samatha* can be gained in the course of one's *vipassana* training, thus obviating the need for the typically long and arduous preparatory exercises in *samatha* and thereby shortening and simplifying the path.

This leads us to the second noteworthy aspect of Mahasi Sayadaw's mindfulness technique: the promise of quick results. If practiced vigorously enough, advocates say, it can lead a person to *nibbana* in this very life. Taking seriously similar statements made in the *Mahasatipatthana Sutta*, Mahasi once said, "It will not take long to achieve the object, but possibly in a month, or 20 days, or 15 days, or on rare occasions even in seven days for a selected few with extraordinary perfection." The "object" to which he refers is nothing other than *nibbana* itself.[15] The initial "taste of *nibbana*" signals the attainment of "stream-entry" (*sotapatti*), the first of the four levels of realization that make the meditator a "noble person" (*ariya-puggala*)[16] destined for liberation from *samsara* within seven lifetimes at the most. The claim that liberation from suffering can be reached within a month or less is an extraordinary one, especially given the widespread view among most modern Theravada traditionalists that it is almost impossible for anyone to become an *ariya-puggala* in modern times.[17] But Mahasi's movement has identified hundreds of his followers as gainers of stream-entry (*sotapannas*), and many are said to have attained the higher three stages as well.[18]

Finally, Mahasi Sayadaw not only provided the Theravada world with a simple meditation method but also was a major force in developing the model of the urban meditation center; this became a catalyst for the spread of meditation among the laity.[19] The impact of this contribution is difficult to overestimate. Buddhists have traditionally maintained that meditation is a difficult and potentially dangerous endeavor that should be undertaken only under proper guidance, usually in the environment of a monk living in a sangha community.[20] Before the modern meditation revival, there were almost no possibilities for householders to engage in meditation; indeed, meditation practice itself was relatively rare even within the sangha. But, in the climate of the Buddhist revival movement, renowned masters hastened to provide facilities for householders to practice, establishing networks of retreat centers led by their disciples, in which laypersons and foreigners could practice meditation alongside ordained monks.[21] This led even the traditionalists to offer meditation courses for their householder patrons.[22] Thus, Mahasi was a force igniting the widespread introduction of meditation for the laity, and this trend was "the greatest single change to have come over Buddhism in Sri Lanka (and indeed the other Theravada countries) since the Second World War."[23]

Missionary Buddhism

Go now, O Bhikkhus, and wander, for the gain of the many, for the welfare of the many, out of compassion for the world, for the good, for the gain, and for the welfare of gods and men. Let not two of you go the same way, Preach, O Bhikkhus, the doctrine which is glorious in the beginning, glorious in the middle, glorious in the end.[24]

Tradition holds that the Buddha gave his monks these instructions in his own lifetime, and thus established Buddhism as a missionary religion from its very beginnings. Buddhist history still recalls the specific monks who brought the faith across the trade routes and mountain passes to span all the regions of Asia. In many places the transmission of Buddhism occurred repeatedly, adding new texts, ritual traditions, and spiritual practices. As for Southeast Asia, between the eleventh and fifteenth centuries the great kingdoms of the region sent missions to Sri Lanka from which monks traveled back to Southeast Asia to establish the now normative Pali Theravada tradition of the Sinhala Mahavihara line.[25]

But, by the late colonial era, Buddhist missionary practice in Asia had become moribund. Mahasi Sayadaw's constant travels to Theravada countries (and sometimes non-Theravada countries) reintroduced a central Buddhist practice, the liberating method of insight meditation (*vipassana*), affirming that the tradition still had great teachers, a missionary ethos, and a compelling spiritual refuge, even for householders. Mahasi referred to his voyages as journeys of *dhamma-vijaya* (victory of the Buddhist doctrine), and they certainly rekindled the revival of the tradition, a movement that his disciples brought to the West.

References

Gombrich, R.F. (1991) *Buddhist Precept and Practice: Traditional Buddhism in the Rural Highlands of Ceylon*, Motilal Banarsidass, Delhi.

Gombrich, R.F. and Obeyesekere, G. (1988) *Buddhism Transformed: Religious Change in Sri Lanka*, Princeton University Press, Princeton, NJ.

Scharf, R.H. (1995) Buddhist modernism and the rhetoric of meditative experience. *Numen*, 42 (3), 228–83.

Silanandabhibumsa, A. (1982) *Venerable Mahasi Sayadaw: Biography* (trans. U.M. Swe), Buddha Sāsana Nuggaha Organization, Rangoon.

Spiro, M.E. (1982) *Buddhism and Society: A Great Tradition and Its Burmese Vicissitudes*, University of California Press, Berkeley.

Swearer, D.K. (1989) Buddhism in Southeast Asia, in *The Religious Traditions of Asia* (ed. J.M. Kitagawa), Macmillan, New York, 119–47.

Swearer, D.K. (1995) *The Buddhist World of Southeast Asia*, SUNY Press, Albany.

Further Reading

Carrithers, M. (1979) The modern ascetics of Sri Lanka and the pattern of change in Buddhism. *Man*, 14 (2), 294–310.

Gombrich, R.F. (1988) *Theravāda Buddhism: A Social History from Ancient Banares to Modern Colombo*, Routledge & Kegan Paul, London.

Ray, R.A. (1994) *Buddhist Saints in India: A Study in Buddhist Values and Orientations*, Oxford University Press, Oxford.

Sayadaw, M. (1971) *The Satipaṭṭhāna Vipassanā Mediation*, Unity Press, San Francisco.

Tambiah, S. (1984) *The Buddhist Saints of the Forest and the Cult of Amulets*, Cambridge University Press, Cambridge.

Notes

1   The details of Mahasi Sayadaw's biography are primarily drawn from Silanandabhibumsa (1982).
2   These practices are known as *dhutangas*, which literally means "the means of shaking off (defilements)." 1. wearing patched-up robes; 2. wearing only three robes; 3. going for alms without exception; 4. not omitting any house while going for alms; 5 eating at one sitting; 6. eating only from the alms bowl; 7. refusing all further food; 8. living in the forest; 9. living under a tree; 10. living in the open air; 11. living in a cemetery; 12. being satisfied with whatever dwelling; 13. sleeping in the sitting position (and never lying down).
3   A Sayadaw, meaning "royal teacher," is a senior monk or abbot of a monastery.
4   Pali: *bojjhanga*.
5   Silanandabhibumsa 1982: 94–5.
6   Silanandabhibumsa 1982: 110.
7   In the mid-1960s, there arose a major controversy brought forth by a group of scholar-monks from Sri Lanka regarding the orthopraxy of Mahasi's mindfulness technique and the results that were claimed for practitioners of it. Their critique will be discussed below.
8   Spiro 1982: 322.
9   Swearer 1995: 47.
10 Swearer 1995: 48.
11 Swearer 1995: 48.
12 Gombrich 1991: 315.
13 Scharf 1995: 255–7.
14 This is the position held by the Sri Lankan scholar-monks who launched the already cited vehement opposition, in the late 1950s and early 1960s, to Mahasi's teaching method.
15 Mahasi Sayadaw cited in Scharf 1995: 256.
16 Scharf 1995: 256.
17 Scharf 1995: 256.
18 Scharf 1995: 256.
19 Scharf 1995: 256.
20 Scharf 1995: 256.
21 Scharf 1995: 257.
22 Scharf 1995: 257.
23 Gombrich and Obeyesekere 1988: 237, as cited in Scharf 1995: 257.
24 *Vinaya Mahavagga* I.112–13.
25 Swearer 1989: 119.

17

Corporal Monk

Venerable Sudinna's Journey from the Sri Lankan Army to the Buddhist Sangha[1]

Daniel W. Kent

Editor's Introduction

This chapter presents the life story of Venerable Sudinna, who fought as a soldier in Sri Lanka's civil war before ordaining as a Buddhist monk. While it is centered on the issue of Buddhism and violence, especially those who support and engage in warfare, Kent's case study on a man who joined the sangha in midlife illustrates one of the meanings of the sangha: being a refuge for individuals. The man ordained as Sudinna after a traumatic injury was sensitized in a profound way to the reality of suffering and the need for "serving the Buddha" by adopting compassion and loving kindness as a new orientation for his life. Through this account of Sudinna's eventual path to join the sangha, we see how the serious reckoning of karma in life is central to the Buddhist worldview. Also noteworthy is how the subject, though enculturated from birth as a Sri Lankan Buddhist householder, had never even heard of the central doctrinal formulation "three marks of existence" (suffering, impermanence, no soul/ego – often featured in introductory college courses) until he had sought advanced understanding of the dharma. The problematic violent expressions of "Buddhist nationalism" hover prominently in the background of this striking biography.

Introduction

The shot that took the young corporal's foot was unexpected. He was not on the front line of a battle against the Liberation Tigers of Tamil Eelam, the rebel group that was seeking a separate independent Tamil nation in the north and east of Sri Lanka. The corporal had fought in the north and had fought in the east, but he had never received as much as a scratch. One day a mortar round had landed right next to him but failed to explode. No, the corporal wasn't injured in battle, but while sitting in his barracks when one of his own comrades accidentally discharged his weapon. The injury didn't seem that bad at first. The foot could have been saved, but a doctors'

Buddhists: Understanding Buddhism Through the Lives of Practitioners, First Edition. Edited by Todd Lewis.
© 2014 John Wiley & Sons, Ltd. Published 2014 by John Wiley & Sons, Ltd.

strike left the hospital understaffed and no one changed his dressings for nine days. It was karma, he explained. The doctors amputated his foot at the calf, ending his career as a soldier and beginning a journey that would lead him, clad in the saffron robes of a Buddhist monk, to the remote and dusty slopes of a hermitage.

The topic of Buddhist involvement in war has received very little attention until recently. Scholars assumed a fundamental disjunction between a Buddhist religion of world renunciation and any acts of intentional killing. This assumption was not without basis: the first precept taken by Buddhist monks and laypeople alike is, "I take the training to refrain from the destruction of life." How could a religion with such a foundation be involved with warfare in any way?

In his widely read introduction to Buddhist thought, *What the Buddha Taught*, Walpola Rahula writes:

> According to Buddhism there is nothing that can be called a "just war" – which is only a false term coined and put into circulation to justify and excuse hatred, cruelty, violence and massacre. Who decides what is just or unjust? The mighty and the victorious are "just," and the weak and the defeated are "unjust." Our war is always "just," and your war is always "unjust." Buddhism does not accept this position.[2]

Paul Demiéville, who was a friend of Rahula, echoed these sentiments in his 1957 article, "Le bouddhisme et la guerre," on Japanese warrior monks. Emphasizing this Buddhist commitment to nonviolence, Demiéville said: "Not killing is a characteristic so anchored in Buddhism that it is practically considered a custom."[3] Rahula's and Demiéville's approaches to Buddhism and war set the tone for future scholarship on the subject; they established Buddhism and war as a contradiction that must be resolved.

Indeed, that is exactly what most contemporary studies of Buddhism and war attempt to do: reconcile the perceived conflict between Buddhism and war. The most comprehensive approach to this problem to date is found in Tessa Bartholomeusz's *In Defense of Dharma*. This work attempts to piece together an implicit just-war theory from canonical and postcanonical Pali texts, Sri Lankan newspapers from the past century, and a small sample of ethnographic interviews conducted over the summers of 1997 and 1999. The primary goal of Bartholomeusz's work is to argue against the simplistic image of Buddhism as a religion of peace. *In Defense of Dharma* provides and refutes the historical background for the creation of a dichotomy between "peaceful Buddhists" and "warlike Christians," demythologizing these polarized conceptions. Locating definitions of Buddhism as a pacifist religion in the anti-Christian rhetoric of late nineteenth-century Buddhists, it deconstructs Buddhism as a monolithic force for pacifism and makes room, for the first time, for a serious discussion of Buddhist participation in war.

Her question "Does Buddhism have a just-war theory?" quickly proves to be ill-suited to the Sri Lankan Buddhist context, however. Early on in her work, one of her informants explains that "just as there is no chicken curry recipe in the Pali Canon, there is no just war ideology."[4] Bartholomeusz presents this anecdote as an example of the resistance she faced during her research, brushing it off as just the ranting of a conservative Sri Lankan scholar reacting to her own status as a Christian Sri Lankan American. Ignoring the repeated protests of her interview subjects, Bartholomeusz presses forward in her quest for a just-war theory implicit in the stories that Buddhists tell about war.

To be fair, it is very difficult to talk about warfare without using the term "justification." The word has a way of slipping in whenever one thinks about the decision made by a state to engage in sanctioned violence. Justification, however, is not the best term for understanding Buddhist participation in warfare. "Justification" presupposes a universal judge or standard by which warfare is made "just." Buddhist thought, however, does not have this ethical standard by which a generalized activity such as warfare can be judged "right" or "wrong." In other words, as I have argued elsewhere,[5] our approach to Buddhist engagement in warfare should not begin with a search for objective "justification" but with an exploration of Buddhist interpretations of war. While Buddhist doctrine may not specifically assign a general moral valuation to war, it does have a tool that lends itself well to the evaluation of individual actions performed during war: karma and *vipaka*, action and consequence. In other words, while Buddhist monks will always judge war in general negatively, as does Rahula, the doctrine of karma allows them the space to evaluate the individual actions of soldiers.

Viewing war through the lens of karma, however, does not help us to resolve the conflict between Buddhist teachings and war. This leads to the larger question of why it must be resolved at all. What if, instead of attempting to resolve this perceived conflict, we accepted Rupert Gethin's assertion that "being human, Buddhists are as capable of hypocrisy, double standards and special pleading as anyone else"?[6] In this chapter, I will present the life story of Venerable Sudinna, who lived the life of a soldier before becoming a monk. Sudinna's biography does not provide us with a solution to the conflict between Buddhism and war, but gives us insight into how one monk perceives the actions of soldiers from a Buddhist perspective. Sudinna does not justify war, but neither does he promote it. He describes his actions in war in karmic terms. Approaching the subject with an attitude of renunciation, viewing it as another flawed aspect of the universe that Buddhists call *samsara*. As one of Bartholomeusz's research subjects opined, "Are you asking if Buddhists can go to war? Yes, to protect the country and to protect the religion. *But war is a matter of karma – that's why when there is war, all bad things done in the past come back to corrupt us – this is why there is war. In the past, too, karma resulted in war.*"[7]

A Forest Monastic Sanctuary

Arannagala is built on a hillside at the end of a long and dusty road through the jungle. At the bottom of the hill sits a *dana salava*, a reception hall, where laity can prepare and distribute alms to the monks of the hermitage. From the reception hall, a red dirt path leads up into the thickly wooded hillside toward the simple red *kuti*, or shelters, where the monks reside. Venerable Sudinna stood out from the monks lined up to receive rice and curry in their begging bowls, walking with the aid of crutches and a plastic prosthetic foot.

Life at Arannagala is quiet. The monks in residence don't hold any large festivals, preaching ceremonies, or classes for the laity. Sudinna, who is the acknowledged head of the community, tries to maintain an atmosphere in which the monks can pursue meditation as suits their own inclination. Sudinna explains that he does not force anyone to meditate, he simply tries to be a "good friend," a *kalyani mitta*, in the pursuit of liberation.

After finishing his alms, Venerable Sudinna led my research assistant and me up the hillside, away from the alms hall, for our chat. We sat on the ground and Sudinna sat on a white plastic chair, an odd site in the wooded surroundings. Sudinna was gregarious but mindful. After I asked a question, he would think a moment and then begin speaking, giving long and detailed answers, peppered with anecdotes and references to the Pali Canon. It was clear that Sudinna would rather speak about Buddhist teachings than himself and I had to frequently bring him back to the topic of his life after he had segued into discussions about the dharma. What follows is an abridged and organized account of our two-and-a-half-hour conversation.

Q: Tell us about how you spend your days here at Arannagala.

A: We ring the bell at 5:00 in the morning. Then everyone comes here to the reception hall and worships the triple gem and chants suttas. At 5:30 or 5:45 the laypeople make gruel for us. We then eat the gruel along with some sweets. After that we spend about 30 minutes cleaning the grounds together. Then we go to our chambers and each person does what he likes. Some perform walking meditation, some read books, and some bathe. Lord Buddha taught that if an obstacle appears in oneself then one must identify it and then act to get rid of it. That action is known as *bhavana*, or meditation. So each person acts accordingly. Then we ring the bell at 10:45, when visitors come from outside. At 11:00 we preach and eat *dana* [alms food]. Then there is cleaning until 12:30 when everyone returns to their chambers. After that there is an *Abhidharma* [systematic philosophy] class from 1:00 until 2:00. Then every day from 2:00 to 2:30 I advise the others how to nurture wholesome dharma and mental happiness. After 2:30 those who didn't bathe in the morning bathe and some monks wash their robes while others read or meditate. Later, the little monks pick flowers and arrange them on the altar. After 5:45 in the evening we ring the bell and everyone gathers here to worship. After worshipping, chanting, and practicing *metta* [loving kindness] meditation, we have an evening snack at 7:00 and go to the hall or to the rock to meditate. Some meditate while sitting and some meditate while walking. After we go to meditate we lose track of time. We might meditate until ten, eleven, one or two in the morning. Some days we even meditate until dawn. Some days if we feel tired, I will read the *suttas* from the *suttapitaka* to the others. I tell them about the value of human life, the ways in which the *arhats* spent their time in *samsara*, and heroic stories of monks.

Q: How did you come to join the army?

A: My mother didn't want me to join the army. I put in my application secretly and left home to join.

Q: How were you injured?

A: I wasn't injured on the battlefield. I went to war. I went everywhere, but I was never harmed there. One day a mortar landed only a few feet away from us, but the fuse had gone out and I was saved. If it wasn't for that, there would have been nothing left of me, but then this happened [pointing at his prosthetic foot], when someone's gun went off while I was working inside. My foot could have been saved, but there was a doctor's strike. They didn't change my dressing for nine days and when they took my dressing off, the whole thing was gangrenous. That's why this happened. It was karma.

After my leg was shot, I had to have it amputated from mid-calf down. I stayed in the hospital for a year for treatment. Back then I still didn't have any ideas about the dharma. I would play games with my friends and just enjoy life. Honestly, I didn't really feel any special *dukkha* [suffering] about life. I wasn't sad. Even though I had lost my leg, I wasn't sad.

I got to go to different courses with the other disabled guys. We were asked to apply for classes so I applied for an electronics class. During the class we stayed at a camp in Colombo. It wasn't just guys from one regiment, but there were disabled people from all regiments there. There were 40 guys in our barracks and we had a lot of fun. On Saturdays and Sundays we didn't have classes so we would go out. Some would go watch movies. I would go to everything.

It was around that time that I met a corporal named Madu, who was very different from the rest. He didn't go to watch movies. He didn't go roaming about. When we would go to watch movies he would go to Keleniya temple with a big bunch of flowers.

Every day I would secretly take the Five Precepts before going to bed. I did it secretly because the other guys would have teased me if they saw. On the days that I drank I wouldn't take the Five Precepts. One day we went to a party at the Second Battalion. We drank a lot that night and the next day I had a big headache. When I went to iron my pants, Madu was already there. While I was waiting with my pants on my shoulder for him to finish, he turned to me and asked, "Why do you drink that fire water?" When asked that, my heart felt like it had been hit. I just went back to my bed without ironing my pants and thought, "Really, why do I drink? What kind of comfort do I get from that? Why do I drink? Do I just drink because other people drink? If I am drinking for comfort, have I received that comfort?" I asked myself those questions. "If I have been drinking for comfort then I should have gotten it by now. How long have I been drinking?" Then I saw that we all are searching for comfort and happiness. However, no one had ever received comfort or happiness. I just sat there by myself and thought, "How can one really receive comfort in this world. One dies. One gets sick. We say that we are Buddhists. We say that the Lord Buddha preached the Four Noble Truths."

In those days I didn't know the Four Noble Truths about suffering and its eradication. I had written about it in tests, but I didn't remember it. Afterward, I wrote in my diary that I would never again take intoxicating substances. I remember it well: it was October 14, 1992.

The next morning, I decided that I should try associating with Madu and stopped going out with the other guys, going to the temple with him instead. When we were going to the temple he started to tell me, "It doesn't matter what we do. Everything is impermanent." Even though he said that, it didn't stick with me. I didn't really understand. One day at Keleniya temple, I heard a layman preach a sermon. He said "There is no 'I,'" "There is no 'mine,'" and "There is no such thing as a soul." I was very surprised to hear that.

Madu didn't eat any meat or fish so I stopped eating them, too. He didn't go drinking so I stopped. He didn't go see movies, so I stopped that too. Now, look at the way that this society is made. Every one of my friends in the barracks started to berate Madu. They accused him of ruining me. They complained that I never went out with them or played cards anymore. Madu didn't pay any attention, though.

While we were in technical school, they would send our food in a basket with our name written on it. What did those rascals do? Once they put a piece of meat underneath my rice before sending it to me. While I was eating they snatched this food and showed it to the other guys. They said, "Look! This guy says that he is taking the precepts, but he's really secretly eating meat!" I just stayed quiet.

Q: Tell us about your ordination.

A: I took the precepts all the time. I would go without vacation and get a pass to take the precepts on the full moon days. Lots of guys teased me. According to my experience, no matter what, if one tries then one can succeed and do wholesome things in society. When I took precepts, some people called me "Lord Monk" or "Mr. Layman." Some days when I got up in the morning, there would be taunts written on the board like, "There is a Buddha alive today!" and "He will tell the future! Bring flowers and lamps!" I didn't get angry at them, but I submitted a letter asking to be transferred to a regiment near my village. After I was transferred, I was able to commute from home to work. I would go to work in the morning and then come home for lunch.

I used to read a lot of novels and stories, but then I stopped and instead started reading the *Tipitika* [lit. "Three Baskets," meaning the three parts of the Pali Canon]. I even started to read philosophy books by Krishnamurti and even Socrates. Later I made a habit of going to work in the morning and then going to the temples in the evening. I wouldn't go home in the afternoon, I would just go straight to the temples. On those days I would stay at the Bodhi Tree in Anuradhapura until 7:00 or 8:00 p.m. Then I would go to my sister's house over there and go back to work from there in the morning. The next day I would go back to the temples and stay at my sister's again. Some days I would go to Ruvanvelisaya at 2:00 in the afternoon. It was so hot, but I would bow down on those hot rocks saying, "May my life be offered for Lord Buddha!"

By then I was taking the precepts on all four monthly Poya days[8] and meditating a lot. My heart was very focused. Even when I was traveling by bus, I wouldn't let my heart stray. However, I still didn't know the importance of the ordained life. I didn't know how important this dharma was for a person's life. Actually, I am not someone who ordained out of great disgust for life. It just came like a wave from my previous habits in *samsara*. Those words by my friend became the cause that led me to this place. He just said a small thing, "Why do you drink that fire water?" but it was those words that led me here, to this place. All he did was say those few words, and even today I treat him as my teacher. He's married now, but I still go to preach to him when I can.

Even then I didn't think about ordaining. No one wanted me to retire from the army back then, but I wanted to be free. Parents don't like it when their children are impoverished so I secretly put in my retirement papers. They wouldn't just give my pension to my mother so I opened a joint account with her and had my pension checks deposited in the bank. After that I gave my mother an ATM card so that she could withdraw the money.

Since my leg was mangled, at first I thought I couldn't ordain.[9] So I just took the Ten Precepts. My mind reached *samadhi*. I didn't have a teacher. My only teacher was the *Tipitika*. So I just looked at the *Tipitika* and acted according to it. I looked at *suttas* and acted accordingly. I think that is why I haven't made any mistakes. When I needed the meaning of the dharma, I looked for it in the *Tipitika*. Sometimes it didn't fit. So I decided that I was wrong. I don't think that there are errors in the *Tipitika*. That is to say, if my idea of the dharma was right then I wouldn't have remained in *samsara* this long. The *Tipitika* can't be wrong. If I continued searching while thinking this way, I would find where my mistake was. I meditated like that for seven months.

Q: Where did you meditate?

A: In our back yard. There was a big forest there. I still wasn't ordained yet, but I lived like an ascetic. After that first seven months, I went to Ritigala to meditate with the monks there. I had visited there while in the army as well. The head monk asked me who my teacher was and I told him that I didn't have a teacher and that I was meditating by myself. The head monk told me that there is a proper lineage in the *sasana*;[10] he said, "You need a teacher. I will ordain you so then you can meditate." Then and there he tied the belt of my robes around my neck and ordained me in accord with the *sasana*. My teacher was criticized a great deal for ordaining me because of my foot.

He's passed away now, but if my teacher were alive today he would be happy because I am doing a great service to the *sasana*. I am the one who teaches all of the monks here. If you try there is nothing in this world that you cannot do. I arrived where I am today through effort. I have another thing to say: when we think about Buddhism, some experience arises. But it is no good to make any decisions based upon that experience alone. That's because you can't say at once whether that decision is correct or not. That's because we have books that have come down to us through a lineage of teachers. We must compare our experiences with the teachings in these books and see whether they match or not.

Q: **How did you come to live here?**

A: When I ordained, I felt that many temple monks don't meditate seriously. While the head monk is out doing external activities, we can't meditate. And it is no good for a student to meditate [unsupervised] while the head monk works. It is no good for us to just do external activities. So a few of us monks got together and created a place in Horana. It was just a temple in the middle of a rubber grove, but it was very busy. Donors came and went. There were too many roads. There were too many houses. It wasn't a big forest. We couldn't calm our minds. So we decided to move to a hermitage and invited another group of monks to take over our temple in Horana. We didn't take anything. We just took a few books. Afterward we went to a place connected to Ritigala. We stayed there, but there were too many outside interruptions there as well. We moved twice more, but it was always too busy. We had to go to almsgivings, chanting ceremonies, and funerals. So we decided to build our own place and came here. At that time there weren't any roads. It was just a forest surrounded on all sides by rice fields. In this forest there were just wood thieves with platforms set up for splitting logs. We took the boards from those platforms, made little beds, and four or five of us monks started to stay here. We received our alms through begging and people gradually started to come to listen to our sermons. The people coming here built these facilities. In the beginning we had to work hard. Now there is a secretary here. I just wanted to make a very basic place. The shelter cells that we have here are enough.

Q: **What sort of advice would you as a monk give your old self, the soldier?**

A: The army is just a job, not one's entire life. That is to say, a person must keep some space for their humanity. I don't think that the army is a place for practicing *metta* meditation. I also can't say that it is good. I don't have the right to say that. However, life is not just that [the army]. I say that no matter what job one does, one must leave some space for virtue and the dharma. No matter if one is in the army or some other job, a person must leave space for virtue. One must keep one's virtue close. One must feel the *dukkha* of others. In that way, one must be a person who believes in the next life. No matter whether one is in the army or somewhere else, one must understand inside one's heart the difference between good and bad. We do everything to avoid *dukkha*. However, we can't be free of *dukkha*. One needs to preserve inside oneself the ability to find the end of *dukkha*. That is my advice. It is wrong to take the army as one's personal identity. That is to say ... It is wrong to think, "I am in the army. Soldiers don't take the precepts." It's like that.

Q: **If I were to come to you and tell you that I was joining the army, what would you say to me?**

A: [laughs] I wouldn't tell someone not to join the army nor would I tell someone to join the army. If someone told me that they were joining the army, I would say, "Do what you can." As a monk, I have no right to say anything about that. As a monk, I have no right to tell you to join or not. However, if a person were to ask me about the dharma, I would explain the dharma. I don't say whether joining the army is wholesome or unwholesome. I don't say that everything that one does as a soldier is wholesome. There are ways of serving in the army by which one can create good karma, in the medical corps, for example.

My friend, Madu, told me this story. He had been to a dangerous area in the northeast. He told me that every day when he picked up his weapon he would think, may no one be harmed by me today. He had that intention. There are characters like that in the army. So, the problem is that not everyone can remain in that mindset. There are some who do that job because of financial problems. There are some for whom the job is their life. We can't say that a person's life is completely wrong. There is also a side that should be seen according to human reality. All I have to say to a person like that is, "Do what you like." I don't say and have no right to approve or disapprove.

Q: If a soldier shoots at the enemy on the battlefield, does a negative karma occur?

A: *Cetana bhikkhave kammam vadami*. Intention becomes karma. You must accept that Lord Buddha has said that if someone makes a mistake in one's life then unwholesome karma occurs. We need to divide this question into parts. There could be a concept that fighting on behalf of one's country is a good thing, but that is not the truth. That is to say, it is not true that unwholesome karma does not collect when one fights on behalf of the country. One must first divide wholesome karma and unwholesome karma. It would be good to think this way. "Can a soldier shoot another person while practicing *metta* meditation?" If he were doing that, how could he kill? Could one kill without obstruction or displeasure? One must not measure something according to the knowledge of a person but according to the dharma. When one goes to perform an action, one must look into the mind in the background. One must look at the thoughts associated with this mind. There is desire, hatred, delusion, and obstruction in it. I think that unwholesome karma occurs when one shoots at the enemy with this kind of mind. One must think of and treat one's enemy as if he were one's only child. In that way, one must spread a mind of loving kindness to one's enemies. If that were the case, would a mother or father shoot their only son? No. So if one were truly in a mindset of *metta* one would not have any enemies. If one does have enemies then they are one's own impure thoughts.

Q: Many other monks I spoke with told me that killing doesn't produce negative karma. Why do you think they said that?

A: It could be ignorance. However, more likely it is because of their own personal beliefs rather than ignorance. That is because they think about the present situation and think that speaking in a nationalist way is good. However, it is my nature to preach the dharma as it is. Otherwise I just remain silent. I would never preach the dharma incorrectly; not for my country, not for myself, nor for my mother and father.

References

Bartholomeusz, T.J. (2002) *In Defense of Dharma: Just-War Ideology in Buddhist Sri Lanka*, Routledge-Curzon, London and New York.

Demiéville, P. (1957) Le bouddhisme et la guerre. Post-scriptum à l'"Histoire des moines guerriers du Japon" de Gaston Renondeau [Buddhism and warfare: postscript to "The history of the monk-warriors of Japan"]. *Mélanges publiés par l'Institut des Hautes Etudes chinoises*, 1, 347–85.

Gethin, R. (2004) Can killing a living being ever be an act of compassion? The analysis of the act of killing in the Abhidhamma and Pali Commentaries. *Journal of Buddhist Ethics*, 11, 167–202.

Kent, D. (2010) Onward Buddhist soldiers: preaching to the Sri Lankan army, in *Buddhist Warfare* (ed. M.K. Jerryson and M. Juergensmeyer), Oxford University Press, Oxford and New York.

Rahula, W. (1974) *What the Buddha Taught*, rev. edn, Grove Press, New York.

Notes

1 The interview on which this chapter is based took place on March 9, 2007 at Venerable Sudinna's hermitage. Given the sensitive nature of this information, personal and place names have been changed to protect anonymity. The research was sponsored by a Fulbright-Hayes dissertation research grant and a Charlotte W. Newcombe Doctoral Dissertation Fellowship.
2 Rahula 1974: 84.
3 Demiéville 1957: 18.
4 Bartholomeusz 2002: 16.
5 Kent 2010.
6 Gthin 2004: 63.
7 Bartholomeusz 2002: 12.
8 These are the full and no moon days, then both eighth lunar days in the waxing and waning moon cycles.
9 It is against Buddhist monastic disciplinary rules to ordain someone who is disabled or disfigured in any way.
10 A Pali term with many meanings, including "Buddhist tradition."

18

The Lure of Renunciation and the Ways of the World
Maechii Wabi of Thailand

Sid Brown

Editor's Introduction

Learning about Wabi's life opens up consideration of just what circumstances draw individuals to seek the monastic life, as well as how difficult it can be for some to remain in the communal setting. The pressure that society exerts on women to be contributors to family life, to settle into marriage, and have their own children is the dominant norm in Asia (and all societies). Even when an individual such as Wabi has direct evidence from her life about the shortcomings of husbands and fathers, and the unequal treatment of women householders, we can see here, as elsewhere in this volume, that family life exerts a strong pull. Serving one's parents is a moral expectation for all Buddhists, including monks.

Wabi's life also helps us to look inside the Theravada Buddhist monastic world, one in which women cannot become fully ordained nuns (*bhikkhuni*) and hence be fully respected and supported monastics. The role that has been created in Thailand is what Wabi's early life led her to, that of a *maechii*. Although new organizations have been created to support these dedicated women in furthering their education, aiding their meditation cultivation, and generating material support, we discover that this semimonastic role is tenuous. Financial resources are still necessary to take the vows and live communally, and *maechii* can find themselves acting as little more than servants for male monastics. Finally, considering Wabi's life demands that we see clearly how Buddhism always exists in specific social and environmental contexts. Gender, socioeconomic status, nationality, and birthplace all contributed not only to Wabi's view of Buddhism but also to her engagement with its institutions. Just as there are many lifestyles that can be taken on by "good Buddhists," we should not be surprised when individuals shift between them as they negotiate their lives.

Buddhists: Understanding Buddhism Through the Lives of Practitioners, First Edition. Edited by Todd Lewis.
© 2014 John Wiley & Sons, Ltd. Published 2014 by John Wiley & Sons, Ltd.

Introduction

The abbess of the *samnak chii*[1] in which I was living in Thailand smiled and nodded in approval when it became clear I was going to spend a lot of time with Maechii Wabi,[2] a light-skinned Thai nun with almond eyes and a ready though shy laugh. Her gentle, humble demeanor was respected in the hundred-person, all-women community; she was known to be pious and careful in her speech and actions. Her seat at the very front of the meditation hall for daily meditation, chanting, and more formal rituals communicated to everyone the relatively lengthy time she had spent committed fully to the Buddhist path. When I met her she had been a *maechii* for ten years.[3]

For months and months I interviewed her; we also spent time working together, in tasks such as cutting the grass of the *samnak chii* with small hand scythes, helping the cooks, working to reestablish a mushroom-growing hut, and going on outings related to my personal and research needs. The central question I returned to all that time and in all those contexts was: why had Wabi become a *maechii*? I returned repeatedly to that central question, going so far as to invite her to make a list and explain to me the most important incidents from her life that she felt had led her to ordain. I also investigated reasons for her ordination about which she might have been less aware, such as those related to social and environmental issues.

The Path to Ordination

The simplest answer to why Wabi ordained is that she was experientially convinced of the value of Buddhist practices. For example, early on, when she was only seven or eight years old, simple versions of the practices (repeating "Buddho, buddho") helped "to calm her heart." She learned this simple form of concentration meditation[4] when she and her mother went to the temple as a traditional practice in Thailand for special lunar days;[5] and, when she ran around playing with her friends, she secretly repeated this word referring to the Buddha and found that it calmed and rewarded her. But this first answer is not a full answer because it does not take into consideration the area in which she was born and raised, in Isaan, northeastern Thailand, a difficult place to live because of its hot, dry climate. While most people in that area then and now farm for a living, its climate is not conducive to bountiful harvests; droughts are frequent, and Wabi's family was not alone when it had to water down its rice to stretch the little food available as far as possible. In addition, her family was quite poor because her father left the family when Wabi was nine years old, leaving her mother to work the fields, care for her children, and do other work such as sell food to make ends meet. Wabi saw family life as an everyday challenge for women like her mother.

The difficulties facing householders in Isaan fell to Wabi herself directly. She was forced to drop out of school at age 12, having completed sixth grade. At that time the government only required its citizens to be educated through fourth grade, so Wabi was lucky to get as much education as she did. Her older brother, however, got more education, despite its cost and the burden it placed on the family. Not only was his work missed in the fields but also his transportation, uniforms, and school supplies drained the family coffers. At the same time, Wabi worked alone in her family's fields every morning. Daily she brought prepared food to sell at the school she had once attended, and daily she cared for her younger siblings, making sure they were safe, fed, and loved. She watched and suffered the results of the gender bias as her brother went off to school while she worked hard every day just to support the family.

This difficult daily round, defined by growing, selling, and eating food, eventually seemed meaningless to Wabi. Alone frequently, or sharing the company only of young children, she grew depressed and often questioned the meaning of this harsh subsistence: Why do these same things day after day? Why live only to grow crops to feed people, in an endless, repetitive round? What else is there? What else could there be?

These questions drew Wabi to explore another aspect of Isaan besides its dry climate and poor agricultural features. This area of Thailand is also known for its rich Buddhist tradition. If you ask any Thai person where in that country one can find those who take Buddhist vows the most seriously and who can best teach about Buddhist meditation from experience, you will be directed to go to Isaan. The Thai forest monastic tradition (exemplified by such internationally famous monks as Ajahn Chah, for example) was born and thrived here. Thus, when Wabi was disenchanted with her family life's harshness, her father's abandonment, and her daily routine of meaningless work, she did not have to look far to see what Buddhism offered in its stead.

The possibility of renouncing family life haunted her; it was, after all, what her father had done to her own family. While the first time he had left Wabi's mother and children he had left to create a householder life with another woman, when he left that family, he ordained as a monk. This renunciant alternative to householder life that played such a role in explaining her family's situation led Wabi to wonder how a renunciant's experience of the world might be different from hers. She wondered whether the life of a renunciant might offer more meaning, more purpose. She wondered whether such a life would nurture her in a way that others seemed to be nurtured by family life.

Another factor in her biography was that, in her teen years, she had recurrent and powerful inner auditory experiences: she repeatedly heard the sound of a razor blade scraping a person's scalp. This sound she associated with ordination since it requires that men and women shave their heads in going forth "to homelessness" as a monastic. Once living as monks and nuns, they must also shave their heads each month on the day before the full moon. She repeatedly asked her mother what the scraping sound was, but her mother would tell her she heard nothing. Others laughed at her for what appeared to them to be foolishness, and this mockery deepened her feelings of loneliness and isolation.

Wabi about this time created an ornate altar in her house, and she started to lead her family and friends in evening chanting in front of it. She started wearing white and following additional Buddhist precepts on the holy day of each week. Many Buddhists periodically take the five basic precepts – not killing, stealing, lying, engaging in sexual misconduct, or taking intoxicants – but, when one desires to increase the intensity of one's practice, an individual such as Wabi can add three or four more such as avoiding taking food after noon, refraining from listening to music, or refraining from watching entertainment. In these ways she was defining a different way of living in this world, a way of finding religious meaning. As she watched other girls her age getting married, she defined herself instead as a Buddhist who seeks meaning beyond the family.

After four years of this hard work and isolation (from the time Wabi was 12 until she was 16), Wabi and her mother took their first and only vacation. They went to a serious meditation monastery and meditated in silence every day for most of their waking hours. It was here that Wabi first went forth as a *maechii*, shaving her head and eyebrows and donning long white robes similar to those of monks. Her mother, more interested in an easier transition back to householder life after their seven days than is provided by the slow growing-in of hair from a state of baldness, took the vows of a *phram*,[6] wearing shorter white robes, not shaving her head and eyebrows, and taking fewer vows. Removed from the householder work that she found so meaningless, Wabi engaged in a simple concentration meditation for seven days. She took a vow of silence and stayed awake many hours to engage fully in meditation. As a result, Wabi bloomed. She had never felt such peace, contentment, and joy.

Those seven days answered the question that her father's abandonment of the family had raised; she now knew why a person like her father would choose to "go forth" as a monk. And she knew, indeed, that she, too, would "go forth." The option of avoiding the default path of marriage and childcare in Thai life that she saw women engaging in every day became more real to her. She had "eaten" the misery of the householder's life and tasted the joys of the religious life, and knew which she would choose. A year later, when a young man became interested in Wabi and she was asked what she wanted, her answer was that, if she were forced to marry him, she would run away. Her mother supported her in her decision, unlike the scenario often heard from *maechii* similarly dealing with marriage and their mothers. Wabi was not forced to marry.

But, as long as she lived outside the *samnak* or temple walls, she would be required by her family to help in the household, and, as the workload increased more and more, so did family tensions. Her older sister had a child, but, since the father of the child did not stay to care for it, not only was there another child in need of care but also the tarnishing of the family reputation by the presence of the out-of-wedlock child troubled

Wabi's older brother. The sister then took up with a new man. Wabi was now expected to take on yet more and more childcare – she walked about, working in the fields and selling food, with her sister's daughter on one hip and her brother's daughter on the other hip. She describes her emotional state at that time as "hot all the time." But by then she'd seen another way – a way out of the seemingly futile work of childcare and money-making and family subsistence. She could become a *maechii*; she grew hungrier every day to "go forth" as one.

There was, predictably, family resistance to her plan. The household needed her help, and going forth as a *maechii* meant less help around the house and farm. Further, her mother in particular would be saddened to lose Wabi's company. Even her father, living as a monk some distance away, could not fully support her in following her dream. He pointed out that women going forth did not enjoy the same respect and education that men going forth as monks received.

It is useful at this point to reflect on the limited exposure of her family to women who live as *maechii*. Wabi's father had only known one; in his temple housing five hundred monks and male novices, there was only one *maechii* and she spent all her time essentially doing the same chores Wabi was doing at home – she worked every day in the kitchen, cooking two meals a day for those hundreds of people. This *maechii* neither meditated nor chanted. As far as Wabi's father could tell, this *maechii* did not engage in any activities furthering her own spirituality besides the very activities that women householders in Thailand are expected to do in their family life: serving the needs of others. Wabi herself had only seen a few *maechii* in her life and had never had a long discussion with one.

With so little contact with *maechii*, how was Wabi to determine how to go about making her new life? She approached her father, whom she had neither corresponded with nor visited for some years, except for one short stay at his temple. Her father, while understanding at least part of her desire to go forth, advised Wabi not to do it. Wabi would only lose status as a *maechii*, he warned. But Wabi convinced him to help her, and in the end he recommended that she go to a temple-monastery near Bangkok. It could be a good fit for her as she had an obvious taste for and appreciation of meditation, and this temple had earned a reputation for its vibrant insight meditation tradition. Insight meditation practice usually follows an individual's experience in concentration meditation, and is viewed by modern Theravadin meditation masters as a critical skill for achieving enlightenment. Through insight meditation, a Buddhist understands that she or he can see how things really are – not in the delusory way we perceive them in daily life, muddied by attachment and anger, but simply as they are, according to the Buddha, as unsatisfactory, as changing, and without any permanent essence.[7]

When Wabi's father offered to take her to this temple in Bangkok, she happily accepted his offer. But neither foresaw a cause for immediate concern: the need for money. Going forth as a monk does not require any money, but it is not the same for *maechii*. When they arrived at the temple in Bangkok, they learned that it would cost Wabi 500 baht a month to stay there. She had arrived with only 155 baht. The immediate roadblock to her plans gave rise to panic. What should she do? Try to find a way to live and work in Bangkok, extracting from its bright lights and materialistic splendor the money she needed to go forth? Or go home to Isaan and her family to work and save more money? Both options frightened and repulsed her; she had finally made the break from householder life, from its weary cycles of meaningless labor, so the last thing she wanted was to be forced back to the place and way of life she'd tried to leave behind. There was the option of going to her father's temple, which would seem like a good option as it would allow her to stay in a monastic institution, but she didn't want to live with monks, mostly serving them, and she didn't want to abandon hope of further education. She wanted to live with women like her who were drawn to the religious life, and she hoped that among these women she might find a way to become more educated.

One *maechii* living at this Bangkok temple gave her advice: go forth as a *phram* and practice meditation for seven days in silence. In the midst of the chaos of her life seeming to go awry, just sit. Wabi took this advice, and her father took his leave of her. Now she was alone for the first time in her life. No family was near, and the only future for her that she was certain about was her next seven days of meditation.

Wabi slipped right into the *samnak* schedule. She arose early and sat with the others for meditation and chanting. While initially deeply panicked by the questions of how and where she might live after the week was over, Wabi put aside concerns for her future; again and again, she brought her mind back to her meditation object. There were moments when terror returned and it seemed that her lack of a certain future would compel her back into the life other Thai women have, tied to a husband and children. When these moments arose, however, she focused her mind on the object of meditation. Again and again she put aside the pressing concerns related to the rest of her life and refocused her mind.

Though Wabi sat in silence, those around her talked together about her predicament; her deep desire to live as a *maechii* was evidenced each day as she silently practiced. How might a solution be found for her money problem?

One day a *maechii*, also from Isaan, approached her. This woman, Maechii Seni, had begun teaching meditation in that *samnak* but also ran her own *samnak* in Isaan. Her problem was that, for the time she spent in Bangkok, she left her elderly father and her sister with intellectual and developmental disabilities in her Isaan *samnak* without proper care. Maechii Seni offered Wabi a deal: she could go forth as a *maechii* and live in Maechii Seni's Isaan *samnak*. For free room and board in the *samnak* and a modest salary, she could follow her dream to go forth as a *maechii*. Once again Wabi was to care for others, but this time in a religious context and among supportive women.

Wabi's voice, when she speaks of her benefactor, quivers. Her eyes fill with tears recounting this offer. At a time when she was among strangers and with neither money nor a place to live nor an endurable future path in life, Maechii Seni had found a way to help her achieve her dream. Wabi cries with sadness, however, when recounting the actual ritual of her going forth. Few attended and there was nothing ornate or celebratory. These were not the aspects of the ritual that troubled her, however. What troubled her was her inability to express her generosity on that important occasion. She had held an ideal that she would be able to give special gifts to the monks on this day of days, but she had no money to do so. Someone donated proper robes for her to wear. A *maechii* she hardly knew cut her hair short and then began shaving her head. While holding a lock of her hair in the traditional manner for both monks and *maechii*, she pondered the life she was leaving and the one she was entering.

There followed seven years of the greatest peace she had ever known. Nine months a year, when Maechii Seni was in Bangkok, Maechii Wabi lived in the *samnak* in Isaan, engaged in the usual tasks of its daily activities as well as caring for Maechii Seni's sister and father. Every day she also chanted and meditated. She cut wood from trees for use as cooking fuel and helped clean and maintain the buildings and grounds of the *samnak*. She studied and earned degrees in various aspects of Buddhism. She made sure the father and sister had lunch and dinner and helped them as they needed. Looking back on this time, Maechii Wabi is filled with nostalgia. It was easy to care for the father and sister; she loved the rhythm of the *samnak*, and the work she did there was imbued with purpose. She studied the dhamma and meditated – she spent many hours in meditation after the father and sister went to bed early. In an arrangement common among the *maechii* I knew in Thailand, she spent three months a year, the rainy season, at other temples and *samnaks*. Maechii Seni came from Bangkok and stayed in her *samnak* then, and Maechii Wabi was thus free to travel, meeting and learning from other teachers.

Her Buddhist education and practices during this time formed Maechii Wabi and rewarded her efforts. Her understanding of Buddhist concepts was not the superficial kind that comes from memorization. Rather, she had particular meditation experiences, such as visions, that helped her understand particular Buddhist concepts in deeply personal, unforgettable ways. For example, one rainy season she was at another *samnak* and she felt anger arise in her very strongly. She was stunned by how much anger she had toward one of her fellow *maechii* back at Seni's *samnak*. Sitting in meditation, a long distance and time from any dealings with that *maechii*, she found herself shaking with anger and wondering why. She understood that of course she might feel anger toward another person but she was surprised by its strength and persistence. How could she understand it?

In some cultures this kind of experience might be explained by Wabi being possessed by some malevolent demon. The solution might be exorcism. Alternatively, her anger might be viewed as related to a habitual cognitive pattern, and the solution would be to substitute another such emotional pattern in this one's place. Wabi, however, understood the arising of such strong anger in the absence of the anger-inducing stimuli to be evidence of the traces of previous rebirths and so caused by karma. She understood that the anger didn't come from nowhere and that it didn't come from someone else. Rather, it came from the intentional thoughts, speech, and actions of her past lives coming to fruition now. There was no need for an outside stimulus to be present because her actions in the past were bound to have their effects, and they came to her clearly in meditation.

Realizing this gave Wabi feelings of lightness, joy, and personal direction. When one is filled with anger, one can counteract it with loving kindness, according to Buddhist tradition. So she sat in meditation and tried to observe as anger arose in her; she then systematically reflected on the kindnesses of this woman, for example how she had helped Wabi's sister and brother find jobs. For weeks Wabi slept very little and kept her focus on observing the waves of anger as they arose, making sure to counteract this anger with thoughts of this woman's goodness.

These meditative practices of careful, mindful observation and loving-kindness concentration meditation also led her to a deepened understanding of the temporariness of emotions. They led her to understand the central Buddhist doctrine of *anicca* (change). This more profound understanding filled Wabi with peace and joy.

One can see in this example how Wabi's commitment to Buddhist meditation and education led to her deepening her understanding of Buddhist teachings. For her now, Buddhist concepts were not of merely intellectual interest; they helped her understand the world in a meaningful way and gave her the spiritual keys to unlock doors to greater personal joy and satisfaction. Buddhist concepts, however, are not the only ones that help us understand her life. Her life is further elucidated by understanding the viable options available to her at any given time – those available to her as a woman, as a person with farming knowledge from a rural area, and as a Buddhist in late twentieth- and early twenty-first-century Thailand.

Wabi spent seven years learning from and living in the *samnak* of Maechii Seni. Then, in her late twenties, troubled by her lack of formal, secular education, by some growing interpersonal challenges in Maechii Seni's samnak, and by profound disappointment in one of her teachers, she moved to another *samnak* in Bangkok, the one where I met her in the mid-1990s. There she belatedly began studying to earn her high-school degree through a program established by the Institute of Thai Maechii.[8] The new *samnak* housed 50 *maechii* and 50 children from all over the country, almost all involved in some way with the Institute's educational programs. She'd been ordained 10 years, was pursuing her high-school degree, and had earned the respect of those around her. She later formed a group of *maechii* who, modeled on what we had done together, wrote short descriptions of their lives, recounting how they had come to be *maechii* and why. These short stories were privately published and distributed, as so much literature is in Thailand.

Just as the Buddha taught that life is constant change, so it was for Wabi. She pursued formal education further, attending college in Bangkok. Unable to meet some of the academic requirements, she had to withdraw, and then she gave up her robes. Despite her adamant insistence when I first met her that she wanted nothing to do with the householder life, she ended up marrying at the age of 28 and having two children. And, despite her early lessons in the undependability of help that women often suffer in the everyday work of raising children, she placed trust in her husband but found that he, like her own father, abandoned the family.

References

Anālayo (2003) *Satipaṭṭhāna: The Direct Path to Realization*, Silkworm Books, Chiang Mai.

Brown, S. (2001) *The Journey of One Buddhist Nun: Even against the Wind*, SUNY Press, Albany.

Griffiths, P. (1981) Concentration or insight: the problematic of Theravada Buddhist meditation theory. *Journal of the American Academy of Religion*, 49, 605–24.

Mohr, T. and Tsedroen, J. (eds) (2010) *Dignity and Discipline: Reviving Full Ordination for Buddhist Nuns*, Wisdom, Boston, MA.

Sole-Leris, A. (1986) *Tranquillity and Insight: An Introduction to the Oldest Forms of Buddhist Meditation*, Shambhala Press, Boston, MA.

Swearer, D.K. (1973) Control and freedom: the structure of Buddhist meditation in the Pali suttas. *Philosophy East and West*, 22, 435.

Further Reading

Brown, S. (2001) *The Journey of One Buddhist Nun: Even against the Wind*, SUNY Press, Albany. (This work describes, analyzes, and contextualizes Maechii Wabee's life; the reader additionally learns about Thai Buddhism, women in Thailand, and the situation of Thai *maechii*.)

Cook, J. (2010) *Meditation in Modern Buddhism: Renunciation and Change in Thai Monastic Life*, Cambridge University Press, Cambridge. (A deep ethnography of a northern Thai monastery informed by phenomenological reflection and including lively descriptions.)

Falk, M.L. (2007) *Making Fields of Merit: Buddhist Female Ascetics and Gendered Orders in Thailand*, University of Washington Press, Seattle. (A thorough ethnography of Thai Buddhist nuns, addressing questions of authority, religious space, and religious legitimacy.)

Kabilsingh, C. (1991) *Thai Women in Buddhism*, Parallax Press, Berkeley, CA. (An introduction to issues relating to the ordination of women in Thailand.)

Mohr, T. and Tsedroen, J. (eds) (2010) *Dignity and Discipline: Reviving Full Ordination for Buddhist Nuns*, Wisdom, Boston, MA.

Muecke, M. (2004) Female sexuality in Thai discourses about maechii ("lay nuns"). *Culture, Health & Sexuality*, 6 (3), 221–38. (This article examines textual, mass media, governmental, and organizational discourses to demonstrate that the social constructions of maechii roles are "grounded in sexuality.")

Tiyavanich, K. (1997) *Forest Recollections: Wandering Monks in Twentieth-Century Thailand*, University of Hawaii Press, Honolulu.

Notes

1 The term *samnak chii* refers to the space of *maechii* within or outside temple grounds – either an area of a temple or a nunnery. *Maechii* refers to a woman who shaves her head and eyebrows, wears white robes, and generally takes eight precepts as opposed to the usual five of householders. She may follow many other rules similar to those of Buddhist monks. She lives as a nun, though many do not recognize *maechii* as full-fledged nuns. For an exploration of this issue, see Mohr and Tsedroen (2010). Note that the term *maechii* is both a noun and an honorific for a woman who is a *maechii*.

2 Pronounced, roughly, "meh-chee wah-bee."

3 For a longer version of this biography, see Brown (2001).

4 There is much scholarly discussion about the differences and relationship between two main kinds of meditation: *samatha*, or calming meditation, and *vipassana*, or insight meditation. Usually calming meditation is understood to focus the mind and to lead to experiences of tranquility; insight meditation is said to lead to experiencing the world as presented in Buddhist philosophy – seeing clearly the roots of unwholesome behavior, for example. See Swearer (1973: 435). See also Sole-Leris (1986) and Anālayo (2003). Griffiths (1981: 605–24) examines the tensions between these forms of meditation.

5 Most weeks have a significant moon-related day – either when the moon is full or at its smallest or halfway between those days – on which traditional Buddhists often visit temples, take more vows, and deepen their understanding of their religion. Now as calendars and work schedules more frequently parallel those of the Christian-influenced West, more people go to temples on Sundays, abandoning the lunar calendar.

6 Sometimes translated as "novice," a *phram* often takes fewer vows for a shorter time but has outward signs of the intensity of commitment to the religion such as wearing white.

7 These "three marks of existence" are taught as primary Buddhist doctrines.

8 This national organization, formed to support *maechii*, holds a national conference yearly and runs educational programs throughout Thailand.

19

Becoming a Theravada Modernist Buddhist in Contemporary Nepal

Lauren Leve

Editor's Introduction

There are many individuals in the West who regard Buddhism as merely a philosophy, saying that originally it was a pure tradition of spiritual practice for meditators; according, this viewpoint goes, only with the passage of time did its essence become distorted, as rituals, superstitions, and other accommodations to the masses distorted its founder's inspiration, turning it into a religion. This interpretation, long rejected by historians and scholars, had its origins in the early interactions between westerners sympathetic to Buddhism and Asian reformers, both of whom wanted the faith to be compatible with modern science and recover its original purity. The former wanted to find a nonmonotheistic religion that was nondogmatic; the latter believed that, if they purified their religion, this would enable them to more quickly shake off the colonial yoke. It was in Sri Lanka that these historical forces converged in the form of "Protestant Buddhism," and exponents of this interpretation found receptive audiences across Asia. Asians who regarded the traditional sangha as corrupt and moribund were eager to support new institutions with uncorrupted meditation teachers to revive Buddhism. The life history found in this chapter, of a young woman from Nepal, provides insight into how Asians eagerly still see Theravada modernism as a life-altering possibility for themselves.

By attending to the arc of Sujata's life, from the rejection of her inherited family Mahayana-Vajrayana tradition to finding inspiration in the Theravada monasteries established by modernists in mid-twentieth-century Nepal and then following her migration to the "pure meditation" institution introduced by the Burmese lay teacher Goenka, we enter into a compelling case study. Through her biography, we can consider what draws individuals to it and how it changed her life, and her entire family's Buddhist orientation. Faced with the limitations to what a woman

---

Buddhists: Understanding Buddhism Through the Lives of Practitioners, First Edition. Edited by Todd Lewis.
© 2014 John Wiley & Sons, Ltd. Published 2014 by John Wiley & Sons, Ltd.

can aspire to in devoting her life to organized Theravada – in which there is no full nun's ordination – Sujata eventually turned back to marriage, motherhood, extended family, and a career; as is universally true, these responsibilities, and satisfactions, leave little time for the demanding *vipassana* practices she savored when young. As in antiquity, and up to the present, young and middle-aged householders face limitations, and meditation is a luxury. Her life allows us to imagine how religious participation may vary over a lifespan, according to one's stage in life and other norms.

It should be noted that the attraction to Theravada Buddhism shown in Sujata's life was abetted by her own social location as a child of an intercaste marriage; the exclusions from participation in traditional Mahayana rituals and the incidents of discrimination based on high-caste superiority she experienced as a child clearly pushed her to find alternatives outside the traditional Newar Buddhist community. Many Newars have been drawn to aspects of this reformist Theravada tradition and the Goenka meditation retreats; but Sujata's journey is not typical of the great majority of Newar Buddhists. The Theravada tradition's impact has not displaced traditional Newar Buddhism but rather has added to the rich marketplace of Buddhism now found in the Kathmandu Valley, now also including many varieties of Tibetan tradition and a growing number of centers dedicated to Japanese Buddhist "new religions."

Introduction

I first met Sujata when we were both in our early twenties. I had just graduated from college and was doing ethnographic research on the rise of Theravada Buddhism in Nepal. She was still in school but close to finishing her bachelor's degree. We spotted each other during a crowded Buddhist ritual at Anandakuti Vihara, an important Theravada Buddhist monastery in the Kathmandu Valley. We stood out to each other because we were both significantly younger than the rest of the crowd. When we spoke, she told me she was there with her grandmother. In fact, they had only recently begun to attend the *vihara* and she didn't really know much about Theravada yet, although she very much wanted to, she said. She also confessed that she was impressed because I seemed to know all the monks. So Sujata was interested in me in part because I seemed to know what she wanted to learn. And I was interested in her because she was interested in Theravada Buddhism. We soon became friends, a relationship that has lasted more than 20 years.

During these two decades, Sujata has undergone a far-reaching religious and personal transformation – to what she calls a "pure Buddhist," and someone I would call a Buddhist modernist. This chapter describes and analyzes the process of her transformation and the ways is has affected her family members' lives. Understanding how Buddhism takes form in individual biographies reveals central aspects of Buddhist modernism, how an individual's practice can shift over 20 years, and how Sujata's identity as a woman affected her spiritual choices and destiny.

Childhood: Newar Buddhist Critic

To understand Sujata's religious transformation, we must begin with a short description of where she began. Sujata is a Newar, the dominant ethnic group in the Kathmandu Valley for at least the past millennium. Speaking a Tibeto-Burman mother tongue (called Nepal Bhasa or Newari), yet with a culture derived largely from South Asia, Newar civilization is rich, vibrant, and socially complex. Existing alongside a variety of Hindu traditions and a variety of Brahmin ritualists, traditional Newar Buddhism has a number of distinctive features. Ritual life defines its Mahayana-Vajrayana tradition; householders participate in complex life-cycle and devotional rituals that are carried out by Vajracaryas, married tantric masters who act as Buddhist priests. Newar society is organized according to a caste hierarchy that elevates the Vajracarya caste as both the most learned Buddhists and the most ritually pure. In additional to a popular Mahayana tradition focused on the worship of *stupas* and the celestial bodhisattva Avalokitesvara, there is, in addition, an esoteric Vajrayana or tantric level of elite practice that is taught to only the highest Newar castes: Vajracaryas, Shakyas, and Uray merchants. Thus, an individual's caste status limits how much and what kinds of Buddhist knowledge are available to whom. On top of all this, celibate monasticism – which is a central institutional feature of Theravada Buddhism – does not exist in modern Newar Buddhism. The role of the monk in Theravada Buddhist societies is played by married householder tantric priests, similar to the Nyingma tradition elsewhere in the Himalayan region.

Sujata was born into a Vajracarya caste lineage. But, compared to other Vajracaryas, her situation was unusual. Her father, Dharma Ratna, was a rebellious, charismatic, and independent man. And, instead of accepting the arranged marriage to a girl of the same caste that his parents prescribed, he eloped with Sujata's mother, who was from a lower caste. As children of an intercaste marriage, Sujata and her siblings weren't considered "full" members of their father's prestigious caste lineage. Although her family was wealthy and enjoyed many economic and educational privileges, they were treated as ritual inferiors by conservative members of elite Newar society.

Looking back, Sujata told me how she resented the way she was treated by the Vajracarya priests who came to her home to perform rituals when she was a child: "I hated the priests' domination. Because we are not 'pure' Vajracaryas, they wouldn't touch us and they wouldn't eat food we had cooked. From deep in my heart, this made me very angry. From this, I felt very negative about [Newar Buddhism]. I had no reverence for the priests. I didn't have any faith in that dharma." Her displeasure with being treated as ritually inferior by the Vajracarya priests was exacerbated by her own ideals of value and cleanliness, which were not based on religious purity and caste ideology but on modern understandings of equality and hygiene that reflected her parents' liberal outlook and the progressive education their children received.

> I thought the Vajracaryas were very dirty. While doing rituals, they would throw things everywhere ... They smoked cigarettes. And after they smoked a cigarette they didn't wash their hands ... [And yet] they behaved as if *we* weren't people ... For my father, it was alright [the way they treated him] but Mother and me ... were discriminated against ... For this reason, I struggled a lot [with Newar Buddhism].

Given her childhood resentment of the Vajracarya priests, it is perhaps not surprising that Sujata found herself attracted to the modernist, egalitarian attitude of reformist Theravada Buddhism when she encountered it in her late teens. Before then, she had not considered herself a religious person. Even when her father constructed a small shrine (*caitya*) in their compound – fulfilling a vow he had made when his father died – she told me that she had remained largely indifferent, focusing mainly on her studies and enjoying time spent with her friends and family. But all this changed when she began to discover Theravada Buddhist teachings.

Theravada Buddhism as a Reformist Movement in Nepal

Although some historical evidence suggests that until 900 CE practitioners of all major Indic schools of Buddhism lived in the Kathmandu Valley, the Sthavira school (ancestor of the Theravada) died out and was not reintroduced into Nepal until the twentieth century. The events that led to the reestablishment of Theravada in Nepal began in Sri Lanka in the late nineteenth century when indigenous and Western Buddhists came together to purify, rationalize, and reformulate customary Sri Lankan Buddhism in ways that appealed to a British-educated colonial middle class. This new tradition of "Protestant Buddhism" incorporated Christian missionary technologies, as well as a Protestant reformist stance vis-à-vis traditional Sri Lankan Buddhism, offering a critique that mirrored this denomination's criticism of Catholicism. The Buddhist modernists retained some traditional features of Theravada orthodoxy, including the ideal of monasticism, the observance of ethical rules, and openness in disseminating the dharma. Other elements and emphases were emphatically new, however, including a broad skepticism toward ritual, a rejection of "superstitious" elements, and an aggressive missionary bent. The Protestant Buddhist movement spread across South Asia and beyond, reaching Calcutta and eventually Nepal.

The first Newars came across this reformed version of Theravada Buddhism in the 1920s and 1930s while in India for travel, business, or study. A few took the step of being ordained as monks or nuns and then returned to Nepal to teach what they had learned. This led to their offering strong critiques of caste hierarchy, animal sacrifice, alcohol consumption, and all forms of social discrimination. They naturally found great fault with Newar Buddhism, focusing especially on the ways that the Vajracarya priests had incorporated the consumption of meat and alcohol into its rituals, sanctioned animal sacrifices in its repertoire of protection rites, and adapted to the caste society found in the Valley's city states, which were ruled by Hindu kings and their Brahmanical courts.

Offering alternatives to the complex rites officiated by Vajracaryas, Theravada monks introduced straightforward ceremonies in which practitioners took refuge in the Buddha, dharma, and sangha; vowed to observe the Five Precepts; and made merit by offering *dana*. And, in direct contrast to Newar Buddhist secrecy, they strove to explain the Buddha's teachings to all, through children's classes, study groups, and sermons. At first, the Theravada reformers encountered fierce resistance both from ordinary Newar Buddhists and the Nepali state. However, many were attracted to the new Buddhist school and they gained adherents over time. Because their confrontational stance against Newar social norms and traditional Buddhism had been greatly softened by the early 1960s, the Theravadins had become a powerful, if minority, voice in the Newar Buddhist landscape by 1980.

In 1990, when Sujata and I met, there were 69 Theravada monks, 82 "nuns,"[1] and 60 novices residing in 71 Theravada *viharas* in Nepal – most of which were located in the Kathmandu Valley. Another dozen or so Nepali monks and nuns were living outside the country, mainly at Buddhist educational institutions in Thailand, Myanmar, and Sri Lanka.[2] We can begin to envision the history of Theravada's growth in Nepal by looking at the history of Anandakuti Vihara. Founded in 1943 in a wooded area behind the historic Svayambhu stupa, the temple grew from a one-room hut to one of the most popular and influential Nepali monasteries; housing from five to nine Bhikkhus and novices, by 1990 it was attracting about 300 worshippers each month for its full-moon-day Buddha puja ceremonies. At the time of its founding, Anandakuti was the second Theravada monastery in the country and the only one exclusively reserved for Theravada monks, who had until then been living in an older, Vajrayana temple-residence (*baha*) alongside other Buddhist renunciants. As the Theravada movement grew, however, other monasteries and nunneries were established in Kathmandu and elsewhere.

Most significant was Dharmakirti Vihara, a nunnery in urban Kathmandu that quickly rose to prominence after its founding in 1965. It grew steadily because of its charismatic and knowledgeable senior nun, Bhikshuni Dhammawati, and its large and effective Buddhist education program, which targeted everyone from young children to middle-aged intellectuals. Like Anandakuti and the other Theravada *viharas*, Dharmakirti has offered regular Buddha pujas and ritual services. But its popularity was also enhanced by the many extraritual activities it sponsors, including a widely circulated Buddha magazine,[3] a women's group that organizes service work such as blood drives and hospital visits, and a youth group that hosts social and intellectual events, including a Buddhist study circle that would play a key role in Sujata's Buddhist development.

Sujata had known about Theravada Buddhism for many years before she became involved herself. A close friend of her father lived next door to a small Theravada nunnery and Sujata often spoke with the elderly nuns and even had tea with them when her father visited his friend. She recalled that they were kind and that they always invited the family to come to Anandakuti, which was only a few minutes' walk from Sujata's home. Yet her father never showed any interest until, one full moon morning when his mother was visiting, he suddenly proposed that they should all go observe a Buddha puja. Sujata's mother was cooking and her sisters were busy, so in the end only Sujata and her grandmother attended. Moreover, they arrived late and missed most of the ceremony. However, they did hear the sermon that came afterward, which began with a tale from the Buddha's previous life (*jataka* story) and ended by discussing the importance of modern moral action. And they were impressed. Thereafter, Sujata and her grandmother attended together every month. At first, she told me, it was awkward. They couldn't understand the chants, which were in Pali, and they didn't know how to act or what to do. But slowly they got to know people and someone gave them a pamphlet that transcribed the chants and explained the ritual. They learned the rest from watching and listening. They eventually found themselves staying on after the Buddha puja and enjoying the collective lunch, which was something that both she and her grandmother had felt uncomfortable about when they first started attending, as it wasn't common for Newars to share boiled rice with people outside their own families.

Within a few months Sujata found that her commitment was growing, along with her conviction that what she was learning was a purer and more worthy type of Buddhism than the one she had known. As she recounts:

> When I first went to a Theravada *vihara*, the main thing that affected me was the Five Precepts [*panca sila*] that the monks and nuns observe. The monks observe many rules, and for this reason, I began to respect them... The *panca sila* is the most important thing for me. Because in Vajrayana, we don't see the *panca sila*... nor any *sila*![4] [Newar Buddhists] drink alcohol when they go to traditional feasts [*bhoj*]. [And] they go to many *bhojs*!

In addition to admiring monastic rules and morality, she was also impressed by the sangha's commitment to sharing Buddhist teachings with everyone and the interpersonal equality that resulted from their rejection of caste hierarchy:

> They don't hide anything at Theravada *viharas*... They explain everything freely. "This is this, this is that," they tell us in detail... They never say they can't teach you things they have learned. They never hide things from your knowledge... They explain whatever we need to know... [Also] there isn't any feeling that you are small, that you are untouchable. I've never seen that [in Theravada Buddhism]. And the teaching thing: they teach very "purely." So when I was learning all this, I came to like Theravada very much.

By the time I met Sujata, she was so deeply committed to the Theravada worldview that it is hard to be sure that her memory of what she found objectionable in Newar Vajrayana Buddhism had not been influenced by her later life and the fact that she had found Theravada superior. Yet, her critique of Newar Buddhism is a common one among Nepali Theravada practitioners.

Becoming a Theravada Devotee

Two important things happened during the first year that Sujata and her grandmother attended Anandakuti. First, the famous Nepali Theravada monk, Bhikshu Amritananda, died in August 1990, sparking a period of intense ritual activity in the Theravada community. Sujata and her grandmother knew Amritananda since he was the head monk at Anandakuti. They had even spoken a few times, she told me, and when he died she shared a sense of loss with the other devotees. This sentiment intensified when she watched the media coverage of his death on television.[5] And, when she stood next to the thousands of other mourners who lined the street for his funeral procession, she told me, she realized that she had begun to feel part of a Theravada Buddhist community.

Second, and even more importantly, she began to attend the youth study group at Dharmakirti Vihara. At Dharmakirti, she became involved with a group of Buddhists roughly her own age and with similar interests, and she began to study Buddhism more seriously. The youth study group drew Buddhists from their late teens through their early thirties. They met every Saturday to study various aspects of Buddhist thought and practice, including monasticism, the role of women in Buddhism, dharma as social service, and *Abhidharma* (systematic philosophy). Each session began with a lecture by a monk, nun, or other expert, followed by a group discussion. Before coming to Dharmakirti, Sujata's main source of information about Theravada Buddhism had been the monthly sermons at Anandakuti. But these sermons were aimed primarily at the older men and women who are the main attendees at Buddha pujas; informative as they had been to Sujata at first, she quickly began to want a deeper, more technical understanding than they offered. She found this intellectual space at Dharmakirti, where she became a regular in the youth study group and, later, a member of the magazine committee as well.

The first time she went to Dharmakirti, she told me, she was very nervous. She had learned about the group from a young monk at Anandakuti who told her she could study Buddha-dharma seriously there. But at that time she didn't know anyone there, nor even its exact location. She got lost the first time she tried to attend! In contrast, most of the group's other members had grown up near the temple and known one another for years. They teased her at first – a Vajracarya girl who knew so little about Buddhism! But, in the end, she felt comfortable there. There were lots of young women so she wasn't alone – plus, everyone seemed to have so much knowledge about the dharma. After her first meeting, they invited her to a youth group picnic; within a few months, she had made friends with everyone in the group. It was intimidating to speak up in class at first, Sujata said, but she made herself ask questions and try to share her thoughts. And thus she began to "learn a little bit of what Theravada Buddha-dharma was about" – that is, to get a serious, academic perspective on Buddhist ethics, history, and philosophy.

Her engagement with the Dharmakirti was to prove crucial for the subsequent direction of her life. First, the knowledge of Buddhism that she gained at the Dharmakirti reinforced her previous belief that Theravada was a truer, purer version of Buddhism than Mahayana-Vajrayana. This not only confirmed her critique but also fueled her faith. As she began to attend the study group regularly, the worldview and community that she developed there grew into a powerful sense of Buddhist identity that came with new activities and friends.

Second, it changed her sense of what a woman could accomplish in Nepal. Dharmakirti Vihara was a nunnery, inhabited and run by Buddhist women. Nepali girls from urban middle-class families like Sujata's are typically expected to marry after completing their education. However, the nuns at Dharmakirti represented a new model: these women could live independently and command respect without being subordinated to the gendered norms and duties that come with married life. And, as Sujata watched each of her friends in the youth group get married, Sujata said, she spoke with her father about becoming a nun. He encouraged her to wait to make any decision; and he agreed to postpone any search for a groom. This decision would have meaningful consequences, since she was almost 34 years old when she eventually did decide to marry – well beyond what is traditionally considered a marriageable age.

Finally, and most significantly in terms of her religious development, it was at Dharmakirti that she first learned of *vipassana*, or mindfulness meditation, the powerful Buddhist practice that she credits for completing her introduction to the highest and truest form of Buddhism. It was *vipassana* practice that inspired the rest of her family to follow the Theravada tradition as well.

Vipassana Meditation and the Practice of "Pure Buddhism"

Sujata unfailingly attended the Saturday study group at Dharmakirti monthly for almost three years. Yet, she later attested, if Theravada Buddhism as practiced by the monks and nuns was superior to traditional Newar Buddhism, it was still inferior to what she discovered when she began to meditate:

> [From going to Dharmakirti] I learned many things. And, while I was learning there, I again went to the meditation center. And the meditation center is even more "pure" [*suddha*] than the viharas, more *suddha*, the most *suddha* in that there isn't even one small defilement! And so, slowly, it was like this [that I learned about Buddhism]. This is the reason I became a pure Theravada Buddhist.
>
> I [learned] a lot at Dharmakirti and I was very good at Buddhist theory ... But I didn't know anything about practice.

When she discovered *vipassana* meditation, Sujata experienced another religious transformation, one that kept her in the Theravada fold but led her away from the *viharas*. She articulates this as her movement from theory to practice. Although she learned about meditation at Dharmakirti, back then it wasn't discussed much by the older people at Anandakuti. But it was a very popular practice among young Buddhists in the 1990s. After she joined the study group, "everyone said, you *must* meditate!"

Again, it was her father, Dharma Ratna, who pushed her to get involved. Sujata had shared what she was learning with her father, who, seeing an advertisement for a lecture on *vipassana* meditation, decided to attend. He brought home a pamphlet describing the teacher, S.N. Goenka, and the nearby center – called Dharmashringa – that his followers had built on the edge of the Kathmandu Valley. Dharma Ratna was unable to enroll in one of the ten-day meditation courses himself, but he encouraged his daughter to attend. At first, she hesitated. As Sujata confessed to me later:

> In my heart, I was so afraid [to go]. I had never left my house [to sleep somewhere else, overnight].[6] I had never left my mother and father in my life. We had always been together. And I didn't know anything about *vipassana*. I knew to say *dhyana* [a general term for "meditation"]. But [otherwise]... I was totally blind. I knew absolutely nothing.

On top of this, she had a shock when she arrived at Dharmashringa:

> When I signed in, I had to write down who had referred me. I wrote down my father's name. And what did [the person who was overseeing the registration paperwork] do? She said it has to be someone who has already done meditation. What could I do?
>
> My father had brought me to the Center on his motorcycle. It was raining *so* hard that morning. Neither of us knew that it was so far and so steep to get there. To go there on a motorbike is hard even when it is not raining. But we went... We didn't know you had to fill out a form [ahead of time]. We didn't know anything. We just opened the door and went inside and asked, "Is this where you do meditation?"

> I didn't know the rules or the time schedule. There were mosquitoes but I hadn't brought repellant. It was cold at night and I didn't have a shawl. I [wrongly] thought I could buy toilet products there. I didn't even know I needed to bring blankets and bedding!

Despite all of this, Sujata completed the course and was so moved by the experience that she immediately enrolled in another. She recalls how she began to recruit her family members:

> After my second meditation retreat, my heart said, "I'm the only one... doing this"... So I decided to convince my siblings... I started with my sisters. I put pressure on them all the time... "Do *vipassana*! Meditate! *Go*!" I said, "If you'll just go once I promise I'll never say anything again... Go! See! Understand!"

Her use of the term "understand" is significant because it indicates a fundamental difference that Sujata sees between text-based Buddhist study and the embodied understanding gained from meditation practice. By the end of the year, each of her siblings had attended at least one ten-day course at the meditation center. Every one of them returned as enthusiastic as she was.

> Our dream, our aim, then, was to get our father to go. He always said, "It's not a good time."... But still, in our hearts, we wanted to force him... And then one day, he said, "I'll go." We were so ecstatic.
>
> After my father went, he was so happy... Before, he'd been thinking, "What is this thing that my children are harassing me to do?" But when he completed his course, he brought his own father to the very next one!

Indeed, *vipassana* proved to have a dramatic effect on the entire family, transforming them into (in their own words) "pure Buddhists" – by which they meant pure *Theravada* Buddhists and, most importantly, *vipassana* meditators. Within days of her father's return from his first course, the family shifted the arrangement of rooms in the house in order to create a designated meditation room where they would sit and meditate together for two hours each day. And, because family members didn't limit themselves to meditating only during those times and no one wanted to disturb another's meditation, the once active home soon became a place of soft steps and whispers. At this time, the family swore off meat and alcohol – which they now perceived as deeply contaminating, prohibited substances – and began to refuse invitations to parties and religious feasts outside the home on the basis that these products would be served there. Indeed, at one party that they didn't feel they could refuse to attend, the family dressed up in their best clothes but sat alone in a small room at the back of the house while the hundreds of other guests – including myself – enjoyed the local alcohol and buffalo meat that are customary parts of Newar ritual feasts.

These ethical changes led to new ritual practices. To Sujata's delight, Dharma Ratna stopped inviting Vajracaryas to conduct Buddhist rituals in the traditional Newar style and started to patronize Theravada monks and nuns instead. When Sujata's grandmother died, the funeral was conducted in Theravada style at a cremation site near Anandakuti. And for the next three years Dharma Ratna either sponsored a ceremony at Anandakuti or invited monks to their home on the anniversary of her death to chant sutras and receive alms – including food, robes, medicine, and money. Similarly, the family stopped celebrating national and Newar Buddhist festivals, which typically involve alcohol and often animal sacrifice. Instead, on these days, they would go meditate at Dharmashringa, maintaining their distance.

If Sujata's discovery of Theravada teachings can be seen as the beginning of her individual Buddhist development, and if her engagement with the Dharmakirti study group represented the next step, Sujata now considers *vipassana* meditation the essence of Buddhism. Soon after she began meditating, she stopped attending the Dharmakirti study group. However much she had previously valued doctrinal understandings of Buddhism, she now took the position of her meditation teacher, S.N. Goenka, that the "practical" knowledge gained from *vipassana* was superior. Nor is she alone in her supreme devotion to meditation: at the time of his death in 2013, Goenka had thousands of Nepali followers who continue to understand and practice Buddhism as he taught them. Since 1989, when the land it sits on was donated for the purpose of establishing a meditation center, Dharmashringa has grown from a wooded piece of land with a single farmhouse to a retreat center capable of housing up to 310 students at a time, with multiple dormitories, dining halls, meditation halls, and even an 84-cell shrine (*stupa*). Four additional centers have also opened in other parts of the country.[7] Almost all of this growth has been funded by local meditators.

For Sujata, the voyage from Newar Buddhism to Theravada Buddhism to *vipassana* meditation was ultimately about religious truth and purity. She saw her religious development as a journey from a highly localized form of Buddhism that had become corrupted by its cultural and historical accretions (Newar Vajrayana Buddhism) to a broader school that revealed what Buddhism was *really* about and exposed her to the original Buddhist doctrine (Theravada), to a universal practice of what the Buddha himself taught (*vipassana* meditation). This way of thinking reflects a particularly Theravada Buddhist outlook and, beyond that, what we might call a meditation bias.[8] Her confidence in it is typical of *vipassana* meditators, rejecting the view of Newar Buddhists, who have traditionally understood Vajrayana as the faster and more sophisticated route to enlightenment.

Remaining a Householder: Marriage and Family Life

For almost ten years after finishing college, Sujata devoted herself to Buddhism wholeheartedly. During this time, she seriously considered becoming a nun. However, as her enthusiasm for Dharmakirti faded and her enthusiasm for Dharmashringa grew, she began to have reservations, citing the fact that nuns sometimes quarreled or gossiped whereas the behavior of volunteers at the meditation center was always, to her mind, "absolutely pure." Once she concluded that it was better for her to practice as a laywoman,[9] friends of the family began to search for a suitable groom. It wasn't as easy as it would have been ten years earlier, nor was she especially eager to marry. But, aside from ordination, there are few options today for meaningful independence for unmarried Newar women.

Eventually one of her uncles learned that a young man he worked with was looking for a bride. The horoscopes matched, so he and some relatives came over to meet Sujata. She was delighted that he was a vegetarian and had taken a Goenka meditation course (even if he hadn't continued to practice). Her future husband, Dipak, was impressed by her intelligence and looks. They were married in an impromptu, hybrid ritual since Dharma Ratna wanted a "pure Buddhist" ceremony and Dipak's family expected a traditional Newar wedding. The events began in Theravada style with monks from Anandakuti and nuns from Dharmakirti chanting sutras and then distributing protective water and string that had been infused with the auspicious words; a gift exchange followed. But, when it became clear that Dharma Ratna now considered the wedding complete, Dipak's family objected that none of the usual rituals had been done. A hasty set of negotiations followed and then Dharma Ratna's family priest – a Vajracarya who had taken to attending ceremonies at the family home in the preceding years, but only as a guest – performed a brief *kanyadan* ceremony, which ritually transferred Sujata from her father to Dipak. After this, the bride and groom returned to his family home, where another Vajracarya waited, and this time Sujata could not avoid the full Newar rites. However, she had told them that she would not consume meat even for the wedding ceremonies, so she did her part using pieces of banana instead. And, although she had to bring cups of alcohol to her mouth many times during the ritual, she told me later she just touched them to her lips and didn't swallow any.

Since the marriage, Sujata's life as a Buddhist has changed greatly. As she and Dipak have gotten to know one another, they have come to love and respect one another deeply. It took several stressful years for them to conceive a child, perhaps because of her relatively advanced age. But since their daughter, Anuji, was born, Sujata tells me, she has been very happy with her life.

The only consistent complaint I've heard from her since the wedding is that domestic life leaves little room for other activities – including Buddhism. Growing up with many sisters, all of whom shared the cooking and chores, she hadn't realized how much time it would take to manage a household alone. Dipak is a government employee and not originally from Kathmandu, so they live as a nuclear family in a rented apartment and she works as a teacher to supplement the family income. But this leaves her little time to complete her household chores, which include cooking, childcare, laundry, and hosting any friends or relatives who might drop by – typically on Saturdays, which is the only time she could visit Dharmashringa. Dipak is supportive of her meditation practice, she says. But the center is far away, she has work, and she enjoys spending time with her extended family.

For the first years of her marriage, Sujata continued to meditate at home for two hours a day, an hour in the morning and an hour in the evening. But, once her daughter was born, things changed:

> I try to meditate in the morning for an hour every day but sometimes I have no time because I have to get up, make food ... [supervise] Anuji and then [prepare for work myself]. It's a lot of work ... And then when I come home, I have to cook again, clean the dishes ... and prepare our child for bed.

> I used to try [at night], but when I'd sit to meditate, I'd doze off instead ... My husband says he's willing to let me go for a ten-day course and my parents will help, but Anuji refuses ... She's still small now. But when she's bigger I will go to Dharmashringa. It's been ten years since I sat for a ... course.

Sujata is fortunate to have support from her husband and parents, and also the friendship of her landlady, whom she knew from Dharmakirti and who is also a *vipassana* meditator. It's the fact that they sit together in the morning that keeps her meditating at all, Sujata told me. She does not resent her domestic duties but she understands their cost: for now, she is unable to volunteer at Dharmashringa or to attend ten-day courses. She hopes to become so again as Anuji ages.

Interestingly, in this situation, Sujata has turned back to the *viharas* that she snubbed when she began to meditate seriously. In 2011, she joined a Pali language course that was being offered on Saturday afternoons and also an *Abhidharma* class taught by a monk from Anandakuti. Because they were held at *viharas* in town, they were much more accessible than Dharmashringa. And she enjoyed the opportunity to resume learning about

Conclusion

Sujata's unmarried siblings continue to meditate, although her second sister is experiencing much the same thing as Sujata now that she is also married and facing new domestic duties. Dharma Ratna is now an active member of Anandakuti and other Theravada *viharas*, while also remaining a passionate meditator. Recent financial difficulties led him to develop hypertension; however, he has found that he can control it with meditation, confirming his confidence in *vipassana*'s power. Meanwhile, Sujata's youngest sister has announced her intention never to marry but to devote herself fully to *vipassana*. At last report (2013), she was receiving training to become an assistant instructor at Dharmashringa. It is she who now encourages Sujata to make time for another course.

What will happen in the future is unclear. Sujata's fiery early commitment led others to *vipassana*, but her move to reformist Buddhist practices has been tempered by childcare, laundry, and other domestic duties. What endures, however, is her rejection of traditional Newar Buddhism and her conviction to live in keeping with reformist Buddhist values and to identify as a "pure Buddhist." My expectation is that she will indeed return to meditation when she is able, albeit probably not as single mindedly as when she was young. As the reformist movement continues in Nepal, it will likely take on new forms; but it will almost certainly remain centered in the spiritually transformative tradition of *vipassana* meditation.

References

Levine, S. and Gellner, D.N. (2005) *Rebuilding Buddhism: The Theravada Movement in Twentieth Century Nepal*, Harvard University Press, Cambridge, MA.

Further Reading

Bechert, H. and Hartmann, J.-U. (1988) Observations on the reform of Buddhism in Nepal. *Journal of the Nepal Research Center*, 8, 1–30.

Hartmann, J.-U. (1993) Some remarks on caste in the Theravada Sangha of Nepal, in *Nepal Past and Present: Proceedings of the France–German Conference Arc-et-Senans, June 1990* (ed. G. Toffin), Sterling Publishers, New Delhi, pp. 73–82.

Kloppenborg, R. (1977) Theravada Buddhism in Nepal. *Kailash*, 5, 301–22.

Lall, K. (1986) *A Brief Biography of Ven. Bhikkhu Amritananda*, Anandakuti Vihara Trust, New Delhi.

Leve, L.G. (2002) Subjects, selves and the politics of personhood in Theravada Buddhism in Nepal. *Journal of Asian Studies*, 61, 833–60.

Leve, L.G. (2014) *Ethical Practice, Religious Reform and the Buddhist Art of Living in Nepal: Seeing Things as They Are*, Routledge, London and New York.

Tewari, R.C. (1983) Socio-cultural aspects of Theravada Buddhism in Nepal. *International Journal of Buddhist Studies*, 6, 67–93.

Notes

1 Technically, these women were designated *anagarikas* (homeless ones), as the ordination lineage of nuns, or the *bhikkuni sangha*, had died out centuries ago in the Theravada countries and the monks across the Theravada world have not agreed to restart it. In recent years, some of Nepal's *anagarikas* have in fact gone on to take full ordination in Chinese nunneries, where, under a different *Vinaya*, ordination lineages for women still exist. This bold move has created controversy and vexation within Nepal's Theravada monastic community, dividing monastics and patrons.

2 By 2001, these numbers had grown to 166 monks and novices, and 115 nuns living in any of 114 *viharas* in Nepal or abroad (LeVine and Gellner 2005).

3   The monks and patrons of the Anandakuti Vihara also publish a widely circulated magazine, the *Anandabhoomi*, and a Buddhist book series. At both Anandakuti and Dharmakirti, publishing activities are overseen by a committee comprising both laypeople and monastics, with both contributing articles and sharing publishing responsibilities.

4   As a generic term in this usage, *sila* means morality or praiseworthy self-restraint. The *Pancha Sila* are five basic moral rules that all Buddhists – and all monks – are enjoined to observe. Simply put, they are: don't kill, don't steal, don't lie, don't engage in improper sexual conduct, and don't consume alcohol.

5   Bkikshu Amritananda was a highly respected monk who was instrumental to establishing Theravada Buddhism in Nepal and became well known both within Nepal and internationally. When he died, his body was carried in procession to the funeral ground as thousands of people lined the streets to view it. This and other events were covered on the radio and television, bringing a lot of public attention to Theravada Buddhism.

6   This is not atypical for a Newar girl from a respectable family.

7   Pokhara, Lumbini, Biratnagar, and Birganj.

8   Sujata's conviction that all Buddhists should meditate and that *vipassana* is the supreme Buddhist practice is somewhat ironic given that historically in the Theravada tradition laypeople were not taught to meditate, although meditation has become a cornerstone of modern Buddhist practice.

9   Goenka's argument – that it is superior to be a lay meditator than a monastic because laypeople can pursue dharma in the same way as monks and nuns but also contribute to dharma (and society) through their economic activities – figured strongly in this decision.

Part IV
Buddhist Lives in the Himalayan Region

20

Tenpe Gyaltsen
The Fifth Jamyang Zhepa

Paul K. Nietupski

Editor's Introduction

In the spectrum of Buddhists surveyed in this volume, this biography of Tenpe Gyaltsen, a monk recognized as an incarnation of his enlightened predecessors, would rank as among the most elite. Buddhism in Tibet evolved in ways not seen elsewhere in Asia. After 1000 CE, the sangha formed transregional schools and its monasteries came to serve as centers of political authority; in over three hundred monasteries, there were monk-abbots who were thought to return to their positions through a series of reincarnations, or *tulkus*. Within a few years of the exalted spiritual lama's death, his disciples would follow clues he left on where to find him in his next rebirth; they would set off in that direction and examine young children, sometimes testing candidates by asking them to identify previous personal possessions (ritual objects, tea cups, etc.) from a set of similar choices. As with the Dalai Lamas (see the 1997 movie *Kundun* for a dramatic portrayal of the current (14th) Dalai Lama's discovery), the candidate Tenpe Gyaltsen was rediscovered as abbot of the Labrang monastery in eastern Tibet, the fifth individual to be called the "Jamyang Zhepa." Assigned to a mentor and regent, at maturity he assumed control over the extensive properties and land holdings (including thousands of acres of pastures and farmlands) of this major institution spread across eastern Tibet. As elsewhere, too, his recognition as a reincarnate lama enabled Tenpe Gyaltsen's family members to wield very large political influence. And, like most other *tulkus* in Tibet, Tenpe Gyaltsen is also regarded as incarnating one or more Mahayana bodhisattvas, enlightened beings who fulfill a vow to return in human form in order to serve their community and all humanity.

What emerges in this biography is a portrait of an extraordinary individual who tried to fulfill traditional expectations of his position while also adapting to the difficult political times into which he was born. For the former, he mastered the traditional academic and praxis curriculum, including an extended pilgrimage to central Tibet; for the latter when the Chinese imperial state had fallen and various regional warlords were challenging new attempts to unify China, Tenpe Gyaltsen had to contend with ethnic neighbors to the north who resisted assimilation. In his position on the periphery of the Tibetan culture region, the Fifth Jamyang Zhepa encountered and actively learned from Western visitors, especially a family of Christian missionaries who settled in his capital. Unlike the conservative Tibetan monastics in Lhasa who resisted westerners and their influences, Tenpe Gyaltsen sought to understand the wider world and acted to open connections with it: building roads and an airport and introducing telegraph connections. He also reformed the legal system and modernized the practices of civil administration. What is evident in the following portrait is the kind of gifted individual who often came to occupy positions of power and spiritual leadership in late traditional Tibet. His early death at 32 left his institution without strong leadership once China was again unified in 1949.

Introduction: 1916–1924

Tenpe Gyaltsen (1916–47), best known by his title, the Fifth Jamyang Zhepa, was a down-to-earth and congenial Tibetan Buddhist monk, regarded by his community as a reborn bodhisattva (*tulku*). He was a ritual expert, a gifted musician, the author of texts and poems, and the inheritor of a huge monastic estate. He was born near Litang, in modern Sichuan Province, then an ethnic Tibetan nomadic community. His family's lifestyle shifted from highland tent dwellers to householders in towns to nobles in monastic estates. Tenpe Gyaltsen spent most of his life in Tibet's Amdo, known today as parts of China's south Gansu, north Sichuan, and Qinghai provinces. It is a predominantly ethnic Tibetan region with communities of Mongols, Muslims, and Chinese – all with their own languages, cultures, and religions – all under the centralized Chinese political bureaucracy.

On this edge of the Tibetan Plateau, low-altitude farming gradually meets high-altitude animal husbandry, an environment that supports abundant and remarkably diverse flora and fauna. Tenpe Gyaltsen lived in these Tibetan highlands, at a time when ancient traditions met modern realities, very often in striking and sometimes violent contrast. This was a time of discovery and of cultural change.

As an adolescent he was largely unaware of the details of the turbulent post-Qing dynasty and early Republican-era politics in the region, and he survived because of his extended family's wits, mobility, and ferocity. The inherited pedigree and humane qualities of his father, Gonpo Dondrup, are noted in written accounts, but his father's reputation as a tough and fearless nomad fighter is often described by those who knew him. Tenpe Gyaltsen's older brother, Apa Alo (Ch. Huang Zhengqing), was like their father tall, rugged, and a fierce fighter, no stranger to high-level negotiations with enemies and allies, an unwavering friend, and a fearsome adversary.

The extended family used their familiarity with their Chinese neighbors, their understanding of nomadic lifestyles, their powerful presence, and their identification with Tibetan Buddhism to their advantage. The family included a central-Tibetan-educated *geshe* (a son who had mastered the complete academic curriculum of Buddhist doctrine), several monks, and, like Tenpe Gyaltsen, another reborn lama, the Fourth Belmang (1918–57); all accepted the authority of religious institutions and observed religious rituals.

Tenpe Gyaltsen was the second of three brothers, with two sisters and later three half-brothers. It was a tough and very unstable political environment, in a rugged mountain region, led by a fierce patriarch and a very tough brother, with sibling monks and a reborn lama and with sisters who formed marriage alliances with neighboring nomad groups. Tenpe Gyaltsen's life experience began in this environment.

His birth is said to have been marked by yellow falling snow and blooming yellow flowers, by the miraculous transformation of the household tea to milk, and by the appearance of Tibetan letters on the baby's body. The sources say that on several occasions the baby said "I am Jamyang Zhepa, the Amdo lama" and that there were numerous other miraculous signs at the time of his birth.[1]

In 1919, at age three, the boy was officially recognized by the Ninth Panchen Lama as the rebirth of the Fourth Jamyang Zhepa and also as an incarnation of the bodhisattvas Vajrapani, Avalokitesvara, and Manjushri and of the saint Milarepa. On August 6, 1920[2] the boy was authenticated as the rebirth of Jamyang Zhepa by Detri and Gungtang, two of the most prominent authorities at Labrang Monastery. The event was marked by showers of flower blossoms falling from the sky, and at the same time the event marks the operation of the Tibetan system of "rebirth," the transference of property and authority from a previous leader to a new one. This is a "sequence of spirit" (*bla brgyud*), not inheritance by genetic identity, and, whether valid or not, served to maintain the continuity of the institution. Tenpe Gyaltsen was subsequently installed on the throne of Labrang, an adolescent into a highly charged position of wealth, power, and religious authority.[3] The family's fortunes were sealed, it seemed, granted legitimacy by leading religious authorities and the community at large.[4]

In 1921, at the age of five, Tenpe Gyaltsen was recognized as the Fifth Jamyang Zhepa, and he went on to take novice vows from the great Amchok lama of the day, Jamyang Kyenrab Gyatso, and was always under the tutelage of Lakho Jikme Trinle Gyatso (1866–1948), one of his key teachers. Even at this young age he began the usual Gelukpa monastic curriculum, studying the five major works of doctrines and philosophies, the sutras, and the tantras, including a Vajra Bhairava tantric initiation.[5] This aggressive teaching of such a young child was typical; he was exposed to texts at a young age, and to elaborate rituals with the understanding that his familiarity and competence would be internalized and enhanced over time.

These religious elements of Tenpe Gyaltsen's life story are prominent in Tibetan *tulku* biographies and evidence a powerful component of Amdo religious and political life. There is also a clear assertion of identity with central Tibetan religious institutions, and when Amdo is mentioned it is very often with regard to the development of Tibetan Buddhist institutions. Religion, and especially Gelukpa-defined Buddhism, colored by local Amdo religious observances, was a major component of Tenpe Gyaltsen's life. The boy was likely not yet fully aware of the turmoil in the greater Amdo communities, however.

Exile: 1924–1927

The boy's life plan was clear, so it seemed, until 1924, when he was eight years old. In that year Labrang was attacked and occupied by the Xining Muslims, so he and his family were forced to flee for nearly four years.[6] The extended family fled to Lanzhou, southern Gansu, and northern Sichuan, protected by the peoples in Labrang's landed estates. Amdo, like neighboring China, was chaotic in those years.

In response to the pressures of the Xining Muslims, Tenpe Gyaltsen's father and brother turned to the Chinese for leverage against Ma Qi, Ma Bufang, and their Xining-based forces. After a series of negotiations with the officers under Chinese warlord Feng Yuxiang, the Tibetans regained control of Labrang in 1927, a watershed year in the young lama's life. The then 12-year-old Tenpe Gyaltsen returned to the throne and resumed his education at Labrang in 1928. All sources note that he went on to excel in his studies of philosophy, meditation, and tantric ritual in this period. He was poised to lead the community forward to unprecedented social and political changes, in a volatile environment.

Early Adulthood: 1928–1937

This period of Tenpe Gyaltsen's life, from ages 12 to 21, was marked by a full schedule of religious and ritual studies. But this 1928–1937 period was also a time of major changes in the region, not least of which were recurring incidents of bloody warfare between local warlords, the Nationalist Chinese, and the Chinese

Communists. Paradoxically, the often catastrophic and far-reaching changes of this decade in China brought new ideas to Labrang and unprecedented exposure to the outside world. In 1927 the Labrang authorities had negotiated assurances of security from the advances of their Hui neighbors with the Chinese under Feng Yuxiang, and later with the Nationalists. Though threatened on several occasions in the 1930s, Labrang was protected from the threats again posed by Qinghai Muslims. Peace at Labrang allowed the development of its markets, some of the few that remained in business in this period, providing all sides with an all-important economic – and ideological – conduit to the outside world. Tenpe Gyaltsen, the religious expert and at least nominal chief authority in the region, benefiting from the support of his powerful brother and father, was among those who welcomed the flow of ideas and goods. The young lama was in the combined classical Tibetan role of religious and lay authority, but with definitions that were adapted to meet the then current events in a newly opened Labrang community.

In this period Tenpe Gyaltsen was very active across the extensive expanse of Labrang's estates, visiting frequently to develop religious, economic, and political ties. His most frequent visits were to southern Amdo, in today's southern Gansu Province, and to sites across Sichuan Province.[7] He also made frequent visits to Gonlung Monastery in Qinghai, where he developed close friendships with the monks there. Unlike in the case of his older brother, Apa Alo, none of the extensive records of this period indicate that Tenpe Gyaltsen engaged directly with the Chinese authorities.

In the late 1920s and 1930s Apa Alo worked closely with the Chinese authorities. But, from about ages 12 to 21, Tenpe Gyaltsen had little contact with Chinese politicians or educators. He did offer support when called on, but his teenage years and early twenties were filled mostly with things Tibetan, and especially Tibetan Buddhism. Tenpe Gyaltsen's enthusiasm for education and social progress was destined to change after his visit to Lhasa, but his enthusiasm was to be colored rather differently, in Tibetan terms, from that of Apa Alo, his powerful older brother, who sought a more plural or integrated Labrang and Tibetan society.[8]

One of the unusual and significant relationships Tenpe Gyaltsen developed in the early 1930s was with the Christian missionaries Blanche and Marion Grant Griebenow. With Labrang Monastery's permission, the Griebenows built a successful mission at Labrang, serving a few converts and a larger number of local peoples in search of medical care and conversations – in local Tibetan dialect – with the curious foreigners. Marion Griebenow in particular befriended Tenpe Gyaltsen, during the Griebenows' stay from 1928 to 1935 and later, after Tenpe Gyaltsen's return from Lhasa in 1940 until the Griebenows' departure in 1945. Detailed written accounts in Tibetan, Chinese, and English by the Griebenows record their contact, and mission newsletters and personal testimonies describe a close friendship and frequent contacts between the Amdo Tibetan lama and especially Marion, the Christian missionary from Minnesota. Marion Griebenow was fluent in spoken Tibetan and he was an engaging individual whose curiosity matched that of the young lama. In the late 1920s and early 1930s, Tenpe Gyaltsen was busy with his studies and the Griebenows were busy gaining familiarity and trust in the local community. Gradually, the lama, though occupied with a regular schedule of rituals several days each week, and the missionary, occupied with local people and his travels in the region, became close friends. Marion Griebenow, though not a highly educated academic theologian, was deeply involved with religion. Tenpe Gyaltsen, well versed in Buddhist scriptures, meditation, and ritual, found some resonance in Marion Griebenow's Christian views of love and compassion, and a great source of information in Griebenow's experience of the world and modern events.[9] The profile of the lama in this period was of an active student, deeply involved in Buddhist ritual, outgoing in his friendships with his Tibetan and foreign friends and actively engaged with his Amdo supporters. While he was certainly aware of Labrang's borderlands location, it does not appear that he was involved in negotiations with Labrang's Muslim and Chinese neighbors in Qinghai and Lanzhou.

Pilgrimage to Lhasa: 1937–1940

In 1937, at age 21, Tenpe Gyaltsen made a three-year trip to central and Western Tibet, returning in 1940. This excursion to Lhasa was normal for Amdo Gelukpa monks; the large majority of Labrang's scholars spent time in Lhasa, usually in Gomang College at Drepung Monastery. For Tenpe Gyaltsen, it was in part the fulfillment of his status as the rebirth of Jamyang Zhepa, and it was also a watershed period in his life.

The lama, some of his family members, and a large retinue of some two hundred escorts and bodyguards left Labrang in 1937, arrived in Lhasa in 1938, and returned to Labrang in 1940. The atmosphere of the lama's 1937 entourage is captured in an account written by Marion Griebenow, who wrote of the

> thousands of horsemen, priests and laymen, driving loaded oxen and mules and horses. The Jamyang Zhepa himself rode in a sedan chair carried on two magnificent mules which were led by a half dozen runners. His chair was always surrounded by hundreds of horsemen and preceded by flagbearers ... on every halt of the journey, camp was made early and in good order – two large circles of white tents spread out in a wide valley, with scores of other smaller circles of tents on every side ... The Jamyang Zhepa often invited me to his tent, or to go with him on picnic trips when stopping for a day or two. Then we frequently spoke of the gospel of Christ ... [and] "Perfect Love."[10]

While in Lhasa, Tenpe Gyaltsen was received with high honors and kept busy with visits, political consultations, and religious teachings at Radreng, Drepung, Ganden, Sera, Drepung, Tashilhunpo in Shigatse, Sakya, the Potala, and several other major central Tibetan monasteries and seats of power. He spent two full years visiting officials, temples, and monasteries, on a diplomatic and religious pilgrimage. Written sources record that he was received as a visiting diplomat and respected religious figure, and was offered large sums of money and other gifts. These offerings can be understood as expressions both of religious piety and of the political diplomacy between Amdo and central Tibetan authorities.[11] By all accounts, and based on his activities on his return to an increasingly evolving Amdo, Tenpe Gyaltsen's Lhasa experience had a profound impact on him. His vision of an increasingly open and progressive Tibetan Amdo was expanded.

Return to Labrang: 1940–1947

When Tenpe Gyaltsen returned from central Tibet in 1940 he was 24 years old and, it appears, charged with enthusiasm for his new vision of Labrang and Amdo.[12] He was quick to resume his life of frequent religious ritual, study, and teaching activities at Labrang, and seemed to at the same time maintain his cheerful and friendly demeanor. This was a committed religious leader but no stern anchorite; he at times disagreed with the traditionalist sensibilities of Labrang Monastery's senior monastic scholars and preceptors. He played jokes on his attendants, and, though a serious ritual master and scholar, he was a congenial friend. Further, consistent with the Buddhist precept that prohibits taking life, and in contrast to the traditional Amdo nomad diet, his personal attendant reports that he ate little meat, preferring instead Chinese-style vegetarian dishes prepared by his Chinese cook.

After his 1940 return to Labrang he quickly renewed his friendship with Marion Griebenow, and with Griebenow as translator often listened to foreign news broadcasts over his short-wave radio. This reveals something of Tenpe Gyaltsen the person; his projects show how he sought to actualize his visions in the Labrang and Amdo community. He took the time to continue playing several musical instruments, the Chinese hammer dulcimer (*yangqin*), harmonium, and Tibetan lute (*sgra snyan*). His love of music led him to sponsor a new monastic music troupe (called *rnam thar*),[13] and to compose words and music to compositions centered on themes from Tibetan history and mythology. Though exposed to English and Chinese languages,[14] Tenpe Gyaltsen chose to work in a Tibetan language medium.

When Tenpe Gyaltsen returned from Lhasa he also quickly started several building projects at Labrang, striving for a more inclusive vision of Labrang's religious community. Inspired by Lhasa's Norbu Lingka, he built Tashi Rapten, a summer residence outside Labrang Monastery with gardens, ponds, pavilions, and a residential compound. He eventually completed the construction of Gyuto College at Labrang in 1941, and wrote the Gyuto College Rulebook (*bca' yig*). He also supported the establishment of the Labrang Medical Clinic in 1940, its 1944 expansion, and the construction of a new nunnery on the west side of Labrang in a property donated by the Mongol Queen Lumantso.

In 1946 Tenpe Gyaltsen and Lama Gortawa, with the help of the Medical College at Labrang, worked to build a permanent Ngakpa College, a community institution with Nyingma and non-Gelukpa roots. This close proximity of Nyingma and Gelukpa monasteries was certainly rare in traditional Tibet. It was named Sangchen Mingye Ling and located in the former residence of the Mongol Prince Kunga Peljor. Tenpe Gyaltsen's personal commitment is clear; oral sources report that he dismantled and offered building materials from the upper story of his own private residence and personally appealed to the major estates at Labrang for support. By 1948 the Ngakpa College had expanded to two buildings.

Other evidence of religious pluralism is in Tenpe Gyaltsen's reported support for the renovation of the Guandi/Amye Nyenchen Temple in Xiahe.[15] This, along with the 1936 rebuilding of the Xiahe mosque and full acceptance of the Muslim community, as well as the lama's acceptance and long friendship with the Griebenow Christian mission, show that Tenpe Gyaltsen was tolerant of diversity, even on monastery property.

The 1940s brought new social developments at Labrang. While many had been started in earlier decades, and others were supported by his brother Apa Alo, their growth was validated and witnessed, if not directly supported, by Tenpe Gyaltsen. His progressive attitude was stimulated in part by his experiences in Lhasa, by his exposure to the Griebenows and other foreigners, and more broadly by the expanding contacts between the Labrang Tibetans and the Chinese Nationalists.

Tenpe Gyaltsen displayed curiosity for what was new, different, modern, and thought provoking. He took a personal interest in the legal system at Labrang, originally called the Tsogdu Marnak, literally the "Crimson Assembly" (*tshogs 'du dmar nag*), and he restructured it on the model of Ganden Podrang court in Lhasa, renaming Labrang's court and general office the Yiktsang (Bureau).[16] The Yiktsang had more extensive legal processes and heard more cases, settled by the consensus of religious and lay authorities. In these years Gyaltsen also became more actively involved with educational initiatives, shown by his encouragement in 1945 for monks to study nonmonastic subjects, including Tibetan calligraphy, music and dance, mathematics, crafts, Chinese language, Tibetan history, and other subjects.[17]

The Tibetans supported the construction of a road for vehicles from Lanzhou to Xiahe, a telegraph and postal office at Labrang, and an airfield in nearby Sangkhok. The years 1944–1947 saw the publication of a free daily newspaper, the *Labuleng jian bao*, largely filled with anti-Japanese propaganda.[18]

The Fifth Jamyang Zhepa was a bright, inquisitive scholar with an appetite for new ideas and new things. He was literate, had imagination and vision, and was involved with his disciples and community. His role in outside politics was rather eclipsed by that of his strong father and brothers, but he nonetheless played an active role in community legal affairs. At age 32 he was struck by smallpox, and on April 14, 1947 the Labrang community suffered a deeply felt loss. An eyewitness, Labrang Jikme Gyatso, said that he endured lesions over his face but in the end he rallied and seemed to get better. "He seemed content; everyone was so pleased, then he just laid down and passed away. We all cried and were so sad."

Why a Biography of Tenpe Gyaltsen?

Tenpe Gyaltsen's life story, though privileged, tells us much about Tibetan society in Amdo. The 1916–24 period shows the operation of the Tibetan system of inheritance by rebirth and how this served to strengthen social institutions. We can see his family's typical Amdo nomad values, their lifestyles, and lifelong interactions with the Chinese in the rugged northeast Tibetan Plateau. The 1924–1927 exile from Labrang shows the gravity of interethnic hostility and negotiations between Tibetans, Qinghai Muslims, Mongols, and Chinese in this important period. In this period too, the solidarity of the greater Labrang community was marked by the support given to the young lama in exile. From 1928 to 1937 we can see Tenpe Gyaltsen in the role of a young Buddhist scholar, in the highest level of Tibetan Buddhist scholarship and ritual at Labrang. These years also brought increasing contacts with the Nationalist Chinese, religious, and ethnic pluralism at Labrang, and the gradual resolution of conflicts with neighboring Muslims. Tenpe Gyaltsen sought to improve his relationships with his revenue-generating estates in this period, illustrating the function of highland Tibetan economics. The lama's pilgrimage to and reception in Lhasa in 1937–1940 shows the crucial sense of solidarity between Amdo and central Tibet and is grounds for understanding Tibetan governance. Finally, the 1940–1947 period illustrates the flourishing in Labrang's community, and real attempts to modernize Tibetan society, in Tibetan terms. Thus, this is a narrative of a privileged Amdo Tibetan man but it is also a narrative of culture in the Amdo highlands of Tibet.

References

Griebenow, M.G. (1938) Traveling with a god of Tibet. *The Alliance Weekly*, May 14, 312–14.

Gyatso, L.J. (1996) *Bla brang bkris 'khyil dang 'brel gtam chos srid gsal ba'i me long* [Tales of Labrang Tashi Khyil], Gomang Academic Publishing House, Kathmandu.

Hansen, M.H. (2005) *Frontier People: Han Settlers in Minority Areas of China*, University of British Columbia Press, Vancouver.

Huang Zhengqing [Apa Alo] (1989) *Huang Zhengqing yu wushi Jiamuyang* [Huang Zhengqing and the fifth Jamyang Zhepa], Gansu People's Publishing Company, Lanzhou.

Huang Zhengqing (1994) *Hwang krin ching blo bzang tshe dbang dang kun mkhyen lnga ba chen po sku mched zung gi rnam thar ba rjes su dran pa zag med ye shes kyi me long (A blo spun mched kyi rnam thar)* [A mirror of stainless wisdom: biographical memories of Huang Zhengqing Losang Tsewang and the omniscient great fifth's family (a biography of the Alo family)] (trans. D. Rinchen), People's Publishing House, Beijing.

Li An-che (1982) *Labrang: A Study in the Field* (ed. and trans. C. Nakane), Institute of Oriental Culture, University of Tokyo, Tokyo.

Nietupski, P.K. (1999) *Labrang: A Tibetan Buddhist Monastery at the Crossroads of Four Civilizations*, Snow Lion, Ithaca, NY.

Nietupski, P.K. (2010) Nationalism in Labrang, Amdo: Apa Alo/Huang Zhengqing, in *Studies in the History of Eastern Tibet: PIATS 2006: Proceedings of the Eleventh Seminar of the International Association for Tibetan Studies. Königswinter 2006* (ed. W. van Spengen and L. Jabb), International Institute for Tibetan and Buddhist Studies, Halle, pp. 179–208.

Nietupski, P.K. (2011) *Labrang Monastery: A Tibetan Buddhist Community on the Inner Asian Borderlands 1709–1958*, Rowman & Littlefield, Lexington, KY.

Rgya zhabs drung tshang skal bzang dkon mchog rgya mtsho (1998) *Thub bstan yongs su rdzogs pa'i mnga' bdag kun gzigs ye shes kyi nyi ma chen po 'jam dbyangs bzhad pa'i rdo rje sku 'phreng lnga'i rnam par thar ba mdor bsdus su bkod pa* [A brief biography of the fifth in the lineage of Jamyang Zhepas, master of all of the Buddhist teachings, the great sun of all-seeing gnosis], in *Rgya zhabs drung tshang gi gsung 'bum: gnas lnga rig pa'i pandita chen po dkon mchog rgya mtsho'i gsung 'bum* [The collected works of Gya zhabs drung tshang: the collected works of Konchok Gyatso, great scholar of the five subjects] (ed. Dor zhi gdong drug snyems blo), Gansu People's Publishing House, Lanzhou, 374–422.

Rgya zhabs drung tshang skal bzang dkon mchog rgya mtsho (2005 [c. 1953]) *Kun mkhyen blo bzang ye shes bstan pa'i rgyal mtshan dpal bzang po'i rnam thar* [A biography of the omniscient Losang Yeshe Tenpe Gyaltsen Pelzangpo], People's Publishing House, Beijing.

Rin chen rgyal po and Reb gong rdo rje thar (1995) *Bla brang bkra shis 'khyil dang rong bo dgon chen gnyis nas dar ba'i bod kyi 'Rnam thar' zlos gar gyi byung ba brjod pa* [A discussion of the origins of the Tibetan drama "biography" that spread between the great monasteries Labrang Tashi Khyil and Rongbo]. *Krung go'i bod kyi shes rig* [The culture of China's Tibet], 2, 94–102.

Rock, J.F. (1956) *The Amnye Ma-chhen Range and Adjacent Regions: A Monographic Study*, Is. M.E.O., Rome.

Sheng Jingxin (1989) Gansu zangqu jixing [Travels in Gansu's Tibetan region], in *Gansu wenshi ziliao xuanji* [Selected materials on Gansu culture] (ed. Meng Guofang), Gansu People's Publishing House, Lanzhou, pp. 1–48.

Yu Cang (1993) Xiahe Bao chuangkan qianhou [Complete edition of *Xiahe News*]. *Xiahe Wenshi Ziliao* [Materials on Xiahe culture], 1, 72–9.

Zhai Yaozhong (1993) Xiahe xian gonglu fazhan gaikuang [A survey of the development of roads in Xiahe county]. *Xiahe Wenshi Ziliao* [Materials on Xiahe culture], 1, 132–59.

Zha Zha (2002) Labuleng si zai Aba tuo zhan jiao qu shi shi shu lue [A brief account of the historical facts of Labrang monastery's expansion in Ngawa], in *Sichuan Zangxue Yanjiu* [Sichuan Tibetan studies research] (5) (ed. Yangling Duoji and Luo Runcang), Sichuan People's Publishing House, Chengdu, pp. 483–505.

Further Reading

Dbang rgyal (1993) Dpon tshang ngo'i jo mo'i sgar: gan lho'i bod brgyud nang bstan dgon sde so so'i lo rgyus mdor bsdus (bar cha) [The nunnery at the lords' estate: brief histories of each of the Tibetan Buddhist monasteries in southern Gansu], *Gannan wenshi ziliao* [Materials on southern Gansu culture], 10, 60–70.

Rgya zhabs drung tshang skal bzang dkon mchog rgya mtsho (1948) *Thub bstan yongs su rdzogs pa'i mnga'*

bdag kun gzigs ye shes kyi nyi ma chen po 'jam dbyangs bzhad pa'i rdo rje 'phreng lnga'i rnam par thar ba mdor bsdus su bkod pa [A brief biography of the fifth in the lineage of Jamyang Zhepa, master of all of the Buddhist teachings, the great sun of all-seeing gnosis], Nanjing.

Notes

1. Rgya zhabs drung tshang 1998: 405; Rgya zhabs drung tshang 2005: 35–6.
2. Huang 1994: 239.
3. Huang 1994: 239.
4. Huang 1989: 2ff; Huang 1994: 5ff.
5. Rgya zhabs drung tshang 1998: 406–7.
6. Nietupski 2011. Joseph Rock met Tenpe Gyaltsen, his family, and escorts in 1926 at Brag dkar Monastery, when the family was in exile from Labrang; see the photo of the Fifth Jamyang Zhepa at age ten, in Rock (1956: Plate XII).
7. Zha Zha 2002: 485–6, 492.
8. Nietupski 2010.
9. Nietupski 1999.
10. Griebenow 1938: 174.
11. Huang 1994: 248–9; Rgya zhabs drung tshang 1998: 413ff.
12. The information in this 1940–1947 section is taken in part from written sources and in part from extended conversations with Labrang Jikme Gyatso (b. 1931), personal attendant to Tenpe Gyaltsen from 1940 to 1947. These interviews date from our first meeting in the mid-1990s, and most recently in September and October 2009 in Kathmandu, Nepal.
13. Rin chen rgyal po and Reb gong rdo rje thar 1995.
14. Tenpe Gyaltsen was obviously exposed to English, by the Griebenows and by radio broadcasts. He was also exposed to Chinese as a young boy, during his visits to Lanzhou and China, and later in visits to Labrang by Chinese delegations. Li Anzhai (Li An-che 1982: 24) reports that he was even tutored in Chinese. However, one of his close personal attendants, Labrang Jikme Gyatso, reported that Tenpe Gyaltsen did not speak English or Chinese. And Li Anzhai worked at Labrang in 1938–1941, largely during Tenpe Gyaltsen's 1937–1940 visit to Lhasa.
15. Hansen 2005: 90–1.
16. Gyatso 1996: 75–6; Nietupski 2011.
17. Gyatso 1996: 73–4.
18. Sheng 1989: 24; Yu 1993.

21
A Female Tibetan Buddhist Diviner in Darjeeling

Tanya M. Zivkovic

Editor's Introduction

There is a tendency for students to focus on literary accounts to imagine how Buddhism is lived, and to neglect the everyday and sensual sphere of popular religious practice. This bias can give the idea that, in the lived reality of this religion, there is a hierarchy that separates the practices of Buddhists into "low" and "high" culture, "little" and "great," "popular" and "elite."[1] The representatives of Buddhism usually presented by scholars – the great abbots, philosophers, saints – can lead to the assumption that these are "typical Buddhists," and that those who are not like them – people little concerned with doctrinal intricacies, or devoted to intensive meditation – are not "true Buddhists." In addition to this assumption being sociologically and historically erroneous, as pointed out in the Introduction to this volume, adopting it entails a bias toward men, since they have dominated in these elite roles.

This chapter features a woman who had an extraordinary experience: she died and returned to life. Labeled in Tibetan as a *delog*, these individuals who relate their death-and-life accounts play an important role in Tibetan Buddhist culture: they testify to the structures of the Buddhist cosmos, through what a person remembers from entering into the death experience and eventually returning to life. A *delog*'s vivid testimony reveals the reality of the realms of hell-beings and hungry ghosts, the liminal world between life and death (*bardo*), and the encounter with Yama, the Lord of Death, whose task it is to process the karmic destiny of an individual's consciousness, the sole enduring connection to the dead that will now find rebirth in a new body. The *delog*'s account often ends with instructions on religious conduct that he or she must convey upon return to those who remain among the living.

This chapter recounts the biography of Mo Sukey, an unlettered woman from the Darjeeling hills of Sikkim, and how she lived her life as a celibate specialist as a distinctly Tibetan diviner, or *mopa*. Although in Tibetan society those who dedicate their lives as *mopa* are thought to represent a category of practitioner morally inferior to the celibate monastic, this biography demonstrates that, in practice, prominent monks revered and respected Mo Sukey and enlisted her service. It shows that in her community there is a single continuous, interconnected field of Buddhist culture and that there are shared sensibilities in day-to-day religious practice that all sectors of society hold in common.

Tibetan tradition is extraordinary in having a genre of hagiographic "liberation tales" (*namthar*) that number in the many hundreds, each recounting the lives of celebrated Buddhist masters. These accounts usually relate how the saint performed miracles and lived an ideal life intermixing spiritual practices, teaching, travel, and accumulating disciples. Few *namthar* are devoted to women. To redress this bias, this chapter focuses on a woman householder whose miraculous return to life led her to a celibate religious career. In her ritual service as a *mopa*, she helps monks and householders of every description to eliminate the obstacles that hinder their lives. Mo Sukey exhibits many traits of an ideal Buddhist life. Considering it in context, the reader can glimpse the common issues and concerns that are central to the religious lives of both the village peasant and the village monks and accomplished lamas.

The details of Mo Sukey's life and her religious encounters did not become distilled into the prototypical "good Buddhist" narrative, as do the lives of the learned (and frequently male) Buddhist exemplars; nor were her descriptions of returning from death (*delog*) previously recorded by a scribe. Although the life history the author presents here is not, she notes, "my attempt to formally present a *namthar* or *delog* narrative," she conceives her contribution here as offering "a particular, albeit limited, insight into the social life of a reclusive human being and the interactions between an unlettered practitioner and the institutional figures of organized monastic Buddhism." Here is an account that invites the reader to smell the incense that wafts through Mo Sukey's dark and humble consulting shack, to see someone who lived to offer her all to the sangha and members of her community.

Introducing Mo Sukey[2]

Mo Sukey was 83 years old when I came to know her during a period of field research that I undertook in the village of Ghum in the Darjeeling Hills, India, in 2004 and 2005. Born in the Kham region of eastern Tibet, she became in her early childhood a *delog* – that is, someone who returns from death – and a *mopa* (diviner). Mo Sukey escaped from the Chinese occupation of Tibet, arriving by foot in India in the 1950s with a group of other refugees. Not interested in family life, she never married or bore children and for 40 years she lived alone in one small room casting divinations and reciting prayers.

Renowned in the Darjeeling vicinity for the accuracy of her predictions, monks and laity alike sought her advice on all manner of issues: the probability of prosperity, health problems, legal proceedings, and the fate of family and friends. Much like a monastic, her primary relationship was with Buddhism, and, as in the case of many religious figures, her patrons considered her especially skilled in the divinatory art of *mo*.

Her "family" was the Buddhist community of lamas and deities under whose tutelage she felt protected and to whom she offered the fruits of her practice.

A short walk away from Ghum's largest monastery and immersed in dense, low-lying cloud, Mo Sukey's home was a regular stop for all those who sought her gift of foresight through the divinatory practice of *mo*. Most Tibetans, when faced with a difficult decision, a long journey, a new job prospect, or a grave illness, will seek out a practitioner of *mo*. Her clients could be an incarnate *tulku*, a lama, or gifted laypeople whose spiritual practice may be conducted in a monastery or at home. Diviners are known locally as *momola*, the Tibetan kinship term for grandmother, or as *mopa*, the term reserved for Tibetan men and women who professionally perform the *mo*. Mo Sukey made her living as the most accurate and reputable diviner in Darjeeling at the time of my fieldwork; her guidance was constantly sought by people from diverse religious and social backgrounds – men and women, monks and laypersons, businessmen and beggars, Buddhists and Hindus, sometimes even foreign tourists – all in search of answers to the problems that plagued them.

Entering the dark and begrimed one-roomed residence, her patrons would carefully maneuver their way around missing floorboards so as not to slip through the colossal cavities, where Mo Sukey urinated and where rodents ran rampant below. They would find the old woman perched on a small bed wearing an unkempt Tibetan-style dress (*chuba*) and a tattered cardigan with an assortment of foreign objects, including money, a handkerchief, and numerous rosaries (*trenga*) conveniently stored inside its folds. There she coughed and spluttered into her surroundings: a tiny room amassed with recycled items – blackened newspapers, thermal flasks, plastic bags, tins, and cardboard boxes – all damp with mold and darkened by the permeating fumes of a paraffin oil cooker, which also stained her walls and ceiling. Textured with a lacquered crust of rancid milk, the metal pan atop the cooker made the tea she drank and hospitably offered to guests. A tiny open window allowed light to strain its way through the dark interior of her home, at times bringing in a moist gray vaporous fog. Her radiant face, bright eyes, and beaded rosary contrasted with the black gaps presented by her toothless gums and with her old hands smudged with grime.

Over time I came to understand something about the biographical details of Mo Sukey. Eagerly I had tried to convey my own researcher status and my interest in her life story in one of our first meetings, but its poor timing prevented further discussion. Mo Sukey opened her door to clients each day but closed it at three in the afternoon so she could eat and then rest. It being near three o'clock I'd hardly arrived before it was time to leave. In an attempt to secure a second visit and since her ailing legs made it difficult to shop for supplies, I asked whether she needed anything from the bazaar in town. My offer of assistance was met with stern rebuff as Mo Sukey condemned my outing, snapping: "It's not enough to sleep near the monastery and spend the days wandering around [*chum chum*] if you want to learn about Buddhism!" I was told that the key to understanding Buddhism is to stay in one place, just as Mo Sukey herself had spent nearly 40 years in one place, practicing Buddhism and not "fluttering around everywhere creating obstacles [*barcha*]." Accompanying her words with large arm movements, a gesture of flippantness, dismissive head shaking, and a discourteous laugh, she followed up by telling me about a nun who stayed nearby, a "*good* practitioner," who "never went *chum chum*. She stayed in her room. You have a room up there next to the monastery, so stay there! That's how you learn about Buddhism." I had been reprimanded. Left stunned, without anything else to say and silenced as she shook her head and rumbled: "Now it is past three o'clock. I have no time to eat." I'd encroached on her mealtime and now I had to leave.

Little by little (and always outside her meal hours) I returned to visit Mo Sukey in the day-to-day context of her religious life, her clients, and her recitation of prayers. Her seeming initial hostility dissipated and she quickly warmed to my project of writing about religious lives, an act she perceived as meritorious, but she also, if humbly, claimed that my writing about her own life could not generate merit for anyone, as it would if I focused on a high lama.

Returning from Death

Mo Sukey's religious biography begins with her relationship with Drolma (Skt. Tara), a female deity who protects her devotees and who can, in at least one of her 21 manifestations, bestow long life. Mo Sukey's personal encounter with Drolma served to both lengthen her life and spark the beginnings of her divinatory ability. As a young child in Kham she regularly accompanied her grandparents to a river where they made offerings and recited mantras to Drolma. On one of these occasions, at the age of eight, she was swept away and adrift by a current and traveled downstream before colliding head first with a rock and dying.

> I was dead. For eight hours I was dead. At this time, many evil water spirits [*lu*] with ugly heads tried to attack me. I felt that I was in battle with them. I made prayers to Drolma, repeating her mantra and pleading for her to help me. Then Drolma descended to me to protect me. When she appeared the *lu* disappeared.

At the request of her family, a local lama performed the rites for the deceased, known as *powa* or the transference of consciousness at the time of death. The lama also made the appropriate funerary offerings for the recently departed. "But," Mo Sukey laughed, "I returned from the dead."

Delog is a Tibetan word used to refer to people who have done just this: returned from death. In some accounts, a person who shows no sign of life for a few hours is a *nyilog*, or someone who returns in a day.[3] A *delog*, by contrast, is a person who for days, even weeks, appears to be dead and then returns to life. Nonetheless, Mo Sukey in her own accounts referred to herself as a *delog*. Typically *delog* narratives, which form a unique and popular Tibetan literary genre, describe a period of illness followed by the person's death and then terrifying journeys to the realms of hell-beings and hungry ghosts. Sometimes the *delog* may tour the multiple domains of various Buddhas, gods, demigods, humans, and animals. The *delog* returns to the living with fearful tales of the liminal worlds between life and death (*bardo*) and the encounter with Yama, the Lord of Death, who calculates both the merits and demerits of the departed and then reanimates their consciousness into new bodies, transmitting instructions on religious conduct that the person returned from death should then bestow upon the living.[4]

Mo Sukey's account does not belong to this literary genre of *delog* stories, however. Neither had she nor anyone else documented her experiences and, in recounting her own death and return, the narrative deviated from this usual sequence of *delog* adventures. Her account is rather unusual, at least from the standpoint of *delog* literature, since it does not contain the usual incidents: an illness that precedes death; a lengthy account of the physiology of the dying process; an appearance of the bodhisattva Avalokitesvara, who often serves the *delog* as a guide or inspiration; scenes of trauma regarding the death, such as seeing the corpse in the form of an animal or not having family members recognize their ethereal embodiment; crossing a bridge over a river to reach the otherworld; a descent to the hell realms; or meeting the ghosts of deceased people known to the *delog*.

However, in line with Pommaret's typology of the *delog* adventure, Mo Sukey did experience "first contact with the other world" through both the frightening water spirits (*lu*) and her familiar protective deity, Drolma, who descended to her that day in the river. Classically, the liminal experiences of the *delog* are epitomized in their crossing a bridge over a river that separates the human from the other world.[5] This motif was also absent in Mo Sukey's account. However, her death and her encounters with the *lu*, as well as Drolma, occurred in a river. The water of the river itself served as a "symbol of transition," thus highlighting the fluidity and "precariousness of passage between the two worlds."[6] Like some other *delogs*, Mo Sukey returned to life with the gift of prophecy: "Drolma came to me that day and then I knew *mo*." These visions of Drolma accompanied Mo Sukey for most of her life and up until her early eighties when, as she interpreted it, they stopped as a result of her taking medicines for physical ailments.

In addition to the art of *mo*, Mo Sukey's experience of returning from the dead taught her not to be attached to her body and to live a religious rather than a married life. In one conversation about being unwedded, she expressed bemusement over family life: "Since husbands drink too much and order their wives about, and since children take their parents' possessions, isn't it better to seek refuge in the Buddha?" Adamant that she would remain financially independent and not marry, as a young woman Mo Sukey took up the low-status female occupation of *chang* (beer) brewer and seller. She made the barley/rice beer in buckets but it only turned out good 50 percent of the time. If she made two buckets of beer using the exact same process for each one, she was able to sell one but the other would turn out bad and had to be thrown away. Frustrated with the result of her labor and an increasingly bad reputation as a brewer, she would cry in desperation as she worked. Eventually, she visited her lama, Khenchen Sangay Tenzin, to seek his advice. It was clear to the lama that the gods did not want Mo Sukey to brew beer and this was their way of telling her to stop making it. From that day, she abandoned her livelihood as a brewer and focused instead on being a professional diviner.

A Professional *Mopa*

As an unmarried and illiterate women, practicing and receiving donations for *mo* was a way in which Mo Sukey could give up on her occupation as a brewer, earn a living, and remain self-sufficient. But, having never studied *mo* or learned how to read scriptures, she was unlike the many lamas in Darjeeling who could cast *mo* from dice in consultation with religious texts. Instead, Mo Sukey performed her divination with a rosary. In sets of two or three, she moved the thread of 108 beads from both ends through her fingers, until she came to the center with one, two, or no beads left and so reached the prediction of an event being unfavorable, favorable, or neutral. Then she elaborated upon the details using her intuitive abilities. Reflecting the plurality of religious traditions in the Darjeeling Hill region, if clients were Buddhist they were commonly instructed to make offerings to the local monastery for the recitation of long-life prayers (*shabten*) by lamas; or, if the clients were Hindu, they were often advised to employ the services of a Brahmin to appease their ancestral deities (*kuladevata*). The recommendations prescribed by Mo Sukey were always intended to eliminate obstacles (*barcha*) to a person's life, and often also to lengthen their lifespan (*tse*).

The recitation of longevity prayers, attending or performing long-life rituals, and a general belief in the ability to extend one's life and the lives of others are widespread in Tibetan Buddhist communities. Mo Sukey could not divine the length of one's life but she could foresee obstacles to one's *tse* through her *mo* divinations. By offering money and requesting longevity prayers from the local monastery, her clients both accumulated merit (by offering donations) and had obstacles to their *tse* removed (through the effects of religious ritual). The accumulation of merit and the elimination of obstacles were practical efforts toward lengthening life. Mo Sukey had great faith in the efficacy of the long-life rituals performed by lamas in their monasteries, just as she herself had gained an extra 36 years to her lifespan through their special ceremonies: a 50-year limit to her life had been calculated by a lama when she was young, so Mo Sukey offered her modest wealth to the monasteries by selling the 100 grams of gold that she had carried with her from Tibet. She then distributed the 50,000 rupees in proceeds to the local lamas in return for their longevity rituals and chanting for her.

Much of Mo Sukey's later earnings were also given to the monasteries. As a young woman she would regularly travel around to visit all of the local lamas to make offerings from her own donations. In later life, she relied on the kindness of others to transport the money on her behalf, the evidence of which was pinned to her wall in the form of piles of receipts recording the relatively large donations that she had made to local monasteries. Mo Sukey's earnings from *mo* were always distributed to the local lamas, and she did not like to receive money from them in exchange for her divinations. In the case of a lama who requested a *mo* to find out whether he should or should not return to Tibet, Mo Sukey lamented the lama's customary offer of a donation for her service:

> I don't need money. When I receive it I never hold on to it. I offer it to the monasteries. I don't need new clothes. I don't need anything. Other people ask who is helping me and I tell them that I don't have any people helping me; everything comes from the dharma.

In response the lama left the money at her bedside and told her that they are the same, "I receive money I don't need for myself. You receive money you don't spend on yourself. What is there to do other than offer [it] to others?"

Devotion to a Lama

Mo Sukey's faith in the abilities of the Buddhist monks crystallized in her relationship with Khenchen Sangay Tenzin, the lama toward whom she had the most devotion and who was the central figure in her relationship with the dharma. In Tibetan Buddhism a high-status lama is often believed to be an incarnation (*tulku*) of a previous lama or the emanation of a deity. Lamas of this caliber are believed to have transcended the habitual cycle of death and rebirth. Enduring beyond death in new forms, the religious relationships they have with their devotees extend beyond singular bodies or lifespans. Khenchen Sangay Tenzin, a renowned local figure and previous abbot of the nearby Sakya Monastery, was able to determine the timing and circumstances of his death and rebirth. Whenever Mo Sukey looked up at her small, faded photo of Khenchen Sangay Tenzin, her bright eyes illuminated a face creviced by its many years. Referring to him as *rinpoche* (a term meaning "precious one" that is reserved for great religious teachers), she explained that, both in his previous and present incarnations, this great lama was "one of the last great lamas from Tibet." She added:

> Before dying he said he would return; he would incarnate as soon as possible ... I used to pray a lot for his incarnation ... When I prayed I would say to Rinpoche, "Please come, please come." ... Then an old lama told me that Rinpoche had come. At that time I already knew because I had a dream that he had come. I had many dreams of his coming so I knew before the old lama ... He came to me and said he would come back quickly. This is how I knew.
>
> Now he is 14 years old and living in the monastic college in Rimbick. Before [in his previous life] he would tell me to never break my devotion to him. After he passed I made offerings to the reliquary [*chorten*] in the monastery containing his relics and made circumambulations on new and full moons. He used to tell me if you face any troubles or undergo any suffering pray to me and you will get well. Now I am sometimes ill but it is never very serious. I am looked after. I receive money and food from people in the area. One day someone gives me some food, another day someone else provides. It is enough for me. This is happening because of the blessings of Rinpoche. The blessings continue ... I have no wish for anything because everything I need is provided and if I died Rinpoche would make prayers for me.

Transactions occur between a monk and the faithful practitioner through devotional acts (including donations) and objects of worship, such as relics, photographs, and reincarnations. Mo Sukey entrusted her life and the means of her own subsistence to this lama, toward whom she dedicated all meritorious activities. This veneration was reciprocated through a constant stream of blessings, which effected states of confidence and health. Merit was also gained and accumulated through gifting to other lamas and monasteries, and the reward was these blessings from the lama in her everyday life.

When I returned to Ghum at the beginning of 2009, I learned that Mo Sukey had recently passed away. She was in her late eighties. Incapacitated, her ailing legs developed sores, becoming increasingly infected until she died, probably from septicemia. Beforehand she told friends that she was ready to go and she knew she had little time left. Mo Sukey died with only the clothes on her back and her *rinpoche* recited prayers at the time of her funeral.

Conclusion

So what can Mo Sukey's individual life tell us about Buddhist tradition more generally?

Biographies of ordinary religious persons like Mo Sukey highlight how "popular religion" pervades both historical and contemporary Buddhist tradition. That the practice of *mo* is conducted for and by householders and monks alike highlights the presence of "popularist" elements in monastic tradition. In a mutually beneficial relationship, Mo Sukey regularly referred her clients to the lamas in the monasteries, where they would make donations in exchange for ritual prayers. In so doing, the monasteries were able to deliver the services to Mo Sukey's clients that she herself was unable to perform. The money that she received from her practice also flowed into the monasteries, supporting the monks and their scholastic pursuits therein.

In this religious circuit of mutual exchange, Mo Sukey – in return for praying to the lama, mantra recitation, divining the future for others, and making donations to the local monasteries – also received blessings, particularly from *rinpoche* and the protective deity Drolma. These blessings she interpreted as the force that sustained her life and livelihood. Without them, she would have been hungry, penniless, and without any profession.

Mo Sukey's devotional practices thus should not be interpreted as separate from "orthodox Buddhism." Her support of monks and contributions to the monasteries demonstrate their interconnection, and these exchanges and their flow from home to monastery and from monastery to home are what sustain Buddhism.

References

Bailey, L.W. (2001) A "little death": the near-death experience and Tibetan *Delogs*. *Journal of Near-Death Studies*, 19 (3), 139–59.

Comaroff, J.L. and Comaroff, J. (1992) *Ethnography and the Historical Imagination*, Westview, Oxford.

Cuevas, B.J. (2008) *Travels in the Netherworld: Buddhist Popular Narratives of Death and the Afterlife in Tibet*, Oxford University Press, New York.

Denzin, N.K. (1989) *Interpretive Biography*, Sage, London.

Epstein, L. (1982) On the history and psychology of the 'das-log. *Tibet Journal*, 7 (4), 20–85.

Pommaret, F. (1997) Returning from hell, in *Religions of Tibet in Practice* (ed. D.S. Lopez, Jr.), Princeton University Press, Princeton, NJ, pp. 499–510.

Samuel, G. (1993) *Civilized Shamans: Buddhism in Tibetan Societies*, Smithsonian Institution Press, Washington, DC.

Spiro, M. (1970) *Buddhism and Society*, Harper and Row, New York.

Wikan, U. (1996) The nun's story: reflections on an age-old, postmodern dilemma. *American Anthropologist*, 98 (2), 279–89.

Zeitlyn, D. (2008) Life-history writing and the anthropological silhouette. *Social Anthropology*, 16 (2), 154–71.

Zivkovic, T. (2010) The biographical process of a Tibetan lama. *Ethnos*, 75 (2), 171–89.

Further Reading

Aziz, B.N. (1976) Reincarnation reconsidered: or the reincarnate lama as shaman, in *Spirit Possession in the Nepal Himalayas* (ed. J.T. Hitchcock and R.L. Jones), Aris and Phillips, Warminster, pp. 343–60.

Cuevas, B.J. (2008b) *Travels in the Netherworld: Buddhist Popular Narratives of Death and the Afterlife in Tibet*, Oxford University Press, Oxford.

Epstein, L. (1982b) On the history and the psychology of the 'das-log. *Tibet Journal*, 7 (4), 20–85.

Gerke, B. (2011) *Long Lives and Untimely Deaths: Life-Span Concepts and Longevity Practices among Tibetans in the Darjeeling Hills India*, Brill, Leiden.

Ortner, S.B. (1995) The case of the disappearing shamans, or no individualism, no relationalism. *Ethos*, 23 (3), 355–90.

Pommaret, F. (1997b) Returning from hell, in *Religions of Tibet in Practice* (ed. D.S. Lopez, Jr.), Princeton University Press, Princeton, NJ, 499–510.

Samuel, G. (1993b) *Civilized Shamans: Buddhism in Tibetan Societies*, Smithsonian Institution Press, Washington, DC.

Tokarska-Bakir, J. (2000) Naive sensualism, docta ignorantia: Tibetan liberation through the senses. *Numen*, 47 (1), 69–112.

Notes

1 E.g., Spiro 1970; Samuel 1993.
2 First, the material was never intentionally collected for the purpose of presenting a life history. The narratives about particular events in the trajectory of Mo Sukey's life were documented over time and through multiple informal visits to her home; they usually occurred in the course of conversations between Mo Sukey and her clients, or between Mo Sukey, myself, and the local Tibetan interpreters who accompanied me during my

visits to her home. Second, something must be said about the presuppositions, cultural underpinnings, and general problems with life-writing. The biographical endeavor has been criticized for resting on ethnocentric assumptions about any cohesive representation of a life course (Comaroff and Comaroff 1992: 25–6), the linear trajectory to which it is usually constrained (Zivkovic 2010), and the interpretive technologies that render it meaningful to the intended audience (Wikan 1996). Scholarly life-writing has attempted to articulate these problems: life histories have been painted as "silhouettes" (Zeitlyn 2008), "fictions" (Denzin 1989), and, more commonly, as "stories." The crafting of Mo Sukey's life story may be best understood as an ethnographic "silhouette: less complete than a biography, but demonstrably based on an individual" and, unavoidably, "limited and incomplete" (Zeitlyn 2008: 168).

3   Bailey 2001: 143.
4   Epstein 1982; Pommaret 1997; Cuevas 2008.
5   Pommaret 1997: 502; Cuevas 2008: 115.
6   Cuevas 2008: 116.

22

Tsultrim Zangmo
A Twenty-First-Century Tibetan Buddhist Woman in South Asia

Tsultrim Zangmo and Michelle J. Sorensen

Editor's Introduction

This life history offers a window into the traditional roots of a young Tibetan refugee and the challenges she faced in South Asia. In an account that she cowrote, Tsultrim Zangmo shares her parents' hardships in their path to exile and recounts the educational opportunities available in the modern state of India for refugee children; it settles into her finding an established and satisfying residence in Pharping, a small town close to a noted pilgrimage center on the edge of the Kathmandu Valley, Nepal.

The biography begins with Tsultrim sent off to and largely ignored in a boarding school in Dharamshala, the Dalai Lama's city of exile, then follows her to Bodh Gaya, India, where she earned a college degree in a Buddhist institute of higher education. The heart of this biography is found when Tsultrim returns to Nepal and shoulders the responsibility of caring for her elderly parents. She finds this role challenging at times but ultimately quite fulfilling, as she cites the traditional teaching that emphasizes that children caring for elderly parents is one of the central and highest forms of Buddhist practice. What is especially exemplary in this relationship is to what extent her own parents, themselves *upasakas*, instilled in her their ritual expertise, advanced teachings, and the strong will to pursue meditation practices. Despite all the setbacks and troubles, we can see how Tibetan Buddhism was a true refuge for them as refugees, at the center of lives that were well lived and spiritually fruitful.

In this biography we also see how Buddhist householders who aspire to advanced spiritual practices everywhere are led to do so by charismatic monks. As Tsultrim makes clear, "Although all the profound teachings are taught and explained in texts, in actual practice, it is our lama who is the one to guide us by showing the path, clearing our doubts." More specific to the Mahayana traditions in the Himalayas, however, is the special devotion focused on this teacher, not just as the source of inspired personal guidance but also as an object of devotion – "viewing one's lama as the Buddha himself," in Tsultrim's words. Also characteristic of the Tibetan tantric tradition is the practice of householders collecting initiations and meditations from various monks who themselves are masters of one or another tradition of practice. Tsultrim does not elaborate on how these have shaped her understanding of her future life but her stated aspiration of being a "hidden yogini" with a husband implies that she hopes to get married and pursue a Vajrayana path to enlightenment.

Homage to the Guru Kyabje Chatral Sangye Dorje Rinpoche,
Embodiment of the wrathful deity, Guru Dorje Doloe in human form,
Who has immeasurable compassion to all beings equally,
In order to liberate them from the ocean of *samsara*,
At your lotus feet I bow.
May we beings receive your kind, blissful blessings
Until we all attain liberation.[1]

Introduction

Tsultrim Zangmo, whose name means "excellent discipline," was born September 3, 1974, in Lhasa, the capital city of Tibet. Her nickname is "Soyang," although she is only called this by family members. Her father was a Nepali businessman who met her Tibetan mother when he worked as a businessman selling Nepali merchandise in the old Barkhor market in the center of Lhasa.

Her family moved to Nepal the winter that Tsultrim was six years old. Shortly thereafter, Tsultrim was sent to boarding school at the Tibetan Children's Village in Dharamshala, India, where the Dalai Lama resides and the Tibetan government-in-exile has been established. The Village is a school for orphans, semiorphans, and newly arrived children from Tibet. Tsultrim has bittersweet memories of her time at the Village. She recalls feeling neglected by her family, who were too busy or distracted to visit her in Dharamshala, or to send her letters or gifts. She was envious of her classmates who received frequent visits from their parents, along with treats. She could seldom return home to visit her family, even for the winter vacation. Tsultrim now reflects that her connection to her family weakened during this period: "Due to such circumstances, my attachment for home lessened."

But Tsultrim did well in school and graduated with grades high enough for her to receive a scholarship to go on to college in India. Since she didn't like the idea of returning home to Nepal, Tsultrim found the idea of going to college very exciting. The summer that she graduated, Tsultrim went home to Nepal to discuss her future with her parents. Her mother did not support her plan of going to college; however, she agreed to allow Tsultrim to study for a degree in Buddhist philosophy at the Central Institute for Higher Tibetan Studies (CIHTS), just outside Varanasi in India. Her mother liked this alternative because Tsultrim would be able to improve her Tibetan language skills and her ability to understand Buddhist texts.

In the summer of 1995, Tsultrim traveled with her mother and her sister to Varanasi in order to apply for admission to CIHTS. They all stayed in the guesthouse of a Chinese Buddhist temple. Her family was shocked at the heat of Varanasi in the summer, where the temperature reached over 110 degrees Fahrenheit, with the sun searing down on the asphalt that they traveled on between their guesthouse and CIHTS. Tsultrim's mother had a contact among the teachers at the Institute and they spoke with him about Tsultrim's application. It was incredibly disappointing to hear from him that they were not accepting any more female students that year and Tsultrim would have to wait another year for admission. But, when her mother asked the teacher whether Tsultrim could board with the teacher and receive tutoring from him in order to prepare for admission the following year, he agreed. So, the next day, Tsultrim moved to a room in his house and her mother and sister returned home.

Tsultrim recalls how sad and abandoned she felt that night, being in a strange place with a strange climate, not knowing anyone, and being alone in her own room for the first time in her life. When it was dark, she became so scared that ghosts or other malicious beings might come to harm her that she left the light on the entire night.

Tsultrim started studying Tibetan grammar with a friend of her family, Lhakpa Kyinzom, who was completing her Acharya degree (equivalent to an M.A. degree) at CIHTS. Tsultrim also started auditing classes at the Institute in order to become familiar with the teachers, their teaching styles, and the subjects being taught. Tsultrim vividly remembers the two days during which she finally took the entrance exam, July 7 and 8, 1996. She took them in Tibetan, which was compulsory, and in Hindi, which was one of two optional languages (the other being English). The results of the exams were to be announced one week after they were completed. In the past, it had been easier to gain admission to CIHTS, since there were fewer students competing for entrance. However, by 1996, competition had become fierce with only 50 people being accepted out of 300 applicants. Among them, ten students would be admitted in each of five sections, divided according to the four Tibetan Buddhist monastic schools (Nyingma, Sakya, Kagyu, and Geluk), and one in the Tibetan Bonpo tradition.

On the day that the examination results were announced, the candidates gathered around the board where the lists of successful applicants were posted. To her despair, Tsultrim did not find her name! She was surprised because she was confident that she had done well in the exams, based on her hard work in preparing for them. Tsultrim asked some of the older students about how the results were posted. They told her the Institute did not list the names of the students who had failed the exams or the names of those who had received a distinction in their exam results. Tsultrim was advised to check with the school's director about her exam results. At the office, the assistant to the director showed her the grades for her exams – she had failed Hindi! "I was terribly shocked because I did well. I couldn't believe it and cried a lot near the office," Tsultrim remembers. She slowly returned to her room, feeling helpless and not knowing what to do next. The teacher at whose house she was staying was away in France on vacation; a woman named Tashi and her husband, who worked in the office at CIHTS, were staying in the same building. Tsultrim told Tashi what had happened; Tashi asked her many times whether she was really sure she had successfully completed the exam and Tsultrim replied each time that she was convinced she had done well. Tashi agreed to help Tsultrim ask for a review of her Hindi exam, for which she would need to file a formal request immediately. Tsultrim rushed to the school with them and her request was approved. In front of the head official of CIHTS, the registrar, and many other people, her Hindi paper was reviewed. The initial evaluation had only been 26 points, but after it was reviewed Tsultrim's exam received a grade of 65! The head official scolded his staff about the error and Tsultrim in the end was admitted to the school for that term.

This was the first of many learning experiences for Tsultrim at her new school, where she would study for more than nine years. One of her strongest memories is of being elected "House Leader" of the girls' hostel on campus. House Leader is a position students can hold in which they are responsible for various campus facilities. Tsultrim did not consider it an honor and remembers how hard she had to work. Not only did she have to miss classes yet take the same exams as students who didn't have such duties but also she received little respect for her efforts. Unfortunately, once you are elected House Leader you are not able to turn down the assignment. Her responsibilities as House Leader included repairing plumbing, fixing electrical problems, ensuring that water was not wasted, carrying meals from the campus kitchen to the hostel for fellow students, helping students who were sick get medical aid, and even making sure that students who were hospitalized had someone stay with them. Because so many students became ill during exam periods, Tsultrim's time for studying was extremely limited; however, she was still able to obtain high grades both semesters in which she served as House Leader.

Tsultrim found it strange that, although students intensively studied Buddhist dharma teachings emphasizing the daily cultivation of loving kindness and compassion for all beings, this was not reflected in their actions: "It was just theory and when it comes to practical action, it seemed as if we had been studying something else."[2] For Tsultrim, "Philosophy means understanding and acquiring knowledge to improve one's way of thinking in order to become a better person." This can happen, she notes, "only when we contemplate what we have studied."

Tsultrim would go on to complete a Shastri degree (equivalent to a B.A.) and receive the title of "Acharya" for completing advanced studies comparable to postgraduate work at a university. She enjoyed studying the various treatises of great Buddhist thinkers and learning the history of Buddhism as it developed in India and Tibet. She was especially impressed by the scholarship of the great translators who made Sanskrit texts available in the Tibetan language. Tsultrim also became interested in the work of scholars who consult various versions of texts in Sanskrit or Tibetan in order to restore missing sections of manuscripts that have been found to be incomplete. As her studies at CIHTS progressed, her interest in translation grew and she wanted to learn how to become an interpreter. Unfortunately, although there were opportunities to interpret for visiting scholars and students, there was no formal training for it, and it was difficult to acquire the skills on one's own. She found this so disappointing that she suggested the development of such a program to school officials before she left CIHTS. Tsultrim thinks of her education at CIHTS as a priceless experience and is thankful for having had the opportunity to study there.

I met Tsultrim in 2005 when I was doing research for my Ph.D. at CIHTS. At that time,

Tsultrim was my tutor for modern Tibetan. Our lessons were often punctuated by discussions of celebrities, clothing, skin care, and fitness. I particularly remember one discussion, initiated by Tsultrim, about how Madonna stayed so fit and youthful. Tsultrim was popular and respected among the students at CIHTS, and young women frequently dropped by to ask for advice on matters both academic and personal.

Return to Her Parents' Home in Nepal

Although Tsultrim had the desire to continue her studies and to pursue her Ph.D., she felt the responsibility to return home to Nepal to live with her parents, who devoted themselves to dharma practices full time in their later years. Since her two sisters had moved to the United States and her parents lived alone, Tsultrim was the child left to shoulder the household's responsibilities. Finding herself in this role, Tsultrim cites the Buddhist teaching that emphasizes that one of the highest forms of dharma practice is serving one's parents in old age and repaying their kindness during one's own childhood. Although she does observe that "living with old age people is really not an easy job at all" and "patience is a must," she is grateful for being able to learn from her parents and to be inspired by their dharma practice.

Tsultrim has fond memories of living in Kathmandu when she was a young girl. Her family home then was in the neighborhood called Chetrapati, near Thamel, an area popular with foreign tourists. In 2000, Tsultrim's family moved to Pharping from Kathmandu, when her parents decided that the city was no longer a good place for dharma practitioners. They bought land and built a three-story house, with a shrine room built on the middle floor for their religious practice and as a space for visiting lamas to stay. Her family lets out rooms to people who come to the area for retreat; at present, a monk and a Sherpa couple are staying with Tsultrim and her mother.

Pharping, known as Yangley shod in Tibetan, is a village 18 kilometers southwest of Kathmandu. It has temples dedicated to the tantric goddess Vajrayogini and the celestial female bodhisattva Tara, and a cave associated with Padmasambhava, the teacher who introduced Buddhism to Tibet in the eighth century.³ Significantly, the root lama of Tsultrim's family maintains a monastery in the area.

Tsultrim remembers her and her siblings' disappointment when they were told that they would be moving to a village, which they thought would be boring; whenever they had the opportunity, they would return to Kathmandu to "hang out," which they loved doing. Their mother would often have to come to retrieve them, scolding them for not returning home.

When considering why her sisters left Nepal to live in the United States, Tsultrim believes they were inspired by her father's desire for his daughters to be independent, to earn their own living, and to live their own lives. Tsultrim was also very close to her father, with whom she would spend time, including watching movies together. Her father was a great dharma practitioner from whom she learned about the lived practice of compassion toward all beings. They also shared a deep love for their family dogs, Sindhu and Tashi. Although Tsultrim's family was vegetarian, Tsultrim and her father used to buy a small amount of cooked meat from a local restaurant to mix with the dogs' food, thinking that it would make them healthier and happier. Since Tsultrim's mother's opinion is that dogs that eat meat will accrue bad karma and its ripening, she would scold her husband and daughter if she caught them hiding the meat in the house or giving it to the dogs. By contrast, Tsultrim's father believed that it was important to feed the dogs well and to treat them with loving kindness, remembering that all beings experience suffering and that it is possible for a person to be reborn as a dog in a future life. From caring for her two dogs, Tsultrim says, "I have learned to be patient and they have now become a part of me. When I go out to town I never forget to feed them and I get worried about them. They have now become like my own kids."

The Loss of a Father

Tsultrim's father suffered from a gastric illness and diabetes for many years. In 2010, he was diagnosed with cancer and scheduled for surgery. The family was scared and asked their lama, Kyabje Chatral Sangye Dorje Rinpoche, to do a divination for them. Kyabje Chatral Rinpoche reported that they should do whatever the doctor said, so they confirmed the date for the surgery and did prayers and made offerings for its success. The operation was successful, although Tsultrim's father was in immense pain. During this time, Tsultrim was responsible for taking care of the house and the dogs as well as making meals and bringing them to her mother and brother, who stayed with her father at the hospital in Kathmandu.

At midnight on the sixth night after the surgery, Tsultrim received a call from the hospital telling her that her father had taken a turn for the worse and that she should return to the hospital the next morning. She was unable to sleep and left early for the hospital. She believes that by this point her father knew he would die because his surgical wound was so deep and, as a diabetic, he would have difficulty recovering; she thinks he lost his courage to struggle and so he passed away around noon that day. Mourning her father was an extremely painful period for Tsultrim, and she credits the dharma for giving her strength in facing impermanence and the reality of death: "Every meeting ends with separation," she says.

She is also comforted by his lifelong spiritual practice. In his late forties, Tsultrim's father became more seriously involved in his Buddhist practice. His tutelary deity was Dorje Sempa (Skt. Vajrasattva), a celestial Buddha in the Mahayana cosmos. Many times daily, Tsultrim's father chanted the Hundred-Syllable Vajrasattva Mantra, which is considered to purify the mind of one who recites it. Tsultrim estimates that, by the time of his death, her father had recited this mantra more than seven million times. Because of this devotion to his daily practice, Kyabje Chatral Rinpoche gave Tsultrim's father higher-level teachings on meditation, and by the time he was in his seventies he was meditating for several hours a day. In Tsultrim's view, her father's devotion to practice and his faith in his lama enabled him to remain in the intermediate realm (*thuktam*) – a state where the consciousness remains in meditation within the body even after the heart has stopped beating – for five days after his physical death.

Mother and Lama as Spiritual Guides

Tsultrim's relationship with her mother is difficult and now she no longer has her father to provide a balance to her home life. She appreciates that her mother, who is now 80 years old, has taught her many things about dharma, including how to perform rituals, recite mantras, do visualization practice, and request blessings from deities. She calls her mother her "guide," and respects how disciplined and hard working she is at following Buddhist teachings. When she was in her later forties, Tsultrim's mother began to learn the ritual songs associated with their family deity, Machik Throma Nagmo. Once she had mastered these songs, she undertook a retreat with the guidance of Kyabje Chatral Rinpoche. Following her retreat practice, she began to teach her dharma friends the rituals associated with Throma Nagmo (Krodha Kali). Like Tsultrim's father, her mother was advised by Kyabje Chatral Rinpoche to increase her practice of meditation in her later life in order to tame her mind and to better understand Buddhist teachings on wisdom and compassion. Tsultrim's mother usually awakens at 3:00 a.m. and washes her face to wake up. After reciting her preliminary mantras for her personal deities, she begins the first of her four daily meditation sessions, each of which lasts around three hours.

Tsultrim's mother is an exceptionally dedicated and strict practitioner, and expects her daughter to live a similarly spiritual lifestyle. Tsultrim is not allowed to see movies, read newspapers, listen to the radio, watch television, go out with friends, go to parties, or wear fancy clothes. She is required to ask her mother's permission before going anywhere; if her mother denies permission, Tsultrim says that she has "no choice but to obey her." Although these restrictions frustrate Tsultrim and she finds living with her mother's demands to be challenging, she makes an effort to trust that her mother has her best interests at heart. She believes that the best option in the face of difficulties is to cultivate a positive perspective.

One particularly memorable episode occurred when Tsultrim's mother was insisting that Tsultrim become a nun. Tsultrim herself did not feel that she was ready to make such a commitment. Her mother repeated her demand several times until one day Tsultrim replied that she would become a nun but that she would go to live in a monastery far away from home. Her mother was alarmed and relented in her request. Tsultrim speculates that part of the reason behind her mother's wish was the desire to be able to tell others that her daughter was a nun with the hope that people would think even more highly of her own dedication as a dharma practitioner. Tsultrim herself feels that such a decision must be undertaken seriously and "is not kid's play." While she has high regard for people who become ordained, respecting that they have sacrificed worldly activities with their vows to spend their lives in service to the dharma, she herself prefers to remain a lay practitioner.

Tsultrim is pleased that she has been able to serve her mother and to support her as she continues her practice to attain enlightenment. She says that she believes that she also will slowly develop "widening spiritual wisdom" and will be able to become like her mother. She continues to learn from her mother, reading the texts her mother recommends and discussing them with her. Says Tsultrim, "The wisdom I am gaining from mom is priceless because nowadays it is quite hard to find people who really know the dharma practically." Tsultrim observes that, while there are many people learned in Buddhist theory, hearing about the experience developed through years of actual practice, particularly in cultivating *bodhicitta*[4] and the meditative awareness of the true nature of the mind as empty, is vital for the student.

Upon returning to Nepal after her studies at CIHTS, Tsultrim began doing *Throma Ngondro* with her mother's guidance; it took her one year to complete this practice. *Ngondro* is a preliminary practice in Vajrayana Buddhism that opens the door for more advanced practices in visualization meditation. The *Throma Ngondro* is focused on the wrathful *dakini* Throma Nagmo, who is an embodiment of wisdom, and originated with the teacher Dudjom Lingpa Rinpoche. As recommended by Kyabje Chatral Rinpoche, Tsultrim received the *Throma* empowerment from another lama, Tulku Theklo. Following the accomplishment of her *Ngondro* preliminaries, Tsultrim undertook two retreats. The first focused on *Nyentsam*, a practice of mantra recitations for Throma Nagmo in order to accumulate merit. The second was *Shagyatsam*, during which she recited mantras intensively for a hundred straight days. Her retreat practice was very strict: Tsultrim had to rise early each morning and begin her practice on time. She followed the retreat instructions closely and with diligence in order to receive profound and powerful blessings. Tsultrim found that being cut off from worldly life was not easy, but for the first time in her life she was able to focus intensely on dharma ritual and learning, through which she gained a more advanced understanding of the dharma. Through these retreats, Tsultrim came to understand that, without the dharma, she was "like a fish without water": she understood that dharma was "the only method that can liberate us from suffering and the only refuge that can give us eternal inner peace."

An average day for Tsultrim now begins at 4:00 a.m. It is hard for her to get up so early, so her mother checks to make sure that she is up. Tsultrim finds it difficult not to doze off first thing in the morning and sometimes loses her place in her recitation of texts and mantras. By 5:00 a.m., she is no longer falling asleep and is able to start her recitations in earnest. She first does her preliminary *Throma Ngondro* practices, then the "Calling the Guru from Afar" prayer for her teacher, Kyabje Chatral Rinpoche. She continues with reciting the instructions she has received from her teacher and then chants various root mantras. At 5:45 a.m., she makes her mother *tsampa* porridge – a staple food for Tibetans made out of roasted barley flour – and offers it to her. At 6:00 a.m., Tsultrim and her mother make incense offerings known as *Riwo Sangchod*, which take 20 minutes; she now knows by heart many of the chants associated with this offering and no longer has to refer to a printed text. Following this practice, she makes tea for her mother to drink with her *tsampa*. Then Tsultrim goes to the shrine room in her family home to do prostrations. When she becomes tired, she recites the *Tsikdhun soldep*, a seven-line prayer she has pledged to recite one hundred thousand times; she has completed over 70,000 recitations since she began several years ago.

At 8:00 a.m. Tsultrim is ready for her own breakfast. Following her meal, if there are bills to be paid or shopping to be done, she takes care of them. If there aren't any such responsibilities, she spends the next couple of hours in her room reading, writing, or reciting texts. At 10:00 a.m., Tsultrim and her mother do a Chutor practice, offering roasted barley and milk diluted in water to the *naga*s (serpent spirits), which takes about 15 minutes. After this, Tsultrim boils milk for her mother and feeds her dogs. The rest of the day is spent in household activities, shopping, and so on. Her religious practice resumes before bed, when Tsultrim does more chanting and also a Chod offering practice.[5]

Every month, Tsultrim and her mother do two *tsok* practices. During a *tsok* offering, practitioners do meditations and visualizations and make offerings of food and drink to a deity. This practice is also considered to be a type of "feast" for practitioners, who enjoy the offerings after the ritual. On the tenth day of the month, Guru Rinpoche Day is observed with a *Throma Tsok*. The 25th day is Dakini Day and another *Throma Tsok* is performed. Tsultrim's mother is now asking her to learn how to make *torma*, tsampa dough that is formed into various shapes and used as an offering to deities. This she plans to begin learning. Tsultrim's family also hangs many prayer flags in holy places and behind their home, and these flags must be changed every year during the celebration of Tibetan New Year. Another annual occasion is *Saga Dawa*, the month during which Tibetan Buddhists believe the Buddha was born, gained enlightenment, and passed into *parinirvana*. Virtuous activities done during this auspicious month are considered to generate more merit for the practitioner than acts performed during other months. Tsultrim observes this month by going to Swayambhu Temple near Kathmandu daily and doing circumambulations.

Tsultrim has received teachings from many highly regarded lamas, all of whom she recalls vividly, including H.H. the Dalai Lama, the late Kyabje Trulshik Rinpoche, the late Kyabje Penor Rinpoche, Kyabje Dungsey Rinoche, Kyabje Dudjom Yangsi Rinpoche, Kyabje Yangthang Rinpoche, and Singdak Rinpoche. Her primary lama is Kyabje Chatral Sangye Dorje Rinpoche. This is the teacher to whom her mother has been devoted for many years and who has guided her mother's retreats in Yolmo.[6] Tsultrim speaks with respect and awe about Kyabje Chatral Rinpoche: "Being our root guru, he is our everything. To us, he is not a human being but a Buddha in human form. Just by receiving his blessing, our obstacles are cleared, and by having an audience with him, our minds are at peace." Because Kyabje Chatral Rinpoche is a vegetarian, Tsultrim's family also follows a vegetarian diet. Tsultrim's perspective on the place of a lama in a Tibetan Buddhist practitioner's life is traditional: "Although all the profound teachings are taught and explained in texts, in actual practice, it is our lama who is the one to guide us by showing the path, clearing our doubts, and it is only through unwavering faith, devotion, diligence, not breaking one's vows, and viewing one's lama as the Buddha himself that we can attain Buddhahood."

Tsultrim is inspired by stories of the many females, both yoginis and *dakini*s, who attained high levels of realization and left many auspicious signs and relics when they passed away. When she reads biographies of great women practitioners, she is encouraged to work hard and strive for her goal of enlightenment. Tsultrim thinks of the women practitioners who, possessing certain qualities and having been prophesied to be *dakini*s, are "taken by lamas as consorts mainly to support the flourishing of the dharma activities." She adds, "some *dakini*s are considered to have the potential to prolong the lifespan of the lama." In Vajrayana Buddhism, a female consort is thought to complement the role of the male practitioner. Tsultrim is aware that some people might be critical of such sexual relationships in a religious context, but she emphasizes that "when lamas take consorts, it is not like from a worldly perspective, but focused on dharmic purposes."

Tsultrim emphasizes that she is happy with the life she has chosen. She says, "I like how I am living because there is a reason to what I am doing." Although her friends have jobs and families, freedoms and luxuries, she appreciates that she is able to live "in an environment where dharma is the key focus, which makes me open my mind with it and slowly immerse myself in it, and experience that this life should be made more meaningful" rather than it being wasted on temporal pleasures and personal material gain. Tsultrim still stays in touch with friends through the internet, and she appreciates that they express support and encouragement for living a life dedicated to her parents and the practice of Buddhist dharma.

Even in a place as remote as Nepal, the sense of her identity being divided is very evident to Tsultrim. She speaks of "experiencing two different worlds simultaneously. At home, I am in the dharma world where mom is the guide." The moment that she steps out of the house to go to the market, to pay bills, or to do any other work her mother assigns her, she is outside in the materialistic world. According to Tsultrim, it is "by the blessing of the supreme dharma that I can be able to equalize and understand the true nature of things"; this ability allows her to think with, as she puts it, "a cool mind."

Tsultrim looks forward to the day that she will have freedom to live her life independently, though her main aim will still be to focus on dharma "because dharma is the only refuge and only hope to free us from this sea of suffering once and for all by not taking rebirth in *samsara*." She says frankly that she is still working on becoming a good dharma practitioner and continues to learn a lot; her confidence in the dharma as a refuge and the possibility for enlightenment if she works hard brings her great joy. Tsultrim can imagine being in a relationship with a man who would be her companion in dharma practice and in life. Due to her desire to devote herself to her dharma practice, she has decided not to have children. In the end, her goal is to become a "hidden yogini," a woman who, despite her great achievements in practicing dharma, maintains humility.[7]

Notes

1. Tsultrim has requested that this prayer to her teacher be placed at the beginning of her biography.
2. This problem intrigued Tsultrim so much that she had hoped to do a Ph.D. thesis on the topic of "Intellectual Dharma and Practical Dharma."
3. The name "Pharping" is said to refer to Pharpingpa, the yogi who, after many years of diligent practice, received a vision of the goddess Vajrayogini. There is a statue of Vajrayogini in Pharping that is not considered to be made by human hands: it is thought to be the manifestation that spontaneously arose in front of Pharpingpa. Pharping also contains sacred sites associated with Tara, a female bodhisattva whose compassionate activity removes obstacles and fulfills wishes and whose image spontaneously emerged from marble rock in the vicinity.

4 A term that means both "the thought of achieving enlightenment" and its goal, "enlightened mind."
5 On this practice, see Chapter 6.
6 A region immediately northeast of the Kathmandu Valley.
7 Tsultrim Zangmo, in August 2012, wrote a final benediction that she requested be placed at the end of her biography: "To my mother, I would like to say, you are the best teacher and guide. You are one of my inspirations in terms of dharma practice and I will do what I can to put all the things you taught me into practice. I may not be the best daughter, but I will do my duty well. I love you, Mom. I also take this opportunity to thank my sponsor friend Toni for being one of the most wonderful friends and for always helping me for all of these years. To my sisters, I thank you as well. I am also grateful to my guy for being supportive in every way and for encouraging me."

23

Bakula Arhat's Journeys to the North
The Life and Work of the 19th Kushok Bakula in Russia and Mongolia

Vesna A. Wallace

Editor's Introduction

Buddhist tradition lists 80 great disciples of the Buddha and 16 celebrated *arhats*, all venerated for their ethical conduct and exceptional spiritual achievements. Among them is the Arhat Bakula, who became legendary as a contemplative hermit who embraced the hardships of an ascetic life and sustained himself on plants, roots, and fruits of the forest. According to the Indian, Tibetan, and Mongolian sources, he never experienced illness, enjoyed an unusually long life, and healed sick monks with medicinal plants. Due to the accounts of his many extraordinary achievements – possessing five extrasensory perceptions (*abhijna*), knowledge of medicinal plants, and healing powers – he became worshipped as a giver of long life who also provided relief to those afflicted with hunger, thirst, material needs, or spiritual obstacles. In Tibet, this *arhat* became the subject of a tradition of perpetual reincarnation; and, in the twentieth century, a nineteenth-century Mongolian prophecy about a future incarnation of this Bakula restoring Buddhism there did indeed come to pass.

In the regions where Tibetan Buddhism was established and its sangha was well supported, the Mahayana belief in the bodhisattva, a being who vows to return to the world repeatedly until all beings are led to enlightenment, evolved to regard extraordinary religious figures as bodhisattvas who return to their monastic position repeatedly, taking human birth to serve their communities with compassion as spiritual leaders. The Dalai Lama, current in his 14th incarnation, is the most famous of these *tulkus*; all but a few are male. Scholars have noted that this system of rule, as seen in the history of the Dalai Lamas, the Panchen Lamas, and the Karmapas, has created countless problems in political terms and in the problem of recognizing the small children proposed as successors. Given the wealth that each *tulku* commands by perpetual ownership of his *labrang* (in buildings, lands, and income) and the power inevitably invested in the regents who manage the youngsters and their *labrang* during their youth, this system has been inherently unstable and prone to corruption. (Only half of the recognized Dalai Lamas reached the age of 40, with poisoning suspected in many situations.)

In this biography of the Kushok Bakula, as with Tenpe Gyaltsen in Chapter 20, we see an example of the system producing individuals who were gifted and successful in nearly everything they undertook. Here, with the life history of the 19th Kushok Bakula, we have an account of one of the most influential monks of the twentieth century. In addition to the usual spiritual responsibilities, we find an extraordinary account of a social activist, politician, and diplomat who worked for the betterment of his native Ladakh and then took a prominent place in the transformation of the former Soviet Union and its satellite, the Mongolian People's Republic, into democratic polities where Buddhist tradition could again freely flourish. Beloved for his spiritual teachings, compassionate nature, and a boundless energy for doing the most for the people, the Kushok Bakula fulfilled his role as the prophesied savior of Buddhism in Mongolia. He lived up to the Tibetan tradition's recognizing him as the bodhisattva incarnation of an *arhat* named Bakula, who lived during the life of Shakyamuni Buddha, and his devotees from Ladakh to Ulan Bator (capital of Mongolia) have remembered him after his death in the classical practice of taking his cremation relics and depositing them in stupas built to enshrine them.

Background

According to a popular Mongolian legend recorded in the nineteenth century,[1] a Mongolian monk (whose name remains unknown) predicted that Buddhism in Mongolia would be assaulted by inimical forces. He further prophesied that, some time after the destruction of Buddhism in the country, Arhat Bakula[2] would come to Mongolia to revitalize the Mongolian Buddhist tradition. He further foretold that, after Buddhism among Mongols received "a crushing blow at the hands of the red barbarians in the early twentieth century," the Mongolian Buddhist cultural heritage would be restored to its previous glory.[3] Then he appealed to Mongolians, saying: "In order to liberate [ourselves] from suffering, [we] must worship Bakula."[4] For that purpose, he composed a prayer in praise of Arhat Bakula, titled *Opening the Door of the Space Treasure of a Compilation of Homage and Worship of the Elders Led by Arya Bakula*, which was read widely in Mongolian monasteries. According to Zava Damdin, leading Mongolian lamas recited that liturgical text of the offering rite to Bakula Arhat, in which he is mentioned as foremost among all the *arhats*.[5]

Following the aforementioned prediction, a *thangka* was made for the sake of worshipping Arhat Bakula. The *thangka* depicts a set of 16 *arhats* of the Buddha, with Bakula Arhat occupying a central position in the painting and holding a mongoose in his hands. He is surrounded by 15 other *arhats* and the Buddha Shakyamuni, who is attended by Shariputra and Maudgalyayana, all depicted above the head of Bakula Arhat. In the upper left and right corners of the paintings are depicted two bodhisattva figures, Tara and Manjushri. At the bottom of the painting are the four Maharajas, the guardians of the four cardinal directions, and on the lower right side, above the fourth Maharaja, there is a representation of the seated Hashang.[6] During the years of the Communist revolution, in every monastery, during daily ritual services, lamas recited the prayer *Salutation and Worship of the Elders*,[7] in which Bakula Arhat is mentioned as learned and holy.[8]

As we will see, a learned monk born in the lineage of Bakula Arhat's incarnations – respected for his strict adherence to the monastic discipline and for his learning, meditative practices, and vegetarian diet, which he adopted in 1925 after hearing that certain villagers slaughtered sheep for his meal – modeled his life work on the celebrated virtues of Bakula Arhat. He eventually made his way to the territories of the Mongols, where in good part he fulfilled their prophecy. But, before venturing to those lands, he had to follow the footsteps of his predecessor, the 18th incarnation of Bakula Arhat, by improving the lives of the local people in his native land, Ladakh. Prior to his death, the 18th Bakula Lobsang Yeshe Tenpa Gyaltsen foretold his next birth, indicating one of the four daughters of his sister as his future mother.

Birth and Early Life of a Reincarnate Lama

On May 19, 1917, a son was born to one of these women; he was recognized as the 19th Kushok Bakula Lobsang Thubten Chognor and confirmed as such when he was six years old by the 13th Dalai Lama. After receiving a preliminary education in Ladakh, at the age of ten he set out overland to attend Drepung Monastery in Lhasa, where he stayed for 14 years and earned the highest monastic degree with honors, the Geshe Lharampa degree. Returning to Ladakh in 1941 at the time of India's transition from its century-long colonial rule to independence, and witnessing the poor social conditions of the people in his home state, the 19th Kushok Bakula (hereafter the Kushok Bakula) applied himself to improving the religious, social, and political welfare of the people of Ladakh. He thus continued the work of his predecessor, the 18th Bakula Lobsang Yeshe Tenpa Gyaltsen, who had also worked for the welfare of the people of Ladakh and ensured a tax exemption for all Buddhist monasteries in the region.

In the 1950s, when the existence of Buddhist monasteries in Ladakh was threatened, the Kushok Bakula established two organizations, the All Ladakh Gonpa Association and the Ladakh Buddhist Association. Both were dedicated to the preservation of the Buddhist monastic life in Ladakh. His concern for the economic wellbeing of the people of Ladakh and for their religion and culture eventually led him to a political career, which lasted 50 years. Trying never to separate his political activism from his Buddhist practice and religious works, he became the first Ladakhi member of the Indian parliament and the first Ladakhi member of the Government Commission for Minorities. There he championed the rights of the people of Ladakh, who were experiencing the hardships of poverty, illiteracy, and abuse from corrupt landlords and governmental officials. His efforts yielded several significant results for his home state: the preservation of the unique identity and Buddhism of Ladakh; the recognition of Ladakh as a part of India in 1948, thereby liberating the state from the longtime neglect by its rulers in the state of Jammu and Kashmir, who hindered its economic development; and the creation of unprecedented educational opportunities for the young people of Ladakh.[9]

Convinced that peace is possible if people genuinely follow the fundamental ethical principles of Buddhism, the Kushok Bakula became committed to nurturing peace and facilitating harmony among different peoples, both within and beyond the modern state of India. As the Vice President of the Asian Buddhist Conference for Peace (ABCP), which he coestablished in 1969 with S. Gombojav, the abbot of Gandantegchenling Monastery in Ulaanbaatar, and later as the President of the ABCP, he helped shape its policies and programs. During the Fifth General Conference of the ABCP, held in Ulaanbaatar, Mongolia's capital, in 1979, the Kushok Bakula expressed his perspective on solving social and political frictions in Asia by stating: "We can overcome all tension if we learn to live in peace, remove all misunderstandings, and get rid of fissiparous tendencies."[10]

Outreach and Missionary Activities in the Soviet Union and Mongolia

The Kushok Bakula persevered in his career as monk and social activist, a politician, and a diplomat not merely because of the difficult social and political conditions that warranted the amelioration in his native Ladakh but also because of the oppressive circumstances of various Mongol ethnic groups in the former Soviet Union and in its client state, the Mongolian People's Republic. Learning about the prohibition of religious expression and of the demise of Buddhism in the countries ruled by Communist governments, he felt compelled to affect positive sociopolitical changes in these regions. He stated often that his "karmic connection" with Buddhists in Russia and Mongolia emerged in 1917, in the same year when the Bolshevik Revolution was victorious in Russia; from that time onward, his desire to visit these countries never waned. While many Tibetan lamas living in India sought to travel to the United State and Europe, where religious freedom allowed the unrestrained spread of Buddhist teachings, the Kushok Bakula chose to journey to the less hospitable northern and northwestern parts of Asia. Speaking of his inner calling, he said:

> A spread of Buddhism to the West was a very important achievement of the twentieth century, which may have a far reaching effect. I myself had a few such opportunities (to set out to the West), but I did not go because in reality I never felt a strong interest in that. However, when the opportunity to leave for Russia was presented, I took it. This may sound strange, but I always passionately endeavored to get there.[11]

Thus, he became the first Buddhist monk to visit the Soviet Union and its regions of Buryatia and Kalmykia, as well as socialist Mongolia and Communist China, where he advocated peace and nuclear disarmament.

In 1968, on the invitation of the Soviet Ministry for Religious Affairs, the Kushok Bakula paid his first visit to the Soviet Union as the head of a religious delegation from India to discuss the creation of the new ABCP. This historic visit also included his travels to Ulan Ude, the capital of Buryatia, and to Leningrad (now St. Petersburg). Bato Tsybenovich Tsybenov, who served as the adviser for religious affairs at that time and accompanied him to Ulan Ude, recounted the excitement stirred by the Kushok Bakula's visit among the Buddhists of Buryatia: large crowds of enthusiastic people hindered his departure by standing in front of the car that was taking him to the airport.[12] After that first official journey, the Kushok Bakula regularly visited various Mongolian ethnic groups living in Buryatia, Kalmykia, and Mongolia.

During a subsequent diplomatic visit to the Soviet Union, he appealed to Soviet leaders to return to Russian Buddhists their temple in St. Petersburg, which had been built by the renowned Buryat Lama Agwan Dorjev (1853–1938) but later vandalized by the Red Army and turned into a zoology institute. He saw the new political movements of Perestroika and Glasnost (1985–1991), which strove to bring economic reforms and democratization of the Communist Party in the Soviet Union, as an opportunity for Russian Buddhists to become socially engaged with the goal of ending the Cold War. In his speech given at the banquet celebrating one thousand years of the Russian Orthodox Church in 1999, the Kushok Bakula pointed out that Perestroika and Glasnost are not a cause for staying quiet but for making a new effort in mobilizing the Buddhist community in a struggle for peace and vigorous resolution.[13]

In 1989, the Kushok Bakula also became the first Buddhist teacher to visit Kalmykia. Commenting on his experiences during that visit, he expressed his empathy and concern for Kalmyk Mongols in these words:

> I made several trips to Kalmykia, to the region of Volga, to the people, who suffered not only from the communist storm, as everyone everywhere did, but who also endured the great pain and humiliation under the rule of Stalin's regime. Not only was their culture destroyed, but also all people were forced to leave the homeland and were forcibly resettled far from the Volga region. Thousands died... In Kalmykia I was struck. I saw a complete erosion of their culture without any sign of the preservation of the remainder of the culture. A strange feeling arose in me, to find myself in the midst of the people of Mongolian origin and to see that they behave more like Russians. But their passionate desire and determination to restore their culture made me happy.[14]

In 1969, a year after his first visit to Russia, the Kushok Bakula made his first visit to Mongolia's capital, Ulaanbaatar. Upon his arrival in Mongolia, he emphasized the urgency of organizing activities related to world peace, with this poetic message:

> In all countries of the world,
> Let all living beings be free from disease and drought.
> Eliminate disaster and war so that
> Peace could prevail, and with peace on the Earth,
> Let all people enjoy a happy life.[15]

During that visit he discovered that the faith of Mongolian Buddhists had not entirely vanished, despite the seven decades of religious repression and Communist ideology imposed by the Mongolian People's Revolutionary Party. Since giving religious teachings in public was still prohibited at the time of the Kushok Bakula's first visit to Mongolia, he quietly offered them to a small group of the faithful in his hotel room. This was the first of his regular visits and teachings in Mongolia through which he enabled Mongolian Buddhists to strengthen their weakened ties to Buddhism. D. Choijamts, the abbot of Gandantegchenling Monastery in Mongolia, who at the time of the Kushok Bakula's first visit to Mongolia was a student at the monastery, remarked on the Kushok Bakula's benefaction to Mongolian Buddhists during that period:

> In spite of the fact that the time was severe and security was rigorous during the socialist regime in Mongolia, we would secretly find opportunities for the faithful to receive teaching and empowerments from our precious teacher, Bakula Rinpoche. These occasions enabled the Mongolian disciples to form a solid and indestructible relationship with our Guru. Then the peaceful transition to democracy in 1990, in the Year of the Horse, gave us the opportunity to enjoy freedom and practice faith and spirituality freely.[16]

Monk-Ambassador to Mongolia

In 1989, just a year before the peaceful democratic revolution in Mongolia, the Kushok Bakula was appointed as the Indian Ambassador to Mongolia. Thus, he became the first Buddhist monk to hold an ambassadorial position and take part in the development of the bilateral relations between India and what soon became a democratic Mongolia. When he presented his diplomatic credentials to J. Batmunkh, who at that time held the post of the Chairman of the Mongolian Parliament, the Kushok Bakula expressed his view that the Buddha Shakyamuni was in fact the first Indian Ambassador to Mongolia;[17] he bewildered the Mongolian governmental officials further by attending the meeting in his monastic robes and presenting them with ceremonial white scarves (*khata*) as an expression of his wishes for their long and prosperous lives. Several months after that, he witnessed the overthrow of one-party rule and the establishment of a new political system that was supportive of human rights, freedom of religious expression, and multiparty democratic elections. The democratic changes in the country allowed the Kushok Bakula to openly assist Mongolian Buddhists in their attempts to revitalize their Buddhist knowledge and devotional practices and to rebuild their temples and monastic institutions. Most of the latter had been razed to the ground under Stalin's influence.

The Kushok Bakula soon began to travel across the extensive, rugged terrains and dusty roads of Mongolia. During his frequent expeditions to Mongolia's rural areas, he visited the rebuilt temples, imparted teachings to Buddhists, performed rituals of blessing and empowerment, and called for the return to Buddhist ethical values, which were neglected during the Communist period. As the Kushok Bakula's popularity grew, Mongolian people from various corners of the country continued to flock to the Indian Embassy, waiting in queues every morning to receive his blessings. He soon became affectionately called *Elchin Bagsh* ("Ambassador Teacher") by the Mongolians. On May 29, 1991, the Kushok Bakula initiated the first public celebration of the Buddha's birthday in democratic Mongolia, which was held at the National Cultural and Recreational Center and attended by thousands of people. Another significance of that event was that, for the first time after seven decades of religious oppression, Mongolian political leaders, headed by the President of Mongolia, participated in a public religious ceremony.

Revitalizing Buddhism in Mongolia

Observing the conditions of Buddhist monasticism, the Kushok Bakula noticed the pressing need for the proper training of Mongolian monks, among whom many did not adhere to monastic regulations for a variety of reasons, one being the lack of monastic institutions that could house monks and provide them with daily necessities and adequate education. He often publicly pointed out the importance of upholding one's monastic vows, which he saw as indispensable for the flourishing of Buddhism in Mongolia. Not long after filling the post of Indian Ambassador, the Kushok Bakula procured Indian visas and funding for Mongolian monks who desired to study in the refugee Tibetan monasteries in India such as Gomang, Sera, the Buddhist School of Dialectics in Dharamashala, the Central Institute for Tibetan Higher Studies, and so on. Until then, it had been virtually impossible for Mongolians to acquire such a visa.[18] More significantly, in 1999, the Kushok Bakula built the Pethub Stangey Choskor Ling Monastery in Ulaanbaatar, which is commonly referred to by Mongolians as Bakula Rinpoche's Monastery. Built in the Tibetan architectural style, it was named after the Kushok Bakula's home monastery in Ladakh. This monastery in Ulaanbaatar became a prominent venue for the training of young monks, public teachings, and ritual empowerments bestowed by the Kushok Bakula himself.[19] Until recently, in addition to Gandantegchenling Monastery, now recognized as the official center of Mongolian Buddhism, Bakula Rinpoche's monastery was the only teaching monastery that provided room and board for the young monks. Prior to granting the novice ordination to young candidates, some of whom came from as far as Buryatia, the Kushok Bakula carefully examined the candidates and their families to determine their motivation and suitability for a monastic life.

At a time when well-trained Buddhist teachers were in great demand in Mongolia, the Kushok Bakula brought highly qualified lamas from Ladakh and Sikkim to educate students in his monastery. To this day, young monks studying in his monastery continue to be educated in Buddhist doctrine, in the classical Tibetan and Mongolian languages, English, mathematics, and geography. Upon graduation, the best students are sent to India for the highest levels of monastic education. With financial assistance from the Tibet Foundation UK, in 2002, a clinic of traditional Buddhist medicine was built on the monastery's grounds; there, Mongolian and Tibetan traditional doctors offer medical care to both the monastic and lay communities. G. Luvsantseren, the head of the Mongolian Buddhist Studies Institute, who worked closely with the Kushok Bakula in the ABCP, in his commemorative speech highlighted the fact that the Kushok Bakula appreciated the uniquely Mongolian form of Buddhist culture and that his "venture was not aimed at Indianizing or Tibetanizing the monks" in Mongolia.[20] As a fervent advocate of human rights, the Kushok Bakula also made sure that the spiritual needs of Mongolian women and their contribution to Buddhism would not be neglected. To that end, he nurtured the creation of the Lay Women Buddhist Organization and gave monastic ordination to women for the first time ever in modern Mongolia.

The Kushok Bakula's various activities dedicated to the restoration of Mongolian Buddhism and culture included his undertaking to convince the Indian government to allow for the relics of the Buddha, kept at the National Museum in New Delhi, to be brought to Mongolia for viewing. As a result of that effort, in August of 1993, the Indian Deputy Minister of Culture brought these relics to Ulaanbaatar. The relics were on display at the Central Cultural Palace for a month and worshipped by tens of thousands of people. Reflecting on that event, Mr. N. Enkhbayar, former President of the Mongolian People's Revolutionary Party and Minister of Culture, said: "For the Mongolian people who had suffered many years of cultural persecution and were denied practice of their faith, the coming of the holy Buddha's relics was like the coming of Lord Buddha to our land."[21]

Since in the early years of Mongolian democracy literature on Buddhist teachings was virtually nonexistent in the modern Mongolian language, the Kushok Bakula encouraged N. Enkhbayar to translate *The Teaching of the Buddha*[22] from English to Mongolian. The book was published in 1995 in Japan and distributed to Mongolian Buddhists free of charge. Yet another inspiration of the Kushok Bakula was to establish the International Buddhist Institute in Mongolia, with the aim to enable international students to conduct research on Mongolian Buddhism. He also invited other eminent Buddhist teachers to come to Mongolia, including the 14th Dalai Lama, who came to Mongolia for the first time in 1992 and gave public teachings and the Kalacakra initiation. The Kushok Bakula's work was nonsectarian: aware of the early contacts between the Mongols and the Sakya order of Tibetan Buddhism – which dates to the thirteenth century, when Kublai Khan brought the Sakya master Phagpa Lama ('Phags pa) to his court from Tibet – the Kushok Bakula made it possible for Mongolians to reestablish their historical connection with the Sakya order by inviting one of the heads of the Tibetan Sakya order, Sakya Trinzin, to Mongolia in 1995. Although the Kushok Bakula belonged to the Gelug order of Tibetan Buddhism, he demonstrated to Mongolian Buddhists his nonsectarian approach to Buddhism and his genuine desire for the development of Buddhism in Mongolia.

While serving as the Indian Ambassador, the Kushok Bakula facilitated India's fruitful cultural relations with Mongolia in ways that enriched the lives of Mongolian people and created new educational opportunities for young people. In so doing, he set up an Indian Cultural Center; equipped with audiovisual materials, books, a performance space, and artwork, the Center has enabled Mongolians to study Indian languages and classical Indian dances. He also helped to establish the Mongolian–Indian Friendship Farm in the city of Darkhan and the Training and Industrial Center in Ulaanbaatar. Likewise, under his initiative, more than 50 Mongolian students were sent for training in Indian colleges and universities under various exchange programs. Ts. Gombosüren, Mongolian Foreign Minister from 1988 to 1996, said this of the Kushok Bakula's ambassadorial service: "There are many major developments that took place in promoting bilateral relations between our two countries [India and Mongolia], and one can clearly see the impact of tremendous contribution made by Kushok Bakula Rinpoche."[23]

Acknowledging the Kushok Bakula's contribution to Mongolian political, social, and religious life when democratic governance in Mongolia was in its infancy, the first democratically elected President of Mongolia, P. Ochirbat, who governed Mongolia from 1990 to 1997, wrote of the Kushok Bakula's constructive inputs in the highest of terms. He pointed out that, by the end of 1990, there were about 50 reopened temples and monasteries sheltering about a thousand monks; but, due to the former restrictive regulations in the country, it was difficult to coordinate the functioning of temples and monasteries. There was no universally recognized leader of Mongolian Buddhists either. The new government dissolved the Council of Religious Affairs that had been set up earlier and replaced it with a supernumerary Religious Council led by a presidential adviser. It formulated a new state policy regarding religion that guaranteed religious freedom and advanced the preservation of the ancient cultural heritage of Mongolia. As all this occurred, noted Mr. Ochirbat, "Bakula Rinpoche advised the people to accept change and maintain peace, harmony, and good will in accord with the cherished values of civilized behavior. Bakula Rinpoche's approach to human psychology brought about desired change, yielding peaceful and meaningful results."[24] N. Enkhbayar underlined the Kushok Bakula's important role in assuring peaceful solutions to political change in Mongolia, which found itself at a crossroad when the country desired a complete departure from the past and a change for the better. He said:

> It was due to our Buddhist heritage and Rinpoche's presence in the country that the transition to democracy in Mongolia, unlike in other socialist countries, was so peaceful. Rinpoche was an integral part of this great transformation and he played an active role in these changes through his advice, assistance, and participation... Young people, including those who actively participated in democratic changes in Mongolia, sought Rinpoche's guidance and help. Many politicians and businessmen also sought audience with Rinpoche to seek his advice... Bakula Rinpoche's advice was simple, yet convincing... If not Bakula Rinpoche, who else could have guided the people through these changes?... In all his interactions with Mongolian people, Rinpoche enthused unity among them and asked the people to work for preserving Mongolia's distinct national identity and independence. And at the same time, he exhorted them to work for the development of the country... For his yeomen service to the nation, the President of Mongolia (P. Ochirbat) conferred upon him "Polar Star," a state award, in 2001.[25]

Not everyone appreciated the Kushok Bakula's council at that time of political turbulence, as certain political circles that resisted change in the country accused the Kushok Bakula of interfering in the domestic affairs of Mongolia, and some even suggested that he be sent back to India.[26] But, on the basis of his accomplishments, most Mongols to this day revere the Kushok Bakula as the fulfillment of the prophesied, bodhisattva emanation of Arhat Bakula. In the year 2008, on the occasion of what would have been the the Kushok Bakula's 91st birthday, distinguished figures in Mongolian political, cultural, and academic spheres wrote of him as a bodhisattva who had brought the nineteenth-century prophecy to reality. Lama G. Purevbat, the most prominent Buddhist artist in Mongolia and the founding director of the Mongolian Institute of Buddhist Art, referred to the Kushok Bakula as "our great teacher Bodhisattva, who made many meritorious deeds to restore and revive Buddhism in Mongolia for the fourth time in the history of our country."[27] Similarly, G. Luvsantseren, the Director of the Mongolian Studies Institute, wrote about the Kushok Bakula's historic role in Mongolia in this way: "Kushok Bakula Rinpoche was a Bodhisattva who dedicated his life for the welfare of all living beings on this earth ... [regarded] as a Great Teacher who had come from India to perform this historic task."[28] The previously mentioned first democratically elected President of Mongolia, P. Ochirbat, wrote this:

> [He] came to Mongolia as a divine messenger at the time of peaceful transformation to democracy and inspired our people ... I always looked to him with prayer in my heart to gain inner strength and confidence when our country was passing through a crucial phase of history in the period of democratic reforms ... Bakula Rinpoche recognized distinctive characteristics of Mongolian democracy and the historic necessity to develop its national culture and traditions, to restore religion to its pristine glory with emphasis on reviving Buddhism as an inseparable part of Mongolian cultural heritage.[29]

During his diplomatic service in Mongolia, the Kushok Bakula traveled to Beijing every two months on his diplomatic mission. During those visits, at the request of Chinese Buddhists, he discreetly offered teachings at a time when giving religious teachings without governmental permission was prohibited. In the year 2000, at the conclusion of his diplomatic service, the Kushok Bakula returned to India, but he regularly visited Mongolia, imparting teachings and empowerments, despite his frail health.

Death, Commemoration, and the Perpetuation of the Tradition

On November 24, 2004, the Kushok Bakula died at the age of 87. His body was kept in Delhi for several days for viewing by many high political and religious dignitaries of India and other countries. On December 7, a special Indian Air Force plane carried the Kushok Bakula's body, covered with a national flag, to Leh, the capital of Ladakh, and it landed in the airport renamed as Bakula Rinpoche Airport. Monks in Leh performed prayers and rituals for 14 days, and on December 16, 2004, the Kushok Bakula's body was cremated with state honors and the police and military men fired shots in the air as an expression of respect. Thousands of monks and laypeople attended the cremation to collect his ashes for blessing. Within a year of the cremation, a gold-gilded, silver stupa measuring 3.5 meters was constructed for keeping his relics and was placed in his monastery in Ladakh. According to the report of Sonam Wangchuk Shakspo, who worked in various capacities with the Kushok Bakula in Mongolia during his time as ambassador, a mongoose[30] appeared in the courtyard of Pethub monastery in Ladakh shortly after the cremation of the Kushok Bakula's body; it ran into the private room of the Kushok Bakula and sat on his cushion. It stayed there for 49 days, behaving like a pet and eating only vegetarian food from the hands of the amused monks. At the completion of the 49th day, it disappeared.[31]

When the news of the Kushok Bakula's death reached Mongolia, crowds of people gathered at Pethub Monastery in Ulaanbaatar to pay homage to their ambassador-teacher. The Prime Minister of Mongolia sent his condolences to the government and people of India, and the Mongolian government dispatched a special envoy to India to offer a floral tribute to the Kushok Bakula. Having obtained some of the Kushok Bakula's relics, his Mongolian disciples placed them in a newly constructed, silver Bodhi Stupa, made with

110 kilograms of white silver, embedded with 1878 precious stones, and measuring 2.5 meters in height. Likewise, a gold plated, life-sized statue of the Kushok Bakula was made by Mongolian artists and ceremonially installed in the same monastery in Ulaanbaatar, with prayers for his swift rebirth. A hanging painting (*thangka*) with a portrait of the Kushok Bakula, which was painted by Lama Purevbat and placed in the monastery, was reprinted in a smaller size (60 × 50 cm) and distributed among Mongolian Buddhists across the country.

A year after the Kushok Bakula's passing, on November 24, 2005, a boy named Thup stan Nga wang was born in Ladakh; he was to be recognized as Arhat Bakula's 20th incarnation and was confirmed as such on February 26, 2008 by the 14th Dalai Lama. As this news reached Mongolia, requests for the young Bakula's visit to Mongolia were made, indicating that the connection between Arhat Bakula and the Mongols that was established by the 18th Kushok Bakula will continue. What form that connection will take will be seen in the future.

References

Enkhbayar, D. (2008) A visionary monk and a statesman, in *In Commemoration of the 91st Birth Anniversary of HH Bakula Rinpoche*, Pethub Buddhist Center, Ulaanbaatar.

Gombosüren, Ts. (2008) A pioneer from Jagar (India), in *In Commemoration of the 91st Birth Anniversary of HH Bakula Rinpoche*, Pethub Buddhist Center, Ulaanbaatar.

Kozhevnikova, M. (2003) *Povesty ob Uchitele: Bakula Rinpoche v Rossii* [A history of the teacher: Bakula Rinpoche in Russia], Nartang, Moscow.

Lkhamsürengiin, K. (1999) *Bakula Rinbüchi Tüvdenchognor (Bakula Rinpoche Thubten Choknor)*, Mongol Uls Shinjlekh Ukhaani Akademi Khel Zokhiolin Khüreelen, Ulaanbaatar.

Luvsantseren, G. (2008) My memoirs about H.H. Bakula Rinpoche, in *In Commemoration of the 91st Birth Anniversary of HH Bakula Rinpoche*, Pethub Buddhist Center, Ulaanbaatar.

Orhcirbat, P. (2008) Bakula Rinpoche who left behind a bright influence in Mongolia, in *In Commemoration of the 91st Birth Anniversary of HH Bakula Rinpoche*, Pethub Buddhist Center, Ulaanbaatar.

Purevbat, G. (2008) A great teacher of Mongolian people, in *In Commemoration of the 91st Birth Anniversary of HH Bakula Rinpoche*, Pethub Buddhist Center, Ulaanbaatar.

Shakspo, S.W. (2008) *Bakula Rinpoche: A Visionary Lama and Statement*, Sonam Wangchuk Shakspo, New Delhi.

Ven Choijamts, D. (2008) Bakula Rinpoche's contribution to the revival of Buddhism in Mongolia, in *In Commemoration of the 91st Birth Anniversary of HH Bakula Rinpoche*, Pethub Buddhist Center, Ulaanbaatar.

Further Reading

Bakkula (1966) in *Encyclopaedia of Buddhism*, vol. 2 (ed. G.P. Malalesekera), Government of Ceylon, Colombo.

Bakkula Sutta (2001) in *The Middle Length Discourses of the Buddha: A Translation of the Majjhima Nikaya*, 2nd edn (trans. Bhikkhu Ñanamoli and Bhikkhu Bodhi), Wisdom, Boston, MA.

Byrne, S. (2005) The ambassador-teacher: reflections on Kushok Bakula Rinpoche's importance in the revival of Buddhism in Mongolia. *Ladakh Studies*, 19 (March), 38–48.

Humphrey, C. and Ujeed, H. (2013) *A Monastery in Time: The Making of Mongolian Buddhism*, University of Chicago Press, Chicago, IL.

Jerryson, M.K. (2008) *Mongolian Buddhism: The Rise and Fall of the Sangha*, Silkworm Books, Bangkok.

Shakspo, S.W. (2006) *Bakula Rinpoche: A Visionary Lama and Statesman*, Sonam Wanghuck Shagspo, New Delhi.

Notes

1. In the records associated with the Eighth Bogdo Gegeen, Jebtsundamba Rinpoche, who was the head of Mongolian Buddhism.
2. Sometimes his name is also spelled as Bakkula, Vakkula, or Bakula. In Pali sources, particularly in the *Majjhima Nikaya* IV, the meaning of his name is derived from the word *dvi-kula* ("two families"), a derivation based on the narrative according to which he was swallowed by a large fish when his nurse tried to bath him in the river Yamuna when he was five days old. A fisherman from Benares, who caught the fish and found the boy alive in it, adopted the child. Having discovered their son alive, the birth parents claimed the child to be theirs, but the king decided that the child should belong to both families. According to the later Tibetan and Mongolian sources, he was named Bakula after the *bakula* tree because he wore clothing made of the leaves and bark of a *bakula* tree during his life as a forest hermit.
3. Purevbat 2008: 84. See also Shakspo 2008: 58. The well-known Mongolian scholar and monk Zava Damdin (1867–1937) makes reference to such a prophecy in his *Golden Book* (*Altan Devter*) but cites the ancient *Manjushrimulatantra* as the original source of the prophecy.
4. Lkhamsürengiin 1999: 85.
5. *Zava Damdin*, I, 47a, 1–3 mentioned by Lkhamsürengiin 1999: 77.
6. The painting is now in the private possession of Dorjiin Damba's family in Ulaanbaatar.
7. gNas brtan phag mchod.
8. Lkhamsürengiin 1999: 77.
9. See Shakspo 2008: 17–27. According to Shakspo, the Indian government provided a hundred scholarships for the higher education of students from Ladakh.
10. Luvsantseren 2008: 76.
11. Kozhevnikova 2003: 14, 17–18.
12. Kozhevnikova 2003: 18.
13. Kozhevnikova 2008: 49.
14. Kozhevnikova 2008: 57.
15. Luvsantseren 2008: 77.
16. Ven Choijamts 2008: 45.
17. Enkhbayar 2008: 35; Shakspo 2008: 62.
18. One of the monks sent to India by Kushok Bakula in 1990 was Lama G. Purevbat, who after completing his studies in Dharamshala became the most prominent Buddhist artist in Mongolia and the founder and director of the Mongolian Institute of Buddhist Art.
19. Luvsantseren 2008: 79. In the present time, Erdene Zuu monastery in Kharakhorum also has a dormitory for young students, which was built a few years ago with financial assistance from the United States.
20. Luvsantseren 2008: 79.
21. Enkhbayar 2008: 35.
22. The translation is based on the English version of *Teachings of the Buddha* published by Bukkyo Dendo Kyokai in Japan and dedicated to the promotion of Buddhism in the world.
23. Gombosüren 2008: 64.
24. Orhcirbat 2008: 57–8.
25. Enkhbayar 2008: 33–4, 37–8.
26. Gombosüren 2008: 66.
27. Purevbat 2008: 86
28. Luvsantseren 2008: 75, 77.
29. Ochirbat 2008: 55–6.
30. A reason for which the appearance of a mongoose was considered miraculous by monks of the Pethub Monastery is that this animal species is not found in Ladakh.
31. This incident was reported to me by Sonam Wangchuk during my field research in Mongolia in the summer of 2009.

24

Hunger, Hard Work, and Uncertainty
Tashi Dondrup Reminisces on Life and Death in a Tibetan Village

Geoff Childs

Editor's Introduction

"Virtuoso spiritual seekers" are a distinct minority in any society and, for a balanced, more nuanced understanding of life in a Buddhist community, it is therefore important to consider the perspectives of all individuals – from venerated saints to humble farmers. In the case of Tashi Dondrup, we see how a poor, socially marginal peasant nonetheless tried his best to live according to the ethics he derived from Buddhist teachings. As in other biographies, this householder struggled with the issue of violence, in this case the inevitable killing of creatures living in the soil he tilled, culling a yak herd of useless males, and eliminating vermin: the lice that infested his body and the rodents that stole his scarce food. Reconciling his Buddhist tradition with the realities of survival as a farmer high in the Himalayas, he tried to remediate the demerit of violence with chants and karmic calculations. Again, Buddhist belief and practice is centered in making good karma and softening the accumulation of bad. Tashi's poignantly rendered biography also illustrates that, in practice, Buddhists try to make final attempts to upgrade an individual's karmic account – determining next-lifetime destiny – through support for old age as a time for more intense religious practices and then, finally, with massive merit-making ceremonies after death, in which merit is transferred to the dead.

Background: Practicing Buddhism and the Complexities of Subsistence Farming

Translating biographies of Tibetan religious practitioners is a common practice nowadays.[1] This is not surprising given that Tibetans are prolific at scribing narrative accounts of their lamas, and Western fascination with Tibet centers disproportionately on Buddhism and Buddhist practitioners. Although the vast majority of Tibetans are versed in the basic tenets of their

Figure 24.1 Tashi Dondrup. Photograph by Geoff Childs. Reprinted with permission.

religion, they regularly encounter predicaments stemming from the incongruity of cultural ideals with economic necessities. Like people in every society, Tibetans must sometimes transgress moral imperatives while side-stepping social reprobation. For example, Buddhism emphasizes nonviolence and consequently frowns upon the killing of any sentient being. However, farmers and herders must atone for the fact that they slaughter innumerable creatures during daily subsistence activities. Recognizing that plowing the earth obliterates soil-dwelling insects, a Tibetan farmer chants a prayer at the end of each furrow to moderate the negative consequences of his action. He is not supposed to harm sentient beings yet must do so in order to feed his family.

Other actions require a bit more finesse to rectify inconsistencies between ethical directives and worldly deeds. I have heard people remark upon learning that Tibetans are enthusiastic consumers of meat, "How is that possible? Aren't Buddhists prohibited from killing animals?" The answer to this apparent cultural contradiction is that (a) Buddhist principles strongly discourage the killing of any sentient being but (b) Tibetans depend on livestock for survival in their arid, high-altitude environment so (c) they engage the services of butchers, a stigmatized class of people who accrue the sins of killing so that others can consume the flesh of domesticated animals.[2] As long as a ruse is maintained that an animal is not killed specifically to feed the meat's eventual consumer, the contradiction is resolved. The rationale boils down to, "I didn't kill it, and it wasn't killed for me, but since it is dead I may as well eat it."

Slaughtering animals to put food on the table is not the only way Tibetans terminate the lives of sentient beings. Villagers need to manage herd sizes and herd compositions. They need animals to plow, transport loads, produce milk and wool, and reproduce the herd. A useful herd consists of yaks, cows, and various hybrids that serve various functions and are adapted to grazing at various altitudes. Whereas some hybrids are highly valued, others are economically useless and need to be culled. *Dzomo* (female cross between a yak and a cow) are a herd's main dairy producers, but their offspring are weak and do not yield much milk. Allowing *dzomo* to breed is important because pregnancy and parturition stimulate milk production. But, as one herder informed me, "There is no benefit if the offspring of a *dzomo* grows up because it will not produce any milk. We do not give milk to such an animal. That would be like giving it our own butter. It just dies."

Note how the man uses the intransitive verb "die" (*shi*) rather than the transitive verb "kill" (*so*) to deflect his own culpability in the demise of bovines. This lexical maneuver disassociates the action (not permitting the newborn animal to suckle) from the outcome (death by starvation). To violently dispatch a newborn calf is an unequivocal sinful act, but to restrict a calf's caloric intake so that it succumbs to a death that appears more natural is ethically ambiguous.

Context and Early Life

I learned these lessons about how Tibetans navigate the complex and often contradictory matrix of moral ideals and economic necessities while living as an anthropologist in Nubri, Nepal, a border region situated on the southern slope of the Himalayas. It was settled at least 900 years ago and is now inhabited by roughly 3500 people. From the mid-seventeenth century until the 1840s, Nubri was controlled by the Tibetan government based in Lhasa, but following a war it was incorporated within Nepal, where it remains today. The people of Nubri adhere to the Nyingmapa and Kargyupa sects of Buddhism; religious life centers on married lamas and their village temples. Until the 1960s a lucrative trans-Himalayan trade route allowed Nubri's inhabitants to prosper. By the time I started conducting fieldwork during the 1990s, however, the decline in trade and other factors had impoverished local communities.

Over the course of numerous visits spanning a decade, I was fortunate to reside with Tashi Dondrup. Born in 1929, he was the illegitimate child of a destitute mother and a father who denied all paternal responsibility. Although the Buddhist moral code condemns improper sexual conduct, Tibetans maintain a remarkably tolerant attitude toward illegitimate children. In an economic environment where labor is always in high demand, additional farm hands are welcome and can find a niche in society. Although Tashi did not bear any stigma associated with his circumstances at birth, he was economically disadvantaged because the basic needs to marry and establish a household – agricultural land, a house, and animals – are passed from a father to his legitimate offspring. Without such assets, people like Tashi Dondrup find it difficult, if not impossible, to marry and have their own families. Hence, he was a lifelong bachelor.

Illegitimacy creates other problems for the individual. Tibetans depend on family for social, economic, and political support. Lacking an extensive kin network renders a person vulnerable in the community. Should troubles arise, one can muster few allies to overcome a crisis or weather a time of need. Tashi's immediate family consisted only of his mother and half-sister (also illegitimate), so he had to carefully cultivate relationships with other people. At the time when Tashi was easing into old age, he even gained a new family member: a foreign anthropologist. We referred to each other using the kinship terms "elder brother" and "younger brother," and through an unstated contract I became the person who provided Tashi with economic support when he no longer had the capability to work for daily subsistence.

Being uneducated and illiterate did not prevent Tashi from comprehending basic Buddhist teachings. After all, he grew up in a Buddhist community, regularly attended a host of rituals, and lived next door to an important lama. Tashi believed in reincarnation and expressed his understanding that we had been brothers in a previous life. He also understood the principles of cause (through a thought or action) and effect (a future consequence of that thought or action), a relationship that is generally termed "karma."

Tashi articulated his understanding of karma by musing that our past actions had brought us together in the present, and that our current sibling-like relationship would make certain our paths would cross in the future. However, similar to his fellow villagers, Tashi's daily religious observances were not geared toward attaining enlightenment or understanding esoteric Buddhist philosophy.

Tashi's devotional activities instead were dedicated to achieving health and economic security in the present and near future. For example, to appease local protector deities, every year Tashi raised a banner inscribed with prayers on the roof of the house. Whenever we departed on a trip he lit a butter lamp and beseeched his *pho lha* (man's god)[3] to guide and protect us. He always made sure to honor the village's mountain-dwelling protector deity by offering a silk scarf, butter, and liquor. Tashi self-identified as a Buddhist and habitually repeated Buddhist prayers in which he vowed to benefit all sentient beings. Yet he never hesitated to crush lice and fleas plucked from his clothing or to kill home-invading rats by enticing them to feast upon poisoned morsels of food. When I asked Tashi whether he should consider adopting a more compassionate demeanor toward these nocturnal visitors, Tashi chortled, "I am a poor man. The rats should take pity on me instead of the other way around!"

Tashi had an unimaginably rough childhood. Yet, despite a disadvantaged position in life, he always maintained an immense capacity for generosity. I surmised that he endured hardships by taking solace in the basic tenets of Buddhism – for example, the knowledge that performing good deeds in this lifetime can help ensure less suffering in future lives. On the other hand, I was always struck by Tashi's pragmatism. He never blamed bad karma for his present predicaments. Rather, he faced obstacles with stoic determination. Here are some details from the life story of Tashi Dondrup, a humble Tibetan villager from Nubri, Nepal:[4]

> As a child I had nothing. You know, I am a *nyelu*, a bastard. My parents never married, and my father never even claimed me as his legitimate son. So my mother and I lived alone, without a home, without fields, and without cattle. Oh, how I suffered as a child! You can never imagine the hardships! But let me start from the beginning.

> When I emerged into the world after spending nine months in my mother's womb, there was nothing to eat, nothing to drink. Food was scarce, so we often ate just boiled vegetables with our *tsampa* [the Tibetan staple, flour made from roasted barley]. When mother worked for other families, they would make corn mush for us. She would eat half, and I would eat half.

> Even though my mother worked hard, I didn't have proper clothing to wear. I wore the old, cast-aside clothing of other people. I wandered about the village looking for whatever scraps could be worn. When it came time for sleeping, I had nothing to cover me beyond the rags that I wore. I didn't even have shoes, so I would pull my knees into my chest and sleep curled up like a ball. Even during the winter I often had no shoes. If I found only a single shoe, I would wear that. It snows a lot during the winter, so my feet were always blistered and cracked. I suffered very much when festering sores developed and bled. With my feet in such a condition, it was difficult to carry salt and barley up and down the valley. But I did so anyway, for this little bit of trade gave us some food.

> We stayed at other peoples' homes, sometimes working as their servants, sometimes living alone if a house was empty. One time we even lived beneath a house in the stable for cattle. Mother was a good weaver, so while she did weaving for other people we would get a place to stay. But living in the homes of others meant that my mother and I always had to sit farthest from the fire, farthest from the warmth. It was not our home, after all. We had no home of our own.

> Most memories [from my youth] are of hunger, hard work, and uncertainty. If only you knew how much I had suffered. Everybody used to say, "Poor Tashi, he is such a good person, but he is so unfortunate." I learned how to work hard, that is why things got better with time.

> My father gave me no inheritance, and beyond that he would not even look at me when we met. When I got older things gradually changed. He told me I was a good worker. Everybody knows this, I always have been one. I asked him for money, barley, or even salt – anything that could be used for bartering. I told him, "If you give me something to trade with, I can do business. How can I do any business without any wealth?" One day he promised to give me some inheritance.

My mother and I never saw the coming of the other woman into his life. When I was 17 or 18, my father married another woman.[5] They had a son, you know him, he is the guy we call Balang [Ox].[6] When Balang was four, his mother died, and when he was eight, our father died. I felt sorry for him, so from that time onward I did much for Balang. Despite my help I still got none of our father's estate. All of the fields, all of the animals, the house where he still lives – all of it went to my half-brother. I received nothing!

We say that my half-brother is a son of the summer, the season of abundance. If that is so, then I am a son of winter. Nevertheless I felt sorry for the boy. I helped him all the time, fed him from our meager supplies, and acted like a true elder brother, or even a father. Yet how has he repaid such kindness?

Since the death of his parents Balang has not accomplished a single virtuous deed. He squandered his entire inheritance; now there is nothing left. Not only that, but you should see the way he treats me! Remember the first months when you lived here? He used to come by all the time, sit there silently like the bovine that he is, and act as if he were king. He ate all our food and treated me like his servant. He never cleaned the dishes or did anything helpful. He treats me like a lowly servant. I acted as his guardian when he was a child. But these days I no longer even speak to him. I have no use for a brother like that.

A Life of Struggle, New Opportunities, Tragedy

Ties of kinship are very important in Tibetan society; family members are supposed to support each other in times of need. That is why Balang's dismissive treatment of his elderly half-brother is such an egregious breach of social ethics. Despite receiving no assistance from his closest kin, Tashi managed to improve his living conditions.

I had neither cattle nor fields, but by working hard I could buy a house. In addition to doing some small trade up and down the valley and working as a servant for others, I once went to Calcutta. I went with a man from Tsum [a valley to the east of Nubri]. Not only did he pay my expenses, but he also gave me about 200 Indian Rupees as a loan so I could do some business on the side. In Calcutta, we stayed with traders from Nyeshang [Manang District, Nepal]. These people had rented a house on the other side of the big bridge over the river. The bridge, this is what I remember most of Calcutta. I heard that there were English people in Calcutta. I never saw them, only scores and scores of Indians. I had never seen such a crowded place in my life!

Anyway, I bought many things in Calcutta, especially precious stones. I brought these back to Nubri, and for a few weeks I went from village to village, from house to house, selling my wares. The profit was very good. I was only about 18 years old at that time, but I understood how to do business. I bought my house with the profits. Yet the house was very dilapidated. Because nobody had lived in it for many years much of the wood was rotting and needed to be replaced. The floorboards were dangerously weak, and all the storage chests were useless. I did much of the work myself. When people helped, I paid them some wages and served food. Wages were low at that time because money had more value. I got the wood for one storage chest from Li, and for those others from Sho.[7] People still make comments when they see these storage chests. They say, "Ah, Tashi Dondrup, where did you get such good wood? How did you build such good chests?" If you do something, you may as well do it right and make it last.

Tashi worked hard to ensure that his mother and sister could live under a roof of their own. But their happiness was short lived, for tragedy soon struck the family.

My sister and I have the same mother, but different fathers. Although much younger, like me she was a *nyelu*, an illegitimate child. Her father was a monk who broke his vows. It was my mother's decision to make her a nun. She was sent to Dagkar Taso Monastery[8] for training. Lopon Zangpo donated some clothing and other items for her. After her ordination at Dagkar Taso, she usually lived with my mother and me in the village.[9] But she had to go to Pungyen during the first month of the year. In the past people still went to Pungyen Monastery[10] for a winter religious retreat. Nowadays they only go during the warmer seasons. Perhaps the monks and nuns are not as dedicated as in former times. Who knows, but at that time people went every winter for a religious retreat during the first month of the year [usually February according to the Tibetan lunar calendar]. The elder ones went to pray and meditate, while the younger ones went to learn reading and writing. When I was 24, she was 13 and was staying at Pungyen Monastery. Eleven people in all were there that winter [1953] when a snowstorm struck.

Among the 11 people staying at Pungyen Monastery, three nuns were killed by an avalanche. My sister was one of them. Of course, at the time we knew nothing, since the monastery is hidden behind that ridge over there. In the afternoon Dawa Tenzin and I were playing dice in the courtyard. A man came running into the village and called to me, "Your sister the nun, she is dead!" I was stunned, not ready to believe what he had said. My mother began to cry.

Several men and I grabbed digging tools and headed up to Pungyen Monastery. We climbed and climbed, anxious to see what had happened and what we could do. The trail is so high and so cold and so difficult to get through due to snow. But now we had to go – we had to see if we could save my sister.

When we got to the temple we found the buildings had been buried under huge chunks of ice. It was a disaster. We started digging furiously – I have no idea where my energy came from. Eventually we found the rubble of the temple, and we found the bodies. Three nuns were dead, including my only sister. That was the saddest day of my life. With heavy hearts we brought the bodies down to the village for a proper cremation. My mother and I sold everything we had in order to perform a merit-making ceremony on her behalf. We were poor, but we had to do this to honor our kin. Later some people managed to dig up most of the statues and other valuable items housed in the temple. The temple has since been rebuilt, but it will never be the same.

People wondered why such a tragedy struck our monastery. Some said that the protector of our village who lives on the mountain must have been angry with us, and even blamed the Japanese mountaineers who had tried to climb Mt. Pungyen during the past autumn, saying that the climbers must have defiled the sacred slopes of the mountain. I don't know if this was the reason. But when the climbers came back the next year for another attempt, we refused to let them go up.

A few years later Tashi's mother passed away. Tashi took pride in the fact that he had provided food and shelter for his mother in her old age, just as she had sustained him through infancy and childhood. With virtually no resources, Tashi had nevertheless fulfilled his filial obligations.

Elder Years and Religious Orientation

When I met Tashi in 1995 he was in his sixties. Although still spry and able to work for other households in exchange for food, he was anxious about the future. For Tibetans, old age is a time that should be dedicated to meritorious acts. In multigenerational households, elderly members do relatively simple chores such as feeding the animals and watching grandchildren. They are freed from more burdensome tasks so they have more time to recite prayers, circumambulate sacred places, and perform other actions that increase their storehouse of merit and enhance their chance of attaining a positive rebirth. Tashi did not have adult children to care for him in old age. Therefore, he had neither the requisite time to prepare for death in a culturally appropriate manner nor people to support him as his physical capabilities declined. But Tashi was a proud man who was reluctant to ask others for favors. He often told me, "I have never been a beggar. Why should I start now?" For a man of principle, death is preferable to the humiliation of beggary.

I once asked, "Tashi, are you afraid of death?" He replied:

Everybody is afraid of death. I am no exception. It is ridiculous for anybody to think he will not die soon. As an old man, I must think about death constantly, for my time is certainly drawing near. Nobody can hold off against death.

We grow old, and meanwhile our time in life expires day by day, month by month. When you are 20 you can look forward to being 30, and when you are 30 you can look forward to being 40. But when you reach 70 there is no longer anything to look forward to. At this point in life I have to wonder what will happen if I become ill again. Who will cook for me? Who will get food for me? Who will light my fire? And what will happen if I go blind? My eyesight is getting worse and worse these days. I am alone. With nobody to care for me, I will die quickly if I go blind. This is my greatest fear – being blind and incapable of taking care of myself. If things get too bad, I will stop eating and just fade away. That would be far better than clinging to the last breath of life and having to endure the indignity of suffering like a helpless child.

I was fortunate to visit Tashi one last time the year before he died. I arrived unannounced, yet Tashi did not seem surprised. He merely shrugged and remarked, "I knew you were coming. I dreamed about it the other night." Proof of his premonition was the vat of spirits distilled to celebrate my arrival.

As was our custom, Tashi sat on one side of his hearth while I sat on the other. We conversed about the usual topics: local culture, politics, and the wellbeing of mutual friends. We recounted past adventures and discussed ways to guarantee he had adequate resources to sustain him after I left. As time passed and the date of my departure grew near, Tashi became morose. During our last evening together we could not bring ourselves to turn in. We chatted deep into the night. Shortly before dawn Tashi asked to see, once again, a video of my daughters. He squinted at the small screen of the camera, watching as two little girls repeatedly bubbled, "Kam sangbo agu Tashi?" ("Are you well, Uncle Tashi?"). After viewing the video one last time, Tashi broke down in tears. He removed a necklace that he had worn since an infant, enfolded it in my hands with his gnarled fingers, and said, "Please give this to your girls." The significance of Tashi's gesture is unfathomable. By giving away the amulet that had protected him over a lifetime, Tashi conveyed that his end was near.

One night I received a telephone call at my home in St. Louis from Purbu Tsewang, my friend who is the headmaster of a school in Nubri. Purbu informed me that Tashi's health was deteriorating rapidly and that his end was near. After returning the phone to its cradle I placed the necklace Tashi had given me around the neck of my elder daughter as she slept with an angelic expression. The next morning, April 7, 2007, I learned that Tashi has passed away.

Tashi Dondrup often told me that we were brothers in a past life and will be brothers in a future life as well. I look forward to seeing him again.

References

Aziz, B. (1978) *Tibetan Frontier Families: Reflections on Three Generations from Ding-ri*, Vikas, New Delhi.

Blo brtan rdo rje with Stuart, K. (2008) *Life and Marriage in Skya rgya, a Tibetan Village*, YBK Publishers, New York.

Childs, G. (2004) *Tibetan Diary: From Birth to Death and Beyond in a Himalayan Valley of Nepal*, University of California Press, Berkeley.

Childs, G. (2008) *Tibetan Transitions: Historical and Contemporary Perspectives on Fertility, Family Planning, and Demographic Change*, Brill, Leiden.

Dargyay, E.M. (1982) *Tibetan Village Communities*, Vikas, New Delhi.

Goldstein, M.C. (1971a) Stratification, polyandry, and family structure in central Tibet. *Southwest Journal of Anthropology*, 27, 64–74.

Goldstein, M.C. (1971b) Taxation and the structure of a Tibetan village. *Central Asiatic Journal*, 15 (1), 1–27.

Goldstein, M.C., Sherap, D., and Siebenschuh, W.R. (2004) *A Tibetan Revolutionary: The Political Life and Times of Bapa Phüntso Wangye*, University of California Press, Berkeley.

Goldstein, M.C., Siebenschuh, W.R., and Tsering, T. (1997) *The Struggle for Modern Tibet: The Autobiography of Tashi Tsering*, M.E. Sharpe, Armonk, NY.

Khetsun, T. (2008) *Memories of Life in Lhasa under Chinese Rule*, Columbia University Press, New York.

Norbu, D. (1987 [1974]) *Red Star over Tibet*, Envoy Press, New York.

Taklha, N.L. (2001) *Born in Lhasa: The Autobiography of Namgyal Lhamo Taklha*, Snow Lion, Ithaca, NY.

Taring, D. (1986 [1970]) *Daughter of Tibet: The Autobiography of Rinchen Dolma Taring*, Wisdom, London.

Thargyal, R. (2007) *Nomads of Eastern Tibet: Social Organization and Economy of a Pastoral Estate in the Kingdom of Dege*, Brill, Leiden.

Tsarong, D.N. (2000) *In the Service of His Country: The Biography of Dasang Damdul Tsarong, Commander General of Tibet*, Snow Lion, Ithaca, NY.

Notes

1 Throughout history Tibetans have penned the vast majority of their biographical literature about venerated saints and lamas. Recently, members of Tibet's former aristocracy have written biographies of laypeople (e.g., Taring 1986; Tsarong 2000; Taklha 2001). Although interesting to read, viewpoints conveyed through the lens of a privileged social class reveal little about the lives of commoners. Meanwhile, scholars have reconstructed the life of the peasantry prior to the 1950s. Such studies do not fit the genre of biography, but they do provide rich details about economic practices, systems of taxation, marriage and family life, religious observances, and the social structure of rural communities before these were dramatically transformed in the 1950s when China reasserted control over Tibet (Goldstein 1971a, 1971b; Aziz 1978; Dargyay 1982; Thargyal 2007; Childs 2008: chapter 3). Several Tibetans have narrated their life stories in recent years. The opening chapters of several works are equally valuable for depictions of life prior to the 1950s (Norbu 1987; Goldstein, Siebenschuh, and Tsering 1997; Goldstein, Sherap, and Siebenschuh 2004; Blo brtan rdo rje 2008; Khetsun 2008). My own book, *Tibetan Diary*, follows the life course of lamas and laymen in historical and contemporary Nubri, Nepal (Childs 2004).

2 Muslims in the large cities of central Tibet have for centuries filled this niche. Even today in rural Tibet, butchers carry considerable stigma. During fieldwork in China's Tibet Autonomous Region, colleagues Melvyn Goldstein, Puchung Wangdui, and I encountered a household that reported no sources of income on our economic survey. Upon inquiry, we discovered that the family made their living by butchering animals for fellow community members. We subsequently invited the household's head to our living quarters and served him tea from our own cups; both actions breach cultural prohibitions against social interactions with butchers. Our gestures put the man at ease and allowed us, through roundabout means, to ascertain how much income his family can derive from butchering animals.

3 The *pho lha* (literally, "man's god") is inherited through the patrilineage, resides on a man's shoulder, and has a special place of worship within every household. By appeasing this deity through offerings, one ensures protection for the household and the lineage against harmful forces.

4 Most of the following autobiographical material is from *Tibetan Diary* (Childs 2004: 50–1, 118–19, 132, 167–8).

5 The timing here is significant. In Nubri a man inherits a portion of his father's land and animals when he marries, usually during his late teens or early twenties. With the promise of an inheritance Tashi could have gotten married. His father's subsequent marriage, and birth of a legitimate son, scuttled any such chance.

6 Tibetans are fond of giving each other nicknames. Balang's nickname plays upon his combination of physical strength and intellectual weakness. His other nickname, Rinyel ("He Who Sleeps in the Hills"), implies that he is more comfortable in the company of wild animals than humans.

7 Li and Sho are two villages in Nubri renowned for their abundant forest resources.

8 This monastery lies high upon a cliff in the valley between Kyirong and Dzongga, Tibet. It was founded at a site where the great saint Milarepa meditated during the eleventh century. Dagkar Taso was an important training center for monks, nuns, and married lamas from the highlands of Nepal.

9 Although it is tempting to imagine that Tibetans become monks and nuns purely out of religious devotion, the reality is more complex. Many illegitimate children are given by parents to monasteries because, lacking economic resources, the clerisy represents one way they can attain a livelihood and social status. In the case of nuns, taking religious vows does not always allow them to fully escape the burdens of family responsibilities. Many girls in Nubri are designated to be nuns not only so they can help care for younger siblings but also in the expectation that they will one day be the primary caretakers for aging parents.

10 Pungyen Monastery is a small temple with meditation huts situated near the base of Mt. Pungyen, the local name for the world's eighth-highest mountain (26,758 ft.), which is more commonly known by its Nepali name, Mt. Manaslu. The mountain is the residence of the local protector deity that the temple honors.

25

Benefiting the Doctrine and Sentient Beings

The Life of a Tibetan Lineage Master and the Ethos of Altruistic Action

Nicolas Sihlé

Editor's Introduction

The subject of this chapter, Ts'ampa Nawang, lives in north central Nepal, where the Tibetan Buddhist Mahayana-Vajrayana tradition is dominant. His extraordinary life as a tantric master allows us to understand how this tradition is lived in a rural high-altitude community. What the author focuses his critical inquiry on in this chapter, however, transcends the particularities of this context, as he considers how the dharma provides a dedicated Buddhist with an ethos, or overall attitude to life itself, and how it instills a sense of personal direction. It is easily noted in reading Mahayana texts that individuals should aspire to be altruistic, even vowing not to enter nirvana themselves until all other beings are established on the path. But, as is often the case in this textbook, we should wonder: what is the relationship between textual ideals and Buddhism as it is lived and practiced? Is such a grand expression of altruism just a trope or a living social reality?

Ts'ampa Nawang's life work in healing using traditional Tibetan medicine opens another important issue in understanding Buddhism. It has long been noted that a medical framework underlies the original formulation of the Buddha's dharma: in his first sermon in the Deer Park, he presented the gist of his teaching, the Four Noble Truths, in a distinctly medical style. He started with a clinical observation (Truth One, the existence of suffering) and proceeded to diagnosis (Truth Two, desire causes suffering), to prognosis (Truth Three, suffering and desire can be extinguished), to prescription (Truth Four, the Eightfold Path). If all beings are bound by suffering, what could be more natural than a Buddhist practicing medicine to relieve it, embodying compassion and altruism. Indeed, the Buddha famously required that members of the sangha be proactive in caring for their sick fellow monastics; and scholars now consider that monks in the Buddhist sangha may have contributed to the advancement in medical practices in South Asia. Indeed, the sangha's serving its surrounding communities through offering healing services may have been an important reason for Buddhism's success as a missionary religion.

As the astute student can notice, it is again kinship ties that bind individuals into their identity and destiny as Buddhists. It was Ts'ampa Nawang's own father who taught him from early on in life the mantras and methods of ritual practice, and who served as his guru in directing him to undergo long retreats and initiations to establish his lifelong spiritual practices. At one key moment of decision in his life, the father commanded his son not to be ordained as a Tibetan monk but to live his life as a married tantric practitioner. In an apt and memorable expression, Ts'ampa Nawang learned that "the vows of the monk are comparable to a fragile crystal vase, whereas those of the tantrist are like a sturdy copper vase, which will not break easily." Advised that if he remained true to his training he would not face difficulties, he moved forward with his life. This is the ethos of the tantric Buddhist, indeed. The exceptionally broad range of religious activities and related altruistic actions undertaken throughout Ts'ampa Nawang's life are testimony to the vitality of this approach to the householder's religious life in the Nyingmapa branch of Tibetan tradition.

One central focus of his religious activism and outreach is the propagation of the "*Mani* mantra" – that is, the repetition of *om mani padme hum* (usually translated "*Om*, Jewel in the Lotus, *Hum*"). This mantra is carved into rocks piled high at village entrances, printed on cloth flags that fly over settlements and mountain passes, and chanted using a rosary or prayer wheel, and Tibetan Buddhists believe that it brings blessings to all living beings, blessing settlements and the entire world. And, on a more advanced level, repeating this mantra while visualizing the most popular celestial bodhisattva in Asia (called Chenrizi in Tibetan, Avalokitesvara in Sanskrit, Kwan Yin in China) is considered a tantric practice that can lead the devotee to enlightenment. Capable of giving complex spiritual teachings to his disciples, Ts'ampa Nawang also considers that the relatively simple task of carving *mani* woodblocks – which can be used to print prayer flags with this mantra on them – is a major altruistic endeavor. His introducing hundreds of devotees to the daily recitation of this *mani* chanting/meditation at home, and at times in large gatherings, is one of many ways that he has found to live a meaningful Buddhist life: spreading the most precious thing in his world, the dharma.

Introduction

When accounts of Buddhist societies stress the core altruistic ideal of the bodhisattva – who works toward enlightenment in order to help all beings to achieve enlightenment themselves – one needs to ask: what is the place of this ideal in the actual lives of Buddhists? What forms does it take? What social processes may lead individuals to actually live up to this ideal in a given Buddhist society? The present chapter examines these very large questions specifically by looking

Figure 25.1 Ts'ampa Nawang. Photograph by Nicolas Sihlé. Reprinted with permission.

at the life of Ts'ampa Nawang,[1] a contemporary Buddhist adept and medical practitioner from Baragaon, a Tibetan-speaking area of northern Nepal.

To do so, we want to steer clear of certain pitfalls. Accounts of Tibet have erred in uncritically embracing popular, romantic fantasies of Tibetan spirituality, in effect projecting textual ideals of wisdom and compassionate altruism into Buddhist societies without anchoring them in lived reality. Some eminent authorities on Tibetan religion who have studied the tradition in practice, however, have expressed serious doubts as to the extent to which the ideal of the bodhisattva has had any effect at all on the lives or communities of Tibetan Buddhists.

According to the pioneering Tibetologist Giuseppe Tucci:

A remarkable characteristic of Tibetan religion is its striking lack of social compassion.... [At the center of Buddhism] is the vow to strive for the good of all beings... but the teachings enshrined in this vow rarely receive more than a vague theoretical assertion. Its simple enunciation brings peace to the soul of a Tibetan, along with the assurance that he has fulfilled his duty as a Buddhist.[2]

Statements such as this are useful antidotes against romantic idealizations of Tibetans; but they may also be misleading in their broad-brush critique. Does a universal altruism directed primarily at *otherworldly* ultimate ends necessarily imply the presence of "*social* compassion"? Any analysis of Buddhist altruism must inevitably be understood according to its own forms and emphases. And should we expect *ordinary* Buddhist monks or laypeople to be *exemplars* of virtue, in societies that encouraged mass monasticism and in which one became a monk most often at a very young age, the decision being actually taken by others? Here again, we need to keep in mind the essential distinction between religious ideals and actual social practices.

In this life history, we will not be concerned with the simplistic questions of *whether*, or *to what degree*, Tibetans in general put Buddhist altruism into practice. Rather, we will be looking more qualitatively at *how* that principle may inform or "color" the lives of certain individuals in Tibetan Buddhist societies.[3]

Methodology and Context

The following account is based on intensive encounters with Ts'ampa Nawang, in and around the Baragaon area, in the mid-1990s, followed by a decade of more intermittent meetings and contacts. In particular, an intensive, one-month period of fieldwork in 1994 was devoted exclusively to biographically oriented work with him. I followed him in all his activities throughout the day, and in the evenings I collected what could be described as the chapters of a life history of a somewhat hybrid nature, inspired in large part by the genre of the Tibetan (auto)biography (*namtar*) and partly also by the demands of my anthropological training.[4]

My communication with Ts'ampa Nawang was always carried out in standard, central Tibetan, a dialect he is one of the few people in Baragaon to have mastered. However, in the second half of the 1990s, I acquired a command of the Baragaon dialect that enabled me to contextualize in a more fine-grained way my understanding of Ts'ampa Nawang's life trajectory. In particular, I lived for a year and a half in Chongkor, the Baragaon village in which he was born and where his prestigious lineage remains the subject of many memories. Ts'ampa Nawang is by now an old friend; we have been meeting less often in recent times, but his generosity and insight have made him over the years into one of the main teachers in my ethnographic career.[5]

Ts'ampa Nawang: The Formative Years

Nawang was born in 1949 in Chongkor, in the Muktinath valley, as the eldest son of Ts'ampa Pembar (1918–78), an esteemed *amchi*, or practitioner of the Tibetan literate medical tradition, the third physician in three successive generations in their family line. As is quite common with *amchi*, both Ts'ampa Pembar and his own father were also "tantrists" (Tib. *ngakpa*). These are nonmonastic religious specialists who most often constitute family lineages, from father to son. They tend to focus more exclusively than monks on tantric practices: rituals that involve visualization (at least in theory), invoking Buddhas and protector deities by reciting powerful mantras. These rituals may have worldly or supramundane aims; they range from rites attracting luck and prosperity, to rituals to heal or exorcise, up to high-level spiritual practices for more advanced adepts.

Before the closing of the border with Chinese-occupied Tibet in the 1950s, Ts'ampa Pembar traveled several times to places in southwestern Tibet to meet religious masters and receive teachings. In particular, over the years, he started following and serving Shangpa Rinpoche, "the Precious One from Shang." This hermit and meditator of the Karma Kagyu tradition, originally from central Tibet, had become an influential figure in parts of southwestern Tibet and especially northwestern Nepal; known for teaching the dharma, he also restored ruined temples and campaigned against local hunting and rituals involving blood sacrifice. One small monastery rebuilt by Shangpa Rinpoche was Kutsap Ternga, which lies atop a hill that overlooks the Jomsom area, just south of Baragaon. After its restoration, Ts'ampa Pembar decided to resettle in Drumba, a village in a small sheltered valley just below Kutsap Ternga Monastery. He saw many precious, sacred associations in that place and moved his family, including his seven-year-old son Nawang, from Chongkor to Drumba.

In these early years, Nawang started learning to read and write in the mornings and evenings, taught by his father and grandfather. Gradually his father also started to teach him the rudiments of religion and medicine. During the day, Nawang would then practice reading and writing, or collect the medicinal plants he already knew while watching over the flocks of sheep and goats – or higher up, the yaks – on the grassy slopes above Drumba. He was the only son of the family at that time, and he started plowing at the age of 11. Nawang always had a keen sense of curiosity; he even learned how to sew, and soon was making clothes and boots for the family.

At the age of 15, following in the footsteps of his father, he embarked upon a retreat of three years and three months, in the somewhat isolated house that had been the residence of the former Kutsap Ternga masters. Throughout this entire period, he was in contact only with two people: an assistant, who would bring his meals, and his father – that is, his religious master. The retreat was devoted primarily to tantric practice, of the Nyingma and Kagyu traditions, along with austerity practices such as fasting, all under the rigorous guidance of his father. Outside the four daily periods of formal practice, Nawang read religious and medical texts, asked his master for clarifications, or copied texts, granting himself little sleep.

At the beginning of this period, Nawang also taught himself the art of carving wooden printing blocks – a skill hitherto absent in the area. Inspired by the particularly beneficial character of the recitation of the *Mani* mantra (*Om mani padme hum*), as extolled at length in various religious sources, and by the possibility of endlessly multiplying its benefits by printing, he resolved to carve a printing block. His first carving instrument was a simple nail. The work quickly became painful, but he persevered, wrapping his fingers in some cloth. When I met him three decades later, the tools and skills had become sophisticated, and he was still carving.

After his retreat, he performed "cutting" (*chod*) practices at various sites recommended for it by tradition: a hermitage, a glacier, a charnel ground, and so on. These tantric procedures involve visualizing one's own body being cut up, transformed into ambrosia, and offered to all beings; as a soteriological practice, they aim at severing ego-clinging, and they are also commonly undertaken in funerary and exorcism rituals.[6] Nawang also started treating patients at this time. As is customary in Mustang, he became known as Ts'ampa Nawang ("Nawang the Retreat Practitioner") after the completion of the three-year retreat; other epithets are applied to him occasionally, such as *amchi*, "the doctor."

A potentially-life-changing moment occurred when, aged 21, he accompanied his father on a pilgrimage to the Kathmandu Valley. As a meritorious activity, they participated in the construction of a Karma Kagyu monastery by offering their labor. Upon the completion of the work, the Karmapa arrived in person and gave teachings to the numerous faithful who had assembled. He then proceeded to ordain monks. Probably strongly impressed by this encounter with a high Tibetan master, and by the grand monasteries of this valley, Ts'ampa Nawang conceived the desire to become a monk and devote his life entirely to the dharma. He who already wore the long hair of the tantrist washed his hair and asked his father and master to grant him leave. His father gave his permission to a codisciple of Nawang who also desired to enter the monastic order but refused his son's request. He told him that he was his only son, and that the way of the tantrist was in no way an inferior one. Their lineage had worked for the good of living beings for generations and, as a result of the accumulated merit, they had never lacked food or other necessities. Their path was that of the profound and unexcelled tantric dharma. It was also that of medicine, with its own levels of excellence. He also taught Nawang that the vows of the monk are comparable to a fragile crystal vase whereas those of the tantrist (the tantric commitments, Sanskrit: *samaya*) are like a sturdy copper vase, which will not break easily. Provided his practice is good, the tantrist will not face difficulties.

Since a disciple does not go against the word of his master, Ts'ampa Nawang thus remained a tantrist. After returning to his home region, he continued his studies with his father and developed his religious and medical activities: carrying out rituals for lay patrons, gathering medicinal plants, treating patients, and so on. His family and their patrons also insisted that he get married: it was necessary to ensure the continuity of the lineage. Desiring to focus on his studies, he resisted for a few years; eventually, in his late twenties, he met a young woman from another village in the Muktinath valley, herself the daughter of a tantrist. After she came to live with them in Drumba, in due course their marriage was celebrated and a son was born. During the winter, Nawang often went on pilgrimage. One year he went to India to assist the Tibetologist David Snellgrove, whom he had met during this scholar's travels in northern Nepal.[7] However, after the untimely death of his first son, in 1982, he put an end to his winter travels for many years. In the following years, altogether three daughters and two more sons were born.

In 1978, when Ts'ampa Nawang was 29, his father died. It was the death of a religious master, who died in a state of meditation. His last instructions to his son were: you have studied and now you must benefit the doctrine and sentient beings. These last words – a classic phrase of Tibetan religious writings – were to remain engraved in Nawang's mind.

Ever Broader Activities

The range of Ts'ampa Nawang's activities steadily widened. Today, on the one hand, he has the life of an ordinary householder, with fields, orchards, and livestock. In 1993, he moved to Jomsom (while still keeping his fields in Drumba) and opened a small hotel right next to the airport. On the other hand, he has developed quite a spectrum of specialist skills and occupations. As a medical practitioner, he collects or purchases medicinal substances on his travels and assembles his own remedies. In 1994, a Japanese NGO created an ecomuseum in Jomsom, with a small section, overseen by Ts'ampa Nawang, that functions as a medical office and museum of Tibetan medicine. The main site of his medical activity, however, is now a clinic he created right next to his residence; he also visits patients who cannot travel. Nawang has also started to experiment with the domestication of certain wild medicinal plants. Finally, in 1998 he was one of the founders of the Himalayan Amchi Association, an NGO aiming to unite *amchi* in Nepal and obtain institutional recognition for their practice.[8]

As a religious and ritual specialist, Ts'ampa Nawang occasionally performs rituals for lay patrons; he also teaches reading and writing in Tibetan, as well as the rudiments of religion, to a few local boys, especially in the winter. Since his move to Jomsom in 1993, Ts'ampa Nawang has started to lead local associations for religious practice, both in Drumba and Jomsom; these assemble yearly on important religious dates, and there he directs the lay participants' practice and provides religious teachings. He engages in related religious activities such as copying texts, carving woodblocks and printing texts, and painting. He has also been one of the key local supporters of the current Shangpa Rinpoche, the reincarnation of his father's master. Finally, Ts'ampa Nawang has occasionally taught in another of the Muktinath nunneries that have the same Kagyu ritual tradition as his own.

Yet another important domain of his activity is that of the literate, educated local notable involved in a variety of projects and institutions. He actively supports literacy and other educational programs, takes part in village administration, and has petitioned development agencies on behalf of local communities. Owing to his literacy, he has been the secretary on many committees; he has often been asked to interpret legal or land-ownership documents, and called to arbitrate disputes. Particularly in association with the Jomsom Ecomuseum, he has also been involved in cultural "preservation" and representation activities.

Although Nawang has for many years voluntarily restricted his travels, he has had intensive contacts with foreigners, in particular with researchers and students as well as with journalists, documentary filmmakers, and tourists. Tibetologists associated with study-abroad programs in Nepal have channeled a steady stream of students toward him for their research projects, and over time his networks have grown. Over the past decade, he has started to travel again, to other Himalayan regions and abroad, as a consultant, as a conference participant, even as a visiting lecturer in a US college. Sometimes he travels to the United States simply to visit his two eldest children, a daughter and a son, who have both migrated there.

Increasingly since the late 1990s, transnational encounters, flows of ideas, and demographically significant migrations have had a profound impact on Ts'ampa Nawang and his surroundings. Former, more localized and isolated communities have been compelled to adapt to a more porous and interconnected world, with its new possibilities and desires but also forms of alienation. The tantrist and *amchi* lineage that for Nawang was a major structural feature, component of his identity, and source of pride in his formative and early adult years will not be carried on fully into the next generation. His elder son will not become a tantrist. His younger son seems to be heading for a career as a Tibetan doctor, and thus in some sense an *amchi* lineage will continue; but he was educated in a Tibetan-medium boarding school in Kathmandu and is now being trained in a formal institution for Tibetan medical studies in India. His life's trajectory might well never turn back toward northern Nepal.

Altruistic Action

The rich, multifaceted (and still unfolding) life sketched above could now be examined further from a variety of thematic or analytical angles. The choice of privileging altruistic action is based on Ts'ampa Nawang's own repeated use of this notion in the autobiographical narratives that I elicited. But are we falling into the trap of mistaking for reality something that might be only a cultural ideal emphasized in our informant's self-representation?[9] Here, the substantial component of actual observation in my work with Ts'ampa Nawang enables us to advance, confident that altruistic action is for him and that his social environment is not just a cliché or an all-too-distant ideal but something more fundamental, which is called an ethos. The exploration of this Buddhist ethos will thus take the shape of unpacking what "benefiting the doctrine and the sentient beings" actually means in Nawang's present context.[10]

Religious activity: the Mani and the spread of the dharma

In his reflections on his past trajectory as well as on his plans for the future, the defining objective of "benefiting the doctrine and the sentient beings" is understood by Ts'ampa Nawang as including far more than just strictly "religious" activities: many of the activities mentioned above participate in this general orientation. This is clearly in line with a key feature of Tibetan, and more widely Mahayana Buddhist, understandings of altruism, namely the concept of "skill in means" (Skt. *upayakausalya*). This is understood as the skillful application of diverse methods, depending on persons and circumstances, of drawing the sentient beings further on the path toward, ultimately, enlightenment.

The single most highly valued component of the above-mentioned core objective remains, for Ts'ampa Nawang, to spread the Buddhist dharma. From a doctrinal perspective, teaching the dharma is the highest form of the gift, and a preeminent mode of altruistic action. Biographies of Buddhist masters often contain chapters entitled "how X benefited the doctrine and the sentient beings," which highlight lists of teachings given to other masters, more modest religious practitioners, or simple laity. In a clearly secondary role, they also show the lama acting compassionately to alleviate human suffering, through ritual and divination, for which there is an incessant demand. In comparison, Ts'ampa Nawang's dharma teaching and ritual activity are limited. He remarks that he prefers to leave the latter to others, as he has many other specialist activities to perform. As for his teaching, it takes place mostly in the context of the yearly meetings of the religious associations he has founded in Drumba and Jomsom. As an adept or master of rather modest stature, compared to heads of prominent monasteries or lineages, he focuses typically on the *Mani* mantra, a major Tibetan theme in teachings for the laity: its correct recitation, the accompanying visualizations, its meaning and benefits, and so on. He also addresses basic tenets such as the preciousness of human life and the law of karmic cause and effect. The larger part of these meetings is then devoted to the collective recitation of prayers and mantras, under his guidance. Ts'ampa Nawang notes that, as a result, a number of people have now started reciting prayers at home, and so he concludes: "This is progress for the dharma."

A similar spread and intensification of the dharma – with the *Mani* tradition playing an important part in his motivation – is his woodblock carving, printing, and copying activities. Over more than three decades, he has made printing blocks for, or copied, altogether several dozen different texts, including an estimated 250 blocks for prayer flags alone, enabling the printing of prayer flags throughout the area, each single flag then producing blessings for all beings in the surroundings. Ts'ampa Nawang emphasizes that, in the context of the persecution of Buddhism in Tibet, this new printing activity in the area is a very precious development.

Finally, another preeminent mode of furthering the dharma consists in contributing to its institutional development, through the founding or restoration of temples, monasteries, and stupas. Following in the footsteps of his father, who assisted the previous Shangpa Rinpoche in such works, Ts'ampa Nawang has been a very active supporter of this lama's present incarnation. He was, for instance, a key local agent in the founding of a Muktinath valley nunnery, for which he rallied community support and oversaw construction. Alone or in consultation with key figures such as Shangpa Rinpoche, he has also been devising or pursuing sometimes ambitious plans, concerning for instance the revitalization of the ancient Kutsap Ternga Monastery.[11]

Another of Ts'ampa Nawang's key projects is to found a proper Buddhist temple in Jomsom that would be associated particularly with the recitation of the *Mani* and the figure of Avalokitesvara, the great compassionate bodhisattva. In his description of the project, the temple's large hall will accommodate 500 people and a large *Mani* wheel will be constructed outside, shielded from the fierce and often cold winds of Jomsom by large glass panes, a design feature that will allow the elderly faithful (in particular) to make their circumambulations and rotate the wheel (thus accumulating merit) while getting exercise and remaining warm. In this project, we can see the conjunction of a compassionate man of religion with a skillful physician.

Medical activity: key religious model and exemplary field of applied Buddhist altruism

From ancient times, medicine has appeared as an exemplary domain with regard to implementing Buddhist altruism.[12] In Ts'ampa Nawang's discourse, it is medicine even more than religious activity that appears as the paradigmatic altruistic activity: the former is fundamentally about *practicing virtue*, the latter about *benefiting others*, as he once put it. According to the foundational treatises of the Tibetan medical system, having the pure mind of a bodhisattva, intent on the good of all beings, is one of the "primordial requirements" (Tibetan: *gyu*) for the ideal physician.[13] Ts'ampa Nawang explains that, without altruism, one could not develop sufficient motivation or perseverance to accomplish the long, very demanding course of medical studies. Additionally, no matter how experienced one becomes, medicine always remains a difficult task: a physician always encounters suffering, and in many guises.

Medical practice also shows other features typical of Buddhist altruism. Ideally, as Ts'ampa Nawang points out, it shares its universal and nondiscriminating character: whether friend or enemy, rich or poor, all patients are treated alike. In the traditional relationship with patients, the physician accepts what a patient wishes to give as payment, according to his or her own estimation and means; not uncommonly, he gives medicine for free, regularly offering the altruistic gift.[14]

Conclusion

A highly regarded expert and enthusiastic participant in scientific projects, Ts'ampa Nawang also takes pleasure in inventing simple new devices and treatments; for example, he designed small cotton pouches filled with strong-scented spikenard (Tibetan: *pangpo*), the soothing virtues of which, he says, help people sleep; this contributes to increasing their lifespan. In medicine as in other domains, his versatile altruistic engagement manifests its distinct blend of core traditional values and creative technical innovation.

It is important to recognize that Ts'ampa Nawang is not a unique phenomenon but rather exemplifies a type of Tibetan practitioner found most notably in the Nyingma tradition. As opposed to the primary emphasis on scholastic reasoning within Gelug monasticism, this type of Buddhist practice creatively mixes textual learning, manual praxis, and empirical experiments; its full expression is the art of the *amchi* doctor. Ts'ampa Nawang belongs to the civilizational lineage of a figure like T'angtong Gyelpo (fourteenth–fifteenth centuries), the religious master who was also a constructor of bridges across Tibet and inventor of the Tibetan opera.[15] Such emblematic figures[16] have linked the way of the bodhisattva and technical activity to serve their communities.

Beyond the strong individual qualities of Nawang and his father, what social factors have contributed to the former's striking engagement in this ethos of altruism? As the descendant of a prestigious lineage, as we have seen, he was under social pressure to reproduce a tradition. More positively, through the early-life daily interaction with his father and grandfather, the lineage provided considerable pedagogical, material, and psychological advantages; this prepared Nawang from a very early age to follow in their footsteps, and enabled him to learn through observation, manipulation, query, and discussion. Additionally, in Tibetan understandings, through the successive generations of the tantrist lineages, blessings (Tib. *chinlap*) grow and accumulate for those who maintain the lineage.

Beyond the immediate examples in his family, more distant models have profoundly influenced Nawang through the reading of texts and the teachings of his father. He recalls that the biography of Padmasambhava, who is viewed by Tibetan historiography as the foundational introducer of tantric Buddhism in Tibet, left a powerful impression on him as a boy. Padmasambhava had practiced all activities, including the ten major and minor sciences: Buddhism, medicine, the technical arts, grammar, logic, and so on. He had also been a king, had founded monasteries, and had benefited all beings. But initially he was only a man, Nawang had reflected; so he, too, should be able to widen and expand the scope of his own activities. This thought provided him with considerable determination and perseverance. It pushed him, he once said, to carve his first *Mani* woodblock as a formidable means of spreading benefits, through the six syllables that, to him, and in accordance with the texts, represented the quintessential beneficial action for the world.

The life of a village tantrist and doctor thus shows us an ethos of altruism with Tibetan Buddhist characteristics: universality, equanimity, and a diversity of applications informed by the notion of "skillfulness in means," located in a community in which perpetuating the dharma is understood as the highest mode of altruistic action. In Nawang we see a tantric master who shows boundless versatility, in which a core ethical imperative fuels action across many fields, far beyond the preeminent domains of medicine and dharma.

References

Besch, N.F. (2006) Tibetan medicine off the roads: modernizing the work of the Amchi in Spiti. Ph.D. dissertation. Ruprecht-Karls-Universität Heidelberg.

Craig, S.R. (2008) Place and professionalization: navigating Amchi identity in Nepal, in *Tibetan Medicine in the Contemporary World: Global Politics of Medical Knowledge and Practice* (ed. L. Pordié), Routledge, London and New York, pp. 62–90.

Craig, S.R. (2013) The many faces of a teacher: portrait of a Himalayan healer, in *Les nouveaux guérisseurs contemporains: Le néo-traditionalisme thérapeutique en biographies* [The new contemporary healers: the biographies of the neo-traditional therapists] (ed. L. Pordié and E. Simon), Anthropos, Paris, pp. 27–47.

Geertz, C. (1973) *The Interpretation of Cultures: Selected Essays*, Basic Books, New York.

Kloos, S. (2010) *Tibetan Medicine in Exile: The Ethics, Politics and Science of Cultural Survival*. Ph.D. dissertation. University of California.

Meyer, F. (1981) *Gso-ba rig-pa: Le système médical tibétain* [Gso-ba rig-pa: the Tibetan medical system], Editions du CNRS, Paris.

Morin, F. (1980) Pratiques anthropologiques et histoire de vie [Applied anthropology and life history]. *Cahiers internationaux de sociologie*, 69, 313–41.

Sihlé, N. (1995) *Pour le bien des êtres et de la doctrine: L'action altruiste dans la culture tibétaine à travers l'exemple du religieux et médecin Ts'ampa Nawang (Jomsom, nord du Népal)* [For the good of others and the doctrine: altruistic action in Tibetan culture through the example of the religious leader and healer Ts'ampa Nawang (Jomson, northern Nepal)]. M.A. thesis. Université de Paris-X Nanterre.

Snellgrove, D.L. (1979) Places of pilgrimage in Thag. *Kailash*, 7 (2), 73–170.

Snellgrove, D.L. (1989) Multiple features of the Buddhist heritage, in *The Buddhist Heritage* (ed. T. Skorupski), Institute of Buddhist Studies, Tring, pp. 28–46.

Stearns, C. (2007) *King of the Empty Plain: The Tibetan Iron-Bridge Builder Tangtong Gyalpo*, Snow Lion, Ithaca, NY.

Stoddard, H. (1985) *Le mendiant de l'Amdo* [The spirit medium of Amdo], Société d'ethnographie, Paris.

Tucci, G. (1980) *The Religions of Tibet*, University of California Press, Berkeley.

Further Reading

Boord, M.J. (1993) *The Cult of the Deity Vajrakila: According to the Texts of the Northern Treasures Tradition of Tibet (Byang-gter phur-ba)*, Institute of Buddhist Studies, Tring.

Craig, S.R. (2012) *Healing Elements: Efficacy and the Social Ecologies of Tibetan Medicine*, University of California Press, Berkeley.

Kohn, R.J. (2001) *Lord of the Dance: The Mani Rimdu Festival in Tibet and Nepal*, SUNY Press, Albany.

Ricard, M. (trans.) (1994) *The Life of Shabkar: The Autobiography of a Tibetan Yogin*, SUNY Press, Albany.

Sihlé, N. (2013) *Rituels bouddhiques de pouvoir et de violence: La figure du tantriste tibétain* [Buddhist rituals of power and violence: the figure of the Tibetan tantrist], Brepols, Turnhout.

Notes

1 The "a" is pronounced like in "Spanish," the "Ng" sound as in the English "sing," and the apostrophe marks an aspirated, breathy "ts" sound.
2 Tucci (1980: 210–11). For a similar pronouncement, see Snellgrove (1989: 12).
3 See for instance Geertz (1973: 126–7).
4 The fullest version of these early data is to be found in Sihlé (1995).
5 In 1993, Ts'ampa Nawang took up residence in Jomsom, the headquarters of the Nepali district of Mustang, which is just to the south of Baragaon and in which the majority of the people are Thakalis, who speak a Tibeto-Burmese tongue only distantly related to Tibetan. Ts'ampa Nawang also speaks this language fluently; I do not at all. Among other limitations, my account of this life on an ethnic frontier zone remains thus rather Tibeto-centric. It should also be mentioned that the more recent, transnational turns of Ts'ampa Nawang's trajectory have received attention elsewhere (Craig 2013); here I will focus more on the early, formative, and middle sections of this very rich life.
6 See Chapter 6, which contains the biography of Ma-chig Lab-dron, the woman who is associated with the origin of this now popular practice.
7 Snellgrove 1979.
8 Craig 2008.
9 "By providing access to the meanings of the subject," the life-historical method enables the researcher, at least in part, to "avoid the pitfalls of his own subjectivity"; however, "the subject's self-justification and self-valuation may lead the researcher to discover an ideal type rather than an actual type" (Morin 1980, reflecting on Bastide's teachings on the matter; my translation from the French).
10 This phrase is far more amenable to ethnography-based analysis than more psychologically oriented Tibetan formulations expressing altruism, such as *shen-phen-gi samlo* (thought turned toward benefiting others).
11 He is motivated here in part by an old prophecy that designates it as an origin for the revival of Buddhism.
12 On recent ideological and political ramifications of this link, see Kloos (2010).
13 Meyer 1981: 195.
14 This is, however, increasingly changing in Tibetan communities in which globalizing capitalist markets and other forces have eroded traditional solidarities (Besch 2006: 218ff.).
15 Stearns 2007.
16 Other examples include Amchi Kunsang (Fernand Meyer, personal communication), whose curiosity led him, among others, to try to produce electricity, and Gendun Chophel, a progressive intellectual and polymath, born in a Nyingma community and educated in Geluk monasteries, and whose taste for constructing technical objects seems to have been spurred by reading sections on the "technical science" in canonical scriptures (Stoddard 1985: 142).

26
Living Practical Dharma
Chomo Khandru and the Himalayan Bon Tradition

Sara Shneiderman

Editor's Introduction

In the Kali Gandaki Valley of central Nepal, Chomo Khandru lived an extraordinary life, beginning as a caravan merchant and then dedicating herself to a career as a ritual practitioner. She was a master of the Bon tradition. This lineage of Tibetan religion has a long and still obscure history; its texts and followers assert that it preceded Buddhism, and that Shakyamuni Buddha was a later incarnation of Bon's founder, Sherab Miwo. Despite Bon's history of marginalization, the 14th Dalai Lama acknowledged Bon as a fifth sect of Buddhism, and the tradition's high lamas are well respected by Buddhist monks and laity. Bon has a long history in places such as the village of Lubra, Mustang, Chomo Khandru's home, and it exists in pockets across the Tibetan cultural region, all the way to eastern Tibet.

Chomo Khandru became an ordained monastic at age 11, accepting the custom of second daughters devoting their lives to religion. Second daughters became *chomo* to ensure that families had at least one member generating religious merit, while also creating a time lag between the marriages of the first and third or younger daughters in a rural, high-altitude environment where resources were sparse.

Chomo Khandru received her religious training from two older *chomo*, who themselves were trained by a Bon lama who came to Lubra 80 years ago and guided them in developing spiritual skills through long solitary retreats. With their guidance, Chomo Khandru learned to read, one of the few women who did so there, memorized basic religious texts, and spent the little free time she had meditating. Through her devotion, she became a highly respected village figure,

Buddhists: Understanding Buddhism Through the Lives of Practitioners, First Edition. Edited by Todd Lewis.
© 2014 John Wiley & Sons, Ltd. Published 2014 by John Wiley & Sons, Ltd.

the only woman ever called to join village lamas in conducting certain rituals in the village temple or individual homes. Although disappointed that she could not master the more philosophical aspects of the dharma, she came to find meaning in serving her village and region through rituals devoted to "practical dharma" that generated merit and protection.

Wherever Buddhism spread, it adapted to the "logic of local life." This chapter offers a detailed and nuanced case study of this truism. It also presents a lucid analysis of how the world that Chomo Khandru was born into has been radically changed, first by the closing of Tibet and then by globalization. Using the case of her great-niece Nhima Bhuti's life choices to sharpen the contrast, we learn that, as trade opportunities moved south, exposure to new languages and places altered worldviews; we also see how the *chomo*'s role lost allure, given the heightened status of ordained, celibate monastics that resulted from the internationalization of Tibetan religion that flowed all the way back to the village. Through these life histories, we are drawn to the life of this strong and dedicated practitioner, even as we are left to witness the end of the tradition she embodied.

Introduction[1]

Chomo Khandru was 80 years old when we met. I was 20. She welcomed me into her home for one night, which soon turned into many. It was 1995, and I had traveled to Nepal's Mustang district to conduct research on the lives of *chomo* – female religious practitioners of the Tibetan Buddhist and Bon traditions who live independently in villages, without the support of an institutional monastic setting.[2] Chomo Khandru was the oldest woman in Lubra, a tiny settlement of 14 houses sheltered in a side canyon of the Kali Gandaki river, and she was arguably the most senior *chomo* in the entire area. She was an old woman with much to teach and no disciples, and I was an eager young student. As I gained her trust, the story of her life as both a celibate ascetic and a worldly trader on one of the historic Tibet-to-India salt-grain trading trails unfolded. With an unusually sharp memory for dates, names, and places, and a down-to-earth way of explaining abstract religious concepts, she was indeed a gifted raconteur and teacher.

Since that first meeting, I have puzzled over how to tell Chomo Khandru's story, an individual life history that recalls the rich collective history of women's religious practice in the village of Lubra as well as that of the larger Himalayan region. It also invokes the intertwined political histories of Nepal, Tibet, and China, and illuminates how living at the intersection of these polities has shaped women's religious experiences over time. Her story also foreshadows the cultural, political, and economic opportunities, and challenges, that Chomo Khandru's descendants now experience as Tibetan religion becomes increasingly globalized. When Chomo Khandru died in November 2002 at the age of 87, a chapter of women's history went with her, and my desire to write about her life grew. This brief biography moves back and forth between the narrative of Chomo Khandru's individual life and a broader analysis of the social dynamics surrounding women's religious practice in the region.

Janice Willis has described women's roles within the historical Tibetan cultural milieu as "dynamic, bustling, diverse, and fluid."[3] I focus here on the tension between such fluidity and fixity in constituting women's religious identities. In Chomo Khandru's life, this dynamic manifested itself as an opposition between the dharma (religion) of action, or "practical dharma," that she saw as her own primary mode of spiritual engagement, and the dharma of study, which she saw as the domain of men within institutional monastic contexts. This opposition was not hard and fast, as Chomo Khandru did have some access to informal religious education, but she saw its role as secondary to meditation and ritual practice in her own spiritual life.

Figure 26.1 Chomo Khandru. Photograph by Sara Shneiderman. Reprinted with permission.

Over the second half of the twentieth century, this local conception of "fluid religious identity" began to come into conversation with more static notions of religious identity. Cultivated by several extralocal entities including the Tibetan monastic establishment in exile, the Nepali state, and foreign charity and development organizations, the definition of religious authenticity based on institutional power and formal learning became increasingly influential during the latter half of Chomo Khandru's life. Idealized extralocal notions of how Tibetan religion "should" be structured have encouraged shifts in local conceptions of religious authority.[4] These trends tend to marginalize the nonmonastic, nonliterate modes of religious practice that were historically most accessible to women in many Himalayan areas. As an example of the flexibility that female practitioners experienced, during Chomo Khandru's youth, celibacy for *chomo* was valued but not strictly enforced. Although both men's and women's potential avenues for spiritual practice have become less flexible in reaction to the ongoing engagement between these varied forces, contemporary women in particular have found it more difficult to follow in Chomo Khandru's footsteps to lead renunciant lives.

Locating Lubra and the Bon Tradition

Lubra is located in the lower half of Mustang District, Dhaulagiri Zone, Nepal. Part of the larger 19-village community known as Baragaon, which stretches along the Kali Gandaki river valley, Lubra is just out of range of the heavily trekked Annapurna Circuit trail.[5] In this sense, it straddles two worlds: it remains relatively isolated and tourist-free in comparison to other Baragaon villages, but its proximity to them furnishes access to the amenities, trade opportunities, and foreign ideas that tourism and development projects have brought. Villager livelihoods depend upon a mixture of subsistence agriculture and cash income from seasonal trade. Over the past two decades, international migration to the United States has also become an important component of familial economic strategies.[6]

The inhabitants of Lubra's 14 houses are descendants of the twelfth-century Lama Tashi Gyalzen, who ventured into the Mustang area from Tibet in search of a spiritual teacher believed to reside there.[7] Upon reaching Lubra, he founded a lineage of noncelibate householder priests that continues today.[8] Lama Tashi Gyalzen fits the description of the "Himalayan frontier lamas" that Joanne Watkins[9] describes in her discussion of women's religious roles in Manang, a Nepali administrative district that lies just to the east of Mustang. Watkins suggests that such eclectic individuals left the rigid religious and political hierarchies found in central Tibet to establish noninstitutional forms of practice in the Himalayan borderland areas. Among other things, the religious traditions that these lamas founded tended to enable greater religious participation for women because they emphasized practical aspects of spiritual development, which could be undertaken in the home, rather than formal study, which required travel and residence in monastic institutions elsewhere.

Tashi Gyalzen was a follower of the Bon tradition, and the villagers of Lubra maintain that identity today.[10] This line of Tibetan religious practice has a long and rather unclear history that has defied clear categorization by cultural historians. Bon's adherents claim that it preceded Buddhism as the earliest form of organized Tibetan religion.[11] The tradition's high lamas are well respected by Buddhist monks and laity, as well as their own lay adherents.[12] In some ways, Lubra's Bon-ness contributed to a sense of "double oppression" for women such as Chomo Khandru, who are not only women but also members of a once marginalized religious sect. Since Lubra is the only entirely Bon village in Mustang, there are far fewer alternatives available to Lubra's women for formal religious practice, since all of the nunneries in the area belong to either the Sakya, Kagyu, or Nyingma Buddhist sects. This is one of the reasons why women's religious practice in Lubra has always been particularly fluid and noninstitutionalized: with the closest Bon monasteries located in eastern Tibet before 1959, and in Kathmandu and northern India afterward, most women had to develop their own forms of spiritual practice as householders. However, Lubra women tend to describe Buddhism and Bon as *experientially* similar, noting only superficial differences in practice, such as the direction of circumambulation or the particular words used in mantras. Krystyna Cech has noted that, for many Bonpos, "Identity is a fluid rather than a rigid concept; it allows for the construction, deconstruction and reconstruction of its aspects."[13] Fluidity is therefore a hallmark of religious identity for both men and women in Lubra, both in terms of the flexibility between Buddhist and Bon identifications and in terms of the particular modes of practice that are available to them. Indeed, many of Lubra's women marry into Lubra from the surrounding Buddhist villages and have therefore experienced both religious traditions. Although Chomo Khandru's life story is first that of a Bonpo woman, it resonates strongly with the experiences of Buddhist women from Mustang and other Himalayan areas.

Life as a *Chomo*: Birthright or Burden?

As we first began to talk, Chomo Khandru had a difficult time understanding my interest in her as a *chomo*. She would direct me to the male village lamas whenever I inquired about her religious practice. Soon I began to realize that, instead of asking questions that focused on her religious activities as a *chomo*, assuming that this was the primary feature of her self-identity, I did better to ask general questions about her life experiences that did not make her feel self-conscious about her lack of formal religious training. The answers to these questions reflected the virtues of the "practical dharma," which Chomo Khandru was initially embarrassed to admit that she practiced. This English phrase best captures a concept that Chomo Khandru and other village women described with various Tibetan and Nepali terms at various times. In short, they contrasted the "dharma of action" with the "dharma of study," associating themselves with the former, which they saw as a lower-status mode of religious practice, and associating men with the latter, higher-status mode.

Born into a family with seven daughters and no sons, Chomo Khandru became a *chomo* at the age of 11. In Lubra, she explained, this was the fate of all second daughters in families with three or more daughters. Economic considerations compelled families to offer their second daughters as *chomo*; first daughters were destined for early marriage, and in certain situations they could also inherit property. Requiring second daughters to become *chomo* ensured that the family would have at least one member focused on generating religious merit, while also creating a time lag between the marriages of the first and third or younger daughters. This tradition enabled the family to save money in between for later dowries and rituals. The local marriage system relied upon fraternal polyandry – meaning that a single woman married two or more brothers simultaneously – in order to maintain the integrity of small plots of land inherited through the male line.[14] Marriage prospects for many women were therefore severely limited in this small community, and a tradition of female renunciation was a good solution to the problem of too many unmarried women. Parents could gain steady religious merit by pledging their daughters as *chomo*, yet maintain the right to their labor rather than lose it to a prospective husband's family. Many middle daughters slated to become *chomo* cursed their fate for keeping them from married life – it was the rare few such as Chomo Khandru who considered themselves fortunate in gaining access to the basic religious training and spiritual practice usually reserved for men.

Chomo Khandru's identity as a dharma practitioner at age 11 was confirmed through a hair-cutting ceremony that took place at the village *gompa* (temple), during which her family made offerings to a visiting high lama and she pledged to devote herself to religious life. However, it is unclear whether this ceremony included formal vows. In any case, such details seemed superfluous, since the community as a whole was well aware of her role and would treat her as a *chomo* whether she had been officially ordained or not. Chomo Khandru then began an informal process of religious training with two well-respected older *chomo*, Tsultrim and Dawa Kunzum. Educated by Yeshe Tenpa Gyaltsen, a Tibetan *tulku* (reincarnate lama) from the eastern Tibetan region of Kham who had spent long periods of time in Lubra during these *chomos*' youth, both women were highly literate in Tibetan and accomplished in meditative practices. Chomo Khandru and other Lubra women spoke of Tsultrim and Dawa Kunzum with great respect: they were the only literate women of their generation and the only village women who undertook extended periods of solitary meditation. These *chomo* passed on their Tibetan literacy skills to Chomo Khandru, but, in her characteristically self-deprecating style, she always told me that she was never able to develop these skills to the high degree that her mentors had.

Although Chomo Khandru had a great desire to engage in spiritual practice, she was compelled by circumstances to work as a trader for many years. Since there were no sons in the family, and she was the only daughter without responsibilities to her own husband and children, she became the heir to her father's trading business. Instead of fostering her religious practice, her identity as a celibate *chomo* required her to serve as the family's missing man, devoting the time she would have spent on religious practice to breadwinning for the family.

One of her primary responsibilities was overseeing the family's concerns in the salt, wool, and grain trade that Himalayan communities have traditionally relied upon. From about 1935 to 1959, when Chomo Khandru was a young woman between the ages of 20 and 45, she worked as a trader. She traveled north to Lo Monthang (the walled city that served as the seat of Mustang's king) at least once a year, carrying Lubra's wheat to trade for Tibetan salt and wool. To go there, she traveled with her male relatives and a train of grain-laden *dzo* (yak–cow crossbreeds). Rarely did any other women accompany them. While trading, she was often frightened that men would attack her and abduct her into a forced marriage, thereby compelling her to give up her religious celibacy. In order to protect herself, she dressed as a man, and, with her hair already cut short as a *chomo*, she could usually pass as one. By her side she carried a *khukuri*, a traditional Nepali knife, and she took turns with her male relatives keeping guard over their hard-won grain. "Sometimes, I was challenged by groups of drunk men we met on the trail," she explained. "They wanted to know whether I was male or female. They wanted me to show them! Of course I didn't!" she chuckled. "I had to wave my *khukuri* to keep them away!" Sleeping out in the open among men who were away from their wives for months at a time, she struggled to maintain her celibacy and the religious honor that went along with it.

Not all *chomo* remained celibate, but her personal commitment to this lifestyle was a source of pride for Chomo Khandru. She was the only *chomo* of her generation who had not given birth, but she still respected the others for their own choices. Her attitude toward celibacy became more sharply defined in her old age, and seemed to highlight a broader social shift on this issue. Due to the influences of both normative Hindu ideals encouraged by the Nepali educational system and the development of Buddhist monasticism, by the late 1990s it was becoming less and less acceptable for women (*chomo* or lay) to bear children out of wedlock: Lubra's villagers had begun to view celibacy for both men and women as a prerequisite to serious religious practice.

Due to the constant fear that her gender subterfuge would be discovered, and given the long periods of time she spent away from Lubra, the trading years were not a happy period in Chomo Khandru's life. At the same time, she was grateful for the freedom from domestic responsibilities that allowed her to travel and visit pilgrimage sites that would have been out of range for most Lubra women, who are generally responsible for maintaining the "home" to which traveling men return. So Chomo Khandru had mixed feelings about the traveling life: on the one hand it allowed her to engage independently with a world that most Lubra women never knew; but, on the other hand, the constant movement kept her from deepening her spiritual practice in a consistent manner. If Chomo Khandru could have had her way, she often told me, she would have stayed at home. But I always wondered whether doing so would have undercut the very foundations on which her reputation as a spiritual practitioner were built – had she stayed at home, she would have been seen as just another woman, without the special, "male" qualities gained through traveling, which gave her the necessary credentials to be well respected as a religious figure in the eyes of the village.

On Writing and Weaving: Gender-Bending Identities

Chomo Khandru's story demonstrates the fluidity of both gender and religious roles in Lubra. As Kim Gutschow describes for nuns in the Zangskar region of northwestern India, the religious agency of *chomo* can be limited by their femininity.[15] In many situations they do not have equal access to the formal religious training that their male counterparts receive. Chomo Khandru's life history also suggests that both gender and religious identities are mutable. The religious role of the *chomo* can enable individuals to bend socially sanctioned gender rules. For example, it can enable a woman to become a symbolic male or, as in the case of Chomo Khandru, to take on certain qualities perceived as man-like. Anthropologist Charles Ramble writes that, in Lubra's Tibetan dialect, "male honorifics are also used of celibate nuns from any rank."[16] This suggests that Chomo Khandru's gender-bending trading activities were not aberrations; rather, women who become *chomo* were perceived to take on male qualities in both the social and spiritual worlds. But there is also a specific kind of maleness that a *chomo* must emulate if she is to command community respect. One lama made it clear to me that it was necessary to read Tibetan to become a fully fledged practitioner; he continued to explain that women were barred from becoming lamas simply because they could not read texts, not because there was anything inherent in their feminine nature preventing them from taking on that role.

Chomos' perceived gender identities shift back and forth between "male" and "female" – although they are clearly women in the biological sense, their ability to read and write marks them with male-gendered qualities. For this reason, *chomo* who cannot read maintain the most ambiguous status: as religious practitioners, they should in theory be literate, therefore becoming honorary men, but without Tibetan literary skills they are stranded between conflicting social expectations and gendered roles.

This state of affairs resonates with Kathryn March's discussion of writing and weaving as gender markers.[17] In Lubra, as in the Tamang community that March describes,[18] weaving stands in opposition to writing as the exclusive province of women. Women weave brightly colored blankets and aprons, the sale of which provides one of the village's few modes of cash income. Chomo Khandru never learned to weave – or perhaps, more accurately, was never taught to weave by her mothers and sisters. Off trading as the "man" of the house, she was expected to write and read but not to weave. Although she learned how to spin – an occupation that men and women share – Chomo Khandru's "male" identity as a trader and religious practitioner prohibited her from taking on the "female" skill of weaving.

One of the ironies of the equation made here between literacy, maleness, and the dharma of study (and its inverse: weaving, femaleness, and the dharma of action) is that the goal of orthodox Tibetan religious practice – both Buddhist and Bon – is to transcend intellectualized understandings of the self as objectively real to reach an experience of the ego as illusory. It is precisely this unintellectualized, embodied aspect of spiritual practice – the dharma of action – that laywomen most often engage in within their daily lives. Their core practices, often repeated many times each day, sometimes while engaged in household or agricultural labor, include mantra recitation with prayer wheels or rosaries, circumambulation, and prostration. As one feminist observer of Tibetan religion has put it, "the *ideals* of these religious systems are often akin to the kinds of experiences women have in day-to-day life. This means that their experiences are perceived to fit in with the ideals of the religion, *even though these experiences are the ones they wish to change.*"[19] In other words, although women are identified with the internal spiritual qualities (embodied in their weaving) that male-dominated religious traditions promote as ideals to attain, women themselves are excluded from the associated institutional structures of the religion precisely because they do not possess the learned skills (such as writing) on which the religion pragmatically relies.

Chomo Khandru and many of Lubra's laywomen seemed to be aware of this tension, although they did not speak in these specific terms. In statements to me, they always accorded their own spiritual attainments through "practical dharma" less value than those of men who engaged in the "dharma of study." Yet they still believed strongly in the importance of "practical dharma," precisely because it was integral to daily life in the village and therefore generated direct, immediate benefits relevant to them as women who spent most of their time at home. This was in contrast to the ostensibly greater, but abstract and unquantifiable, merit generated by monks in faraway institutional settings.

For instance, I was told by several people that one of the reasons there was no strict rule of celibacy for Lubra's *chomo* was because having the experience of childbearing and rearing enabled them to empathize more fully with laywomen's experiences, and this enabled them, therefore, to meditate more fully on motherhood as an experience of great compassion as one plank of their spiritual practice. Tsultrim and Dawa Kunzum – the two literate *chomo* who taught Chomo Khandru – both bore illegitimate children (neither was married), but this did not compromise their reputation as spiritual practitioners. If anything, motherhood strengthened their ability to engage with the dharma at the practical level and serve as role models and teachers to other women. In this, they inhabited an intermediary space between male and female identities: they could read and write like men, yet they never received more formal education or institutional support because they were women. When at home they lived like women who worked with their families and cared for children, yet they periodically left for pilgrimage or business trips that took them away, like men. This intermediate position was socially acceptable in the village context, allowing them to maintain a fluid identity that did not depend upon institutional legitimization.

Changing Religious, Economic, and Educational Landscapes

Chomo Khandru's trading work came to an unexpected halt when the crossborder trade between

Nepal and Tibet was disrupted after the Chinese asserted control over Tibet in the 1950s. This political shift allowed her to devote the latter part of her life to the religious practice that had eluded her in youth. Finally, she had time to read texts and sit in meditation. Of course, she still had work to do – she became an indispensable help to her sister Palsang, who was raising six children. When I met her, she was still working alongside her sister, serving as a second grandmother to her nephew's two small sons and doing a full share of fieldwork and housework. Domestic labor dominated her days – she once said sarcastically in response to a question about why she had not engaged in more formal religious training: "Every day we have work. Only when we die, we don't have work!"

Nevertheless, Chomo Khandru could work hard at home or in the fields during the day and spend her evenings reading by flickering candlelight. Through her obvious devotion to the dharma, she became a highly respected village figure, the only woman ever called to join village lamas in conducting certain rituals in the village temple or individual homes. She memorized basic religious texts and spent the little free time she had meditating, but she was never able to study at the more advanced philosophical level that she desired. By the time she was 50, her eyesight was beginning to fail. Slowly, over the next ten years, the world receded into a fog, and she could no longer study new texts. She had committed the most important works to memory and could still chant them with the lamas when she was called. But slowly these too faded. "My dreams of becoming enlightened are still just dreams. I am old now, and cannot undo all of the bad karma I have accrued in this life. It is too late," she said remorsefully one evening as we sat around the fire. Although venerated by the villagers for her age and experience, her prayers were no longer thought to be as effective as those offered by younger monks trained formally in the new monastic centers of India and Kathmandu, places that Chomo Khandru had never visited.

Such institutions began to develop after the Tibetan flight into exile after 1959, often with support from the growing numbers of Western practitioners of Tibetan Buddhism and Bon.[20] Although the people of Lubra were citizens of Nepal, the political shifts north of the border changed the terms of their religious practice. The itinerant lamas from Tibet who had provided the focal point of Lubra's religious life no longer came; the center of religious authority for the people of Lubra and other Himalayan villages shifted from Tibet to the exile towns of India and Nepal, where many lamas reestablished their monasteries after the Dalai Lama and many other Tibetans fled into exile. The people of Lubra had never previously needed to visit monasteries in Tibet; the lamas had always come to them. Now they were bypassed. Lubra became ever more constrained by its out-of-the-way location. Ironically, the transnational development of Tibetan religion further isolated Lubra from religious and cultural centers.

This shift had grave effects for the women of Lubra. No longer could they receive religious teaching from high lamas at home. Instead, they had to travel to faraway places. While boys were now sent off for study, girls rarely were. Menri Gompa, which had been the most important Bonpo *gompa* in Tibet, was reestablished in 1969 as the seat of the Bon tradition in exile at Dolanji, in Shimla, Himachal Pradesh, India.[21] Funded in part by foreign donations, the Dolanji monastery began offering full scholarships for studies up to grade eight to children from Himalayan villages such as Lubra. Although in theory these scholarships were open to boys and girls, parents rarely felt able to send both their daughters and sons, and ultimately boys received priority.

Instead, girls were kept home and sent to study at the Nepali government school established in the village in the late 1980s. Although this was certainly a positive step forward in the overall educational level of village women, the *type* of education had unexpected effects on women's abilities and motivations for religious practice. Most importantly, although girls gained literacy in Nepali, this opportunity in fact curtailed their ability to learn the Tibetan they would need for serious religious practice. With the time limitations placed on girls by their domestic responsibilities, they could barely manage to study one written language, let alone two. Further, the school provided a false sense of educational security, and even the one lama who had previously tried to provide some education in Tibetan for village girls ceased these activities after the establishment of the school. Most importantly, education in Nepali provided younger women with access to the world of trade and commerce. Many girls, including those intended to be *chomo*, began leaving the village to become businesswomen elsewhere.

From Chomo Khandru's perspective, Lubra's younger generation of women had been converted to the "religion of money." She attributed this in part to the emergence of Nepali-language education in the vacuum left after the itinerant lamas stopped coming to teach after 1959. However, Chomo Khandru herself had spent years as a trader and was not untainted by worldly concerns. So what was her critique of the young women? She felt that her own engagement in business was not out of choice but of necessity, whereas the younger women wanted nothing more than to leave the village for commercial pursuits. Chomo Khandru claimed that, in her time, trade was a necessary evil that she was pushed into by her family for economic survival, while she would have chosen to stay home to focus on spiritual practice if given the option. At the same time, as mentioned above, traveling did afford Chomo Khandru a certain freedom to visit pilgrimage sites; in contrast, the women of her great-niece's generation had little interest in religious practice and saw traveling and trading as ends in themselves, often leaving the village against the wishes of their families. Further, they traveled southward to the Nepali city of Pokhara and onward to India, rather than northward to Tibet. This shift was in large part caused by the disappearance of northern trade opportunities after 1959, but there was no question that Nepali education had also contributed to shifting the younger generation's orientation.

Continuing the Lineage

Over the past two decades, I have returned to Lubra many times. In 1999, I became *mithini* (Nepali), or *drogmo* (Tibetan) – "ritual sister" – with Chomo Khandru's eldest great-niece, a young woman exactly my age named Nhima Bhuti. Nhima was one of the young woman traders who spent much of her time outside the village, selling sweaters in India for the months of October through February. I empathized with Nhima when Chomo Khandru constantly berated her for succumbing to the religion of money; Nhima was just like any other young woman in the 1990s anywhere in the world, seeking new experiences and independence from her family. In many ways, she was just like me.

I began to suspect that Chomo Khandru's harsh attitude toward Nhima's cohort belied a sense of personal responsibility for failing to provide the young women with a better religious education, or to inculcate her successors with a greater sense of spiritual commitment. Nhima was in fact very similar to Chomo Khandru herself – a strong, self-confident woman who cared about her village and family but did not want to be tied down and valued the freedom that travel brought. Yet she was not a *chomo*, did not read Tibetan, and was only nominally religious. Nonetheless, she had taken on many of the gender-bending attributes that defined Chomo Khandru's youth: Nhima was the oldest child of six, and, since her father had died young and her mother was chronically ill, Nhima had become the honorary man of the family, just as her great-aunt had before her. Now in her late thirties, Nhima has chosen to remain unmarried.

When I asked Nhima why she did not become a *chomo*, since I thought this might have added some social legitimacy to her otherwise unusual single status, she chuckled. "The *chomo* tradition is not about the future, it's about the past." She continued:

> It's the worst of both worlds: they are not full monastic practitioners, so no one respects them, but they also don't get to enjoy married life or the freedom and excitement of trade like I do, because they are always worried about if they are doing enough dharma. There is no point in having *chomo* any more – if women want to practice religion they should become proper nuns in one of the big places, and if they want to stay unmarried they can just be businesswomen like me.

Nhima's attitude shows that, while general social expectations of women have become more liberal (in Chomo Khandru's time it was virtually impossible to remain unmarried without becoming a *chomo*), religious expectations of women have become more conservative. Appreciation of the "practical dharma" that Chomo Khandru exemplified has diminished as the "dharma of study" has taken precedence. Women who could previously gain respect as lay practitioners by taking teachings in their home village and demonstrating their commitment to dharma through an embodied commitment to practices such as circumambulation, prostration, and mantra recitation must now leave the village to join a monastic institution elsewhere if they wish to be considered authoritative practitioners. The problem with this equation is that there are few Bon institutions that offer formal religious education for women in Nepal or India, so Lubra women who want to be nuns must give up their Bonpo identity to join a Buddhist institution. While some women have done this in recent years, many more have decided to eschew religious practice altogether and take up the trading life like Nhima. While most travel only as far as India, the more adventurous have migrated to the United States. At least in these roundabout ways they can maintain their lay Bonpo identity (which they would have to give up in order to become a formal nun), and, by virtue of their economic successes, gain a status level within the community much higher than that of a *chomo*. For all of these reasons, the highly fluid religious identities that women held in Chomo Khandru's time have given way to a more limited set of possibilities that have been shaped by outside actors such as the Nepali state, exiled Tibetan monastic institutions, and foreign interests.

When Chomo Khandru died in 2002, the Bonpo *chomo* tradition of Lubra went with her.

References

Campbell, J. (1996) *Traveller in Space*, George Braziller, New York.

Cech, K. (1993) The social and religious identity of the Tibetan Bonpos, in *Anthropology of Tibet and the Himalaya* (ed. C. Ramble and M. Brauen), Ethnological Museum of the University of Zurich, Zurich, pp. 39–48.

Childs, G. (2004) Culture change in the name of cultural preservation. *Himalaya: Journal of the Association of Nepal and Himalayan Studies*, 24 (1–2).

Craig, S. (2002) Place and identity between Mustang, Nepal and New York City. *Studies in Nepali History and Society*, 7 (2), 355–403.

Gutschow, K. (2004) *Being a Buddhist Nun: The Struggle for Enlightenment in the Himalayas*, Harvard University Press, Cambridge, MA.

Karmay, S. (1972) *The Treasury of Good Sayings: A Tibetan History of Bon*, Oxford University Press, London.

Karmay, S. (1998) *The Arrow and the Spindle: Studies in History, Myth, and Ritual in Tibet*, Mandala Book Point, Kathmandu.

March, K. (1984) Weaving, writing, and gender. *Man*, 18, 729–44.

Moran, P. (2004) *Buddhism Observed: Travelers, Exiles and Tibetan Dharma in Kathmandu*, RoutledgeCurzon, London.

Ramble, C. (1983) The founding of a Tibetan village: the popular transformation of history. *Kailash*, 10 (3–4), 267–90.

Ramble, C. (1984) *The Lamas of Lubra: Tibetan Bonpo Householder Priests in Western Nepal*. D.Phil. thesis. University of Oxford.

Samuel, G. (1993) *Civilized Shamans: Buddhism in Tibetan Societies*, Smithsonian Institution, Washington, DC.

Schuler, S. (1978) Notes on marriage and the status of women in Baragaon. *Kailash*, 6 (2), 141–52.

Schuler, S. (1987) *The Other Side of Polyandry: Property, Stratification, and Nonmarriage in the Nepal Himalayas*, Westview Press, Boulder, CO.

Sihlé, N. (2002) Lhachö [*Lha Mchod*] and Hrinän [*Sri Gnon*]: the structure and diachrony of a pair of rituals (Baragaon, northern Nepal), in *Religion and Secular Culture in Tibet: Tibetan Studies II* (ed. H. Blezer), Brill, Leiden, pp. 185–206.

Skorupski, T. (1981) Tibetan g-Yung-Drung Monastery at Dolanji. *Kailashi*, 8 (1–2), 25–43.

Snellgrove, D. (1980) *The Nine Ways of Bon*, Prajna Press, Boulder, CO.

Watkins, J.C. (1996) *Spirited Women: Gender, Religion, and Cultural Identity in the Nepal Himalayas*, Columbia University Press, New York.

Willis, J.D. (1989) Tibetan Ani-s: the nun's life in Tibet, in *Feminine Ground: Essays on Women and Tibet* (ed. J.D. Willis), Snow Lion, Ithaca, NY, pp. 96–117.

Further Reading

Gutschow, K. (2004) *Being a Buddhist Nun: The Struggle for Enlightenment in the Himalayas*, Harvard University Press, Cambridge, MA.

Khandelwal, M., Sondra, L.H., and Gold, A.G. (eds) (2006) *Women's Renunciation in South Asia: Nuns, Yoginis, Saints and Singers*, Palgrave Macmillan, New York.

Ramble, C. (2007) *The Navel of the Demonness: Tibetan Buddhism and Civil Religion in Highland Nepal*, Oxford University Press, New York.

Snellgrove, D. (1957) *Buddhist Himalaya*, Bruno Cassirer, London.

Watkins, J.C. (1996) *Spirited Women: Gender, Religion, and Cultural Identity in the Nepal Himalayas*, Columbia University Press, New York.

Notes

1 An extended version of this biography was previously published, as "Living Practical Dharma: A Tribute to Chomo Khandru and the Bonpo Women of Lubra Village, Mustang, Nepal" in *Women's Renunciation in South Asia: Nuns, Yoginis, Saints and Singers* (ed. M. Khandelwal, S.L. Hausner, and A.G. Gold), Palgrave Macmillan, New York, 2006, pp. 69–93. I am grateful to the editors and publisher for permission to reprint this adaptation here. I also thank Sienna Craig, Ann Gold, Nhima Bhuti Gurung, Sondra Hausner, Meena Khandelwal, Charles Ramble, Pat Symonds, Mark Turin, Mark Unno, and the people of Baragaon for their invaluable contributions to my work on this topic.

2 There are two Tibetan etymologies for this word: *chos mo* literally means "woman of the dharma," while *jo mo* means "noblewoman" or "woman of high rank." Both meanings inform indigenous understandings of the term. Although the term is often translated as "nun," I prefer to use *chomo* throughout, since "nun" suggests an individual who has taken formal vows within an institutional setting, which is usually not the case for *chomo*.

3 Willis 1989: 100.
4 Ramble 1983.
5 Ramble 1984.
6 Watkins 1996: 200.
7 See Sihlé (2002) for a general discussion of the increasing monasticization of ritual practices in the Mustang area. In an analysis of "culture change in the name of cultural preservation" in Nubri (an ethnically Tibetan area in Western Nepal's Gorkha district, just east of Mustang), Childs (2004) states that, "an unintended consequence of foreign patronage for Buddhist monasteries in exile has been a loss of Tibetan cultural diversity in Himalayan highland communities."

8 Baragaon means "twelve villages" in Nepali. The Nepali government officials who gave it that name misconstrued the locally defined boundaries of the larger community, excluding seven of the member villages.

9 Craig 2002.

10 Earlier scholarly works in English generally used an umlaut over the "o" – "Bön" – to approximate the Tibetan pronunciation of the word, but more recent works have dropped the umlaut. For simplicity's sake I follow the latter convention.

11 For more detailed information on Bon, see Karmay (1972, 1998); Snellgrove (1980); and Samuel (1993).

12 Noting these similarities, Geoffrey Samuel suggests that "the modern Bonpo are to all intents and purposes the followers of a Buddhist religious tradition, with certain differences of vocabulary from the other four major traditions of Tibetan Buddhism, but no major difference in content" (1993: 326).

13 Cech 1993: 42.
14 Schuler 1978, 1987.
15 Gutschow 2004.
16 Ramble 1984: 133.
17 March 1984: 729.
18 The Tamang are an ethnic population living in Nepal's middle hills who speak a Tibeto-Burman language and practice their own form of Buddhism.
19 Campbell 1996: 156.
20 Moran 2004.
21 Skorupski 1981.

27

Excavating the Stories of Border-Crossing Women Masters in Modern Buddhism
The Oral Biography of Pelling Ani Wangdzin and Her Family

Amy Holmes-Tagchungdarpa

Editor's Introduction

There is a scarcity of accounts of Tibetan women in the Buddhist historical archive. As we noted in the biography of Mo Sukey (Chapter 21), this has marginalized women due to a combination of androcentric record-keeping practices and the tendency of scholars to focus on the monastic exemplars from central Tibet, who are all men. Joining the biography of Mo Sukey, here is another oral history of a woman, Pelling Ani Wangdzin. This life history also sheds light on the rapid changes occurring between the nineteenth and twentieth centuries in the eastern Himalayas, facts of life that affected rural Buddhist practitioners.

Born in the tiny eastern Himalayan kingdom of Sikkim, Pelling Ani Wangdzin studied in a monastery with her brothers and then traveled extensively, taking advantage of the new technologies of mobility, which allowed her to cover distances more quickly. Her life was shaped by her family, as the Buddhist identity of her father and her brothers opened up avenues for her. Funded by her father's successful businesses, new possibilities opened up that Pelling Ani Wangdzin fearlessly embraced. Here again, it is merchant families and their wealth that led to Buddhist innovation.

Especially noteworthy in this spiritual biography is the role of pilgrimage in the formation of this practitioner and eventual master. From within the tradition, she won blessings from connecting with the powers found across her Buddhist world:

from newly rediscovered Bodh Gaya, where the Buddha was enlightened, to the Kathmandu Valley's great *stupas*. Pelling Ani Wangdzin then made her way to Bhutan and Central Tibet, where she worshipped at all the major temples and monasteries. In search of a religious master, Tokden Shakya Shri (1853–1919), she also completed one of the greatest, and most arduous, pilgrimage routes in all Tibet, done only every 12 years in Kham, circling the Crystal Mountain, Tsari. This arduous passage, which requires venturing from high-altitude trails clinging to the mountain to low jungle trails, promises the blessing of spiritually purifying the pilgrims, as each must engage in practices over a one-month course that include prostrations, prayers, and offerings to local deities.

Aside from adapting to British colonial presence, the resulting travel technologies, and new business networks, what is clear is that, rather than disrupt the Sikkim Buddhist traditions, the new wealth earned by householders allowed Himalayan Buddhists to continue, even strengthen, their older traditions. Most borderland Buddhists were no longer isolated, and Wangdzin's life gives an idea of the opportunities available for women at this time. Underwritten by her family's wealth and position, she gained a tantric education during her travels that allowed her to return to her home state to become a renowned community leader and teacher, and the founder of a unique community outside a monastery that brought together a variety of ethnicities and forms of Himalayan Buddhism in a shared space of tantric yogic and meditative practice.

Introduction

Despite the fascinating nature of her life story and the rich context it provides us for studying modern Buddhism in the Himalayas between East and South Asia, a figure such as Pelling Ani Wangdzin[1] would normally remain off the radar. This is because, unlike the most famous male religious spiritual figures, whose disciples had written life stories, Pelling Ani Wangdzin never had a written biography devoted to her.[2] Her story remains in an oral archive, possessed by her descendants and people who lived in the villages around her birthplace and practice center in Western Sikkim. Members of her family remain deeply proud of her achievements and inspired by her tale of spiritual achievement, which has been mirrored by a number of her nieces and nephews who still survive today and still remain part of Sikkim's diverse Buddhist landscape. Significantly as well, the last few of her students only died in the past decade, which has meant that information about everyday life in her community was still available until very recently. I have assembled the following biography from among these three groups during the past eight years. Like many oral biographies, it remains incomplete, with tantalizing and frustrating gaps in the particulars. Rather than dismissing the stories of Pelling Ani Wangdzin's adventures on these grounds, however, these gaps can instead be seen as possibilities for the imagination to fill in details. The details that we do know remain as important disruptions to the limitations in the archive related to women, rural Buddhist communities in the Himalayas, and the Tibetan and Himalayan experience of modernity more generally. Compiling an oral biography provides us with methodological challenges, but the richness of possibility and the alternative perspective that such biographies provide us with make up for these challenges, and allow us to explore alternative trajectories in the creation of Himalayan Buddhist communities. The following is assembled from those details, with an attempt to bring them together from contextual sources.

Sikkim: Religious and Historical Context

Pelling Ani Wangdzin was born sometime in the 1870s in the eastern Himalayan kingdom of Sikkim. Nestled between the kingdoms of Nepal and Bhutan, Sikkim remained a stronghold of Vajrayana Buddhist practice based on the Nyingmapa tradition of Tibetan Buddhism. The kingdom played a special role in the broader Tibetan Buddhist imagination due to its being viewed historically as a "hidden land" (*sbas yul*), a geographical space identified to be efficacious for spiritual development by the Tibetan saint Guru Rinpoche, and sealed off to be discovered at a time of need by the spiritually realized.

Beginning a thousand years ago, various Tibetan groups migrated into the area, and they interacted with the Lepchas, an ethnic community indigenous to the area. According to popular legend, one Tibetan chief named Khye Bumsa settled in Sikkim, and his descendants and their communities later became known as the Lhopos.[3] By the seventeenth century, one of these clans, headed by Phuntsok Namgyal, was enthroned as the first king in the Namgyal dynasty, supported in this by a charismatic Tibetan lama named Lhatsun Namkhai Jigme (1597–1653). He also founded monasteries and began traditions of unique meditative practices in Sikkim.[4]

As part of the political changes that took place in the seventeenth century, a number of Lhopo and Lepcha families rose in prominence due to their being assigned territories and lands to administer by the king of Sikkim. Pelling Ani Wangdzin was born in the late nineteenth century into one of these families, the Takchungdarpa clan, which administered large tracts of land in the Singyang area of Western Sikkim. Her father, Aphur, was known popularly as Nordak (*Nor bdag*), or "the holder of wealth," due to his large territories but also due to his business acumen.

Darjeeling and the nearby border town of Kalimpong to the south of Sikkim both became vital for trans-Himalayan trade, which had been opened by the British colonial rule, and, as a result, a number of enterprising Lhopo, Lepcha, and Nepali Sikkimese attempted to create new economic opportunities for their communities. While this part of Western Sikkim was known for its fertile land and traditional agriculture, Pelling Ani Wangdzin's father, Aphur, was successful due to three business ventures. The first was the operation of a dairy, where he employed local villagers and laborers to produce cow milk and cheese, staples of the Sikkimese diet. The other two businesses were unusual, however, in that they adapted to the rapid changes taking place in and around Sikkim. Aphur produced two items that became sought after in eastern Himalayan trade: the first was large cardamom, which he cultivated on his steeper forested land, a spice that after 1900 became widely sought after and of which Sikkim was the major supplier; the other venture was sheep wool and to produce it Aphur controlled the entire production, from herders and shearers to transport to Kalimpong, where it was carded and distributed throughout the region's wool trade network, one that spread as far as Britain.[5] These three business ventures, which fused traditional agricultural practices, trade-route transport, and modern commodity networks, gave Aphur his Lhopo-language nickname but also gave him a widely known Nepali-language moniker, Aphur Mahajan (Aphur the Rich Man).

With his wealth, Aphur established his other legacy, as a generous patron of Buddhism. Tibetan Buddhists believed that patronage of Buddhism through donations to Buddhist institutions and individuals in materials and food would generate merit, which would help them move along the path to enlightenment even if in their current lifetime as laypeople they could not dedicate themselves full time to practice. Aphur became a crucial patron, or *jindak*, to the major monastery of Western Sikkim, Pemayangtse. As the royal monastery of Sikkim, which had been founded by Lhatsun Namkhai Jigme, its lamas were connected to the royal court and had the vital role of carrying out the coronation and legitimating the kings of Sikkim, for whom they also acted as advisers and ritual specialists. The Pemayangtse lamas were uniquely recruited, composed of representatives from the 14 Lhopo clans in Western Sikkim. Even more unique was that, by the late nineteenth century, the sangha of Pemayangtse was almost entirely noncelibate tantrikas (*ngak pa*). As such, they were therefore still involved in agriculture and trade, and families would take several sons to be admitted to the monastery, allowing them to decide once they got older whether they would complete their ritual training or engage in vocations outside. Admitting a son to the monastery accrued merit, but, more importantly, it provided the most comprehensive education available in Sikkim until the late nineteenth century. While Aphur did not take admission in the monastery, he sent several of his sons to do so, and used his financial resources to ensure they were able to remain engaged in religion and learning while his other children assisted him in the family businesses.

Two of Aphur's sons became prominent lamas in the Pemayangtse community. Yab Gyatso became the Discipline Master (*Tshul thrims pa*) of the monastery. Even more famous, however, was Yab Gyatso's older brother Osel, who became renowned for his mastery of Buddhist learning and for this was awarded a position in the palace temple in Gangtok. Here he came to the attention of the 11th king of Sikkim, Tashi Namgyal (1893–1963), who employed him as his private secretary (*'bri gnyer chen po*); there he excelled until he passed away at the young age of 40.

Aphur was not only dedicated to his sons, however. He was also concerned about providing his daughter, Wangdzin, with an education. He would encourage his sons to take her with them to Pemayangtse, where she would sit with them learning how to read Tibetan texts. There were no nunneries in Sikkim, and, because of the lack of secular educational opportunities, girls had limited access to formal learning. Learning to read Tibetan books (*pecha*) with their fathers, uncles, and brothers in monasteries was the main form of education for many girls, who could become highly literate and able to carry out their own household religious rites as well as keep records of household transactions.

The concern for Wangdzin's education was representative of broader attitudes toward women in Lhopo society, which traditionally afforded women high status and autonomy. There was no traditional preference for male children and no dowry system. Instead, girls were given their own wealth upon marriage, and remained eligible to inherit family land and own it in their own name. The Lhopo community did practice arranged marriage, particularly within the 14 clans, and fathers and brothers sought marital partners who had landed assets and were therefore financially stable for their daughters and sisters.

When Wangdzin came of age, however, her father did not seek a husband for her, despite many seeking her hand and through it a marital alliance with the powerful Aphur Mahajan. Although many of his sons married, Wangdzin did not. Instead, she remained committed to her reading and writing and to the spiritual practices she had learned at the monastery and from her father. Her dedication and promise led her father to make a different type of investment in his daughter, whereby he began to sponsor Wangdzin's going off on pilgrimages. This has been a very popular practice throughout the Tibetan world, due to the belief that sacred sites (*gnas*) associated with the historical Buddha and important Buddhist masters were thought to contain a special type of power (*byin rlabs*) that could be conferred on visitors and that would lead them to better rebirths and heightened spiritual powers.[6] By the late nineteenth century, wealthy Lhopo and Lepcha Buddhists were active on broader South and East Asian pilgrimage circuits that saw them visit sacred sites in Bhutan, Kathmandu, Tibet, and Indian sites such as Bodh Gaya. The particularly wealthy or cosmopolitan individuals also visited more distant Chinese sites such as Wutai Shan. Sikkimese Buddhists appear to have had a long history of pilgrimage to these areas, and would arrange trade trips so they could visit new places. By the nineteenth century, there was increased participation in these circuits, largely due to the new print and transport technologies (trains, buses), which spread information about them and allowed for shorter traveling times. During her youth, Wangdzin visited Lhasa a number of times to see the sacred centers of central Tibet, as well as nearby Bhutan. In those days before passports, she had easy border crossings and, due to her father's patronage and support, had more than enough resources and connections to facilitate easy travel and the opportunity to gain merit through substantial monetary donations at the major sacred Buddhist sites.

Wangdzin's father and brothers also made another investment in her, in providing her with the opportunity for a Buddhist education. Sometime in the first decade of the twentieth century, Aphur passed away. His devastated children allowed for their pious sister Wangdzin to carry his ashes to the sacred sites of Indian Buddhism in order to gain him a better rebirth. Wangdzin first traveled with several family members by train to Bodh Gaya, the site of the Buddha's enlightenment. Here, beneath the Bodhi Tree, the family sponsored rituals from various Buddhist traditions, including Tibetan and Sri Lankan. By the early twentieth century, Bodh Gaya was a booming pilgrimage site. While Tibetan Buddhists had traveled there for many centuries,[7] the early twentieth century was a time of renewal. The British Government's Archaeological Survey of India was engaged in renovating the site, which had been "rediscovered" by British civil servants in the late nineteenth century. Buddhists flocked there from throughout Asia, and it became a significant networking point and crossroads for various forms of Buddhism. Wangdzin also traveled to nearby Varanasi, where she immersed part of her father's ashes in the Ganges, as was traditional among Sikkimese Buddhists because of the spiritual efficacy of the river.

After these trips, Wangdzin traveled by train again up to the Nepal border, where she then joined a group of other pilgrims heading to the Kathmandu valley by horse. In Kathmandu she made offerings in her father's memory at the Three Stupas of Kathmandu Valley: Svayambhu (Tib. Phakpashingkun), Bauddha (Charungkhashor), and *Namo Buddha* (Takmolujin). These large *stupas* were all associated with celestial Buddhas and bodhisattvas, and therefore considered some of the most important sites in the Tibetan Buddhist world.

Until this point, Wangdzin was part of broader pilgrimage networks and roads well traveled by other Buddhists. What happened next was not so typical, however. During her travels, Wangdzin had heard of a great meditation teacher in Tibet, who people said possessed miraculous powers due to his realization and mastery of different forms of meditation. Aristocrats, traders, farmers, and nomads flocked to his base in eastern Tibet for the opportunity to meet with him and study meditation, and his reputation and stories of his accomplishments were circulated far and wide by traders and wandering yogis. It is likely Wangdzin met one of these figures in Bodh Gaya or Kathmandu, or perhaps she had even heard of this remarkable yogi back in Sikkim, where lamas competed with each other to travel further and gain their education from Buddhist centers mysterious and remote, beyond the great monasteries of the plateau. Wangdzin was intrigued by these stories, and, inspired by her father's piety, decided to set out to meet this teacher. Some sources say she walked over land for six weeks from Kathmandu to southeastern Tibet; others say it took her between three and five months to reach the hilly mountains. When she arrived, however, she was not disappointed.

Wangdzin arrived in the eastern Tibetan province of Kham excited at the prospect of learning meditation in one of the most stimulating Buddhist environments of her day. Eastern Tibet remained largely politically autonomous throughout Tibetan history, with a variety of different forms of political administration throughout its valleys. Some areas were ruled by lamas, reincarnated masters, and monasteries; others by chieftains or kings. In the nineteenth century there had been considerable political turmoil when an ambitious chief named Gonpo Namgyal attempted to unite Kham and threatened to take over central Tibet and even China.[8] The political turmoil of the period inspired religious response and a move against religious sectarianism. It led to a period of cultural and religious efflorescence in religious communities in Kham, where older practices were circulated alongside new ones by religious masters attempting to avoid violence and develop alternative visions of community for the culturally diverse region.

The yogin Tokden Shakya Shri (1853–1919) was but one of the masters involved in these broader networks of practice and transmission. Born into a humble nomadic family, he started his religious career as a cook in a monastery before embarking on a lifelong dedication to meditation. He was never ordained, instead preferring to practice along with his family, which included two wives and ten children and a spiritual family of students that quickly developed and by the early twentieth century included members from as far west as Kinnaur and Ladakh and as far east as Arunachal and Bhutan. The members of his community included students from all sections of Tibetan and Himalayan society, who came to visit his community, which spanned two sides of a valley in Kham. On both sides of the valley, students lived in yak-hair tents and built huts, and spent their days in silent retreat, broken only by the ringing of a bell at Shakya Shri's residence that signified meal times and lecture times. It was an idyllic environment for the spiritually determined, but was hard living and scared off many who came just to be associated with the master.[9]

It is not clear when Wangdzin initially went to Kham, or how long she stayed there. One indication of the general time period is that Ani Wangdzin took part in the pilgrimage called Tsari Rongkhor Chenmo, literally "the great circumambulation of the valleys"), a physically grueling and spiritually challenging pilgrimage that entails going the entire way around Tsari mountain in southeastern Tibet, through jungles and over mountain tracks.[10] This pilgrimage was considered to spiritually purify its participants, as they engaged in practices along the way including prostrations, prayers, and offerings to deities who dwelled in the landscape. Even if the experience was not spiritually transformational, it certainly was a physically difficult experience, as participants fought off leeches, snakes, and hostile local inhabitants in the region who possessed arrows and guns; they also often had to hang off the sides of cliffs and scramble on hands and knees, clinging to vines and bushes to get through some of the tougher terrain. Due to the scale of this pilgrimage, it was only staged once every 12 years, during the Year of the Monkey in the Tibetan calendrical cycle. Considering that Ani Wangdzin only lived until her fifties, only three of these events took place in her lifetime: in 1884, 1896, and 1908.[11] Assuming that she did the Rongkhor in 1908, while she was in her teens or twenties, it seems likely that she studied with Shakya Shri around that time. Shakya Shri also had a community based at Tsari, though stories state Wangdzin definitely studied with him in Kham.

It is also not clear what exactly Wangdzin learned during her time in eastern Tibet. She eventually left Kham to return to Sikkim, where she built a simple retreat hut on land above the small town of Pelling, near Pemayangtse Monastery. Here in the jungle, students began to gather around this distinctive woman who wore her hair long in a topknot and dressed in the red robes of a nun. She became known as Pelling Ani, the Nun of Pelling. Her community was made up of a variety of ethnic groups – Lhopo, Lepcha, Gurung, Tamang, and Rai, among others – and both men and women. With her, they studied the physical yogas of manipulating the inner wind channels, the meditation systems of Dzokchen and Chakchen, and forms of prayer and purification practice. One popular practice she taught was Nyungne (*Smyung gnas*), a fasting practice dedicated to Avalokitesvara. As part of this practice, students would fast and prostrate on alternate days, making offerings to the bodhisattva of compassion with the goal of self-transformation.[12] Her ability to teach this wide range of practices suggests she learned a great deal during her time in Kham but had also accumulated her learning during the many years before that in which she had traveled and studied. When Pelling Ani Wangdzin passed away in her fifties in Pelling in the early 1920s, practitioners both monastic and nonmonastic, female and male, came to accompany her body back to her home of Singyang, where her grieving brothers honored their extraordinary sister with a ceremony that went on for many days. They built stupas in her memory up near her retreat house, and in the decades that followed many other masters came to stay in retreat there in the space sanctified by Wangdzin's practice.

At some point, however, the masters stopped coming. The local landowners sold the land to the government, who built a helipad there in the 1990s to cater to tourists, and in the first decade of the 2000s the exact site of Wangdzin's hut was completely cleared to make way for yet another luxury hotel, which will join the crowded concrete conclave that Pelling has become. Now, all that remains from Pelling Ani Wangdzin's time period are trees planted by her community; but even they are being felled to make way for development, disappearing just as the memory of this great local woman saint grows faint. As her older descendants and original students pass away, even the lineage practices she passed on have now all but disappeared. Her story demonstrates the fragility of the oral narratives. It also illustrates the very real importance of preserving such biographies. Pelling Ani Wangdzin's story also suggests alternate understandings of the impact of modernity on local, rural Buddhist communities in various parts of Asia, and the importance of border-crossing in the creation of these communities,[13] which would indicate that few communities, even in the most remote areas, were completely isolated.

References

Allione, T. (ed.) (2000) *Women of Wisdom*, Snow Lion, Ithaca, NY.

Bessenger, S. (2010) *Echoes of Enlightenment: The Life and Legacy of Sonam Peldren*. Ph.D. dissertation. University of Virginia.

Bhutia, K.D. (2007) Sikkimese lay practitioners: Mani Amlas, Gomchen, and alternative paths for laypeople in the religious landscape of Guru Rinpoche's hidden land, in *Proceedings from the Chong-ji Buddhist Order Forum on Lay Buddhists in Society, Seoul, 2007*, Chong-ji Buddhist Order Education Centre, Seoul, pp. 120–41.

Bogin, B. (2005) The life of Yol mo Bstan 'dzin nor bu: a critical edition, translation and memoirs of a seventeenth-century Tibetan Buddhist lama. Ph.D. dissertation. University of Michigan.

Cox, L., Bocking, B., and Turner, A. (2010) Beachcombing, going native and freethinking: rewriting the history of early Western Buddhist monastics. *Contemporary Buddhism*, 11, 125–47.

Diemberger, H. (2007) *When a Woman Becomes a Religious Dynasty: The Samding Dorje Phagmo of Tibet*, Columbia University Press, New York.

Gyatso, J. (1998) *Apparitions of the Self: The Secret Autobiographies of a Tibetan Visionary*, Princeton University Press, Princeton, NJ.

Guarisco, E. (trans.) (2011) *Togden Shakya Shri: The Life and Liberation of a Tibetan Yogin Marigar*, Edizioni Shang Shung, Italy.

Harris, T. (2013) *Geographical Diversions: Tibetan Trade*, Global Transactions, University of Georgia Press, Athens.

Holmes-Tagchungdarpa, A. (forthcoming) *The Social Life of Tibetan Biography: Textuality, Community and Authority in the Lineage of Tokden Shakya Shri*, Lexington Press, Lanham, MD.

Huber, T. (1999) *The Cult of Pure Crystal Mountain: Popular Pilgrimage and Visionary Landscape in Southeast Tibet*, Oxford University Press, New York.

Huber, T. (2008) *The Holy Land Reborn: Pilgrimage and the Tibetan Reinvention of Buddhist India*, University of Chicago Press, Chicago, IL.

Jacoby, S. (2007) Consorts and revelation in Eastern Tibet: the auto/biographical writings of the treasure revealer Sera Khandro (1892–1940). Ph.D. dissertation. University of Virginia.

Lopez, D.S., Jr. (2005) *The Madman's Middle Way: Reflections on Reality of the Tibetan Monk Gendun Chopel*, University of Chicago Press, Chicago, IL.

Lopez, D.S., Jr. (2013) *Gendun Chopel: Tibet's First Modern Artist*, Serindia and Latse Library, Chicago, IL.

McKay, A. (1998) *Pilgrimage in Tibet*, Routledge, London.

Mthu stobs rnam rgyal and Ye shes sgrol ma (2003 [1908]) *'Bras ljongs rgyal rabs* [History of Sikkim], Tsuklhakhang Trust, Gangtok.

Pitkin, A. (2009) "Like pouring water into water": Buddhist lineages, modernity, and the continuity of memory in the twentieth-century history of Tibetan Buddhism. Ph.D. dissertation. Columbia University.

Quintman, A. (2006) Milarepa's many lives: anatomy of a Tibetan biographical corpus. Ph.D. dissertation. University of Michigan.

Rinchen Lhamo (1985 [1926]) *We Tibetans*, Potala Publications, New York.

Schaeffer, K. (2004) *Himalayan Hermitess: The Life of a Tibetan Buddhist Nun*, Oxford University Press, Oxford.

Taring, D. (1986 [1970]) *Daughter of Tibet: The Autobiography of Rinchen Dolma Taring*, Wisdom, London.

Van Spengen, W. (2000) *Tibetan Border Worlds: A Geohistorical Analysis of Trade and Traders*, Kegan Paul, London and New York.

Willock, N. (2010) A Tibetan Buddhist polymath in modern China. Ph.D. dissertation. Indiana University.

Yamamoto, C.S. (2012) *Vision and Violence: Lama Zhang and the Politics of Charisma in Twelfth-Century Tibet*, Brill, Leiden.

Yudru Tsomu (2006) Local aspirations and national constraints: a case study of Nyarong Gonpo Namgyel and his rise of power in Kham (1836–1865). Ph.D. dissertation. Harvard University.

Further Reading

Balicki-Denjongpa, A. (2008) *Lamas, Shamans and Ancestors: Village Religion in Sikkim*, Brill, Leiden.

Blackburn, A. (2010) *Locations of Buddhism: Colonialism and Modernity in Sri Lanka*, University of Chicago Press, Chicago, IL.

Huber, T. (1999) *The Cult of Pure Crystal Mountain: Popular Pilgrimage and Visionary Landscape in Southeast Tibet*, Oxford University Press, New York.

Jha, P.K. (1985) *History of Sikkim (1817–1904): Analysis of British Policy and Activities*, OPS Publications Private, Calcutta.

Kathog Situ (2009) *Togden Shakya Shri: The Life and Liberation of a Tibetan Yogin* (trans. E. Guariso), Shang Shung Institute, Merigar.

McKay, A. (1998) *Pilgrimage in Tibet*, Routledge, London.

Notes

1. *Ani* is a term used for female ordained religious practitioners that is now commonly regarded as pejorative. While I generally support the removal of the term from discourse regarding ordained women in Tibetan societies, I will persist in using it here since Wangdzin was generally known as Pelling Ani Wangdzin in her community in Sikkim, and because the use of "Ani," a term for "maternal aunt" in the Tibeto-Burman dialect used in Sikkim, may in fact reflect an actual kinship tie that many in the region claim with her. It is noteworthy that information regarding ordination lineages for women in Sikkim is extremely sparse, and therefore it has not been absolutely established that Wangdzin was ordained, though she did wear robes and never married.
2. Important recent studies that focus on life-writing in the Tibetan Buddhist context include Gyatso (1998), Bogin (2005), Quintman (2006), Pitkin (2009), Willock (2010), and Yamamoto (2012). These studies all focus on prominent male masters. Some of the studies related to female masters include Allione (2000), Schaeffer (2004), Diemberger (2007), Jacoby (2007), and Bessenger (2010). Nonreligiously-focused biographies and autobiographies also remain scarce, and include Rinchen Lhamo (1985) and Taring (1986).
3. Today people of this ethnic group are known as Bhutias.
4. This early popular history is taken from Mthu stobs rnam rgyal and Ye shes sgrol ma's *History of Sikkim* (2003).
5. Van Spengen (2000) and Harris (2013) provide overviews of these trade networks.
6. The essays in McKay (1998) act as an excellent introduction to pilgrimage practices in Tibetan cultural areas.
7. Toni Huber (2008) explores the Tibetan fascination with Bodh Gaya and the history of Tibetan pilgrimage there.
8. Yudru Tsomu (2006) covers the nineteenth-century history of Kham.
9. This summary of Tokden Shakya Shri's life and community comes from his biography, which has been translated by Guarisco (2011) and is studied in Holmes-Tagchungdarpa (forthcoming).
10. On this extraordinary tradition, see Huber (1999: 128ff).
11. Huber 1999: 128.
12. Bhutia (2007) is a detailed overview of Nyungne in Sikkim.
13. In the Tibetan cultural area, Gendun Chophel remains paradigmatic as a modern Buddhist, due to his travels throughout South Asia and experimentation with various literary and artistic forms. For more on him, see Lopez (2005, 2013). Recent work done by Brian Bocking, Lawrence Cox, and Alicia Turner on the early Irish monk U Dhammaloka has revealed the alternative versions of modern Buddhist history that appear when nonelite sources are used. See Cox, Bocking, and Turner (2010) for more on methodological considerations related to the recovering and writing of these various histories.

Part V
Buddhist Lives in East Asia

28

The Life of a Contemporary Japanese Buddhist Priest

Protecting the Dharma and Ensuring Its Flow with All of One's Strength

Naoyuki Ogi

Editor's Introduction

As Buddhism spread from India across the world, it absorbed elements it encountered from the various societies and their cultures that it encountered. There are major differences that distinguish Japanese priests from other countries' Buddhist monks. Today a majority of Japanese Buddhist priests marry, have families, and retain ownership of their own lineage temple. Most Japanese priests are nonvegetarian.

One of the dominant Buddhist sects in Japan is Jodo Shinshu (hereafter Shin Buddhism). It was founded during the twelfth and thirteenth centuries by Shinran (1173–1263). He was one of Japan's most controversial priests of his time, and yet his contributions and interpretation of the Buddhist teaching are still with us today, bringing comfort and life meaning to millions of followers throughout the world.

Traditionally, the central practice of Pure Land Buddhism is the *nembutsu*, a recitation of the name Amida Buddha, one of the many Buddhas revealed by Shakyamuni Buddha in early Mahayana texts. (The name "Amida" comes from "Amitabha" or "Amitayus" in Sanskrit and means "immeasurable light" or "immeasurable life.") Therefore, Amida Buddha is the "Buddha of Immeasurable Light and Life." Adherents of the Pure Land school express gratitude for this existence, saying *Namo Amida Butsu* (I revere Amida Buddha). The Shin Pure Land Buddhist school is the most popular in Japan today. Part of its popularity is due to its tradition of moderation, which doesn't demand that its followers, including priests, abide by monastic religious precepts or many dietary restrictions.

This biography is centered on a rural 250-year-old monastic temple, Daikenzan Choshoji, located in rural southwest Japan. This historic temple, with its miraculous

Buddha image, is itself a character in this biography, as its priest, Rev. Ogi, has throughout his life struggled with how to raise the funds to repair the buildings and ensure the material continuity of Buddhist ritual traditions and other services. Throughout Japan, migration to large urban centers has gradually depopulated the rural hinterland, so that the former systems of tithing and deriving priestly income in exchange for ritual services can no longer support the life of a married Shin Buddhist family. As hereditary priests have faced this reality, they have had to take training and jobs in the outside world; under these circumstances, it is easy to see why there are hundreds of Buddhist sanctuaries in Japan that are vacant and inactive.

Among the various Pure Land schools, today there are roughly ten thousand temples of the Jodo Shinshu Hongwanji-ha subsect of Shin Buddhism throughout Japan. This most popular school of Japanese Buddhism, Pure Land, is represented in the narrative of Keishin Ogi, a contemporary priest; it is conveyed in the voice of his son, who will one day face a new array of similar challenges to sustain Buddhist tradition in Japan's rural countryside.

Introduction

In a small village in the west of Japan, there is a priest who continues the Shin Buddhist tradition as the 13th-generation hereditary-lineage priest of his temple. His name is Rev. Ogi, Keishin (hereafter Rev. Keishin, secular first name: Megumi), and he is the current head priest of Daikenzan Choshoji temple. I have come to have much respect for him as a contemporary Shin Buddhist priest. Rev. Keishin's life is unusual but typical of the distinctive life of a Shin Buddhist priest in today's Japan.

Pure Land in the Context of Modern Japanese Buddhism

After the Warring States era ended in the seventeenth century, the Japanese government issued a law decreeing that each person in the nation had to be registered as a member of a Buddhist temple. The rulers knew that Buddhism could be a useful force in controlling society since it had spread to every part of Japan and since it wanted to stamp out the European missionary-led conversions to Christianity from earlier centuries. As a result, all Buddhist temples had to maintain membership records and submit them to the government every year.

In 1868, the Meiji Restoration returned the emperor to power, ending Japan's feudal era. The nation's new ruling class tried to create a new political system based on the Shinto religion and the supreme authority of the emperor as a Shinto god. As a result, many Buddhist temples and Buddhist statues were destroyed. Buddhist authority in society was reduced and deprived under a government-led movement that initially attempted to abolish Buddhism. Buddhist leaders had to find some way to survive in society and its leaders succeeded to some degree in eventually softening the government's opposition.

Some Buddhist sects changed their doctrines so that their teachings could be merged into Shinto and offered teachings such as "Buddha and the Shinto gods are the same" or "Our primal teaching is to protect the emperor as divine." However, in spite of the tremendous pressure, Buddhism survived in this new nationalist climate by focusing on funeral rituals, a task that Shinto avoided. But this change in Buddhism's role in Japanese society was the cause of Buddhist temples coming to deal almost exclusively with funerals and memorial services, leading some historians to label the Japanese Buddhist tradition in the twentieth century "Funeral Buddhism."

After World War II, the roles of state and religion were separated by the new Japanese constitution. Buddhism was once again free to do all kinds of Buddhist activities without restrictions from the government. However, the idea that Buddhism was only for funeral rituals became ingrained in both the Buddhist priests and the people, and this perception continues in the minds of many right up to the present day.

Today, Buddhism in Japan mainly focuses on funeral and memorial rituals, and is also known for the selling of talismans and amulets for prosperity and other wishes, and for conducting prayer rituals for happiness and safety. These activities provide the main sources of income for most modern Buddhist temples. But, realizing the declining position and shrunken role of Buddhism in contemporary Japan, some Buddhist priests are trying to introduce new activities and ideas to revitalize the teaching of Buddha, especially in ameliorating contemporary suffering in Japanese society. Some schools, for example, have established Buddhist hospices and nursing homes and provide round-the-clock counseling services. In addition, young Buddhist priests are trying to create innovative activities and programs to reach out to the younger generation using skillful means: among these are Buddhist "hip hop" chanting contests, a Buddhist priests' vestments fashion show, and the production of anime DVDs on Buddhism. They are trying to leap beyond the centuries-old perception that Buddhism is only a conservative tradition.[1] It is in this context that the biography of our modern Pure Land priest should be centered.

The Life of Rev. Keishin Ogi

Rev. Keishin was born the second son to Rev. Zengyo and his wife Ritsuko on March 4, 1944 in a small village called Kishimi Tokuji, in Yamaguchi prefecture in southwest Japan. Rev. Keishin was born into a temple family that as of this writing has been protecting and has been responsible for the noted temple Daikenzan Choshoji for over 350 years – a very unusual circumstance.

This temple was established as a result of a mysterious series of events. In 1490, a piece of wood that looked like a Shakyamuni Buddha image was discovered in a well under the Daikenzan Ara Shinto shrine.[2] Ouchishi, a local feudal lord, believed this to be an omen of fortune and established a new temple, Daikenzan Sennoji, for the worship of the discovered wooden Shakyamuni Buddha statue.[3] According to historical records, the Sennoji temple fell into disuse. However, the Hongwanji Pure Land Buddhist priest Ejun (d. 1687) came to the temple in 1659. In 1660 he rededicated it as a Shin Buddhist temple, which he renamed Choshoji.[4] In 1694, Choshoji was recognized as an official Shin temple by the head temple of the Jodo Shinshu Hongwanji-ha sect in Kyoto.

When Rev. Keishin was born in 1944 as the second son, both his family and the temple sangha members expected that he would become the 13th head priest of the temple. Accordingly, it seems that he was raised very strictly and so describes the early days of his life as follows:

> What made me so sad during my childhood was that my family would not buy me any toys or equipment for sports such as running shoes, soccer balls, etc. As a child, I was quite sports minded but my family tried to shy me away from having any interest in sports. They did allow me to practice judo but even that I was forced to quit after having an appendicitis attack. Anyways, my parents made me focus just on my studies and priestly calling.

When he was young, he said that he honestly did not want to become a priest. He confessed the complicated feelings he had during his student days:

> I grew up in the extremely poor economic conditions of postwar Japan. The Choshoji temple had about 50 family members who were mainly poor farming families. Although my father, Rev. Zengyo, worked for the temple as the 12th head priest, my mother worked outside the temple as a government employee because the temple's membership was too small to support our family and the temple financially. Our small Buddhist temple with its straw-thatched roof had been progressively and seriously damaged through natural disasters over the past centuries. I wondered, "How long under these terrible conditions can we ensure the survival of our temple and protect it?" I dreamed, "How long until I can reconstruct this temple for the future?" I had a strange feeling, something along the lines of melancholic apprehension, just thinking about the time when I would become the next head priest of this poor and dilapidated temple.

When he had to choose a university to attend, Rev. Keishin was given two options: the local university in the countryside or going to a Pure Land-affiliated institution called Ryukoku University in Kyoto. His decision was easy:

> Kyoto is a much bigger city than my hometown, so it didn't take me long to make my decision! Ryukoku University was the biggest and best academic institution for me to learn about Shin Buddhism. I enrolled in the department of Shin Buddhist studies at Ryukoku and majored in Buddhist doctrine and history. I especially enjoyed my studies on the concept of *shinjin* [faith or awakening], developed in the Shin Buddhist path, and how human beings can be saved just as we are through Amida Buddha's intervention, and this became the basis for my B.A. thesis. Actually it was these studies that led me to realize that I wanted to live my life as a Buddhist priest and share this teaching with others. While at Ryukoku University, I encountered many great teachers who impressed upon me just how important this concept and the teachings were in life and step by step I came to realize the wonderfulness of the Buddhist teachings. I received ordination to become a Shin Buddhist priest when I was in my junior year.

As this slow transformation occurred during college, Keishin's thoughts turned to his broken-down home temple and what might be done to revitalize the community. In the end, he realized that he needed additional training and skills in order to be able to earn more income:

> After much consideration, I started to study to become a government employee along with being a Buddhist priest. This was the only way for me to maintain my temple and a family after I returned to my village. To be honest with you, I wanted to work at a manufacturing or electronics company, but I had to give up these thoughts due to my responsibility to the Choshoji temple.

There is a common saying among Japanese Buddhist temple families that goes: "Returning to *gobuppan* [the rice for Buddha]." In Japan, there is the time-honored custom that temple members annually donate rice to the temples, and this rice is then offered every day to the Buddha. For the Japanese, rice is the most important staple food in sustaining life. Therefore, they first offer rice to the Buddha before partaking in their own meals. This offering is a reflection of the fact that people's lives are sustained not only by their own efforts but also as a result of countless other causes, both visible and invisible, and countless sacrifices made by others. Buddhist temple families can also consume the rice that the members donate for the Buddha. So, Buddhist temple families can survive because of this *gobuppan* rice. In return, temple family members have the responsibility to work for Buddha by protecting the temple and spreading the teaching of Buddha. Realizing his life's purpose, Rev. Keishin made a commitment and would not discard this responsibility.

After returning to his hometown from Kyoto in 1966, Rev. Keishin started to work at several junior high schools in Yamaguchi city and Kawakami village as a temporary Social Studies teacher. It seems that he had also earned a secondary teacher's license during his university days. However, in light of his financial responsibilities toward his family and his university studies, he began to work in the child welfare section at the Yamaguchi Prefectural Office in 1967. Through his dedication and interest in social-welfare issues, he eventually rose to be in charge of the entire social-welfare program for Yamaguchi prefecture.

In 1972, he married Kazuko Shigaki (who later became Rev. Keiwa Ogi), who had been born into a lay Shin family in Kumamoto prefecture. Buddhist priests can marry a person from another Buddhist sect or religion but they usually marry someone who grew up in the same sect. Often, the temple family seeking a spouse will conduct formal marriage interviews to find a prospective spouse/partner in order to ensure the continued prosperity of their temple. Rev. Keishin came to love and marry Kazuko, who had grown up in a Shin Buddhist family. His partner would need to be open-minded and someone who could understand and accept his unusual life path, combining both secular and religious elements. After their marriage, Kazuko became an ordained priest in her own right to support and assist Rev. Keishin.

In 1982, Rev. Keishin officially became the 13th head priest of Choshoji temple after his father, Rev. Zengyo, the 12th head priest, passed away. By that time, his family had grown to include three children, and the temple family membership had increased to about 120 families. However, even with this growth, this membership was still too small to support the temple financially, and Rev. Keishin and his wife continued to work outside the temple on weekdays. Rev. Keiwa found work in the court system and Rev. Keishin, working in the prefectural government, was promoted to direct the prefectural senior-citizen nursing-home care system, called Tokubetsu Yogo Rojin Homu Tojujien, a position he held until 2011. For them, their temple work is a part-time job mostly done on weekends. Indeed, nowadays most Japanese Buddhist temples hold services for the temple parishioners on weekends since most lay followers work at companies or in agriculture and have no time to come to the temples on weekdays.

The life of Rev. Keishin prompts the question of what the difference is between a Shin Buddhist priest and a layperson or lay follower. In the Shin Buddhist tradition, there is a significant term, *hisohizoku*, that means "neither a monk nor a layperson." It was coined by Shin Buddhism's founder, Shinran.[5] Rev. Keishin interprets this term in relation to his life as follows:

> As a public servant in the provincial nursing-home care system I am able to share and spread the teaching of the Buddha. I wanted to personally engage with society and spread the teaching of Buddha through my daily actions and in my administrative work. At the same time, I wanted to protect and maintain the temple building for the people who wish to encounter the teaching of Buddha without imposing upon my temple members with financial burdens. I believe this is my way of following the path of a Buddhist priest's life, which Shinran called "the path of *hisohizoku*." Now that I am retired from my public-servant government work, I can share my life experiences accumulated in 40 years of government administration work with my temple members, who have faithfully supported me, my family, and our temple.

Over the years, many nonmembers have come to trust Rev. Keishin and Rev. Keiwa and have come to Choshoji temple to seek advice and support when trouble and problems arise since they have much experience and possess worldly knowledge that other Buddhist priests may not have. Not only are their perspectives rooted in the ideals of the Buddha's teachings but they are able to apply them to the realities of today's complicated societal and family life.

While they could just have stayed at the temple and focused on responsibilities such as conducting memorial services and speaking at various temples, Reverends Keishin and Keiwa came to question how to apply and disseminate the Buddha's teachings. And they have chosen to actively engage in society, becoming bridges between the Buddha's teaching and the people of Yamaguchi. They found a path enabling them to spread the dharma through their actions in daily life and, at the same time, protect and maintain the traditional place where people can formally find the Buddha's teachings. This is the difference between a Shin priest and a layperson. It is hard to imagine how difficult and challenging it has been for Reverends Keishin and Keiwa to manage their many responsibilities in life.

In 2003, as a result of the dedicated efforts of Reverends Keishin and Keiwa and with support and donations from their members and followers, a new and beautiful Choshoji temple was rebuilt. In reflecting back on the celebration of the new temple building, Rev. Keishin stated:

> As I quietly sat in front of the Amida Buddha statue placed in the center of the Buddha Hall during the ceremony, I had flashbacks of my life's pathways and its many adventures, trials, and tribulations. Although I initially thought that it was my efforts throughout my life that had made this terrific day possible, I realized that all of this was only possible due to the infinite visible and invisible causes and sacrifices of so many. At the same time, I reflected that I, who was born at this temple, was nurtured by my loving parents. While others may see me as a gentle man, my true character is that I am irritable and vengeful. I, myself, realize that I have many undesirable personality flaws. I used to have quarrels with my sister and friends when I was young, so I was often disliked. However, it was this kind of person who was still able to fulfill my sincere wish to rebuild the temple while serving as the abbot and being a public servant at the same time. But, this was only possible due to the relentless support of my family, temple members, and coworkers, who warmly surrounded me all these years. When I reflected on these realizations, the name of Amida Buddha naturally sprang forth from my mouth with tears of joy, appreciation, and gratitude. The only thing I could do was recite *"Namo Amida Butsu, Namo Amida Butsu, Namo Amida Butsu"* in my deepest gratitude for this life I have been given.

Through this wonderful life experience, Rev. Keishin was able to realize that he had been saved by the power of Amida Buddha. Without this realization, he would have continued to live in uncertainty and darkness, wondering whether his way of life as a priest was correct or not. But he realized that this way of life itself was his salvation. Now, Rev. Keishin looks ahead to his only son, who will, he hopes, assume responsibility for protecting the dharma, thus continuing the family tradition into its 14th generation and prolonging the family's three-hundred-year history of serving the Choshoji community. As he stated:

> During my tenure as head priest of the Choshoji temple, I am sorry that I was not able to sufficiently propagate the teaching of Buddha to all of my temple members due to my having to maintain two responsibilities, as a public servant and priest. However, I have intended to raise my successor without burdening him with the sad feelings that I had when I was young. I've let my son do whatever he wants to do such as sports and studying abroad for long periods of time. Also, I have tried my best to develop and enhance the functions of our temple building during my term as head priest. During my responsibilities as a public servant, I intentionally focused on gaining construction-related knowledge and technology, which would become useful to me in the eventual reconstruction of Choshoji temple. Because of this knowledge, I was able to tackle the temple-rebuilding project with the construction companies with confidence. Through innumerable people's support, I was able to rebuild our over-three-hundred-year-old temple, which was in a dilapidated condition. I would like my successor to focus on studying the dharma, which I was not able to accomplish as I had wished.
>
> With this new temple we were able to construct, I want him to strengthen his confidence in the propagation of Buddhism, which I was not able to do due to my inadequacies. It is my hope that our temple members will strive to learn even more about Buddhism and that the wonderful teachings of Buddha can once again have a positive influence on society through the efforts of my successor and this temple.

The subtitle of this chapter features the words "Protecting the Dharma," and I believe the life and work of Rev. Keishin exemplify the responsibility of a priest to protect the dharma. However, in reality, his way of life is not so special in the rural regions of Japan. In fact, many Buddhist priests and their families are today facing the same financial limitations and the gradual loss of population in the countryside. Nowadays it is quite easy to close down a Buddhist temple, but it is very difficult to build a new one. Many Buddhist priests are trying to protect and maintain their temples for the sake of their followers and to honor their ancestors who supported the temple before them; they explore new ways to do so for the sake of future generations, who will still live in this world of suffering and will need to hear the teachings of the Buddha.

As the future 14th head priest of Choshoji temple and as a Buddhist priest of the Jodo Shinshu Hongwanji Shin sect, it is my sincerest desire to fulfill my father's ardent commitment to protect this historical temple that is the object of innumerable people's memories; as such, it is a landmark of their former sacrifices to pass on the Buddha's dharma. My dharma name is Shojun (尚順). My father and I both incorporated one Chinese character from the name of the first head priest of our temple, Ejun 惠順, into our own Buddhist names. By doing so, this became our personal expression of our promise to accept the responsibility to carry on the tradition established by Ejun over 350 years ago. I promise with all my life's strength to protect and pass on the dharma to future generations and the world.

References

Makino, C. and Ogi, N. (2009) Japan: Buddhist priests use pop culture to win back faithful. *IPS*, October 2, www.ipsnews.net/2009/10/japan-buddhist-priests-use-pop-culture-to-win-back-faithful (accessed January 27, 2014).

Ogi, N. (2008) "Neither a monk nor one in worldly life" (*hisōhizoku*) and "foolish/stubble-haired" (*gutoku*): understanding Shinran's social consciousness. *The Pure Land*, 24, 189–206.

Ogi, N. (2011a) Dharma diva shows bopping to Buddha done better by nun. *Majirox News*, September 28, www.majiroxnews.com/2011/09/28/dharma-diva-shows-bopping-to-buddha-done-better-by-nun (accessed January 27, 2014).

Ogi, N. (2011b) Japan's first online Buddhist temple. *Majirox News*, July 10, www.majiroxnews.com/2011/10/07/japans-first-online-buddhist-temple (accessed January 27, 2014).

Tokujichoshi, H.I. (2005) *Tokujichōshi*, Omura Insatsu Kubushikigaisha, Yamaguchi.

Further Reading

Blum, M.L. (2002) *The Origins and Development of Pure Land Buddhism: A Study and Translation of Gyonen's Jodo Homon Genrusho*, Oxford University Press, New York.

Hirota, D. (2000) *Toward a Contemporary Understanding of Pure Land Buddhism: Creating a Shin Buddhist Theology in a Religiously Plural* World, SUNY Press, Albany.

Nelson, J. (2013) *Experimental Buddhism: Innovation and Activism in Contemporary* Japan, University of Hawaii Press, Honolulu.

Payne, R.K., Getz, D.A., and Glassman, H. (eds) (2003) *Approaching the Land of Bliss: Religious Praxis in the Cult of Amitabha*, University of Hawaii Press, Honolulu.

Notes

1 Concerning the activities of current young Buddhist priests, see Makino and Ogi (2009); Ogi (2011a, 2011b).
2 Tokujichoshi 2005: 163.
3 Tokujichoshi 2005: 160. This historical piece of wood is enshrined in a place of honor at the Choshoji temple even today.
4 Tokujichoshi 2005: 636. Although the Tokuji Chohi village records says that Ejun passed away on March 20, 1687, the historical record of Choshoji marks April 23, 1687 as his date of passing and I trust the latter data.
5 See also Ogi 2008.

29

Toshihide Numata
Igniting the Flame of the Dharma

Naoyuki Ogi

Editor's Introduction

The subject of this chapter, a scion of a modern Japanese industrialist, follows in the line of other biographies in this volume that have drawn attention to the significance of merchants in the history of Buddhism. As we have seen elsewhere, too, family history and the individual's commitment to fulfilling filial duty to his or her parents figure prominently. The subject of this chapter, Toshihide Numata, inherited both the family business and the modern Buddhist organization his father founded, the Bukkyo Dendo Kyokai (Society for the Promotion of Buddhism, BDK). The BDK was created in 1965 to propagate Buddhist wisdom and the cooperative spirit found in the Japanese culture. To that end, it has sponsored many cultural activities and academic programs. In 1985, Toshihide Numata became the leader of this organization, and thus this biography focuses on the leader of one of the most influential Buddhist foundations in the world today.

The precise Buddhist context for this life history is Japan's Hongwanji branch of the Pure Land school, which descends from the thirteenth-century monk Shinran. Once Toshihide Numata had focused his life on the BDK, he studied for and became a member of the married clergy of this school. Although he frames his own identity and daily practice firmly in Pure Land Buddhism – involving chanting the *nembutsu* ("*namo Amida Butsu*") daily, citing the motivation to promote Buddhism as responding to Amida's grace – the work of the BDK and its many projects also reflects his conviction that modern Buddhist activism, both in Japan and internationally, should be nonsectarian.

Interestingly, although he does hold the view that his current life circumstances are the product of good karma from past lives, Rev. Numata states strongly that the BDK's efforts are *not* for the purpose of creating merit; rather, he notes, the work of the BDK is an opportunity for him to share his "heart of realization" and "appreciation for the many blessings in life he has had bestowed on him due to the grace of Amida Buddha." This perspective of unconcern for merit is atypical for most Buddhists worldwide but is common for Pure Land adherents. Consistent with this school's doctrine of humanity's spiritual decline in what is now a decadent age (*mappo*), only Amida's grace is truly effective in altering individual and collective destiny. Also typical of modern Buddhist organizations in Japan, the group expresses a central goal of working for world peace.

Background

Have you ever seen or read the book *The Teaching of the Buddha*, which is often placed in hotel rooms? Many people who have traveled and stayed at hotels in Asia and around the world would say "yes." But they might not be familiar with the story of this book, one of the most published Buddhist works in history, and who donated it to the hotel and sees to its distribution globally. Translated into 46 languages, there are over 8 million copies printed and placed in more than 11,000 major hotels, libraries, schools, and prisons in more than 60 countries. It is published by the Bukkyo Dendo Kyokai (BDK), one of the largest private Buddhist foundations in Japan. The BDK was established in 1965 by the late Rev. Dr. Yehan Numata (1897–1994), the founder of Mitutoyo Corporation, the world's leading manufacturer of precision-measurement instruments. Toshihide Numata's Buddhist life was decisively shaped by his family history, and the work of his father to found the BDK. Some background on them is helpful to understanding his biography.

Toshihide's father, Rev. Dr. Yehan Numata, was the founder of Mitutoyo, a corporation that has manufactured precision-measurement instruments since 1934. His idea from its inception was that some of the proceeds of his company would be used to promote an understanding of Buddhism throughout the world. Numata firmly believed that the success of an enterprise depended on the harmonious association of heaven, Earth, and human, and that the perfection of the human mind was attainable only through a well-balanced coordination of wisdom, benevolence, and valor. He did everything he could to create the best measuring instruments and felt that they could contribute to the development of the human mind; he also believed that the attainment of world peace would be possible only when this development of the mind was enhanced by the teachings of the Buddha. Therefore, along with managing his business enterprise, he exerted his efforts toward the spreading and modernization of Buddhist teachings and culture.

In December 1965, he incorporated a foundation with his private funds to engage in the propagation of Buddhism, and at the same time to work for world peace. Thus, he initiated the BDK as a public organization. The BDK has been financially supported by Mitutoyo based on its founder's fervent wish to spread the teaching of Shakyamuni Buddha throughout the world. From its founding, the BDK has been diligently translating and distributing copies of *The Teaching of Buddha* with the support and cooperation of like-minded individuals and organizations.

In addition, the BDK has undertaken the task of creating an English translation of the Taisho Tripitaka, the Chinese Buddhist canon. This project began in January 1982, when the late Yehan Numata established the Editorial Committee of the English Tripitaka Translation Project. For the purpose of transmitting the Buddhist teachings to the English-speaking world, Dr. Numata felt it necessary to translate the entire Taisho Buddhist canon into English, an immense project. In order to facilitate this prodigious project, a Publication Committee was established at the Numata Center for Translation and Research in Berkeley, California, in the United States. As of 2013, 75 works have been translated in 45 volumes to make up the "English Buddhist canon." The remaining works are being translated by Buddhist scholars throughout the world.

Yehan Numata also established the Numata Program in Buddhist Studies at 15 leading universities in North America and Europe; this is its other major project to introduce and promote the understanding of Buddhism to the world. The first "Numata Chair in Buddhist Studies" was established at the University of California, Berkeley, in January, 1985; since then, the program has grown to include 15 major universities in North America and Europe.

Early Life and Formative Influences

Toshihide was born in 1932 in Yokohama, Kanagawa Prefecture, the eldest son of eight children to Yehan and Shizuko Numata. When he was nine years old, he became ill and was in frail health and had to spend about three years recuperating at a child healthcare facility in the natural setting of Lake Yamanakako in Yamanashi prefecture. Since then, he has always felt grateful for the good health he has since enjoyed.

Even though Toshihide grew up in wealthy circumstances, his lifestyle was not by any means extravagant. Although his father could afford to do and buy anything he wanted, he was always frugal. It was this example that instilled in Toshihide that the simple and natural way of life was best for him. Up to this day, Toshihide resides in an old and simple traditional Japanese house that was built by his father five decades ago. His usual meals are also simple and healthy, not costly. Only when dining with a guest does he partake in fancy meals as a courtesy in hosting his guest. From time to time, when I have the opportunity to grab a beer or enjoy sake with him, he encourages me to drink and eat whatever I want, but he himself enjoys eating simple dried sardines called *mezashi*, which are his favorite, or plain cucumber pickles.

Toshihide speaks favorably of his early childhood memories of his father, who became the model for his own way of life:

> My father was born in 1897 in a small town called Shiwa in Higashi Hiroshima City as the third son of the resident priest of the Jorenji Temple, a Shin Buddhist temple in the Hongwanji tradition. This area was historically famous for very devout Shin Buddhist followers, and this circumstance greatly influenced my father's deep spiritual faith in Buddhism and was well reflected in his way of daily life. For example, even though my father was always preoccupied with the direction and management of Mitutoyo Corporation, he still made time every morning to lead our family tradition in reciting a sutra in front of our family Buddhist altar, which enshrined a statue of the Amida Buddha, every morning before breakfast.

> My father would recite, "Thanks to the protection of the Buddha and the support of my fellow human beings, I am blessed to have awoken from a peaceful sleep, which has given me renewed strength to devote myself wholeheartedly to my chosen work, promising to practice the Four Gratitudes the Buddha has shown me."

> It seemed this recitation gave him renewed energy to encounter the new day. To be honest with you, I could not understand the meaning of these words at all when I was young. But in time, I came to memorize these same words unconsciously through our daily recitation and now the image of my father facing the altar, and his deep and clear voice, is deeply embedded in my mind even to this day.

What is clear is that Toshihide grew up in the surroundings of a traditional Japanese Buddhist family but, unlike his father, he was not that interested in Buddhism when he was young. He mentioned that his father and mother influenced him in his Buddhist identity through their model behavior in daily life, such as eating everything served, not behaving arrogantly, always being modest, and exhibiting self-restraint and kindness to others. He noted that his parents demonstrated how to behave in concert with the Buddha's teachings. He knew about the Eightfold Noble Path, the doctrine of seeing all beings as interrelated and acting consciously in our lives.

These influences doubtless led him to study Asian philosophy, and Buddhism, at Tokyo's Waseda University, from which he graduated in 1956. As soon as he graduated, Toshihide entered Mitutoyo Corporation and put aside his academic interests to focus on learning the business. In 1964, at his father's recommendation, he married Keiko, who came from a very famous Shin temple (Hoonji Temple) with historical ties to Shinran, the founder of Shin Buddhism. Unfortunately, she passed away at a fairly young age, when Toshihide was in sixties.

In 1971, he was appointed president of the Mitutoyo Corporation and he served in that position for ten years; in 1985, he passed the president's position on to his younger brother Yoshiteru while he assumed the position of Chairman of BDK, replacing his elderly father. In making this transition, Toshihide describes the personal insight he gained when he took over as the Chairman of BDK:

> I felt, if I could be freed from this responsibility, I would be happy to pass the title and position on to Yoshiteru. This was my honest gut feeling. But then, I was so surprised with my father's next command, "Now will you take over leading the BDK," was what he then told me.
>
> Until that time, I looked upon BDK as my father's hobby. I did not know what to say since I did not posses any knowledge or understanding of Buddhism except for our morning family tradition. Also, as a Mitutoyo employee, I had even questioned why Mitutoyo had to support BDK.
>
> After I was appointed as Chairman of BDK, I was bothered by the fact that, when I would attend a meeting with Buddhist priests and organizations, I had no idea of what they were talking about because they used technical Buddhist terms. Additionally, I was not familiar with the traditions and norms of the Buddhist world, so I would often just smile even if I did not understand any of what was being said and inferred during the meetings and in conversations.

This would change. Under these circumstances, Toshihide took it upon himself to deepen his understanding of the teachings of the Buddha and by doing so developed a great respect and personal conviction regarding supporting his father's wish to promote Buddhism. As a result of his personal conviction, Toshihide went to Nishiyama Betsuin Seminary in Kyoto, which provides a several-day intensive Buddhist program on Shin Buddhist chanting, ritual, and doctrine, to be ordained into the Hongwanji priesthood in 1997. He reflects on his ordination as follows:

> After becoming involved with the various activities of BDK, I came to understand why my father wanted to promote the teaching of Buddha to the world. And I also realized that my father established Mitutoyo Corporation to enable him to engage in the promotion of Buddhism. It all began with his personal experience during his days at the University of California, Berkeley, when he was a student. He led an effort to publish an English-language magazine called *Pacific World* to introduce Asian culture in general to key and prominent Americans in an attempt to reduce the anti-Japanese sentiment of that time. However, he faced the harsh reality of the world and realized that, no matter how good an undertaking might be, in this economically driven world, nothing could be achieved without sufficient funding support. It was this realization that led my father to establish a company from which the profits could be used to support the promotion of the teachings of Buddha.
>
> Secondly, I learned why my father selected the name "Mitutoyo" for his company. The *mitu* means "three" and the *toyo* signifies "abundance." According to my father, the "three abundances" (*mitu-toyo*) express several key significant ideals. First, the three abundances needed for human growth are wisdom, benevolence, and valor; second, time-honored tradition tells us that "heaven, earth, and man" are significant in this world for success in business, and for Buddhists the Buddha, dharma, and sangha represent the three key points of the Buddhist teaching that are required to create world peace. Thus, in his selecting the name "three abundances" for his company, we can see that his Buddhist spirit is reflected in the company too.

His shifting the center of his life to the BDK altered his understanding of "right livelihood" in the Buddhist world. As he noted, "Before coming to BDK, I just focused on the business end of things, which just pursued economic profits for Mitutoyo. However, after coming to the BDK, I realized the benefit that Mitutoyo could truly make in this world was greater than just economic profits. In time, I marveled at the opportunity I had been given to assume responsibility for helping to achieve my father's dream."

Toshihide also felt that involvement with the Pure Land school transformed his outlook profoundly:

> After I became an ordained priest, I could start to feel that the Buddhist path was *my* way of life and I now had the opportunity to protect and advance my father's wish and to further develop it during my lifetime. I am sure there are Mitutoyo employees who are also wondering why they have to work so hard to support BDK and Buddhism just as I once did. Fortunately, I have an advisory

position at Mitutoyo, so I want to make the answer clear to them through my life's work. I feel this is what my father wanted to ask of me as his oldest son.

Toshihide understands that this life path ignited his own Buddha nature, which was lying dormant in him. However, this dedication and spirit were originally developing in his heart without his realization. In all that the BDK is doing to promote Buddhism across the world, he feels great satisfaction to be expanding its scope. He has added programs to support the academic study of Buddhism in Japan and abroad; created cultural and book awards for special achievements; sponsored Buddhist seminars and lectures to aid scholarship; and developed religious educational facilities for kindergartens, preschools, and other institutions.

A recent BDK initiative is the Mugen Project Foundation, which will make available a vast Buddhist studies database for textual and curriculum materials in various major languages of the world. The BDK has also created a lecture series for businesspeople and the general public and is now involved in the relief effort to help those affected by the Great East Japan Earthquake.

In spite of the BDK's great efforts to promote an understanding and appreciation of Buddhism, Toshihide does not think about the merit made possible by his family's business being used to support the dharma. He is the first to admit that he was moved to use his family's business in this way when he finally realized that he had been completely surrounded by the immeasurable kindness of countless others throughout his life, and this realization enabled him to understand that he, too, wanted to live his life as a practicing Buddhist who could share this philosophy and realization with others. At the same time, he comprehends the responsibility that has been passed on to him by his father and sees that it is his filial duty to continue this institution and have the family business venture truly realize the promotion of Buddhism.

In his typically modest manner, Toshihide emphasizes that this effort is not at all the result of his efforts alone: "All of the funding support that enables the BDK to continue on its mission is due to the hard work of Mitutoyo employees throughout the world. Reflecting on this, I try to always be mindful that this is only possible due to the Buddha and Mitutoyo."

In thinking about the modern tradition in Japan, Toshihide shares his father's conviction that Japanese Buddhism is too sectarian. He often uses the metaphor of climbing a mountain to convey his thoughts of Japanese Buddhism:

Through my work with the BDK, what concerns me is the degree to which Japanese Buddhism has segregated itself. Although there are 13 traditional schools and 56 sects which are registered with the Japan Buddhist Federation today, each school including my own affiliated school, Shin Buddhism, does not try to understand each other's traditions and history.

Of course, I do not mean to criticize each tradition's own understanding of Buddhist teachings and rituals, but what I want to emphasize is that the starting point and goal of all Buddhists, regardless of tradition, are the same. It is like climbing a mountain. The final goal is to reach the peak of the mountain, which for all Buddhists is to attain nirvana. But, as we ascend to the top of the mountain, there are many paths or ways by which to reach the top of the mountain. There is not only one way to reach the peak. Likewise with Buddhism, just as there are many ways to reach the peak, there are many paths of Buddhism to reach the goal of enlightenment or nirvana.

Accordingly, all Buddhist schools should realize this common goal we all share and reach out to help all people in need.

For Toshihide, Buddhism is founded on compassion and compassion means to think about and respect each other. This is exactly what his father was trying to promote through the establishment of the BDK nearly 50 years ago.

Toshihide is now 81 years young and is still serving actively as Chairman of the BDK. He does not have any special daily practice, but whenever he passes in front of a temple, either on foot or in a car, he puts his hands together and bows toward it. Also, whenever he receives something from another individual, he places the item in front of the Buddhist altar and bows since this gift was bestowed upon him and made possible through countless karmic influences. He expresses this heart of appreciation by frequently reciting the name of Amida Buddha, Namo Amida Butsu.

The fervent fire of the dharma received from his father can be seen in Toshihide's great smile as a father and grandfather. Toshihide has two children, who graduated from Shin Buddhist high schools, and five grandchildren. Every one of them has now memorized the morning sutra chanting because they chant together with their grandfather every morning before breakfast, just as Toshihide did with his parents and, likewise, his own father chanted with his parents. Toshihide hopes his son Yoshiaki, current Executive Director of Mitutoyo, will take over his position at the BDK in the future and continue the family tradition. However, he says that he does not have any intention to force his son to do so. He is just warmly wishing for it in his heart.

The BDK will observe its 50th anniversary in 2015. Looking to the BDK's future, Toshihide comments:

> I believe the BDK has the responsibility and role to make this intersectarian dialogue possible. In today's contemporary world, there are many people in need of the teachings of Buddha. I would like to create a bridge between those in need and Buddhism through our BDK activities.
>
> Additionally, I truly believe that Buddhism's role in the world will become even more significant in the future. Under today's harsh, uncertain, and ever-changing conditions in this materialistic world, I imagine that more people will seek meaning, hope, and strength for their lives through Buddhism. The upcoming 50th anniversary of the BDK will be a good starting point for the further development of the BDK and our potentiality to pass on the teaching of the Buddha throughout the world.

What is boundlessly impressive and still a mystery is where such a great wish, vision, and burning desire comes from to enable this 81-year-old man to devote his life to the promotion of Buddhism. But what is clear is that dharma inspiration, first ignited by his father's dream, is definitely burning in him; and it seems certain as well that this light in the endowment of the BDK will continue to brighten the lives and hopes of many people throughout the world with the blessings of the dharma in the days and years to come.

Further Reading

Bloom, A. (ed.) (2004) *Living in Amida's Universal Vow: Essays on Shin Buddhism*, World Wisdom, Bloomington, IN.

Bloom, A. (ed.) (2013) *The Shin Buddhist Classical Tradition: A Reader in Pure Land Teaching*, World Wisdom, Bloomington, IN.

Dobbins, J.C. (2002) *Jodo Shinshu: Shin Buddhism in Medieval Japan*, University of Hawaii Press, Honolulu.

Kyokai, B.D. (2012) *The Path with Saint Shinran*, Bukkyo Dendo Kyokai, Tokyo.

30

Seno'o Giro
The Life and Thought of a Radical Buddhist

James Mark Shields

Editor's Introduction

In the collision between Asia and the colonizing Western nations, Buddhism adapted according to the logic of each country's own traditions and the circumstances created by each nation's historical response to this challenge. In countries that were under direct colonial rule (Sri Lanka, Burma, Cambodia, Vietnam), Buddhist reformers linked the revival of their tradition to the struggle to throw off colonial rule. Japan, however, retained its independence by closing itself off from the outside world; once it reopened after restoring the emperor to power in 1868, its leaders sought to ensure its sovereignty by westernizing and modernizing as quickly as possible. The country was mobilized under an encompassing nationalism based on loyalty to the ruler; after threats of closing temples and strong urging that monks marry, Buddhists were under great pressure to conform to this situation. Most did so. The biography of Seno'o Giro here represents a circle of Buddhist leaders in early twentieth-century Japan who refused this compromise and who looked to their own tradition to both critique the status quo of exploitative imperial capitalism and critique the Buddhist elite who had knuckled under to nationalism and its growing militarism.

Like other Buddhist thinkers across Asia, Seno'o Giro's attempted to link the compassionate teachings of the Buddha with the utopian doctrines in modern socialist and Marxist thought. Seno'o Giro's connections to the distinctively Japanese Nichiren School naturally proved suitable for this purpose. This school arose in the tumultuous Kamakura period (1185–1333), when its founder, Nichiren (1222–1282), developed a unique and influential interpretation of the relationship between religious practice and social affairs. Like many of his contemporaries, Nichiren was convinced that the chaos of his times meant that the world had

---

Buddhists: Understanding Buddhism Through the Lives of Practitioners, First Edition. Edited by Todd Lewis.
© 2014 John Wiley & Sons, Ltd. Published 2014 by John Wiley & Sons, Ltd.

reached its "latter days," a Buddhist teaching about a period known as *mappo* when the dharma would begin to decline and eventually disappear. Nichiren felt that it was incorrect to retreat to seek enlightenment in meditation (as in Zen) or to focus on chanting and cultivating faith to secure rebirth in another world (as in the Pure Land schools); he taught that individual and national "salvation" could only be found within society itself – remade according to the teachings of the *Lotus Sutra*. He did insist on chanting the name of the title of this text as his school's main ritual. But his school also sought to inspire visionary leaders who would work for social reform, so that a "Buddha land" would be created on earth in which there would be both peace and prosperity. This school, and its offshoots such as the Soka Gakkai (see the biography of Soka Gakkai member Keiko Yonamine in Chapter 31), continue up until the present to focus actively on advancing economics, education, and political activism to engage in what can be called "Buddhist mass politics." In this biography of Seno'o Giro, we can witness the power of Buddhist teachings to inspire individuals to create a compassionate world on a large scale; we can also see that the prophetic voice of Nichiren heard eight hundred years ago has continued to inspire selfless and courageous lives up until the present.

Buddhism is nothing but the truth of development and change.

Seno'o Giro

Introduction

On a rainy afternoon on April 5, 1931, an extraordinary meeting was taking place in a small room on the third floor of the Young Men's Buddhist Association dormitory at Tokyo Imperial University. With some 30 lay Buddhists in attendance, most in their twenties and early thirties, along with four watchful uniformed police officers, Seno'o Giro (1889–1961) inaugurated the Youth League for Revitalizing Buddhism (Jp. Shinko Bukkyo Seinen Domei), an experiment in Buddhist social activism that set itself up as a vanguard of socialist protest against poverty, injustice, colonialism, and imperialism.

The following are a few highlights from the League's inaugural proclamation, read publicly that afternoon:

> The modern era is one of suffering. Brothers who want to share fellowship are engaged in conflict beyond their control, while the general public is forced to beg for scraps of bread. Whether you run or you fight, the present age is one of chaos and distress. In such an age, what do Buddhists see, and what contributions are they making? Drunk with their own peace of mind, the majority of Buddhists do not see a problem… They say: "Religion is above this; religion values harmony." And yet, the fact is that religion is playing the role of an opiate, imposed upon the people. Unless the righteous indignation of young Buddhists is aroused, nothing will be done about this. The present condition is not one that those of pure heart can endure…
>
> As for us, we cannot help but firmly call for a revitalized Buddhism… Recognizing that most of the current suffering has its origins in the capitalist economic system, a revitalized Buddhism pledges to collaborate with the people to make fundamental reforms in the interest of social welfare. It is a Buddhism for the people – whose aim is to revolutionize the bourgeois Buddhism of the present… Young Buddhists! Now is the time for us to rise up! Let's throw all conventions aside at once and return to the Buddha. And, beginning with our own personal experience of the Buddhist spirit of love and equality, let's boldly turn to a restructuring of the capitalist system. Let's make every effort to construct our ideal Buddhist society![1]

With its relative openness, the short-lived Taisho period (1912–25) witnessed a blossoming of Marxism and left-wing activism in Japan – in philosophical, political, and literary forms.

Figure 30.1 Seno'o Giro (front row, middle) and his associates. Reproduced by permission of Iwanami Shoten, Publishers, Tokyo.

Despite these developments, by the early Showa period (1926–1989), tides had begun to turn decisively against progressive politics, religious or otherwise. By the late 1920s, while Buddhist institutions in Japan were claiming neutrality in the growing struggles between labor and management, Buddhist leaders knew on which side their bread was buttered – or, perhaps, who was supplying the soy sauce. So-called "[Buddhist] factory evangelists" would parrot the government mottos about strength, harmony, and unity, while denouncing "socialist agitators."[2] It was in this context that Seno'o Giro established the Youth League for Revitalizing Buddhism, based on the simple but disarming premise that the capitalist system generates suffering and, thus, violates the spirit of Buddhism.

Early Life and Its Context

But who was Seno'o Giro? Let us turn back the clock to 1889, the year of his birth. The late 1880s was a time of great transformation in Japanese society. In fact, one might say that the previous two decades saw unparalleled change, with the collapse of the centuries-old rule by the *shogun* of the Tokugawa family (in concert with regional warlords). The country then experienced, in short order, a new government and the "restoration" of the Imperial Throne (in 1868), followed by a period of remarkable openness to Western ideas and technologies, accompanied by a brief but intense and traumatic persecution of Buddhism. In 1889, a new constitution was proclaimed, quickly followed by the Imperial Rescript on Education, which helped lay the ideological foundations for twentieth-century Japanese nationalism and imperialism.

Seno'o Giro was born on December 16, 1889, in the village of Tojo, in the Nuka district of Hiroshima prefecture (now part of Shobara city).[3] His father Tamejiro, a sake-brewer, died while Seno'o was still young. His mother Haru, who claimed ancestral ties to the once-mighty Ashikaga samurai clan, was well known for her kindness. As the fourth male child in a family of nine children, the young Giro was never at a loss for companionship. According to later reminiscences of his sister Noriko, he was a kind but passionate (and occasionally hot-headed) youth. In 1908, the year of the Akahata or "Red Flag Incident," in which dozens of left-wing activists were rounded up following a street demonstration, Giro entered the English Law Department at the First Higher School (Ichiko) in Tokyo, Japan's most prestigious prewar college preparatory school. Among his fellow students were Kawai Eijiro (1891–1944), who would emerge as an outspoken liberal (and anti-Marxist) in the 1930s, as well as future luminaries: prominent political scientists Kamikawa Hikomatsu (1889–1988) and Takagi Yasaka (1889–1984), art historian and museum director Yashiro Yukio (1890–1975), politician and wartime finance minister Kaya Okinori (1889–1977), and Yakushi Shiko (1889–1984), the lawyer who would defend Seno'o at the time of his arrest in 1936. It was an eclectic group, but one that, as Inagaki Masami notes,[4] shows remarkable consistency with respect to future individual social engagement.

The primary influence on Seno'o's education was Nitobe Inazo, the well-known Quaker writer and author of *Bushido: The Soul of Japan*, who served as Headmaster of the First Higher School from 1906 to 1913, a period during which Nitobe was regarded – at least among students – as "the most popular man in Japan."[5] From Nitobe, Seno'o gained an appreciation for Western principles of equality and individual dignity, through his exposure to thinkers such as Whitman, Longfellow, and Tolstoy. Yet it was not the famed Nitobe but rather an elderly local tofu maker, Matsuzaki Kyutaro (1852–1920), who would introduce Seno'o to the *Lotus Sutra*, the ancient Buddhist scripture that would shape his thinking and activities for the rest of his life. Like his more famous contemporary the writer and rural activist Miyazawa Kenji (1896–1933), who was also raised in a Pure Land household (Jodo Shinshu), Seno'o would eventually turn toward Nichiren Buddhism, the Japanese school that reveres the *Lotus Sutra* above all other texts.

Early in his second year of high school, Seno'o was diagnosed with bronchial catarrh (in addition to anemia), and in December 1909 he was forced to drop out of school and return home to Tojo, to be nursed by his mother and sister-in-law. Despite several attempts to return to Ichiko, Seno'o spent the bulk of the next two years in a state of prolonged convalescence, eventually withdrawing from school in September 1911. To make matters worse, at around the same time, the family sake-brewing business began to fail. After his 16-year-old sister died of lung disease in June 1911, upon the recommendation of his newfound acquaintance Matsuzaki, Seno'o turned to the *Lotus Sutra*, as well as the Bible, for consolation and strength. Over the next few months Seno'o spent much time at a local Nichiren sect temple, where he participated in ritual readings of the *Lotus Sutra*. He became familiar with the head priest of the temple, and was encouraged to read the writings of the founder, the thirteenth-century Japanese Buddhist reformer Nichiren (1222–1282). He also read texts of the Tendai school (Ch. Tiantai), which was transmitted from China in the early ninth century CE by the Japanese monk Saicho (767–822, also known as Dengyo Daishi).

Education and Formative Influences

During his long convalescence, Seno'o spent much time walking in the countryside. Upon finally regaining his health in November 1911, he took up a position as English and composition instructor at his local alma mater, the Tojo First Normal Higher Elementary School. Though he continued in this position for two years, these were not happy times for Seno'o. While he greatly enjoyed teaching the young children, he found the pedagogical approaches of his fellow teachers stilted and mechanical. During this same period an interest in Christianity sparked, though he still remained wedded to the *Lotus Sutra* and the teachings of the Nichiren sect.

In August 1913, Seno'o left Tojo Elementary to apply for admission to the East Asian Common Cultural College (Toa Dobun Shoin), a school established in 1900 by the Japanese foreign ministry in Shanghai in order to promote good relations between the two modernizing countries. It seems that Seno'o applied to this overseas school on a whim, though the prospect of free tuition – and the possibility of foreign adventure – no doubt played a role. Along with three others, Seno'o successfully passed the admissions test and gained acceptance to the academy, but he was unable to travel to Shanghai due to the fact that the school's buildings had been burned down in the aftermath of China's 1911 Revolution. Until the Shanghai academy was rebuilt, Seno'o and the others were sent to Nagasaki on the southern Japanese island of Kyushu to undertake Chinese-language training. Over the next few months, in the midst of recurring health troubles, no doubt exacerbated by his sparse lodgings at a local Nichiren temple, Seno'o once again turned to the *Lotus Sutra*. He quickly made the acquaintance of the temple head priest, who taught Seno'o "basic Buddhism" (i.e., the Four Noble Truths, the Eightfold Path, the 12 stages of dependent origination) as well as the specifically Mahayana teachings of the bodhisattva's six "perfections" (Skt. *paramita*), the doctrine of Buddha nature (i.e., the "spark" or "seed" of awakening in all sentient beings), and the Tendai doctrine of the nondualistic interpenetration of all things (Jp. *inchinen sanzen*). Although the Shanghai academy was soon ready for its new Japanese recruits, Seno'o's continuing health problems compelled him to give up the journey to Shanghai. While his companions set off for China in late 1913, he returned home to Tojo, now 24 years old but still without much direction in terms of his life's course.

Things were no better at home – that fall, the family lost its entire stock of sake and was facing financial ruin. At this time, Seno'o's elder brother, who had run the business since the death of Seno'o's father, also fell ill. In order to relieve the family of some of its burden during this difficult time, Seno'o decided to spend some time abroad. In spring 1914 he sailed to Taiwan, then a Japanese colony, where he took up a position in a patent office in the city of Chilung. Once again, however, illness cut short the young Seno'o's plans. In March 1915, upon doctor's orders, he reluctantly returned to Japan, where he was diagnosed with pulmonary tuberculosis, an inflamed appendix, and pleurisy.

Immersion in the Nichiren Buddhist Tradition

Despite (or perhaps because of) his seemingly endless battles with illness, in September of that same year, 1915, Seno'o made the bold decision to embark on a nationwide pilgrimage to the thousand most significant temples of the Nichiren sect. Known as the Sengaji, this difficult pilgrimage ends at Kuonji, the Nichiren temple headquarters located on the slopes of Mt. Minobu, a sacred mountain not far from Mt. Fuji, in central Japan. Even for healthy persons, the Sengaji normally takes many years to perform. Somewhat to Seno'o's surprise, the first few temples he approached in Okayama prefecture refused him lodging, making his early journey very difficult. At this point, however, he was told of a small temple called Shakuson Shuyoin in the town of Soja, run by a Nichiren priest named Shaku Nikken (b. 1875?). Recognizing that Seno'o was in no condition to complete his pilgrimage, the priest and his wife, Myozenni, asked him to stay at Shakuson. Accepting the offer, Seno'o repaid the couple by acting as an instructor for 30 orphans under their care, reading them books (such as *Aesop's Fables*) and drawing cartoons for them. Seno'o also actively engaged in Nichiren religious practice, including daily chanting of the *daimoku* (i.e., repetition of the name of the *Lotus Sutra*): "*Nam-myoho-renge-kyo*." The views of Shaku and Myozenni would have a profound effect on the young seeker, so much so that, in December 1915, at the age of 26, Seno'o entered the Nichiren priesthood at Myohonji. And yet, what he learned from Abbot Shaku was not entirely "orthodox"; the older man was a maverick who had little respect for many aspects of institutional Buddhism and was fiercely critical of the character of most priests. Thus, even while deepening his commitment to the ideas and practices of Nichiren Buddhism, Seno'o was simultaneously charting a path toward independence from the traditional Buddhist establishment.

In early 1916, just as Seno'o felt well enough to continue his pilgrimage to Mt. Minobu, his mother Haru became ill, and he returned to Tojo to assist with her care. After she died in late July, Seno'o spent the next two years in Tojo, where he became increasingly involved in the Nichirenist (Jp. Nichirenshugi) lay movement, which had been established several decades before by Tanaka Chigaku (1861–1939). While rooted in the teachings of sect-founder Nichiren, Tanaka sought in "Nichirenism" a more socially and politically engaged form of Buddhist practice, one that was also skeptical of monastic institutions. By the 1890s, under Tanaka's charismatic leadership, Nichirenism had taken on a profoundly nationalistic hue, combining some of Nichiren's ideas on protecting the nation with the emerging imperialist ideology known as State Shinto. Seno'o had been introduced to Tanaka's work some years before, and now he formed a club, called the Society for Respecting and Revering Nichirenism (Nichirenshugi Sangyokai), in order to further study Tanaka's ideas.

In the summer of 1918, with his health substantially improving, Seno'o left Okayama for Tokyo in order to put his Nichirenist ideals into practice.[6] To his dismay, his request for direct assistance from Tanaka's Nichirenist academy, the National Pillar Society (Kokuchukai), was refused. Seno'o took this rebuff personally, blaming the size and "bureaucratic" nature of the society, which in his estimation led to a bias against followers coming from rural areas. He then turned his attention to the work of another significant teacher in the Nichirenist movement, Honda Nissho (1867–1931), who had recently published his own interpretation of the *Lotus Sutra* (*Hokkekyo no shinzui*, 1917). Though less overtly political than Tanaka's quest for "world unification" (Jp. *sekai toitsu*) under the *Lotus Sutra*, Honda looked for a unification of all Buddhist sects, and, also like Tanaka, questioned the traditional division between monastic and lay Buddhism. Finally, he sought a Buddhist solution to the deepening class rifts (and social unrest) occasioned by Japan's unbridled capitalism. These ideas appealed to Seno'o. He began to attend weekly meetings of Honda's Toitsudan (Unification Group), and, after an encouraging meeting with Honda in May 1918, dedicated himself to working for Nichirenist ideals as a layman. At the age of 28, it must have seemed to Seno'o that he had finally found his calling.

In 1919, Seno'o began working full time at Toitsudan, preparing for the society's weekly meetings and proofreading Honda's numerous publications. Honda's Sunday lectures drew hundreds of mostly working-class men and women seeking solace from their economic woes. In November 1919, under Honda's guidance, Seno'o established a group called the Greater Japan Nichirenist Youth Corps (Dainippon Nichirenshugi Seinendan), which brought together young Nichirenists – men and women – from across Tokyo. In September of the following year, Seno'o published an article in the inaugural issue of *Wakodo* (Youth), the group's organ, making the case for a recovery of the "humanist" element within traditional Nichiren thought to be an antidote to the increasing alienation people felt in modern society.[7] That same month, at the age of 30, Seno'o married Saito Fumiyo, a colleague from his time teaching at Tojo Elementary School. Seno'o's new bride subsequently gave birth to their first child, Tetsutaro, named in honor of Sato Tetsutaro (1866–1942), a prominent military theorist and admiral in the Japanese navy. The fact that Seno'o named his first-born son after a military ideologue shows that he was, at this point, still very much enmeshed in the nationalistic ideology of Nichirenism.

In general, these were good years for Seno'o. He spent his time writing for and editing the youth corps journal, traveling around the country lecturing on Nichirenism, and caring for his small family. However, hints of dissatisfaction with his chosen course – and specifically with some of the ideals and practices of the Nichirenist movement – were beginning to surface. One historical event that would have a lasting effect on Seno'o's thought – and had no small effect on his turn toward radical politics – was the Great Kanto Earthquake of September 1, 1923. This great tragedy, which devastated the city of Tokyo and caused the deaths of over 140,000 ordinary Japanese, drove home for Seno'o the Buddhist doctrine of impermanence and the brute reality of suffering in this world. Perhaps even more significant, however, was the aftermath, which unleashed massive scapegoating of foreigners, particularly Koreans. This made Seno'o question the conceits of liberal progressivism regarding the natural goodness of humanity while driving home the necessity of *active* compassion over contemplation or meditation.[8] In other words, he began to wonder whether it was enough to simply espouse the personal ideals of "liberty" and "progress" without aiming for a more fundamental transformation of society.

New Movements: Merging Nichiren Buddhism and Western Radical Traditions

By 1926, Seno'o was starting to entertain serious doubts about the justice of the capitalist system, and began to consider socialism as a practical foundation for his thoughts on social and religious reform.[9] This turn seems to have been prompted by his increasing contact (and sympathy) with both tenant farmers and factory workers. He began reading the work of left-leaning writers, both Japanese – e.g., Kawakami Hajime (1879–1946), Yamakawa Hitoshi (1880–1958), and Hosoi Wakizo (1897–1925) – and European – e.g., Romain Rolland, Bukharin, Lenin, Marx, and Engels.[10] Although this turn to socialism represents a move away from the specific political leanings of Nichirenism, it could also be understood as a differential extension of the fundamental insights of Tanaka and Honda with regard to the fusion of religion and politics. Indeed, although he would come to renounce the Nichiren sect as an institution, the establishment of the Youth League for Revitalizing Buddhism in 1931 was an attempt to bring about a form of Buddhism that Nichiren himself would have advocated had he been alive in Seno'o's own day.[11]

As one of a number of popular new "reform" movements that arose during the tumultuous Kamakura period (1185–1333), the Nichiren sect developed a unique and influential interpretation of the relationship between religious practice and social affairs. Accordingly, Nichiren taught that it is incumbent upon visionary leaders to work for social reform, so that a "Buddha land" on earth can be created in which there is both peace and prosperity.[12] This includes involvement in what we would today call mass politics, as well as economics, education, and various aspects of culture. The underlying premise behind this religiopolitical vision is that:

> The self and society are mutually intertwined, and, together as one, shape reality. Thus, in conjunction with one's own transformation and salvation, the surrounding environment will also change and be saved, which in turn will again have an impact on one's own transformation.[13]

Perhaps unsurprisingly, however, there is little in Nichiren's writings to suggest what modern scholars would call "historical consciousness" of, and imperative to address, "structural suffering" in society and the need for sociopolitical change. Seno'o rectified this problem by developing the concept of *hansei* (critical reflection or meditation) as fundamental to Buddhist social and political reform. *Hansei* is a deeply penetrating form of self-reflection that must be grounded in one's existence with and among others.

For Seno'o, the state itself must undergo constant *hansei* as one of the primary qualities of rulership, along with humaneness and moral practice. Seno'o went so far as to suggest that these three virtues were the true meanings behind Japan's Imperial Regalia, or *Sanshu no jingi*: the mirror, jewel, and sword that traditionally have been understood as symbols attesting to the divine authority of the emperor. In similar fashion, Seno'o offered a reinterpretation of the Three Jewels/Refuges of traditional Buddhism, in which Buddha represents the manifest human ideal, dharma the law of selfless love, and sangha a new society, free of exploitation.[14]

Seno'o and the Youth League were fighting a war of interpretation on two fronts: on the one hand against conservative, co-opted Buddhist institutions and on the other against anti-Buddhist and antireligious forces.[15] This required a delicate balance of apologetics and criticism. In general, Seno'o's Youth League interpreted Buddhism as an atheistic, humanistic, and ethical religion. Their rejection of existent forms of Buddhism is also reminiscent of these earlier movements; their critique of the capitalist system – and the more explicit emphasis on material wellbeing – was new.

In addition to its journal, *Under the Banner of Revitalized Buddhism*, the Youth League held an annual national conference, called "Revitalized Buddhist Youth." Here various positions were proclaimed and debated. For example, at the third conference, held in January 1933, the League asserted its opposition to nationalism, militarism, warfare, and the annexation of Manchuria; the fourth conference, held in January 1934, stated their commitment to building a "cooperative society," promoting internationalism, and bringing about a mutually productive unification of all Buddhist sects; and at the fifth conference, held in January 1935, the League explicitly proclaimed its intent to restructure the capitalist system, vigorously challenge "reactionary religious sects," and allow each person to reach a state of perfection through inner purification.[16] Needless to say, most if not all of these positions were in conflict with the trends and views of the political elite of the time, and so the Youth League began to draw critical attention to the movement.

At the same time, Seno'o became an active participant in various leftist and labor organizations, including the proletarian Social Masses Party, which he joined in 1932, and no fewer than three separate antifascist groups, with which he became involved in 1933 – not coincidentally, the very year that Hitler's Nazi party established power in Germany. Seno'o was first arrested in 1934, for taking part in a strike organized by the Social Masses Party. In April 1935, at the invitation of Kato Kanju (1892–1978) and Takano Minoru (1901–1974), leaders of the National Council of Trade Unions, Seno'o became editor of *Rodo Zasshi* (Journal of Manual Labor), whose aim was the establishment of a popular front.[17] In 1936, he participated in Kato's Convention of Proletarian Workers, later known as the Proletarian Party of Japan. He also stood, unsuccessfully, as that party's candidate in the Tokyo municipal elections.

Repression, Imprisonment, and Postwar Activities

At just this time, the government began to increase its repression of left-wing groups and liberal thought. By 1936, membership in the Youth League had reached nearly three thousand, and, although this made it an object of concern for the government, it was Seno'o's active involvement with the broader left-wing popular front that would lead to his eventual arrest. Along with hundreds of members of all these organizations, including Kato Kanju, Seno'o was arrested on December 7, 1936 and charged with treason, under the auspices of the Peace Preservation Act of 1925. After five months of relentless interrogation, Seno'o finally confessed his crimes and pledged his loyalty to the emperor in May 1937. In Japanese, this is called *tenko*, and refers to a person's "ideological conversion" to nationalism. The Youth League for Revitalizing Buddhism dissolved after a roundup of over two hundred members, many of whom were arrested on the "evidence" of Seno'o's confession. Sentenced in August 1939 to five years hard labor (subsequently commuted to three), he was released due to ill health on July 27, 1942, and, after spending two further months in a hospital, returned home in September 1942.

After the war, Seno'o quickly resumed his work for peace and social justice.[18] In May 1946 he helped found the Buddhist Socialist League (Bukkyo Shakaishugi Domei); in April 1947, he established the Shinano Buddhist Youth League (Shinano Bukkyo Seinen Domei); and, in April 1949, he became Chairman of the newly formed All Japan Buddhist Reform Alliance (Zenkoku Bukkyo Kakushin Remmei). He joined the Socialist Party in December 1949, and in the early 1950s took on leadership roles in a number of secular pacifist organizations, such as the Assembly of Citizens United for Peace, the Japan–China Amity Association, and the Japan–North Korea Amity Association. Finally, in 1959, he became a member of the Japanese Communist Party. Yet, while Seno'o remained active in left-wing politics until his death at the age of 71 in 1961, he was never able to forgive himself for his 1937 *tenko*.[19]

A quarter-century ago, in one of the first and only Western studies on Seno'o Giro and the Youth League for Revitalizing Buddhism, Whalen Lai made the case that the changeability of Seno'o's life effectively "recapitulated the whole dilemma of Japanese Buddhism since the Meiji Restoration ... and highlights well the unresolved conflicts at the heart of modern liberal Buddhism."[20] This was echoed a few years later by Stephen Large, who remarked that "Seno'o Giro exemplified a tradition of protest within Japanese Buddhism which merits further examination in future research to provide a more balanced perspective on Buddhism as a political force in modern Japanese history."[21]

It is indeed important to examine Seno'o's life in the broader traditions of Buddhist doctrinal interpretation, and the Japanese historical tradition of reform and social criticism, as well as in relation to the post-1868 movements in Buddhist and Japanese thought (the Kyoto School, Critical Buddhism, and Engaged Buddhism). Only then can we see the lingering tensions within Buddhist ethics that were perhaps present from the tradition's origins: between the "materialist" desire to create a more just society and the "spiritual" quest for personal liberation. For Seno'o Giro, this tension was acutely felt and a central thread in his biography. Whether or not he fully resolved it, his life stands as a testament to the problems as well as the possibilities of engaged Buddhist activism.

References

Davis, W. (1992) *Japanese Religion and Society: Paradigms of Structure and Change*, SUNY Press, Albany.

Honma, Y. (1971) Hanshūkyō undō [Antireligious movements], in *Nihon shūkyōshi kōza* [Course in Japanese religions], vol. 4 (ed. S. Ienaga), San'ichi Shobō, Tokyo, pp. 66–103.

Inagaki, M. (1974) *Budda o seoite gaito e: Seno'o Giro to Shinkō Bukkyō Seinen Dōmei* [Carrying Buddha on their backs: Seno'o Giro and the Youth League for Revitalizing Buddhism], Iwanami Shoten, Tokyo.

Kashiwahara, Y. (1990) *Nihon bukkyōshi: Kindai* [Japanese Buddhist history: modernity], Yoshikawa Kōbunkan, Tokyo.

Kimura Noriaki (2000) Seno'o Girō ni kan suru Ikkō-satsu: Honda Nisshō no Eikyō [Reconsidering Seno'o Giro: the influence of Honda Nissho]. *Risshō Daigaku Nichiren Kyōgaku Kenkyūjō* [Research group for the study of Nichiren's teachings, Risshō University] 27.

Lai, W. (1984) Seno'o Girō and the dilemma of modern Buddhism: leftist prophet of the Lotus Sutra. *Japanese Journal of Religious Studies*, 11 (1), 7–42.

Large, S. (1987) Buddhism, socialism, and protest in prewar Japan: the career of Seno'o Girō. *Modern Asian Studies*, 21 (1), 153–71.

Machacek, D.W. and Wilson, B.R. (eds) (2000) *Global Citizens: The Soka Gakkai Buddhist Movement in the World*, Oxford University Press, Oxford.

Matsune, T. (ed.) (1975) *Senō Girō to "Shinkō Bukkyō Seinen Dōmei"* [Seno'o Giro and the "Youth League for Revitalizing Buddhism"], San'ichi Shobō, Tokyo.

Nichiren (1990) Risshō Ankoku Ron [On establishing correct teachings for the peace of the nation], in *Selected Writings of Nichiren* (ed. P.B. Yamplosky), Columbia University Press, New York, pp. 11–49.

Ōtani Eiichi (2001) *Kindai Nihon no Nichirenshugi undō* [The Nichirenist movement of modern Japan], Hōzōkan, Kyoto.

Seno'o, G. (1975) *Seno'o Girō shūkyō ronshu* [Collected religious writings of Seno'o Giro], Daizō Shuppan, Tokyo.

Shields, J.M. (2012) A blueprint for Buddhist revolution: the radical Buddhism of Seno'o Girō (1889–1961) and the Youth League for Revitalizing Buddhism. *Journal of Japanese Religious Studies*, 39 (2), 333–51.

Tamamura, T. (1980) *Nihon bukkyōshi: III* [Japanese Buddhist history: III], Hōzōkan, Tokyo, pp. 129–32.

Further Reading

Sawada, M. (1996) *Tokyo Life, New York Dreams: Urban Japanese Visions of America, 1890–1924*, University of California Press, Berkeley.

Notes

1 Inagaki 1974: 3–6, my translation.
2 Davis 1992: 177.
3 The following account of Seno'o's early life (1889–1915) has been adapted from various sources but especially Inagaki (1974: 40–53) and Kimura (2000: 48–50).
4 Ingaki 1974: 33.
5 *Oriental Review*, November 10, 1910: 451.
6 The following account of Seno'o's involvement with Nichirenism, and Honda in particular, relies on Inagaki (1974: 57–75) and Ōtani (2001: 269–70).
7 See Matsune (1975: 24–45), Tamamura (1980: 393–411), and Large (1987: 155).
8 Seno'o 1975: 197–220.
9 Kashiwahara 1990: 214.
10 Inagaki 1974: 78–89.
11 Seno'o 1975: 260–2; Inagaki 1974: 11.
12 See Nichiren 1990.
13 Machacek and Wilson 2000: 103.
14 Seno'o 1975: 384–7.
15 See Honma 1971. For a more detailed analysis of the ideas of Seno'o and the Youth League, see Shields 2012.
16 Kashiwahara 1990: 215.
17 Large 1987: 163.
18 The following data on Seno'o's postwar activities are drawn largely from Kimura (2000: 52–4).
19 Large 1987: 171.
20 Lai 1984: 7.
21 Large 1987: 168.

31

Building a Culture of Social Engagement
Nichiren Buddhism and Soka Gakkai Buddhists in Japan

Anne Mette Fisker-Nielsen

Editor's Introduction

This chapter's subject, a lifelong member of the Soka Gakkai, a twentieth-century householder organization and an offshoot of Nichiren Shoshu, provides a fine example of this influential Japanese Buddhist group's vivid emphasis on compassionate service and especially political activism. Now a global school found in 190 countries, Soka Gakkai is the largest Buddhist group in Japan, one of the many sects that emerged from the thirteenth-century Buddhist priest Nichiren (1222–82).

Drawing on one of the most authoritative Mahayana Buddhist texts, the *Lotus Sutra*, this group seeks to proclaim and spread ideals that uplift the human condition; like Mahayana Buddhists elsewhere, but organized with skillful modern techniques, Soka Gakkai exhorts disciples to summon courage and apply their wisdom to take compassionate action, putting service at the center of their lives. Nichiren also advocated the chanting of the five Chinese characters that had come to represent the title of the *Lotus Sutra* – *Myoho-renge-kyo* (in Japanese), adding to it *namu* (honor).[1] Chanting and daily ritual respecting the calligraphic *honzon*[2] is thought to empower a person to act in the world based on the perspective of Buddhahood. Soka Gakkai members engage in daily morning and evening chanting whether individually or in groups.

The term "human revolution" is Soka Gakkai's notion of achieving enlightenment in this lifetime, a process of self-transformation that empowers the individual to rise to the challenge of finding a positive and mutually beneficial outcome in the social world. This interpretation of Buddhism steps outside most forms of Japanese Buddhism, which have tended to focus on merit-making, rituals, and afterlife destiny.

Soka Gakkai members have placed special emphasis on seeking to have members of the organization's own political party, the Komeito, elected to the Japanese parliament, and this commitment as an expression of Buddhist peacemaking is a central thread in Keiko Yonamine's Buddhist life history. Formed in 1964, Komeito opposed the political elitism, corruption, and bureaucratization entrenched in the Japanese political system and political culture.

Nichiren Buddhism in Practice: The Experience of Keiko Yonamine

Keiko Yonamine[3] was born in June 1972, just after Okinawa was returned to Japan after having been under US jurisdiction since 1945, when Japan lost World War II. The youngest of six siblings, Yonamine's parents were members of Soka Gakkai. Soka Gakkai discussion and study meetings took place regularly at her home as she was growing up. Her most poignant memories from her childhood are of the many happy people coming to her house to chant and discuss Buddhism. It was natural for her as a young child to join the family in their daily chanting of *Nam-myoho-renge-kyo* and recitation of the *Lotus Sutra*. Every morning and evening her parents would sit down in front of their altar where the *gohonzon* (the group's distinctive symbol) was enshrined, recite the sutra, and chant for about half an hour, often longer. Sometimes the children would join in. As they got older, they would also stay to listen to their parents reading or discussing short passages from Nichiren's writings. Yonamine had good relations with her parents although it was not until she was older that she understood the principles by which her parents tried to live. Yet she tells laughingly that, as far back as she can remember, there was always something she admired about them despite normal family disputes.

But, living in a small and not-well-insulated house, their chanting was audible outside. Yonamine recounts how at times neighbors gathered to listen, wondering what her family was doing. It wasn't always fun at the time, as she sometimes felt intimidated by the people around her and by the neighbors' prying eyes. She knew that most people were somehow different from her parents, and there were moments when she wished her family's religious practice would simply constitute the occasional visit to a local temple or shrine so as not to be so conspicuous. Peers at school would sometimes tease and even bully her because her family were members of a group seen by the wider society as a controversial Buddhist organization because of its political involvement. However, her friends liked the chanting and were impressed by her ability to read the difficult Chinese characters in which the *Lotus Sutra* is written. Although there was animosity toward Soka Gakkai, "It was a happy childhood, growing up within the Gakkai," something Yonamine appreciates even more now as an adult because, she says, it taught her "to live a life of value."

By the early 1980s, Soka Gakkai had 7–8 million members. "Of course as children we could not read the daily Soka Gakkai newspaper, the *Seikyo Shinbun*, that our parents read, but I learned about Buddhism as I participated in the Primary School Group." This group had its own bimonthly newspaper, written and organized by young people. Yonamine tells that they did not always read it despite their mother urging them to do so, but she greatly enjoyed the activities. These were more than formal explanations of Buddhism, as she explains:

> Ikeda-Sensei [Daisaku Ikeda] used to send us songs and messages such as "We are waiting for you to grow up [to be fine adults]" or "The world is waiting for you, so never give up." I was amazed to think that the world was waiting for *me*! I never heard such messages anywhere else, not in school, nor from my parents.

As Yonamine moved into secondary school and became part of the Soka Gakkai Future Group for young people aged 13–18, the idea that she was in charge of and responsible for the direction of her life began to take shape. This was also when she began participating in the Soka Gakkai brass band, and when she began to think about her Buddhist practice more independently.

> Of course our parents wanted us to succeed, and did what they could for us, loved us, encouraged us and so on, but the idea that people were waiting for *us* to grow up, waiting for us to contribute to the world stuck with me. It really made me think about how I chose to live my life ... I have a deep sense of gratitude for having grown up in that environment, always full of hope. I was encouraged by people who themselves struggled to achieve their dreams and to do their human revolution.

As Yonamine entered a wider group of young teenage Buddhists, she began to think more specifically about the philosophy itself. She explains that the modern-day term they use for "enlightenment" – "human revolution" – is mainly about inner change, a process she describes taking place as she continues to chant and study Buddhism, participate in Soka Gakkai activities, and reflect upon her own actions and reactions. "It is a life based on finding the spirit of nobility," she explains. Her Buddhist practice does not end with chanting itself, which clearly makes her feel full of positive energy and resolve, but rather entails what she sees as taking humanistic actions. It is a daily process that starts in the morning with chanting as well as reading one of the Soka Gakkai news organs, even if only for a few minutes. This sets her off for the day thinking about how she is going to approach her work or her family with the spirit of trying to create value. "Proof of the state of the 'greater self' is really at the moment of interception with others," she explains.

Meetings of small groups of people are held to discuss or study Nichiren Buddhism, and Yonamine often attends these in the evening. Such individual practice and participating in meetings are the mainstays of this sect's Buddhist practice. Although she now works full time in nursing care in a hospital and is the mother of two young children, Yonamine can always be seen at Soka Gakkai meetings with her children playing next to her. Her husband is usually there as well. As one of those responsible for meetings and members in her area, she often prepares study points on Buddhism. For instance, one evening she talked about the importance of changing oneself and respecting others. She used this quote: "In a passage of the 'Record of the Orally Transmitted Teachings,' the Daishonin observes, 'When you bow to a mirror, the reflected image bows back.'"[4] She explains, by quoting Ikeda, "People who respect others are respected by others in turn. Those who are unstinting in their compassion and concern for others are also protected and supported by others. Our environment is essentially a reflection of ourselves."[5]

Yonamine explains that the first time she chanted seriously (with resolve) to achieve something was when she entered the brass band around the age of 13. She laughs thinking back to that time, "Practice in the brass band was not easy for me; certain musical parts were really difficult. I became frustrated because I could not play the way I wanted." So she chanted and practiced assiduously. Every day she would chant, read Ikeda's guidance (which always encouraged her to believe in herself and her own potential), and then practice her instrument full of resolve to succeed.

> On the day of the performance, I played so well that even my band members were astonished. This was my first experience of really chanting with determination to achieve something. It made me practice harder and I had to stretch myself beyond my own ability ... we learned to believe in ourselves and to encourage others through our music.

From this musical creativity, she first experienced real joy because she had challenged herself and expanded her state of life.

Another example occurred when Yonamine was preparing for her university entrance examination:

> I was desperately trying to memorize everything in such subjects as History, English, Japanese, working very hard every day. One of my seniors in the Young Women's Division[6] saw how desperately I was trying to memorize everything, and she told me to pause for a moment and to think for myself. Studying so hard just to pass an exam was meaningless. Instead, she encouraged me to think about for what purpose and with what kind of determination I was studying. Thinking for yourself is not usually something you are encouraged to do in the Japanese school system ... I realized my aim should not simply be to fit into

the system, but to find my own objectives in life, find my own purpose. I wanted to develop into a person who contributes to others. Prioritizing this as important is something I learned from Ikeda-Sensei's writings and from my seniors, who encouraged me to look at myself as having a significant social role to play in society.

Yonamine continued:

> Rather than studying I had enjoyed the activities in the brass band. I found the topics in my studies not very interesting, but only something I needed to learn to pass the exam. So I chanted to work for kosen-rufu ["wide proclamation" (of world peace)], the ideals expounded by Nichiren Daishonin and Ikeda-Sensei, including the happiness of my friends and for a more humane society. When I passed the entrance exam, I gained more self-confidence. At university, I made many great friends. I found that many young people were suffering or distressed in some way about their life. Meeting these friends, who are still my friends today, I thought, was the main reason why I had come to study.

Yonamine graduated in March 1993, a time when Japan was experiencing financial crisis. Unemployment was rising, and "Not being able to find a job became the norm," she explains. During this time, she was busy volunteering as a member of the official campaign team for the Komeito candidate Taiichi Shiraho, who was standing as a representative for Okinawa in the Lower House. She says laughingly:

> I was around 21, and being part of the campaign team for Shiraho we were driving around in campaign vans, announcing policies, and seeking name recognition. Now it is more formal, but at that time, it was more like being in a soccer team really, singing things like "Oley, Oley, Oley Oley," dancing, like real Okinawa style, which is always very festive with drums and singing. We were Shiraho's "soccer" team ... Of course, now soccer is very popular in Okinawa, it wasn't then. So we danced and danced and I have never sweated so much. You know Okinawa is very hot, and in that weather dancing until Shiraho or some guests came was hard work. But it was great fun. Then he lost the election. This was hard, because we did so much to promote his policies. Some of the women's division members encouraged us by stressing that the experience of losing when still so young would definitely make us into great women.

Yonamine and the other young people who had campaigned so actively in the election were reminded of the idea that, even when you lose, there is an opportunity to win, to turn poison into medicine, and to develop strength of character in the process. "I did feel deflated by the loss, because I had worked so very hard and believed that Shiraho-San was a great candidate who would work really hard for the people." While she had been busy with the election, she had not stopped looking for a job, and she says, "I found one and began the very next day after the election. I was exhausted, but happy to be starting a new job as an office assistant."

Over the years, Yonamine has continued to canvass for the Soka Gakkai-connected Komeito Party at election times, not as part of the official campaign team but through her personal efforts to call friends and family to talk to them about Komeito. Observing how busy she was with canvassing for the party during the 2009 Lower House and 2010 Upper House elections while simultaneously working full time, managing two young children, and continuing to engage in Soka Gakkai activities and her daily one-hour chanting practice, I asked how she mustered the enthusiasm. She replied, "From a young age, I watched my parents engage in election activities. Their objective was to have sincere and honest politicians who represented ordinary people and who could improve their life."

Living on one of the smaller islands outside the main island of Okinawa, her parents keenly felt the opposition to the change they were promoting. Within a conservative, patriarchal mentality in which family connections formed the route to social security and political power, it was not easy to introduce Komeito politicians, who stood for broader social concerns such as state provision of welfare, human rights, equal opportunity, and protecting the environment. "My parents used to say that, to change the way of thinking on the island, they worked hard to introduce people to the issues Komeito stands for."

This was not easy as Soka Gakkai was viewed as an outside religion, an intruder into local religious traditions, which caused some tension in the local community, as elsewhere in Japan.

However, I grew up seeing my parents coming home joyful from having talked with people about such meaningful political issues. While many continued to oppose them, some of them did come to support what Komeito stood for. As a child I couldn't quite understand these political issues, but I could see my parents were happy. My parents talked to me a lot about why they were so busy both with Gakkai activities and in supporting Komeito candidates. I grew up feeling my parents worked for our future, for a better society for us children.

Yonamine believes that, "The philosophy Ikeda-Sensei expounds maintains that, if we work for others' happiness, society will definitely change. If we don't only think of ourselves, we will definitely improve the society we live in." Certainly, Yonamine and many of her Soka Gakkai friends are still volunteering much of their time to canvass for Komeito during election time. However, more of their time is spent on specific Buddhist activities such as study or discussion meetings. They also engage in peace-related public activities such as raising awareness of the importance of environmental protection or nuclear disarmament. But mostly the dialogues are inconspicuous daily conversations with friends about life, and not necessarily related to an election. "To think that everything will be okay and not do anything to change the issues confronting our world is the cause of failure for future generations." Buddhism here is a way not to separate oneself from social action but to focus on taking action to create a better and equal world in which people care for each other.

When Yonamine was younger, people at times got angry when she talked about politics.

But now both my friends and I have matured. They are more interested in politics now that they have children. For instance, many problems have arisen because of attention deficiency syndrome. Another problem has been autism. My own child has a bit of autism. Even though children go to different schools, some of my friends have such problems with their children. When I tell my friends that they should talk to local Komeito politicians and make them listen to their problems, they are at first very surprised; they have never thought of going to see their local representative. When these women meet with Komeito local politicians they are impressed because they feel they are being listened to.

This approachability of many Komeito politicians, who themselves usually come from the ranks of ordinary people, seems to be the real power and attraction of Komeito. People who have grown up in Soka Gakkai learn to view politicians as ordinary people. Indeed, Komeito politicians tend to be friendly and down-to-earth people, as Yonamine stresses:

If I had not grown up in Soka Gakkai, I probably would not have had such an experience, of working to get such a kind of politicians elected. I would probably have been the kind of person who complains at the hairdressers, not knowing any means to address my problems. I am thankful that I have learned how I can link the wider social problems up to the level of policies and people who make decisions on a wider scale so that they can try to change things. There is a relationship of trust and confidence in people. For example, our municipal politician is very close, he lives just around the corner, and he is just like an ordinary person. Normally in Japan when someone becomes a politician, you refer to them as teacher (*sensei*), but with Komeito politicians, we always refer to them as Mr. or Ms. (*san*). We have confidence in them because we know that their basic spirit is to work for the people, and we feel safe consulting them.

Many people who grow up in Soka Gakkai learn to view politicians as people whose job it is to work for others' welfare. This is not surprising as even national-level politicians can be found going to small groups of 10–15 people to explain their policies and listen to what people have to say. Considering the usual formality of such social gatherings in Japan, at such meetings between politicians and their supporters, people are surprisingly direct in inquiring why politicians are making certain decisions, and in making it clear if they feel politicians are not living up to their stated political ideals. Yonamine is thankful that she has learned to link wider social problems to the level of policies or the kind of politics that shapes wider issues. She feels a sense of ownership of the political system that is empowering.

Yonamine changed her job a few years ago and became a caretaker in a hospital. Both her husband, who is also an active Soka Gakkai member, and her mother were working in nursing care, which she says is probably why she decided to change careers when her company in Okinawa closed down. Although she was offered a job at the company's head office in Aichi prefecture, in consideration of her husband's work and the desire to stay in Okinawa, she changed her job.

"My husband is also a member, and so is his mother, but his father is not religious at all. In the past, he was really against Soka Gakkai, but not now. Now he supports Komeito, and has come to our cultural centre, shown around by his grandchildren." Her husband is the friend of her elder brother, and is a person she has known since she was a child. Her husband is often visible at the Soka Gakkai cultural centre. "So I married him, having known him most of my life." She sees the importance of husband and wife sharing the same faith, "Otherwise I don't think he would understand the reasons for all my activities and how inspired I feel by Ikeda-Sensei." Her husband was also born into Soka Gakkai practice, and he is, she says, "her best friend." Not all the women in her Buddhist group have supportive husbands, however, and Yonamine explains that sometimes problems arise for new members when they want to attend a meeting at seven o'clock in the evening.

> Many husbands [in Japan] think their wives should be at home looking after them, and find it difficult to understand why they are busy doing things outside the home. Although their husbands may come to support Komeito, it is sometimes difficult for those wives to participate in Soka Gakkai activities if their husbands are not … It is great when husband and wife have the same objectives and are working together. My husband never complains about the house looking like this!

She looks around her large house and smiles, but then more seriously explains how she continues with her daily Buddhist practice:

> My son was born with heart problems. Overcoming that made me most happy. So I pray every day to repay my depth of gratitude. I have been so encouraged by Ikeda-Sensei's words that, as a disciple, I also want to work hard to create a better world with the same spirit as my mentor. There are still many points I want to improve in my life, and the way Ikeda-Sensei encourages us through his many writings on Nichiren Buddhism and his own many dialogues with people, I feel a power well up, and the sense that I cannot give up. This brightens my own spirit. Work might be hard, bringing up children raises various challenges, issues with friends may come up, but through all those vicissitudes, every day after I read the *Seikyo Shinbun* and chant I am encouraged and excited about life.

Yonamine sums up with a quote from Ikeda:

> A life lived without purpose or value, the kind in which one doesn't know the reason why one was born, is joyless and lacklustre. To just live, eat and die without any real sense of purpose surely represents a life pervaded by the world of Animality. On the other hand, to do, create or contribute something that benefits others, society and ourselves and to dedicate ourselves as long as we live to that challenge – that is a life of true satisfaction, a life of value. It is a humanistic and lofty way to live.[7]

Conclusion: Religion as a Life Philosophy and Practice of Value-Creation

One key truth for Soka Gakkai members is the importance of believing in "the Buddha nature" in oneself and others, and always striving to enhance human dignity and creativity. The "path of Buddhahood" thus entails overcoming whatever undermines the human condition as one of nobility and equality. Soka Gakkai seeks to have its members adopt a lifestyle that aims to correct social injustice and human suffering. A most significant achievement of Soka Gakkai as an organization has been the more than half-a-century-long social and political engagement of so many ordinary people who concern themselves with wider social issues of common concern.

Buddhahood is not perceived as a static entity or an end point in itself; rather, it is part of a larger world of experience from which a desire to act wisely and with compassion, and in consideration of the wider world, arises. Striving to act in this way, individuals may slip from one moment to the next – indeed, many Soka Gakkai members such as Yonamime testify to the "slips" – but these must not deflect one from keeping a forward-looking attitude that aims at self-transformation and wider social change.

The more concrete this good becomes – such as in the form of conspicuous support for a political party – the more controversial it is seen to be in Japan. However, as a socially engaged form of Buddhism, it also poses new questions about "religion" and "politics." Soka Gakkai Buddhism for the householder goes beyond adherence to externally imposed moral codes and embraces a creative approach to social engagement. For active Soka Gakkai members such as Yonamine, Buddhism is about inner transformation and a wider conceptual transformation of society that is enacted through grassroots conversations about public issues.

References

The Writings of Nichiren Daishonin (1999) Soka Gakkai, Tokyo.

Ikeda, D. (1996) *SGI Newsletter* [Tokyo: Soka Gakkai], 2816.

Nichiren Daishonin Gosho Zenshu (1952) Seikyo Shinbun, Japan.

Further Reading

Bocking, B. (1995) Of priests, protests and protestant Buddhists: the case of Soka Gakkai International, in *Japanese New Religions in the West* (ed. B.P. Clark and J. Somers), Curzon, London, pp. 117–31.

Dolce, L. (1999) Criticism and appropriation: Nichiren's attitude toward esoteric Buddhism. *Japanese Journal of Religious Studies*, 26 (3–4), 349–82.

Earhart, H.B. (1984) *Religions of Japan*, Harper and Row, New York.

Fisker-Nielsen, A.M. (2010) The making of representations of the religious adherent engaged in politics. *Fieldwork in Religion*, 5 (2), 162–79.

Fisker-Nielsen, A.M. (2012) *Soka Gakkai Youth and Komeito: Religion and Politics in Contemporary Japan*, Routledge, London.

Heine, S. and Prebish, C. (eds) (2003) *Buddhism in the Modern World: Adaptations of an Ancient Tradition*, Oxford University Press, New York.

Hurst, J. (2000) A Buddhist reformation in the twentieth century: causes and implications of the conflict between the Soka Gakkai and the Nichiren Shoshu Priesthood, in *Global Citizens* (ed. D. Machacek and B. Wilson), Oxford University Press, Oxford, pp. 67–96.

Metraux, D.A. (1994) *The Soka Gakkai Revolution*, University Press of America, Lanham, MD.

Reader, I. (2005) Historical, new, and "new" new religions, in *A Companion to the Anthropology of Japan* (ed. J. Robertson), Blackwell, Oxford.

Sato, H. (1999) Nichiren's view of nation and religion. *Japanese Journal of Religions Studies*, 26 (3–4), 319.

Stockwin, J.A.A. (1999) *Governing Japan: Divided Politics in a Major Economy*, 3rd edn, Blackwell, Oxford.

Tamaru, N. (2000) Soka Gakkai in historical perspective, *Global Citizens* (ed. D. Machacek and B. Wilson), Oxford University Press, Oxford, pp. 15–41.

Notes

1. Derived from the Sanskrit word *namas*.
2. *Honzon* is usually preceded by the honorific prefix *go*, making it *gohonzon* (see *The Writings of Nichiren Daishonin* 1999: 366). Nichiren calligraphically depicts the treasure tower described in the *Lotus Sutra*, which he takes to represent the "absolute."
3. Not her real name.
4. *Nichiren Daishonin Gosho Zenshu* 1952: 769.
5. Ikeda 1996: 14.
6. The Young Women's Division is for unmarried women in their twenties and thirties.
7. Ikeda 1996: 2.

32

Blood and Teardrops
The Life and Travels of Venerable Fazun[1]

Brenton Sullivan

Editor's Introduction

This chapter looks at the life of a twentieth-century pilgrim-translator, the Chinese monk Fazun, whose life stands as a case study for the visceral, difficult, and still ongoing process of transmitting Buddhism. It provides a reminder of the primary way that Buddhism was transmitted across Asia over the past two millennia: by small groups of monks who traveled alone or together with caravans of merchants or soldiers, traversing passes through the towering Himalayas and the mountain ranges of central Asia, or enduring long, frightful sea voyages to reach their destinations. The character of Buddhism as the world's first missionary religion (beginning with the Buddha's first converts) did not end back then. In the case of thousands of others in subsequent millennia such as Fazun, after immersing themselves in their studies, the lucky ones returned home or ventured out; infused with the fervor to spread the dharma, and with a spirit of personal adventure, they carried scriptures on their backs and new understandings in their minds to serve their tradition. To complete their transmission of the dharma, most also had another challenge to surmount: the formidable difficulty of crossing linguistic boundaries to compose translations to complete their task.

Wu Tai Shan, the Buddhist sacred mountain region in Shanxi Province, northwest of Beijing, is part of Fazun's biography. It became an important center of international Buddhist pilgrimage as far back as the Tang dynasty (618–906), from which records survive indicating that pilgrims as far as India traveled all the way there for the promise of having visions of the celestial bodhisattva Manjushri. From the Mongolian Yuan dynasty onward (1271–1368), this valley center surrounded by the Wutai Shan peaks became a center where numerous Tibetan lineages established monasteries. Chinese monks such as Fazun could find refuge there for spiritual practice and access to Tibetan masters who passed on their distinctive Buddhist traditions.

Buddhists: Understanding Buddhism Through the Lives of Practitioners, First Edition. Edited by Todd Lewis.
© 2014 John Wiley & Sons, Ltd. Published 2014 by John Wiley & Sons, Ltd.

Fazun ultimately became the most prolific translator of Tibetan Buddhist literature into Chinese. In the 1920s and 1930s, he twice traveled to Tibet and studied for about a decade under some of the most renowned Tibetan Gelug masters of his day. Crossing forbidding, dangerous terrain and enduring limited food and medical care, Fazun wore away his own skin, shed many tears, and lost blood, driven by an insuppressible zest to give his life fully to his missionary cause. The fruit of his toils is a massive body of literature, much of which still serves today as the textual bedrock for the scholastic study and ritual practice of Tibetan Buddhism in China and Taiwan. His life and travels give us a glimpse into the concerns of Chinese Buddhists in the early twentieth century and the spread of lineages of Tibetan Buddhism across China. As seen in the biography of Auntie Li (Chapter 33), Chinese interest endures in Tibetan lineages of Mahayana-Vajrayana Buddhism. Chinese teachers in these lineages continue to spread in modern China up to the present day, complicating the relationship between China and traditional Tibet in our historical imagination.

The heart of this chapter is the author's clear rendering of portions of Fazun's life in his own words, as the Chinese monk adopted the common practice among noted Tibetan lamas – and hardly seen elsewhere in the Buddhist world – of composing an autobiography that shares the vicissitudes of his life. Clearly conveyed in his own words are a Chinese monk's determined adaptation to a diet based on the acquired taste of buttered tea and barley flour, his reverence and respect for the learned Tibetan masters, and his appreciation of the richness of central Tibet's Buddhism-infused civilization. We see how he recalls early translator-pilgrims and their suffering to keep himself going. What is not lost in this account, either, is the Chinese identity of this bicultural author, whose narrative in the early days comments on incidents of pettiness and competition among fellow monks yet whose love of his homeland is unmistakable when he meets other Chinese in Tibet so far from home.

Introduction

The Chinese monk Fazun (1901–80) dedicated his life to a single goal: seeking out, translating, and disseminating the dharma, or the teachings of the Buddha. Fazun was the most prolific translator of Tibetan Buddhist literature into Chinese of the twentieth century and, it would seem, of all time. He had as his role models some of the paradigmatic pilgrim-translators of earlier generations, such as Faxian (340–?), Xuanzang (600–64), and Yijing (635–713), who had traveled through numerous Buddhist countries and ultimately to India in search of the sutras. For most pilgrims such trips ended in death. As Yijing once said, "Those who set out are equal to a hundred; those who come back are not even ten. Those who come later learn in ease, [while] those who go ahead face difficulties."[2] Moreover, these journeys often lasted decades – 15 years in

Figure 32.1 Venerable Fazun. Photograph from *Haichaoyin* 17 (4). Reproduced by permission of Haichaoyin Publishers.

the case of Faxian, 16 years for Xuanzang, and 24 for Yijing. Fazun's two journeys to Tibet lasted close to a decade.

By the end of his life, Fazun is said to have penned over 120 articles, treatises, translations, and lectures. As one account states: "With Tibetan Buddhism as his specialty, he mastered both exoteric and esoteric traditions and nearly covered every aspect of Buddhist studies, including *Vinaya*, Perfection of Wisdom, Madhyamaka, Mind Only, Stages of the Path to Enlightenment, Stages of the Esoteric Path, Logic, History, and Philology."[3]

In the 1950s, following the Communist takeover of China, Fazun served as the assistant director of the Chinese Buddhist Academy. In the early years of the Cultural Revolution (1966–1976) he was branded as a reactionary, and he had to serve time doing forced labor. Despite this, he continued translating up to the moment he passed away at the age of 79, shortly after having been elected to serve as the director of the newly reopened Chinese Buddhist Academy.[4]

Fazun rose to lofty heights from a rather typical or even disadvantaged position, and he did so at the price of much toil and suffering. He writes:

> I was born in 1902. While [still] a lay person I only had three years of education. I was very uncultured. In 1919, because of the [financial] difficulties that my family faced, I went to Baoding Prefecture to study leather shoe-making. Due to long-term illness, I was unable to complete my studies, and in the spring of 1920, having grown weary of the world, I fled to Mount Wutai and renounced lay life.[5]

The same year Fazun became a monk, he met the first of his three principal teachers, Ven. Dayong (1893–1929). Dayong took part in the Chinese craze for esoteric Buddhism of the 1920s and 1930s by traveling to Japan to study and receive initiation. After he returned, however, his interests took a fateful turn, when the Mongolian lama Bai Puren (1870–1927) convinced him that the Tibetan traditions of esoteric Buddhism were more complete than their Japanese counterparts. Thus it came to pass that Dayong organized and led the Team to Study the Dharma Abroad in Tibet (Chi. *Liu Zang xuefa tuan*). Fazun joined this group of 20-odd members, and in the summer of 1925 he began his first perilous journey through Tibet.

Fazun's journeys to "the roof of the world" were fraught with illness, death, brigands, and a crude lifestyle to which he was unaccustomed. The story of these journeys thus provides a glimpse of the caldron in which a scholar-monk is fired and made. Fazun himself wrote: "the years that I studied abroad in Kham [i.e., eastern Tibet] and Tibet must be considered as the most exciting and satisfying 'portrait' of my life."[6]

I have selected and translated five passages from Fazun's account of his time spent in Tibet.[7] The first recounts the years leading up to Fazun's departure for Tibet. It reveals just how complex the Buddhist religious bureaucracy there was, and it shows how important *guanxi*, or "connections," are for a young monk trying to secure an education. The second passage relates the time right before Fazun and his team plunged entirely into the Tibetan cultural world. Here, Fazun recounts the awe and inspiration he felt after having read Yijing's account of his journey to India via the South China Sea. The third passage gives a candid account of Fazun's daily life during the nine years he spent living and studying in eastern Tibet and Lhasa (1925–1933 and 1936). The fourth passage describes the great difficulties Fazun faced when traversing the Himalayas from Kalimpong to Tibet on his second trip (in 1935) in order to bring his Tibetan master, Amdo Geshe,[8] back to China. The final passage reveals Fazun's disappointment in his failure to bring Amdo Geshe back to China. However, the final note is still one of hope and determination.[9]

Translations of Fazun's Autobiography

Competition for recognition and admittance[10]

In the spring, summer, and autumn of the tenth year of the Republican Period [1921] I again received a lot of instructions from Ven. Dayong. In the winter, at Fayuan Monastery in Beijing I was fully ordained under the Elderly Venerable Daojie. Also in the winter Ven. Dayong left for Japan to study esoteric Buddhism. Then, in the middle of the 12th lunar month, I received the kindness of my ordination masters and the eight officers of Mount Baohua, who helped us three Northern disciples get into Mount Baohua to study monastic discipline.[11] ...

[In the summer of the following year] I just managed to be present for Master Taixu's[12] opening of the Buddhist Academy in Wuchang. One of my ordination brothers wrote to me saying that, [at the Wuchang Institute], each day a scripture is lectured on for six hours and there is independent study for two or three hours. When I saw that letter I was just like a small child waiting in anticipation for New Year's. I was so happy I did not even know what to do! Right then I made going there my purpose, but I did not have anyone to introduce me nor did I have anyone to act as a guarantor. How would I be able to go? Just then a coincidence occurred, which was right at the time that Mt. Baohua's ordainees from last year were entering upon the monastery's roster as instructors. We three were ordainees from Beiping, and according to the old rules of Mt. Baohua, it is difficult to enter the monks' hall [ban tang][13] and get one's name on the rosters as an ordination instructor; but our "threshold was a little tougher" [menkan laide ying xie; i.e., they had a richer background]: the Great Master of Mt. Baohua was none other than our senior ordination instructor; and the first few ahead of us on the rosters for the east and west monks' halls were none other than our ordination instructors. When I entered the monks' hall [roster] I preceded Mt. Baohua's own ordainees by half a year, and they fell behind us. The monastery's own ordained were obviously not very happy ... [since] they wanted to have the superior position on the monastery's instructors' rosters. Who could have guessed that circumstances would go against their wishes? The instructors' roster ultimately had me listed first. This immediately revealed their burning envy, which [flamed] up higher than the sky. I could not but jeer uncontrollably in public and in secret, saying "although my rank is higher than yours, I won't be staying here long! Yet [you] how is it that you all lose face in this way?"[14] Less than ten days later I received a reply from Dayong from Japan. He very compassionately consented to giving me an introduction and to vouch for me [in going to the Wuchang academy]. I immediately went to the masters of Mt. Baohua and did a ceremony of temporary resignation. I had an effortless trip west and arrived in Wuchang, paid a visit to Master Taixu, and enrolled in classes at the Buddhist academy.

Academic training and guidance from one's "enlightened forebears"

In the summer of ... [1925] we took the summer retreat at Mt. Emei and while there carried out a five-week ritual assembly for the pacification of disasters. That fall while at Wulong Monastery in Jiading I read [from] the *Vinaya* [i.e., the collection of codes and narratives pertaining to monastic conduct] and [Yijing's] *Record of the Inner Law Sent Home from the South Seas*.[15] I began to have a truly faithful and respectful interest in Tripitaka Master Yijing and I felt as if all these scriptures of ours in China came about at the cost of our enlightened forbears having sacrificed limitless lives, resources, toil, and sweat, and, further, by their having suffered limitless pain, worry, sorrow, and tears. In other words, I felt as if every character and stroke [of the brush] was the product of a drop of blood and a teardrop. They came about as the result of the requests and translations our enlightened forebears made through acts of great compassion and great fearlessness and through making great vows and selfless sacrifices. When we later students take these [scriptures] we should at least think about the great aspirations, causes, sacrifices, and kindness of our enlightened forbears, and we should not criticize and slander [others] while thinking ourselves too clever, forgetting the kindness [of our forebears], and turning our backs on their gift. Even though we may have never been able to add to the fortune and wisdom that has come through the suffering and causes of our enlightened forebears, nevertheless we must also never lose that [very] ... wisdom that has come through their efforts ...

It says in Ven. Yijing's verses of the "Eminent Monks Who Searched for the Dharma,"[16] "Those who set out are equal to a hundred; those who come back are not even ten. Those who come later learn in ease, [while] those who went first faced great difficulties."[17] When I read those two verses my eyes were no doubt red, because the size of [my] teardrops was that of grapes. He also says, "Talented Ones who follow, if they do not understand the meaning of this, will frequently take the scriptures to be easy to read!" I was stimulated by that elder's words, and at the same time they impacted me emotionally. With regard to Talented Ones of old I definitely do not dare give rise to the slightest bit of condescension. I certainly do not dare look upon the causes of [our] enlightened forebears as in the slightest way easy.

I admire to the utmost this spirit of great compassion, kindness, and fearlessness of all of our enlightened forbears. I too want to sacrifice everything to go study, to study [our] enlightened forebears. As for the classic texts of Tibetan Buddhism, none of them exist in Inner China, and I vow to study and translate all [of them] to compensate for this lack. In particular, I really want to supplement and complete the *Vinaya* translated by Ven. Yijing. The esoteric religion of Tibetan Buddhism, of course, does not stand on its own; thus, I also aspire to study worldly things such as geography, history, the arts, medicine, politics, literature, and so on. However, the energy and lifespan of a single individual are very limited. Whether or not I will be able to reach my goal is very hard to predict.

Living as a Tibetan monk

What were the circumstances of my life during these years like? The first year I was in Kandze (Ch. *Ganzi*; Tib. *dkar mdzes*; see Figure 32.2) I ate together with Dayong; the eating, of course, was not bad at all. In the second year after having split up, I began to use a large ceramic thermos. I would fill it with cold water, and at night right before going to bed I would gently place it on a ceramic pot filled with [lit.] yak dung, and then I would cover it with some worn-out wool blankets to keep out the cold. The smoke from the yak dung in the ceramic pot would gradually heat it [i.e., the thermos] up until it would boil over. In the morning I would get up and first pour a little to clean my face. In the rest I would throw in a handful of coarse tea and half a handful of "barbarian [rock] salt." This is what one calls [in Chinese] "barbarian tea."

On my bed I would recite and memorize my morning lesson. Then for breakfast I would move it [i.e., the tea] to in front of the bed, get out a wooden bowl, a small sack of barley flour [*tsampa*[18]], a chunk of butter, and some slices of fresh radish. After breakfast I would go to the teacher's place to await his teaching. At noon I would return [to my room] and again drink a few cups of leftover tea. I would knead a bowl of *tsampa* to eat, and in the afternoon I would go again to class. In the evening I would casually eat a few things, and that would be a day. On the second day it would be "the same prescription for picking up the medicine."[19] For 360 days a year it would be "the same chess move." Although life was very difficult, my spirit was extremely happy to the point that sometimes, while reading and

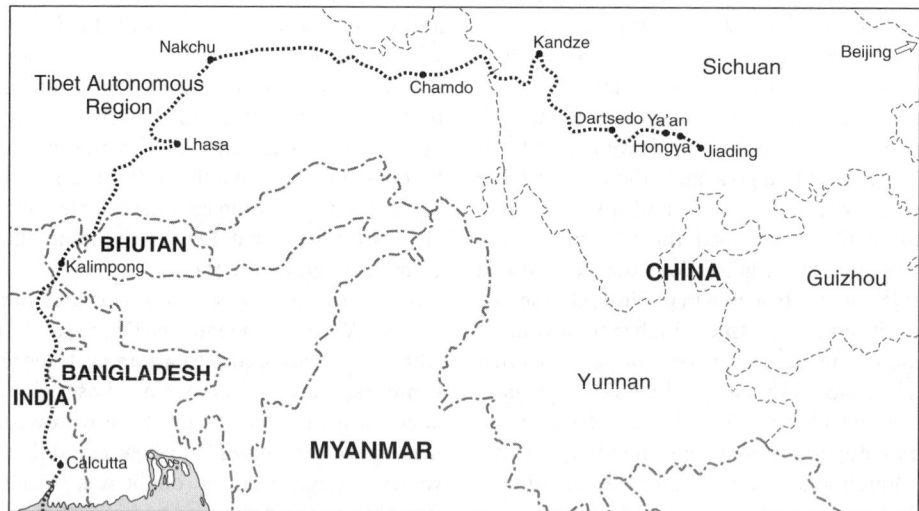

Figure 32.2 Places visited by Fazun on his journeys to Tibet along with present-day national and Chinese provincial borders.

writing, I would be so happy that I would forget to sleep. The marvel of it all is inexplicable!

The few years I lived in Lhasa were more or less like this. Being busy reading books and reciting scriptures, I would rise early and retire late. Even eating required that I specifically take away time from my rest. Over the course of the days and nights of these eight or nine years I was able to acquire a basic understanding of the fundamentals of Tibet's exoteric and esoteric doctrines. It's likely due to this that I'm indifferent to [the material necessities of] clothing, food, and shelter.

Traversing the Himalayas

On the 18th [of the 12th lunar month of 1935], together with a Mr. Ye Zenglong, I hired a team of mules to [again] enter Tibet. In order to avoid being seen by the [road]blocks set up by the British, every time we approached a mountain pass we had to hide. In the middle of the night we would sneak through. Due to the fact that I had not hiked in over a year and since my new leather boots were too small, by the afternoon of the 19th the heels of both my feet had been rubbed raw and three toenails had fallen off. It hurt so bad it was extremely hard to bear. I ground my teeth with each step. That night we stayed at Sanglingquka. I couldn't take even one more step. I thought to myself, "This is the first time in this life that I have received this kind of punishment. I know that all [enlightened] forebears who sacrificed for the dharma also 'ate' this kind of suffering. In my past lives I was compelled by greed, anger, and ignorance, and the pain I suffered as a result of my pursuing the five pleasures must have been a hundred times greater than this. In this life I renounced domestic life, and if I suffer a little because of my wish to invite [Master Amdo] Geshe to disseminate the dharma, then it truly must be something I ought to bear. In the three [Buddhist] worlds [of desire, form, and formlessness] there are many beings who suffer this kind of pain and even greater pain. They are truly very pitiable. On top of the pain I am suffering I should accept all the sufferings of all sentient beings. My only wish is that no being ever again suffers." By thinking thus for just a moment I forgot about the pain in my foot and body.

When sleep would come I would fall into a dark sleep until daylight. The next day I would try to walk a few steps. Like this I walked with pain and accompanying sickness until the 24th when we got to Pari[20] and stayed at [an inn named] Heng Sheng Gong (Forever Prosperous Country), where we were received graciously by Mr. Ma Yicai. We rested for a few days. On the 28th we hired two mules [from] Bai Yucang. Zenglong and I went together on to Tibet. On the first day of the first month we passed the new year in the middle of our trip at the highest and coldest Kala (Ch. Kalu).[21] On New Year's Day eve (Ch. *chuxi*) Zenglong boiled some porridge and gave it to me to eat. My illness lasted a long time: along the way I was completely dependent upon Zenglong's care, and I came to completely understand and feel an emotional bond of [being] fellow countrymen. He would tell jokes, saying "later on, when you're celebrating happy new years, don't forget us here today!" In this way I endured ten days until the morning of the ninth day of the first month of the 25th year of the Republican Period [1936], when we reached Lhasa.

All of my fellow countrymen who were living in Tibet came to the [city's] outskirts to welcome me – encountering one's fellow countryman in a foreign land seems to be an even more affectionate [occasion] than the relationship between genuine brothers. On the tenth I met up with Amdo Geshe's attendant who delivered two handwritten letters from Amdo Geshe telling me that he would be traveling by a roundabout way and that he wasn't coming to Lhasa. He told me to ask in Lhasa for the books I need and some pack animals and to return directly to Pari where we would meet up and head back to the East. After having had the pleasure of reading this I was so overjoyed that my jaw dropped to the ground and my spirit was invigorated. Even the pain from my ailments half disappeared.

On the morning of the 14th I was startled when I saw the attendant coming hurriedly with a face of panic. I immediately asked him what was the matter, and he said a special envoy had come [from] Nakchu and that, on the 12th, the eminent master had passed into nirvana. Oh! Good Heavens! Oh, my! Such defeat! It seemed as if I had a mouthful of blood and it rushed directly upwards. Fortunately it quickly went away and I did not faint. I heaved a small sigh and then hurried off to the temples in every place to offer lamps. I then sent a telegram notifying donors back in Inner China.

On the 16th I followed the attendant and others to Nakchu. At the border of Drigung (*Zhigong*; Tib. '*bri gung*)²² we encountered multiple feet of snow that had fallen. Later, near the end of the journey, it was a world of ice and snow. Plus, we were eating and sleeping in the open air. This then aggravated an old spasm in my leg and on top of that added some dysentery. At the start of the 30th we arrived at Rongpo Monastery (*Rongbo si*; Tib. *rong po dgon*),²³ the place where [Amdo] Geshe passed into nirvana. I recuperated at the monastery for a few days before joining the group responsible for [Amdo] Geshe's arrangements. On the 13th of the second month, the date of [Amdo] Geshe's cremation, everybody unanimously nominated me to officiate at the services. So, he was cremated employing the *Ritual Fire Offerings to Yamanataka*.²⁴ On the 19th we collected his ashes, and among them we found several relics. After having completed the 49 days of ritual services, we made offerings to the dharma protector deities for several days.

On the third of the third month, a group of three of us headed back to Lhasa. On the way we again ran into a lot of snow and we again camped in the open air – [both] more than on the previous occasion. When coming [to Nakchu], because we were assisted by government horses, along the way we could still find accommodations [by] the pastures. On the return trip all our horses were private horses, so we could only let the horses roam around the wild fields and [we] would search for firewood to cook. We did this up until the evening of the 18th when we reached Lhasa.

Completion of the journeys

After returning to the Sino-Tibetan Buddhist Studies Institute [outside Chongqing], I really wanted to rest and recuperate for a few days. However, I have vowed to sacrifice on behalf of the Buddha-dharma, and the work going on at the institute was very busy. Plus, I had been away from the institute for a year and had burdened Weifang by asking him to direct everything. The [Office of] General Affairs had gone through several people. Fortunately Brother Miyan had taken responsibility for managing it, [even though] this burdened him. Brother Yanding was largely the one who taught the graduate students' curriculum. [So,] I was all the more thankful. Each of the rest of the teaching and administrative staff took responsibility for his [respective] tasks. There was not one [individual] who did not inspire great gratitude in me.

As for myself, I had run back and forth in vain, wasting more than a year's time [to invite the now-deceased Amdo Geshe]. It was truly and unimaginably shameful. I had failed to bring back a teacher, and I would still have to carry out the [necessary] tasks. My shoulders would have to toughen up some, and my back would have to straighten out a little. Every day, besides teaching for the undergraduate and graduate classes, I still had to lecture some on *Vinaya* and on esotericism for the monks. Then, if I had free time I could do the translation work that I personally desired to do. As long as I am able to make a real contribution to the Buddha-dharma, translate books, teach classes, and cultivate pupils, then I [will be attending to] my duties.

References

Chandler, S. (2004) *Establishing a Pure Land on Earth: The Foguang Buddhist Perspective on Modernization and Globalization*, University of Hawaii Press, Honolulu.

Chen Bing (2008) The Tantric revival and its reception in modern China, in *Images of Tibet in the 19th and 20th Centuries*, vol. 1 (ed. and trans. M. Esposito), Études thématiques 22, École française d'Extrême-Orient, Paris, pp. 387–427.

Chen Guangsheng and An Caidan (2004) *Changjian Zangyu renming diming cidian* [Dictionary of common Tibetan personal and place names], Waiwen chubanshe, Beijing.

Dibeltulo, M. (2005) Il testi della scuola dGe lugs pa nelle parole di Fazun fashi: traduzione annotata e studio della sezione Biepo Weishizong nel Ru Zhonglun Shanxian Miyi Shu di Lama Tsongkhapa [The Texts of the dge lugs pa school in the words of Fazun fashi: an annotated translation and study of the Biepo Weishizong section of the Ru Zhonglun Shanxian Miyi Shu by Lama Tsongkhapa], Università Ca' Foscari di Venezia, Venice.

Fazun (1937) *Xiandai Xizang* [Modern Tibet], Han Zang jiaoli yuan, Chongqing.

Fazun (1990a) Fazun fashi zishu [Autobiography of Ven. Fazun], in *Fazun fashi foxue lunwen ji*

[Collected Buddhist studies writings of Ven. Fazun] (ed. Lü Tiegang and Hu Heping), Zhongguo fojiao wenhua yanjiusuo, Beijing, pp. 372–6.

Fazun (1990b) Zhuzhe ru Zang de jingguo [This author's experiences entering Tibet], in *Fazun fashi foxue lunwen ji* [Collected Buddhist studies writings of Ven. Fazun] (ed. Lü Tiegang and Hu Heping), Zhongguo fojiao wenhua yanjiusuo, Beijing, pp. 358–71.

Long Darui (2000) Humanistic Buddhism from Venerable Tai Xu to Grand Master Hsing Yun. *Hsi Lai Journal of Humanistic Buddhism*, 1, 53–84.

Long Darui (2007) Venerable Taixu's interpretation of Chan: the revival of Buddhism in early 20th century. *Indian International Journal of Buddhist Studies*, 8, 131–52.

Lü Tiegang and Hu Heping (eds) (1990) Bian houji [Editor's afterword], in *Fazun fashi foxue lunwen ji* [Collected Buddhist studies writings of Ven. Fazun], Zhongguo fojiao wenhua yanjiusuo, Beijing, pp. 212–25.

Pittman, D.A. (2001) *Toward a Modern Chinese Buddhism: Taixu's Reforms*, University of Hawaii Press, Honolulu.

Sullivan, B. (2007) Venerable Fazun and his influence on life and education at the Sino–Tibetan Buddhist Institute. M.A. thesis. University of Kansas.

Takakusu Junjirō and Watanabe Kaigyoku (1924) Taishō shinshū daizōkyō, 85 vols, Taishō Issaikyō Kankōkai, Tokyo.

Tuttle, G. (2005) *Tibetan Buddhists in the Making of Modern China*, Columbia University Press, New York.

Tuttle, G. (2006) Tibetan Buddhism at Ri bo rtse lnga/Wutai shan in modern times. *Journal of the International Association of Tibetan Studies*, 2 (August), 1–35.

Wang-Toutain, F. (2000) Quand les maîtres chinois s'éveillent au bouddhisme tibétain: Fazun: le Xuanzang des temps modernes [When a Chinese master sought Tibetan Buddhism: Fazun, the Xuanzang of modern times]. *Bulletin de l'École française d'Extrême-Orient*, 2 (87), 707–27.

Welch, H. (1967) *The Practice of Chinese Buddhism, 1900–1950*, Harvard East Asian Studies 26, Harvard University Press, Cambridge, MA.

Welch, H. (1968) *The Buddhist Revival in China*, Harvard University Press, Cambridge, MA.

Yijing (1986) *Chinese Monks in India: Biography of Eminent Monks Who Went to the Western World in Search of the Law during the Great Tang Dynasty* (ed. and trans. L. Lahiri), Motilal Banarsidass, Delhi.

Further Reading

Sullivan, B. (2008) Venerable Fazun at the Sino–Tibetan Buddhist Institute. *Indian International Journal of Buddhist Studies*, 9, 199–241.

Notes

1 The origins of this chapter lie in the work I did several years ago for my master's thesis while at the University of Kansas. Thus I am especially grateful for the guidance given to me by my adviser at Kansas, Professor Daniel Stevenson. I am now at the University of Virginia, where I have benefited greatly from professors and peers. Dr. Jann Ronis helped in the very early stages of this paper by helping me identify the Tibetan names of several of the titles, place names, and person names in Fazun's writing. Since then I have learned Tibetan myself, but I have still turned to Jann on numerous occasions with questions I have been unable to answer. Chien I-ling has also met with me numerous times to help me figure out the meaning of puzzling and idiomatic Chinese passages. Professor Paul Groner read through a less than polished draft of this chapter and provided crucial critical comments and suggestions. Professor Todd Lewis is to be commended for taking the time to organize the present volume and for patiently working through my modest contribution. All errors and faults in this chapter are due, of course, to my own mistakes and shortcomings.

2 See note 17.
3 Lü and Hu 1990: 408.
4 This corrects an avoidable mistake I made in my thesis (Sullivan 2007: 25), where I incorrectly said that Fazun had been the director of both the Chinese Buddhist Academy *and* the Chinese Buddhist Association.
5 Fazun 1990a: 372.
6 Fazun 1937: 16.
7 This is based on a section of my thesis. After completing my thesis I learned that Martino Dibeltulo (2005) had earlier translated Fazun's travelogue into Italian in his master's dissertation. Other studies in Western languages that examine Fazun include Françoise Wang-Toutain (2000) and Gray Tuttle (2005, 2006). See also Chen Bing (2008).

8   Wang-Toutain (2000: 716) and, following him, Monica Esposito suggest that Amdo Geshe's full name is 'Jam dpal rol pa'i blo gros (1888–1935).
9   Fazun's account of his journeys in Tibet were originally published in chapter one of his 1937 book *Modern Tibet* (*Xiandai Xizang*). At that time he had only recently returned, demoralized, from his second trip to Tibet, and he had resumed his duties as the acting director of the Sino-Tibetan Buddhist Studies Institute (Han Zang jiaoli yuan) outside Chongqing. *Modern Tibet* no doubt found an eager audience of readers who had followed his earlier articles and translations in major Buddhist publications, such as the journal *The Sound of the Ocean Tide* (*Haichao yin*). A second edition of the book was published six years later, in 1943.
10 This and the following subtitles are not in the original text. I have added them here to help orient the reader.
11 Baohua Mountain was one of the preeminent monasteries in China for the study of the precepts and proper deportment that are supposed to guide a monk's life. See Welch (1967: 287–9).
12 Taixu (1889–1947) was one of Fazun's three principal teachers (the other two being Dayong and Amdo Geshe). He is often referred to as a modern, reformist monk and as the creator of "humanistic Buddhism" (*rensheng fojiao*) – that is, Buddhism adapted to and engaged with the needs of modern society. For more on Taixu see Welch (1968), Long (2000, 2007), Pittman (2001), and Chandler (2004).
13 I am grateful to I-ling Chien and Ven. Fazhao, who helped me reach the conclusion that here *ban tang* can refer to any hall in the monastery in which an officer carries an incense board (*xiang ban*, 香板) used to prod and encourage dozing and day-dreaming monks. For an illustration and more thorough explanation of incense boards, see Welch (1967: 66).
14 Another reading of this line suggested to me is: "Although on the outside I remained calm, on the inside I jeered uncontrollably."
15 *Nanhai jigui zhuan* (T. = *Taisho shinshu daizokyo*; Takakusu and Watanabe 1924). As is rather standard, the number before the period is the volume number whereas the number after the period is the text's title number. Any additional numbers would indicate line numbers.
16 (Takakusu and Watanabe 1924: T. 51.2066) *Da Tang Xiyu qiufa gaoseng zhuan*. For an English translation see Yijing (1986).
17 I have not been able to find this verse here. The earliest appearance of it seems to be a Song dynasty text (Takakusu and Watanabe 1924: T. 54.2131:1178a09–10).
18 *Tsampa* is a staple in the Tibetan diet. It is roasted barley flour that is usually mixed with butter and milk tea, rolled up, and eaten with one's hands.
19 Dibeltulo 2005: 72n413.
20 T. Pha ri; Ch. Pakeli. My thanks to Tundrup Tendzin for helping me quickly identify this place name.
21 Dibeltulo 2005: 79n441.
22 See Chen and An (2004).
23 See Chen and An (2004).
24 Dibeltulo 2005: 80n445.

33

A Modern Chinese Laywoman
Dumplings, Dharani, and Dedication – Honest Auntie Li Tries to Be a Good Buddhist

Alison Denton Jones

Editor's Introduction

Although no individual can embody the lived tradition of Buddhism in China today, many aspects of this biography illustrate the lives of Chinese who are part of the Buddhist revival there. In Auntie Li with her dumpling shop we can see how she "does Buddhism" as a householder and how this entails struggle to be a "good Buddhist." She wants to practice more but needs to make money to support her family; while doing so, she also wrestles with the question of how to live up to her Buddhist ideals when they impact her business and conflict with unsavory aspects of contemporary Chinese society. In her life as an urban migrant far from home, Auntie Li has not inherited a local Buddhist tradition and teacher, but she chose among the marketplace of alternative masters and schools, creating her own "package" of teachings and practices as she has opted to live her life "doing Buddhism." In this, she comes up with her own elective path to the dharma, like millions of new urban migrants across Asia.

In this account, we can witness the universal two-fold division of tradition that Buddhism offers individuals and communities: pragmatic, "this-worldly" benefits such as health, success, and wealth; and the transcendental blessings concerned with merit, rebirth destiny, spiritual growth, and progress toward enlightenment. Both benefits have been present since the origin of Buddhism; in this account, we see that Auntie Li is troubled by her own and others' attraction to the worldly blessings side of the tradition. This is a modernist perspective that is widespread, even though, as we saw in the Introduction, the Buddha praises householders who attain wealth if it is rightly gained. Modern Buddhists across the world, including many in the West, agree with Auntie Li in finding these traditions inferior and not really

---

Buddhists: Understanding Buddhism Through the Lives of Practitioners, First Edition. Edited by Todd Lewis.
© 2014 John Wiley & Sons, Ltd. Published 2014 by John Wiley & Sons, Ltd.

to be pursued by a "true Buddhist." The author of this chapter sensitively conveys other realms where this householder struggles to do business and be true to Buddhist ethical norms.

What is specific to China in this biography is the shaky ground that Chinese Buddhists must occupy to live a Buddhist life today. It is hard to balance the political and cultural realities in their milieu, as the past is not entirely gone: during the Maoist period from the 1950s to 1976, the Communist state first restricted then completely banned religion; at the same time, it embarked on a series of campaigns to promote atheism through the schools and in Party propaganda. These efforts disrupted traditional ways of passing on and teaching Buddhism, both by monks in monasteries and through families. Now, though the Chinese state tolerates religious practices and institutions, it still periodically attempts to discredit them as cultural phenomena, labeling those monks and monasteries it doesn't like as "backward," "superstitious," or "corrupt." So, religion in China today (including Buddhism) still faces both legal and cultural handicaps. These create tensions for lay Buddhists such as Auntie Li that are specific to China, joining with tensions that are faced by householders everywhere as they strive to adapt their Buddhist practice to a changing world.

Auntie Li is a good example of how householders bring together certain Buddhist practices, relationships, and values into a personally satisfying "package." The relationship between business and Buddhism also deserves attention not only because Auntie Li herself was preoccupied with it but also because this has been a perennial tension for lay Buddhists throughout history. That this tension was important from early times is especially clear in one Mahayana Buddhist text, the *Vimalakirti Sutra*. It is centered on a Buddhist householder who is a man of the world but nonetheless is an exemplar of Buddhist practice, morality, and teachings. Among other things, the sutra reassures householders that it is possible to be a "good" Buddhist while living "in the world." Since the great majority of Buddhists today are householders, the future of the tradition is centered in individuals like Auntie Li.

Introduction

Tucked down a bustling alley of a large city in Southeast China, dumpling connoisseurs flock to "Honest Auntie's" tiny restaurant.[1] Known for fresh ingredients and excellent customer service, the restaurant also discretely displays Buddhist images and phrases: one inside wall is covered with a mural of lotus flowers; signs on the outside door spell out Buddhist sentiments and show hands positioned in Buddhist *mudras*.

In 2007, while I was conducting dissertation research on urban lay Buddhism, friends brought me to "Honest Auntie's," knowing I was always looking for restaurants with a good vegetarian selection. They were unaware of the store's connection to my research topic. Soon, our group sat down to steaming plates of freshly cooked dumplings stuffed with egg and leeks, squash, and tofu-tomato. (The carnivores could have pork dumplings.) After dinner, I settled our bill with the owner, a diminutive woman in her late thirties. Unable to restrain my curiosity, I asked her, "I see this lotus mural and the signs outside. Is there a connection between this restaurant and Buddhism?" "No connection," she replied, "It's just that I practice esoteric Buddhism." She had to rush off to attend to other customers and check on the kitchen, but she agreed to speak to me later about her Buddhist involvement as part of my research project. Over the course of several one-on-one, in-depth interviews, Auntie Li told me about how she got involved in Buddhism, her practices, and her business enterprise, and many other stories.

In this chapter, we follow her story not only to see, objectively, how she "does Buddhism" but also to hear through her words how she tries to be a "good Buddhist." Buddhist involvement in China today is not always smooth sailing, and Auntie Li represents many lay Buddhists as she wrestles with how to practice as a Buddhist when that is sometimes in tension with her business or other aspects of Chinese society. This chapter will focus on four dimensions of this question as they play out in Auntie Li's story. First, we look at Auntie Li's *practices* to see what she does when explicitly "doing Buddhism." Second, we examine her *pathway* into Buddhism: her story of how she got involved not only represents a typical path but also reveals some important anxieties and tensions around (third) *how to define and embody a "good Buddhist"* in post-Socialist China. Fourth, Auntie Li tells us how she negotiates the *tensions between business and Buddhism*: how to be a "good Buddhist" with the hectic pace and moral ambiguities of living a "normal" lay life – especially as a small entrepreneur?

How regular Chinese people find their way into Buddhism, make sense of their Buddhist involvement, and balance it with the rest of their lives are all not straightforward matters in today's China. During the Maoist period from the 1950s to the late 1970s, the Communist state first restricted and then completely banned religion. At the same time, it embarked on a broad campaign to promote atheism through the education system, propaganda, and other political institutions. These efforts disrupted traditional ways of passing on and teaching Buddhism both in temples and through families. Now, though the Chinese state no longer outlaws religious practice, it still attempts to restrict it to the private sphere and to discredit it as a cultural phenomenon. Chinese are guaranteed "freedom of belief," but not the freedom to practice or proselytize religion in public places. In addition to these legal restrictions, the effort to label religion as "backward" and "superstitious" has strongly impacted the thinking of many regular Chinese city-dwellers, not only government officials. So, religion in China today (including Buddhism) still faces both legal and cultural handicaps. These create tensions for lay Buddhists such as Auntie Li that are specific to China, to go along with tensions that are faced by lay Buddhists everywhere as they strive to put Buddhism into practice.

Introducing Auntie Li

Before examining her Buddhist involvement, it will be helpful to know that Auntie Li is an example of one "common character" found in China today. She is part of the emerging urban middle class, and specifically part of the large group of small entrepreneurs that has played an important part in the economic reforms that got into gear in the early 1990s. She was born in the mid-1970s into a large and tight-knit family in a major northeastern city. She graduated from a technical college, which puts her solidly in the middle class by education, though this is not as high in status as a bachelor's degree from an academic college. She first worked several low-status white-collar jobs in service and sales. Then, about a year before our interview, Auntie Li had moved to the southeastern city to try her hand at small business with a dumpling restaurant. Although no one in their family had ever been in the restaurant business, she and her brother decided there was a niche because "people in [this city] are not good at making wheat-dough noodles and baked goods [which are a regional specialty of her native city]. Also, they are lazy about cooking. They don't make things at home." So the two worked together to start the dumpling restaurant, although Auntie Li was the one responsible for most of its management.

Auntie Li was born after the height of the Maoist period, but, despite missing the Cultural Revolution's severe repression of religion, she did not grow up with religion in the family. It took decades for religion to rebound in Chinese cities, and she represents many of her peers in telling me that "it was only in the 1990s that people in my family started to get involved with Buddhism."[2] If her family had been involved with religion in previous generations, she was unaware of it. Auntie Li herself began to get involved with Buddhism in 2003, over four years before I met her. In the next but one section of this chapter, we will examine her pathway into Buddhism in more depth. First, let's take a look at how she "does" Buddhism.

Practicing Buddhism

Auntie Li's practice of Buddhism can be understood as falling into three areas: identification with a *teaching tradition* that defined her regular *practices*; the *relationships and communities* she has developed through Buddhism; and the role of *doctrinal study versus self-cultivation* in Buddhist practice.

At the broadest level of categorization, Auntie Li primarily practices esoteric Buddhism rather than Pure Land or Chan (Zen), which are more common in modern China.[3] Asked about the difference between esoteric and other schools of Buddhism, she explained, "non-esoteric Buddhism is like taking a boat from China to the US, while esoteric is like taking a plane to the US. Esoteric has methods to get you [to liberation] faster." However, for Auntie Li, esoteric versus other schools of Buddhism is a matter of the personal fit and effectiveness of practices and the teachers she met, not a matter of strong self-identification. We can say that, like most other Chinese lay Buddhists, Auntie Li does not think of herself as "an esoteric Buddhist" as opposed to "a Pure Land practitioner," but simply as a lay Buddhist who follows a particular teacher and his style.[4] Unlike the typically strong boundaries between, and identification with, denominations in Christianity, most lay Buddhists in China today (and in the past) take a pragmatic, inclusive view toward the teachings and practices of various Buddhist schools.

Like most Buddhists, Auntie Li follows a daily routine of practice that includes some form of morning and evening ritual. After waking and washing, she burns incense and offers wine and water to the Buddha. She spends five or six minutes reciting mantras. Then it is off to work. The "assignment" given by her teacher is to recite her mantra one thousand times each day, which she says is "only very little," but she still has trouble keeping up. She is so busy that she has to squeeze in some time to practice while on the road to and from work, as well as at work. "Usually, you should do the recitations with a rosary," she tells me, "but I'm afraid that isn't appropriate at work, and that [this] might be bad for business. So, I have gotten one of those little mechanical counters that people use to count money or entrances to parks or whatever. When I'm in public or in the restaurant, I use the counter to keep track of my recitation, instead of beads." She gets home very late at night because of work and tries to fit in her evening devotions. At night, "I will repent any bad stuff from the day, and share the merit[5] from any good things that day to my parents and to all living beings." She explains that this kind of practice is part of esoteric Buddhism's focus on self-observation and paying attention to your deeds. Throughout the day, she says, you should also make an offering before eating each meal.

In addition to these daily practices, Auntie Li engages in two more occasional types of practice, both common in China today. First, she observes the "Eight Vegetarian Precepts." You are supposed to observe these on four days throughout the Chinese lunar month,[6] she says, but she only does it once a month, and does a simplified version. "On this day, you should be like a bodhisattva: no singing, dance or entertainment. No scented products like soap, toothpaste, makeup. Don't eat after noon, and you must only eat vegetarian food." "Sometimes I forget," she admits, "but at night, if you weren't able to keep the precepts, you should repent. The next morning, you share the merit for the previous day of precepts." Although the Eight Vegetarian Precepts is a common practice across various schools of Chinese Buddhism, most urban Chinese I met did not try to observe them until they were retired. As Auntie Li notes, it is hard to keep these more strict observances while conducting a "normal" social and work life.

Second, she participates in communal rituals by sending money to her family in her home city to help support the cost of the offerings for rituals in the local monastery and to underwrite the monks who preside over them. As in the case of her father's illness, these may be directed at generating merit to help a specific individual with a mundane problem, or may be used for a more general promotion of Buddhism and merit for all living creatures.

However, with the exception of this, mostly "virtual," participation in communal rituals sponsored by her family, Auntie Li's Buddhist involvement lacks communal practice, either in local temples or with a lay group where she lives. She very rarely attends rituals or holidays at temples in her city, nor does she participate in any group study or practice. In this, she is somewhat unusual among lay Buddhists in China today.

In large part this gap is a matter of time – the restaurant is open seven days a week for lunch and dinner and she is very busy keeping it going. It is also the case that she has stronger ties to collective practices in her home city, where most of her family still lives. However, another piece of the puzzle here relates to a larger issue for Buddhists in urban China today: Buddhist holidays, communal rituals, and temple-based cultivation sessions are still mostly organized according to a traditional lunar schedule, which does not correspond to current weekends and official holidays. Like Auntie Li, most working-age urban Chinese cannot take time off work to attend several days of temple holiday or cultivation sessions. Thus, these activities are mainly attended by retirees. This fact further discourages many younger, more educated, or professional Buddhists from attending communal activities, because of the cultural and generational distance they feel from the "old ladies" who frequent temples.

Some of the other younger Buddhists I spoke with made up for their lack of temple participation by finding or forming lay groups of like-minded people to study or practice Buddhism together on a more feasible schedule. Auntie Li does not do this, not only because her Buddhist community is primarily her family in another city but also because her Buddhist involvement is strongly centered on a one-on-one relationship with her monastic teacher back home.

The relationship with her teacher is so important that she says, "He is the most important person in my life now, like parents, like the Buddha. I follow him and have confidence in him. I send offerings to support him every month, no matter what." Her teacher is not only a guide for her practice of Buddhism but also acts as a personal counselor. Auntie Li stressed that anyone practicing Buddhism must have a strong relationship with a teacher who can help them navigate the complexity of Buddhism, assign practices (or study texts) appropriate for that particular individual, and keep them from going astray into dangerous areas.[7] In addition, Auntie Li looks to her teacher for advice on business decisions, shares personal and psychological confidences, and turns to him to help her make sense of tragedy and injustice in the world. She sums up the importance of this relationship thus:

"Without his blessings, I would not have today." Having such a close relationship with a teacher is the ideal of most lay Buddhists in China today, and is in fact the traditional structure of Buddhist spiritual mentoring for both clergy and laity. However, in contemporary China, the severe shortage of qualified Buddhist teachers (especially of ordained monks) makes it difficult for most lay Buddhists to achieve the kind of active guidance from a teacher that Auntie Li enjoys.[8] In this, then, she is not typical of urban Chinese lay Buddhists but she represents a mode of Buddhist involvement that is not only well recognized but also highly desirable.

The preceding description reveals that Auntie Li's practice of Buddhism is primarily focused on cultivating herself as a better human being in this life rather than studying Buddhist doctrine. She hardly ever reads Buddhist sutras or even reads magazines or watches DVDs of contemporary Buddhist teachers expounding the dharma. When the subject of the many different schools and teaching traditions within Buddhism came up, she named several but admitted, "honestly, I don't pay that much attention to the schools and haven't tried to learn about them. I don't need to pay attention to those, but can just cultivate my own practices. Even the teachers have trouble explaining it all clearly." She sees these scholarly differences as irrelevant to her goals of personal cultivation and self-improvement. For Auntie Li, Buddhist practice is crucially about cultivating oneself to be more selfless, humble, and disciplined, as well as cultivating one's faith in, and progress toward, the Buddhist goal of liberation. She had this in mind when she explained to me her view of the "Fundamentals of Buddhism."

> The first fundamental is the "heart of confidence." You must believe that if you keep studying Buddhism, you will advance [toward liberation]. Second, you must maintain a "heart of respect" for Buddhism and for all living beings. You should not be selfish; you should think of others first. Third, you must have a "heart of offering." If someone gave me a piece of clothing, I would first offer it to the Buddha before wearing it. Any good things or good thoughts and moods should be offered to Buddhism. It doesn't matter if you have money or not; you can offer anything you think is good in your life to Buddhism.

Auntie Li is one example of how urban Chinese bring together certain Buddhist practices, relationships, and values into a personally satisfying "package." Many of the elements in this are common in contemporary China; others, such as the strong relationship with a teacher in contrast to little communal practice, are less typical but still widely shared by urban lay Buddhists. An interesting feature of Chinese Buddhism today is the great variety of packages that are found among laypeople; there is a great deal of flexibility for "mixing and matching" elements of Buddhist practice and doctrine. This is in part because Buddhist teachings themselves acknowledge that people vary, and allow that study and practice should be individualized. For this reason, Mahayana Buddhist texts claim to offer "ten thousand doors to the dharma," or individual packages. With all of this variety, the question of how to be a "good Buddhist" is not simple indeed! We have seen how Auntie Li has assembled her package – with the guidance of her teacher – but she still has some anxiety over whether she is really a "good Buddhist," as we will see.

Pathway into Buddhism

Auntie Li's story of how she got involved in Buddhism sheds light on two important dimensions of being Buddhist in contemporary China. On the one hand, the objective experience of her encounter with Buddhism is a common pathway in urban China today but exhibits important changes from religiosity in traditional China. On the other hand, the way that Auntie Li tells her story exposes important subjective understandings and anxieties she holds about what a good Buddhist should be. Let us begin by listening to the story in her own words.

"I initially became interested in Buddhism for selfish reasons," Auntie Li told me quite frankly. "Most people start from superstition and selfishness, from wanting to get protection or blessings from a Buddha. They don't start from wanting to better themselves through cultivation, or to reach enlightenment. Of all the people around me, all the Buddhists I know, only one person got started in Buddhism with the goal of liberation and cultivation." In Auntie Li's case, this "selfishness" was on behalf of her father. He became seriously ill in 2003. Her whole family was trying everything they could think of to save him, from conventional medicine to religious intervention. Friends told them that they could help their father's health if they stopped eating meat, burned certain offerings in rituals, and financed a large-scale "Release of Living Creatures" ceremony. (All are common Buddhist practices in China.) Although the family had no previous history of such religious involvements, they did all of these things. In the Release of Living Creatures ritual, they purchased and then freed into the wild about a thousand animals (birds, fish, etc.) as part of this common Buddhist ritual. It symbolizes compassion, the goal of liberation, and is thought to create a largess of merit that can be redirected to, for example, an ailing relative.

"My father actually got better after we did these things, for whatever reason," Auntie Li explained.

Through these attempts to save him, we came into contact with Buddhism and got to know a particular Buddhist teacher [a monk]. This teacher tried to get us to understand more about Buddhism and start studying it. There were actually a lot of Buddhist teachers in the city at that time; and esoteric Buddhism was really starting to become more popular. Many friends took me around to visit different teachers, some were from Tibet and some were Han Chinese in either esoteric or conventional [exoteric] traditions. Eventually, I decided that the first teacher I had gotten to know, a Han Chinese teacher of esoteric Buddhism, was best for me. Any teacher is capable of guiding your study of Buddhism, but you have to decide which clothes look good on you – the fit has to be right.

On the more objective level of Auntie Li's experience, her story is representative of an important characteristic of urban lay Buddhism in China today – people's pathway to Buddhism is not the "traditional" one. That is, in most times and places across the world, people have adopted the religious traditions of their families through a relatively straightforward process of socialization. Until recently, active choice among religious affiliations (including no affiliation) was the exception. In modern China, the suppression of all religious activity during the Maoist era was combined with the dominance of political propaganda praising atheism, both combining to interrupt the traditional, unproblematic "inheritance" of religion through families. Among my interviewees, most were like Auntie Li: she did not grow up with any religion, and whatever folk religious involvement prior generations in her family may have had was not an important factor in starting her on the pathway to Buddhist involvement.

This break in religious tradition is important for several reasons. From a comparative dimension, it means that Auntie Li's experience – and that of many other urban Chinese Buddhists – may be more comparable to the experience of Buddhist "converts" in the West and other historically non-Buddhist societies than it is to lay Buddhists in historically Buddhist societies where family transmission is still predominant. Moreover, when religious involvement becomes a relatively conscious choice, it focuses attention on the question of motivations.

Thus, turning to Auntie Li's subjective perspective, her account makes it clear that she is quite preoccupied with this question of whether people have instrumental (selfish) motivations for Buddhist involvement or higher/transcendent motivations that focus on self-cultivation and the aspiration for enlightenment. Auntie Li began her story of how she got involved with Buddhism with this distinction, and it came up again and again in our conversations. It was clearly an important aspect of how she categorized Buddhist householders, as well as how she chose to present it to a (sympathetic) outsider. She gave many examples of relatives who turned to Buddhism for instrumental benefits: a brother who set up a Buddha altar because he wanted to become an official (he did); a cousin who started practicing Buddhism after a mugging cracked her skull; and cancer and tumors that disappeared after taking refuge in Buddhism, reciting sutras, and/or performing Release of Living Creatures rituals.

Auntie Li emphasizes that all of these people started on the pathway of Buddhism because they had a problem they thought Buddhism could help solve, not because of a real desire to learn and practice Buddhism. Some of them, in fact, have never gone beyond using Buddhism for problem-solving. Her brother who is now an official has not learned more about Buddhist teachings or started practicing self-cultivation; he only continues to pay respects to the Buddha statue he installed, out of gratitude and hope for continued benefits. For most of the others, as for Auntie Li herself, Buddhism's ability to solve their problem was a gateway into a more concerted study and practice of Buddhism. In fact, her claim that most people in urban China start on the pathway to Buddhist involvement for instrumental reasons is borne out by my research. The elements of Auntie Li's narrative – first contact through a Buddhist ritual or practice that successfully solves a mundane problem, with this positive impression then leading the person to explore Buddhism further – are common to many of the lay Buddhists I interviewed.

Defining a "Good Buddhist"

In her story, we can see Auntie Li's definition of a "real" lay Buddhist: someone who goes beyond using Buddhism for problem-solving to studying its teachings and/or putting its teachings into practice in self-cultivation. In fact, this definition corresponds closely to scholarly definitions of the boundary between folk and lay Buddhists.[9] Auntie Li's story further reveals that she feels a great deal of anxiety around these categories. After all, this is not just about abstract definitions but also about status: status as a "good" (selfless) Buddhist versus a selfish one, status as an intellectual (or not), status as rational versus superstitious thinker.

It is illuminating here to disentangle and discuss these three tensions around how to be a "good" Buddhist that Auntie Li's story demonstrates. First, Auntie Li places a value judgment on the *motivations for* engaging in Buddhist practice. Although most people may start on the path for instrumental reasons, she sees those who accept and begin working toward the Buddhist goals of self-cultivation and enlightenment as "the real Buddhists" with purer motivations. Second, she privileges certain *modes of* practicing Buddhism. She regards more intellectual modes that involve studying texts as higher than the moral self-cultivation that she herself focuses on. This distinction is connected to a long-standing dimension of Chinese literati culture that values literacy and textual study as very high status.

Third, her story contains a *criticism of superstitious or magical thinking*. For Auntie Li, superstition is bad for several reasons. First, it is connected with selfish motivations for studying Buddhism because of the miraculous way its rituals solve problems. Second, superstition as a mode of practice is opposed to higher-status, scholarly engagement with Buddhism. Third, "superstition" is now a highly charged, and negative, label in modern China. On the one hand, it is a major factor determining the official boundary between legal religion and illegal "cults." On the other hand, labeling a person as superstitious, rather than rational and modern, places them in opposition to China's modernization effort. Thus, the attempt by Auntie Li and others to be a "good Buddhist" has had to take into account the dangers surrounding what others might view as "superstition."

However, Auntie Li is conflicted about "superstition," because she also believes that miraculous action is possible and that Buddhist ritual has the power to intervene in the world. She believed I would be skeptical of her stories – as would many urban Chinese – but she also believed she had witnessed many examples of Buddhist tradition's powers of healing and bringing mundane benefits. Moreover, her belief in the immanent, pragmatic power of Buddhism has strong roots not only in traditional Chinese understandings of the powers and connections present between human and spirit worlds but also in Buddhist teachings. In fact, Auntie Li's perspective – that although Buddhism is truly capable of bringing mundane benefits these benefits are not the ultimate goal of Buddhist involvement – is shared by all of the lay Buddhists I talked to in China, including those who were more educated or white collar than she. Therefore, most lay Buddhists I spoke with shared her anxiety and conflicted perspective on the "superstitious" dimensions or elements in Buddhism.[10]

Balancing Business and Buddhism

Auntie Li's description of her practices reveals a second set of tensions that she experiences as she tries to be a "good Buddhist": negotiating the relationships between her Buddhist commitments and the demands of her business. The tensions surrounding her business emerged as the second major issue in our interview, as she returned to them at many points. The relationship between business and Buddhism deserves attention not only because Auntie Li herself was preoccupied with it. The tension between business and Buddhism – or, more generally, between the demands of making a livelihood as a layperson and Buddhist study and practice – is a perennial tension for lay Buddhists throughout the ages and across the world. If one is not going to take the tonsure as a monk or nun in order to devote one's life to the study and practice of Buddhism, how does one adhere to the values and find time for the practice of Buddhism while leading a "regular" life?

More specifically, one of the steps on the Noble Eightfold Path is "right livelihood." This enjoins Buddhists to make sure that their work is in accord with Buddhist principles, including no killing, no untruths, and so on. As an obvious example, Buddhists should not work as butchers. Even commercial business in general is somewhat suspect to many Buddhists as it often involves self-promotion, advertisement that borders on deception, underhanded competition for customers, and (at its most basic) grasping for money. These aspects of business conflict with many Buddhist teachings: humility, not telling untruths, helping the wellbeing of others, eschewing worldly success, and not grasping.

Auntie Li told me about three kinds of problem she saw in the relationship between Buddhism and her business: a moral or karmic problem, a reputation problem, and a time problem. The first problem is straightforward – her restaurant sells meat-filled dumplings along with the wide vegetarian selection that I enjoyed, and serving meat requires killing animals. Although Auntie Li and her employees do not kill the animals themselves, so they are not directly contradicting Buddhist precepts, she feels that the dependence of her business on killing is a problem, creating negative karma for herself and others.[11] She asked her teacher what to do, and "he told me to get an automatic prayer wheel to set up inside the restaurant, to help counteract the negative karma that comes from killing animals. And though we serve meat, all of our dumplings follow the Buddhist prohibition on eating onions and garlic – we don't use those ingredients. Also, we buy good quality meat and run a clean business." In fact, these practices attract Buddhists and other customers who value the focus on quality and sanitation.

Yet, Auntie Li has been ambivalent about making the Buddhist connection of the restaurant public. "At first, we didn't want the customers to know that it was Buddhist, because we were worried about misunderstanding and superstition. Eventually my brother decided to paint the mural and door couplets. We figured that only Buddhists would recognize the Buddhist references." As explained above, in China, religion is restricted to the private sphere and it is illegal to proselytize in public spaces. The line between proselytizing and simply the public display of religious symbols, as at the dumpling restaurant, is fuzzy, hence her concern. She does not want to get in trouble with the authorities, nor does she want potential customers who are atheists to avoid the restaurant based on the Buddhist connection. Further, she says, "if you are a good Buddhist, you shouldn't broadcast it; it isn't humble."

Finally, as we have already heard, Auntie Li's biggest concern about the relationship between her business and Buddhism is that the former takes time away from the latter. "I hope to get the restaurant to the point of being self-sufficient soon, or to get someone else to run it on a daily basis, so that I have more time to practice. I'm the least dedicated person in my family with regards to Buddhism. Some of them have time to study many hours each day." As noted above, it is not merely a matter of time, but the lack of time restricts her Buddhist involvement to basic self-cultivation and does not allow her to get more in-depth in the study of Buddhist doctrine. This brings us back to her feeling that people who practice Buddhism in a more intellectual mode are "better" Buddhists.

Auntie Li's business presents these several problems to her Buddhist involvement, but there are also some positive dimensions to the relationship. Her business offers several opportunities to practice Buddhist compassion in helping others, humility, and spreading the dharma. First, the business presents a karmic opportunity to help others. Some of its profits are used to support her family as well as her hometown monastery. The display of the Buddhist symbols painted above the door can benefit others as well: "My master said that if we put the symbols there, it will help get rid of the bad karma of every customer who passes under it. We have a lot of customers, so this can help a lot of people." Further, the fact that the food adheres to Chinese Buddhist proscriptions against eating garlic or onions is good for the karma of customers. Introducing other people to Buddhism is highly valued in the religion. Introducing others to Buddhism not only is believed to help those people get on the path to liberation but also could earn merit for Auntie Li.

In addition, Auntie Li explains that she brings Buddhist principles into her customer service, which coincidentally helps the reputation of the business more generally. "During the snow storms, we didn't raise prices even though our costs rose, because that's not how to take care of customers, that would show that you don't understand gratitude" (a Buddhist principle). She also credits her Buddhist practice with making her better at customer relations (as well as other interactions). "Buddhism has had a big influence on my life. I've always gotten angry easily. Buddhism helps me control my temper and have a better attitude when interacting with people. Now I speak less sharply to others."

Finally, Auntie Li tentatively states that Buddhism may be good for her business in another way. "I won't take this for granted, but I do feel that maybe the business is being protected by the Buddhas and bodhisattvas, because things have been so smooth. We have had no problems with sanitation or health [inspectors], with law suits or accidents or anything."

Auntie Li's story shows that, although business can be a site for putting Buddhist values and self-cultivation into practice, as well as possibly for introducing others to the religion, pursuing business can also create problems when trying to be a "good" Buddhist. Some of these problems are the result of tensions inherent in the need for lay Buddhists to simultaneously work in the world and try to transcend it. Other problems Auntie Li describes are caused by the particularities of the political and social climate in contemporary China. Many of my interviewees shared similar stories and concerns about how to be "good Buddhists" while making a livelihood and maintaining a social life in the highly competitive economic and social environment of contemporary China.

Conclusion

Auntie Li's story illustrates one way to do Buddhism. We have examined her objective experiences in terms of her explicitly Buddhist practices and her pathway into Buddhist involvement. We have also heard her discuss subjective dimensions of trying to be a "good Buddhist." The chapter explored two of the main tensions that she has experienced: first, how to negotiate the boundaries of a "good Buddhist" and the place of "superstition" in that, and second, balancing the relationship between one's livelihood and Buddhist practice. Auntie Li is typical of many urban Chinese lay Buddhists today along both objective and subjective dimensions of her Buddhist experience.

References

Jessup, J.B. (2010) The householder elite: Buddhist activism in Shanghai, 1920–1956. Ph.D. dissertation. University of California.

Jones, A.D. (2010) A modern religion? The state, the people, and the remaking of Buddhism in urban China today. Ph.D. dissertation. Harvard University.

Jones, A.D. (2011) Contemporary Han Chinese involvement in Tibetan Buddhism: a case study from Nanjing. *Social Compass*, 58 (4), 540–53.

Ter Haar, B.J. (2001) Buddhist-inspired options: aspects of lay religious life in the Lower Yangzi from 1100 until 1340. *T'oung Pao*, 87, 92–152.

Tuttle, G. (2007) *Tibetan Buddhists in the Making of Modern China*, Columbia University Press, New York.

Further Reading

The following works may be consulted for more information on religion and Buddhism in Contemporary China.

Ashiwa, Y. and Wank, D.L. (2009) *Making Religion, Making the State: The Politics of Religion in Modern China*, Stanford University Press, Stanford, CA.

Fisher, G. (2012) Buddhism in China and Taiwan, in *Buddhism in the Modern World* (ed. D.L. McMahan), Routledge, New York, pp. 68–88.

Goossaert, V. and Palmer, D.A. (2011) *The Religious Question in Modern China*, University of Chicago Press, Chicago, IL.

Ji, Z. and Goosaert, V. (2011) Social implications of Buddhist revival in China [special issue]. *Social Compass* 58 (4).

Yang, F. and Tamney, J.B. (eds) (2005) *State, Market, and Religions in Chinese Societies*, Brill, Leiden.

Notes

1. All names are pseudonyms.
2. All conversations were conducted in Mandarin Chinese by the author, and were not audio-recorded. Quotes are translations by the author, reconstructed from detailed notes at the times of interviews and observation.
3. Esoteric Buddhism is sometimes also referred to as tantric Buddhism, by its Sanskrit name of Vajrayana. In China, most of the teaching traditions among Han Chinese for the past several hundred years have been exoteric Mahayana rather than esoteric. Over the past centuries, Tibetan Buddhist teachers and monastic schools spread under the patronage of the Qing dynasty and attracted Han men and women who joined their monasteries (Tuttle 2007). In Auntie Li's case, her teacher is an ethnic Han Chinese who studied esoteric Buddhism in a Tibetan lineage. This is unusual; most teachers in the esoteric tradition in China today are ethnic Tibetans.
4. For more on the rise of esoteric Buddhism among ethnic Han Chinese in contemporary China, see Jones (2011).
5. In Buddhism, positive actions of many sorts (prayer and ritual, helping others, donating to temples or clergy, etc.) are believed to generate "merit." Merit is essentially a spiritual currency that can be directed to help oneself, specific loved ones or people, or even all living beings. This help can be mundane (curing illness, protection, doing well in school) or intended to help the individual advance in his or her Buddhist study and progress toward enlightenment/liberation.

6   The full moon, new moon, and two eighth days of the waxing and waning lunar cycle.
7   Particularly in esoteric Buddhism, it is believed that cultivation can lead to special powers but that these can be dangerous.
8   This shortage was mainly caused by the break in training during the state suppression of religion in the Maoist period (mid-1950s to early 1980s). For more on the shortage of qualified Buddhist teachers in contemporary China, see Jones (2010).
9   Ter Haar 2001; Jessup 2010.
10 See chapter 4 in Jones (2010) for an extensive discussion of the variation in lay Buddhists' strategies for dealing with critiques of the "superstitious" elements of Buddhism.
11 Within the esoteric Buddhist tradition, vegetarianism is not required, but people must not kill animals themselves.

Index

Abhidhamma Foundation, 154
Abhidharma, 6–7, 148, 149, 150, 152, 183
   philosopher-monk, 2–3
   studies, 154–155
accumulation of extraordinary merit, 151
Adicca, U, 158
Against the Stream, 108, 113
Against the Stream Buddhist Meditation Society, 113
Agwan Dorjev, Buryat Lama, 221
Akahata or "Red Flag Incident," Japan, 283
Akhu Donpa *see* Donpa, Uncle
All Japan Buddhist Reform Alliance (Zenkoku Bukkyo Kakushin Remmei), 287
All Ladakh Gonpa Association, 220
altruism, Buddhist, 238–239, 244
Amaro, Ajahn, 107, 111, 112
Amdo practices, 195, 196
American Zen Teachers' Association, 137
Amida Buddha, 269, 271, 275, 276, 278
   nembutsu, 267, 274
Amitabha Buddha, 82, 84, 97, 101
Amritananda, Bhikshu, 183
Anandakuti Vihara, 180, 182
Anathapindika, 29, 147
   in the *Upasaka*, 30–34
ancestor worship, 43, 124, 272
   Brahmins and 43, 44
   Chinese, 80, 83, 85, 149
   monks and, 24
   Thailand, 49, 52, 152–153
Anguttara-nikaya, 5, 22

anicca, 177
Apa Alo (Ch. Huang Zhengqing), 194, 196, 198
Aphur (Nordak *Nor bdag*), Aphur Mahajan, 259, 260
   pilgrimages, 257, 260
Arannagala, 167–168
Archaeological Survey of India, 261
Asanha Bucha day (Asalha Puja day), 150
Asian Buddhist Conference for Peace (ABCP), 220, 221, 223
Assembly of Citizens United for Peace, 287
Atisha, Vikramasila monastery, 64
Auckland Zen Centre, 134, 136
Auntie Li, 297, 305–314
   "doing Buddhism", 307, 308
   on fundamentals of Buddhism, 309
   on relationship with teacher, 309
avadanas, 4
Avalokitesvara, 26, 55, 65, 181, 195, 243

baby-boomers and Buddhism, 134, 137, 138
Ba Khin, U, 162
Bakula Arhat, 218–226
   reincarnation of, 220, 225
   revitalising Mongolian Buddhism, 219
   see also Kushok Bakula
Balang (half-brother of Tashi Dondrup), 232
Batmunkh, J., 223
Beat movement, 115, 116
Bhadda Kundalakesa, 21–27
   achieves *arahant*, 24
   joins Jain order, 23–24

Buddhists: Understanding Buddhism Through the Lives of Practitioners, First Edition. Edited by Todd Lewis.
© 2014 John Wiley & Sons, Ltd. Published 2014 by John Wiley & Sons, Ltd.

Bhadda Kundalakesa (*continued*)
   and Kundalakesa, 24
   and Sattuka, 23
   verses of, 25
Bhagavad Gita, 48
Bhaisajyaguru, 80
Bhaisajyu (Bhaisajyara), 82, 84, 85
Bhallika, 30
bhikkhuni see nuns
Black Crown ceremony, 99
Black Yajurveda, 45
Bodh Gaya, 261
bodhicitta, 214
bodhisattva, 7, 134, 261, 284, 313
   bodhisattva path, 120
   bodhisattva vow, 101, 116
   and Chod, 62
   concept in Tibetan Buddhism, 97, 103, 193, 218, 238, 243–244
   depictions of, 41
   and Eight Vegetarian Precepts, 308
   ideal of 237, 238, 243–244, 308
   Mongolia, 219, 225
   and Uncle Donpa, 52, 53, 56
   worship of, 41
   see also under names of bodhisattvas
Bon tradition, 246–254
   absence of training for women, 254
   lamas in, 249
   and vegetarianism, 82
   worship of, 84
boun (merit), 92
Brahmanism and women, 25
   and Buddhism, 43, 46
Buddha, 2
   and bell curve of belief, 2–3, 7
   and Brahmins, 44–45
   celebrations in Mongolia, 222
   as a communalist, 4
   doctrine of Buddha nature, 284
   historic context, 14
   and householders, 305
   as human ideal, 286
   and Kundalakesa, 24
   and laypeople's gifts, 147
   and Mallika, 14, 15–16, 17–18
   and medical framework of teachings, 236–237
   and men, 21
   and merchants, 29–30
   and missionary activity, 163
   and Pali Canon, 74
   pilgrimage sites, 151–152
   preaching to kings and courtiers, 14
   previous incarnation, 16–17, 183
   and ritual offerings, 6
   and role of monks, 44
   on significance of loyalty and devotion, 16–17
   and significance of rebirth, 5, 16
   Sujata's gift to, 147
   teachings in Japan, 269, 275, 284
   in the *upasaka*, 30–37
   and vegetarianism, 82
   and women, 21
   words of, 4–5
Buddhadasa, Ajahn, 150
Buddha-dhamma, 127, 128, 129, 130–131
   limitations of, 130
Buddhaghosa, 3, 5
Buddha Land, 281, 286
Buddhism
   American, 108–113, 117, 119, 120, 121, 133–134
   and anti-war counter-culture, 115
   basis of, 3
   and Bon, 246, 249
   and Brahmanism, 42, 43, 44–45, 46, 48
   and caste, 181
   in China, 80–88, 296–298, 305–314 *see also* China
   Chinese laic Buddhism, 85–86
   Chinese monasticism, 80
   complexity of, 7, 261
   contemporary, 141, 179, 180
   counterculture and, 139
   critical Buddhism, 287
   defining a "good Buddhist", 311–312
   diversity of, 7, 41, 155
   doctrines, 6
   "doing Buddhism", 6
   early Buddhism, 22
   and education, 47
   elite Buddhism, 135–136
   engaged Buddhism, 137, 287
   female practice, 21–27
   focus of, 289
   gender and Buddhism, 153–154
   global, 125
   and Hinduism, 44, 45
   householders, 161
   impact on social structures, 58
   incorporation of local gods, 58
   in India, 14, 21, 39–50, 74, 267–272 *see also* India
   in Indonesia, 160
   influence on Asian society, 2
   influences within Buddhism, 7
   in Israel, 124–131 *see also* Goenka, Satya Narayan; Israel; Tovana
   in Japan, 267–272, 274–279, 280–288, 289–295 *see also* Japan
   Jodo Shinshu, 267, 268, 269, 272
   Judaism and, 116–117, 129–130
   and karma, 3
   and killing animals, 229–230
   Ladakh Buddhism, 220

in Laos, 87–94 *see also* Laos
"later spread", 63–64
lay Buddhism, 258
Mahayana Buddhism, 40, 44, 66, 136
Mallika and, 14
mappo period, 281
in Mathura, 40, 41, 43–44
merchants and spread of Buddhism, 274
and mind cultivation, 3–4
missionary Buddhism, 163, 237
modernistic forms, 135–136, 281–288
modification of, 124
in Mongolia, 219–220, 221–225 *see also* Mongolia
in Nepal, 179–188, 230, 250 *see also* Nepal
in New Zealand, 134–141 *see also* New Zealand
and Palestinian-Israeli conflict, 130
perceptions of, 2
and personal responsibility, 91
popular and elite components, 201
practices, 47
Pragmatic Buddhism, 4–5, 84–85
Protestant Buddhism, 157, 179
in Sikkim, 259 *see also* Sikkim
and social compassion, 238–239, 244
spread and promotion of, 1, 7–8, 46–47, 272, 274, 275–275, 276, 277, 296 *see also* Bukkyo Dendo Kyokai
in Sri Lanka/Ceylon, 78, 165–171, 179, 181, 182 *see also* Sri Lanka
study of, 2
tantric, 244
teachings, 284
terminology, 1
Thai Buddhism, 7, 149–155, 172–175, 182
in Tibet, 56, 62–68, 96–104, 129, 134, 193–199, 201–207, 212–213, 228–234, 236, 247–254, 296–302 *see also* Tibet
Tibetan Buddhism in China, 296–298
Tibetan Buddhism and the West, 115, 118, 134, 253
Tibetan Buddhist split, 101, 150–153
Tibetan laic Buddhism, 62, 67
Tibetan monasticism, 62, 63, 64 *see also* Tibetan Buddhism
Tibetan women, 257–262
traditions of, 298
Transcendental Buddhism, 4–5
in the United States, 88, 100, 101, 115, 121, 134, 136 *see also* United States
violence and Buddhism, 165, 166
war and Buddhism, 166, 167
West and Buddhism, 3, 221, 280
Western Buddhism, 73–79, 87, 97, 98, 103, 108, 134, 141, 158
Western stereotypes and perceptions, 6, 149, 179

women and, 14–15, 63, 76, 134, 141, 216 *see also specific women*
Zen Buddhism, 47
see also Bukkyo Dendo Kyokai; esoteric Buddhism; karma; meditation; monks; Newar Buddhism; Nichiren Buddhism; nuns; Pure Land Buddhism; Theravada Buddhism; United States; Vajrayana Buddhist practices; *other specific types of Buddhism*
Buddhist factory evangelists, 283
Buddhist Herald, 78
Buddhist Liturgy, The, 83
Buddhist Lodge of the Theosophical Society, 77
Buddhist mass politics, 281
Buddhist Modernism, 102
Buddhist School of Dialectics in Dharamashala, 223
Buddhist Socialist League (Bukkyo Shakaishugi Domei), 287
Buddhist Society, 77
Buddhist tradition, 1
   in Britain, 76–77
   liturgy, 47
   monuments, 1
   ritualism, patronage and ethical principles, 40
   texts, 1
   see also particular countries
Bukkyo Dendo Kyokai (Society for the Promotion of Buddhism, BDK), 274–279
   and promotion of Buddhism, 272, 274, 275–276, 277, 278
Bun Phra Wes festival, 147
Burma (Myanmar), 74, 152, 182, 280
business and Buddhism, tensions between, 307, 312–313

Cakrasamvara Yogini-Tantra teachings, 99
Camadevi of Haripunjaya, Queen, 153
Cambodia, 88, 152, 159, 280
Cease Fire of the Heart, 130
Central Institute for Higher Tibetan Studies (CIHTS), 210–212, 214, 223
Ceylon *see* Sri Lanka
Ch'an (J. Zen) meditation, 85
Chah, Ajahn, 174
   Ajahn Chah forest lineage, 111
chanting, 48, 83, 173, 174, 176, 274, 291, 292
   chanting contexts, 269
   chanting ritual, 277, 279, 281, 284
   chanting services, 140, 168, 170, 291
   chanting sutras, 187
   and the *Lotus Sutra*, 289, 290
   mantra chanting, 83
   and meditation, 237
   Uncle Donpa and, 56
Chatral Sangye Dorje Rinpoche, Kyabje, 213, 214, 215–216

China
  1920s, 195–196
  Buddhists in, 80–88, 296–298, 305–314
  Communist takeover, 298
  Kushok Bakula and, 221, 225
  and religion, 307
Chinese Buddhist Academy, 298
Chinese–Tibetan relations, 52
Chod Hair-tip Wisdom Teachings, 68
Chod tradition and practices, 62, 67, 68, 215, 240
Chogyam, 100
Choijamts, D., 223
chomo (Tibet), 246, 247, 249
  gender fluidity of, 251
Chomo Khandru, 246–254
  access to religious life, 250
  becomes ordained monastic, 246, 250
  biography, 250–251
  and changing women's identities, 247, 249, 250, 251, 252
Christianity, 75, 125, 137, 138, 268
  anti-Christian rhetoric, 166
  and "Protestant Buddhism", 181
  in Tibet, 194
class and clan, 42–43
colonialism and Buddhism, 74
concentration meditation, 173–174, 175, 177
Confucius, 83
Convention of Proletarian Workers/Proletarian Party of Japan, 287
Cosmopolitan Greetings, 120
counterculture, 110, 115, 126, 133, 134, 139
"Crazy Wisdom" school, 116
Critical Buddhism, 287
Crystal Mountain, Tsari, 258
Cultural Revolution (China 1966–76), 298, 307

Daikenzan Choshoji, 267–268, 269
Dalai Lama, 193, 215, 218–219
  13th incarnation, 220
  14th incarnation, 218
  and Arhat Bakula, 226
  and Bon, 246
  flight from Tibet and exile, 209, 210, 253
  inheritance of authority issues with reincarnation, 219
  and Karmapa, 102
  visit to Denmark, 100
  visit to Mongolia, 224
  see also Tibet
dana (generosity), 4, 129, 151
delog, 201, 204
demerit (*pap*), 4, 13, 204
  and violence, 228
Denmark and Buddhism, 101
Dhammacarya, 159

Dhammapada, 17, 150
  Bhadda and, 26–27
  commentary on, 26
Dhammawati, Bhikshuni, 182
dharma, 3, 79, 104, 130, 150, 278, 279, 301
  Buddha and, 5, 14
  conception of, 6, 169, 183
  decline of and "latter days", 281
  developments in, 127
  dharma of action, 247, 251–252
  dharma path, 133, 310
  dharma of study, 247, 249, 251, 252
  dissemination of, 18, 64, 81, 112, 133, 182, 297, 301, 313
  effect of, 205, 213, 236
  festivals, 6
  in Israel, 130
  in Japan, 267–272, 279
  and military, 170, 171
  and monastic vocation, 161
  practical dharma, 247, 249, 254
  practicing of, 91, 212, 213, 216
  preaching of, 4–5, 171, 214
  promotion of spread, 124, 125, 242–243, 296
  protecting dharma, 267–272
  and punk, 112, 113
  recitation of, 63
  ritual 215
  sacrifice for 301
  significance of, 168, 169
  spreading of, 124, 125, 134, 271
  teachings, 212, 309
  and Theravada Buddhism, 182
  Tibet, 237, 244
  transmission of, 136, 239
  and Triple Jewels, 2, 7, 14, 88, 94, 182, 277, 286
  Ts'ampa Nawang and, 242–243
  understanding, 161, 165, 184, 206
  women and, 65, 214, 216
  see also Ginsberg, Allen; Mallika
Dharma Buddha, 101, 184
Dharmakirti Vihara, 182, 183–185
Dharma Punx, 108, 113
Dharma Punx (Levine biography), 108
Dharmashringa, 186
dhutangas, 158, 160
Diamond Way, 96, 97, 99, 100–103
  and renaming of buddhas and bodhisattvas, 103
  see also Nydahl, Lama Ole
Dispeller of Disputes, 46
Dondrup, Tashi, 228–235
  biography, 230–232
Don-drup Zang-po (Prince Mon-lam Drup), 68
Donpa, Uncle (Akhu Donpa), 7, 52–60
  as common man's hero, 53, 54–56, 58
  as "mad" yogin, 53, 56, 57, 58

misogynistic aspects of, 54, 59
modern interpretations, 58–60
nature of stories, 52
as proto-Communist, 59–60
as protomodernist, 59
roles of, 53–54
as saint in disguise, 56–58, 59
scatological nature of stories, 52, 53, 54
as trickster, 52
Dorje Sempa (Skt. Vajrasattva), 213
Drolma (Skt. Tara), 204, 207
Drukpa Kagyu, 57
Drukpa Kunle, 57–58
Dudjom Rinpoche, 118
Dudjom Yangsi Rinpoche, Kyabje, 215
dukkha, 170
Dungsey Rinoche, Kyabje 215

Eightfold Path, 3, 111, 236, 276, 284, 312
Eighth Karmapa, 99
elite representations of Buddhism, 2, 136
   and Buddhist texts, 1, 2
   dharma and nirvana and, 4
   and modernist Buddhism, 135, 141
   monastic, 153, 160
   as only one perspective, 3, 201
   tantric level and teaching, 181
   Uncle Donpa and religious elites, 52, 54–56, 57, 58
emptiness, concept of, 42, 66, 67, 127
   absorption into, 45
   and the Buddha, 47
   emptiness of, 66
   and Japanese nationalism, 280, 286
   Madhyamaka school, 39
   Mahayana arguments, 42, 44, 118
   meditation and, 66, 67, 214
   Nagarjuna's argument 42, 44, 45, 47
Engaged Buddhism, 287
Engaged Dharma blog, 130
English Tripitaka Translation Project, 275
Enkhbayar, N., 223, 224
enlightenment, 2
Entering the Diamond Way (1999), 98
esoteric Buddhism, 231, 298, 306, 308, 310; *see also* Tantric traditions; Vajrayana Buddhist practices
Evans-Wentz, Walter Y., 98, 99

Fa Yue Monastery, Hong Kong, 80
Fa Yue Temple, UK, 81, 82
Fazun, Venerable, 296–302
   biography, 298–302
   as translator, 297
Feng Yuxiang, 195, 196
Fifth Jamyang Zhepa *see* Tenpe Gyaltsen
First Noble Truth, 112

Five Precepts (*panca sila*), 78, 150–151, 153–154, 168–169, 174
   and Theravada Buddhism, 182, 183
five ritual offerings (*bali*), 5
fluid religious identity, concept of, 247–248
fortune-telling, 85
Four Conditions, 5
Four Foundations of Mindfulness, 159
Four Good Deeds, 5
Four Gratitudes, 276
Four Noble Truths, 4, 6, 91, 111, 284
Fourth Jamyang Zhepa, 195
Fulder, Dr. Stephen John, 124–131
   background, 126
   and funding of Tovana, 129
   on Jewish-Buddhist interaction, 129–130
Funeral Buddhism, 268–269

Gandhi, Mahatma, 126, 127
Gang-pa (Chod practitioners), 68
Gelek Rinpoche, 120, 121
Gelukpa-defined Buddhism, 195, 243
Geshe, Amdo, 298, 301, 302
Ginsberg, Allen, 101, 115–122
   Blake vision, 117–118
   and Buddhist lack of a creator, 117
   influence, 116
   and Jewish–Buddhist interaction, 116–117
   poetry, 118
   Snowmass incident, 119, 120
Ginsburg, Louis, 117, 121
Giro, Seno'o, 280–287
   biography, 282–284
   parents Tamejiro and Haru, 281–282, 284
   sister Noriko, 282
   socialist views, 286
Goenka, Satya Narayan, 125, 128–129, 131, 179, 186
   move to exclusivity, 129
Golden Rule, 14
Gradual Path (*anupurvikatha*), 3, 4
Greater Japan Nichirenist Youth Corps (Dainippon Nichirenshugi Seinendan), 285
Great Naropa Poetry Wars, The, 120
"Great Perfection, the" (*rDzogschen*), 47
Great Speech Chapter (*Bka' tshoms chen mo*), 66–67
Griebenow, Blanche and Marion Grant 196, 197
Guru Rinpoche, 259, Guru Rinpoche Day, 215
Guru-Yoga path, 115
Gyalwa Karmapa, 16th, 96, 98, 99
Gyuto College, Labrang, 197, 198

Hartung, Caty, 101, 103
Heart Sutra (*Prajnaparamitahrdayasutra*), 66, 83
higher knowledge (*khippabhinna*), 22
Hikomatsu, Kamikawa, 283
Himalayan Amchi Association, 241

Hinduism, 44, 45
Horner, Isaline B., 73, 75–79
    legacy, 14–15, 78–79
    and meditation, 78
householders, 29–37
    bonds among householders, 151
    and Buddhism, 1, 4, 17, 150, 165, 186–188
    Chinese, 306
    female (*upasika*), 14, 15, 147, 148, 172
    interrelationship between monastic tradition and householder devotees, 80, 161
    king as householder, 46–47
    Mahayana-Vajrayana tradition, 181
    and meditation, 163
    and merit, 5
    and minor precepts, 82
    and Nydahl, 100
    religious life, 237
    spiritual practices, 210
    tantric priests, 181
    Tibetan, 6–32, 246
    and wealth, 305
    see also Ma-chig Lab-dron
Hridaya, Chittadhar, 30
Humphreys, Christmas, 77
Hundred-Syllable Vajrasattva Mantra, 213
hungry ghosts, 20, 47, 201, 204
    worship of, 5, 6, 82, 84

Ikeda-Sensei (Daisaku Ikeda), 290, 291, 293
In Defense of Dharma, 166
India, 152, 160, 209
    British Rule, 74
    and Buddhism, 21, 74, 267
    Ladakh becomes part of India, 220
    at time of Buddha, 14
Indian Cultural Center, Mongolia, 224
Insight Meditation Society, 128
Institute of Thai Maechii, 177
International Buddhist Institute in Mongolia, 223
International Buddhist Study Group in Ceylon, 78
Israel, Buddhism in, 124–131
    Buddha-dhamma courses, 127–128
    historical basis, 125
    Jewish–Buddhist interaction, 129–130
    regional development, 128
    see also Fulder, Dr. Stephen John
Israel Vipassana Trust, 126, 128, 129

Jainism, 25, 43
Jamyang Zhepa (Tenpe Gyaltsen), 193–198
Japan
    Buddhism in, 267–272, 274–279, 280–288, 289–295
    Christianity in, 268
    focus of, 269
    invasion of Burma, 159
    Jodo Shinshu, 267, 268, 269, 271, 272
    Marxism in, 281
    rural depopulation, 268
    sectarian aspects of, 278
    see also Shin Buddhism
Japan Buddhist Federation, 275
Japan–China Amity Association, 287
Japanese Communist Party, 287
Japan–North Korea Amity Association, 287
jatakas, 4, 6, 15
Jetavana monastery, Shravasti, 29
Jetsun Rigdzin Chonyi Zang mo, 68
Jeweled Garland, 46, 47
Jewel Heart organization, 120, 121
Jewish–Buddhist hybridity, 117
    interaction, 116–117, 124
Jigme, Lhatsun Namkhai, 259
Jodo Shinshu Hongwanji-ha sect, 267, 268, 269, 271, 272
just war concept and Buddhism, 166–167

Kaew (temple of the Emerald Buddha, Thailand), 148, 149
Kagyupa association, 100
Kalacakra Stupa, 104
Kalmyk Mongols, 221
Kalu Rinpoche, 99, 100
Kapleau, Roshi Philip, 133, 136
karma, 19, 92, 93, 177, 230
    karmic calculations, 228
    karmic seeds, 148
    negative karma, 312, 313
    and its ripening (*vikalpa*), 14, 151, 213
    and war, 166, 167
Karma Kagyu community (*bKa' brgyud*), 96, 100, 102, 103, 104
    succession dispute, 97
Karma Kagyupa Association (KKV), 100
Karmapa, 219
    16th, 96, 97, 98, 99, 100, 101, 102
    17th, 97, 104
    death, 98
    in Rumtek, 99
Kassapa Buddha, 22
Keiko Yonamine, 290
Kerouac, Jack, 115, 116
Khandru, Chomo, 246–254
    biography, 250–251
kings, and Buddhism, 46–47
    responsibilities, 47
Kitthivuttho, Phra, 154
Kjolhede, Roshi Bodhin, 133, 135, 136
Komeito, 290, 292, 293, 294
Kornfield, Jack, 112
Kosala Sutta, 19

Index

Krishna, 48
Ksitigarbha, 80, 82–83, 85, 86
Kublai Khan, 224
Kumarajiva, 44
Kummasapinda Jataka, 15
Kunzum, Tsultrim and Dawa, 250, 252
Kushok Bakula, 19th, 219
 appointed Ambassador to Mongolia, 223
 death, 225
 influence in Mongolia, 221–225
 outreach, 220–222
Kutsap Ternga monastery, 239, 240, 243
Kwan Yin, 80, 81, 82, 83, 86, 237
 veneration of, 84, 85
Kyoto School, 287

Labrang Medical Clinic, 197
Ladakh, 220–221
Ladakh Buddhist Association, 220
Lakho Jikme Trinle Gyatso, 195
lamas, 52, 54, 60, 205–206
 defining lamas, 251
 Tibet, 247
Laos, 87, 88, 94, 152
 establishment of the Lao People's Democratic Republic, 90, 91, 92
 US aid to, 89
Lay Meditation Movement, 162–163
Lay Women Buddhist Organization, 223
Levine, Noah, 107–113
 amalgamating punk and Buddhism, 108, 111–113
 biography, 108–109
 and Buddhism, 110–111
 spiritual awakening, 109–110
Levine, Stephen, 109, 111–112
Li, Auntie, 297, 305–314
 "doing Buddhism", 307, 308
 on fundamentals of Buddhism, 309
 on relationship with teacher, 309
liberation narratives and tales" (Tib. *namthar*), 101, 103, 202
Liberation Tigers of Tamil Eelam, 165
Life of Nagarjuna, 44
Lion Roar of Srimaladevi, 47
London Buddhist Vihara (LBV), 77, 78
longevity rituals, 205
Lotus Sutra, 281, 283, 284, 285, 289, 290
Lubra, Nepal, 248–249
 fluidity of gender and religious roles in, 251, 252, 254
Lumantso, Queen, 198
Lung-mo Bum-chen, 65
Luvsantseren, G., 223, 225

Ma-chig Lab-dron, 62–68
 biography, 64–66
 and Chod tradition, 62, 67, 68

commentary on Heart Sutra, 66
emphasis, 62
legacy, 68
on Negative Forces, 66, 67
Machik Throma Nagmo, 214
"mad" yogin (*naljor nyonpa/rnal 'byor smyon pa*), concept of, 52, 53, 56, 57–58
Mahabharata, 48
Mahajanapada, 14, 153
Mahakala, 96
Mahapajapati, Queen, 13
Mahasamghika sects, 42
 monasteries, 41
Mahasatipatthana Sutta, 160, 161f
Mahasi, Sayadaw, 157–163
 biography, 158
 mindfulness techniques, 162–163
 missionary work, 160
 treatises on *Visuddhimagga*, 159–160
Mahavastu, 5
Mahayana Buddhism, 39–40, 210, 242, 310
 Avalokitesvara, 26, 55, 65, 181, 195, 243
 belief in bodhisattvas, 218
 bodhisattva Manjushri, 56, 84, 195, 219, 296
 Heart Sutra (*Prajnaparamitahrdayasutra*), 66, 83
 Mahayana-Vajrayana tradition, 179, 181, 236, 297
 meditation, 62, 97,
 merit-making in, 215, 225, 233, 249–250, 259–260, 274–275, 278
 monastic traditions, 44, 181
 Nembutsu practice, 267, 274
 Perfection of Wisdom (Prajnaparamita) literature, 42, 44, 62
 pilgrimage traditions, 96, 101, 118, 196–197, 257, 258, 261, 284, 296
 Pure Land Buddhism, 82, 84, 97, 101, 269, 271, 275, 276, 278
 and skill in means, 242
 Sutra on the Past Vows of the Earth Store Bodhisattva, The, 85
 Svayambhu Stupa, Kathmandu, 99
 Tara (Tib. Drolma), 204, 207
 in Tibet, 64, 65, 99, 104
 tathagatagarbha doctrine, 47–48
 Vimalakirti Sutra, 306
 Zen, 85, 115, 117, 136, 281
Maitrayani Upanishad, 45
Maitreya Buddha, 85
Malayky, 87–96
 biographical details, 89–91
 on Buddhism, 88, 92–94
 resettlement in US, 91–92
Mallika, 13–19
 biography, 14–16
 and Buddha, 14
 and the dog, 14, 16

Mallika (*continued*)
  historical context, 14
  and husband, 14, 16, 17–18
Mallika Sutta, 18
"*Mani* mantra", 237, 240, 242
  tradition, 242–243
Manjushri, bodhisattva, 56, 84, 195, 219, 296
Manorathapurani, 22, 25, 27
Manual of Vipassana Meditation, 159
Mara, 66
Margarethe, Queen of Denmark, 99, 101
Mathura, 40–41
Maudgalyayana, 219
Maya, Queen, 13
Meditate and Destroy (2007), 112
meditation, 40, 88, 134, 148, 149, 157, 175–176, 285
  Burma, 157–158, 159, 179
  Cakrasamvara meditation, 97
  Ch'an (J. Zen) meditation, 84, 85
  as characteristic of Buddhism, 78
  Chod, 67
  as component of Buddhist development, 3–4
  Diamond Way, 97, 99, 100
  and emptiness, 67
  forms of meditation, 2
  hansei, 286
  and health issues, 88, 93, 134
  insight meditation, 158, 160, 161, 175
  and Judaism, 124, 129, 130
  laity and, 99, 148, 159, 162, 210
  Mahasi Sayadaw and, 162–163
  Mahayana, 62, 97, Tibet, 64, 65, 99, 104
  mani, 237
  and mantras, 84
  metta meditation, 170, 171
  mindfulness meditation, 108
  modern, 179, 180, 201
  and modern world, 107, 108
  and nirvana, 6, 7
  and perception of truth, 40
  practical meditation, 94
  and religious, 2, 43, 84, 135, 162–163, 168, 169, 173, 174
  and ritual, 6
  sitting meditation, 136, 176
  tantric, 102
  traditions, 8
  tsok and, 215
  Venerable Sudinna and, 167–168
  vipassana meditation, 124, 125, 126, 184–185, 186
  visualization meditation, 214
  walking meditation, 167
  Western meditation, 127, 158
  Western style, 100, 101, 102, 133, 134, 149, 151
  women and, 154–155, 172
  yogic, 45
  see also Levine, Noah
merit-making, 7, 25, 36, 147, 205, 206, 233, 240, 250, 305, 308
  accumulation of, 5, 88, 151
  act of transferring merit, 5, 92, 94, 154, 228, 308, 310, 313
  BDK and, 274–275, 278
  and death, 204, 228, 233
  demerit (*pap*), 4, 13, 204, 228
  and dharma, 4, 62, 247
  and "doing Buddhism", 6
  donations and, 3, 4, 7, 151, 259, 260
  earning merit, 80, 82
  effect of, 13, 15
  and householder practice, 150
  impact on health, 151
  Japan, 289
  Mongolia, 225
  Nepal, 240
  and old age, 233, 243
  and pilgrimages, 151, 152
  and recitations of texts, 62, 65, 214
  and religious activity, 151, 182, 203, 205, 206, 240, 246, 249, 252, 260
  rituals, 6
  and sangha, 151
  Sikkim, 259–260
  in Thailand, 151, 154
  Tibet, 215, 233, 249–250, 259
  women and, 151, 153
  Yama and, 204
Merwin, W.S., 119, 120
Metteyya (Maitreya), 6
Middle Way, 118, 160
Middle Way, The, 78
Mi la'i rnam thar (gTsang smyon He ru ka), 98
Milarepa, 55, 98, 195
Mind Body Awareness Project, 113
Mind Breaths: Poems, 1972–1977, 116
mind cultivation, 3–4
mindfulness, 3–4, 93, 112, 125, 134, 160, 184
  mindfulness cultivation, 159
  mindfulness meditation practices, 157–158
Mitutoyo Corporation, 275, 276
mo (Tibetan practice) and *mopa* (practitioners), 202, 203, 204, 205
monasteries, sectarian affiliations, 41, 42
  donations, 42–43
  Mahayana-Vajrayana tradition, 44, 181
  in Mathura, 42–44
  monastic practices, 299
  monastic vocations, 43
  rituals, 83–84
  in Tibet, 193

Mongolia
    Buddhism in, 219–220, 221–222
    revitalizing Buddhism in, 223–225
    women in, 223
    see also Kushok Bakula
Mongolian Buddhist Studies Institute, 223
Mongolian–Indian Friendship Farm, 224
monks, 3
    alms rounds, 151
    Buddhist writers, 1
    and doctrine, 44
    gifts to and merit, 150
    and medical developments, 237
    Monastic Ordination and Ascetic Practices, 160–162
    Mongolian, 223
    motivations for becoming, 160
    and religious ideals, 239
    as symbol, 149
    war monks, 166
    Zen, 2
Mon-lam Drup, Prince (Don-drup Zang-po), 68
moon, significance of full and new, 30, 42, 84, 169, 174, 182, 206
moral instruction (*shila*), 4
Mugen Project Foundation, 278

Nagarjuna, 39–48
    diversity of narratives about, 39, 40
    and Mahayana movement 39–40
nagas cults, 41, 43
    advice to sovereigns, 46
    in Andhra Pradesh, 45–48
Nakchu, 300, 301, 302
namthar, 97, 101, 103, 202
Naone, Dana, 119, 120
Naropa, 121
Nawang, Ts'ampa, 236–244
    and altruism, 242
    biography, 239–241
    medical activities, 238, 239, 240, 241, 242, 243, 244
    shift from monk to tantric practitioner, 237
Negative Forces, and Negative Forces with and without Obstruction, 66, 67
nembutsu, 267, 274
Nepal, 179, 182, 209, 210, 212, 230, 238
    Buddhism in, 179–188, 230, 250
    Theravada Buddhist, 181–183
    women in, 184, 246, 247, 249–250
    women's changing role in, 253–254
Newar Buddhism, 180–181, 182, 183, 184, 188
    ritual, 186, 187
New Zealand, 134–141
    Zen in, 136
    see also Sensei, Amala
Nhima Bhuti, 247, 254

nibbana, enlightenment, 91, 162
Nichiren Buddhism, 280–281, 283, 284–287, 289–295
    study of, 291
    and Western radicalism, 285–287
    see also Soka Gakkai
Nichirenist (Jp. Nichirenshugi) lay movement, 284
nirvana, 4, 6, 7, 158, 160, 162
Nonsectarian (Tib. *ris med*) center, 100
Nu, U, 159
Numata, Toshihide, 274–279
    biography, 276–277
    see also Bukkyo Dendo Kyokai
Numata, Dr. Yehan, 275, 276, 277
Numata Program in Buddhist Studies, 275–276
nuns (*bhikkhuni*), 3
    "elder nuns" (*theris*), 22
    Theravada, 180, 182
    Tibetan, 2
    and Uncle Donpa stories, 52, 53, 54, 55, 59
Nydahl, Hannah, 97, 98, 101, 103
Nydahl, Lama Ole, 96–104
    attitude toward sexuality, 100
    charismatic aspects of faith, 100, 104
    and schism, 102–103
    teaching career, 100
    and Tibetan Buddhism, 96, 97, 98, 99, 101
    travels in Tibet, 96, 100–101
    see also Diamond Way

Ochirbat, P., 224, 225
Ogi, Rev. Keishin (Megumi), 268–272
    biography, 269–270
    role in prefectural government, 271
    role as Shin priest, 270–272
Ogi, Rev. Keiwa, 270–271
Opening the Door of the Space Treasure of a Compilation of Homage and Worship of the Elders Led by Arya Bakula, 219
Orlovsky, Peter, 121

Pa-dam-pa Sang-gye, 64, 65, 68
Padmasambhava, 68, 212–213
Padumuttara, Buddha, 22, 25
Palestinian–Israeli conflict, 130
Pali Canon, 44, 92, 148, 162, 167, 169
    and Bhadda, 26–27
    and Brahmins, 44
    commentaries on, 5, 127, 159
    and just war concept, 166
    Mallika, 18
    material for instructors, 4
    printing of, 159
    and questions for novices, 26
    "taking refuge" verses, 88
    and Theravada Buddhism, 74
    translation, 76–77, 78, 192

Pali Canon (*continued*)
   Vinaya, 76
   and the West, 78
   and women, 22
   see also Abhidharma; *Anguttara-nikaya*; Horner, Isaline B.
Pali literature, 22, 92, 147, 158, 166
Pali Text Society (PTS), 75, 76–77
Panchen Lama, 219
   ninth, 195
Parama, Sayadaw U, 158
Pasenadi, king of ancient Kosala (Skt. Prasenajit), 13, 15, 16, 17
Pathet Lao, 90
Pawinee Bunkhun, 147–155
   Abhidharma studies, 154–155
   biography, 149
   Buddhist householder practices, 149–150
   classifying difficulties, 151
   impact of gender, 153–154
   religious practices, 152–153
Pemayangtse Monastery and lamas, 259–260, 262
Pembar, Ts'ampa, 239, 244
People to People workshops, 130
Perfection of Wisdom (*Prajnaparamita*) literature, 42, 44, 62
   Chod, 62
   Ma-chig and, 64–65, 66
Pethub Stangey Choskor Ling Monastery, 223
phowa ('*pho ba*, conscious dying), 60, 97, 101
pilgrimage, 64, 111, 152, 257
   and Buddha's landscape, 151–152, 260, 261
   Japan, 284, 296
   Sengaji, 284
   Tibet, 96, 101, 118, 196–197, 257, 258, 261
Piyajatika Sutta, 17, 19
Pragmatic and Transcendental Buddhism, 4–7
prajna, 4
pratimokshas, 42
punk, 107–108, 112
punya, 4
Pure Land, 97, 101
Pure Land Buddhism, 149, 267, 268–269, 274–275, 277, 281
   China, 308
Purevbat, Lama G., 225, 226
Purva Arama ("Eastern Monastery"), 13, 29

"Queer Dharma", 118

Raja, 19
Rajuvula, King, 41
Rang byung rig pa'i rdo rje (16th Karmapa), 97
Ratna, Dharma, 186, 187
rDzogschen, 47

reciprocity and Buddhism, 18–19
reincarnation, 193, 206, 218, 230
"Release of Living Creatures" ceremony, China, 310
religious virtuosi, Buddhist, 1–2
Rhys Davids, Caroline Augusta Foley, 75, 76
Rhys Davids, Thomas William, 74–75
Riding the Tiger (1992), 98, 101
rituals, 6
Rochester Zen Center (RZC), 133, 134, 136, 137, 140
role of enlightenment and Buddhist societies, 237–238
Root Verses on the Middle (*Mula Madhyamaka Karika*), 40, 41–42, 45, 46
royal land grants (*brahmadeyyas*), 45
Russia, Buddhists in, 218, 221

Saicho (Dengyo Daishi), 283
saints, Buddhist, 7
Salutation and Worship of the Elders, 220
Samantabhadra, 85
Sambula Jataka, 17
Sammitiyas, 42
samsara, 4, 14, 58, 167
samyak sambodhi see enlightenment
San Francisco Zen Center, 112
sangha, 2, 7, 14, 29, 82
   "fourfold sangha", 30
   and Theravada Buddhism, 182
Sangharakshita, 97
sanzen, 127
Sariputta, 24, 26
Sarvastivadin doctrines, 41, 42
Satipatthana Sutta, 118
satire, limitations of, 55
satori (enlightenment), 2
Sattuka, 22–23, 25, 27
Sayadaw, Ledi, 162
Sayagyi U Ba Khin, 126
Sayamagyi Daw Mya Thwin (Mother Sayamagyi), 126
Sengaji pilgrimage, 284
Sensei, Amala (Charlotte Wrightson), 133–141
   background, 134
   on conversion, 137–138, 139–140
   as Zen teacher, 133, 137
sesshin, 2
Shagyatsam, 214–215
Shakyamuni Buddha, 6, 41, 42, 85, 219, 246, 267
Shakya Shri, Tokden, 261–262
Shamarpa (Red Hat Karmapa), 102
Shambhala Mountain Center in Colorado, 121
Shangpa Rinpoche, 239, 241, 243
Shariputra, *219*
Shigaki, Kazuko (Rev. Keiwa Ogi), 270–271
Shinano Buddhist Youth League (Shinano Bukkyo Seinen Domei);, 287
Shin Buddhism, 267, 270, 271, 276, 278
Shinran, 267, 276, 271

Shinto, 268, 285
Shrisura Arya, King, 68
Sikkim, 99, 202, 223, 257, 258, 261, 262
    Buddhism in, 259
    cardamom production, 259
Sino-Tibetan Buddhist Studies Institute, 302
Sixth Theravada Council, 160, 161
sngon 'gro, 100, 102
Snyder, Gary, 115, 117
Sobhana, Ashin, 158–159
Society for Respecting and Revering Nichirenism (Nichirenshugi Sangyokai), 285
Soka Gakkai, 281, 289–295
    core beliefs, 294
    Soka Gakkai Future Group, 290
Soviet Union, 221
Spirit Rock Meditation Center, Woodacre, California, 112
Sri Lanka, 3, 74, 76, 78, 152, 160, 165–171
    and Protestant Buddhism, 179, 181, 182
Sthavira school, 181
Straight Edge movement, 110
Sturmer, Richard von, 136, 137, 138–139, 140
Sudinna, Venerable, 165–171
suffering, cause of, 19
Sugata Saurabha, 30
Sujata, 13, 147, 179–188
    becoming a Theravada devotee, 183–186
    biography, 180–181
    family life, 186–187
Sujata Jataka, 16
Sukey, Mo, 202–207, 257
Surikit, Queen, 153
Sutra on the Past Vows of the Earth Store Bodhisattva, The, 85
Svayambhu Stupa, Kathmandu, 99

Taisho Tripitaka, 275
Taiwan, 284
Taixu, Master, 299
Takyu, 80–88
Takyu Sik (Wai), Venerable, 81–86
Tantric traditions, 99, 181, 195, 237, 240
    deities, 64, 88
    lamas and priests, 96, 181
    lineages, 242, 244
    meditation, 101, 102
    practitioners, 121, 181, 236, 239, 240, 259
    rituals, 103, 195
    tantric education, 119, 258
    in Tibet, 244
    traditions, 97, 210
    yoga, 99
    see also Vajrayana Buddhist practices
Tara, 65, 68, 219
Tashi Namgyal, king of Sikkim, 260

tathagatagarbha doctrine, 47–48
Teaching of the Buddha, The, 81, 223, 275
Teaching of the Perfection of Wisdom in Eight Thousand Lines, 66
Team to Study the Dharma Abroad in Tibet (Chi. *Liu Zang xuefa tuan*), 298
Tendai school (Ch. Tiantai), 283, 284
Tenpe Gyaltsen (Fifth Jamyang Zhepa), 193–199, 219
    biography, 194–195
    and construction projects, 198–199
    exile, 195
    support for religious pluralism, 198, 199
    trip to Lhasa, 196–197, 199
Ten Precepts, 81, 169
Tenzin, Khenchen Sangay, 205, 206
Tetsutaro, Sato, 285
Thailand, 7
    Buddhism in, 7, 149–155, 172–175, 182
Theklo, Tulku, 214
Theravada Buddhism, 76
    Abhidharma, 148, 154
    aspirations, 92
    bifurcation into learning and praxis, 161
    in Burma, 74
    in Cambodia, 159
    centers of, 74
    in Ceylon/Sri Lanka, 74, 77, 159, 163
    compared to other types of Buddhism, 184, 186
    development of, 152, 159
    history of, 161
    in India, 159
    "insight cultivation" (*vipassana-bhavana*), 158
    in Japan, 160
    in Laos, 89
    London monastery, 77
    meditation, 162
    modern Buddhism, 159, 162–163, 179–188
    monks, 158, 160, 162, 172, 179–188
    in Nepal, 181–184
    nuns and renunciants, 151, 153, 186
    rituals, 6, 88, 91–92, 149, 161
    syncretistic aspects of, 181–182
    texts and Pali Canon, 74, 78, 161
    in Thailand, 149, 150, 159
    and Tovana, 128
    writings, 159
Theri-Apadana, 22, 25–26
Therigatha (Verses of Elder Nuns), 13, 22
    on Bhadda, 26–27
    commentary on, 26
    Kundalakesa, 24–25
theris, 13, 22
Three Pillars of Zen, The, 136, 138, 139
Three Refuges, 19, 78, 94
Three Stupas of Kathmandu Valley, 261

Throma Ngondro, 214, 215
Thubten Chognor, 19th Kushok Bakula Lobsang, 220
Tibet, 52–60, 209–216, 247
    attitudes towards illegitimacy, 230
    beliefs about women, 63, 251–252
    borders with China, 239
    Buddhist teachings, 47, 209
    and China, 194
    Chinese assertion of control, 253
    Chinese rule over, 58–59, 97, 202
    criticism of elites, 55
    during "later spread" of Buddhism, 63–64
    goal of religious practices, 251–252
    literacy in, 63
    misperceptions about, 238–239
    nineteenth century, 261
    relations with China, 52
    religious practitioners, 228–229
    society, 53
    subsistence farming, 228–230
    views of society, 55
    women, 257–262
Tibetan Buddhism, 97, 193–199, 218–226, 228–234
    and Bon tradition, 246–254
    killing of animals, 229–230
    Ma-chig Lab-dron's influence, 62
    Mahayana-Vajrayana tradition, 236
    and meat consumption, 229–230
    Nyingmapa tradition, 259
    and patronage of Buddhist institutes, 259
    split, 102
    see also Dalai Lama; Donpa, Uncle; Drukpa Kagyu
Tibetan Children's Village, Dharamshala, India, 210
Tibetan refuge formula, 103, 104
Tibetan Yoga and Secret Doctrines (1935), 99
Tibetan Youth Congress, 59
Tibet Foundation, UK, 223
Tipitika (Skt. *Tripitaka*), 169
Titmuss, Christopher, 127, 129, 130
Toitsudan, (Unification Group), 285
Tokden Shakya Shri, 258
To-nyon Sam-drub (Snowman of Sham-pogang), 68
Toshihide, Yoshiteru, 277, 279
Tovana, 125, 127, 128, 130
trance, 3
tranquility meditation (*samatha*), 162
trickster figures, 52, 53 *see also* Donpa, Uncle
Triple Jewels/Gems, 2, 19, 152
Tri Ratna, 14
Trulshik Rinpoche, Kyabje, 215
Trungpa, Chogyam, 100, 115, 116, 117, 118, 120
Tsari Rongkhor Chenmo, 262
Tsechu, Rinpoche Lopon, 99, 103
Tsogdu Marnak (Crimson Assembly)
tsok offering, 215
Tsultrim Allione, 68

Tsultrim Zangmo (Soyang), 209–216
    biography, 210
    Throma Ngondro, 214–215
Tulku, Ayang, 99, 100

U Ba Khin, Sayagyi, 125, 127, 131
udana, or "inspired utterance", 18
United States, 91, 94, 116, 121, 125, 140
    Buddhism in, 88, 100, 101, 115, 121, 134, 136
    meditation, 160
    migration into, 249, 254
    see also Ginsberg, Allen; Vietnam War
Upanishad, 45
upasaka and *upasika see* householders
upaya (skilful means), 134

Vajra Bhairava, 195
Vajradhatu, US, 100, 101, 115
Vajrayana Buddhist practices, 259
    concept of guru devotion, 119
    and female consorts, 216,
    tantric level of elite practice, 181
Vajrayogini, 65
value of reaching heaven (*svarga*), 4
Vasabha, Queen, 17
vegetarianism and Buddhism, 81–82, 84, 150, 216, 220, 306
    "Eight Vegetarian Precepts", 308
Vessatara *jataka*, 147
Vientiane, 90, 91
Vietnam, 280
Vietnam War, 88, 92, 115, 118–119
vikalpa, 14
Vimalakirti Sutra, 306
Vinaya, 78, 80, 150, 153
vipassana, 67, 112, 162, 184
    in Israel, 124, 129
    Vipassana Meditation and the Practice of "Pure Buddhism", 184–186
    and war, 166
    see also Tovana
Vishakha, 13, 29, 34–37, 147
Visuddhimagga ("The Path to Purification"), 5–6, 159–160
Voice of the Silence, The, 77

Wabi, Maechii, 172–175
Wai (Venerable Takyu Sik), 81–86
Wangdzin, Pelling Ani, 257–262
    biography, 260–261
Wat Mahathat, 148, 152, 154
Wat Pah Nanachat, 111
Wat Pho, 149
Wat Phra Kaew, 149
Wat Traimit, 154

Weber, Max, 1
Wesak Day, 85
Western Karma Kagyu lay movement, 102
Western scholars and Buddhism, 74–75
    immigration and Buddhism, 87–88
What the Buddha Taught, 166
"womb of the Buddha", doctrine, 47
women and Buddhism, 21, 22, 26, 27, 134, 216, 253
    and Brahmanism, 25–26
    and Chinese Mahayana tradition, 81
    difficulties faced in undertaking advance practices, 63
    and enlightenment Tibet, 68
    householders, 14, 15, 172
    in India, 22
    and issues with ordination Tibet, 65
    in Japan, 281
    in Nepal, 183, 184, 247, 248, 253
    religious roles in Tibet, 251–252, 257–262
    in Thailand, 153–154
    women *arhats*, 13
    women's wisdom, 27
Woods, John, 126
"word of the Buddha" (*Buddha-vacana*), 44
Wrightson, Charlotte *see* Sensei, Amala

yaksa cults, 41
Yama, Lord of Death, 201, 204
Yasodhara, 13
Year to Live, A: How to Live This Year as if It Were Your Last, 112
Yeshe Tenpa Gyaltsen, 18th Bakula Lobsang, 220, 250
Yijing, Ven, 299–300
yogas, 159
yogic practice, 45
Yonamine, Keiko, 281
Youth League for Revitalizing Buddhism (Jp. Shinko Bukkyo Seinen Domei), 281, 286, 287

Zang-ri Kar-mar cave and Ma-chig, 66
zazen (sitting meditation), 2, 117, 135, 139, 140
Zeidner, Hannah and Ernest, 125
Zen Buddhism, 85, 115, 117, 136, 281
    in China, 308
    doctrines, 47
    elite, 135
    in Israel, 125
    in Japan, 136
    reforms, 136
    Western, 133, 134–135, 136, 140
    see also Sensei, Amala
Zhi-je method, 65–66